Additional Praise

T0272688

Hezbollah: The Global
of Lebanon's Party of God

"Levitt's comprehensive work contributes significantly to our understanding of one of the most dangerous and sophisticated terrorist groups in the world. Through rigorous research written in approachable, sometimes poetic language, Levitt takes us on a journey through the worldwide activities of Hezbollah." —*Middle Eastern Studies*

"A meticulously detailed examination. . . . The book sheds new light on the targeting of Western and Israeli interests in Lebanon and abroad."
—*The Washington Times*

"Levitt's coverage of Hezbollah's illegal and criminal operations on American soil mightily increases the value of this useful, well-written book." —*Choice*

"A wide-ranging portrait of Hezbollah's activities on five continents and its actions." —*Library Journal*

"A compelling account of the global terror group's operations . . . as rich in detail as it is in storytelling. . . . The compelling narrative leaves readers wondering how it is possible that this organization has grown so powerful and influential with few repercussions." —*The Jerusalem Post*

"This book's meticulous documentation of Hezbollah's terrorist and criminal enterprises makes it required reading for all those concerned about understanding its true nature." —*Perspectives on Terrorism*

"Authoritative and immensely important new book." —*Commentary*

"Levitt's book makes a major contribution to the literature and we should be grateful to him for his forensic skill in mapping . . . Hezbollah's 30-year embrace of violence." —*International Affairs*

HEZBOLLAH

HEZBOLLAH

The Global Footprint
of Lebanon's Party of God

Updated Edition

MATTHEW LEVITT

GEORGETOWN UNIVERSITY PRESS
Washington, DC

The publisher is not responsible for third-party websites or their content. URL links were active at time of publication.

Library of Congress Cataloging-in-Publication Data

Names: Levitt, Matthew, 1970- author.
Title: Hezbollah : the global footprint of Lebanon's Party of God / Matthew Levitt.
Description: Updated edition. | Washington, DC : Georgetown University Press, 2024. | Includes bibliographical references and index.
Identifiers: LCCN 2024025711 (print) | LCCN 2024025712 (ebook) | ISBN 9781647125325 (paperback) | ISBN 9781647125332 (ebook)
Subjects: I CSH: Hizballah (Lebanon) | Islam and politics—Lebanon. | Terrorism. | Lebanon—Politics and government.
Classification: LCC JQ1828.A98 H62534 2024 (print) | LCC JQ1828.A98 (ebook) | DDC 324.25692/084—dc23/eng/20240717
LC record available at https://lccn.loc.gov/2024025711
LC ebook record available at https://lccn.loc.gov/2024025712

∞This paper meets the requirements of ANSI/NISO Z39.48-1992 (Permanence of Paper).

25 24   9 8 7 6 5 4 3 2 First printing

Printed in the United States of America

Cover design by TG Design.

For my parents,
who made it all possible

And my wife and children,
who make it all worthwhile

Contents

Preface to the Updated Edition, 2024

IT HAS BEEN MORE THAN A DECADE since the publication of the original, hardcover *Hezbollah*, but the trends and themes laid out in the book remain as accurate today as they did then. An afterword was added to the book when the paperback edition was released in 2015, focusing on Hezbollah's ongoing international plots and its entry into the Syrian civil war next door. Since then, Hezbollah has continued to carry out terrorist operations around the world—including plots since the book was first published—in Thailand (2014), Belgium (2017), Chile (2019), Cyprus (2021), Colombia (2021), and Brazil (2023), among others—and its illicit financial activities continue unabated. These alone, however, would not warrant the release of a new paperback edition of the book today. It should not surprise anyone that Hezbollah would continue carrying out the kinds of activities it has pursued for decades at home and around the world. But two new trends warrant this edition with a new epilogue, which will update the reader on some of these more recent plots and activities.

The first trend is Hezbollah's growing role as a regional actor throughout the Middle East, acting in tandem with and at the direction of Iran's Islamic Revolutionary Guard Corps (IRGC). Hezbollah today helps Iran manage the sometimes-contentious relationships between and among Iran's various proxy groups in the region. Hezbollah trains recruits from these proxy groups, deploys its own troops to foreign battlefields that have nothing to do with Israel, and engages in a wide array of illicit financial, cyber, procurement, and other activities.

The second trend—Hezbollah's commitment to resume attacks against Israel, now that it has largely withdrawn from Syria—thrust itself to the forefront after the Hamas terrorist attacks of October 7, 2023, when Hezbollah quickly began firing rockets into northern Israel on a near daily basis in solidarity with the Hamas attacks to Israel's south. These attacks led to the internal displacement of nearly 100,000 Israeli civilians from communities in northern Israel and brought the area, as of this writing, to the brink of a regional war. While Hezbollah appears not to have known that Hamas would carry out its attack on October 7, it certainly knew Hamas was preparing such an attack, which came straight out of the

Hezbollah playbook. For at least two years, Hamas and Hezbollah maintained a "joint operations room," as they called it, in Beirut.[1] And just three months before the October 7 attacks, Hezbollah released a video of a simulated Hezbollah attack on an Israeli military base on the Israel-Lebanon border.[2] Indeed, even before the October 7 attacks, Hezbollah actively sought to find ways of changing the informal rules of the game governing the shadow war between Hezbollah and Israel, looking for opportunities to hit Israel that fell below the threshold for a severe Israeli retaliation.

Today, these two trends combine to make Hezbollah a much more complicated and significant threat. The group's acts of international terrorism and criminal enterprises have continued apace, but Hezbollah now also plays a central role in events that will determine not only whether Iran and its proxies will dominate the Middle East but also whether they will destabilize the region to the point of a regional war. For more on this, please read the new epilogue to this book. For additional resources, see my open-access map and timeline of Hezbollah worldwide activities,[3] and my podcast, *Breaking Hezbollah's Golden Rule*.[4]

Matthew Levitt
April 2024

Notes

1. Jonathan Schanzer, "Iran-Hezbollah Intelligence Center May Help Hamas Target Israel," *Foreign Policy,* September 13, 2022, https://foreignpolicy.com/2022/09/13/iran-hezbollah-hamas-israel-beirut-lebanon-intelligence-sharing-center/.

2. "Hezbollah Publishes Video of Simulated Attack on Israeli Outpost," in *Lebanese Hezbollah Select Worldwide Activity Map*, Washington Institute for Near East Policy, July 16, 2023, www.washingtoninstitute.org/hezbollahinteractivemap/#year=2023&id=1863.

3. "Lebanese Hezbollah Select Worldwide Activity Map," Washington Institute for Near East Policy, March 5, 2024, www.washingtoninstitute.org/hezbollahinteractivemap/.

4. Matthew Levitt, *Breaking Hezbollah's Golden Rule*, Season 2, September 18, 2023, www.washingtoninstitute.org/policy-analysis/podcast-breaking-hezbollahs-golden-rule-season-2.

Acknowledgments

THIS BOOK IS THE PRODUCT of a decade of research and writing, based on interviews with officials and experts from five continents, declassified intelligence reports, court documents, and much more. Some people spoke on the record, but more spoke on background or not for attribution, either because they still work in government or because they feared putting at risk their future access to people in Lebanon. Many people also helped me obtain documents that, though unclassified (or declassified), were not necessarily accessible to the public. I have thanked these people privately, and do so again here—the reader will not know their names, but they know who they are and will recognize themselves in this acknowledgment all the same.

Special thanks are due to my friends and colleagues at The Washington Institute for Near East Policy, where I am a senior fellow and direct the institute's Stein program on counterterrorism and intelligence. I am especially grateful for the support of the institute's executive committee, board of trustees, and executive director Robert Satloff. The institute's senior research staff was a constant source of support, and I am a wiser person for having the opportunity to be a part of this truly remarkable intellectual community.

I owe a special thanks and acknowledgment to the various research assistants and interns at The Washington Institute who at some point over the past few years put their hearts and souls into this study, including David Bagby, Ben Freedman, Shoshana Haberman, David Jacobson, Julie Lascar, Jake Lipton, Julia Miller, Michael Mitchell, Jonathan Prohov, Aaron Resnick, Guive Rosen, Gabriela Rudin, Nick Shaker, Melissa Trebil, and Kelli Vanderlee. As researchers, data organizers, fact checkers, editors, formatters, sounding boards, and partners in crime, the institute's cadre of researchers have been second to none throughout this project.

But among the research assistants who worked on this book with me, four stand out for the amount of time and energy they invested in the project. Samuel Cutler, Stephanie Papa, and Becca Wasser each spent over a year organizing material, scheduling interviews, drafting timelines, and so much more. These three saw me through the long haul of organizing the massive quantity of material I collected into a coherent, usable archive so that I could start drafting chapters. All told, Divah Alshawa will have spent over two years on this project, including many rounds of "final" editing, fact-checking, and formatting. I often had to kick her out of the office at the end of the day, only to find that she'd gone home and worked on the manuscript there too. Any errors or typos that may have slipped through are mine alone, but the reason there will be so few, if any, is that Divah made sure that would be the case. Many thanks to Kelsey Segawa who worked on the afterword for the English-paperback and Spanish versions of the book.

Special thanks to Jason Warshof, editor extraordinaire, who invested countless hours working with me on each draft chapter. When the final manuscript submission came out well over the expected word count, Jason stepped in to help trim the fat and keep the book as lean and focused as possible without losing key content.

I want to thank the academic peer reviewers selected by Georgetown University Press who gave generously of their time to review the manuscript in its entirety and offered tangible comments and guidance. A host of other, informal readers reviewed sections of the book, and I am very grateful to them as well. My editor at Georgetown University Press, Don Jacobs, was a calming influence when I needed him to be and gently prodding when he had to be. Always supportive and with the patience of Job, he encouraged and supported me throughout the project as it crept along, sometimes at a snail's pace. Once submitted, the manuscript was expertly prepared and promoted by the press staff. It was a stroke of genius on the part of my literary agent, Robbie Hare, to match me with Don and Georgetown University Press. Robbie is a valued friend and an exceptional agent, and from the moment she read the early proposal that became this book was its most ardent supporter.

Finally, I recognize how tremendously blessed I am to be a part of such a loving, supportive family. I am truly grateful to my family—including my parents, in-laws, children, and my incredible wife, Dina—for their love, support, and patience.

Introduction

Researching Hezbollah's Clandestine Activities

IN MAY 2003 I PARTICIPATED in a conference for current and former US law enforcement and intelligence personnel on Lebanon. Sponsored by the US government and featuring speakers from the United States and Lebanon, each of the conference panels was chaired by a US official. Strikingly, when participants on several panels insinuated that Hezbollah had never engaged in an act of terrorism or that there was no such person as Imad Mughniyeh (Hezbollah's late operations chief)—both concepts being American or Israeli fabrications—the US officials chairing the respective panels said nothing. The issue was put to rest once the session was opened up to questions from the audience, but the experience left me convinced of the need for a serious study focusing on Hezbollah's clandestine activities worldwide to complement the already rich literature on the party's overt activities in Lebanon.

"Due to the secretive nature of [Hezbollah's terrorist wing], it is difficult to gather information on its role and activities," an Australian government report acknowledges.[1] Hezbollah, to be sure, goes to great lengths to hide its covert and illicit activities, severely complicating the prospect of conducting open source (i.e., unclassified) research on the subject. As a former FBI agent put it, groups like Hezbollah "are well aware of our interest in them and what our intentions are" and therefore "they have become experts in the art of concealing their activities."[2] It should therefore not surprise that this book is the product of almost a decade of painstaking research. Collecting publicly available material only underscored the dearth of detailed information available on even such well-known incidents as the 1992 and 1994 bombings in Buenos Aires. As for other incidents, like the failed 1994 attempt to bomb the Israeli embassy in Bangkok, the vast majority of people—among both the general public and professionals in the field—had no idea these events had occurred at all.

So over the course of several years I interviewed officials and collected reports from all over the world. I met with journalists, academics, and current and former government officials—policymakers, intelligence officials, law enforcement officers, analysts, and more—everywhere from Australia to Germany and from Jordan to Singapore. My travels took me from the Los Angeles garment district to the salon of a Kuwaiti intellectual, and from a Belgian steakhouse to innumerable coffeehouses and government offices. I interviewed former undercover agents in the most unlikely places, and when a face-to-face meeting could not be arranged I conducted interviews over the phone.

The tale of international intrigue that poured forth from these meetings amazed me at first, though over time I grew accustomed to scribbling pages and pages of notes that knew no geographic bounds. In one instance a couple of investigators mapped out a case that involved petty crime and massive fraud, radical ideology and nationalistic fervor, all interwoven with arms procurement, document forgery, counterfeiting, and fundraising schemes. More astounding still were the stops in that one story: from the United States to Argentina, Azerbaijan, Belgium, Germany, Iran, Iraq, Lebanon, Paraguay, Slovakia, and Syria.

Most interviews led to several others, over the course of which I methodically bounced ideas off people who came from a wide array of backgrounds, and ultimately I sifted through the vast amounts of raw material to form the contents of this book. A great deal of information I collected did not make the cut. From time to time, interviews are cited directly in the notes. But the greatest value of the interviews was in confirming material from the many reports, investigations, declassified intelligence assessments, and other documents I collected along the way and which are more commonly cited here.

This book benefits from extensive field research, including hundreds of interviews; primary source material, including newly released documents, declassified intelligence, court documents, and official reports; and supplementary material which I worked hard to vet and confirm from press reports and the existing academic and other literature. The documents I collected include declassified reports from the CIA and FBI, the Canadian Integrated Threat Assessment Centre (ITAC), the Israeli Shin Bet and Mossad, and agencies of the governments of Argentina, Chile, Germany, the Philippines, and Singapore, among others. The documents include case files from local law enforcement agencies, congressional testimonies, press releases, government affidavits and reports, and much more.

Because of the sensitivity of the subject matter, and since many of the people I interviewed were current or former government officials, many of these interviews were conducted on a not-for-attribution basis. "Anonymous sourcing is widely recognized as necessary when researching clandestine militant groups," as a colleague put it in the introduction to his own study.[3] But the necessary practice makes the vetting of materials and exploitation of as much publicly citable material as possible all the more important. To that end, I used each interview not only as an opportunity to collect new information but also to vet and confirm information I obtained in other interviews or documents. What I write here is based on this research, not any special knowledge of my own. I direct the reader to the notes for further information on the source of information for any given fact or statement. It should be assumed that persons or entities accused of illicit conduct of any kind within the documents I cite dispute those charges. But with the source information provided here, readers can and should draw their own conclusions.

The book is structured along geographic and loosely chronological tracks. It opens with Hezbollah's birth and its first forays into violence targeting Western interests, first at home in Lebanon and then abroad. It then follows the trajectory of Hezbollah's operations abroad, first in Europe and the Middle East, then South America and Southeast Asia. Hezbollah's activities in North America pre–September 11 come next, moving to the Persian Gulf where the group played a role in the bombing of a US military barracks building in Saudi Arabia. The book then takes a look at the Hezbollah unit dedicated to supporting Palestinian militant groups, at Hezbollah's activities in Africa, and at the group's activities in post–Saddam Iraq. A chapter on Hezbollah's activities in North America post–September 11 follows, taking advantage of the significant amount of information gleaned from investigations of Hezbollah in the United States and Canada over the past few years. The book concludes with a look at Hezbollah's role in Iran's shadow war with the West, including plots targeting civilians around the world.

This book is not intended to be the final word on Hezbollah's global reach, nor does it pretend to be a comprehensive study of Hezbollah's worldwide presence and capabilities. This book is, however, the first study of its kind focused specifically on Hezbollah's clandestine activities worldwide. I look forward to the conversation that follows.

Notes

1. US Department of the Treasury, "Hizballah External Security Organisation." Attorney General's Department, Australian Government, May 16, 2009 (document last modified November 8, 2010).
2. Hamilton, "Hezbollah's Global Reach."
3. Tankel, *Storming the World Stage*, 7.

1

The Party of God Is Born

FOR A WHILE, the two Hezbollah operatives sat in their car, scoping out the Israeli embassy in Baku, Azerbaijan. Concentrating on their stakeout, the operatives were unaware that police were watching them watch the building. When the operatives finally realized they were under surveillance, they pulled into traffic, but not quite quickly enough, and were caught fleeing the scene. Police inspected their car, where they found explosives, binoculars, cameras, pistols with silencers, and pictures from earlier surveillance runs. Police arrested the two Lebanese men, later identified as Ali Karaki and Ali Najem Aladine, raided several safe houses, and arrested four local militants recruited by Karaki and Aladine to work for them.[1]

Working closely with Iranian intelligence agents and local operatives—some Islamist extremists, others criminals—the Hezbollah operatives had methodically planned a series of spectacular terrorist operations for spring 2008. The planned attacks reportedly included multiple and simultaneous car bombings around the Israeli and US embassies, kidnapping the Israeli ambassador, and blowing up a radar tower.[2] None of this was to take place in Lebanon, where Hezbollah is based, or in Israel, the primary target of Hezbollah's ire, but some 900 miles away, in the remote capital of Azerbaijan, just north of Iran.

Hezbollah operatives had been caught plotting in Azerbaijan before. In fall 2001 six suspects reportedly tied to Hezbollah were arrested near the Iranian border.[3] Over the next few years Azerbaijani authorities exposed several cells tied to Iran that were said to be plotting attacks against Israeli or other Western targets there. In 2006 fifteen Azeris were accused of plotting attacks against Israeli and Western targets, reportedly after receiving training and direction from Iran. As a result of the increased surveillance tied to that case, police uncovered the 2008 plot when local militants were found to be in contact with Karaki, described as a "veteran of Hezbollah's external operations unit," and Aladine, a "lower ranking explosives expert." Using Iranian passports and staying in luxury hotels, the two traveled among Azerbaijan, Iran, and Lebanon in early 2008. Together they recruited a network of local operatives, several of whom eluded arrest—along with some other Lebanese and Iranian suspects—by driving south across the border into Iran.[4]

The investigation determined that the men received orders from Hezbollah's international terrorist wing, alternatively known as the Islamic Jihad Organization (IJO) or the External Security Organization (ESO). Iran's Islamic Revolutionary Guard Corps (IRGC) provided the explosives and other support, including facilitating the foreign cell members' entry into Azerbaijan on Iranian passports.[5]

In their plots focused on the Israeli and US embassies, the suspects intended to park as many as four cars filled with explosives near the sites and detonate them simultaneously. The location of the Israeli embassy in the Hyatt Tower, a complex that also housed the Thai and Japanese embassies, apparently did not dissuade the plotters from going forward. Once arrested, Karaki and Aladine were detained for more than a year before they were charged in June 2009 with treason, revealing secret information abroad, espionage, preparing acts of terrorism, drug trafficking, and arms smuggling.[6]

During the trial Ali Karaki, identified as the cell leader, admitted that he had served as Hezbollah's representative in Iran since 2003, earning $900 a month. In Iran, Karaki also worked with tour groups that gathered near Tehran's al-Nabi mosque, where he was approached by someone from Iran's Ministry of Intelligence and Security (MOIS) and ultimately put on its payroll as well. Among his responsibilities, Karaki admitted, were collecting information on the Jewish Cultural Center in Baku and investigating Iranians (presumably Iranian Jews) suspected of "help[ing] Israel."[7]

Karaki and Aladine were reportedly tasked with the operation by Hezbollah officials in Lebanon before traveling to Iran, where IRGC agents helped them cross the border into Azerbaijan in 2007. During their multiple visits to Baku in 2007 and early 2008, they first recruited local operatives and then conducted surveillance of potential targets. One such target was the Qabala radar station, which is leased by the Azeris to Russia and manned by Russian personnel—a seemingly odd target for Hezbollah or Iran.[8]

But Hezbollah and Iran had a reason to keep their eye on the radar station. To begin with, it is likely that the original operational concept had been limited to surveillance alone, just in case either party ever needed to carry out a future attack. Also, Russia had offered to staff the radar station jointly with the United States in lieu of deploying the US missile shield in Poland and the Czech Republic. Russia made the offer in June 2007, not long before the surveillance began.[9] Hezbollah and Iran did decide to operationalize at least the part of the plot focused on the Israeli embassy and ambassador, however, in reaction to the February 2008 assassination in Damascus of Hezbollah's chief of external operations, Imad Mughniyeh.

Three months later Karaki and Aladine were caught red-handed with explosives and weapons at the ready. In October 2009 the six defendants, including Karaki and Aladine, were convicted of preparing attacks targeting the Israeli and American embassies, as well as the radar station. The two Hezbollah operatives were sentenced to fifteen years in prison.[10] A few months later their families complained that they neither received Hezbollah stipends nor saw any effort to secure Karaki and Aladine's release. "Had Imad Mughniyeh been alive," some grumbled, "he would not have treated the families in this indecent way."[11] Less than a year after their convictions, they were both released to Iran and repatriated home to Lebanon in a prisoner trade that secured the freedom of an Azeri scholar jailed in Iran.[12]

Avenging the Death of Hajj Radwan

Exiting a meeting with Syrian intelligence on the evening of February 12, 2008, Imad Mughniyeh—also known as Hajj Radwan—climbed into his Mitsubishi Pajero and was killed instantly when an explosive device, reportedly inserted into the driver's seat headrest, went off, causing a massive explosion.[13] For years Mughniyeh had successfully evaded capture by international intelligence agencies (he reportedly altered his appearance with plastic surgery), so the assassination shocked Hezbollah, Iran, and Syria alike, leading officials from Syria's various intelligence agencies to blame one another for the intelligence failure. Meanwhile both Hezbollah and Iranian intelligence lacked faith in a unilateral Syrian investigation and pressed to have their own officers included in the investigation.[14]

According to media accounts, US diplomatic cables reported that the Saudi ambassador to Lebanon told US diplomats that Hezbollah suspected that Syria was behind the assassination. By this account the Iranian foreign minister, who personally attended Mughniyeh's funeral, made the trip "to calm down Hezbollah and keep it from taking action against Syria."[15] In time Iran and Hezbollah concluded that Israeli intelligence had carried out the attack, based on information gathered by Palestinian and Syrian recruits.[16] Hezbollah engaged in a counterintelligence investigation of its own, leading the group to terminate activities it feared may have been compromised and led to Mughniyeh's identification (see chapter 11).

Hezbollah denied Mughniyeh's existence altogether while he lived but openly embraced him in death.[17] A major street in Hezbollah's stronghold in Beirut's southern suburbs was renamed Imad Mughniyeh Avenue, complete with a memorial to the Hezbollah commander in the median.[18] Hezbollah posted a glowing memorial to Mughniyeh on its website, noting that the group's secretary-general, Hassan Nasrallah, had posthumously awarded him the "exceptional title" Leader of the Two Victories, referring to Israel's withdrawal from southern Lebanon in May 2000 and Hezbollah's July 2006 war against Israel.[19] His tomb became a shrine, part of Hezbollah's string of militant-themed tourist sites.[20]

From the outset there was little question that Hezbollah would seek to avenge Mughniyeh's death. In a fiery eulogy delivered by video link from a secure location, Nasrallah spoke to the crowds gathered for the commander's funeral. "Zionists," he threatened, "if you want this sort of open war, then let the whole world hear, so be it!" In a pledge to his followers, Nasrallah promised, "The blood of Imad Mughniyeh will make them [Israel] withdraw from existence."[21] Since its self-described "divine victory" against Israel in July 2006, Hezbollah had already begun to engage in what the National Counterterrorism Center would later describe as "an increasingly aggressive terrorist campaign"—likely a reference to both the group's militant actions at home targeting fellow Lebanese and its support to other militants abroad, especially in Iraq but also in Somalia (see chapters 9 and 10).[22] Within weeks Hezbollah attempted the first of several plots—the foiled plot in Baku—intended to make good on Nasrallah's threat.

More plots followed, the first of which was exposed by the September 2008 arrest of key members of a Hezbollah network in Egypt that was funneling weapons to Palestinian terrorist groups in Gaza and reportedly was planning a string of attacks in Egypt. Another was foiled in January 2009, this time in an unnamed European country.[23] In September–October 2009 Turkish authorities disrupted a plot in which Hezbollah and Iranian agents posing as tourists intended to attack Israeli, American, and possibly local Jewish targets. By one account a cell led by Abbas Hossein Zakr was looking to strike Israeli tourists, Israeli ships or airplanes, or synagogues in Turkey.[24] Turkish police arrested Hezbollah operatives traveling on Kuwaiti and Canadian passports who reportedly smuggled a car bomb into the country from Syria.[25] The thwarted plot, combined with an assessment that Hezbollah sought to kill an Israeli diplomat to avenge Mughniyeh's death, led Israeli officials to heighten security for Israeli officials traveling overseas.[26]

Sources close to Hezbollah, embarrassed by its failure to retaliate for Mughniyeh's assassination, as Nasrallah had promised two years earlier, couched the group's failed attacks in terms of divine will. "The divine factor is necessary in all actions," they explained, adding that "the attempts . . . were unsuccessful because the time had not yet come for an opportunity reflecting the divine wish."[27] Hezbollah also posted a poem on its website implying that while no attacks had succeeded, part of the group's revenge was keeping the threat of an impending attack hanging over Israel's head. Titled "Mughniyeh Haunts 'Israel,' Every Day, Every Year," the poem reads, in part,

> With every rising sun he asks revenge / With every passing month he asks revenge / And with every passing year, they ask themselves when, where, and how they will taste his revenge / This year, like last year, like the year before, his killers warn their supporters: Beware Mughniyeh! / Wherever you are, beware Mughniyeh.[28]

The absence of an attack, then, was not a sign of failure but part of a master plan. Later that year Hezbollah produced a hit list of prominent Israeli officials it held responsible for Mughniyeh's death. Mimicking the US military's deck of cards featuring wanted Iraqi insurgents, Hezbollah's own deck featured the head of Israel's Mossad intelligence service, the Israel Defense Forces (IDF) chief of staff, the prime minister, and others.[29]

Meanwhile, despite its operational failures abroad, Hezbollah had much to celebrate at home in Lebanon. In July 2008 Hezbollah secured a blocking third in the new Lebanese cabinet as part of the Doha (Qatar) agreement reached by opposing Lebanese factions that May to end the country's protracted political crisis. The one-third-plus-one representation of Hezbollah and its allies within the thirty-member cabinet effectively undercut any legislative means to disarm the group's military wing as required under UN Security Council Resolution 1701.[30] At the time, then–UN secretary-general Kofi Annan stated, "Dismantling Hezbollah is not the direct mandate of the UN." Commenting on the continued flow of weapons from Iran to Hezbollah through Syria, Annan made it clear that the UN force would not stop the transactions. "The understanding," he added, "was that it would be the Lebanese who would disarm [Hezbollah]."[31]

Israeli intelligence officials reported that Hezbollah had tripled its supply of rockets since the summer 2006 war. More disturbing, the quality of the rockets had improved along with the higher numbers. Hezbollah now had "serious weapons," a French diplomat reported, "not just Katyushas."[32] According to an Israeli security official, Hezbollah could now fire rockets on Tel Aviv from north of Lebanon's Litani River and hit as far south as Dimona from southern Lebanon.[33]

Hezbollah also appeared to have overcome the political setbacks incurred by the massive damage caused to Lebanon's infrastructure in the July 2006 war. Despite underwriting the reconstruction of homes and more in southern Lebanon with financing provided by Iran, Hezbollah suffered significant domestic criticism for igniting the war by kidnapping Israeli soldiers and firing thousands of missiles into northern Israel. Local criticism arose again in May 2008, after Hezbollah militants briefly seized control of part of West Beirut, turning onto fellow Lebanese citizens the weapons the party claimed were maintained strictly to resist Israel. The fighting broke out after the Lebanese government announced intentions to curb Hezbollah's intelligence activities at Beirut International Airport and shut down its private "military telecommunications network."[34]

But by July 2008 Hezbollah had every reason to expect that its reconstruction support and military successes would translate into political gain. In particular Hezbollah negotiated a prisoner exchange that secured the release of five Lebanese militants held in Israeli jails as well as the remains of several other Hezbollah and Palestinian fighters. This, the party felt confident, would catapult the group and its leader, Hassan Nasrallah, back into the limelight as the spearhead of resistance against Israel. Among the slogans plastered along coastal roads from the Israeli border to Sidon was Nasrallah's refrain: "Thanks to the weapons of the resistance, we will free our prisoners."[35] Hezbollah posters referred to the exchange as the "Radwan Operation"—framing the prisoner release itself as part of the group's revenge for Mughniyeh's assassination.[36] The Israel-Lebanon frontier, however, remained eerily quiet. Even when Israeli forces fought a pitched battle with Hamas in Gaza over three weeks in 2008–9, not a single Hezbollah rocket or fighter brought the fight to Israel's northern border. While Hezbollah declared victory in the July 2006 war, the devastating Israeli military response appears to have deterred Hezbollah from entering the fray two years later.

Campaigning at Home, Exposed Abroad

As the Hezbollah-led March 8 coalition campaigned ahead of Lebanon's June 2009 elections, the group was forced to contend with the unexpected exposure of its covert terrorist activities within Lebanon and internationally. At home, Hezbollah stood accused by a UN tribunal of playing a role in the assassination of former Lebanese prime minister Rafiq Hariri. Abroad, a series of law enforcement actions targeted Hezbollah support networks operating across the globe. Together these activities posed what Hezbollah leader Hassan Nasrallah described as "the largest and most important and serious challenge" facing the party.[37]

Mughniyeh's funeral—where Nasrallah threatened open war—occurred on the third anniversary of Hariri's assassination. These two events became even more intimately intertwined several months later, in May 2009, when the German weekly *Der Spiegel* revealed that the UN Special Tribunal for Lebanon (STL) investigating Hariri's assassination had implicated Hezbollah operatives in the murder. Citing Lebanese security sources, the report referred to cell phones linked to the plot and found that "all of the numbers involved apparently belonged to the 'operational arm' of Hezbollah." The report described a principal suspect, Abdulmajid Ghamlush, as "a Hezbollah member who had completed a training course in Iran." The investigation of Ghamlush, who reportedly purchased the mobile phones, led officials to Hajj Salim, the alleged mastermind of the assassination plot and commander of a special operational unit reporting directly to Nasrallah.[38]

It would be another two years before the STL issued formal indictments to Lebanon's state prosecutor calling for the arrest of four Hezbollah members. While two of the suspects—Hasan Aneisi and Asad Sabra—appear to have been low-level musclemen, the others—Salim Ayyash and Mustapha Badreddine—were senior members of the IJO, Hezbollah's famed terrorist wing, with international connections. Ayyash was described as a US passport holder who headed the cell that carried out the assassination. Meanwhile, Badreddine, Mughniyeh's brother-in-law, was a longtime partner in Mughniyeh's terrorist plots dating back to the Beirut bombings in the early 1980s and succeeded Mughniyeh as head of Hezbollah's external operations.[39]

Nasrallah took to the airwaves condemning the tribunal as an American project based on fabricated communications data from Israeli spies embedded in Lebanon's telecommunications industry. Israel was behind the assassination, he claimed, as he exhorted the Lebanese people not to cooperate with its investigators.[40] But even before the formal indictments were issued, Hezbollah reportedly conducted quiet surveillance of the tribunal's headquarters in The Hague. The Netherlands considers Hezbollah a terrorist group, and Dutch intelligence was already conducting bimonthly assessments of potential threats to the tribunal. While they found no plots in the works, they did note periodic surveillance of tribunal headquarters. In particular before the tribunal occupied its newly refurbished building, a Lebanese camera crew was caught taking suspicious pictures and video of the unfinished facility.[41]

Back in Lebanon Hezbollah followed tribunal investigators on the ground and intimidated them overtly. The group reportedly collected information on tribunal officials entering and leaving the country through airport surveillance, creating an environment in which investigators did not feel safe.[42] The January 25, 2008, assassination of Lebanese Internal Security Forces captain Wissam Eid, who was detailed to the Hariri investigation, underscored those fears. According to a Canadian Broadcasting Corporation report, the investigation of Eid's murder—which also fell under the tribunal's jurisdiction—implicated two additional Hezbollah officials, Hussein Khalil and Wafiq Safa.[43]

Meanwhile, in April 2009 Egyptian authorities announced the November 2008 arrest of a cell of Hezbollah operatives and several dozen local recruits accused of funneling arms to Hamas and targeting Israeli tourists and shipping through the Suez Canal. As long as the arms smuggling network only ran weapons into Gaza, Cairo looked the other way. But local authorities took offense when Hezbollah leaders tasked its Egypt cell with also collecting intelligence for a possible attack on Israeli interests on Egyptian soil. According to Egyptian prosecutors the operatives were instructed to collect intelligence from villages along the Egypt-Gaza border, at tourist sites, and at the Suez Canal. Nasrallah himself confirmed that one of the men arrested was Sami Shihab, a Hezbollah member who was on "a logistical job to help Palestinians get [military] equipment."[44]

The cell reportedly established commercial businesses as fronts for its operational activities, purchased apartments in el-Arish and on the Egyptian side of Rafah for use as safe houses, and contacted criminal elements in Egypt to procure forged Egyptian passports so that members could leave Egypt as needed and purchase or rent apartments. Some of the cell members reportedly worked for the Egyptian bureau of al-Manar, Hezbollah's satellite television station, as cover for their activities in Egypt.[45] Following the exposure of the Hezbollah cell operating in Egypt, UN special envoy Terje Roed-Larsen noted "a growing concern that Hezbollah has engaged in clandestine and illegal militant activities beyond Lebanese territory."[46] The Baku plot was made public that May, prompting senior State Department officials to comment that the foiled plot "illustrate[d] the group's continued disregard for the rule of law, both inside Lebanon and outside its borders."[47]

Hezbollah's Operation Radwan continued apace as the group mobilized operatives to carry out attacks to avenge Mughniyeh's assassination. In April 2009 Israeli officials issued warnings to Israeli businesspeople traveling to Europe in response to what was described as "pinpoint" intelligence of a specific threat.[48] In August 2008 Israel had issued similar warnings of a pending Hezbollah attack targeting Israelis in Africa.[49] A few weeks later senior Israeli officials confirmed that five attempts by Hezbollah operatives to kidnap Israeli citizens abroad had been thwarted.[50] In May 2009 the US Treasury Department issued a press release adding two Africa-based Hezbollah supporters to its list of Specially Designated Global Terrorists (see chapter 9).[51]

Halfway across the world, pressure on Hezbollah continued to build as Argentine prosecutors issued an international arrest warrant for Samuel Salman al-Reda, who was charged with involvement in the 1994 bombing of the Asociación Mutual Israelita Argentina (AMIA) Jewish community center (see chapter 4).[52] Within days Nasrallah gave his final major address before the Lebanese elections. In the speech Nasrallah bemoaned what he described as an Israeli effort to "return to the strategy of introducing Hezbollah as a terrorist organization that attacks countries and peoples and threatens world security." Even worse, Nasrallah said, was "the attempt to accuse Hizballah of assassinating [the] martyr Rafiq Hariri in order to foment a sectarian sedition in Lebanon."[53]

While the Hezbollah coalition would underperform in the July 2009 election, by early 2011 it led a coalition government and held the reins of power in Beirut. In the interim Hezbollah attacks continued. According to leaked diplomatic cables cited by Israel's *Ha'aretz* newspaper, IDF chief of staff Gabi Ashkenazi informed the United Nations envoy to Lebanon of intelligence indicating that Hezbollah was behind the January 2010 bombing of an Israeli diplomatic convoy in Jordan.[54] By then, six different Hezbollah plots, each intended to exact revenge for Mughniyeh's assassination, had reportedly been foiled.[55] While the Israeli diplomats were unhurt, Hezbollah continued to threaten revenge, with Hezbollah second-in-command Naim Qassem stating in February 2010 that the "commitment exists" but that "the (attack) period and specifications [will] come in due time."[56]

And so even as it was crowned as the dominant political force in Lebanon, Hezbollah's illicit activities were highlighted by a series of international criminal investigations. "Since 2008," the government of New Zealand would later conclude in its decision to ban Hezbollah's military wing, the Islamic Resistance (IR), "there is clear evidence that IR has re-engaged with planning terrorist attacks against Israeli interests abroad."[57] What started out as a desire by Hezbollah to avenge Mughniyeh's assassination would, by early 2010, evolve into a larger shadow war between Iran and the West in which Hezbollah would play a central role (see chapter 12).

Hezbollah's Multiple Identities

Hezbollah—Lebanon's Party of God—is many things. It is one of the dominant political parties in Lebanon, as well as a social and religious movement catering first and foremost (though not exclusively) to Lebanon's Shi'a community. Hezbollah is also Lebanon's largest militia, the only one to maintain its weapons and rebrand its armed elements as an Islamic resistance in response to the terms of the Taif Accord, which ended Lebanon's civil war and called for all militias to disarm.[58] While the various wings of the group are intended to complement one another, the reality is often messier. In part that has to do with compartmentalization of the group's covert activities. But it is also a factor of the group's multiple identities—Lebanese, pan-Shi'a, pro-Iranian—and the group's multiple and sometimes competing goals tied to these different identities.

Hezbollah is also a pan-Shi'a movement and an Iranian proxy group, rounding out the foundation and context for the group's radical Shi'a ideology. In 1985 Hezbollah's original political platform included the establishment of an Islamic republic in Lebanon as a central pillar, although this emphasis has since been downplayed.[59] Also prominent in this document are the fight against "Western imperialism" and the continued conflict with Israel. A source of inherent conflict associated with Hezbollah is its ideological commitment to Ayatollah Ruhollah Khomeini's revolutionary doctrine of *velayat-e faqih* (guardianship of the jurist), which holds that a

Shi'a Islamic cleric can also serve as the supreme head of government. The group is thus committed simultaneously to the decrees of Iranian clerics, the Lebanese state, its sectarian Shi'a community, and fellow Shi'a abroad. Hezbollah's other (often competing) goals have included resisting Israeli occupation of Lebanese territory and contesting, and ultimately seeking to eliminate, Israel's very existence; promoting the standing of Shi'a communities worldwide; undermining Arab states with Shi'a minorities in an effort to export the Iranian Shi'a revolution; and serving as the long arm of Iran in coordination with the IRGC–Qods Force. The consequences of these competing ideological drivers was clear after Hezbollah dragged both Israel and Lebanon into a war neither state wanted by crossing the UN-demarcated border between the two countries in July 2006 and killing three Israeli soldiers while kidnapping two more.

The literature on Hezbollah's political, social welfare, and militia activities in Lebanon is rich. Much has been written on the group's ideology, its provision of charity and cradle-to-grave services, and its military structure and tactics—to include standing and reserve members of its formidable militia and an arsenal of tens of thousands of rockets—all within Lebanon. But when it comes to the group's international activities—from financial and logistical support networks to procurement agents and terrorist operatives—the literature is remarkably thin. Most books on Hezbollah make some mention of the group's terrorist activities, especially those in Lebanon in the early and mid-1980s and better-publicized attacks like the bombings in Argentina in 1992 and 1994. But even those references tend to be made in passing, rarely occupying more than a few paragraphs or pages.

To be sure, Hezbollah cannot be truly understood without an appreciation for its political, social, and military activities in Lebanon, underscoring the importance of the existing literature on the group. But its activities outside Lebanon are equally fundamental, including its criminal enterprises and terrorist networks. These sectors, even more than its militia activity at home and its wars with Israel, have led countries around the world to task their law enforcement and intelligence agencies with countering Hezbollah's activities.

Because of Hezbollah's involvement in international terrorism, the US Treasury Department listed the group as a Specially Designated Terrorist entity in 1995.[60] Two years later the US Department of State designated Hezbollah as a Foreign Terrorist Organization.[61] In 2001, in line with Executive Order 13224, the United States named Hezbollah as a Specially Designated Global Terrorist entity. In an interview on Lebanese television just months after the designation, US ambassador to Lebanon Vincent Battle reiterated the US position that "Hezbollah is on the list of terrorist organizations because it is considered an organization that carries out terrorist acts and is capable of staging them [with] vast global reach."[62]

In addition to blacklisting the organization, the United States named several Hezbollah individuals as Specially Designated Global Terrorists, including Sheikh Mohammad Hussein Fadlallah, described as Hezbollah's spiritual leader; current secretary-general Nasrallah; former secretary-general Subhi al-Tufayli; late military chief Imad Mughniyeh; his successor (and brother-in-law) Mustapha Badreddine;

and current IJO chief Talal Hamiyeh. Other US-designated Hezbollah entities comprise financial institutions, including the Islamic Resistance Support Organization, Bayt al-Mal, Yousser Company for Finance and Investment, and al-Qard al-Hassan; communication outlets, including the Lebanese Media Group, Radio al-Nour, and al-Manar television, among others; and foundations, such as the Martyrs Foundation, which provide financial and operational support.[63]

In Europe and elsewhere in the West the approach to Hezbollah has been varied. Many European governments have resisted international efforts to designate the organization as a terrorist group by distinguishing between Hezbollah's political and military wings. The United Kingdom distinguishes among Hezbollah's terrorist, military, and political wings and banned both the terrorist and military wings in 2000 and 2008, respectively.[64] Similarly, only the ESO terrorist wing was banned by Australia in 2003.[65] However, the Netherlands designated Hezbollah a terrorist entity in 2004 without distinguishing between the group's political and military wings. A 2004 Dutch intelligence report highlighted investigations that show "Hezbollah's political and terrorist wings are controlled by one co-ordinating council."[66] Canada does not distinguish among Hezbollah's different wings either and banned the entire organization in 2002.[67] Israel banned Hezbollah as a terrorist group in June 1989.[68]

In May 2002, the European Union froze the assets of a non-European terrorist group for the first time by adding seven Hezbollah-affiliated individuals, including Imad Mughniyeh, to its financial sanctions list for terrorism. However, it did not sanction Hezbollah as an organization.[69] On March 10, 2005, the European Parliament passed a nonbinding resolution recognizing that "clear evidence exists of terrorist activities on the part of Hezbollah" and calling on the EU Council to take "all necessary steps to curtail them."[70]

And yet despite all these actions, for journalists and scholars alike, researching Hezbollah's political, social, and military activities is a far more accessible endeavor than examining its terrorist and other covert activities. Hezbollah's leaders, members, and supporters are more likely to speak openly and honestly about the group's overt activities than about its covert, often blatantly illicit, ones. Nor is it a simple matter to identify the overlap and interconnectivity of the overt and covert activities of a multifaceted group like Hezbollah.

But upon closer inspection the ties that bind Hezbollah's political leadership with its international illicit activities become unmistakable. According to the CIA, even before Hassan Nasrallah rose to the position of secretary-general in 1992, he was "directly involved in many Hizballah terrorist operations, including hostage taking, airline hijackings, and attacks against Lebanese rivals."[71] His personal envoys as far afield as South America and Africa have been linked to explicitly apolitical activities (see chapters 4 and 9). And according to information made public by the US government, it was Nasrallah who oversaw Hezbollah's support for the Syrian regime of Bashar al-Assad in its efforts to crush the Syrian rebellion.[72]

Consider two less well-known cases in the United States (discussed in detail in chapter 12). At the same time that Ali Karaki was planning a Hezbollah attack in

Baku, his brother, Hassan Karaki, was helping to lead a broad criminal conspiracy to sell counterfeit and stolen currency to an undercover FBI informant posing as a member of the Philadelphia criminal underworld. In a parallel plot overseen by Hezbollah politician Hassan Hodroj, Hezbollah sought to procure a long list of sophisticated weapons in a black market scheme involving Hezbollah operatives across the globe.[73]

As senior State Department officials have testified on numerous occasions, while "Hezbollah attempts to portray itself as a natural part of Lebanon's political system and a defender of Lebanese interests . . . its actions demonstrate otherwise."[74] In particular, when Israel withdrew from southern Lebanon in 2000 in compliance with UN Security Council resolutions, Hezbollah quickly filled the political vacuum left in the long-established security zone along the Israel-Lebanon border. Some expected that Hezbollah, having achieved its goal of ending the Israeli occupation of southern Lebanon, would give up its arms and focus on development and civil society. Yet despite calls for the group to disarm under UN Security Council Resolution 1559, the group did quite the opposite. And overall Hezbollah sees its social welfare, political, militant, and international terrorism activities as equally legitimate means of accomplishing its goals, which transcend threats to Lebanon's territorial integrity.

The Party of God Is Born

Founded in the early 1980s by a group of young Shi'a militants, Hezbollah was the product of an Iranian effort to aggregate under one roof a variety of militant Shi'a groups in Lebanon, themselves the products of the domestic and regional instability of the time. On the one hand, Hezbollah was the outgrowth of a complex and bloody civil war, during which the country's historically marginalized Shi'a Muslims attempted to assert economic and political power for the first time. Hezbollah was also a by-product of Israel's effort to dismantle the Palestine Liberation Organization (PLO) by invading southern Lebanon in 1982.[75] Decades later, former Israeli prime minister Ehud Barak noted: "When we entered Lebanon . . . there was no Hezbollah. We were accepted with perfumed rice and flowers by the Shia in the south. It was our presence there that created Hezbollah."[76]

Although Hezbollah first emerged following the 1982 Israeli invasion, the organization did not coalesce into a centralized party until a few years later.[77] According to Hezbollah's deputy secretary-general, Naim Qassem, the 1982–85 period was foundational "for the crystallization of a political vision, the facets of which were harmonious with faith in Islam as a solution" and for the establishment of "an effective jihad operation as represented by the Islamic Resistance forcing Israel's partial flight from Lebanon in 1985."[78]

Many of Hezbollah's founders originally belonged to Amal, the military arm of a Lebanese political party founded by an influential Shi'a cleric named Musa al-Sadr. The cleric, who disappeared in Libya in 1978 and has long been presumed dead, urged the Lebanese Shi'a community to improve its situation both economically and politically. He also intended for the Shi'a militia he established to fight against Israel as part of the Lebanese army. But other armed factions representing various interests in Lebanon emerged after al-Sadr's death, and many Shi'a were disappointed by Amal's moderate policies and the willingness of al-Sadr's replacement, Nabih Berri, to accommodate Israel politically rather than confront it militarily. As a result, disaffected Amal members joined with other Shi'a militant groups—including the Muslim Students Union, the Dawa Party of Lebanon, and others—and established their own umbrella militia, Hezbollah.[79]

The paramilitary networks that made up Hezbollah in its early years revolved around clans such as the Musawis and Hamadis.[80] While these groups agreed on strategic goals such as the creation of an Islamic state in Lebanon, they often diverged on tactical and operational measures.[81] In the early 1980s, the Islamic Dawa Party in Lebanon became a "core component in the establishment of the Hezbollah movement," joined by other radical Shi'a groups.[82] The formation of a revolutionary Shi'a movement under the Dawa Party, according to a CIA account, was advocated early on by Ayatollah Mohammad Hussein Fadlallah, later a "spiritual guide" for Hezbollah.[83] Ultimately Iran's Qods Force (or Pasdaran) drew from the coalition of Shi'a militant groups and, working with the Iranian embassies in Lebanon and Syria, "sired the creation of Hezbollah in Baalbek."[84]

Indeed, Iran played a central role in Hezbollah's founding. Shortly after the Israeli invasion, approximately 1,500 IRGC advisers set up a base in the Bekaa Valley as part of its goal to export the Islamic Revolution to the Arab world.[85] All Hezbollah members were required to attend IRGC-run camps in the valley, according to Naim Qassem, which taught them how to confront the enemy.[86] In 1985, Hezbollah identified its ideological platform: "We view the Iranian regime as the vanguard and new nucleus of the leading Islamic State in the world. We abide by the orders of one single wise and just leadership, represented by 'Waliyat el Faqih' and personified by Khomeini."[87] Over the past three decades, Hezbollah has remained Iran's proxy, and the Pentagon estimates that Tehran provides Hezbollah with weapons and spends up to $200 million a year funding the group's activities, including its media channel, al-Manar, and operations abroad.[88] By other accounts, Iran may provide Hezbollah as much as $350 million a year.[89]

In addition to Iran, Syria's regime under Hafiz al-Assad has been tied to the group's founding. Not only did mutual Iranian-Syrian support for Hezbollah serve to maintain Syria's alliance with Iran, but it also allowed the Assad regime to retain influence over Lebanon and remain a threat to the United States and Israel. In early 2004, four years after Bashar al-Assad succeeded his father as president of Syria, Damascus and Hezbollah further solidified their alliance. Ali Shamkhani, then Iranian defense minister, placed Hezbollah under Iran's direct protection by signing a memorandum of understanding with Syria, a move that signified an Iranian commitment to protect the Syrian regime against an attack by either Israel or the United States—and that extended to Hezbollah strongholds in Lebanon.[90] A year later, after the assassination of Lebanese prime minister Rafiq Hariri and the subsequent Syrian withdrawal from Lebanon, Hezbollah declared its full support for and "gratitude" to Syria.[91] Hezbollah would soon side with the Assad regime in its violent crackdown against Syrian citizens.

The Party of God initially identified its main objectives on February 16, 1985, in an open letter addressed "to all the Oppressed in Lebanon and the World." First, the letter pledged to expel all colonialist entities—the Americans, the French, and their allies—from Lebanon. Second, it committed to bringing the Phalangists to justice for the crimes they had committed against Lebanese Muslims and Christians alike. Last, although it professed to permit "all the sons of our people to determine their future and to choose in all the liberty the form of government they desire," the letter encouraged Lebanon to install an Islamic regime, the only type of government that could "stop further tentative attempts of imperialistic infiltration into our country." Moreover, party officials did not attempt to hide the militaristic aspect of their organization. Hezbollah's guiding document professed, "Our military apparatus is not separate from our overall social fabric. Each of us is a fighting soldier."[92] At the center of the group's insignia is not a map of Lebanon but a globe alongside a fist holding an AK-47 rifle.

According to the CIA, in the first few years following its founding, Hezbollah "established what is virtually a radical Islamic canton in the Bekaa Valley, despite Syria's military presence there." In areas under Hezbollah's control, the CIA reported in 1987, strict Islamic rule was implemented: "Sale or transport of liquor are prohibited, women are forbidden from interacting with men in public and must adhere to a strict dress code, civil crimes are punished according to the Koran, and Western education and influences are prohibited."[93]

Since 1982, Hezbollah has built an extensive global network that relies on operatives and supporters mainly from Lebanese Shi'a diaspora communities. Throughout the 1980s, Hezbollah targeted Western interests within Lebanon, including bombing embassies and military barracks, kidnapping Westerners, and hijacking aircraft. By the 1990s operatives expanded their reach. Hezbollah operatives were involved in attacks as far afield as South America and Europe. Attacks like those targeting the Israeli embassy and the AMIA Jewish Community Center in Buenos Aires in 1992 and 1994, respectively, highlighted Hezbollah's capability to mobilize operatives far from home.[94]

But where this covert network fits within the overall overt structure of Hezbollah is a matter of debate. "Little is known about [the Hezbollah military wing's] internal command hierarchy," a Western government report noted in 2012, "due to its highly secretive nature and use of sophisticated protective measures." Still, before 2006 Hezbollah's Islamic Resistance militia was believed to field 400 to 800 full-time fighters plus 5,000 to 10,000 part-time reservists or village guards. These numbers are believed to have increased significantly since the July 2006 war.[95]

The structure and manpower of Hezbollah's external operations wing, which is responsible for its financial and logistical as well as terrorist operations abroad, is similarly opaque. Sometimes referred to as the Special Security Apparatus (SSA) or the External Security Organization (ESO), it is referred to here as the Islamic Jihad Organization (IJO, or Islamic Jihad)—not to be confused with the Palestinian Islamic

Jihad (PIJ)—the name under which Hezbollah's international wing was formally founded in 1983 when Mughniyeh fled to Iran after the Beirut bombings (see chapter 2).

This much is clear: Since its founding, the group has developed a sophisticated organizational and leadership structure. The overall governing authority, the Majlis al-Shura (Consultative Council), wields all decision-making power and directs several subordinate functional councils. Each functional council reports directly to the Shura Council, which, according to Hezbollah deputy secretary-general Qassem, is "in charge of drawing the overall vision and policies, overseeing the general strategies for the Party's function, and taking political decisions."[96] US assessments echo Qassem's description: "Hezbollah has a unified leadership structure that oversees the organization's complementary, partially compartmentalized elements," according to a Congressional Research Service report.[97]

The secretary-general, currently Hassan Nasrallah, presides over the Shura Council and functions as the group's leader under the authority of the "Jurist Theologian," Iran's Supreme Leader Ali Khamenei. Five administrative bodies, organized around thematic responsibilities, run Hezbollah's political, military (jihad), parliamentary, executive, and judicial activities.[98] The Shura Council considers all elements of the group's activities, including its political and military wings, as part of one holistic entity. In the words of Naim Qassem,

> If the military wing were separated from the political wing, this would have repercussions, and it would reflect on the political scene. But Hezbollah has one single leadership, and its name is the Decision-Making Shura Council. It manages the political activity, the Jihad activity, the cultural and the social activities. . . . Hezbollah's Secretary General is the head of the Shura Council and also the head of the Jihad Council, and this means that we have one leadership, with one administration.[99]

The Executive Council manages daily operations and oversees all cultural, educational, social, and political affairs.[100] The Political Council administers Hezbollah's external relations, oversees the group's relations with the other political forces in Lebanon, and organizes public information and propaganda efforts through a series of subcommittees.[101] For example, the recruitment and propaganda organ runs Hezbollah's radio stations and al-Manar television station.[102] The Political Council continuously seeks to foster "relationships with the various political powers and parties" in Lebanon, according to Qassem. The Parliamentary Council coordinates the activities of the party's parliamentarians and studies proposed legislation brought before the government, while the Jihad Council coordinates "resistance activity."[103] The Jihad Council, Qassem explains, "comprises those in charge of resistance activity, be that in terms of oversight, recruitment, training, equipment, security, or any other resistance-related endeavors."[104]

The Jihad Council is responsible not only for Hezbollah's formal militia activity (the Islamic Resistance) but also for its covert activity—at home and abroad—under the auspices of the IJO. To accomplish its mission the Jihad Council is divided into several smaller units in charge of protecting the leadership, carrying out internal and external surveillance, and overseas operations. The party security branch is further divided into three subgroups: central, preventive, and overseas security. In 2000 a dedicated counterintelligence branch was reportedly founded as well.[105]

Under this structure Hezbollah's militia, terrorist wing, and security organ all report to the Jihad Council.[106] Unlike its sister councils, the Jihad Council enjoys strategic ambiguity such that neither the majority of its officials nor the party's elected parliamentarians are aware of the details of Hezbollah's covert military and terrorist activities, which are decided upon by the party's most senior leadership. According to the US government, while these activities are "executed" by the leadership of the Islamic Resistance (led today by Mustapha Badreddine) and the IJO (led today by Talal Hamiyeh), they are "overseen" by Secretary-General Nasrallah.[107]

Until he was killed, Mughniyeh was Hezbollah's "top militant commander" and reportedly led the Jihad Council himself.[108] By some accounts he held a seat on the Consultative Council as well, which would be typical for the party's standing military commander.[109] According to Deputy Secretary-General Qassem, "a limited circle of individuals was aware of resistance operations. Only those directly involved with planning and execution within the tactics set by the military command formed part of this circle."[110]

Some have construed Qassem's account—itself to be taken with a grain of salt, since a leader of his stature would have every incentive to obfuscate—to mean that Hezbollah's covert military apparatus "exists as a distinct entity from the main body of the organization."[111] No matter how one understands Hezbollah's structure, such a conclusion is a leap too far. The same report that asserts the IJO is a "distinct entity" somehow also upholds its status as the group's "foreign intelligence unit specializing in espionage, counter-intelligence, and dispatching operatives overseas to infiltrate diaspora communities [and] business and criminal networks, and carry out terrorist attacks."[112]

Some governments, such as Canada, differentiate between Hezbollah's efforts to work with foreign individuals, organizations, and communities that are sympathetic to the group, which are carried out by Hezbollah's Foreign Services Department (FSD), and the group's foreign logistics, procurement, and terrorist operations, which fall under the IJO. The FSD, Canadian intelligence assesses, is responsible for setting up front organizations and other platforms in foreign countries, serving as talent spotters, and organizing local Shi'a communities to support Hezbollah and Iran. Canadian authorities—who describe Hezbollah as "one of the most technically capable terrorist groups in the world"—investigate both entities but see the FSD's mission as propaganda, financing, and support, and the IJO's as procurement and terrorism.[113] Still, Canada proscribed the group in its entirety in 2002.

US officials have also long acknowledged, respected, and feared Hezbollah's terrorist network, not only because of its devastating attacks on US interests abroad, such as the early 1980s bombings of the US Marine barracks and embassy in Lebanon and the 1996 bombing of the Khobar Towers in Saudi Arabia, but also because of

Hezbollah's active presence in the United States. In 2007 the US National Intelligence Estimate on the threat to the US homeland noted that Hezbollah's operational capabilities extend to the United States. The report warned of an increased likelihood that Hezbollah could attack on US soil if it (or Iran) felt threatened by the United States.[114]

Such concerns are warranted, given CIA reports observing Hezbollah operatives "actively casing and surveiling [sic] American facilities" and noting "extensive contingency plans" for attacks.[115] The key question, however, is under what conditions Hezbollah might target US interests abroad or in the homeland. One consideration is Hezbollah's own perception of threats to its interests and whether the group sees a US hand behind such threats. A second, and at least equally important, consideration involves Hezbollah's intimate relationship with Iran—a relationship in which the Tehran regime has long used Hezbollah as a militant extension of its foreign policy. The increasingly tense standoff between Iran and the West over Iran's nuclear program could therefore play a central role in Hezbollah's operational calculus. A June 2006 British intelligence report warned of "an increased threat to the UK from Iranian state-sponsored terrorism should the diplomatic situation deteriorate."[116] And that it has.

Today, Hezbollah shows no signs of moderating its commitment to violence. At home the party continues to dominate Lebanese politics, even as its support for the brutal Assad regime in Syria threatens to undermine the party's support and popularity and spark a sectarian conflict pitting Sunni against Shi'a across the Syria-Lebanon border. Meanwhile, the party continues its campaign to shape a culture of resistance within Lebanon that glorifies violence and perpetuates hate. In February 2012, for example, Hezbollah's al-Manar television station aired a segment in which Imad Mughniyeh's grandson, a child no more than five years old, says he wants to be "in the resistance" and then handles his grandfather's gun.[117]

Hezbollah not only continues to seek vengeance for the 2008 assassination of Mughniyeh. As tensions escalated over Tehran's nuclear weapons program, the group embarked on an international terrorism campaign as part of Iran's larger shadow war with the West. "The last year," the Treasury Department reported in September 2012, "has witnessed Hezbollah's most aggressive terrorist plotting outside the Middle East since the 1990s" (see chapter 12).[118] But let us start at the beginning, Beirut in the 1980s.

Notes

1. Government of New Zealand, "Statement of Case to Designate Lebanese Hizbollah's Military Wing, al-Muqawama al-Islamiyya ('The Islamic Resistance') as a Terrorist Entity," October 11, 2010.

2. Yossi Melman, "Hezbollah, Iran plotted bombing of Israeli embassy in Azerbaijan," *Haaretz* (Tel Aviv), May 31, 2009.

3. Wilhelmsen, "Islamism in Azerbaijan," 731.

4. Sebastian Rotella, "Azerbaijan Seen as New Front in Mideast Conflict," *Los Angeles Times*, May 30, 2009.

5. Government of New Zealand, "Case to Designate Lebanese Hizbollah's Military Wing."

6. Ibid.; Rotella, "Azerbaijan Seen as New Front."

7. Valiyev, "Alleged Iranian and Hezbollah Agents on Trial."

8. Ibid.

9. Ibid.

10. Agence France Presse, "Azerbaijan Jails Two Lebanese for Embassy Plots," October 5, 2009. In an odd twist, the court spokesman said the cell was tied not only to Hezbollah and Iran but to al-Qaeda as well—possibly an attempt to put the plot into the context of the global "War on Terror."

11. "Families of Najmeddin and Karaki Complain about Hezbollah Treatment," As-Seyasseh (Kuwait), February 10, 2010.

12. Ben Hartman, "Azeri-Iranian Prisoner Trade Draws Fire," Jerusalem Post, August 16, 2010.

13. Smadar Peri, "Explosion," Yediot Ahronot (Tel Aviv), February 6, 2009; Gordon Thomas, "Mossad's Most Wanted: A Deadly Vengeance," Independent (London), February 23, 2010.

14. Ian Black, "WikiLeaks Cables: Syria Stunned by Hezbollah Assassination," Guardian (London), December 7, 2010.

15. Ibid.

16. "Qassem: Syrian-Palestinian Agents Tipped Mossad to Murder Mughniyeh," Naharnet (Beirut), March 31, 2010.

17. Palmer Harik, Hezbollah: Changing Face of Terrorism, 173; Martin Kramer, "Imad Who?" Middle East Strategy at Harvard (blog), February 14, 2008.

18. "Hajj Imad Moghnieh Avenue," Hezbollah's official English website, February 18, 2010.

19. "Who Is Hajj Imad Moghniyeh," Hezbollah's official English website, February 12, 2010.

20. Robert F. Worth, "Hezbollah Shrine to Terrorist Suspect Enthralls Lebanese Children," New York Times, September 2, 2008; Agence France Presse, "Hezbollah Shows Off Weaponry in Lebanon 'Tourist Complex,'" Ynetnews (Tel Aviv), May 21, 2010.

21. "Hezbollah Chief Threatens Israel," BBC News, February 14, 2008.

22. Statement of Matthew G. Olsen, Homeland Threats and Agency Responses.

23. "Israel Thwarted 'Major Terror Attack' in Europe," Media Line (New York), January 29, 2009.

24. Daniel Edelson, "Hezbollah Plans Attacks on Israeli Targets in Turkey," Ynetnews (Tel Aviv), October 20, 2009.

25. Sebastian Rotella, "Before Deadly Bulgaria Bombing, Tracks of a Resurgent Iran-Hezbollah Threat," ProPublica and Foreign Policy, July 30, 2012.

26. Yaakov Katz, "Shin Bet Boosts Protection for Officials Traveling Abroad," Jerusalem Post, January 20, 2010.

27. "Sources Close to Hezbollah: Retaliation Linked to 'Divine Opportunity,'" Al Rai al-Aam (Kuwait), February 16, 2010.

28. "Moghniyeh Haunts 'Israel,' Every Day, Every Year," Hezbollah's official English website, February 15, 2010.

29. Roee Nahmias, "Hezbollah Prepares Hit List to Avenge Mughniyeh Killing," Ynetnews (Tel Aviv), September 15, 2010.

30. Robert F. Worth, "More Power for Hezbollah in Lebanon's New Cabinet," *New York Times*, July 12, 2008; UN Security Council, *Security Council Resolution 1701 [on full cessation of hostilities in Lebanon and on extending and strengthening the mandate of the UN Interim Force in Lebanon (UNIFIL) to monitor ceasefire]*, S/RES/1701 (2006), August 11, 2006.

31. "Kofi Annan Dismantling Hizbullah Is Not the Direct Mandate of the UN," *Jerusalem Post*, August 16, 2006; UN secretary-general Ban Ki-moon, press conference with EU Representatives, Brussels, Belgium, August 25, 2006.

32. Author interview, Ludovic Pouille, Paris, March 26, 2008.

33. Author interview with Israeli counterterrorism officials, June 3, 2008.

34. Government of New Zealand, "Case to Designate Lebanese Hizbollah's Military Wing"; Tom Perry, "Beirut Cabinet Challenges Hezbollah, Tension Rises," Reuters, May 6, 2008.

35. Agence France Presse, "Hezbollah Preps South Lebanon for Prisoner Return," *Now Lebanon*, July 12, 2008.

36. Agence France Presse, "Nasrallah Appears in Person at Beirut Celebration," *Al Arabiya News* (Dubai), July 17, 2008.

37. Hassan Nasrallah, "Resistance and Liberation Day," address at Hezbollah rally in the Bekaa Valley, Lebanon, May 29, 2009 (transcript available via *Now Lebanon*, http://nowlebanon.com/NewsArchiveDetails.aspx?ID=96217).

38. Erich Follath, "New Evidence Points to Hezbollah in Hariri Murder," *Der Spiegel* (Hamburg), May 23, 2009.

39. Prosecutor for Special Tribunal for *Lebanon v. Mustafa Badreddine et al.*, STL-11-01/I/PTJ, June 10, 2011; Neil Macdonald, "Who Killed Lebanon's Rafik Hariri?" *CBC News* (Canada), November 21, 2010.

40. Elias Sakr, "Nasrallah Calls Tribunal 'Israeli Project,'" *Daily Star* (Lebanon), July 17, 2010; United Press International, "Nasrallah Calls for STL Boycott," October 29, 2010.

41. Author telephone interview, Dutch intelligence official, March 9, 2010; author interview, Washington, DC, March 25, 2010.

42. Author telephone interview, Dutch intelligence official, March 9, 2010.

43. Macdonald, "Who Killed Lebanon's Rafik Hariri?"

44. "Hezbollah Denies Egypt Accusations," *Al Jazeera* (Doha), April 11, 2009.

45. Israel Intelligence Heritage and Commemoration Center, Intelligence and Terrorism Information Center, "Exposure of a Hezbollah Network in Egypt," April 28, 2009, 2–7.

46. Barak Ravid, "Hezbollah: UN Envoy Biased in Favor of Israel," *Haaretz* (Tel Aviv), May 9, 2009.

47. Statements of Daniel Benjamin and Jeffrey Feltman, *Assessing the Strength of Hezbollah*.

48. Roni Sofer, "Mossad Warns Businessman: Hizbullah May Target You," *Ynetnews* (Tel Aviv), April 23, 2009.

49. Amos Harel, "Hezbollah Planning Attack on Israelis in West Africa," *Haaretz* (Tel Aviv), August 4, 2008.

50. Itamar Eichner, "Israel Foils 5 Attempted Abduction by Hizbullah," *Ynetnews* (Tel Aviv), September 2, 2008.

51. US Department of the Treasury, "Treasury Targets Hizballah Network in Africa," press release, May 27, 2009.

52. "Colombian Sought in 1994 Argentina Attacks," *CNN.com*, May 21, 2009.

53. Nasrallah, "Resistance and Liberation Day."

54. Barak Ravid, "IDF Chief Reported: Hezbollah Was Involved in Attack on Israeli Convoy in Jordan," *Haaretz* (Tel Aviv), December 8, 2010.

55. United Press International, "Israelis Brace for Hezbollah's Revenge," January 25, 2010.

56. "Qassem: Hizbullah Still Seeking Revenge for Mughniyeh's Assassination," *Naharnet* (Beirut), February 14, 2010.

57. Government of New Zealand, "Case to Designate Lebanese Hizbollah's Military Wing."

58. Addis and Blanchard, *Hezbollah: Background and Issues for Congress.*

59. Fadhil Ali, "New Hezbollah Manifesto."

60. US Department of the Treasury, "Treasury Targets Hizballah Financial Network," press release, December 9, 2010.

61. US Department of State, Public Notice 2612, Designation of Foreign Terrorist Organizations, October 2, 1997, 62 Fed. Reg. 195 (Oct. 8, 1997).

62. "Embassy Row," *Washington Times*, December 12, 2001.

63. Addis and Blanchard, *Hezbollah: Background and Issues for Congress*; US Department of the Treasury, "Twin Treasury Actions Take Aim at Hizballah's Support Network," press release, July 24, 2007.

64. "UK Ban on Hezbollah Military Arm," *BBC News*, July 2, 2008.

65. Australian Government, Attorney General's Office, "Hizballah External Security Organisation," May 11, 2011.

66. Government of the Netherlands, Ministry of the Interior, "Annual Report 2004: General Intelligence and Security Service."

67. Government of Canada, "Currently Listed Entities," Public Safety Canada website, last modified August 20, 2012.

68. Israel Ministry of Defense, Terrorist Organization Decrees, www.mod.gov.il/pages/general/teror.asp (רשימה הכרזות וצווים).

69. Statement of James Phillips, *Adding Hezbollah to the EU Terrorist List.*

70. European Parliament, "Texts Adopted at the Sitting of Thursday, 10 March 2005," March 10, 2005.

71. US CIA, "Lebanon's Hizballah," 9.

72. US Department of the Treasury, "Treasury Targets Hizballah for Supporting the Assad Regime," press release, August 10, 2012.

73. Author interview with law enforcement officials, March 11, 2010.

74. Benjamin and Feltman, *Assessing the Strength of Hizballah*; see also statement of Frank Urbancic Jr., *Hezbollah's Global Reach.*

75. Universal Strategy Group, *Directed Study of Lebanese Hezbollah*, produced for the United States Special Operations Command, Research and Analysis Division, October 2010, p. 3.

76. Norton, *Hezbollah: Short History*, 33.

77. Government of New Zealand, "Case to Designate Lebanese Hizbollah's Military Wing."

78. Qassem, *Hizbullah: Story from Within*, 98. Augustus Richard Norton disputes the founding timeline of Hezbollah leadership, but his version of events appears to contradict not only Hezbollah's own account by those of the CIA as indicated in declassified CIA

reports referenced later in this book. According to Norton, "Although its leading members refer to 1982 as the year the group was founded, Hezbollah did not exist as a coherent organization until the mid-1980s. From 1982 through the mid-1980s it was less an organization than a cabal." See Norton, *Hezbollah: Short History*, 34.

79. Sami Hajjar, "Hizballah: Terrorism, National Liberation, or Menace?" Strategic Studies Institute, August 2002, 5.

80. Magnus Ranstrop, "Hezbollah Training Camps in Lebanon," in *The Making of a Terrorist*, ed. James Forest, vol. 2: *Training* (Westport, CT: Praeger, 2005), 252.

81. US CIA, "Lebanon: Prospects for Fundamentalism."

82. Wright, *Sacred Rage*, 95.

83. US CIA, "Lebanon: Prospects for Fundamentalism."

84. Wege, "Hizballah Security Apparatus."

85. Byman, *Deadly Connections*, 82.

86. Qassem, *Hizbullah: Story from Within*, 66.

87. As cited in the Center for Special Studies, Intelligence and Terrorism Information Center special information bulletin, "Hezbollah," June 2003.

88. Viola Gienger, "Iran Gives Weapons, $200 Million a Year to Help Lebanese Hezbollah Re-Arm," *Bloomberg*, April 20, 2010.

89. "Iran Cutting Financial Aid to Hezbollah," *Daily Star* (Beirut), October 12, 2011.

90. Rabil, "Has Hezbollah's Rise Come at Syria's Expense?" 43–51.

91. Hassan Fattah, "Hezbollah Declares Full Support for Syria," *New York Times*, March 6, 2005.

92. "An Open Letter: The Hizballah Program," *Jerusalem Quarterly* 48 (Fall 1988).

93. US CIA, "Lebanon: Prospects for Fundamentalism."

94. "Backgrounder on Hezbollah," *Council on Foreign Relations*.

95. Government of New Zealand, "Case to Designate Lebanese Hizbollah's Military Wing"; Rabil, "Hezbollah: Lebanon's Power Broker."

96. Qassem, *Hizbullah: Story from Within*, 64.

97. Addis and Blanchard, *Hezbollah: Background and Issues for Congress*.

98. Ibid.; Government of New Zealand, "Case to Designate Lebanese Hizbollah's Military Wing"; Qassem, *Hizbullah: Story from Within*, 63–64.

99. Naim Qassem, interview with al-Mustaqbal, December 31, 2000, as cited in Center for Special Studies, Intelligence and Terrorism Information Center special information bulletin, "Hezbollah," June 2003.

100. Rabil, "Hezbollah: Lebanon's Power Broker," 48–49.

101. Deeb, "Shia Movement in Lebanon," 683–98.

102. Hamzeh, "Lebanon's Hizbullah."

103. Qassem, *Hizbullah: Story from Within*, 63.

104. Ibid.

105. International Crisis Group, "Hezbollah: Rebel without a Cause?" Middle East Briefing, July 30, 2003, 3; Rabil, "Hezbollah: Lebanon's Power Broker," 4–8; Ranstorp, "Hezbollah Training Camps in Lebanon," 251.

106. Rabil, "Hezbollah: Lebanon's Power Broker" 4–8.

107. US Department of the Treasury, "Treasury Designates Hizballah Leadership," press release, September 13, 2012.

108. US Department of the Treasury, "Treasury Designates Hizballah Leadership," press release, September 13, 2012; Rabil, "Hezbollah: Lebanon's Power Broker," 6.

109. International Crisis Group, "Hezbollah: Rebel without a Cause?" 3.

110. Qassem, *Hizbullah: Story from Within*, 69–70.

111. Government of New Zealand, "Case to Designate Lebanese Hizbollah's Military Wing."

112. Ibid.

113. Government of Canada,"Currently Listed Entities," *Public Safety Canada*, reviewed December 22, 2010; author interview with Canadian officials, Ottawa, January 12, 2010.

114. Office of the Director of National Intelligence, National Intelligence Council, National Intelligence Estimate, "The Terrorist Threat to the U.S. Homeland," July 2007.

115. Tenet, *National Security Threats to the United States*.

116. United Kingdom, Intelligence and Security Committee, *Annual Report 2005–2006*, Cm 6864 (June 2006) 5.

117. The Middle East Media Research Institute TV Monitor Project, "Family of Slain Hizbullah Terror Mastermind 'Imad Mughniyah, Encourages His Grandson to Follow in His Footsteps," originally aired on al-Manar TV (Lebanon), February 16, 2012.

118. US Department of the Treasury, "Treasury Designates Hizballah Leadership."

2

Branching Out

Targeting Westerners in Lebanon and Beyond

BEIRUT, A CITY BATTERED BY WAR, was experiencing a period of relative calm in fall 1983. US diplomats and soldiers were still coming to terms with the suicide bombing that struck the US embassy in April, and US Marines wore their combat uniforms everywhere they went—even to social events and diplomatic functions. But to the US Marine commander on site, the threat environment seemed to have eased somewhat. The embassy bombing was seen as an outlier event. Marines were free to roam the city and were interacting with Lebanese children in public without fear of ambush.[1] Beirut was under a cease-fire, and hopes were high for Syrian reconciliation talks. It was the quiet before the storm.

In the early hours of October 23, 1983, a young Lebanese man from a Shi'a family awoke, said his morning prayers, and drank tea. In a suburb overlooking the marine barracks, his superiors shared a few final thoughts with him, after which a senior cleric blessed him before he drove off in a yellow Mercedes truck.[2] At 6:22 AM, he rammed the explosive-laden truck through the guard post at the entrance to the US Marine Battalion Headquarters Building in Beirut. The blast decimated the four-story, concrete, steel-reinforced structure—considered one of the strongest buildings in Lebanon at the time. A dense, gray ash cloud engulfed the area as emergency vehicles rushed to the scene.[3] Those soldiers lucky enough to escape serious injury quickly mobilized to rescue their fellow marines, sifting through "dust-covered body parts, moaning wounded and dazed survivors."[4] Seconds later, a nearly identical attack targeted the French Multinational Force (MNF) building less than four miles away.

Lebanon's devastating civil war, which lasted from 1975 to 1990, hardened divisions among the country's various sectarian communities. Against this backdrop, the 1982 Israeli invasion and subsequent occupation of southern Lebanon created the space in which Iranian diplomats and agents could help fashion the unified entity Hezbollah from a motley crew of Shi'a militias and groups. Another turning point in the 1980s involved militants targeting not only fellow Lebanese but also the international forces dispatched as peacekeepers to provide the war-torn country with a measure of security. Over time, Hezbollah and Iran's interests in driving foreign forces out of Lebanon would expand from attacks targeting Western interests in Lebanon to attacks on Western interests abroad.

Over a nine-month period in 1985, the CIA calculated, Iran's Lebanese proxy groups were responsible for at least twenty-four international terrorist incidents.[5] Such targets were popular given Iran's efforts to dissuade countries from arming and supporting Iraq in its ongoing, costly war against the Islamic Republic. Heeding Iran's call to carry out attacks beyond Lebanon's borders, Hezbollah would engage in plots throughout the Middle East. By February 1985 the CIA would warn that "Iranian-sponsored terrorism" presented the greatest threat to US personnel and facilities in the region.[6] Inevitably some of the Hezbollah operatives sent to conduct attacks in places like Kuwait were caught, leading Hezbollah to plot bombings, hijackings, and other operations in places as diverse as Germany and the Republic of the Congo in an effort to secure the release of jailed comrades.

In Lebanon three spectacular attacks targeting US interests over an eighteen-month period defined the group's relationship with the United States for years to come. The US embassy was bombed on April 18, 1983, killing sixty-three, including seventeen Americans. The driver of the explosive-filled van entered the embassy compound, slowed to navigate a sharp left turn down a cobblestone lane, and then accelerated and crashed into the embassy's front wall. The seven-floor embassy complex was engulfed in clouds of black smoke that hid the bodies of Lebanese security guards and American government workers torn apart by the blast. Among the dead were the top American intelligence officials stationed in Lebanon, including the CIA's chief Middle East analyst, Robert C. Ames.[7]

Then came the nearly simultaneous attacks of October 23, 1983, targeting the US Marines and French army barracks, both compounds under the aegis of the Beirut-based Multinational Force sent to Lebanon as peacekeepers to oversee the evacuation of the Palestine Liberation Organization (PLO) from Beirut.[8] Those attacks left 241 Americans and 58 French dead. Less than a year later, on September 20, 1984, the US embassy annex was bombed, killing 24.

The US government had little doubt about who was behind the 1984 attack, even before crime-scene analysis and sensitive source reporting began to flow in. Writing just days after the second embassy bombing, the CIA noted that "an overwhelming body of circumstantial evidence points to the Hizb Allah, operating with Iranian support under the cover name of Islamic Jihad." For one thing, the suicide vehicle-bomb employed had become a trademark of the group. And, the CIA added at the time, "Shia fundamentalists are the only organized terrorists in Lebanon likely to willingly sacrifice their lives in such an attack." Following the bombing, two callers claimed responsibility in the name of Hezbollah's Islamic Jihad Organization (IJO). Several times in the year to follow, the CIA noted, anonymous callers in Beirut warned that the IJO planned to continue attacking US interests.[9]

FBI forensic investigators determined that the marine barracks bombing was not only the deadliest terrorist attack then to have targeted Americans, it was also the single-largest non-nuclear explosion on earth since World War II.[10] Composed of at least 18,000 pounds of explosives—the equivalent of six tons of dynamite—the bomb demolished the four-story building on the fringe of the Beirut Airport campus, leaving behind a crater at least thirteen feet deep and thirty feet wide.[11] So many marines, sailors, and soldiers perished that day that the base ran out of body bags.[12] At the French MNF building, the deaths of fifty-eight French paratroopers marked the French military's highest death toll since the Algerian war ended in 1962.[13] The eight-story building where the paratroopers were staying was literally upended by the blast.

Imad Mughniyeh, the Hezbollah operational leader and terrorist mastermind, and his brother-in-law and cousin, Mustapha Badreddine, reportedly not only watched the marine barracks bombing through binoculars from a perch atop a nearby building overlooking their neighborhood but also coordinated it.[14] In February 1998, Lebanon's highest court announced plans to try Hezbollah's first secretary-general, Subhi al-Tufayli, for his role in the marine barracks bombing, among other crimes. At the time, the CIA assessed that Iran, Syria, and Hezbollah would likely help Tufayli escape so he could not "implicate them in a variety of illegal activities, including terrorist operations against US citizens." He was never tried.[15] Another suspect was Mohammad Hussein Fadlallah, a leader of the Lebanese Shi'a community often described as one of Hezbollah's founding spiritual figures.[16]

Lebanon's Khomeini?

In 1986, the CIA reported that Fadlallah "has long been recognized as the spiritual leader of and political spokesman for Lebanon's Shia Hezbollah." Fadlallah's stature, the CIA added, grew "along with Hizballah's political and military influence." Fadlallah "benefited from and contributed to the growing extremism in the Shia community by his bold sermons attacking Israel and, later, the presence of the Multinational Force in Lebanon." Lebanese Shi'a were inspired by the Iranian revolution to seek an Islamic state in Lebanon, and Fadlallah valued his ties to Iran, in large part because of the significant military, financial, and political assistance Tehran provided to Hezbollah. This assistance helped forge a powerful and potent militant Shi'a group out of several smaller groups.[17]

But over time Fadlallah's relationship with Iran changed. Fadlallah never fully embraced the Iranian revolutionary concept of *velayat-e faqih* (rule of the jurisprudent), which, according to a 1986 US intelligence report, "virtually equates Khomeini with the Mahdi—the 12th Imam who is in occultation."[18] As much as Fadlallah sought an Islamic state in Lebanon, US intelligence analysts concluded he also recognized the need to maintain the country's religious diversity within an Islamic context. But other, more radical voices within Hezbollah, like the up-and-coming security official Hassan Nasrallah, the CIA warned, promoted a maximalist program in which an Islamic republic in Lebanon would presage a pan-Islamic movement spanning the entire Muslim world. "In our view," the analysts wrote in 1988, "Nasrallah does not represent the mainstream of the movement."[19] Four years later Nasrallah would rise to the leadership of Hezbollah, moving the group's mainstream sharply to the right.

Mohammad Hussein Fadlallah was born in Najaf, Iraq, in 1935, but his father was a Shi'a cleric from Lebanon. Educated by some of the day's elite Shi'a scholars, he was ordained a Shi'a clerical jurisprudent by Ayatollah Abu al-Qasim Khoi. In the 1960s he relocated to his ancestral village in Lebanon, where he amassed a large following by ministering to the needs of local Shi'a. He moved to East Beirut in 1966, where he founded a religious center and charity that would serve as the model for future grassroots efforts focusing on religious and charitable institutions. In 1976, when the Nabaa quarter of East Beirut fell to the Christian Phalangist militia, Fadlallah briefly moved to southern Lebanon only to return to the Shi'a slums in Beirut's southern suburbs. Living in the Bir al-Abid quarter, Fadlallah served as the local representative of his Iraqi teacher, Ayatollah Khoi, and founded schools, mosques, and other institutions.[20]

Though he studied in Najaf under Ayatollah Khoi, a major figure in the quietest tradition of Shi'a Islam, Fadlallah was radicalized by his experience in Lebanon. Between the discrimination suffered by Lebanese Shi'a and the hardships of the civil war, Fadlallah increasingly saw the Muslim world, and Shi'a in particular, as a victim of oppression and injustice at the hands of imperialism and Zionism. "The rise of Imam Musa Sadr in the Shia community [in Lebanon] coincided with Fadlallah's gradual conversion to the more activist school," the CIA reported. Sadr preached an explicitly activist message even before the 1979 Iranian revolution, but for Fadlallah the turn away from Ayatollah Khoi's teaching—and Khoi's rejection of clerical involvement in politics—came with the revolution in Tehran and his announcement that Ayatollah Khomeini was the "source of authority."[21]

Back in Lebanon Fadlallah's role in politics was most clearly evidenced by his founding of the Muslim Student Union, a group of Shi'a students inspired by the Iranian revolution that met often in Fadlallah's home. He was also instrumental in the creation of the Lebanese branch of the Dawa Party. Both groups were among the key constituent movements that would later coalesce into Hezbollah.[22]

Ultimately, Fadlallah's transformation from quietest to activist led him to support suicide bombings in Lebanon on religious grounds. "There is no difference between dying with a gun in your hand [and] exploding yourself," he stated. "What is the difference between setting out for battle knowing you will die after killing ten [enemies], and setting out to the field and knowing you will die while killing them?"[23] According to US intelligence analysts, what guided Fadlallah and other Hezbollah supporters as they considered backing violent attacks was "the degree to which the foreign presence threatens the Shia community—and its Hezbollah vanguard." Through Hezbollah, the CIA assessed in 1986, "Fadlallah reveals the darker side of his political ideology, as well as a realistic appraisal of the Lebanese political situation: the use of violence is a necessity."[24]

Fadlallah's exact role in Hezbollah has been debated by scholars and intelligence officials alike. In a 1985 assessment titled "Lebanon's Khomeini: Muhammad Husayn Fadlallah," the CIA reported that "Fadlallah plays an important role in the Hizballah terrorist network. . . . Besides serving as a spiritual leader, he coordinates radical Shia activities in Beirut." Analysts assessed Fadlallah to be particularly dangerous "because he operates successfully as a fundamentalist religious leader and masks his role as [a] coordinator of terrorism."[25] By 1987 the CIA characterized the murky nature of his evolving relationship with Hezbollah as follows: "The key figure in the Islamic fundamentalist movement is Shaykh Muhammad Husayn Fadlallah, who is considered by most Lebanese as the spiritual guide of Hezbollah—the most powerful radical group in Lebanon—although he is not himself part of the organization's leadership."[26] But the very next year the agency appears to have come to a starkly different conclusion, stating that "Fadlallah's emphasis on his religious role is intended to hide his decision making role in Hezbollah."[27]

When it came to actual operations, in August 1986 the CIA concluded that "Fadlallah would have approved of the suicide bombings of the US Marine barracks and similar attacks against the MNF in Beirut because their presence constituted a clear threat to the Hizballah and the Shia community."[28] But former CIA officer Bob Baer insisted Fadlallah offered no such approval. Fadlallah "wasn't our friend, let's get that straight, but that doesn't mean he was a master terrorist. I can guarantee you, and I have seen every bit of intelligence, that Fadlallah had no connection [to the attacks]. He knew the people carrying out the terrorism attacks, but he had no connection in ordering them."[29] Whatever his ties to the Beirut bombings or others who carried them out, by 1986 the CIA predicted, "If the Hezbollah continues on its present path, Fadlallah will be clearly identifiable as the Lebanese equivalent of Khomeini."[30]

But as Fadlallah's relationship with Iran changed, so did his relationship with Hezbollah. Iran did not appreciate Fadlallah's interference in operational planning, such as when Fadlallah prevented Hezbollah from following through on Iranian orders to attack Syrian security forces after their February 1987 takeover of West Beirut.[31] Tehran, in turn, took to circumventing Fadlallah and dealing directly with Hezbollah officials through the Iranian embassies in Beirut and Damascus or through the Islamic Revolutionary Guard Corps (IRGC) contingent in the Bekaa Valley. Iran also established the Council of Lebanon, a nine-member body including the Iranian ambassadors to Beirut and Damascus and the local IRGC commander as well as several Lebanese clerics, but not Fadlallah. Hezbollah's intimate ties to the IRGC were further cemented by its reliance on the IRGC's Sheikh Abdullah Barracks in the Bekaa Valley. The barracks served as Hezbollah's "most important facility, serving as a primary garrison, base, and communications center," even as it remained the IRGC's headquarters in Lebanon. For his part, Fadlallah—whose influence remained significant as the head of the Lebanese Dawa Party, a key constituent element within Hezbollah—took to holding informal meetings with Lebanese Shi'a clerics and security officials as a means of circumventing Iran.[32]

Even as Fadlallah's ties frayed with Iran and likewise Hezbollah, he would always be revered by Lebanese Shi'a. He remained the most prominent Shi'a spiritual leader in Lebanon, having championed the use of violence to expel Western and Israeli forces from the country and dedicated his life to improving the lot of its Shi'a community. His charities remained sources of financial revenue for Hezbollah, as evidenced by US government action targeting such charities over the years, and he continued to have personal relationships with Hezbollah operatives, including a cell caught in Charlotte, North Carolina.

However revered or marginalized Fadlallah might have been, by 1985 someone wanted him dead. On March 8, 1985, a car filled with 250 kilograms of explosives detonated near Fadlallah's home in Bir al-Abid, killing 80 people and wounding more than 250 others.[33] Fadlallah, who was leaving his mosque at the time, escaped unscathed, but several of his bodyguards—including Imad Mughniyeh's brother Jihad—were killed. (Another of Mughniyeh's brothers, Fuad, would be killed in 1994 when a bomb exploded outside a market Fuad owned near Fadlallah's mosque.) Fadlallah's followers hung a banner reading "Made in USA" in front of one of the blown-out buildings.[34]

But was the United States involved? According to *Washington Post* reporter Bob Woodward, former CIA director William Casey admitted on his deathbed to arranging Fadlallah's assassination plot in conjunction with the Saudis, who worked through back channels to fund Lebanese hired guns. Fadlallah "had been connected to all three bombings of American facilities in Beirut," Woodward wrote. "He had to go." But in a twist, Casey's family denied Woodward ever visited Casey in the hospital. The Saudi press office and President Reagan also denied any involvement in the operation.[35] In a letter to the *Washington Post*, responding to an article alleging an "indirect" CIA connection to the car bombing, the agency denied any ties to the attack and cited the findings of an investigation conducted by the US House of Representatives Select Committee on Intelligence (HPSCI), which found "no evidence that any U.S. intelligence agency—any U.S. Government agency—has encouraged or participated in any terrorist activity in Lebanon."[36]

Such a complete exoneration, however, appears to be a stretch too far. In a 2001 interview a former chief of operations at the CIA's Counterterrorism Center explained that following the Beirut bombings the US government helped the Lebanese security service become a more professional intelligence entity in the hope the Lebanese would better deter terrorists on their soil. But according to the former operations chief, the Lebanese service "proved to be totally independent, non-responsive to CIA human rights guidelines. And they went out and killed people." The attempt to kill Fadlallah did not occur with US encouragement or direction, he added, but it was carried out by this CIA-trained Lebanese security service.[37]

In any event, Fadlallah laid blame for the attack squarely on the United States and pledged that Hezbollah would exact revenge by targeting US or other Western interests in countries like Bahrain, Kuwait, or Jordan. Iranian agents were already in place in several Gulf countries, Fadlallah warned, and Lebanese Shi'a agents would be sent to Jordan if an attack there were deemed feasible.[38] By one account the Saudis, who facilitated the back-channel CIA payments to the Lebanese, subsequently paid Fadlallah $2 million to act as an "early warning system for terrorist attacks on Saudi and American facilities." Fadlallah was reportedly never tied to acts of terrorism after this deal. "It was easier to bribe him than to kill him," Saudi Prince Bandar allegedly quipped.[39]

In 1995, a decade after the Bir al-Abid bombing, the United States listed Fadlallah as a Specially Designated Terrorist, presumably for the continued financial ties between his foundations and Hezbollah.[40] But Fadlallah's charities continued to attract US attention. In 2003, for example, Lebanon's finance minister, Fouad Siniora, was prohibited from entering the United States due to a donation he had made to one of Fadlallah's charities. The charity, al-Mabarrat, had an office in Dearborn, Michigan, that the FBI raided in 2007.[41]

The Fox Who Never Sleeps

According to the CIA, Hezbollah's most infamous terrorist mastermind, Imad Mughniyeh, was a Fadlallah disciple. "Fadlallah aims to bring forth defenders of the faith who are indifferent to intimidation, contemptuous of foreign influence, devoted to Shia Islam, and whose self-control borders on fanaticism," according to a 1986 CIA report. "Hajj Imad Mughniyeh, Fadlallah's former bodyguard, spiritual disciple, and Hezbollah's security official," the report continued, "may well be an example of Fadlallah's handiwork—a cunning, resourceful, coldly calculating adversary for whom virtually any act of violence or revenge performed in the name of Shiism is permissible."[42]

Nicknamed "the Fox" and "the One Who Never Sleeps," Mughniyeh reportedly escaped to Iran after watching the bombing of the marine barracks from a rooftop with Mustapha Badreddine. According to the Australian government this trip led to the formal creation of the Islamic Jihad Organization (IJO), or what the Australian and British governments refer to as Hezbollah's External Security Organization (ESO).[43] He returned to Lebanon regularly, traveling on a false Iranian diplomatic passport, according to Lebanese officials. At some point in the late 1980s or early 1990s, once he was tied by name to the Beirut bombings and kidnappings, he reportedly moved his family to Tehran.[44]

Little is known about Imad Fayez Mughniyeh's early life. According to former CIA officer Robert Baer, "Mughniyeh systematically had all traces of himself removed. He erased himself. He had his records removed from high school, and his passport application was stolen. There are no civil records in Lebanon with his name in them."[45] Yet we know that he was born in the village of Tir Dibba in southern Lebanon in 1962 and that his family fled to the slums of south Beirut in the wake of Israeli attacks targeting Palestinian militants in the late 1970s. Growing up in the Ayn al-Dilbah neighborhood near the Beirut airport—within eyesight of the marine barracks he would later help destroy—he was deeply affected by the tumultuous times. Syria invaded Lebanon when he was thirteen years old. Five years later, when he was an engineering student at the American University of Beirut, Israel invaded. The following year the Israeli army laid siege to Beirut in an effort to expel the PLO from Lebanon, by which time Mughniyeh was already active in Yasser Arafat's Fatah militia.[46]

A clearer picture of Mughniyeh's early years would emerge from the unlikely city of Buenos Aires, where the Hezbollah mastermind was indicted for his role in the 1994 bombing of a Jewish community center.[47] Argentine prosecutors would learn of the American University graduate's reported fluency in Arabic, English, Farsi, French, and German and his training by Arafat's Fatah movement during Lebanon's civil war. Mughniyeh later became a member of Arafat's personal security detail, Force 17. According to the CIA, "Many Hezbollah leaders began their careers as Fatah militants before the Israeli invasion in 1982."[48] That year, when the PLO left Lebanon, Mughniyeh joined Hezbollah.[49] He quickly became a central player in the group's most sensitive activities. By 1982 or 1983, he reportedly joined Fadlallah's Muslim Student Union, described as the student branch of the Dawa Party, and soon served as Fadlallah's bodyguard. Not long after he played direct roles in the 1983–84 bombings of the US embassy and marine barracks in Beirut.[50]

Appointed to Hezbollah's Majlis al-Shura, or consultative council, in 1986, he would serve in multiple security posts and ultimately as chief of Hezbollah's IJO, overseeing Hezbollah kidnapping operations together with Abdelhadi Hamadi and spearheading the group's overseas operations in coordination with Iranian security and intelligence services.[51] Not one to shy away from serving on the front lines, Mughniyeh was reported by the CIA to have served as a military commander in southern Lebanon as well.[52] According to the former Middle East unit chief in the FBI's Counterterrorism Section, Mughniyeh ran Hezbollah's "terrorist side—not the guerilla arm, the terrorist arm."[53] A European Hezbollah expert described Mughniyeh as "an architect who unleashes violence on special occasions."[54] Together with Hassan Nasrallah, Mughniyeh represented the radical wing of Hezbollah. When Hezbollah first engaged in Lebanese politics, the CIA speculated that if such a move came at the expense of militancy, more radical elements like Nasrallah or Mughniyeh could split off.[55] But Hezbollah averted such an outcome not only by maintaining its military and terrorist activities even as it engaged in politics but also because Nasrallah's rise to the position of secretary-general ensured the group would remain on the radical track.

While Hezbollah's relationship with Syria would later become very close, in the 1980s it was often contentious. In 1987, Mughniyeh and other senior Hezbollah security officials were recalled to Tehran to prevent their capture following Hezbollah attacks against Syrian forces in West Beirut. Both Imad Mughniyeh and Abdelhadi Hamadi reportedly underwent training while in Iran as they waited for the security situation in Lebanon to improve. That likely took some time, considering Syria issued a warrant for Mughniyeh's arrest in 1988.[56]

Senior Hezbollah operatives would seek refuge in Iran for security reasons many more times over the years. For example, Mughniyeh and Hamadi fled to Iran twice in 1994, first after Israeli commandos kidnapped Hezbollah ally Mustafa Dirani in May and then after Mughniyeh's brother, Fuad, was assassinated in December.[57] Mughniyeh played a central role in the Hezbollah terror campaign carried out in Lebanon and Europe in the 1980s. Indeed, Mughniyeh and a small group of his lieutenants were the "senior commanders of the Hezbollah operations in Europe."[58]

Over the years the Fox would evade capture on several occasions. The first such evasion reportedly came in Paris in November 1985, when officials intercepted a voice frequency sample of Mughniyeh, who was tracked to a luxury hotel on Paris's Champs Elysées, just around the corner from the US embassy. That same month, a US grand jury issued a sealed indictment against Mughniyeh and three other Hezbollah operatives for their roles in the hijacking of TWA flight 847 five months earlier. Why

Mughniyeh was in Paris remains unknown, though speculation abounds that his presence involved negotiations over the release of four French hostages. Mughniyeh was traveling on a false identity, but the CIA provided French officials with a copy of the passport he was using. Instead of detaining him, French intelligence officials reportedly met Mughniyeh several times over a six-day period and allowed him to leave the country in return for the release of a French hostage.[59]

A decade would pass before US intelligence would get another opportunity to capture Mughniyeh. In 1995, intelligence indicated that Mughniyeh was traveling under an assumed name on a flight from Khartoum to Tehran that was scheduled to make a stop in Jeddah, Saudi Arabia. US officials asked their Saudi counterparts to detain Mughniyeh, which they did not do, while FBI agents jumped on a plane to arrest him. But Saudi officials denied the FBI plane landing rights, allowing the Fox to slip away once more.[60] The following year, a month after Hezbollah helped its Saudi affiliate bomb the Khobar Towers military barracks near Dharan, Saudi Arabia, information arose suggesting Mughniyeh was aboard the *Ibn Tufail*, a boat sailing in the Arabian Gulf. Navy ships trailed the *Ibn Tufail* while a team of navy SEALs prepared a snatch-and-grab operation to be executed the following day off the coast of Qatar. The operation was called off, however, when senior American decision makers deemed the intelligence insufficient to warrant such a risky operation.[61]

A decade earlier, in June 1985, the now infamous photo of Mughniyeh holding a gun to the head of the pilot of hijacked TWA flight 847 had made Hezbollah a household name (see chapter 3). Although it was only in the weeks following the September 11 attacks that Mughniyeh was added to the FBI's new list of Most Wanted Terrorists, in large part based on the TWA hijacking indictment, US intelligence agencies were already keenly focused on him for his role in the Beirut bombings and the kidnappings that followed. US intelligence reports from the 1980s through at least 1991 refer to him as "hostage holder Imad Mughniyeh" and as "leader of the Islamic Jihad Organization (IJO)."[62] By the time he was killed in a Damascus car bombing in February 2008, Mughniyeh not only was considered the second most important figure in Hezbollah after Secretary-General Hassan Nasrallah, he was believed to simultaneously hold a formal commission in the IRGC.[63]

Mughniyeh frequently consulted with Iranian intelligence and IRGC officials, according to US intelligence sources. An Iranian official sat on the Hezbollah Shura Council in 1992, and around the same time two Iranians—including the deputy commander of the IRGC—were members of Hezbollah's military committee. The IRGC ran Hezbollah's intelligence planning section until 1989, when a Lebanese candidate was finally deemed capable of doing the job. Over the years, senior IRGC Qods Force and Ministry of Intelligence and Security (MOIS) officials would periodically visit Lebanon to work with Hezbollah and assess the group's security.[64] And when Mughniyeh wanted to target US interests, he would seek Iranian consent. For example, in December 1991 the CIA worried over intelligence suggesting that Hezbollah planned to attack US interests in Beirut in the ensuing weeks. Iran would likely oppose more Hezbollah kidnappings, the CIA assessed, since Tehran wanted to preserve its political capital from the recent release of some hostages.

However, the agency warned, "It is possible that Tehran has approved low-level terrorist operations against US interests—such as sniper attacks—to allow Hezbollah elements to vent their animosity toward the United States. These Hezbollah elements may include former hostage holder Imad Mughniyeh." Other sources, the CIA added, suggested Hezbollah was planning a car bomb attack targeting the US ambassador, attacks targeting CIA officers in Beirut, and a plot to attach an explosive device to an embassy employee's car or nearby vehicle.[65]

Solid Gold Intelligence

Two decades after the marine barracks bombing, a civil suit brought against the Islamic Republic of Iran by the family members of the soldiers killed and wounded in the attack established that the bombings were carried out by Hezbollah with Syrian and Iranian oversight. According to the testimony of former US military officials, two days after the bombing—on October 25, 1983—the chief of naval intelligence notified Adm. James Lyons, then deputy chief of naval operations, of an intercepted message from September 26, 1983, just a few weeks before the barracks bombing. Sent from MOIS in Tehran, the message instructed the Iranian ambassador in Damascus, Ali Akbar Mohtashemi, to contact Husayn al-Musawi, the leader of Islamic Amal (a key precursor to Hezbollah), and to direct him to "take spectacular action against the United States Marines" and the multinational coalition in Lebanon.[66] In the words of Col. Timothy Geraghty, commander of the marine unit in Beirut at the time of the bombing, "If there was ever a 24-karat gold document, this was it. This is not something from the third cousin of the fourth wife of Muhammad the taxicab driver."[67] US signals intelligence had caught Iranian officials instructing a Hezbollah leader to carry out an attack targeting US Marines in Lebanon, but the military bureaucracy prevented that information from getting where it needed to be in time to prevent the attack.[68]

Lawyers for the families in the marine barracks bombing suit found a former Hezbollah member—referred to as Mahmoud—who testified that Ambassador Mohtashemi followed orders and contacted an Islamic Revolutionary Guardsman named Kanani, who commanded the IRGC's Lebanon headquarters.[69] Imad Mughniyeh and his brother-in-law Mustafa Badreddine were named operation leaders after a meeting that included Kanani, Musawi, and then–Hezbollah security official Hassan Nasrallah. Planning meetings were held at the Iranian embassy in Damascus, often chaired by Ambassador Mohtashemi, who helped establish Hezbollah in the first instance.[70]

The operatives involved in the attack monitored the US Marine barracks for months, noting delivery times and routes, the marines' late wake-up on Sunday mornings, and even the color of the delivery trucks.[71] The red van that slammed into the French barracks was identical to a delivery van used by a vegetable vendor in the neighborhood.[72] The vehicle to be used in the US barracks attack was fitted with explosives, likely at or near the shared Hezbollah-IRGC headquarters at the Sheikh Abdullah Barracks in the Bekaa Valley, but was delivered to Beirut only a few days before the attack.[73] Ten days after the bombings of the US and French installations, a similar truck bombing targeted the Israeli military headquarters building in Tyre, killing twenty-nine Israelis and injuring more than thirty, the second attack on that facility.

A 1983 Department of Defense report on the October bombing revealed that US forces in Lebanon were aware of the threat. The MNF's intelligence support issued more than a hundred reports warning of terrorist bombing attacks between May and November 1983. But while there was a lot of noise, the US investigation concluded, the reports held no specific intelligence that could have successfully been acted upon to thwart the attack. The assessment continued: "The fact that political and sectarian affinity is reinforced by family and clan solidarity, particularly among radical Shiites, makes timely intelligence penetration problematic at best."[74] The Defense Department report was released just two months after the October 1983 marine barracks attack. But before the lessons could be learned, Hezbollah struck again.

Attacking the US Embassy . . . Again

At 11:30 AM on September 20, 1984, a truck carrying more than a thousand pounds of explosives ripped off the front of the new, five-story US embassy building in Beirut, killing twenty-four and injuring scores more. The embassy had opened just weeks earlier, following the destruction of the previous embassy in April 1983. The US ambassador, although buried under the rubble, escaped with only minor injuries.[75]

Islamic Jihad again claimed responsibility in a telephone call "for blowing up a car rigged with explosives which was driven by one of our suicide commandos into a housing compound for the employees of the American Embassy in Beirut." The operation underscored Hezbollah's pledge "not to allow a single American to remain on Lebanese soil." The caller also warned people "to stay away from American institutions and gathering points, especially the embassy," since more attacks could follow.[76]

The new embassy had been described as Fortress America, a supremely secure facility supposedly immune to the kinds of attacks that flattened the previous embassy and marine barracks.[77] But the embassy had been hurriedly relocated from West Beirut to the city's northeast fringe. The protective steel gate had not yet been installed, and rooftop cameras were not yet activated.[78] Now, with the six-week-old embassy evacuated, the ambassador's residence in East Beirut became the temporary embassy, complete with antiaircraft guns and a no-fly zone above. Gradually, the American diplomatic corps left Beirut by way of helicopters to Cyprus. A year after the second embassy bombing, Lebanon held new elections, by which point the once-strong force of 190 American diplomatic officials had shriveled to 6.[79]

There is no question that Iran directed the Beirut bombings. According to the testimony of a former Hezbollah member, the suicide bomber who drove the truck that October morning was Iranian. "The Iranians took no chance that Hezbollah in its formative stages would not cooperate and instead had the truck actually driven by an Iranian," lawyers concluded based on the Hezbollah member's testimony.[80]

FBI agents investigating the 1984 embassy bombing found traces of pentaerythritol tetranitrate (PETN) explosive on a piece of concrete rubble at the scene. The FBI determined the PETN was produced in Iran, one of several factors that led a US federal judge to find Iran "liable" for the bombings in a 2003 ruling.[81]

Between 1983 and 1988, Iran's government spent $50 million to $150 million financing terrorist organizations in the Near East, focusing its efforts on Lebanon in order to spur the withdrawal of Western forces from the country.[82] In 1983, according to testimony, Hezbollah acted "almost entirely . . . under the order of the Iranians and [was] financed almost entirely by the Iranians."[83]

Prowling for Hostages

Although it ultimately became a strong, unified movement, Hezbollah in its early years resembled a secretive cluster of Shi'a militant groups more than it did a structured sociopolitical organization.[84] Various Shi'a militant cells or factions took Westerners hostage, as did other groups not affiliated with Hezbollah. The tradition of kidnapping in Lebanon runs deep, as explained by one Lebanon watcher: "There was no 'kidnapping-central' but a cabal of militants, some certainly linked to Hezbollah, others in various other gangs and groups, including some that were in the hostage business, selling and trading hostages for profit."[85]

According to Magnus Ranstorp, who wrote the definitive work on Hezbollah and the Western hostage crisis, decisions relating to hostage taking had to be cleared first by the organization's highest leadership command, despite the many competing sectarian militias, the clerical factionalism within many of these groups (including Hezbollah), and the fact that some abductions were carried out by specific clans for their own interests. Such clearance helped Hezbollah ensure that "all acts of hostage-taking also coincided with the collective interest of the organization as a whole," no matter who carried them out—or why.[86] Once hostages were captured, however, different Hezbollah clans or family factions had significant input on their release. "Hezbollah does not speak with one voice on this issue," the CIA noted in 1991. "Last-minute maneuvering and reversals by individual [Hezbollah] leaders appear to have derailed agreements on more than one occasion." In the context of one prisoner swap effort, the CIA noted that Mughniyeh "had been uncharacteristically quiet during this latest round of hostage-related activity, so he presumably is not opposed to it."[87] The reference to Mughniyeh, never known for speaking publicly, being "uncharacteristically quiet" suggests that US intelligence had other means of listening to his chatter.

The "core group of kidnappers of Western hostages," later investigation and the testimony of former hostages would reveal, involved only "a dozen men from various Hezbollah clans, most notably the Mughniyeh and Hamadi clans."[88] This helps explain why Western intelligence found it so difficult to crack what they assumed were larger and disparate kidnapping networks. Based on familial and religious bonds and personally and ideologically committed to Hezbollah, this small band of kidnappers made itself very difficult to infiltrate. At the time, however, the CIA was busy sorting out what it described as "the numerous quasi-independent Shia funda-mentalist gangs that prowl the streets of West Beirut."[89]

"Hizbullah has never been involved in or responsible for any of these [kidnapping] incidents," Sheikh Naim Qassem, Hezbollah's deputy chief, wrote in 2005.[90] In fact the group diverted attention from itself by using a variety of aliases or fictitious names to claim responsibility in calls to media outlets. The ruse enabled Hezbollah to avoid retaliation and confuse investigators.[91] Released hostages later revealed that their own kidnappers had kidnapped others using different cover names.[92] The aliases most frequently used to claim responsibility for the kidnappings were Islamic Jihad, the Revolutionary Justice Organization, the Oppressed on Earth, the Holy Fighters for Freedom, and the Defense of the Free People.[93]

By 1984, Lebanon had the highest number of international terrorist incidents in the world, an unenviable honor it would hold for four consecutive years.[94] Between Janu-ary 1982 and August 1988 approximately 40 percent of international kidnappings worldwide took place in Lebanon. Hezbollah claimed responsibility under various cover names for fifty-one of these ninety-six kidnappings, which targeted American, French, British, Soviet, West German, Saudi, Cypriot, Kuwaiti, Swiss, Iraqi, and In-dian citizens.[95] Beirut, the CIA concluded in 1987, had become a "terrorist Mecca" serving as a "key terrorist headquarters" in the region.[96]

The kidnappings drew attention to the Shi'a cause but also convinced many for-eigners to leave or avoid Lebanon, fulfilling one of Hezbollah's primary objectives of "expel[ling] the Americans[,] the French and their allies definitely from Leba-non, putting an end to any colonialist entity on our land."[97] In the process the West began to view Hezbollah "as a crazy and fanatic religious group, bent on martyrdom through suicide-operations, and engaged in the random abduction of foreigners, under the assumed strict control and direction of Iran's clerical establishment."[98]

Throughout the 1980s, Hezbollah's actions were influenced, if not directed, by the Iranian regime. In fact the organization's founding letter states, "We obey the orders of one leader, wise and just, that of our tutor and *faqih* (jurist) who fulfills all the nec-essary conditions: Ruhollah Musawi Khomeini. God save him!"[99] Over time Hezbol-lah became somewhat more independent from its state sponsor, but at the time the group was run as a virtual extension of Iran's Revolutionary Guards. David Jacobsen, the head of the American University of Beirut Medical Center, kidnapped in 1985, would later recall that after he had reached out to Fadlallah in a "private initiative," Fadlallah had explained that "only the Iranian chargé d'affaires could release those held." Fadlallah described the Hezbollah captors as "nothing more than the Iranian 'hunting dogs.'"[100]

In June 1986, the US government got its first direct acknowledgment from an Ira-nian official that Tehran held sway, if not complete control, over the kidnappers. An American envoy asked Ali Akbar Hashemi Rafsanjani, then–speaker of the Iranian parliament (Majlis), "what sign of sincerity Iran required from the United States" for Tehran to use its influence over Hezbollah to win the release of US hostages. After launching into a tirade against US policy, Rafsanjani implied that Iran would consider future discussions with the United States if Washington adopted "a new atti-tude." In a memo summarizing international efforts to secure the release of US hostages in Lebanon, the CIA director's "Hostage Location Task Force" concluded that the meeting was "noteworthy in that Rafsanjani acknowledged that Tehran had influence with the captors."[101]

And yet that influence was limited, as the chief of the CIA's Office of Near Eastern and South Asian Analysis noted in a memo penned two years later. "We continue to believe that Iran is unable unilaterally to order the release of Western hostages and must bargain with Hezbollah on the terms of any release." The key, the memo concluded, would be sweetening the deal for the key hostage holder, Imad Mughniyeh. "Mughniyeh," the CIA assessed, "may be willing to release one or a few U.S. hostages in exchange for ransom money or Iranian promises of assistance in future operations against Kuwait."[102] The CIA understood the central role Mughniyeh still played in the hostage drama and the limitations of Iran's influence over him when it came to his prized bargaining chips. "The last two hostages who have been freed were held by Imad Mughniyeh's Islamic Jihad Organization (IJO)," the CIA noted in March 1991. "Mughniyeh most likely would resent Iranian efforts to secure the release of another IJO hostage at this time, viewing any such request as an Iranian effort to draw down his pool of hostages first."[103]

The adoption of kidnapping reflected the judgment that taking Western hostages provided Hezbollah—and, by extension, Iran—significant leverage over Western governments. Often, Hezbollah kidnapped Westerners in order to pressure the hostages' governments to secure the release of incarcerated Shi'a. In other cases hostages were taken as a means to pressure Western governments against funding or arming Iraq in its war against Iran. They later became pawns in the arms-for-hostages Iran-Contra affair. When kidnappings failed to sufficiently pressure foreign governments or secure a desired response, Hezbollah would threaten hostages' lives to increase pressure on their governments to negotiate for their release.[104] Nonetheless, only five Westerners died or were executed while held hostage by Hezbollah between 1982 and 1992.[105] According to former hostage David Jacobsen, when fellow captive William Buckley—the CIA station chief in Beirut—died in captivity, reportedly from drowning in his own lung fluids as a result of torture, it "really shook up our kidnappers."[106]

Late 1983 saw a lull in kidnappings over several months, until early 1984, possibly because Hezbollah was distracted by its efforts to expand beyond the Bekaa Valley to southern Lebanon and Beirut. And what operational resources the young movement had available were being used to carry out the more spectacular Beirut bombings. Many more kidnappings would follow, but not before Hezbollah and other pro-Iran Shi'a militants carried out a string of attacks on Western targets in Kuwait at Iran's behest. Those events would shape the Western hostage crisis in Lebanon for years to come.

The Kuwait 17

On December 12, 1983, terrorists carried out a series of seven coordinated bombings in Kuwait, all within two hours, at the American and French embassies, the Kuwaiti airport, near the Raytheon Corporation's grounds, at a Kuwait National

Petroleum Company oil rig, and at a government-owned power station. The seventh
explosive, outside a post office, was defused.[107] Six people were killed and some
eighty-seven wounded in the attacks.[108] The string of bombings was executed at
Iran's behest by Lebanese and Iraqi Shi'a militants.[109] In a 1986 report the CIA assessed that while Iran's support for terrorism was meant to further its national interest, including dissuading Kuwait from supporting Iraq militarily in the Iran-Iraq
War, this support also stemmed from the clerical regime's perception "that it has a religious duty to export its Islamic revolution and to wage, by whatever means, a constant struggle against the perceived oppressor states."[110] The Kuwait bombings
were the first in a long chain of such attacks.

   In these attacks, senior Hezbollah operatives, joined by their Iraqi compatriots,
acted in the explicit service of Iran rather than in the group's immediate interests. But
in the aftermath of the bombings, Hezbollah would carry out many more attacks, at
home and abroad, seeking the release of members jailed in Kuwait. Though he later
denied the group played any role in the kidnappings of Westerners in Lebanon, Hezbollah deputy chief Naim Qassem once acknowledged that the Kuwait episode "was
the starting point for the idea of hostages, to impose pressure for the release of prisoners in Israel and elsewhere."[111]

   The bombings took Kuwaiti officials by surprise, but the damage could have been
much worse had the bombs been properly wired. As it happened, faulty engineering
prevented three quarters of the explosives planted at the American embassy compound from detonating, saving many lives.[112] Shoddy planning also reduced the de-
structiveness of the attacks: a truck carrying 200 gas cylinders primed to explode at
the National Petroleum Company site went off 150 yards from a refinery and just a
few yards shy of a pile of flammable chemicals. More adept operational planning
might also have resulted in the destruction of Kuwait's primary water-desalination
plant, located within the premises, leaving the desert nation nearly devoid of fresh
water.[113]

   Credit for the bombings went to the Iraqi-based Dawa group, as well as the IJO,
which claimed responsibility in a call to a French news agency in Beirut. By then,
Islamic Jihad was already recognized as a cover name Hezbollah used in such calls.[114]
Dawa, a group of Iraqi Shi'a established in 1968, was one element in an amorphous,
Iran-sponsored Shi'a network particularly active in and around Lebanon in the mid-
1980s. Still composed primarily of Iraqis, Dawa carried out most of its activity, and
was headquartered, in Iran.[115] Signaling the intimate links between Dawa and Hezbollah, Sheikh Subhi al-Tufayli, one of Hezbollah's founders, acknowledged that
"Hezbollah is in essence the Dawa party."[116] Fadlallah, meanwhile, headed the Lebanese branch of the Dawa Party.

   Six days after the attacks the Kuwaiti government accused twelve Shi'a—nine
Iraqis and three Lebanese—of playing a role in the plot. Abdul Aziz Hussein, then
Kuwait's minister of state for cabinet affairs, identified all twelve as Dawa members,
including the operative who drove the explosives-laden truck into the US embassy
compound, Raad Mouchbil.[117] The discovery of one of Mouchbil's thumbs—the
sole piece of his body still intact following the explosion—provided just enough

evidence for Kuwaiti authorities to apprehend, and eventually try, some of his accomplices.[118]

While the bombings appear to have been orchestrated by Dawa, the group had called on the expertise of the three arrested Lebanese operatives. One, Hussein al-Sayed Yousef al-Musawi, was the first cousin of Husayn al-Musawi, leader of Islamic Amal (which merged with Hezbollah).[119] Another was Mustapha Badreddine, Imad Mughniyeh's brother-in-law and cousin, who was in Kuwait under the Christian-sounding cover name Fuad Saab. The last was Azam Khalil Ibrahim.[120]

In total twenty-five suspects were charged (four in absentia).[121] Ultimately they were charged with "belonging to a group bent on demolishing the basic values of society through criminal means," charges diluted significantly from the initial accusations of membership in the banned Dawa organization or practicing terrorism.[122] Despite multiple references to "another state," the charges made no explicit mention of Iran.[123] For its part, Iran denied any involvement in the plots, insisting that "attribution of these attacks to Iran is part and parcel of a comprehensive plot by the United States of America and its agents against the Islamic revolution."[124]

After a six-week trial the court handed down six death sentences (three in absentia), seven life sentences, and seven sentences of five to ten years in jail. Excepting the five found not guilty and the three convicted in absentia, seventeen convicted terrorists were jailed in Kuwait—thus the moniker "the Kuwait 17," or the "Dawa 17."[125] Mughniyeh and the IJO would spend the next few years carrying out kidnappings, hijackings, and other attacks aimed at securing the release of the Kuwait 17, Badreddine in particular. When a Kuwaiti court sentenced Badreddine to death in March 1984, Hezbollah threatened to kill some of its hostages if the sentence was carried out (it was not).[126] Discussing prospects for the release of US hostages, a CIA memo noted that "Mughniyeh has always linked the fate of his American hostages to release of 17 Shia terrorists in Kuwait, and we have no indication he has altered this demand."[127]

"Wild, Wild West Beirut"

By the spring of 1985, US intelligence described West Beirut's transformation from a commercial and cultural hub of the Arab world—the Paris of the Middle East—into "a lawless militarized zone contested by confessional and ideological factions." The CIA titled an analytical report on the subject *Wild, Wild West Beirut*, noting that "turf battles, terrorism, rampant street crime, and the lack of central authority have made the city extremely dangerous for both local residents and foreigners."[128]

Hezbollah's successful expansion from the Bekaa Valley into Beirut, at Amal's expense, enabled the group to carry out kidnappings and other plots in the city with greater ease. Hezbollah gunmen had become so comfortable in the city that they were notorious for harassing women wearing Western-style clothing and raiding restaurants that served alcohol. Noting the lack of security, poor economic conditions, prospects of unemployment, and social alienation facing many young Lebanese men, especially in the Shi'a communities, intelligence analysts correctly assessed that "the strength of the Hezbollah fundamentalists in West Beirut is likely to grow."[129]

Against this backdrop, the Western hostage crisis stretched on until 1992, with Westerners and, on occasion, other foreigners being abducted in stages that, in retrospect, can be loosely tied to specific Hezbollah causes. Magnus Ranstorp breaks down the Western hostage crisis into nine stages, starting with Hezbollah's expansion from the Bekaa Valley into Beirut and southern Lebanon and its terrorist operations aimed at ridding the country of foreign forces and ending with the release of the last American hostages, a closer relationship with Iran based on converging interests, and the election of Hassan Nasrallah as secretary-general. Each of these periods focused on some particular goal, though certain themes—like securing the freedom of Shi'a militants jailed abroad or kicking Israeli and Western forces out of Lebanon—remained constant. For example, the abduction of CIA Beirut station chief William Buckley in March 1984, as well as several other kidnappings in the second half of 1984, was a direct response to the arrest and sentencing of the Kuwait 17 bombers.[130]

To be sure, some kidnappings were carried out by Hezbollah factions or clans—each with its own alias—in an opportunistic fashion to secure, for example, the release of a jailed relative. Others involved poorly trained muscle to grab people off the streets; several people were kidnapped because they were mistaken for American or French citizens. Captors assigned to guard the Western prisoners were often "unsophisticated but fanatic Muslims," as one captive put it.[131] In contrast, the abduction of William Buckley indicated careful target selection and operational surveillance, likely supported by Iranian intelligence. According to one account, some of the intelligence Hezbollah used to identify Buckley as the local CIA chief was provided by Iran based on materials seized during the US embassy takeover in Iran in 1979.[132]

As for Buckley, he was sent to Beirut in 1983 to set up a new CIA station after the previous one had been decimated in the April US embassy bombing.[133] His kidnapping was a devastating blow to the CIA. "Bill Buckley being taken basically closed down CIA intelligence activities in the country," commented one senior CIA official.[134] But the CIA had adequate sources to determine within six months that Hezbollah was holding Buckley.[135] For CIA director William Casey, finding Buckley was an absolute priority, the CIA official added. "It drove him almost to the ends of the earth to find ways of getting Buckley back, to deal with anyone in any form, in any shape, in any way, to get Buckley back. He failed at that, but it was a driving motivation in Iran-Contra. We even dealt with the devil . . . the Iranians, who sponsored Hezbollah, who sponsored the kidnapping and eventual murder of Bill Buckley."[136]

A year after Buckley's abduction, Hezbollah kidnapped American journalist Terry Anderson, with Islamic Jihad claiming responsibility in a call to a Western press agency. The caller issued a "final warning to foreigners in the Lebanese capital against involving themselves in subversive activities." Like Buckley's, this kidnapping was clearly planned. Anderson was with an Associated Press (AP) photographer at the time of his abduction, but only he was taken. In addition, Anderson had been followed by a green Mercedes for two days prior to the kidnapping, suggesting he had been subjected to preoperational surveillance. The Islamic Jihad claim of responsibility was ultimately confirmed by the CIA, proving somewhat of an embarrassment for Hezbollah. Despite their earlier surveillance, the kidnappers were apparently unaware that Anderson had interviewed Sheikh Fadlallah at his home earlier that day. Fadlallah told the AP he considered the kidnapping a matter of "my own honor," suggesting that his hosting of the reporter would have precluded his initiating or approving of his abduction.[137] After 2,454 days in captivity, Anderson was ultimately released in December 1991.

Frustrated with its inability to achieve its goals through hijackings and kidnappings, Hezbollah sent pictures of six hostages to several Beirut newspapers in May 1985. "All of the hostages in the photographs looked fairly healthy," the CIA noted, "except U.S. embassy political officer Buckley who has been held longer than any of the others."[138] A year after Buckley's capture, the agency was still fiercely protective of his cover—even in its own, classified reporting—for fear that revealing his CIA affiliation would cause him harm. This assessment was right except that Hezbollah already knew he was a CIA official—indeed, this was why he was targeted. Buckley was tortured, reportedly by both Lebanese and Iranian interrogators.[139] Hezbollah reportedly sent three different videotapes of Buckley being tortured to the CIA, one more harrowing than the next.[140] Another hostage, David Jacobsen, later recounted that Buckley occupied a cell separated from his own by a thin wall. "It was apparent that he was very sick. I could hear him retching between coughs." Another hostage held with the two men recalled Buckley hallucinating. Once, in the bathroom, Buckley apparently announced, "I'll have my hot cakes with blueberry syrup now."[141]

By some accounts Buckley was moved through the Bekaa Valley and transferred to Iran; others say he was buried in an unmarked grave in Lebanon.[142] Islamic Jihad announced it had killed Buckley in October 1985, but fellow hostages would later reveal he had died months earlier as a result of the torture he endured, possibly at the hands of Imad Mughniyeh himself.[143]

Once taken hostage, American, French, and British citizens were held for an average of 782 days.[144] The first few months of captivity were generally spent in total isolation, with hostages reportedly chained to a wall or a bed and blindfolded. Some former hostages said they had been beaten. They also reported very poor sanitary conditions, with cells located in the cellars of houses in Dahiya in the southern Shi'a suburb of Beirut, or in the Sheikh Abdallah barracks near Baalbek. Captives were frequently transferred from one location to another, hidden in coffins for the journey to prevent their discovery and rescue.[145]

Not all kidnapping plots went smoothly. On September 30, 1985, four Soviet diplomats were taken hostage in Beirut in an attempt to pressure the Soviet Union to end pro-Syrian activity against an Islamic movement in Tripoli, evacuate its Beirut embassy, and retract all Soviet citizens from Lebanon's capital.[146] In response to these demands, levied by Islamic Jihad and the so-called Islamic Liberation Organization, more than half of the Soviet diplomatic staff withdrew from Beirut over the course of a month.[147] During that time one of the Soviet hostages was shot in the head and his body dumped near a stadium in West Beirut.[148] In response, the KGB reportedly mobilized its clandestine Alpha counterterrorism unit and, with the help of local Druze informants, identified the Hezbollah kidnappers, their clans, and their families.[149] From this point on, accounts of the secretive operation vary, though each reveals the KGB's merciless efforts to retrieve the three remaining Soviet hostages.

In one retelling, the KGB kidnapped a relative of the hostage-taking organization's chief, cut off the relative's ear, and sent it to his family.[150] In another, the Alpha unit abducted one of the kidnapper's brothers and sent two of his fingers home to his family in separate envelopes.[151] Still another version has the Soviet operatives kidnapping a dozen Shi'a, one of whom was the relative of a Hezbollah leader. The relative was castrated and shot in the head, his testicles stuffed in his mouth, and his body shipped to Hezbollah with a letter promising a similar fate for the eleven other Shi'a captives if the three Soviet hostages were not released.[152] The final scene could not have been better scripted: "That evening, the three diplomats, emaciated, unshaven, barefoot, and wearing dirty track suits, appeared at the gates of the Soviet embassy."[153] Never again would Hezbollah or any other militant Shi'a group target Soviet officials in Lebanon. As for the Islamic Liberation Organization, the group never resurfaced, feeding suspicions that it never existed in the first place.[154]

"Hezbollah has a notorious history of taking Western hostages during Beirut's civil war," the FBI summarized in a 1994 report. "Between 1982 and 1991, Hezbollah abducted and held at least 44 Western hostages, including 17 U.S. persons, three of whom died while in captivity." By the time this report was written, Hezbollah had moved on to more spectacular terrorist operations, often well beyond Lebanon's borders. "Hezbollah leaders now believe that taking Western hostages is counterproductive," the FBI noted, adding the caveat that "certain elements within the group continue to argue for the resumption of the kidnappings."[155]

Kuwait in the Crosshairs

Many Western hostages were kidnapped for reasons unrelated to the fate of the Kuwait 17, but the Kuwait 17 would play a major role in the expansion of Hezbollah's focus from foreign elements in Lebanon to Western interests far beyond Lebanon's borders. Those attacks, especially in the early 1980s, were conducted at Iran's behest—such as the Kuwait bombings or attacks in Europe (see chapter 3). And the resulting capture of many of these Hezbollah operatives only led the group to carry out more international attacks in an effort to punish those countries and seek their operatives' release.

Such logic applied to the Hezbollah hijacking of Kuwait Airways flight 221 from Kuwait to Karachi, Pakistan, via Dubai—a flight that was diverted to Tehran. On December 3, 1984, four armed hijackers easily slipped through security at Dubai International Airport, where Britain's Princess Ann was scheduled to depart the same morning and security was busy ensuring her timely departure. No more than fifteen minutes into the journey, a group of young men commandeered the Kuwait Airways flight and took its 162 passengers hostage, including three American auditors employed by the US Agency for International Development (USAID).[156] One of the USAID employees was shot dead after the plane landed in Tehran. "Minutes after the shooting was heard," Iran's news agency reported, "the main door was opened and the half-dead body of one of the passengers was thrown out." Once on the tarmac, the body was shot twice more.[157] Forty-four passengers were released in Tehran, where the hijackers demanded the release of the Kuwait 17, who, they insisted, had been tortured by "the joint butchering machine" of Kuwait, the United States, and France.[158] Despite the hijackers' threats to destroy the aircraft if their demands were ignored, the Kuwaiti government refused to accede.[159] Three days into the standoff the captors murdered another American and dumped his body on the tarmac as well. The man was so badly disfigured that Swiss officials had trouble identifying him despite the detailed information American officials had passed on about the four US citizens on board.[160]

Surviving passengers described how the hijackers singled out the Americans and Kuwaitis on board and were particularly abusive toward the Americans. Not only were the Americans separated from the rest of the passengers, moved to the first-class section, and bound to their seats, but they were forced to lie on their backs as the hijackers stood on them and shouted anti-American slogans. They were interrogated with lit cigarette butts held to their face and hands, and threatened with pistols held to their heads.[161] As the crisis entered its sixth day, Iranian police seized control of the plane, arrested the Hezbollah operatives, and freed the remaining captives. But the rescue was apparently a farce, engineered by Iran to give the hijackers a way out. In fact, authorities "suspected that the hijackers were acting in league with leading members of the Iranian regime."[162]

A US official explained that the plan for the rescue—sending Iranian agents onto the plane disguised as a cleaning crew that the hijackers had requested—was puzzling, to say the least. "You do not invite cleaners aboard an airplane after you have planted explosives, promised to blow up the plane and read your last will and testament," he said. "That is patently absurd."[163] The fact that the Iranian team was so sure of its success—the members entered through only one door and tossed so many smoke bombs that no one could see whether or not the hijackers showed any sign of resistance—led the head of the US State Department's counterterrorism office to conclude, "We feel there is a great deal of sympathy [for the hijackers], if not support and active collusion, on the part of the Iranian government."[164] In the end the Hezbollah hijackers escaped despite requests for their extradition to Kuwait, and the Kuwait 17 remained in prison.[165]

Undeterred, Hezbollah struck again one year later, this time against a far more sensitive target: the Kuwaiti emir himself. On the morning of May 25, 1985, an explosives-filled car rammed into Sheikh Jaber Ahmad al-Sabah's royal motorcade as it traveled to his office from the residential palace. The attack, which struck the convoy's lead car carrying security personnel instead of its desired target, killed two of the emir's bodyguards and a pedestrian and injured twelve others, including

Sheikh Jaber, who suffered only minor lacerations.[166] The driver of the car bomb, believed to be an Iraqi Dawa member working with Hezbollah's Islamic Jihad, apparently waited at a gas station along the procession route and rammed a limousine into the motorcade as it passed by. Within hours an anonymous caller to a Western press agency in Beirut claimed Islamic Jihad was behind the attack: "We hope the Emir has received our message: we ask one more time for the release of those held or all the thrones of the Gulf will be shaken."[167]

Three years later on April 5, 1988, Hezbollah operatives hijacked Kuwait Airways flight 422, which was carrying 111 passengers from Bangkok to Kuwait. The hijackers redirected the plane to land in Mashhad, Iran, and issued their by-now familiar demand: the release of the Kuwait 17.[168] Fifty-seven passengers were released over the next three days before the plane departed for Larnaca, Cyprus.[169] Four days into the hijacking the assailants shot a Kuwaiti passenger when their deadline for having the plane refueled passed. Another Kuwaiti passenger was then released as a goodwill gesture, which reportedly led Cypriot authorities to allow the Hezbollah operatives and the remaining passengers to fly out of Cypriot airspace.[170] They flew to Algiers, where negotiations among the hijackers, Kuwaiti officials, and the Algerian government took place over eight days.[171] On April 20, fifteen days after the initial flight from Bangkok was commandeered, the last passengers were freed. And still the Kuwait 17 remained in jail.[172]

Despite the many terrorist attacks Hezbollah executed in an effort to secure the release of the Kuwait 17, the Kuwaiti government never shortened the sentences of the convicted terrorists behind the 1983 bombings. Nor, however, did the Kuwaiti emir ever sign the six death sentences, so the convicts sat in jail.[173] Two served out their sentences and were released in 1989. The others escaped in the tumult of the Iraqi invasion in 1990. Even then, the Western hostage crisis persisted for more than a year longer.

Although Hezbollah failed to secure the release of the Kuwait 17, the group did successfully push Western forces out of Lebanon. The lesson both Hezbollah and Iran appear to have learned from the experience is that terrorism works. Hit hard enough, they surmised, and America would pick up and run. Pointing to the withdrawal of American and French forces from Lebanon in the wake of the Beirut bombings, Osama bin Laden would later come to the same conclusion.[174]

Lebanon's foreign hostage crisis ended when Iran—in desperate need of foreign investment and improved relations with the West after the Iran-Iraq War—and Syria—aiming both to compensate for flagging Soviet support by wooing the United States and to solidify its control over Lebanon—pressured Hezbollah to accept a political and military agreement with Amal in January 1989.[175] A September 1990 US intelligence report declared, "The hostages have been a major obstacle to ending Iran's international isolation and attracting foreign investment."[176] And once the Kuwait 17 escaped from prison, Hezbollah agreed to facilitate the release of its remaining foreign hostages in return for being allowed to remain armed as a resistance movement in Lebanon despite calls for all Lebanese militia to disband under the 1989 Taif Agreement, which laid out the terms for ending the civil war in Lebanon.[177]

By this time the CIA was concerned not only with Hezbollah's ongoing plots targeting US interests in Beirut but also with its efforts to strike at US interests internationally. In December 1991, when the CIA assessed the presence of a series of threats to US interests in Beirut, it also reported on the possibility of Hezbollah attacks outside Lebanon. Apparently still sensitive today, that section of the report remains redacted in full in the declassified version.[178] The concerns were clearly well placed, however, given Hezbollah's track record of carrying out attacks not only in the Gulf but in Europe as well.

Notes

1. D. Peterson et al. v. The Islamic Republic of Iran, Ministry of Foreign Affairs and the Ministry of Information and Security, United States District Court, District of Columbia, Docket No. CA 01-2684, March 17, 2003, pp. 24–25.

2. Jaber, Hezbollah: Born with a Vengeance, 83; US Department of Defense, "Report of the DOD Commission on Beirut International Airport Terrorist Act, October 23, 1983," December 20, 1983, 32.

3. Geraghty, Peacekeepers at War, 92.

4. Ibid., 95.

5. US CIA, "Iranian Support for Terrorism in 1985."

6. US CIA, "Middle East Terrorism: The Threat and Possible US Responses."

7. Wright, Sacred Rage, 16; "Terrorist Attacks on Americans, 1979–1988: The Attacks, the Groups, and the U.S. Response," PBS Frontline, 2001.

8. Jaber, Hezbollah: Born with a Vengeance, 77.

9. US CIA, "Lebanon: The Hizb Allah."

10. Kirit Radia, "Beirut U.S. Embassy Bombing 25 Years On," ABC News, April 28, 2007; Wright, Sacred Rage, 70.

11. Jaber, Hezbollah: Born with a Vengeance, 77; D. Peterson et al. v. The Islamic Republic of Iran, p. 17; Wright, Sacred Rage, 70.

12. Geraghty, Peacekeepers at War, 101.

13. Wright, Sacred Rage, 72.

14. Jaber, Hezbollah: Born with a Vengeance, 83.

15. US CIA, "Planning to Prosecute Shaykh for Bombing."

16. Jaber, Hezbollah: Born with a Vengeance, 80.

17. US CIA, "Lebanon: Theology of Power."

18. Ibid.

19. US CIA, "Lebanon: Hizballah at the Crossroads."

20. US CIA, "Lebanon: Theology of Power."

21. Ibid.

22. Ibid.

23. David Kenner, "The Sheikh Who Got Away," Foreign Policy, July 6, 2010.

24. US CIA, "Lebanon: Theology of Power."

25. US CIA, "Lebanon's Khomeini: Muhammad Husayn Fadlallah."

26. US CIA, "Lebanon: Prospects for Islamic Fundamentalism," 7.

27. US CIA, "Lebanon: Hizballah at the Crossroads [redacted]," 23.

28. US CIA, "Lebanon: Theology of Power."

29. Kenner, "Sheikh Who Got Away."

30. US CIA, "Lebanon: Theology of Power."

31. US CIA, "Lebanon: Prospects for Islamic Fundamentalism."

32. Ibid.

33. US CIA, "Shia Extremists Taste Own Medicine."

34. Blanford, *Warriors of God*, 74.

35. Woodward, *Secret Wars of the CIA*, 396; Richard Zoglin, Jay Peterzell, and Bruce van Voorst, "Did a Dead Man Tell No Tales?" *Time*, October 12, 1987, 23.

36. George V. Lauder, letter to the editor, *Washington Post*, June 21, 1985.

37. Vincent Cannistraro, interview by Target America, *PBS Frontline*, September 2001.

38. US CIA, "Western Government Installations Targeted by Shia Terrorists."

39. Woodward, *Secret Wars of the CIA*, 397.

40. US Department of the Treasury. "Specially Designated National List Changes," January 10, 1995.

41. Associated Press, "Treasury Acts against Hezbollah Financing," *Washington Times*, July 25, 2007; Kenner, "Sheikh Who Got Away."

42. US CIA, "Lebanon: Theology of Power."

43. Australia, Attorney General's Department, "Hizballah External Security Organisation," Listing of Terrorism Organisations, November 8, 2010; Borzou Daragahi and Sebastian Rotella, "Hezbollah Warlord Was an Enigma," *Los Angeles Times*, August 31, 2008; Simon McGregor-Wood, "U.S. Wanted Terror Suspect Killed in Syria," *ABC News*, February 13, 2008.

44. Barton Gellman, "West Pursues Terror Camp's Possible Link to Saudi Bombing of U.S. Troops," *Washington Post*, December 1, 1996.

45. Jeffrey Goldberg, "In the Party of God: Hezbollah Sets Up Operations in South America and the United States," *The New Yorker*, October 28, 2002.

46. James Risen, "Before bin Laden, One of the World's Most Feared Men," *New York Times*, February 14, 2008; Baer, *See No Evil*; Tim Llewellyn, "Imad Mughniyeh: Hizbullah Chief High on the US-Israeli Hitlist," *Guardian* (London), February 13, 2008.

47. Buenos Aires, Argentina Judicial Branch, AMIA Indictment, Office of the National Federal Court No. 17, Criminal and Correctional Matters No. 9, Case No. 1156, March 5, 2003 (hereafter cited as AMIA indictment).

48. US CIA, "Lebanon: Prospects for Islamic Fundamentalism."

49. Elisabeth Smick, "Profile: Imad Mugniyah," *Council on Foreign Relations*, February 13, 2008.

50. Goldberg, "In the Party of God: Hezbollah Sets Up Operations."

51. Ranstorp, *Hizb'Allah in Lebanon*, 68.

52. US CIA, "Inching toward a Hostage Release."

53. Smick, "Profile: Imad Mugniyah."

54. Ibid.

55. US CIA, "Lebanon: Hizballah at the Crossroads."

56. Ranstorp, *Hizb'Allah in Lebanon*, 71, 85–86.

57. Ibid.

58. AMIA indictment; Ranstorp, *Hizb'Allah in Lebanon*, 69.

59. Edward Cody, "Lebanese Suspect in Past Attacks on U.S Makes FBI List," *Washington Post*, October 31, 2001; Blanford, *Warriors of God*, 76; Jacobsen, *Hostage*, 250; Diaz and Newman, *Lightning Out of Lebanon*, 68.

60. Cody, "Lebanese Suspect in Past Attacks"; Diaz and Newman, *Lightning Out of Lebanon*, 68.

61. Diaz and Newman, *Lightning Out of Lebanon*, 68.

62. Cody, "Lebanese Suspect in Past Attacks"; US CIA, "Inching toward a Hostage Release."

63. McGregor-Wood, "U.S. Wanted Terror Suspect Killed in Syria"; Caroline B. Glick, "Hizbullah Mastermind's True Legacy," *Jewish World Review*, February 15, 2008.

64. James Risen, "U.S. Traces Iran's Ties to Terror through a Lebanese," *New York Times*, January 17, 2002.

65. US CIA, "Hizballah Terrorist Plans against U.S. Interests."

66. *D. Peterson et al. v. The Islamic Republic of Iran*, p. 53.

67. Ibid., 55.

68. US CIA, "Hizballah Terrorist Plans against U.S. Interests."

69. *Peterson v. Islamic Republic of Iran*, Memorandum Opinion, pp. 6–7.

70. Ibid., 6–7; Jaber, *Hezbollah: Born with a Vengeance*, 82.

71. Jaber, *Hezbollah: Born with a Vengeance*, 83.

72. Wright, *Sacred Rage*, 88.

73. Jaber, *Hezbollah: Born with a Vengeance*, 82–83.

74. US Department of Defense, "Report of the DOD Commission on Beirut International Airport Terrorist Act, October 23, 1983," December 20, 1983.

75. US Department of State, "Department Statement, Sept. 20, 1984," *US Department of State Bulletin*, November 1984; "1984: US Embassy Blast Kills 20," *BBC News* (On This Day), September 20, 1984.

76. Wright, *Sacred Rage*, 107–8.

77. Ibid., 108.

78. Ibid.

79. Ibid., 110.

80. *D. Peterson et al. v. The Islamic Republic of Iran*, p. 17.

81. Ibid., 18; "Iran 'Liable' for Beirut Bomb," *BBC News*, May 31, 2003.

82. *Peterson v. Islamic Republic of Iran*, Memorandum Opinion, p. 4.

83. Ibid.

84. Norton, *Hezbollah: Short History*, 34.

85. Ibid., 73.

86. Ranstorp, *Hizb'Allah in Lebanon*, 64–65.

87. US CIA, "Inching toward a Hostage Release."

88. Ranstorp, *Hizb'Allah in Lebanon*, 64.

89. US CIA, "Western Hostages in Lebanon."

90. Qassem, *Hizbullah: Story from Within*, 232–33.

91. Ranstorp, *Hizb'Allah in Lebanon*, 62.

92. Ariel Merari et al., "INTER: International Terrorism in 1987," JCSS Project on Low Intensity Warfare, *Jerusalem Post*, 1988, 36; Ranstorp, *Hizb'Allah in Lebanon*, 64.

93. Ranstorp, *Hizb'Allah in Lebanon*, 63.

94. Ariel Merari et al., "INTER 85: A Review of International Terrorism in 1985," Project on Terrorism, Jaffee Center for Strategic Studies, *Jerusalem Post*, 1986, 5.

95. Ibid , 62–69.

96. US CIA, "Beirut: Terrorist Mecca."

97. "An Open Letter: The Hezbollah Program," *Jerusalem Quarterly* 48 (Fall 1988): 3.

98. Ranstorp, *Hizb'Allah in Lebanon*, 60.

99. "Open Letter: The Hezbollah Program," 1.

100. Jacobsen, *Hostage*, 290.

101. US CIA, "Release of US Hostages in Lebanon," 3.

102. US CIA, "Iran and the U.S. Hostages in Lebanon."

103. US CIA, "Playing Politics with Western Hostages."

104. Merari et al., "INTER: International Terrorism in 1987," 36.

105. Ranstorp, *Hizb'Allah in Lebanon*, 6.

106. Jacobsen, *Hostage*, 53.

107. Shaked and Dishon, *Middle East Contemporary Survey*, 405.

108. Judith Miller, "Driver in Embassy Bombing Identified as Pro-Iranian Iraqi," *New York Times*, December 17, 1983; Shaked and Dishon, *Middle East Contemporary Survey*, 405.

109. Ranstorp, *Hizb'Allah in Lebanon*, 117.

110. US CIA, "Iranian Support for International Terrorism."

111. Jaber, *Hezbollah: Born with a Vengeance*, 129.

112. Wright, *Sacred Rage*, 112.

113. Ibid., 113.

114. Ibid., 122.

115. Shaked and Dishon, *Middle East Contemporary Survey*, 407; Ranstorp, *Hizb'Allah in Lebanon*, 91.

116. Jaber, *Hezbollah: Born with a Vengeance*, 54.

117. Associated Press, "12 Iraqis and Lebanese Accused in U.S. Embassy Blast in Kuwait," December 19, 1983; Miller, "Driver in Embassy Bombing."

118. Wright, *Sacred Rage*, 124.

119. Al-Musawi, whose Islamic Amal ultimately merged with other radical Lebanese Shi'ite groups to form Hezbollah, had been suspected of organizing the October 1983 attacks on the American and French Multinational Force barracks in Beirut. See Ranstorp, *Hizb'Allah in Lebanon*, 91; Jaber, *Hezbollah: Born with a Vengeance*, 80.

120. *The Prosecutor Special Tribunal for Lebanon v. Mustafa Amine Badreddine, Salim Jamil Ayy Ash, Hussein Hassan Oneissi & Assad Hassan Sabra*, Case No. STL-11-01IIfPTJ, June 10, 2011, p. 4.

121. Ranstorp, *Hizb'Allah in Lebanon*, 91.

122. Wright, *Sacred Rage*, 124–25.

123. Ibid., 125.

124. "Iran Denies Kuwait Blast Role," *New York Times*, December 14, 1983.

125. Wright, *Sacred Rage*, 125.

126. Ranstorp, *Hizb'Allah in Lebanon*, 92.

127. US CIA, "Iran and the U.S. Hostages in Lebanon."

128. US CIA, "Wild, Wild West Beirut."

129. Ibid.

130. Ranstorp, *Hizb'Allah in Lebanon*, 86–108.

131. US CIA, "Western Hostages in Lebanon."

132. Jaber, *Hezbollah: Born with a Vengeance*, 118.

133. "William Francis Buckley," Arlington National Cemetery website, last modified April 23, 2006.

134. Cannistraro, interview, *PBS Frontline*.

135. US CIA, "Lebanon: Hizb Allah."

136. Cannistraro, interview, *PBS Frontline*.

137. US CIA, "New Rash of Kidnappings."

138. US CIA, "Lebanon: 'Islamic Jihad' Goes Public."

139. Jaber, *Hezbollah: Born with a Vengeance*, 118.

140. Gordon Thomas, "William Buckley: The Spy Who Never Came in from the Cold," *Canada Free Press*, October 25, 2006.

141. Jacobsen, *Hostage*, 51–52.

142. Thomas, "William Buckley."

143. James Sturcke, "Car Bomb Kills Hizbullah Chief in Syria," *Guardian* (London), February 13, 2008.

144. Ranstorp, *Hizb'Allah in Lebanon*, 2.

145. Jacobsen, *Hostage*, 54.

146. Israel, Intelligence and Terrorism Information Center, "Hezbollah (part 1): Profile of the Lebanese Shiite Terrorist Organization of Global Reach Sponsored by Iran and Supported by Syria," June 2003; Ariel Merari et al., "INTER 85: A Review of International Terrorism in 1985," 98; Ariel Merari et al., "INTER: International Terrorism in 1987," 54.

147. Ibid.

148. Davies and Tomlinson, *Spycraft Manual*, 108.

149. Ibid.; Fisk, *Pity the Nation*, 613.

150. Ariel Merari et al., "INTER 85: A Review of International Terrorism in 1985," 99.

151. Fisk, *Pity the Nation*, 613.

152. Woodward, *Secret Wars of the CIA*, 416.

153. James S. Robbins, "Holding Us Hostage Speaking Their Language," *National Review Online*, April 12, 2004.

154. National Consortium for the Study of Terrorism and Responses to Terrorism, University of Maryland, "Islamic Liberation Organization," 2012.

155. US Department of Justice, FBI, "International Radical Fundamentalism."

156. John Kohan, Johanna McGeary, and Barry Hillenbrand, "Horror aboard Flight 221," *Time*, December 17, 1984.

157. Wright, *Sacred Rage*, 134.

158. Kohan, McGeary, and Hillenbrand, "Horror aboard Flight 221."

159. Evan Duncan, "Terrorist Attacks on U.S. Official Personnel Abroad, 1982–84: Iran," US Department of State Bulletin, April 1985.

160. Wright, *Sacred Rage*, 136.

161. Ibid.

162. Paul Wilkinson, "Hezbollah: A Critical Appraisal," *Jane's Intelligence Review* (August 1993): 369.

163. Wright, *Sacred Rage*, 140.

164. "Facts for Your Files: A Chronology of U.S. Middle East Relations," *Washington Report on Middle East Affairs*, December 17, 1984.

165. Duncan, "Terrorist Attacks on U.S. Official Personnel Abroad."

166. Shaked and Rabinovich, *Middle East Contemporary Survey*, 404.

167. US CIA, "Lebanon: 'Islamic Jihad' Goes Public."

168. "1988: Hijackers Free 25 Hostages," *BBC News* (On This Day), April 5 1988.

169. Associated Press, "Hijacked Plane in Cyprus After 7 Hours of Air Terror," *Los Angeles Times*, April 8, 1988.

170. Associated Press, "Chronology of Events in Hijacking of Kuwait Airways Flight 422 with AM-Hijack Bjt," AP News Archive, April 12, 1988.

171. Sam Allis Larnaca and David S. Jackson, "Terrorism Nightmare on Flight 422," *Time*, April 25, 1988.

172. Times Wire Services, "Hijackers Free Hostages, End 16-Day Ordeal," *Los Angeles Times*, April 20, 1988.

173. Jaber, *Hezbollah: Born with a Vengeance*, 129.

174. National Commission on Terrorist Attacks upon the United States, *9/11 Commission Report*, released July 22, 2004, 48.

175. Ranstorp, *Hizb'Allah in Lebanon*, 125.

176. US CIA, "Keenan's Release a Victory," 5.

177. Ranstorp, *Hizb'Allah in Lebanon*, 105.

178. US CIA, "Hizballah Terrorist Plans against U.S. Interests."

3

Hezbollah's European Debut

"WE'VE GOT A HIJACK," flight engineer Christian Zimmermann told the captain, John Testrake, as he reached for the cockpit fire ax by the bulkhead door. Who knew what weapons the hijackers had, or what weapons the crew might be able to use? Either way, Zimmermann thought, better to hide the ax. TWA flight 847 had just taken off from Athens on a short flight to Rome, with continuing service to the United States. But the routine trip became a terrifying, 8,500-mile journey around the Mediterranean aimed at securing the release of Lebanese Shi'a militants from Israeli and other jails. The hijacking also introduced the world to its mastermind, Imad Mughniyeh, who was famously photographed leaning out the cockpit window over Captain Testrake with his gun pointed at the tarmac.[1]

As soon as the flight engineer turned off the seat belt sign, the hijackers rushed the cockpit door. The flight crew first heard banging from the main cabin, then heavy pounding on the cockpit door. The door's bottom panel was kicked out, flying into the cockpit. The hijackers kicked lead flight attendant Uli Derickson in the chest and held a gun to her head while screaming, "Come to die! Americans die!" Derickson called the captain on the intercom: "We're being roughed up back here! Please open the door!" As Zimmermann unlocked the door, two hijackers stormed in, one gripping an automatic pistol and the other a couple of hand grenades, and demanded the plane head for Algeria. As he planned a new course for Algeria, the captain mused to himself how "they were well-groomed, average-looking guys who didn't look like they could be hijackers or killers."[2]

Aware they were vastly outnumbered, the two hijackers, later identified as Hezbollah operatives Mohammad Ali Hamadi and Hasan Izz al-Din, quickly established authority and control over the 153 passengers and crew. They burst in and out of the cockpit and ran up and down the aisles hitting passengers on the head, Hamadi holding the gun and Izz al-Din the grenades. Some crew members were pistol-whipped by Hamadi, while Izz al-Din took to pulling the pins out of his grenades and playing with them nervously. In an effort to reduce threats to the hijackers, men were seated by the windows and women and children moved to aisle seats. The area near the cockpit was cleared of passengers, who were crammed into the back of the aircraft, where passengers now sat four across in each three-seat row. They were instructed to sit silently with heads down and hands clasped over their heads. Those who made a noise or complained were beaten. Such precautions were wise; members of the crew and several US military officers on board each considered confronting the hijackers but thought better of it. At one point the pilot even considered flying the plane to Tel Aviv and landing before the hijackers realized what he had done.[3]

Neither hijacker spoke English, and the crew spoke no Arabic, but Hamadi and Uli Derickson both spoke German. Hamadi would wave his gun and bark orders in German for Derickson to translate, while Izz al-Din "kept jumping up and down making threatening gestures."[4] Through Derickson the crew explained to Hamadi that the plane lacked the fuel to fly to Algeria, nearly twice the distance of the flight's planned route to Rome. The hijackers first settled on Cairo as an alternative but quickly changed their minds, yelling, "Beirut! Beirut! Fuel only!" At this point the hijackers demanded the fire ax on seeing its empty storage space. The crew insisted the plane just didn't have one, so the hijackers found another way to smash the doorknob off the cockpit door, which now swung open. With the flight under their control and now headed to Beirut, the hijackers sent Derickson to collect passengers' passports and identify all the Jews. Instead, Derickson shielded passengers with Jewish-sounding names.[5]

US Navy divers Robert Stethem and Clinton Suggs were seated in the last row of the plane, tired after a week's work repairing an underwater sewer line at a US naval communications station in Greece and eager to get home. Soon after taking their seats they fell asleep, waking to passengers' screams as the hijackers ran up and down the aisles hitting people on the head. When Derickson and Hamadi came by collecting passports, Suggs whispered that he and Stethem only had their military identity cards and hesitated before handing them to her. Seeing this interaction, Hamadi demanded they hand over their identification, which they did.[6]

Ten or fifteen minutes later, Hamadi barreled down the aisle holding the two divers' military ID cards. "You, marine?" Hamadi asked after hitting Suggs on the head with his pistol. "No, US Navy," Suggs replied. Hamadi turned to Stethem, told him to stand up, and led him to the front of the plane. After another five or ten minutes, Hamadi returned to pistol-whip Suggs once more and take him to the first-class section as well. There, Suggs saw Stethem with his hands tied behind his back and his head between his knees. Hamadi tied up Suggs too, adding, "If you move, I kill you." He pulled an armrest off a chair, dragged Stethem into the open cockpit doorway, and used the armrest—with screws still sticking out—as a club to beat Stethem. Soon it was Suggs's turn to be beaten, and from time to time the hijackers also hit members of the crew, especially Zimmermann, the flight engineer, whose face was quickly bloodied. But Stethem took most of the punishment.[7]

As the plane passed over Cyprus, the crew radioed Beirut air traffic control for permission to land. "I am sorry," the controller replied, "but we are closed, and you will not be allowed to land." Frustrated and under tremendous stress, the first officer made it clear the flight was landing in Beirut, like it or not. "These people are armed and dangerous," he stressed. "And they are ordering us to land at Beirut." The captain chimed in, noting that the aircraft was low on fuel, and in distress he declared an emergency and demanded clearance to land. As the flight entered its final approach to the Beirut airport, the unnerved controller finally relented: "Very well, sir, you are cleared to land. Land quietly please."[8]

Insecurity at Beirut International Airport

As the hijackers' primary means of communication, Derickson found herself at the center of the drama. She occasionally calmed Hamadi by singing him a German song he requested, successfully negotiated for the release of some of the passengers, and repeatedly came to the defense of passengers and crew. "Don't you hit that person!" she would shout. At one point, one of the hijackers asked her to marry him. She would later be honored for her bravery and would be the subject of a made-for-TV movie. But at the time she thought not of fame or honor, just survival.[9]

Derickson was immersed in the third Middle East hijacking in four days, and she could only have hoped this affair would end as well and as quickly as the other two. All three hijackings involved Beirut International Airport, which had become a preferred transit point for terrorists on the move. It was now, the CIA reported days after the TWA hijacking, "the site of a considerable number and variety of terrorist activities, especially skyjackings."[10]

The first of that week's hijackings took place three days before the TWA 847 saga began, when six Shi'a gunmen stormed a Jordanian airliner at the Beirut airport and forced the Swedish pilot to fly to Cyprus, then Italy, and then back to Beirut, where the passengers were released and the plane was blown up. Over the twenty-eight hours during which the plane hopped around the eastern Mediterranean, the hijackers, who called themselves the "Suicide Brigade of Imam al-Sadr," lashed out at a recent Arab League statement supportive of the plight of Palestinians in Beirut's refugee camps. The camps had been under attack from Shi'a militants over the past few weeks, part of an effort to drive the Palestinians out of Lebanon and undermine the Palestine Liberation Organization (PLO). After airing their grievances and destroying the plane, the hijackers sped off into the Shi'a neighborhoods of South Beirut near the airport.[11] One of the hijackers would issue a statement in the name of the "Martyrs of the Lebanese Resistance," a Hezbollah cover name.[12] It would not take long for more concrete ties to emerge between this hijacking and that of TWA flight 847.

Some of the passengers of this hijacked Jordanian flight were able to book themselves on the first available flight out of Beirut, a Middle Eastern Airlines flight to Cyprus the next day. But as the plane landed at Larnaca, a Palestinian militant pulled out a hand grenade and threatened to blow up the airplane to protest the previous day's hijacking. He was talked out of that idea, however, and allowed to fly to Amman, where he was arrested on arrival.[13]

The hijacking of TWA flight 847 by Hamadi and Izz al-Din took place two days later, kicking off a seventeen-day crisis far more severe than the week's earlier two hijackings. Airport hijackings involving Beirut International Airport, the CIA concluded, were "a particular problem." The agency recorded thirty-six hijackings involving the airport, part of a "sorry 15-year record" underscoring the "chronic security problem there."[14]

Airport employees, the CIA noted, did not try to keep terrorists out of the facility. In fact, sympathetic workers helped terrorists pass through the airport covertly. "Most of the airport employees are Shias," the CIA reported, "and there is evidence that customs clerks, porters, and taxicab drivers constitute a network of collaborators for Shia groups hoping to kidnap foreigners or Lebanese notables going to or from the airport."[15] Against this background Derickson and everyone else aboard flight 847 must have taken little comfort from the fact that the flight to Rome had finally landed—in Beirut.

"They're Beating the Passengers!"

Fearing an ambush, the hijackers initially refused to allow the airplane to taxi to a refueling area. When a truck came onto the runway to lead the plane to the refueling area, one of the hijackers leaned out of the cockpit window and waved his gun until the truck drove off. Once the pilot explained they could not refuel—and therefore not fly on to Algeria, as the hijackers demanded—without taxiing to the refueling area, the hijackers relented. Even so, as the captain guided the plane down the runway, a hijacker held his cocked pistol to the captain's head. In his other hand he held a hand grenade with its pin pulled, right in front of the pilot's face, blocking his view of the runway.[16]

Relieved to have reached the refueling area safely despite the distractions, the pilot parked the aircraft and waited for someone to refuel to plane. But the wait enraged the hijackers, who took their anger out on Robert Stethem. "The sounds of the blows were sickening," the pilot later recalled. As the hijackers beat Stethem with the armrest, the first officer radioed to the tower: "They're beating the passengers! We demand fuel!" Then another voice added, in broken English, "The plane is booby-trapped. If anyone approaches, we will blow it up. Either refueling the plane or blowing it up. No alternative." Though it still took some time, a crew eventually arrived and refueled the plane. When Hamadi left the cockpit to check on conditions in the cabin, Uli Derickson asked him in German to release the women and children. Seventeen women and two children were freed, and then the plane took off for Algiers, some four hours away.[17]

Once the plane was in the air, the hijackers dragged Stethem back into the first-class cabin, where Suggs was still sitting. Suggs saw that Stethem was in bad shape, leaning his head, which was covered in blood from a wound on the side of his head against the wall. He begged for someone to untie his hands, saying the pain was unbearable. Looking over, Hamadi said, "Let the American pig suffer!" Uli Derickson untied him anyway and moved him into the coach-class section.[18]

As the plane approached Algeria, the hijackers took over the radio and began to make long, impassioned speeches to authorities on the ground. From the hijackers' angry reactions, it appeared they were not getting what they wanted. As in Beirut,

Algiers flight controllers insisted the airport was closed. "We are going to land, we have no choice," the first officer replied. "They have told us they will blow up the airplane if we do not land in Algiers!" Besides, the plane lacked enough fuel to fly anywhere else. When a runway was opened for the flight, it was surrounded by Algerian military personnel and armored vehicles.[19]

To compel Algerian authorities to approach the plane and negotiate over their demands, the hijackers threatened to start shooting passengers. For the next few hours the hijackers negotiated with airport officials, giving the crew a first glimpse of their demands: the release of Lebanese Shi'a prisoners, including 766 prisoners in Israel, two arrested in Spain in September 1984 after attempting to assassinate a Libyan diplomat, and the Kuwait 17.[20] But at that moment, what the hijackers wanted more than anything else was more fuel, though they did not yet know where they wanted to fly next.[21]

Negotiations, conducted mostly through the cockpit window, apparently were not going well because the hijackers dragged another passenger, Maj. Kurt Carlson, US Army Reserve, into the first-class section and started beating him as well in order to bargain for fuel. "They're beating and killing Americans. We need fuel right now," the pilot pleaded. Hamadi yelled out the window, "Ten minutes, not more, and one American will die."[22]

When he first discovered Carlson was traveling on an official US government passport, Hamadi pointed his weapon at Carlson's face, yelling, "CIA, FBI!" Seeking to defuse the matter, Uli Derickson explained that he was just a reserve officer returning from a one-week civil engineering assignment in Egypt. Yet needing leverage, the hijackers continued abusing Carlson, who was already blindfolded with a bandana reeking of vomit, his hands tied behind his back. They proceeded to shove him just inside the cockpit and kick and beat him with a steel pipe. Over and over they screamed, "One American must die!" As horrible as Carlson's screams were, the pilot held the microphone close so that the control tower would hear and take the hijackers seriously. For about ninety minutes the beating of Carlson continued, until finally the pilot announced a fuel truck was coming.[23]

Events then veered briefly into the absurd. When the fuel truck arrived, the driver shouted something toward the cockpit window. "I think this guy is asking for a credit card," an exasperated crew member exclaimed. Not sure he heard correctly, the pilot asked, "You mean he wants us to pay for fuel so we can hijack ourselves?" Derickson took out her purse, mumbling as she removed her wallet, "He wants a credit card." Once the driver had her card he began pumping to the tune of $6,000. Meanwhile the hijackers brought Carlson back to his seat and resumed beating Robert Stethem. They left him unconscious in the doorway but let an additional twenty-one women and children deplane in Algiers.[24]

The flight took off, and only then was the crew told they were heading back to Beirut. By now it was clear to the captain: "This was no ordinary, run-of-the-mill hijacking. We were being held for ransom."[25] A flight that was never intended to leave Europe was now bouncing around the Middle East, the latest in a growing trend of Middle East terrorism spilling over into Europe.

Mideast Terror "Spillover" into Europe

"International terrorists had a banner year in 1985," the State Department conceded in its annual terrorism report, which included the hijacking of flight 847.
Terrorists' focus on softer, civilian targets, and international transportation in particular, "gave pause to international travelers worldwide who feared the increasingly
indiscriminate nature of international terrorism." Not only had international terrorist incidents risen by 30 percent since the previous year, but attacks by Middle
Eastern terrorists accounted for nearly 60 percent of all attacks in 1985. And whereas
most attacks by Western European terrorists were designed to avoid casualties, the
State Department reported, attacks by Middle Eastern groups were frequently intended to cause maximum casualties. It was therefore all the more disconcerting
that Middle Eastern terrorist groups, including Hezbollah, increased their level of
activity abroad—especially in Europe—in 1985.[26]

Several factors help explain the Middle Eastern terrorist spillover into Europe,
including the desire by Middle Eastern terrorists to gain the release of comrades
jailed in European countries. But operationally, too, Europe made for an attractive
venue. Few travel restrictions existed at the time among European countries, and
some had special arrangements with Middle Eastern countries to facilitate guest
workers. While Western installations were well protected in the Middle East, security was still relatively lax back home in Europe, where targets abounded. And the
open nature of European society made operating there easy. Finally, the State Department noted, "large numbers of Middle Easterners—many of whom comprise
expatriate and student communities—live and travel in Western Europe and provide cover, shelter, and potential recruits."[27]

"They've Just Killed a Passenger!"

Nearing Beirut, the crew received a now familiar message from the control tower: "I
am sorry, but the airport is closed." Barricades were obstructing the runways, suggesting airport officials were serious about fending off the problem of TWA flight
847. When the captain himself explained over the radio that the plane was in distress, the controller replied, "I sympathize with you, sir. But unfortunately my superiors do not care about your problems." Turning to one of the hijackers, the captain
explained that no runways were open and that if he attempted to land, he would
crash the airplane. "Good," the hijacker replied. "That will save us the trouble of
blowing it up!" Circling overhead the airport, the captain continued to press the
controller to open a runway while the crew prepared the passengers for a crash landing. Ultimately a runway was opened—possibly influenced by the hijackers' threat
to crash the plane into the control tower or the presidential palace—and the flight
landed. But the relief of a safe landing was short-lived.[28]

After stopping the plane in the middle of the runway, and thereby precluding a
sneak approach by rescue teams, the hijackers dragged Stethem and Suggs to the
front of the plane. Then, Suggs later testified, "everything went crazy." The hijackers

were screaming into the radio, and the officials in the tower appeared to be scream-ing right back. The hijackers demanded that the Amal militia get involved in nego-tiations over the release of the Shi'a prisoners and became enraged when the Amal leadership failed to respond. They also wanted some of their Beirut-based compa-triots to join them on the airplane.[29]

As the screaming continued, the hijackers resumed beating a now severely injured Robert Stethem. Suddenly, Hamadi jerked Stethem to his feet and shot him. Suggs recalled hearing Stethem, still alive, say, "Oh God! Oh God!" Suggs remembered feeling the change in pressure and the wind as the plane door was opened and a sec-ond shot rang out, with Stethem's body falling to the tarmac.[30] "They've just killed a passenger!" the first officer yelled into the radio. "There will be another in five minutes," Hamadi threatened, demanding the plane be refueled immediately. Meanwhile he resumed beating Suggs.[31]

The captain was told to taxi to the refueling area, which he did—carefully, to avoid running over Stethem's body. The body remained there for hours until a search by a Red Cross ambulance that night. About a half hour after arriving at the refueling area, the two hijackers were joined by five more heavily armed militants, one of whom was Imad Mughniyeh. With Mughniyeh was Fawaz Yunis, who had hijacked and blown up the Jordanian airplane just two days earlier at this same air-port.[32] Years later, American authorities would tie the TWA flight 847 hijacking back to not only Mughniyeh—who would be indicted in US court for his role in the attack—but also Iran. The *New York Times* would later cite US intelligence stating that an Islamic Revolutionary Guard Corps (IRGC) officer, Feirud Mehdi Nezhad, was at Beirut International Airport—with Mughniyeh—during the seventeen-day standoff at the airport.[33]

As their comrades boarded the plane, Hamadi stopped beating Suggs, who later remembered hearing people running on board with weapons.[34] The arrivals hugged the hijackers and quickly removed several US military personnel and others with Jewish-sounding names from the plane. A secondary crisis thus arose, whereby some hostages were held in safe houses across Beirut and others remained on the plane. The military hostages were held in a twelve-by-twenty-foot basement cell with a steel door and bars on the window.[35] "The hijacking was engineered by Hizballah official Imad Mughniyah," a CIA memo noted several days into the crisis, adding that "Mughniyah still holds at least four of the Americans."[36] Confirming the CIA's information, inves-tigators would later find Mughniyeh's fingerprints on the plane's lavatory walls.[37] According to US prosecutors, Mughniyeh personally took part in the beatings that continued over the course of the crisis.[38] Nor, during the crisis, were the hijackers discreet about their affiliation. Witness interviews conducted by the FBI after the hostages were released made clear "that one of the hijackers said that he and the other hijackers were from Hizballah."[39] Then–national security adviser Robert McFarlane would later testify that he heard "various foreign communications intercepted by the United States" that confirmed Hezbollah was behind the hijacking.[40]

The hijackers now demanded food and fuel, and said they wanted the runway cleared for takeoff at dawn. They also demanded that Greek authorities release their comrade Ali Atwa, the third hijacker, who had been arrested at the Athens airport. Failure to reunite Atwa with the rest of the hijackers in Algiers, they warned, would lead them to execute the eight Greeks on the plane, including singer Demis Roussos. This presumably would have come as a surprise to Roussos, who reported after his release that his captors were "nice people" and even gave him a cake to celebrate his birthday on June 15.[41]

Algiers and Back

The flight's arrival back in Algiers was clearly prenegotiated, because the airport was open and the landing uneventful. A doctor was allowed on board and three passengers suffering from heat exhaustion were released.[42] Meanwhile Hamadi escorted a crew member around the plane to check on the jet's engines. Pointing to the plane's door, where the aircraft was streaked with Stethem's blood, Hamadi bragged about killing the navy diver.[43] The plane sat on the tarmac for almost twelve hours, during which the hijackers periodically negotiated by radio with local authorities, reprising their familiar demand for the release of Shi'a Lebanese prisoners in Israel and elsewhere and blaming America for "just about every evil in the world." Eventually, Ali Atwa—who was flown to Algiers from Athens—was brought to the plane and fifty-eight more passengers and crew members were released. The only remaining hostages on board were American men.[44]

Among the new militants who boarded the plane in Beirut was the group leader—likely Mughniyeh—who went by the alias Jihad. He spoke fluent English and was clearly more educated than the original hijackers. In the morning Jihad entered the cockpit with a young passenger. "We want to play a little game here," he told the remaining crew. "We need to convince the airport to bring us fuel." On cue, the young passenger screamed into the microphone as if he was being beaten, but his performance was lackluster. The first officer tried next, and was more convincing. As he screamed Jihad politely asked the captain to open the window and quickly squeezed off three or four rounds from his chrome-plated, pearl-handled pistol. Within minutes the fuel truck arrived, but it was driven by the same employee as in the last Algiers episode and again he wanted a credit card. The crew refused this time, but Jihad's earlier gunshots were apparently enough to convince the driver to start pumping fuel. Unsure of where they wanted to fly next, the hijackers first chose Aden, Yemen, but the distance would be too far without a stop. After considering Iran, they settled on returning a third time to Beirut.[45]

Landing in Beirut, the crew faked engine failures and convinced the hijackers the plane could fly no more. For the next few hours the hijackers talked perpetually with people in the control tower. A sick passenger was released at one point, and later on several more armed militants boarded. In the middle of the night more militants arrived and woke up all the passengers. Within a half hour everyone was off the plane except the pilot, first officer, and flight engineer. Over the next sixteen days dozens of Shi'a militants would come and go while the crew remained on board. The passengers were held in locations around Beirut.[46]

Two crises now unfolded, one in the plane and a second in safe houses around Beirut, both in the context of the larger hostage crisis involving hostages taken before the 847 hijacking. The terrorists demanded that Amal leader Nabih Berri negotiate on their behalf, which he ultimately agreed to do. Amal had put its forces on combat alert the previous day and sealed the airport in response to the arrival of both an aircraft carrier, the USS *Nimitz*, and a guided-missile destroyer, the USS *Kidd*, off the coast of Lebanon. Unconfirmed reports claimed further that American Delta Force commandos had been sent to the Middle East. And several days later, three warships carrying 1,800 US Marines arrived off the Lebanese coast.[47]

Back in the United States, the hijacking crisis was covered on live television and captivated both the American public and government officials. A dedicated element within the CIA's Counterterrorism Center worked on the issue, focusing on efforts to penetrate Hezbollah. In at least one instance, the FBI tried to help uncover the locations of the TWA flight 847 and other hostages in Beirut by tapping existing investigations of Hezbollah supporters in the United States but was thwarted by Washington bureaucracy.[48]

After more than two weeks of captivity, the remaining thirty-nine hostages were freed on June 29 and sent to Damascus. Israel gradually released Shi'a prisoners, though it claimed their release was in no way connected to the release of the TWA hostages. On November 14, 1985, the United States indicted Ali Atwa, Mohammad Hamadi, Hassan Izz al-Din, and Imad Mughniyeh on fifteen counts, including conspiracy to commit aircraft piracy, hostage taking, and murder.[49] While the three escaped into the slums of Beirut after the hijacking, their names would reappear in relation to Hezbollah's campaign of international terror. Izz al-Din was later linked to the 1988 hijacking of Kuwait Air flight 422 from Bangkok, and Hamadi was arrested in West Germany in 1987 after attempting to carry liquid explosives onto a plane departing from Frankfurt.[50]

Europe in the Crosshairs

The first recorded operation carried out by Hezbollah on European soil occurred on November 13, 1983, when bombs exploded at a train station and aboard the express train from Paris to Marseilles, attacks for which Islamic Jihad claimed responsibility. Almost a year later to the day, Swiss police arrested Lebanese national Hussein Hanih Atat at the Zurich airport when several pounds of explosives were discovered in a cloth belt around his waist and arming devices were later found in his luggage. An accomplice escaped detection, though police later discovered his luggage, which contained an additional five pounds of explosives.[51]

Atat was attempting to board a plane to Rome at the time of his arrest; further interrogation revealed the presence of an Islamic Jihad cell in the seaside resort town of Ladispoli, twenty-four miles north of Rome.[52] Almost two weeks later, Italian police arrested the cell of seven Lebanese students, which was then planning an attack against the US embassy in Rome. A search of the members' apartment revealed a map of the embassy, with arrows marking guard and television camera positions, and pro-Iranian and Islamic Jihad literature. Pillars and concrete barriers constructed at the embassy in the wake of the Beirut marine barracks as protection against truck bombings and the time of the marine guards' shift changes were also documented. A caller claiming to represent Islamic Jihad first denied participation in the cell's activities, but a second asserted Islamic Jihad's role, stating, "It seems the Italian government has started following the ways of American imperialism and desperately defending its devilish role."[53]

The arrests in Rome occurred just four days after a meeting in Tehran between the al-Dawa al-Islamiyya and Islamic Amal parties and Ayatollah Hossein Ali Montazeri—a key regime figure tasked with spreading the Islamic Revolution—where a decision was made to launch a wave of "armed resistance" against Saddam Hussein's allies in the Gulf and to begin an anti-American campaign in Western Europe.[54] The group wasted no time in jump-starting its European campaign. On April 12, 1985, a bomb ripped through the El Descanso restaurant in Torrejon, Spain, a favorite spot of Americans stationed at a nearby air base. The attack killed eighteen Spaniards and wounded eighty-two, including fifteen Americans. Several groups claimed responsibility, including the Basque separatist groups Basque Homeland and Liberty (ETA) and First of October Anti-Fascist Resistance (GRAPO); however, the most credible claim came from Islamic Jihad.[55] Despite the attack in Spain, few were prepared for the plethora of events that would follow two months later.

Believing that his role in the TWA hijacking was unknown to Western intelligence, and convinced of the secrecy of his movements, Mughniyeh was said to have traveled to Paris in November 1985, just five months after the TWA hijacking. Lebanese security officials became aware of Mughniyeh's travel through communication intercepts and informed US authorities. US officials implored French police to arrest the Hezbollah leader. Instead, French agents reportedly interrogated him several times over a six-day period before releasing him, apparently in return for the release of a French hostage in Lebanon.[56]

In July 1985 in Copenhagen, Hezbollah planted bombs at the office of the US-based Northwest Orient Airlines and at Scandinavia's oldest synagogue. The bombs injured twenty-two people, including Americans, and damaged a Jewish home for the elderly. In a telephone call to a news agency in Beirut, an anonymous caller claimed the Islamic Jihad Organization (IJO) had carried out the attacks to avenge an Israeli attack in Lebanon. No longer would Hezbollah limit its operations to the Middle East, the caller warned; they would now "be aimed at every Zionist, American or reactionary establishment in various parts of the world."[57]

Next on Hezbollah's hit list was France. Between December 1985 and September 1986, Hezbollah operatives bombed fifteen targets in Paris. The first bombing took place December 7, 1985, when explosives were placed at both Galerie Lafayette and Galerie Printemps, injuring forty-three people.[58] At the time, despite claims of responsibility by Islamic Jihad and the Palestine Liberation Front, French authorities did not consider Middle Eastern terrorists prime suspects because of the bombs' rudimentary nature.[59] Struggling continuously against the radical leftist Action Directe network, French authorities assumed the unsophisticated bombs pointed to domestic actors. But the focus would soon shift to Lebanon.

On February 3, a bomb went off in a shopping gallery on the Champs Elysées, injuring eight people; a second bomb was later found and defused at the Eiffel Tower. A group calling itself the Committee of Solidarity with the Arab and Middle East Political Prisoners (CSPPA) claimed responsibility and demanded the release of several Lebanese terrorists held in France, including Anis Naccache, a convert to Islam who was a close friend of Ahmad Khomeini, Ayatollah Khomeini's son, and Mohsen Rafiqdust, the IRGC commander in Lebanon. Most important, Naccache had served in Fatah's Force 17 and was said to be a good friend of Imad Mughniyeh. After Mughniyeh's death in 2008, Naccache spoke glowingly of the Hezbollah leader to the Associated Press, calling him the "top architect" of the 2006 war with Israel.[60]

The deadliest of the fifteen Paris bombings occurred September 17, 1986, in front of Tati, a clothing store. Seven were killed and more than sixty were wounded, with the CSPPA again claiming responsibility.[61] The mastermind of this and the other bombings, most of which employed the same type of C4 explosive used in the 1983 bombing of the French embassy in Kuwait, was identified as a Tunisian named Fouad Ali Salah. According to the Associated Press, "French authorities said the terrorist network he led was controlled by Hezbollah." Additionally intelligence officials concluded that "Iran ordered the attacks through Hezbollah to curb French support for Baghdad in the Iran-Iraq war."[62] Still further investigation revealed that while Salah organized the network and selected targets, Hezbollah dispatched an explosives expert from Beirut to execute the attacks on the orders of senior Hezbollah leader Abdelhadi Hamadi.[63] Confirming Hezbollah's role in the attacks, Hussein Ali Mohammed Hariri, who would hijack an Air Afrique flight in 1987 (see chapter 9), would later acknowledge during his interrogation that "all the organizations that you know in France under various names are all dependent on Hezbollah. The actions are decided by the board of operations of Hezbollah in collaboration with the secret services of the Party of God."[64]

As Salah's wave of terror continued throughout 1986, it was unclear if French investigators would ever identify the responsible party. Fear gripped Paris as bomb after bomb exploded and the investigation saw little progress. Only a string of lucky breaks revealed the full extent of the cell's operations to French police. In January 1987, Mohammad Ali Hamadi of TWA flight 847 was arrested at the Frankfurt airport, where he was found carrying methyl nitrate, an extremely potent liquid explosive, and an address book with the name of a Tunisian later discovered to be Salah. Another name found in Hamadi's address book was that of Hussein Mazbou, one of Salah's Lebanese bomb makers.[65] Hamadi was reportedly en route to France to resupply Salah's group with the more potent methyl nitrate for use in another wave of more deadly attacks. Further, Hamadi's group in Germany was reportedly tasked with providing Hezbollah's European cells with both arms and drugs supplied by a network run by one of Mohammad Hamadi's brothers in Lebanon.[66]

Then, in February 1987, a Tunisian approached French police in the Loire Valley and indicated that he had information regarding the bombings. He was assigned the cover name Lofti and agreed to function as a mole, feeding information to French intelligence.[67] Lofti had previously studied in Qom, Iran, before traveling to France as an agent for the Iranian intelligence services and reportedly earned $30,000 a year from the Iranian government to convert fellow North Africans in France to Shi'ism.[68] Lofti agreed to let French intelligence wiretap his conversations, which led them to the cell. According to a French intelligence report, the details of which were published in the French daily *Libération*, top Iranian officials were responsible for the wave of bombings. The report went further still, claiming that Ayatollah Khomeini himself ordered the bombings through a fatwa.[69] For his cooperation with the French government, Lofti was paid about $178,000 and later traveled to the United States.[70]

On March 21, 1987, seven other suspects were arrested along with Salah, including five Tunisians and two Lebanese with French citizenship, one of whom was Salah's wife. During the raid, French police seized two automatic pistols, ammunition, and twenty-six pints of methyl nitrate contained in bottles of arrack liquor. Six and a half kilograms of heroin were also found in the cache, allegedly to be used to finance the network. After the arrests Tunisia broke diplomatic relations with Tehran, accusing Iran of recruiting Tunisians to carry out terrorist acts, and claimed that the six Tunisians were members of Hezbollah's IJO. Salah was charged by a special antiterrorist court in France in November 1987 and found guilty in 1992 of murder, attempted murder, and conspiracy and sentenced to life in prison.[71]

Salah's trial was memorable, among other things, for his courtroom theatrics. Following one outburst, he loudly proclaimed, "My name is Death to the West" and "War, holy war!"[72] Thereafter, he was ejected from the court. In another statement Salah described his motivation for the attack. "I am a fighter advocating for the Islamic cause," he declared. "The stronghold of Islamism is Iran, and our enemies are all those countries who fight against Iran. By helping Iraq against Iran, your country, France, becomes our enemy.... Our main goal is to make France aware of what it is doing to us through violence."[73]

Mohammad Mouhajer, one of the Lebanese men arrested in connection with the bombings, was the nephew of Hezbollah leader Sheikh Ibrahim al-Amin.[74] As a cover for his activities Mouhajer operated an Islamic bookstore in Paris. He, along with Salah, also frequented an Islamic cultural center named Ahl al-Beit, which was operated by Sheikh Fadlallah's brother Mohammad Bakir. According to Hezbollah expert Magnus Ranstorp, Mouhajer "occupied a senior position as coordinator of the French pro-Iranian network and Hizb'allah in Lebanon." Mouhajer's release in 1988 coincided with the release of several French hostages, leading some to conclude that French law enforcement had averted normal legal proceedings against him in order to minimize the risk of further terrorism in France and obtain the release of French nationals held by Hezbollah.[75]

Salah's cell in France received its marching orders from both Hezbollah Special Security Apparatus chief Abdelhadi Hamadi and Wahid Gordji, a translator and unofficial second-in-command at the Iranian embassy in Paris. Gordji, who had been responsible for obtaining Salah's scholarship to study at Qom, served as Tehran's primary contact with the Paris cell.[76] In June 1987, Paris accused Iran of "instigating the 1986 bombing campaign and of giving support to a cell of North African terrorists," and the French investigative team demanded that Gordji submit to questioning related to the bombings.[77] His refusal to answer the summons and subsequent confinement to the Iranian embassy in Paris triggered a diplomatic row. After French police cordoned off the Iranian embassy to prevent Gordji from leaving the country, Tehran responded by blockading the French embassy in the Iranian capital. On July 18, France officially severed ties with Iran, leading to a warning from a French lawyer for the Iranian government that unruly crowds could storm France's embassy and seize staff. Hezbollah's IJO also issued a communiqué threatening to immediately execute two French hostages, Marcel Fontaine and Marcel Carton, though the two were eventually released in 1988. The dispute ended with the release of Gordji, who returned to Iran, in exchange for the release of the French consul Paul Torri.[78]

The 1986 bombing campaign resulted from a convergence of interests between Hezbollah and Iran. Hezbollah sought the release of its imprisoned members, while Iran desired to make France pay for its support of Iraq and other anti-Iranian policies.[79] Despite Salah's arrest and the destruction of his network, the terror campaign of 1986 accomplished many of its goals. In July of 1986, Masoud Radjavi, leader of the Iranian opposition movement Mujahedin-e Khalq (People's Mujahedin of Iran, or MEK) also known as the National Council of Iranian Resistance, was expelled from Paris along with his organization and forced to transfer its headquarters to Iraq. In 1988, France also agreed to repay $300 million of the $1 billion loan from Iran to the French nuclear consortium Eurodiff, a deal dating from before the Islamic Revolution aimed at financing the construction of a nuclear plant.[80] In return for these goodwill gestures, overt attacks against French targets and the kidnapping of French nationals in Lebanon ceased. However, Europe overall remained an arena for Hezbollah's attacks against Israeli, Jewish, and American targets.

The Long Arm of the Hamadi Clan

It would not be long before Mohammad Hamadi followed up on the hijacking of TWA flight 847 with further European attacks. The Hamadi clan had long been part of the core of Hezbollah—there at its founding and central to its IJO. A July 1987 CIA report tied "Hizballah's success in the Bekaa" to Shi'a clans in the valley, in particular "the Musawi, Tufayli, and Hamadi clans."[81] The agency had no mere parochial interest in the Hamadi clan—the family's members were popping up in a series of international Hezbollah plots.

Around the time of Mohammad Hamadi's 1987 arrest at the Frankfurt airport, another Hezbollah operative was arrested in Italy, indicating the group was "apparently preparing the logistic grounds for future terrorist attacks," according to the CIA.[82] Meanwhile, Abbas Hamadi, who returned to Lebanon after being briefly detained along with his brother, helped kidnap two West German businessmen in an attempt to pressure the West German government to release his younger brother, Mohammad. The eldest Hamadi brother, Abdel, was chief of security for Hezbollah in the Beirut suburbs and the de facto leader of an operational network that went by the name "Freedom Fighters" and which claimed responsibility for three kidnappings in West Beirut following Mohammad Hamadi's arrest in Germany.[83] When these actions failed to secure Mohammad's release, Abbas took the fight to Germany, but—just twelve days after his initial release—he was arrested at the Frankfurt airport again.[84]

Mohammad might have been the youngest Hamadi brother, but his star burned brightest given his role in the TWA flight 847 hijacking. So when Mohammad was caught in Frankfurt, the retribution was high: not just the kidnapping of two Germans in Lebanon but also that of two Swedish journalists (thought to be West Germans) on February 11, 1987, in Beirut. Once the kidnappers realized they had grabbed Swedes, not Germans, the captives were promptly released. These kidnappings closely followed the January 27 capture of another West German hostage, also taken in an effort to secure the Hamadis' release. Two years later, Hezbollah operatives kidnapped two German charity workers in southern Lebanon, the day before Mohammad Hamadi was convicted and sentenced to life imprisonment in Germany in May 1989.[85] The Hezbollah hijacking of a flight in 1987, led by Hussein Ali Mohammad Hariri, was also aimed at securing the release of detained Hezbollah operatives, chief among them the Hamadi brothers (see chapter 9).

Hezbollah saw Europe in general and Germany in particular as a permissive operating environment, however, and had bigger plans than just kidnapping Germans in Lebanon. According to a US Senate report, Hezbollah leveraged the acumen and connections of sympathetic Lebanese businessmen in Europe to build a "web of import-export companies in Western Europe as part of its dormant network." The purpose of this network: "to insert large quantities of explosive and related equipment into target countries."[86] The Hamadi brothers' operational plans had been thwarted with Mohammad's arrest and conviction, but other Hezbollah operatives were ready to pick up where the Hamadis had left off.

Casing Targets in Germany

In 1989, Hezbollah operative Bassam Gharib Makki was apprehended in Germany, where he was planning to carry out a bombing attack. Makki was found in possession of preoperational intelligence about Israeli, Jewish, American, and other targets in Germany, and Arabic bomb-making instructions were discovered in his apartment in Darmstadt, in the southwest part of the country.[87]

Born on July 25, 1967, in Bint Jbeil, in southern Lebanon, Bassam Makki first arrived in Germany on December 2, 1985, and filed an asylum claim. However, after learning he could not attend university under asylum status, he flew back to Lebanon and later returned under the auspices of a church group. In April 1988, Makki received his residency permit and began studying physics at the Institute of Technology in Darmstadt, on a full scholarship from the Hariri Foundation.[88] However,

Makki's interest in higher education was merely a cover for his real mission in Germany, which was to case American, Israeli, and Jewish targets.[89]

On September 23, 1988, German authorities intercepted a package sent by Makki to his contact in Lebanon containing an atlas of the Rhine-Main area and thirteen color photographs of Israeli targets. It also contained an odd letter referring to various BMW cars that he claimed to have located, with a particular focus on the BMW 320 and 520 models. The Germans intercepted another package en route to Lebanon on May 31, 1989, which contained a list of twenty Mercedes cars and a statement from Makki that buying larger models such as the 450 and 480 would be difficult. If there were some "marks or checks," he added, he would be willing to buy the cars.[90] Investigators would make sense of the letters only later, when they found Makki's codebooks and realized the references to cars were code for his operational planning.

When Bassam Makki was apprehended by German authorities on June 22, 1989, he was found in possession of a letter identifying all his targets.[91] A search of his apartment revealed codebooks hidden in a suitcase and behind a picture frame as well as instructions on the use of explosives. The codebooks were simple but effective. For example, the sentence "I have found a car in good condition" indicated he had discovered a good bombing target. "BMW" referred to Israeli and Jewish targets, and "Mercedes" indicated an American target. The combination 320 and 520 BMW referred to the Israeli religious community at Reichensbachstrasse 27, while the numbers indicated that both injuries to persons and property damage could be achieved. For this reason, it was considered the best target. The references to the Mercedes 450 and 480 implied difficulty scouting out special buildings or people. And "marks or checks" referred to the weapons or explosives needed to make feasible an attack on the targets.[92]

During his trial Bassam claimed that he had been coerced into conducting reconnaissance by a man named Jozef, an Arab who appeared in his apartment in September 1988 and threatened his family unless Bassam complied with his demands. "Jozef," also the name signed to the letters seized en route to Lebanon, was determined by the German court to be a fabrication.[93] "For an undetermined time," the court concluded, "he has had connections with similarly-minded persons or organizations in Beirut, Lebanon, who engage in or have an interest in preparing and executing bomb attacks against Israeli, Jewish, or American installations" in Germany.[94]

Makki was sentenced to two years in prison on December 22, 1989, and deported to Syria on July 22, 1990.[95] This was hardly the end of his involvement with Hezbollah, however; Makki turned up again in South America several years later under incriminating circumstances (see chapter 11).

Iran's Dissident Hit List

Immediately following the founding of the Islamic Republic, the Iranian leadership embarked on an assassination campaign targeting individuals deemed to be working against the regime's interests. Between 1979 and 1994, the CIA reported, Iran "murdered Iranian defectors and dissidents in West Germany, the United Kingdom, Switzerland, and Turkey."[96] Overall, more than sixty individuals were targeted in assassination attempts.[97] In many cases Hezbollah members functioned as the logistics experts or gunmen in these plots.

The first successful assassination of an Iranian dissident in Western Europe occurred in 1984. On February 7, Gen. Gholam Ali Oveissi and his brother were fatally shot on a Paris street by what French police described as "professional assassins." Police claimed there were "two or three men involved and that one or two of them had fired a 9-millimeter pistol at the victims who were walking on Rue de Passy."[98] Oveissi, the former military governor of Tehran under the shah who was known as the Butcher of Tehran, distinguished himself by responding to protests with tanks. Just before his death, Oveissi claimed that he had assembled a small counterrevolutionary army to retake Iran. Hezbollah's IJO and another group, the Revolutionary Organization for Liberation and Reform, claimed responsibility for the killings. The day after the attack, the Iranian government described the event as a "revolutionary execution."[99]

Oveissi's assassination ushered in a period of great danger for Iranian dissidents in Europe. On July 19, 1987, for example, Amir Parvis, a former Iranian cabinet member and the British chairman of the National Movement of the Iranian Resistance, suffered a broken leg, cuts, and burns when a car bomb exploded as he drove past the Royal Kensington Hotel in London. Several months later, on October 3, Ali Tavakoli and his son Nader, both Iranian monarchist exiles, were found shot in the head in their London apartment.[100] Both attacks were claimed by a previously unknown group, the Guardians of the Islamic Revolution, which according to a March 3, 1989, report by the *Times* of London, "is believe[d] to be closely linked to the Hezbollah extremists in south Beirut, but all its London-based members are Iranian."[101]

A year later, on July 13, 1989, Dr. Abdolrahman Ghassemlou, secretary-general of the Kurdish Democratic Party of Iranian Kurdistan (PDKI); Abdollah Ghaeri-Azar, the PDKI's European representative; and Fazil Rassoul, an Iraqi Kurd serving as a mediator were assassinated in a Vienna apartment while meeting with a delegation from the Iranian government. Although forced underground after the 1979 revolution, Ghassemlou and the PDKI were informed after the Iran-Iraq War that the Iranian government was open to conducting talks. On December 30 and 31, 1988, Ghassemlou met with an Iranian delegation headed by Mohammad Jafari Sahraroudi, the head of the Kurdish Affairs Section of the Iranian Ministry of Intelligence. The two met regularly until July 13, when a meeting was held that included Sahraroudi; governor of the Iranian province of Kurdistan Mostafa Ajoudi; an undercover Iranian agent, Amir Mansour Bozorgian; and the victims. At one point during the meeting, Rassoul and Ghassemlou proposed a break and suggested that the negotiations resume the next day. Soon after, gunshots were heard. In the shooting the three Kurds were killed and Sahraroudi was injured. Investigators found a blue baseball cap in Ghassemlou's lap, the same call sign that was left at the scene of the murder of an Iranian pilot, Ahmad Moradi Talebi, in 1987 and the 1990 murder of resistance leader Kazem Radjavi.[102] Bozorgian was taken into custody; however, he was later released and fled the country, along with several other suspects.[103]

Just one month after the Vienna assassination, on August 3, 1989, Mustafa Mahmoud Mazeh died when an explosive device he was preparing detonated prematurely inside the Paddington Hotel in London. His target was Salman Rushdie, whose 1988 publication of *The Satanic Verses* prompted Ayatollah Khomeini to issue a fatwa condemning the writer, his editors, and his publishers to death, and to place a $2.5 million bounty on his head. Mazeh, a Lebanese citizen born in the Guinean capital of Conakry, had joined a local Hezbollah cell in his teens. Though he was being watched by security agencies, he succeeded in obtaining a French passport in Abidjan, Ivory Coast, from an official later arrested by the French authorities in Toulouse. Mazeh apparently went to Lebanon and stayed in his parents' village before traveling to London through the Netherlands.[104]

Later, speaking about Khomeini's fatwa against Rushdie, a Hezbollah commander would tell an interviewer that "one member of the Islamic Resistance, Mustafa Mazeh, had been martyred in London."[105] According to the CIA, attacks on the book's Italian, Norwegian, and Japanese translators in July 1991 suggested "that Iran has shifted from attacking organizations affiliated with the novel—publishing houses and bookstores—to individuals involved in its publication, as called for in the original *fatwa*."[106] Today, a shrine dedicated to Mazeh still stands in Tehran's Behesht Zahra cemetery with an inscription reading, "The first martyr to die on a mission to kill Salman Rushdie."[107]

Less than a year after the Vienna assassinations and the abortive attempt on Rushdie's life in London, Kazem Radjavi, former Iranian ambassador to the UN and brother of the leader of the MEK, was assassinated. On April 24, 1990, his car was forced off the road in Coppet, Switzerland, by two vehicles, after which two armed men exited one of the vehicles and opened fire. Again, a blue baseball cap was left at the scene, marking the third use of this call sign at the site of a suspected Iranian assassination.[108]

According to the report of the Swiss investigating judge, evidence pointed to the direct involvement of one or more official Iranian services in the murder. All in all, there were thirteen suspects—all of whom had traveled to Switzerland on official Iranian passports.[109] One report indicated that "all 13 came to Switzerland on brand-new government-service passports, many issued in Tehran on the same date. Most listed the same personal address, Karim-Khan 40, which turns out to be an intelligence ministry building. All 13 arrived on Iran Air flights, using tickets issued on the same date and numbered sequentially." International warrants for the thirteen suspects' arrests were issued on June 15, 1990.[110]

No death, however, shook the Iranian expatriate community more than the assassination of Chapour Bakhtiar, former Iranian prime minister and secretary-general of the Iranian National Resistance Movement. On August 6, 1991, Bakhtiar and an aide were stabbed to death by Iranian operatives in Bakhtiar's Paris apartment.[111] Previously, in July 1980, Bakhtiar had been targeted in another assassination attempt led by Anis Naccache that killed a policeman and a female neighbor. One reason Hezbollah abducted French citizens in Lebanon was to secure the release of Naccache, who was imprisoned in France for the attempted killing.[112]

In a 1991 interview Naccache recalled, "I had no personal feelings against Bakhtiar. . . . It was purely political. He had been sentenced to death by the Iranian Revolutionary Tribunal. They sent five of us to execute him."[113] Hezbollah, for its part, pushed hard for Naccache's release following its various kidnappings and terrorist acts and on July 28, 1990, finally got its wish. Naccache was sent to Tehran, with his pardon granted in a bid to improve relations with Tehran that would lead to the release of French hostages held in Lebanon.[114]

Death at the Mykonos Restaurant

The most daring and public assassinations Hezbollah carried out at the behest of its Iranian masters occurred September 17, 1992, when operatives gunned down Dr. Sadegh Sharafkandi, secretary-general of the PDKI—the biggest movement of Iranian Kurdish opposition to Tehran—and three of his colleagues at the Mykonos restaurant in Berlin.[115]

In its findings, a Berlin court ruled that the attack was carried out by a Hezbollah cell by order of the Iranian government. In delivering the opinion, presiding judge Frithjof Kubsch said the judges were particularly struck by Iranian leaders' assertions that they could "silence an uncomfortable voice" any way they pleased. To strengthen his point, he cited a television interview given by Iran's intelligence minister, Ali Fallahian, one month before the Mykonos attack, in which Fallahian bragged that Iran could launch "decisive strikes" against its opponents abroad.[116] Furthermore, on August 30, 1992, Fallahian admitted in an interview with an Iranian television reporter that Iran monitored Iranian dissidents both at home and abroad: "We track them outside the country, too," he said. "We have them under surveillance. . . . Last year, we succeeded in striking fundamental blows to their top members."[117]

Much of the information surrounding the Mykonos plot was relayed by an Iranian defector named Abolghasem Mesbahi, who claimed to be a founding member of the Iranian Security Service. According to him, the decision to carry out the attack was made by the Committee for Special Operations, which included President Rafsanjani, Minister of Intelligence Fallahian, Foreign Minister Ali Akbar Velayati, representatives of the Security Apparatus, and, most significantly, Supreme Leader Ali Khamenei.[118]

The "attack group," organized by Fallahian, arrived in Berlin from Iran on September 7, 1992. It was headed by Abdolraham Banihashemi (also known as Abu Sharif, an operative for the Ministry of Intelligence and Security who trained in Lebanon), who also served as one of the attack's two gunmen and who has been implicated in the August 1987 assassination of a former Iranian F-14 pilot in Geneva.[119] The operation's logistics chief, Kazem Darabi, was a former Revolutionary Guard and Hezbollah member who had been living in Germany since 1980 and belonged to an association of Iranian students in Europe. According to Argentine prosecutors,

"[Association of Islamic Students in Europe] UISA and the associations that belonged to it worked closely with extremist Islamic groups, particularly Hezbollah and Iranian government bodies such as the embassy and consulate. UISA was the main organization from which Iran's intelligence service recruited collaborators for propaganda and intelligence activities in Iran."[120]

In a statement to German prosecutors, Ataollah Ayad, one of Darabi's recruits, made clear that Darabi was "the boss of Hezbollah in Berlin."[121] Moreover, Darabi would also be linked to an attack at the 1991 Iran Cultural Festival in Dusseldorf. Before the festival, German intelligence reportedly intercepted a telephone call in which Darabi was instructed by someone at the Iranian cultural center in Cologne with ties to Iran's Ministry of Intelligence to enlist some "Arab friends" from Berlin and head to Dusseldorf. Armed with pistols, gas, guns, and mace, Darabi and his accomplices assaulted members of the Iranian opposition group MEK, who were exhibiting books and pictures at the festival. Several MEK members were seriously injured. Eyewitnesses later testified that Darabi appeared to be the leader of the assault.[122]

Already concerned about Darabi's activities in their country, German officials attempted to deport him in June 1992. However, the Iranian government intervened and asked Germany to allow Darabi to remain in the country.[123] The second gunman, Abbas Rhayel, and one of the co-conspirators, Youssef Amin, "were members of Hezbollah," according to Argentine prosecutors, adding they received training at an IRGC center near Rasht in Iran.[124] According to German prosecutors, when the "Hit Team" arrived in Berlin and command was transferred from Darabi to Banihashemi, two of the co-conspirators who were not members of Hezbollah "were shut out of the immediate involvement in the act."[125]

The operational stage of the Mykonos attack began on the morning of September 16, when Rhayel and Farajollah Haider, another Hezbollah member of Lebanese origin, received an Uzi machine gun, a pistol, and two silencers. The source of these arms was never identified but was suspected to be linked to Iranian intelligence. German investigators later traced both the pistol and silencer to Iran. On the next morning, September 17, Rhayel and Haider purchased the bags they would use to conceal the weapons as they entered the Mykonos Restaurant.[126]

On the night of September 17, Banihashemi and Rhayel entered the restaurant at 10:50 PM, while Amin waited outside to block the door. Haider and an Iranian known only as Mohammad, who had previously been tasked with keeping the targets under surveillance, waited several blocks away with the getaway car. The car had been purchased several days earlier by Ali Dakhil Sabra, who had served with Amin and Rhayel in Lebanon and then come with them to Germany. When the targets emerged into view, Banihashemi shouted, "You sons of whores" in Persian and opened fire. Rhayel followed Banihashemi inside and shot both Sharafkandi and Homayoun Ardalan, the PDKI's representative in Germany. Between the two assassins, thirty shots were fired. The assailants then fled on foot to the getaway vehicle.[127]

The police investigation quickly revealed Iranian involvement in the attack. On September 22, the bag containing the weapons and silencers was discovered, and tests revealed significant similarities between these weapons and those used in the assassination of Iranian dissidents Akbar Mohammadi in Hamburg in 1987 and Bahman Javadi in Cyprus in 1989. The police also matched the serial number on the pistol used by Rhayel to a shipment delivered by a Spanish dealer to the Iranian military in 1972. Rhayel's palm print was discovered on one of the pistol magazines, the blood of one of the victims was identified on the pistol itself, and Amin's fingerprints were found on a plastic shopping bag inside the getaway vehicle.[128]

According to German prosecutors, Abdolraham Banihashemi "left the city by airplane after the crime and went via Turkey to Iran. There, he was rewarded for his role in the attack with a Mercedes 230 and participation in profitable business transactions."[129] The others were not so fortunate. Darabi and Rhayel were sentenced to life in prison in Germany in April 1997, while Amin and Mohammad Atris, a document forger who assisted the attackers, were given terms of eleven and about five years, respectively.[130] While Amin and Atris served out their shorter terms, in December 2007 Darabi and Rhayel were released from prison and returned to Iran. Germany's *Der Spiegel* suggested they were released in exchange for a German tourist arrested in Iran in November 2005. Germany, it appears, was not the only country seeking collateral for Darabi and Rhayel's release; Israel had hoped to bargain for an early release in return for information about Ron Arad, an Israeli aviator shot down over Lebanon in 1986.[131]

The brazen assassination in public of four Iranian dissidents at Mykonos, in the opinion of Germany's highest criminal court, signaled culpability for terrorism at the highest levels of the Islamic Republic. The court judgment rejected the premise that the attack was executed by "mavericks," concluding that "the assassination [was] put into action much more through the powers in Iran." By identifying President Rafsanjani and the Supreme Leader himself as the orchestrators of the assassination, the judgment found that "Iranian powers not only allow terrorist attacks abroad . . . but that they themselves set in action such attacks." When the Tehran regime encountered political opposition, the court determined, its solution was simply to have the opponents "liquidated."[132]

Yet the ruling would not translate into durable and tangible action against Iran or Hezbollah. Iran responded to the placement of a plaque memorializing the victims of the Mykonos attack by displaying one of its own near the German embassy in Tehran denouncing Germany for arming Saddam Hussein with chemical weapons during the Iran-Iraq War. Apparently concerned over the diplomatic ramifications, the German ambassador to Iran distanced his government from the original plaque's assertion of Iranian responsibility for the Mykonos attack.[133] While many European nations withdrew their ambassadors from Iran following the ruling, this diplomatic freeze lasted only months. And along with the release of perpetrators Darabi and Rhayel, none of the Iranian leaders identified in the court judgment—Rafsanjani, Fallahian, Velayati, or Khamenei—were ever held to account for their roles in the attack.

Hezbollah's emergence as a terrorist force operating in Europe, well beyond the confines of the Middle East, elicited neither a unified nor a coherent strategy by

European capitals. Hezbollah was undeterred, and its European operations marked only the beginning of its rapid transformation from a regional threat into a global terrorist network. The European Union would repeatedly refrain from designating Hezbollah as a terrorist organization, in whole or in part. The consequence would be felt not only in Europe but around the world.

Notes

1. Testrake, *Triumph over Terror,* 67.

2. Ron Eschmann, "Terror on Flight 847," *The Officer* 79, no. 7 (October 2003): 23; Testrake, *Triumph over Terror,* 67–68.

3. Eschmann, "Terror on Flight 847"; Testrake, *Triumph over Terror,* 69–71.

4. Eschmann, "Terror on Flight 847."

5. Testrake, *Triumph over Terror,* 70–71; Associated Press, "Slain Navy Man Bravely Endured Beatings, TWA Attendant Says," September 20, 1988; Jennifer Bayot, "Uli Derickson, 60, Flight Attendant Who Helped Airline Hostages, Dies," *New York Times,* February 24, 2005.

6. *Richard L. Stethem et al. v. The Islamic Republic of Iran et al.,* Plaintiff's Proposed Finding of Fact and Conclusion of Law, Case No. 00-CV-00159, United States District Court, District of Columbia, December 31, 2001.

7. Testrake, *Triumph over Terror,* 71–72; *Stethem et al. v. The Islamic Republic of Iran et al.*; Associated Press, "Slain Navy Man Bravely Endured Beatings, TWA Attendant Says," September 20, 1988.

8. Testrake, *Triumph over Terror,* 74.

9. Jennifer Bayot, "Uli Derickson, 60, Flight Attendant Who Helped Airline Hostages, Dies," *New York Times,* February 24, 2005; Jon Thurber, "Uli Derickson, 60; Was Lead Flight Attendant on Hijacked Jet," *Los Angeles Times,* February 25, 2005.

10. US CIA, "Terrorist Use of Beirut International Airport."

11. US CIA, "Terrorist Use of Beirut International Airport"; William E. Smith, "Terror Aboard Flight 847," *Time,* June 24, 2001.

12. US CIA, "Two Jordanian Jets Hijacked"; Smith, "Terror aboard Flight 847."

13. US CIA, "Terrorist Use of Beirut International Airport"; US CIA, "Two Jordanian Jets Hijacked"; Smith, "Terror Aboard Flight 847."

14. US CIA, "Terrorist Use of Beirut International Airport."

15. Ibid.

16. Testrake, *Triumph over Terror,* 74–75.

17. Ibid., 75–77; Smith, "Terror Aboard Flight 847."

18. Testrake, *Triumph over Terror,* 77; *Stethem et al. v. The Islamic Republic of Iran et al.*

19. Testrake, *Triumph over Terror,* 77–78.

20. Ranstorp, *Hizb'allah in Lebanon,* 95; Ariel Merari et al., "Review of International Terrorism in 1985," Project on Terrorism, Jaffee Center for Strategic Studies, *Jerusalem Post,* 1986, 89.

21. Testrake, *Triumph over Terror,* 78–79.

22. *Stethem et al. v. The Islamic Republic of Iran et al.*; Testrake, *Triumph over Terror,* 78–79.

23. Eschmann, "Terror on Flight 847."

24. Testrake, *Triumph over Terror*, 79–81.

25. Ibid., 78.

26. US Department of State, *Patterns of Global Terrorism: 1985*, Washington, DC, October 1986, 2.

27. Ibid., 11–14.

28. Testrake, *Triumph over Terror*, 83–85; Smith, "Terror Aboard Flight 847."

29. Testrake, *Triumph over Terror*, 85–87; *Stethem et al. v. The Islamic Republic of Iran et al.*

30. *Stethem et al. v. The Islamic Republic of Iran et al.*

31. In his memoir, Captain Testrake recalls just a single shot, not two. Testrake, *Triumph over Terror*, 85; Eschmann, "Terror on Flight 847"; Smith, "Terror Aboard Flight 847."

32. Clarridge, *Spy for all Seasons*, 350; Testrake, *Triumph over Terror*, 86–87.

33. James Risen, "U.S. Traces Iran's Ties to Terror through a Lebanese," *New York Times*, January 17, 2002.

34. *Stethem et al. v. The Islamic Republic of Iran et al.*

35. Eschmann, "Terror on Flight 847."

36. US CIA, "Status of TWA Hijacking/Hostages."

37. Isabel Kershner, "The Changing Colors of Imad Mughniyah," *Jerusalem Report*, March 25, 2002; *United States of America v. Ali Atwa et al.*, United States District Court, District of Columbia, No. 85-0405, November 14, 1985; Shaked and Rabinovich, *Middle East Contemporary Survey*, 87.

38. *USA v. Ali Atwa et al.*

39. US FBI Special Agent [name redacted] affidavit, "In Re: Hizballah, aka Islamic Jihad Organization," June 8, 1997.

40. *Stethem et al. v. The Islamic Republic of Iran et al.*

41. Reuters, "Captors 'Nice People' Greek Folk Singer Says," June 19, 1985; Smith, "Terror Aboard Flight 847"; Testrake, *Triumph over Terror*, 88.

42. Testrake, *Triumph over Terror*, 88.

43. *Stethem et al. v. The Islamic Republic of Iran et al.*

44. Testrake, *Triumph over Terror*, 88–89; *USA v. Ali Atwa et al.*

45. Testrake, *Triumph over Terror*, 90–91.

46. Ibid., 98.

47. "Chronology of Hostage Crisis," *Washington Post*, June 30, 1985.

48. Clarridge, *Spy for all Seasons*, 339; "Victoria Toensing: FISA Fears Shielded 9/11 Plotters," *Newsmax.com*, January 24, 2006.

49. *USA v. Ali Atwa et al.*

50. Elaine Sciolino, "U.S. Links Hijacker on Kuwaiti Plane 1985 Air Piracy," *New York Times*, April 16, 1988; James M. Markham, "Brother of Suspected Hijacker Arrested," *New York Times*, January 28, 1987.

51. United Press International, "Seven Lebanese Questioned in Embassy Bombing Plot," November 29, 1984; Janet Stobart, "Italians Foil Possible Terrorist Attack on US Embassy in Rome," *Christian Science Monitor*, November 29, 1984.

52. United Press International, "Seven Lebanese Questioned in Embassy Bombing Plot"; Stobart, "Italians Foil Possible Terrorist Attack on US Embassy in Rome."

53. Hoffman, *Recent Trends and Future Prospects*, 16; Stobart, "Italians Foil Possible Terrorist Attack," November 29, 1984; "Callers Warn Italy on Plot Probe," *Washington Post*, November 29, 1984; "Italy: Disaster Averted," *Time*, December 10, 1984.

54. Hoffman, *Recent Trends and Future Prospects*, 20; Ranstorp, *Hizb'allah in Lebanon*, 93.

55. "Islamic Jihad Admits to Blast in Spain," *Globe and Mail*, April 15, 1985; US Department of State, *Patterns of Global Terrorism: 1985*, 11.

56. Edward Cody, "Anti-Terror Efforts Revive Interest in an Old Enemy—FBI List Includes Lebanese Suspect in Past Attacks on U.S.," *Washington Post*, October 31, 2001.

57. Government of New Zealand, "Case to Designate Lebanese Hizbollah's Military Wing"; Times Wire Services, "3 Copenhagen Blasts Injure 22: Vengeance for Lebanon, Islamic Jihad Declares," *Los Angeles Times*, July 23, 1985.

58. *France v. Saleh Fouad Ben Ali*, Cour d'Appel de Paris, 1ère Chambre d'Accusation, March 4, 1991.

59. Diana Geddes, "Panic over Paris Store Bombs," *Times* (London), December 9, 1985.

60. Scheherezade Faramarzi, "Mughniyeh Was a Key Hezbollah Commander, Insider Says," Associated Press, February 27, 2008.

61. US Department of State, *Patterns of Global Terrorism: 1986*, Washington, DC, 38.

62. *France v. Saleh Fouad Ben Ali*; Associated Press, "Terrorist Mastermind Sentenced to Life for Paris Bombings," April 14, 1992.

63. Agence France Presse, "Pro-Iranian Terrorists Sentenced Over Paris Bomb Attacks," April 14, 1992.

64. Translated from *France v. Saleh Fouad Ben Ali*.

65. Youssef M. Ibrahim, "Trial of Accused Mastermind in Bombings Begins in Paris," *New York Times*, January 30, 1990; Didier Bigo, "Les attentats de 1986 en France: Un cas de violence transnationale et ses implications," *Cultures & Conflicts* 4 (Winter 1991): 5.

66. Ibid.

67. William Echikson, "How France Links Iran to Terror," *Christian Science Monitor*, July 31, 1987.

68. Brian Moynahan, "French in Crisis Talks as Embassy Deadline Nears," *Sunday Times* (London), July 26, 1987.

69. Moynahan, "French in Crisis"; Richard Bernstein, "French Report on Terrorism Raises Suspicions about Iran," *New York Times*, July 24, 1987; Bigo, "Les attentats de 1986 en France."

70. Ibrahim, "Trial of Accused Mastermind."

71. "Tunisian Given Life Sentence in Series of Paris Bombings," *New York Times*, April 15, 1992.

72. Ibrahim, "Trial of Accused Mastermind."

73. Buenos Aires, Argentina Judicial Branch, AMIA Indictment, Office of the National Federal Court No. 17, Criminal and Correctional Matters No. 9, Case No. 1156, March 5, 2003, (hereafter cited as AMIA indictment), 186–87.

74. Ranstorp, *Hizb'allah in Lebanon*, 97.

75. Ibid., 155.

76. Bigo, "Les attentats de 1986 en France," 5.

77. US CIA, "Iranian Support for Terrorism in 1987," 13.

78. Paul Lewis, "France Breaks Iran Ties and Isolates Embassy," *New York Times*, July 18, 1987; Ariel Merari et al., "Review of International Terrorism in 1987," JCSS Project on Low Intensity Warfare, *Jerusalem Post*, 1986, 52; Ranstorp, *Hizb'allah in Lebanon*, 123.

79. Ranstorp, *Hizb'allah in Lebanon*, 97; Federal Court of Canada, *Mohamed Hussein Al Husseini*, Annex E. October 23, 1993, 9.

80. Ranstorp, *Hizb'allah in Lebanon*, 124; Shay, *Axis of Evil*, 176.

81. US CIA, "Lebanon: Prospects for Islamic Fundamentalism."

82. US CIA, "Prospects for Hizballah Terrorism in Africa."

83. Ihsan Hijazi, "Kidnapping Suspect Helps Syria," *New York Times*, June 1, 1988.

84. Hoffman, *Recent Trends and Future Prospects*, 28.

85. Marc Fisher, "Bonn Condemns Threat by Shiites," *Washington Post*, July 26, 1991; Martin Kramer, "Will Germany Release an American-Killer?" *Sandstorm*, January 27, 2004.

86. US Senator John Kerry and US Senator Hank Brown, "The BCCI Affair," A Report to the Committee on Foreign Relations United States Senate, 102nd Cong., 2nd sess., December 1992, 445.

87. Bergman, *Secret War with Iran*, 191; Statement of Matthew Levitt, *Islamic Extremism in Europe: Beyond al-Qaeda—Hamas and Hezbollah in Europe*.

88. Munich, German Judicial Branch, Judgment of the 1st Criminal Chamber of the Munich Landgericht I, Gz. 1 KLs 112 Js 3948/89, December 22, 1989, 4–5.

89. Diaz and Newman, *Lightning Out of Lebanon*, 102–3; *United States of America v. Bassam Gharib Makki*, Presentence Investigation Report, United States District Court, Southern District of Florida, Miami Division, CR 98-334-01, February 12, 1999, p. 7.

90. Munich, German Judicial Branch, Judgment of the 1st Criminal Chamber of the Munich Landgericht I, Gz. 1 KLs 112 Js 3948/89, December 22, 1989, 5–10.

91. "West Germans Arrest Suspect in Bomb Plot," *Anchorage Daily News*, July 7, 1989.

92. Munich, German Judicial Branch, Judgment of the 1st Criminal Chamber of the Munich Landgericht I, Gz. 1 KLs 112 Js 3948/89, December 22, 1989, 8–10.

93. Ibid., 12–14.

94. *USA v. Bassam Gharib Makki*.

95. Munich, German Judicial Branch, Judgment of the 1st Criminal Chamber of the Munich Landgericht I, Gz. 1 KLs 112 Js 3948/89, December 22, 1989, 22; *USA v. Bassam Gharib Makki*.

96. US CIA, "Iranian Support for Terrorism in 1987," 13.

97. Thomas Sanction et al., "The Tehran Connection," *Time*, March 21, 1994.

98. John Vinocur, "Exiled Iranian General Is Killed with Brother by Gunmen in Paris," *New York Times*, February 8, 1984.

99. Vinocur, "Exiled Iranian General Is Killed"; "Murder of Iranian Exile Underlines Risk of Paris," *Globe and Mail*, February 9, 1984.

100. Michael Horsnell and Hazhir Teimourian, "Two Iranians Shot Dead in London," *Times* (London), October 3, 1987.

101. Hazhir Teimourian and Nicholas Beeston, "Iranian Extremist Cell in UK Could Number under 12," *Times* (London), March 3, 1989.

102. Argentina, Buenos Aires, Investigations Unit of the Office of the Attorney General. *Office of Criminal Investigations: AMIA Case*. Report by Marcelo Martinez

Burgos and Alberto Nisman, October 25, 2006 (hereafter cited as Burgos and Nisman), 25.

103. Iran Human Rights Documentation Center, "No Safe Haven: Iran's Global Assassination Campaign," May 2008, 26.

104. Anthony Loyd, "Tomb of the Unknown Assassin Reveals Mission to Kill Rushdie," *Times* (London), June 8, 2005.

105. Chehabi and Abisaab, *Distant Relations*, 292–93.

106. US CIA, "Iran: Enhanced Terrorist Capabilities."

107. Loyd, "Tomb of the Unknown Assassin."

108. Burgos and Nisman, 24–25; Sanction et al., "Tehran Connection."

109. US Department of State, *Patterns of Global Terrorism: 1990*, Washington, DC, April 1991, 15.

110. Sanction et al., "Tehran Connection."

111. Burgos and Nisman, 31; US Department of State, *Patterns of Global Terrorism: 1991*, Washington, DC, April 1992, 30.

112. Patrick Marnham, "Jailed Iranian Puts Pressure on France," *Independent* (London), February 3, 1989.

113. Robert Fisk, "Two Faces of an Unlikely Assassin," *Independent* (London), October 27, 1991; Ranstorp, *Hizb'allah in Lebanon*, 95.

114. Ibid.

115. Burgos and Nisman, 33; Agence France Press, "Iran Ordered Slaying of Kurdish Leaders: German Prosecutor," May 27, 1993.

116. William Drozdiak, "German Court: Tehran Ordered Exile Killings; Verdict Blaming Top Iranians Ruptures Ties," *Washington Post*, April 11, 1997.

117. Rick Atkinson, "Killing of Iranian Dissenters: Bloody Trail Back to Tehran," *Washington Post*, November 21, 1993.

118. Burgos and Nisman, 37.

119. Burgos and Nisman, 37; Ely Karmon, "Iranian Terror in Switzerland against Opposition Activists," IDC Herzliya, International Institute for Counter-Terrorism, April 20, 2009.

120. Burgos and Nisman, 38–41.

121. Mykonos Urteil [Mykonos Judgment], Urteil des Kammergerichts Berlin vom 10. April 1997 [Judgment of the Court of Appeal of Berlin on April 10, 1997], OLGSt Berlin, (1) 2 StE 2/93 (19/93).

122. Iran Human Rights Documentation Center, "Murder at Mykonos: Anatomy of a Political Assassination," March 2007.

123. Burgos and Nisman, 70–71.

124. Ibid., 38–39.

125. Mykonos Urteil [Mykonos Judgment], Urteil des Kammergerichts Berlin vom 10. April 1997.

126. Iran Human Rights Documentation Center, "Murder at Mykonos," 2–8.

127. Ibid., 8–11.

128. Ibid., 12.

129. Mykonos Urteil [Mykonos Judgment], Urteil des Kammergerichts Berlin vom 10. April 1997.

130. Drozdiak, "German Court: Tehran Ordered Exile Killings."

131. "Germany Releases 'Mykonos' Assassins," *Der Spiegel* (Germany), December 11, 2007.

132. Germany, Judgment of the Court of Appeal of Berlin on April 10, 1997, OLGSt Berlin, (1) 2 StE 2/93 (19/93), 50.

133. DW Staff, "Germany and Iran Embroiled in Diplomatic Spat," *Deutsche Welle* (Germany), April 28, 2004.

4

Bombings in Buenos Aires

IT WAS AROUND 9:45 AM ON JULY 18, 1994, and Monica Lucía Arnaudo was in her bedroom, which looked out onto Pasteur Street. As she watched television, Monica heard a car outside speed up and then slam on the brakes. "The tires creaked," she would later recall, "and then [there was] a sort of a crash or collision." She sat upright in bed, just in time to hear a tremendous explosion and feel "something like sand and dust" bursting in through her window.[1] It was 9:53 AM.

What Ms. Arnaudo had actually felt and heard were the shock waves and debris from the explosives-laden van that had just blown the face off the Asociación Mutual Israelita Argentina (AMIA), just across the street—the community center for the largest Jewish community in South America. The Renault Trafic van carried 300 to 400 kilograms of explosives composed of ammonium nitrate, combined with aluminum, a heavy hydrocarbon, TNT, and nitroglycerine. The explosion killed 85 people and wounded some 150 more. The force of the blast instantly destroyed roughly 2,000 of the AMIA building's 4,600 square meters, killing many instantly and trapping others beneath the rubble.[2]

Within forty-eight hours of the attack, the United States sent thirteen International Response Team (IRT) investigators to help investigate the bombing—including FBI investigators; Alcohol, Tobacco, and Firearms (ATF) explosive experts; and State Department Diplomatic Security agents.[3] By Friday, July 22, Israeli forensic police, part of a Disaster Victims Identification group, arrived in Buenos Aires as well.[4] For twelve days, the American IRT members worked side by side at the bomb site with their Israeli and Argentine police and emergency response counterparts sifting through the debris for pieces of the bomb, the van, and the victims.[5] The attack was classified as a double aggravated homicide owing to its nature as a "racial or religious crime" carried out in a manner intended to create "public hazard" and kill and wound as many people as possible.[6]

Within weeks, Argentine federal police had released the composite sketch of the suicide bomber to the local press from testimony that included a door-to-door survey of neighborhood residents shortly after the bombing. Other sketches were publicized of the person who parked the van used in the bombing in a nearby garage three days before the attack.[7]

But as quickly as authorities produced these sketches, and as useful as they would later be in definitively identifying the perpetrators as members of a Hezbollah hit team, they were too late to help apprehend them before they escaped the country. The Iranian diplomatic support network left the country in waves in the weeks leading up to the attack.

The exception was Mohsen Rabbani, an Iranian who lived in Argentina for eleven years. Rabbani, the primary architect of the AMIA plot, reportedly had come from Iran for the express purpose of heading the state-owned al-Tauhid mosque in the Floresta neighborhood, but he also served as a representative of the Iranian Ministry of Agriculture, which was tasked with ensuring the quality of Argentine meat exported to Iran.[8] Prosecutors would later conclude that Rabbani was "the driving force behind these efforts [to establish an Iranian intelligence network in Argentina]. . . . From the time of his arrival in the country in 1983, Mr. Rabbani began laying the groundwork that allowed for the later implementation and further development of the [Iranian] spy network."[9]

Rabbani had never traveled abroad before this assignment but wasted no time establishing himself as a religious leader in the local Muslim community. Rabbani's political views permeated his religious and cultural activities to the point that congregants described his religious activities as a "mask" used to promote the Iranian revolution and condemn Zionism. By one account, for example, several students at the mosque told another congregant that on many occasions, Rabbani exhorted them to "export the revolution," stressing to them, "We are all Hezbollah."[10]

It was widely known within the local Muslim community that the network of followers Rabbani cultivated proactively collected intelligence on his behalf for Iran; they were commonly referred to as "the antennas." Rabbani deployed trusted members of his network as spotters to scout potential Jewish and American targets.[11] Some, like intelligence agent Mohammad Reza Javadi-Nia, went so far as to work as taxi drivers to better carry out the surveillance, targeting, and other intelligence functions assigned by Rabbani.[12] According to an FBI report, Javadi-Nia was believed to be an agent of Iran's Ministry of Islamic Culture and Guidance (Ershad), which, together with other Iranian government agencies such as the Ministry of Intelligence and Security (MOIS), the Cultural Bureaus, and the Foreign Ministry, along with the Qods Force, was believed to have provided cover for Iranian intelligence activities. In the case of Ershad, these activities would have occurred under the guise of religious activity. Previously, the FBI determined, Javadi-Nia had served in similar capacities in Belgium, Spain, Colombia, and Brazil in the mid- to late 1980s. Then, from 1988 to 1993, he served as a cultural attaché at the Iranian embassy in Buenos Aires, before Rabbani took over that position in 1994.[13]

Just four months before the attack, Rabbani suddenly was named an official Iranian diplomat, complete with diplomatic credentials and immunity. As for the Hezbollah operatives brought in to execute the bombing, Argentine law enforcement and intelligence officials would later determine that they left the country about two hours prior to the actual explosion.[14] Some of the operatives, including the suicide bomber, entered the country at Argentina's highly unregulated border crossings in the tri-border area, where Argentina meets Brazil and Paraguay. Others arrived—presumably with false documents—at Ezeiza International Airport in Buenos Aires on July 1, 1994, and left the morning of the attack through Jorge Newberry Metropolitan Airport, also in Buenos Aires, some on flights to the tri-border area.[15] Investigators would later trace phone calls placed from pay phones at these airports, as well as calls from pay phones near the AMIA building during the operatives' stay, to a cellular phone in Foz do Iguaçu, on the Brazilian side of the Friendship Bridge spanning the Parana River in the tri-border area. From Foz, as it is locally known, a network of Hezbollah supporters coordinated the activities of the terrorist cell members operating in Buenos Aires. Frequent calls were made between phones in Argentina and the cell phone in Foz as preparations for the bombing progressed. Then, the day of the attack, the flow of calls suddenly stopped.[16]

Ultimately, Argentine authorities would conclude that "the decision to carry out the AMIA attack was made, and the attack was orchestrated, by the highest officials of the Islamic Republic of Iran at the time, and that these officials instructed Lebanese Hezbollah . . . to carry out the attack."[17]

From the outset, the Argentine investigation into the AMIA attack was poorly handled. Argentine president Nestor Kirchner would later describe it as a national disgrace.[18] The only people convicted of crimes related to the attack were corrupt police officers involved in the sale of the Renault Trafic van used in the attack. Judge Jose Galeano, the judge appointed to serve as chief prosecutor in the AMIA case, originally maintained his full caseload while overseeing this major case. Then, once he took on the AMIA investigation full time, he was caught attempting to bribe a defendant—himself an accused corrupt police officer—to falsely accuse other police officers of involvement in the case. This and other "irregularities" led a grand jury to impeach Galeano in December 2003 for official misconduct. Other irregularities included the charge that then–president of Argentina Carlos Saúl Menem had long maintained close ties to Iranian intelligence and accepted a $10 million bribe from Iran to cover up the Islamic Republic's role in the attack.[19]

Eventually, Judge Rodolfo Canicoba Corral would take over the case and assign a team of experienced federal prosecutors to the investigation. Led by Alberto Nisman, the team reinvestigated the AMIA bombing from scratch, despite the passage of more than a decade since the crime was committed. The investigation covered hundreds of files, produced 113,600 pages of documentation, leveraged telephone intercepts, and incorporated material from the Secretariat of Intelligence of the Executive Branch (SIDE, formerly the Federal Secretariat of Intelligence), which was ordered declassified by then president Nestor Kirchner. Some material the prosecutors sought was no longer available, such as certain financial records destroyed by banks after ten years, as required by local law. Other information the prosecutors sought was, to their dismay and surprise, never maintained in the first place, such as detailed immigration records. Until 1996, all immigration records were recorded manually—a slow bureaucratic process. As the prosecutors dryly concluded in their

2006 report, "it is well known that at the time of the AMIA attack, the Argentine immigration control system suffered serious deficiencies."[20]

While concluding that the evidence did not suffice to call for the indictment and arrest of some of the individuals indicted by Galeano in March 2003, prosecutors determined in 2006 that several additional suspects should be indicted. Moreover, the prosecutors' report reserved particular criticism for Galeano's findings regarding Iran and Hezbollah. While Galeano concluded that the AMIA bombing was the work of "radicalized elements of the Iranian regime," Nisman's team determined "that the decision to carry out the attack was made not by a small splinter group of extremist Islamic officials, but was instead a decision that was extensively discussed and was ultimately adopted by a consensus of the highest representatives of the Iranian government."[21] Regarding the role of Hezbollah, Nisman's report was clearer still: "Whereas Judge Galeano made a point of stating that there was no need to determine whether Hezbollah is a 'terrorist movement, or a movement that is resisting Israel's illegal occupation of Lebanon,' it is obvious to us that the 'terrorist movement' characterization is the correct one."[22]

Even though a claim of responsibility for the AMIA attack was issued under one of Hezbollah's known affiliated names, Galeano concluded that "no evidence has come to light as yet indicating that Hezbollah could have known of the plans, and subsequent to that, could have been implicated in the consequences."[23] To be fair, some of the material available to Nisman's team emerged only after Galeano was excused from the case. By some accounts, the flaws in Galeano's investigation were exacerbated by SIDE's failure to share key intelligence related to the AMIA attack, such as details about the links among Iranian officials suspected of playing various roles in the bombing plot. This included information gleaned from telephone intercepts as well as social network analysis of key addresses where many of the suspects lived at one time or another.[24]

Yet Galeano's indictment includes substantial information about the role of Hezbollah in the attack, including that of Hezbollah's chief of international operations, Imad Mughniyeh, and Hezbollah supporters based in the tri-border area. Coming on the heels of the 1992 Hezbollah bombing of the Israeli embassy in Buenos Aires, this role should not have come as much of a surprise. According to the FBI, as early as summer 1993, "a number of reports from various sources indicated that Hizballah was planning some sort of spectacular act against Western interests, probably Israeli but perhaps against the United States."[25]

Hezbollah Comes to South America

The first waves of immigration from Lebanon and Syria to South America, particularly Argentina and Brazil, came in the 1880s. According to records from the Argentine Immigration Directorate, more than 80,000 immigrants from Arabic-speaking countries arrived from 1882 to 1925. Most were considered "Turks," since they came from countries within the declining Ottoman Empire, and they carried Ottoman identity and travel documents.[26] Lebanese communities in South

America saw another large influx of immigrants during the Lebanese civil war of 1975–1990.

According to a study conducted for US Special Operations Command, "Hezbollah clerics reportedly began planting agents and recruiting sympathizers among Arab and Muslim immigrants in the TBA [tri-border area] at the height of the Lebanese Civil War in the mid 1980s."[27] The result was the establishment of more formal Hezbollah cells in the region beyond the comparably amorphous networks of individuals of Lebanese descent, particularly Shi'a Muslims, who provided some measure of financial support to Hezbollah. This was one of the "opportunities" Rabbani was sent to South America to pursue in 1983.[28]

According to witness testimony, known Hezbollah militants would sometimes stay at mosques associated with Rabbani. One former "Hezbollah fighter," who stayed at both the Canuelas and al-Tauhid mosques in the early 1990s, seemed depressed. According to a mosque official, this former fighter was upset because nine of his ten siblings had died in combat, but he was denied the opportunity of martyrdom. Congregants found the visitor's stay strange; he spoke only Arabic, no Spanish, and looked very weak.[29]

But Buenos Aires was always more Rabbani's base of operations than the center of the Hezbollah support network in the region. That distinction was then and remains today the claim of the tri-border area, located some 800 miles north of the Argentine capital. The transformation of the tri-border area from a backwater into a center of economic activity began in the early 1970s when Brazil and Paraguay reached an agreement to build the Itaipu hydroelectric dam. Around the same time, several South American countries joined together to form the Common Market of the South (Mercosur), which created a series of regional free trade zones, including one in Ciudad del Este. Already Paraguay's second largest city, Ciudad del Este quickly grew into the biggest commercial center in South America.

Sandwiched between Brazil and Argentina, Ciudad del Este has been described as "the United Nations of crime," a "jungle hub for [the] world's outlaws," a classic "terrorist safe haven," and a counterfeiting capital, where "just about everything that is not biodegradable is fake."[30] The State Department's 2009 annual report on global terrorism summarized global concerns about terrorist supporters and a flourishing black market economy being collocated in the tri-border area. Terrorist supporters "take advantage of loosely regulated territory" in the tri-border area "to participate in a wide range of illicit activities," State reported, including "arms and drugs smuggling, document fraud, money laundering, trafficking in persons, and the manufacture and movement of contraband goods through the TBA."[31]

As the Muslim community in the tri-border area grew, so did its need for educational, cultural, and religious institutions catering to the local Arab and Muslim communities. One such institution, the Profeta Mahoma mosque in Ciudad del Este, was reportedly built by a prominent member of the local Arab community, Mohammad Yousef Abdallah, who had been living in Ciudad del Este since July 1980. According to Argentine intelligence officials, Abdallah was one of the first Hezbollah members to settle in the tri-border area, though they did not know it at the time.[32] Only four years later, in April 1984, would the Argentine Federal Police see the first indications of a Hezbollah network in the tri-border area.[33] By mid-2000, experts would put the estimated number of Hezbollah operatives living and working in the tri-border area at several hundred.[34] The number of supporters or sympathizers who are neither trained operatives nor official group members but provide services or support—out of a more general affinity or to improve the lot of their families back home in Lebanon—is believed to be much larger.

Hezbollah's Tri-Border Support Hub

Early reports from Argentine intelligence following the AMIA attack informed that "the main activists" suspected of being members of an Islamist terrorist organization included Mohammad Youssef Abdallah, Farouk Abdul Omairi, and Samuel Salman el-Reda, among others.[35] As the investigation into the AMIA bombing progressed, it focused increasingly on these three Hezbollah operatives.

A US district court sentencing memorandum for a convicted Hezbollah terrorist in 1999 revealed that the FBI had been running a confidential informant—a Lebanese immigrant—in the tri-border area.[36] According to the informant, Mohammad Abdallah was regarded as "the principal leader of Hezbollah in the region"; his brother, Adnan Yousef Abdallah, functioned as his deputy. As the "second most important Hezbollah figure in the tri-border area," the FBI reported, Adnan "oversees the clandestine extremist activities of the Abdallah clan."[37] Only much later, in December 2006, would the US government publicly designate Mohammad Abdallah as a Hezbollah terrorist.[38]

According to Argentine intelligence and the reports of a protected witness, Farouk Omairi maintained regular contact with the Iranian embassy in Buenos Aires and with the city's al-Tauhid mosque, where Omairi lived briefly. Along with his business partner, Mohammad Abdallah, he was closely tied to the Husseinia mosque and the Islamic Charitable Association.[39] Prosecutors were especially interested in Omairi's contacts with the recently minted Iranian diplomat Mohsen Rabbani.[40] In time, these connections would be leveraged by Rabbani to help execute the AMIA bombing, as demonstrated through telephone calls traced to and from the travel agency co-owned by Omairi and Abdallah, Piloto Turismo. Intelligence officers would later determine that Piloto Turismo was not just a business that provided convenient cover for illicit conduct but rather that it was opened with start-up funds supplied by Hezbollah and that it was meant explicitly to serve as a Hezbollah front company.[41]

Uniquely positioned to provide cover for a wide array of illicit activities, travel agencies like Piloto Turismo enabled the subjects of terrorism-support and criminal investigations to obtain false documents, such as fake passports and residency documents. This positioned the travel agencies as de facto points of contact for individuals overseas, especially in Lebanon and elsewhere in the Middle East, seeking to enter the tri-border area surreptitiously. As cash-heavy businesses, the travel agencies could also serve as underground currency exchangers and alternative money remittance services. As their investigations progressed, Argentine law enforcement authorities quickly found additional cases to corroborate their initial findings. For example, the Interpol office in Brazil reported that the communities of Middle Eastern immigrants in Foz do Iguaçu and Ciudad del Este appeared to have ties both to Hezbollah and to Palestinian extremists.[42]

The result of these activities was that Hezbollah built formal and informal support networks in the tri-border area, a process made easy thanks to the large Lebanese and Shi'a populations. Hiding in plain sight, the Hezbollah operatives brought over through Piloto Turismo and other travel agencies found themselves in an ideal operating environment to raise funds, provide logistical support, and engage in operational activities in the region. This included, according to a protected witness, the formation of sleeper or "dormant" cells operating under strict operational security guidelines such that members of one cell were not aware of members of another. To avoid attracting attention, they reportedly settled and worked among friends and relatives in Ciudad del Este, where they used businesses, schools, and mosques to help establish their cover.[43]

After the AMIA attack, Omairi would run a new travel agency for a time before authorities arrested him and his son on charges of using the travel agency and a money-exchange business to falsify documents and launder drug money.[44] The arrests were the result of a 2006 Brazilian Federal Police counternarcotics investigation dubbed Operation Camel, which determined that Omairi provided travel support to drug mules transporting cocaine and that he had obtained Brazilian citizenship illegally.[45] The arrests came within months of the US Treasury Department's designation of Omairi and Abdallah as Hezbollah operatives. Omairi, Treasury stated, served as a regional coordinator for Hezbollah and procured false Brazilian and Paraguayan documentation with which he helped people obtain Brazilian citizenship illegally. He was also involved in trafficking narcotics between South America, Europe, and the Middle East.[46] Omairi and Abdallah were key pillars of the "Barakat network" in the tri-border area; the extent of the network's criminal support for Hezbollah was staggering. Abdallah's role included personally carrying monies raised in the region to Hezbollah in Lebanon, where he met with senior Hezbollah officials and members of Hezbollah's security division, Treasury revealed. Sometimes money flowed in the reverse direction, and Hezbollah would send Abdallah back with funds intended to support the Hezbollah network in the tri-border area.[47]

As the personal representative of Hezbollah leader Sheikh Hassan Nasrallah to the tri-border area, Assad Ahmad Barakat commanded respect. Even as of late 2001, he reportedly traveled to Lebanon and Iran annually, meeting with both Nasrallah and Fadlallah.[48] This proved important for maintaining unity among the tri-border area's Hezbollah supporters, some of whom, like Barakat, were closer to Nasrallah, while others, like Abdallah, were closer to Fadlallah. (Abdallah's cousin was Fadlallah's spokesman.)[49] At times when the two Beirut-based Hezbollah leaders were vying for leadership of the group, tensions would quickly reverberate across oceans and time zones all the way to their respective supporters in South America. In the late 1990s, for example, tensions rose to such a level that a member of the Hezbollah network with familial and business ties to both the Abdallah and Barakat clans,

Hussein Ali Hmaid, served as a liaison between the two rival clans.[50] In an effort to demonstrate the high regard in which the Hezbollah leadership in Lebanon held its tri-border support network and to foster unity within the local Hezbollah community, Fadlallah reportedly traveled to Ciudad del Este in 1994 on an Iranian passport bearing another name to bless the Profeta Mahoma mosque, which Abdallah owned and ran.[51]

Barakat first arrived in Paraguay with his father, a former chauffeur for a Lebanese politician, in 1985.[52] Though only eighteen years old at the time, Barakat soon became a prominent businessman within the Lebanese community in Ciudad del Este.[53] Like so many other Hezbollah supporters, Barakat lived primarily on the Foz do Iguaçu side of the Friendship Bridge but traversed the bridge regularly on his way to his various businesses based in Ciudad del Este. Among these was an electronics wholesale store, Casa Apollo, located in the Galeria Page shopping center, that authorities determined served "as a cover for Hezbollah fundraising activities and as a way to transfer information to and from Hezbollah operatives." He used another of his companies, Barakat Import Export Ltd., to raise money for Hezbollah "by mortgaging the company in order to borrow money from a bank in a fraud scheme."[54] The extent of Barakat's criminal activity in support of Hezbollah was impressive. From distributing and selling counterfeit US dollars to shaking down local shopkeepers for donations to Hezbollah, Barakat was accused by the Treasury Department of engaging in "every financial crime in the book" to generate funds for the group.[55]

"Barakat is more than a financier," explained a Paraguayan investigator.[56] According to Argentine authorities, Barakat was a card-carrying member of Hezbollah's Islamic Jihad Organization (IJO) terrorist wing.[57] He and his network collected sensitive information about the activities of other Arabs in the tri-border area, including those who traveled to the United States or Israel. This was of particular interest to the group and duly collected and passed along to Hezbollah's Foreign Relations Department in Lebanon.[58] Even in his fundraising role, Barakat's heavy-handed tactics underscored that he was no mere fundraiser. His threats to shopkeepers were a case in point: instead of threatening local store owners themselves, Barakat threatened that family members in Lebanon would be put on a "Hezbollah blacklist" if they did not pay their quota to Hezbollah through Barakat.[59]

Residents knew to take such threats seriously. In the fall of 2000, Barakat reportedly attended a meeting where Hezbollah members in the tri-border area discussed assassinating Israelis and former members of the recently disbanded South Lebanon Army (SLA).[60] A year and a half later, Michael Youssef Nasser, a former SLA member and cousin of SLA commander Antoine Lahad, was gunned down in São Paulo in a carefully planned assassination. While the case was never fully resolved, it should not surprise that suspicions pointed to Hezbollah.[61] Given his history and personal ties, Barakat's participation in discussions about violent activities is no anomaly. Some law enforcement officials, for example, maintain he was a "close collaborator" of Hezbollah hijacker Mohammad Ali Hamadi, who participated in the 1985 hijacking of TWA flight 847 and the murder of US Navy diver Robert Dean Stethem.[62]

The day after the September 11 attacks, a SWAT team descended on the Galeria Page shopping center in Ciudad del Este and raided Assad Barakat's Casa Apollo electronics shop. Barakat either was away on business or, according to one account, had fled home to Foz do Iguaçu on the Brazilian side of the border. Either way, while he evaded capture, two of his employees were arrested and his shop shuttered.[63] Among the items found during this initial search was a letter from Hezbollah acknowledging receipt of $3,535,149 from Barakat in 2000.[64] The following month, thirty masked Paraguayan antiterrorism police raided Casa Apollo once more, netting still more incriminating documents, videos, and computer files and arresting Barakat's executive assistant, Sobhi Fayyad.[65]

Investigators found hundreds of receipts, often from Hezbollah's Martyrs Foundation. "The money goes to charities," explained the head of Paraguay's antiterrorism unit, "and the Martyr Foundation is managed by Nasrallah so it is obviously suspicious." Speaking in 2003, he noted, "We believe he [Barakat] sent some $50 million to Hezbollah since 1995."[66] But one letter in particular, signed by "brother Hassan Nasrallah," was especially damning. In the letter, the Hezbollah leader expresses his gratitude for Barakat's collaboration with the "protection program for brothers and martyrs."[67]

The sixty or so seized videos included footage of militants and speeches inciting people "to armed struggle and revolution, and [arguing] that it was better to die and become a martyr than be subjected to the whims of Israel and the U.S."[68] On one computer police found a video of Hezbollah military operations, including operatives detonating explosives and the ensuing deaths. Another file detailed "Hezbollah military orders for each town and village in southern Lebanon."[69] When ultimately detained and questioned, Barakat played down the significance of the seized material, claiming he merely supported Lebanese charities and collected videos that are commonly available on Hezbollah's al-Manar television station. Authorities found his protestations unconvincing, however, especially given the attention then being paid to his activities elsewhere.

Branching out from the tri-border area, Barakat's import-export business took him to other regional free trade zones like Iquique, Chile, where authorities observed Barakat, Mohammad Abdallah, and other members of their clans open import-export companies, conduct lengthy meetings, and engage in a range of suspicious activities. Paralleling its Paraguayan counterpart's investigation into Barakat's illicit financial activities and links to Hezbollah, the Chilean Ministry of the Interior initiated an investigation into what it suspected was "illicit association for the purpose of committing terrorist acts." Barakat's financial activities in Chile, it seemed to investigators, were an extension of his Paraguay-based schemes, which were aimed at supporting "relatives fallen in terrorist acts and the economic strengthening of Hezbollah."[70] According to Chilean intelligence, in March 2001 Barakat set up two fictitious businesses in Iquique, Saleh Trading Limitada and Importadora/Exportadora Barakat Limitada, for the purpose of laundering money earned through his criminal enterprises in Ciudad del Este, Paraguay.[71]

Barakat's business ties extended to Miami and New York as well, and were alleg-edly established as cutouts to receive international shipments of goods that could then be re-exported to the tri-border area.[72] Traveling on a multiple-entry US visa, Barakat acknowledged making a half dozen trips to the United States. Although theoretically he could have entered the United States on false documents of the kind his network was known to produce, the last entry stamp into the United States on Barakat's Paraguayan passport was in April 2001, when he visited Miami. The visa was reportedly revoked later that year when "his name appeared on the US Department of State's list of suspected terrorists."[73]

As a result of evidence collected during the 2001 raids of Barakat's store, Brazil-ian police eventually arrested Barakat in June 2002 on tax evasion charges, just as Barakat was making plans to flee to Angola. The arrest prompted a leader of the Husseinia Iman al-Khomeini mosque in Foz, where Barakat served as deputy finan-cial director, to ban all non-Hezbollah members from attending services.[74] As for Barakat's Africa plans, they were far from original. According to Brazilian police, Hezbollah accomplices were known to move about Africa on forged Paraguayan travel and identity documents of the kind Barakat's network produced.[75]

As Barakat sat in a Brasília prison, investigators uncovered evidence that his net-work had partnered with Hong Kong Mafia barons to receive and distribute a broad array of pirated goods, including knockoff Barbie dolls and other toys. Raids of in-coming shipping containers netted goods valued at half a million dollars, leading prosecutors to add trademark counterfeiting to Barakat's charge sheet.[76] Barakat's legal troubles took another turn for the worse in May 2003, when Argentine prose-cutors issued their own warrants for Barakat's arrest, this time for his roles in the 1992 bombing of the Israeli embassy in Buenos Aires and the 1994 AMIA bomb-ing.[77] Finally, in November 2003, Barakat was extradited to Paraguay. He was ulti-mately convicted of tax evasion and sentenced to a six-and-a-half-year prison term. In 2007, he was also stripped of his naturalized citizenship based on evidence that he operated as a "financial agent" of Hezbollah.[78]

The Barakat network continued to function, however, leading the US Treasury Department to add Assad Barakat and two of his companies—the Casa Apollo shop in Paraguay and Barakat Import Export Ltd. in Chile—to its list of Specially Designated Global Terrorist entities. Targeting a "key terrorist financier," the Trea-sury designation aimed to disrupt the Barakat network by denying these companies access to their US-based re-exporters, pressuring local governments to take action of their own targeting this hybrid criminal-terrorist network, and signaling such behavior was now in the US government's crosshairs.[79] Shaking the tree, as law en-forcement officials would describe it, often forces criminals to scramble about to protect other assets from being targeted and can provide valuable intelligence if authorities are properly prepared to watch how members of the criminal network react to any given public action.

And react they did. A host of other members of the Hezbollah network stepped in to assume responsibility for various activities, from running parlor-meeting fund-raisers to extorting businessmen with Mafia-style strong-arm tactics to carrying out counterintelligence activities and overseeing counterfeit currency operations, drug running, and more. Two of Assad Barakat's brothers, Hamzi and Hatim, took over Assad's Galeria Page storefront and his business activities in Chile. His cousin Muhammad took over responsibility for the Barakat network's overall finances in the tri-border area, held fundraisers for Hezbollah, and arranged the transfer of funds to the Middle East. Barakat's successor as leader of the tri-border Hezbollah network, Ali Muhammad Kazan, additionally helped oversee the group's counter-intelligence activities in the region. Muhammad Chamas and Saleh Fayyad served as counterintelligence operatives providing "security information" on local residents. Chamas, who was also Mohammad Abdallah's private secretary, maintained daily contact with Hezbollah officials in Lebanon and Iran. Meanwhile, Assad Barakat's assistant Sobhi Fayyad served as the local Hezbollah community's liaison to the Iranian embassy in Buenos Aires, met Hezbollah leaders in Lebanon and Iran, and was a "professional" Hezbollah operative who received military training in the group's camps in Iran and Lebanon.[80]

The four-story Galeria Page shopping center in Ciudad del Este, which Abdallah and members of the Barakat network co-owned with other Hezbollah operatives, was described by Argentine police as the "regional command post for Hezbollah."[81] The shopping center, the US Treasury Department concurred, "is locally considered the central headquarters for Hizballah members in the TBA." Mohammed Abdallah not only maintained ties to senior Hezbollah officials and met with members of Hezbollah's security division, according to the US government, but managed day-to-day operations at Galeria Page and paid a regular quota to Hezbollah from profits earned at the shopping center.[82]

Coordinating Sleeper Cells

According to telephone call records obtained by Argentine intelligence, by fall 1993 Assad Barakat was in touch with Samuel Salman el-Reda, a "Hezbollah contact person" who had lived in Foz but also maintained a residence in Buenos Aires, and where he lived for long periods over the seven years before the AMIA attack.[83] Based on phone call records and the protected testimony of a Hezbollah operative referred to in the AMIA indictment only as "Witness A," authorities pieced together evidence pegging el-Reda as "an active member of Hezbollah" who coordinated the activities of the Hezbollah attack squad in Buenos Aires and maintained communication with Hezbollah leaders in Lebanon and the operation's logistics command in the tri-border area.[84]

El-Reda, prosecutors concluded, "was the coordinator of [Hezbollah] sleeper cells" in Buenos Aires and the tri-border area.[85] As the AMIA plot took shape, el-Reda and Assad Barakat kept in touch. Investigators tracked additional telephone calls between the two in January and June 1994.[86] Investigators determined further that it was around 1993–94 that el-Reda settled in Foz, "from where he provided all the necessary support to perpetrate the terrorist attack against the [AMIA] building."[87]

Samuel el-Reda was first radicalized within the extremist, pro-Iranian community Mohsen Rabbani built around himself and the al-Tauhid mosque. A Lebanese citizen born in San Andres, Colombia, el-Reda reportedly left Colombia after getting involved in a "huge street fight" that led to two murders. He moved to Argentina around 1987, seven years prior to the AMIA bombing, and married Silvina Gabriela Sain, an Argentine woman from a Lebanese family, two years later. After a brief return to Colombia, el-Reda moved his family in September 1992 to the tri-border area, where they lived on the more comfortable Brazilian side of the bridge. El-Reda commuted to his job in Ciudad de Este at a business in the Galeria Page shopping center. While in the tri-border area, he developed a reputation as an "Arab from the mafia" and a Hezbollah member.[88]

El-Reda's brother married Sain's sister and they, too, were close followers of Rabbani. The sisters, described by authorities as "zealot Islamist militants," were both active members of the al-Tauhid mosque, where they worked with Rabbani.[89] During this period el-Reda apparently returned to Lebanon at least once, where he spent time as a Hezbollah fighter in the south.[90]

In Buenos Aires el-Reda's friendships with the likes of Mohsen Rabbani and Mohammed Reza Javadi-Nia help explain investigators' finding that he was involved with the "most radical core" elements within the local Muslim community in Buenos Aires.[91] According to investigators, telephone calls like the one placed from el-Reda's home in Foz to the al-Tauhid mosque on May 26, 1994, underscore el-Reda's ties to Rabbani in the period leading up to the AMIA attack. For his part, both before and after the AMIA bombing, Rabbani was in regular contact with a wide array of Hezbollah-related personalities, including Sheikh Mohammad Hussein Fadlallah's secretary in Beirut, according to a call on April 3, 1992. On August 2, 1994, just a couple of weeks after the bombing, Rabbani met with a Brazilian national and suspected Hezbollah operative named Ghazi Iskhandar. Iskhandar was presumably from the tri-border area, and his name was found in the appointment calendar of Bassem Harakeh, described by authorities as a "Hezbollah terrorist" who was at the time under detention in Norway.[92]

Plotting the AMIA Bombing

Hezbollah would later link the AMIA bombing to the capture of Hezbollah militant Mustafa Dirani by Israeli commandos. But in May 1993—a full year prior to Dirani's capture by Israeli commandos—and again in November 1993, Rabbani visited car dealerships to inquire about purchasing a Renault Trafic van, according to Argentine intelligence. No purchase was made at the time, though authorities grew suspicious when they learned that Rabbani gave each car salesperson a different story explaining his interest in the purchase. Then, in a television interview following the AMIA bombing, Rabbani would deny having inquired about buying a van at all, insisting he was looking for a sedan all along despite the detailed testimonies of several salespersons at multiple dealerships.[93]

Further investigation would reveal a much earlier start date for Rabbani's fieldwork in support of the AMIA bombing. From the time he first arrived in the country in 1983, investigators found, Rabbani recruited local Shi'a scouts to assess potential

Jewish and American targets in the city, providing the basis for surveillance and targeting reports that Rabbani drafted and passed along to senior intelligence officials back in Iran. According to prosecutors, Rabbani's surveillance reports would later prove to be "a determining factor in making the decision to carry out the AMIA attack."[94]

With Rabbani's reports in hand, senior Iranian officials meeting in Mashhad, in northwest Iran, would select the AMIA building from a list of potential targets on August 14, 1993.[95] The testimony corroborating the occurrence of this meeting by intelligence defector Abolghasem Mesbahi, prosecutors noted, was particularly useful "by virtue of his having worked for [Iran's Ministry of Intelligence and Security, MOIS], his participation in operations similar in nature to the AMIA bombing, and his close relationship with the then–second in command of [MOIS], Said Eslami."[96] Around the time of this August meeting, intelligence reports indicated Hezbollah was "planning some sort of spectacular act against Western interests, probably Israeli but perhaps against the United States."[97]

A subgroup of Iran's Supreme National Security Council, the Committee for Special Operations, made the final decision to approve the attack. That meeting reportedly included Supreme Leader Ali Khamenei, President Rafsanjani, Minister of Intelligence Ali Fallahian, and Foreign Minister Ali Velayati. Also present, all the way from Argentina, were Mohsen Rabbani and Ahmad Asghari, the latter a suspected IRGC official stationed at the Iranian embassy in Buenos Aires under diplomatic cover whose real name, according to Abolghasem Mesbahi, was Mohsen Randjbaran. Based on their firsthand knowledge and experience, Rabbani and Asghari were present to advise the committee about the target selection, their logistical and intelligence support networks, and the political and security environment in Argentina.[98]

According to Argentine intelligence, once the committee reached its decision, Supreme Leader Khamenei issued a religious edict—a fatwa—sanctifying the operation as a sacred duty aimed at exporting the revolution. Intelligence chief Ali Fallahian was then given overall operational responsibility for the attack, and Qods Force commander Ahmad Vahidi was instructed to provide any necessary assistance. Under Fallahian, three critical assignments were made, according to Argentine intelligence. First, "Fallahian instructed [Hezbollah's] Imad Mughniyeh to form an operational group, which then took charge of executing the attack."[99] Next, Rabbani was put in charge of local logistics for the attack, including all details pertaining to the purchase, hiding, and arming of the van to be used in the bombing, and liaising with the Hezbollah operatives on the ground in Argentina. Finally, Asghari was placed in charge of activating Iran's "clandestine networks" in support of the operation.[100]

Rabbani helped by activating his own local networks too. Argentine intelligence confirmed that Rabbani left for Iran on June 18, 1993, and returned four months later on October 29. He returned to Iran in late February 1994, presumably to receive his diplomatic credentials. The decision to accredit Rabbani as a diplomat just months before the AMIA bombing enabled him "to go about providing material support for the operation with relative ease, while at the same time guaranteeing him diplomatic immunity following the attack."[101]

In time investigators would uncover records of phone calls between the Iranian embassy in Buenos Aires—where Asghari and now Rabbani were both employed— and suspected Hezbollah operatives in the tri-border area operating out of a mosque and a travel agency.[102] Even the trained Hezbollah operatives who would soon follow Rabbani and Asghari back to Argentina to carry out the actual attack are presumed to have been directly tied to Iran. According to expert opinions provided in the AMIA investigation, Hezbollah prefers outside operatives to local contacts when running its major operations in other countries. These operatives generally are more trustworthy and better trained, more often than not in Iranian terrorist training camps.[103]

Intelligence and Logistics Support for the AMIA Bombing

Within weeks after the meeting in Mashhad at which Iranian officials approved the AMIA bombing based on Rabbani and Asghari's briefings, Iranian diplomats started requesting diplomatic visas for visits to Argentina. Visas were requested in October 1993 for Ministry of Islamic Culture and Guidance (Ershad) undersecretary Ali Janati and Ahmad Alamolhoda, the director of the Cultural Department at the Ministry of Foreign Affairs. Coming on the heels of Rabbani's appointment as cultural attaché, these officials' proposed six-day visit raised concerns among investigators— not least because of Janati's seniority and witness descriptions of his brother as a Revolutionary Guard official and "a well-known terrorist and member of the hard line faction."[104] For reasons unknown, this trip never happened. Nearly simultaneous visa requests would later be submitted for Alamolhoda at the Argentine embassies in The Hague and Berlin on June 7 and 8, 1994. Alamolhoda arrived in Argentina within days, and despite specifically requesting a thirty-day visa, he departed just four days later for Madrid, site of the MOIS regional office that oversees activities in Latin America.[105]

Next, on June 18, Ahmad Abousaeidi, the first secretary at the Iranian embassy in Uruguay, arrived in Argentina on a ninety-day visa.[106] At least six other Iranian officials traveled to Buenos Aires for short visits in June 1994, including Iranian ambassador to Uruguay and suspected MOIS operative Mohammad Ali Sarmadi-Rad, who had made a similarly suspicious trip to Argentina in the lead-up to the 1992 embassy bombing.[107] Another group of Iranian diplomats entered Argentina the weekend prior to the AMIA bombing and left just two days later.[108] Looking back on the bombing, investigators highlighted a variety of suspicious behaviors related to this group. Several group members reportedly traveled on fictitious names. Masoud Amiri, an attaché in the Iranian embassy in Brasília, provided the Sheraton Hotel as his local address on his immigration form on arrival in Argentina, but the hotel had no record of anyone by that name ever staying there.[109]

Argentine authorities would also note in hindsight that many of the passports used by the various Iranian government officials who arrived in Argentina in June and July of 1994 were brand-new, issued in April and May, just ahead of this travel. Many of these officials had existing passports in good standing, suggesting they specifically sought new passports for this trip. In several cases, investigators later determined, the officials' new passports featured sequential or nearly sequential numbers.[110] These findings confirmed for prosecutors that the "new diplomatic cover was granted" expressly to create confusion "concerning the identity of these envoys."[111]

As for the funding of the AMIA bombing, much appears to have flowed through bank accounts controlled by Rabbani. In December 1993, two months after he returned from the go-ahead meeting in Mashhad, Rabbani opened an account at a local branch of Deutsche Bank. He already had two active bank accounts, one opened at Banco Sudameris in April 1989 and another at Banco Tornquist opened in March 1992, but the new account was to serve a very specific purpose. Just four months before the AMIA bombing, a total of $150,812 was deposited in Rabbani's new bank account. Rabbani withdrew a total of $94,000 from this account in the period leading up to the July 18 bombing, and another $45,588 was withdrawn within two months following the attack. These funds arrived through international bank transfers, at least three of which were sent from Iran's Bank Melli through Unión de Bancos Suizos.[112] Only later, in October 2007, would the US government reveal that Bank Melli was an established financial conduit through which Iran purchased sensitive materials for its nuclear and missile programs and moved money for the IRGC and Qods Force.[113]

Rabbani apparently received funds from Iran in his Banco Tornquist account as well. According to Argentina's federal tax office, there is no evidence that funds deposited into that account originated in Argentina. Prosecutors believe that "Rabbani used the funds from the aforementioned account to defray various expenses related to the execution of the AMIA attack."[114] Over the course of 1994—both before and after the attack—Rabbani withdrew a total of $284,388 from his accounts, underscoring Mesbahi's testimony that "Rabbani was the main person in charge of the local logistics for the operation."[115]

Alongside Iran's use of diplomatic cover to build an intelligence network in Argentina, Tehran likewise provided cover stories and day jobs to Hezbollah operatives. A close contact of Imad Mughniyeh's, the New Yorker reported, "is a sheikh named Bilal Mohsen Wehbi, a Lebanese who was trained in Iran, and who reports to the Iranian Cultural Affairs Ministry."[116] This ministry, along with the Ministry of Islamic Guidance and the Foreign Ministry, effectively embedded agents abroad to support Hezbollah plots. At the Foreign Ministry, for example, the director for Arab affairs, Hossein Sheikh al-Islam, coordinated with the IRGC "to place its members in Iranian embassies abroad and participate in Hezbollah operations," according to Hezbollah expert Magnus Ranstorp.[117] Members of the IRGC's Qods Force also played key support roles in the AMIA attack, according to a Defense Department report on Iran's military power.[118]

In addition to dispatching intelligence officers under diplomatic cover, Iran's intelligence services ran operatives under nonofficial cover. The lack of diplomatic cover made for a riskier proposition—but in other ways a more effective one, given such operatives' freedom from the embassy walls and bureaucracy. Take, for example, Hossein Parsa, who replaced the IRGC intelligence agent Seyed Jamal Youssefi at the Iranian government–owned Government Trade Corporation (GTC). GTC "had two missions," according Abolghasem Mesbahi, the Iranian intelligence official who defected: "generating income; and manipulating sources and providing them with ample cover." Whereas Youssefi's activities focused on intelligence collection and other preoperational activities, Parsa positioned himself in the right place at the right time to provide logistical support for the AMIA attack. Three months before the AMIA bombing, Parsa rented an apartment that was notable principally because its rear windows were completely obscured by a massive billboard. The contract for the apartment was signed at the Iranian embassy in April 1994, with embassy personnel serving as the official witnesses. From the outside, no one could see what was going on in the apartment. But telephone records would reveal that calls were placed from this apartment to the Ministry of Reconstruction in Iran, including one the day before the AMIA attack.[119]

Two days before the attack, as the explosives-filled van was being parked in a garage near the AMIA center, Mohsen Rabbani placed calls to GTC from his cell phone. Cell tower logs confirm Rabbani was in the vicinity of the parking garage and the AMIA at the time. This drew the attention of investigators, not only because GTC was believed to be a front for Iranian intelligence but also because the Ministry for Reconstruction "was used as a cover for activities by Quds Force representatives."[120]

Did Hossein Parsa's apartment function as an operational safe house for the AMIA plotters? Investigators simply say that "further work remains to be done" in terms of investigating Parsa's activities. Prosecutors took note, however, of testimony stressing that "the first priority in selecting a safe house is security, and the second is distance." Prosecutors noted further the importance safe houses played in the botched Hezbollah bombing in Bangkok earlier that year and in other cases, such as in Croatia, where police raids of Hezbollah safe houses turned up arms and explosives.[121]

Whatever the function of Parsa's apartment for this network, Argentine intelligence took note when, two months after the AMIA bombing, he abruptly left Argentina with a year and a half remaining on his rental agreement.[122] The Iranian embassy also withdrew Khalil Mashoun, the commercial representative of GTC, that same month.[123] Authorities suspected GTC of functioning as an intelligence front even after the AMIA attack. While the company failed to submit tax filings most years, it reported no commercial activity at all in its filing for the period of January–September 1995. Authorities believe GTC conducted no business of any kind over this nine-month period because it was primarily a front for Iranian intelligence that benefited from a permanent Iranian government subsidy, not a commercial enterprise.[124] Interviewing witnesses and investigating GTC and other companies, investigators found that Mohsen Rabbani maintained such close ties with Iranian front companies that he often determined whom they employed. In one intercepted telephone call, the head of one suspected front company, South Beef, was overheard explaining that "Rabbani was the one who provided all the personnel for the companies" and therefore hiring new employees was not up to him.[125]

While Rabbani attended to the necessary logistical details in Buenos Aires, Hezbollah operatives in the tri-border area planned the operation itself. These two groups stayed in close touch as the plot slowly came together. On only two occasions, tri-border plotters called Rabbani at home, reflecting either sloppy tradecraft or perhaps an especially pressing operational need. One of those calls, placed from Farouk Omairi's Piloto Turismo travel agency, was immediately preceded by a succession of brief calls to other numbers, which the FBI determined "could demonstrate a possible pattern of calls of coordination in preparation for the call to Rabbani's residence."[126]

Shuttling between safe houses in Buenos Aires, where he was then living, and a red brick house in Foz, Samuel el-Reda coordinated the Hezbollah operation in the weeks leading up to the attack.[127] He coordinated the arrival of the Hezbollah operational squad in the country some seventeen days before the attack, saw to the logistics of their stay in Buenos Aires, and oversaw the departure of the Hezbollah strike force on a flight to the tri-border region some two hours prior to the attack. El-Reda, as the primary local logistician for the attack, kept the chief operational coordinators based in the tri-border area apprised of the Hezbollah cell's progress throughout the attack's final phases.[128] It would take years, but in June 2009, prosecutors would issue a warrant for el-Reda's arrest on charges of being a central coordinator for the AMIA bombing operation.[129]

Several tri-border-based Hezbollah operatives played central roles in the AMIA bombing, but the actual coordinator may have been Imad Mughniyeh himself.[130] Following the Mashhad meeting, according to Argentine intelligence, Mughniyeh acted on Iran's orders to assemble the operational group that carried out the attack.[131] According to Israeli intelligence, Mughniyeh oversaw the operation and provided the explosives used in the attack.[132]

Mesbahi's testimony, meanwhile, indicated that the person chosen by Intelligence Chief Fallahian to head the operation (whether Mughniyeh or not) went by the cover name "Ahad." To oversee the attack, Ahad traveled to Argentina some five or six days before the bombing on an authentic Greek passport refitted with a false name. He left the country on that same passport two or three days after the attack. Mesbahi further explained, "[Ahad] can be found in the area of Baalbek, Lebanon, Iman Hossein headquarters, where he is now the Commander in Chief of the Hezbollah's Army." Based on Mesbahi's description, Argentine authorities made a police sketch of Ahad that was circulated to several other countries as well as Interpol and provided to the media in an effort to identify him. That effort proved fruitless, an unsurprising result given the dearth of public pictures of Mughniyeh.[133] Ahad has never been proved to be Mughniyeh, despite strong suspicions to this effect; even Mesbahi could not state the tie definitively. But whether he was there in person or oversaw the operation from abroad, investigators believe Mughniyeh masterminded the

AMIA bombing. "Mughniyeh would be the ultimate [suspect]," AMIA prosecutor Nisman would admit in 2002, "that is our target."[134] The following year, prosecutors would issue arrest warrants for both Imad Mughniyeh and Assad Barakat.[135]

Whoever coordinated the attack on the ground, whether Mughniyeh or someone else, that person carried the full weight and authority of the Hezbollah leadership back in Lebanon. According to one witness interviewed by investigators, an order was handed down from Hassan Nasrallah himself to Abbas Hijazi and Farouk Omairi that Hezbollah members in the tri-border area were to provide members of the Barakat network with "everything they needed to realize" the AMIA attack. To that end, the witness continued, Hijazi and Omairi provided the "Barakat brothers" with high-quality forged passports and identity cards, money, maps of the region and of Buenos Aires, and "information concerning the persons they were to contact in Buenos Aires to carry out the operation," including at least one person at the Iranian embassy.[136]

On average, one call a month was placed to Iran from Omairi's travel agency, according to phone records the FBI reviewed. One Iranian number was called more than others and stood out because it was called from multiple locations in the tri-border area, including a phone number registered to Farouk Omairi at the Iguazú Falls mosque.[137] Taken together, the telephone records amount to "evidence of coordination between the Triple Frontier area and 'sleeper cells' in Buenos Aires," Argentine investigators concluded.[138]

In an attempt to shield from potential eavesdropping, Iran routed calls between field agents at diplomatic posts and MOIS in Tehran through what they thought was a secure network. Calls, for example, from the Iranian embassy in Buenos Aires to Department 240—a cutout established to liaise with the Iranian Foreign Ministry and MOIS—were run through an Iranian military switchboard that triangulated them to prevent their being detected. According to Argentine intelligence, the Iranian embassy in Buenos Aires started using this communications cutout the day before the bombing of the Israeli embassy, on March 16, 1992, and continued using it until July 6, 1994, twelve days before the AMIA bombing. Having identified this technical cutout, Argentine intelligence was able to track calls before and after the Israeli embassy bombing, including calls placed from Ambassador Hadi Soleimanpour's cell and home phone lines.[139]

More than a communications hub, the tri-border area is known as a travel facilitation hot spot through which people can come and go across the region's multiple and loosely controlled borders. While investigators were unable to definitively identify who accompanied the AMIA suicide bomber, Ibrahim Berro, on his trip from Lebanon to South America, they are convinced a Hezbollah operative traveled with him—and that he entered Argentina through the tri-border area. In the opinion of one FBI agent who investigated the AMIA attack, "any participation in the AMIA attack on the part of elements in the Triple Border area would have involved logistics, obtaining explosives and money, and helping operatives to enter and leave Argentina."[140] Investigations determined that Berro and whoever accompanied him passed through Europe on their way to the tri-border area, whereupon they "entered Ciudad del Este using false European passports; and after a stay in this area, during which time they received new logistics support for purposes of carrying out their mission, [they] left for their final destination, which was Buenos Aires."[141]

In January 2003, an Argentine intelligence report concluded that the C4 plastic explosive Hezbollah used in the AMIA bombing came to Buenos Aires through Ciudad del Este.[142] According to one Israeli intelligence official, the C4 explosive was smuggled into the country from Iran via an Iranian diplomatic pouch.[143] The C4 formed the core of the bomb, which was assembled in the tri-border area before being delivered to Buenos Aires.[144] Evidence collected by police suggested either parts of the explosive or the detonator came from Foz do Iguaçu.[145]

Bombing the AMIA Building

Iran's ambassadors to Argentina, Uruguay, and Chile all returned to Iran in the weeks leading up to the AMIA bombing. The Iranian ambassador to Buenos Aires, Hadi Soleimanpour, departed for Tehran by way of Miami on June 30. Though Soleimanpour and his fellow Iranian heads of the mission would later claim they were coincidentally all taking vacation at that particular time, other officials interviewed would report they were recalled to Iran for a meeting of regional ambassadors. The Iranian ambassadors to Uruguay and Chile boarded the same flight from Santiago, Chile, to Frankfurt, Germany, on July 17, the day before the bombing.[146] After the sharp increase in diplomatic visits to South America leading up to the AMIA bombing, the sudden absence of the senior Iranian officials in the region when the bombing took place was hard to miss.

According to Argentine intelligence, Ambassador Soleimanpour had a track record of engaging in espionage under cover of diplomatic activity and working with spies operating under cover of accredited Islamic Republic News Agency (IRNA) journalists. Prior to his posting in Buenos Aires, Soleimanpour served as chargé d'affaires and then ambassador in Spain from 1985 to 1989.[147] "During this period," investigators determined, "Soleimanpour was instructed by the Iranian government to take charge of the collaboration of a group of five residents of Spain with a view to providing Pasdaran [IRGC] with support in the event a reprisal action was carried out against the U.S. and Israel."[148]

Meanwhile, in the two-and-a-half-week period between the departures of Soleimanpour and his fellow ambassadors, the influx of Hezbollah operatives and the staggered departure of Iranian officials continued. About a month before the bombing, Samuel el-Reda's wife departed for Lebanon.[149] The morning of July 1, Samuel el-Reda made his way to Buenos Aires's Ezeiza International Airport to meet a group of Hezbollah operatives arriving for the sole purpose of executing the AMIA bombing. From the airport, el-Reda placed a call at 10:53 AM to a cell phone in Foz—registered under the cover name Andre Marques and used by the Hezbollah operative who coordinated the attack from the tri-border area—to report that the

Hezbollah operatives had arrived as planned.[150] According to investigators, the Marques cell phone "belonged to the Agencia Piloto tourist [agency] and currency exchange agency owned by Farouk Abdul Omairi."[151]

The Marques cell phone, it warrants noting, received calls from Buenos Aires from July 1 to July 18, never before and never again. The last call to this phone from Buenos Aires came at 7:41 AM on July 18, just two hours before the attack and about forty minutes before the Hezbollah hit squad and el-Reda boarded a flight from Jorge Newberry Metropolitan Airport to Puerto Iguazú in the tri-border area. El-Reda, prosecutors determined, was a busy man over this short period of time.[152]

El-Reda called the Hezbollah coordinator in Foz on the Marques cell phone once again four hours later from a pay phone at the airport, likely to report that the Hezbollah operatives had deplaned and were about to depart for one of el-Reda's safe houses in Buenos Aires. That evening, the Marques phone received a third call from Buenos Aires, this one placed from a pay phone about a mile from the AMIA building. Six minutes later, a call was placed to a Hezbollah operative in Foz from another pay phone in the same area. Finally, just nine minutes after this call, yet another call was placed from the same pay phone in Buenos Aires to a telephone subscriber in Beirut identified by investigators as "the head office of Hezbollah in Beirut."[153]

All these calls, investigators believe, were placed by el-Reda. The calls, for example, were all placed to numbers that el-Reda also called from his home landline in Foz on other occasions. Moreover, the call to the Hezbollah head office in Beirut was immediately followed by a call from the same pay phone to a member of el-Reda's family in Germany. In fact, el-Reda apparently dropped his guard and, ignoring the operational security protocols for which Hezbollah is well known, called his wife or parents several times immediately after placing calls to Hezbollah operatives, including call sequences captured by investigators on July 8, 9, and 15.[154]

Calls from el-Reda frequently led to a flurry of telephone traffic within Hezbollah circles. For example, at 9:28 AM on July 8, el-Reda placed a call from a pay phone near the AMIA building to the cell phone of "the coordinator of the operational group," presumably the same person in Foz who used the Marques cell phone. Over the next nineteen minutes, authorities would later learn, this one call initiated a chain of more than twenty additional calls made to people in Lebanon who, according to Argentine intelligence, were members of Hezbollah. Such calls, investigators determined, "involved an extensive exchange of information." Tellingly, this particular telephone chain occurred on the day that Ahmad Asghari, having successfully run Iran's clandestine networks in the area in support of the bombing plot, abruptly left Argentina for good despite being scheduled to remain at his post for another three months. Asghari did not give the standard diplomatic notice of his intent to exit his posting, leaving Argentine authorities to surmise that "Asghari left not of his own volition, but in response to a direct order from his boss in Tehran, namely [Iranian foreign minister] Ali Velayati."[155]

Interestingly, on July 1 a call was placed from the pay phone near the AMIA building (presumably by el-Reda) to a New York City telephone number. Two minutes later a call was placed from the same pay phone to the Marques cell phone. Eleven days would go by, and on July 12 another call was placed to the New York City number, this time from a pay phone less than two miles west of the AMIA building. Seven minutes later, the call to New York was followed by a call to the Marques cell phone. A third call was placed to the New York number on July 17, the day before the bombing, followed minutes later by a call to the Marques cell phone. In one instance a call was placed from the same pay phone to a line "identified as a Hezbollah communication center in Beirut." These calls and others reveal what investigators concluded was a command-and-control communication system among Hezbollah operatives on the ground in Buenos Aires, coordinators in the tri-border area and New York, and Hezbollah operatives in Beirut.[156]

Approximately a week before the AMIA bombing, a walk-in intelligence source warned Argentine, Brazilian, and Israeli officials of a pending terrorist attack in Argentina similar to the March 1992 attack on the Israeli embassy. Wilson Dos Santos, a Brazilian citizen, contacted these countries' consulates in Milan around July 8, asking not for money but for protection. He was clearly nervous, but nobody believed his story that he was having an affair with an Iranian spy and prostitute who confided to him that she was involved in both the 1992 bombing and another that was about to strike Argentina.[157] "Something big is going to happen," he warned, but his story was deemed too farfetched.[158] Years later Dos Santos would recant his timely prediction, telling Brazilian investigators he had only approached authorities about knowledge of the 1992 bombing, not the soon-to-be-executed AMIA attack. Yet an investigation carried out in the wake of the AMIA bombing corroborated much of Dos Santos's story. It also determined that Narim Mokhtari, Dos Santos's girlfriend, had a "highly suspicious" history. The home address in Iran she provided on her application for Argentine citizenship was tracked to a cemetery. The references she gave on the application denied knowing her. And the addresses where Dos Santos claimed Mokhtari met her Iranian colleagues were identified by investigators as "places suspected Iranian intelligence agents met," including the home of a person whose nephew Argentine intelligence considered to be an Iranian intelligence agent.[159]

Iranian and Hezbollah agents, unaware of how close their plot came to being disrupted, continued coordinating the logistical support for the final phase of the operation. The actual Hezbollah suicide bomber, Ibrahim Berro, arrived in Buenos Aires via the tri-border area within the last few days before the attack. Details emerged in a report from a "collateral unit" of Argentine intelligence: "Berro made this trip [to the tri-border area] in the company of a Paraguayan resident by the name of Saad. Berro stayed at the home of the brothers Fuad Ismael and Abdallah Ismael Tormos, who had arrived in the Triple Border area in 1992 and are thought to have been members of Hezbollah."[160]

According to an Argentine intelligence source, Saad, a military coordinator of a group of supporters of the Lebanese Shi'a Amal Party in the tri-border area, maintained a romantic relationship with a female law enforcement officer at the Tancredo Neves Bridge, whom he described as being "fat with short hair" and who allowed people to cross the border into Argentina unchecked in exchange for gifts or money.[161] FBI and press reports describe a woman named Nora Gonzalez, also known as Fat Nora, who at one time ran the Argentine customs station at the bridge and who allegedly helped people and goods cross the border illicitly.[162]

The Trafic van that Berro would ultimately drive into the AMIA building had a bad paint job and damaged roof. It likely came as a pleasant surprise when the seller, a police officer named Carlos Telleldin, found a buyer the very day he placed his ad. As it happens, neither chipped paint nor a dented roof presented much of a problem for a truck bomb. The buyer gave the name Ramon Martinez, provided what was later determined to be a false address, and said he was buying the vehicle for someone else. According to Telleldin, Martinez wore a hat and glasses, spoke with a Central American accent, and had difficulty operating the vehicle.[163]

The van would not be seen for five days, during which time it was fitted with 300 to 400 kilograms of explosives, a new set of rear-axle shock absorbers, and extra-large rear wheels to carry the extra weight. Just a few weeks earlier, and halfway across the globe, Hezbollah operatives had made the same modifications to the truck used in a Bangkok bombing plot (see chapter 5).[164] Investigators never could determine where the mechanic work in Argentina was done. But on July 15, just five days after Telleldin's ad appeared in the newspaper and only three days before the bombing, the explosives-filled Trafic van was driven to the Jet parking lot, located a mere 400 meters from the AMIA building.[165]

According to prosecutors, the man who parked the car gave his name as Carlos Martinez, although his true identify remains unknown. The parking lot operators described the driver as a short, dark-skinned man in his thirties who wore a brown suit. "Martinez" claimed to be visiting a sick relative and staying at the Hotel de las Americas. This statement seemed odd since the hotel was located nowhere near the Jet parking lot. Another anomaly the parking lot employees noticed was that Martinez struggled to park the van, which had stalled. A second individual, who walked over on foot, parked the car for Martinez and left after the two exchanged hand signals. Martinez told the parking lot attendant he wanted to park the car for four or five days, during which time he would need to remove the vehicle once or twice. In the end, he paid $100 cash for a fifteen-day pass, the same as the higher daily rate for just a few days. Apparently nervous, Martinez entered a wrong license plate number on the parking registration form.[166]

By 6:00 PM, the van was parked in the lot. About ten minutes later, Mohsen Rabbani placed a call on his cell phone from the vicinity of the Jet parking lot to Samuel el-Reda at the al-Tauhid mosque. The call lasted a mere twenty-six seconds, "just the amount of time," prosecutors would later comment, "that would have been necessary to confirm the success of a key phase of the operation."[167] Informed that the car bomb was successfully parked at the lot just blocks from the AMIA building, el-Reda left the mosque within minutes of taking the call from Rabbani and walked to a nearby phone booth. At 7:18 PM, he received instructions (presumably in the form of a call to that pay phone) to pass along the news that the car bomb had arrived at the parking lot. This he did, calling Khodor Barakat, who was back in the tri-border area.[168]

On the morning of July 18 around 7:41 AM, el-Reda again called his contact in the tri-border area on the Marquis cell phone. El-Reda's final assignment was to escort the rest of the Hezbollah hit team back to the airport and see that they caught their flight to Puerto Iguazú in the tri-border area. According to investigators, this final call to the Hezbollah coordinator in Foz was to inform him that the Hezbollah team was checked in for their flight, which took off forty minutes after the call.[169] By the time the flight landed, eighty-five people were dead, and emergency responders were tending to the wounded and dying victims of the AMIA bombing.

According to Israeli sources, the suicide bomber Ibrahim Berro called home to his family in Lebanon just a few hours before the bombing and informed them he was "about to join his brother," an apparent reference to Assad Hussein Berro, a brother who carried out a Hezbollah suicide bombing targeting Israeli soldiers in Lebanon in August 1989.[170] Proof was slow in coming, however, and Hezbollah claimed Ibrahim was killed in a Hezbollah operation in Lebanon. In 2005, with evidence pointing to Berro as the AMIA suicide bomber, FBI agents and Argentine officials interviewed two of Ibrahim's brothers, Abbas and Hussein, both naturalized US citizens, in Dearborn, Michigan.

At the interview, held at the Berro's home on April 26, 2005, the Berro brothers confirmed that another of their brothers, Assad, had died carrying out a Hezbollah suicide attack on Israeli troops in southern Lebanon on August 3, 1989. Still another, Ali, worked at a hospital run by Hezbollah. The family was unaware, however, that Ibrahim had also been active in Hezbollah. According to Abbas, "When he died, my parents were told . . . that he had died fighting in Lebanon. We didn't know at this point that he was a member of Hezbollah." But Abbas, who lived with Ibrahim in the period leading up to the AMIA bombing, also noted that "Ibrahim was often away for lengthy periods of two to three months, and when the family learned of his death, he'd been away for a while." The brothers flew in from the United States for the funeral, which Hezbollah leader Hassan Nasrallah personally attended. According to Hussein, he learned of his brother's role in the AMIA attack only in 2003, when his teenage son came across press reports about the attack on the Internet.[171]

Abbas added that their mother felt extreme sadness over her son's death and, with the passage of time, had come to doubt the story Hezbollah leaders told them of Ibrahim's death in southern Lebanon. Despite its initial claim of responsibility for the AMIA bombing under an affiliated name, Hezbollah quickly retracted the statement in a new communiqué. According to an account in the Argentine press, "The communiqué issued by the Islamic guerilla group maintains that 'the martyr Ibrahim Berro' was part of a group of fighters who 'died during a clash between the Islamic Resistance (the armed wing of Hezbollah) and Israeli occupation forces in southern Lebanon.'"[172] The brothers provided the FBI with two pictures of Ibrahim, which were compared to the police sketch. Based on expert analysis, prosecutors determined that the person at the wheel of the Trafic van that rammed into the AMIA building was, in fact, Ibrahim Berro.[173]

The 1992 Embassy Bombing

The 1992 attack that preceded the AMIA bombing occurred on the afternoon of March 17, when a Ford F-100 panel van filled with explosives drove up onto the sidewalk in front of the Israeli embassy in Buenos Aires and blew up, destroying the front of the building along with the entire consulate building. Twenty-three people were killed and another 242 injured. Most of the casualties were in the embassy, but some were pedestrians, including a priest from the Roman Catholic Church across the street and children at a nearby school.[174]

As it happened, Yaacov Perry, then director of the Israel Security Agency (Shin Bet), had visited Argentina just a week before the embassy bombing for liaison meetings with his intelligence counterpart. At a polo match and luncheon, the intelligence chiefs discussed "the menace posed by terrorists," though neither had any idea how close the menace was or how soon it would be realized. Within days, Israeli counterterrorism teams would be back in Buenos Aires investigating the embassy bombing alongside Argentine and American law enforcement and intelligence experts.[175] Yet Argentine political leaders seemed intent on concluding the investigation as quickly as possible. Early reports suggested the explosion may have erupted inside the building; others contended the attack did not involve a suicide bomber. Both were definitively proven false in detailed forensic accounts by US and Argentine explosives experts.[176] American and Israeli investigators reportedly decided not to cooperate fully with their Argentine counterparts; it would take years for confidence to be built.[177]

In time investigators would determine that the Ford van had been parked in a lot just a couple of blocks from the Israeli embassy for the hour and a half immediately preceding the bombing—to be precise, from 1:18 PM to 2:42 PM, according to the stamped parking ticket.[178] Three minutes later, the vehicle bomb exploded outside the embassy.

In its claim of responsibility, delivered to a Western news agency in Beirut, Hezbollah's IJO declared "with all pride that the operation of the martyr infant Hussein is one of our continuing strikes against the criminal Israeli enemy in an open-ended war, which will not cease until Israel is wiped out of existence." Hussein was the five-year-old son of Hezbollah leader Abbas al-Musawi, both of whom were killed in an Israeli air strike on Musawi's car on February 16, 1992.[179] Following this initial admission of responsibility, an individual claiming to represent the IJO called a news agency denying the group's involvement in the bombing. But shortly thereafter, the release of surveillance video by the group with footage of the Israeli embassy proved the IJO's claim of responsibility.[180] Releasing such a video, the State Department's counterterrorism coordinator testified, is itself a Hezbollah trademark.[181]

While the Musawi assassination would not lead Hezbollah to resume kidnapping Westerners in Lebanon, as some feared it might, Sheikh Fadlallah issued a statement warning "there would be much more violence and much more blood would flow."[182] The CIA noted in a July 1992 intelligence report that Hezbollah held the United States and Israel equally responsible for Musawi's death and threatened to target American interests in retaliation. According to the CIA, his was no empty threat: "Hezbollah elements began planning a retaliatory operation against US interests in Lebanon shortly after Moussawi's death." Hezbollah, the CIA reminded policymakers in a July 1992 report, had executed two successful attacks targeting US interests in Lebanon the previous year—firing missiles at the US embassy on October 29, 1991, and destroying the administration building at the American University of Beirut in a car bombing on November 8, 1991.[183]

These plans never did materialize, perhaps because Hezbollah was supremely focused on avenging Musawi's killing beyond Lebanon's borders. Just eight days after the assassination, the vehicle used in the embassy bombing was purchased in Buenos Aires by an individual with a Portuguese accent who signed documents with a last name different from the one on his identification.[184] Three weeks later, the embassy was in ruins. The actual speed at which the operation was executed is easier to understand, however, in light of evidence that Iran had decided to carry out an operation in Argentina well before Musawi was killed. Mohsen Rabbani, the same operative who coordinated the AMIA attack, spent ten months in Iran from January to December 1991.[185] Five days after his return to Argentina, Buenos Aires suspended shipment of nuclear material to Iran due to "concrete indications that Iran had non-peaceful plans for its nuclear capacities."[186] According to Argentine prosecutor Alberto Nisman, Hezbollah used the Musawi assassination to justify the embassy bombing to its supporters, but the attack was carried out at the behest of Tehran in response to Argentina's suspension of nuclear cooperation with Iran.[187] Iran was positioned to facilitate such an attack because it invested over time in the patient construction of an extensive intelligence base in South America, beginning in the early to mid-1980s.

Around the same period, security measures were enhanced at the Iranian embassy in Buenos Aires. Correspondingly, in the days leading up to the attack, Iranian officials arrived in Argentina. One prominent arrival was Jaffar Saadat Ahmad-Nia, an attaché at the Iranian embassy in Brasília, who arrived in Buenos Aires as a diplomatic courier on January 21, 1992, staying just that one day. He returned on March 16, the day before the bombing, and departed the day after the attack.[188]

Embassy Bombing: The First Strike in a Broader Campaign

According to Argentine intelligence, Samuel el-Reda headed the Hezbollah operational group that carried out the embassy bombing based on preoperational intelligence collected by MOIS agents in Buenos Aires. This finding, prosecutors noted, is corroborated by the testimony of Witness A, a former Hezbollah fighter. According to Witness A, the embassy bombing drew on the logistical support of local Hezbollah cells.[189]

It is worth noting that in the two years prior to the 1992 embassy bombing, Assad Barakat made numerous trips to Lebanon and Iran, at which time he met with Iranian government leaders. In an apparent effort to obfuscate his whereabouts, he traveled to Lebanon on a Lebanese passport and onward to Iran on a Paraguayan passport.[190] Several Hezbollah operatives reportedly entered the country through the tri-border area, transiting through London and Ciudad del Este on their way from the Middle East to Buenos Aires.[191]

The Argentine Supreme Court investigation into the embassy bombing identified IJO chief Imad Mughniyeh as "one of the persons that was responsible for the attack." The evidence in the case, the court concluded, "supports the contention that the March 17, 1992, attack on the Israeli embassy in Argentina was organized and carried out by the terrorist group known as Islamic Jihad, the military wing of Hezbollah."[192] American intelligence concurred: "Master terrorist Imad Mughniyah's Islamic Jihad Organization (IJO)—an element of Hezbollah with a long history of spectacular terrorist operations—claimed responsibility for the operation less than 24 hours after the attack."[193] It would take several years, but on September 2, 1999, Argentine authorities issued an arrest warrant for Mughniyeh for his role in the embassy bombing. One piece of key evidence—handwriting on the paperwork for the purchase of the truck used in the attack—was tied to known Hezbollah operatives.[194]

According to both Witness A and the Iranian intelligence defector, Mesbahi, Imad Mughniyeh was behind the Israeli embassy bombing. Mughniyeh, Witness A added, personally accompanied Imad Ghamlush, whom he identified as the suicide bomber, to Brazil in February 1992.[195] Ghamlush may or may not be the suicide bomber's actual name, but it rings truer than the IJO's contention in its claim of responsibility that the suicide bomber was an Argentine convert to Islam named Abu Yasser.[196] Investigators found no evidence to substantiate this latter claim.

Interpol, Argentine intelligence, the CIA, the FBI, and the US State Department all concurred that Hezbollah was behind the embassy bombing—a determination later officially confirmed by Argentine investigators.[197] Revealing communications intercepts captured in the wake of the embassy bombing appear to have reinforced these coordinated findings. These include a conversation in which the estranged wife of Iamanian Khosrow, an Iranian diplomat and suspected MOIS agent, threatened to expose her husband's terrorism-related activities.[198] Other such intercepts included a revealing exchange between Tehran and the Iranian embassy in Moscow alluding to a forthcoming attack, and similarly telling messages from the Iranian embassies in Brasília and Buenos Aires.[199]

By one account, American intelligence intercepted a communication between Tehran and the Iranian embassy in Moscow three days prior to the Israeli embassy bombing indicating "an awareness of an impending attack on an Israeli legation in South America." Unfortunately, it was only translated sometime after the bombing. Messages from the Iranian embassies in Brasília and Buenos Aires also reportedly included coded references to a nearing attack. The United States subsequently provided Israel with hard evidence of Hezbollah's role in the attack, including reference to a phone conversation between Mughniyeh and a senior Hezbollah official, Talal Hamiyeh. The two reportedly were "heard rejoicing over 'our project in Argentina' and mocking the Shin Bet, which is responsible for protecting Israeli legations abroad, for not preventing it."[200]

Two weeks after the bombing, on April 3, 1992, Mohsen Rabbani placed a call from his home phone to Sheikh Fadlallah's secretary. Argentine intelligence detected the call, and prosecutors pointed to it as timely evidence of Rabbani's relationship with the Hezbollah leader and the fact that one of Rabbani's primary responsibilities in Argentina was "being in charge of Hezbollah."[201]

Iran, for its part, appeared quite pleased with Rabbani's performance leading up to the Israeli embassy bombing. In fact, the embassy not only covered the costs of Rabbani's mosques but also underwrote the bombing of the Israeli embassy, according to Argentine investigators. On May 16, 1992, two months after the attack, Iranian ambassador Hadi Soleimanpour traveled to Foz do Iguaçu, Brazil, together with a senior official from the Iranian Foreign Ministry, an officer from the Iranian embassy in Chile, and a small group of tourists. The officials stayed for three days, met with the Iranian ambassador to Brazil, and left a day before the rest of the tour group. The meeting and tour, however, were apparently a cover for the true purpose of the trip: "to make a payment due in connection with the bombing against the Israeli Embassy in Buenos Aires." [202]

Rabbani, however, was not the only such agent to be dispatched to South America. Not long after Rabbani arrived in Argentina, he was followed by Mohamed Taghi Tabatabei Einaki, who arrived on a thirty-day visa. Like Rabbani, Einaki worked as a chicken and meat inspector. According to Argentine intelligence, Einaki "launched Hezbollah's activities in Brazil in the 1980s." So concerned were the Saudi and Iraqi governments that they protested to Brazilian authorities that Einaki was radicalizing Lebanese Shi'a in communities across Brazil. Hezbollah's new Brazilian recruits, they warned, could be mobilized as terrorist cells.[203]

Such activities were reason for still greater concern as Nasrallah replaced Abbas al-Musawi as Hezbollah's leader after Musawi was killed in February 1992. In the wake of the embassy bombing, the CIA raised concerns that with Nasrallah's selection as Musawi's replacement, the leadership of Hezbollah might take on a more direct role in terrorist operations that were previously tasked to "autonomous security groups" like Mughniyeh's IJO. "Nasrallah was directly involved in many Hezbollah terrorist operations, including hostage taking, airline hijackings, and attacks against Lebanese rivals," the CIA noted. "Nasrallah's terrorist credentials," the CIA warned, "may lead him to bring terrorist-related matters under the control of the Leadership Council."[204] Looking back, the CIA's warning seems prescient.

Two years later, in May 1994, speaking in the wake of the Israeli kidnapping of Shi'a militant and Hezbollah ally Mustafa Dirani, Hezbollah's Sheikh Fadlallah would allude to the Israeli embassy bombing in Buenos Aires as part of Hezbollah's response to Musawi's assassination: "The enemy has said that they have a long reach but when Abbas Moussawi was assassinated, the Islamic fighters proved that they can reach all the way to Argentina. The battlefront has spread throughout the world, and the battle is unfolding as time goes on."[205]

Hezbollah Activities Continue Unabated

The day after the AMIA bombing, as cleanup crews were clearing away the debris, terrorists struck again, this time in Panama. On July 19, a twin-engine Embraer commuter plane operated by Atlas Airlines exploded shortly after takeoff from Colón on its way to Panama City. Of the twenty-one passengers and crew, most were businessmen working in the Colón Free Trade Zone; all were killed instantly. Amazingly, given the small size of the Jewish community in Panama, twelve of the passengers were Jewish, including four Israelis and three Americans. Coming just after the AMIA bombing, the tragedy shook the Panamanian Jewish community. The community's fears were quickly confirmed when Panama's president-elect announced that the crash "was not an accident but a planted bomb."[206] Investigators would determine that the attack was executed by a suicide bomber who was never identified beyond the Middle Eastern name with which he purchased his ticket and that appeared on the flight manifest.[207]

Within days, Hezbollah claimed responsibility for both the AMIA bombing and the Panama airline bombing in a leaflet distributed in the Lebanese port city of Sidon. The claim of responsibility was issued under Ansar Allah, or Partisans of God, a well-known cover name for Hezbollah's IJO.[208] Authorities never conclusively determined who was behind the bombing of the Panamanian commuter plane, despite Hezbollah's claim of responsibility. But according to a November 1994 FBI report, both the AMIA bombing and the Panama airline downing—as well as two other bombings in London on July 26 and 27 (both near Israeli targets)—were all "highly suspected of being perpetrated by Hizballah."[209]

Not long after the AMIA and Panama aircraft bombings, still in 1994, Uruguayan police disrupted a Hezbollah-run weapons smuggling operation with ties to the tri-border area. The following August, Paraguayan police arrested three members of a Hezbollah "sleeper cell" with possible links to the 1992 Israeli embassy bombing.[210] Imad Mughniyeh himself was reported to have concocted a plot during the mid-1990s to purchase a large quantity of beef from Paraguayan cold-storage companies and poison the meat before shipping it for resale in Israel. Paraguayan police reportedly intercepted the shipment and prevented it from leaving the country.[211]

Following the AMIA attack, law enforcement and intelligence agencies in Brazil, Argentina, and Paraguay launched a coordinated effort, in tandem with US agencies, to disrupt the activities of Middle Eastern terrorists groups in the region. Dubbed Operation Double Top, the strategy was to target the illicit logistical and financial activities for which such groups had become infamous. "We realized the best way was to hit their dirty businesses in the region," one former Argentine official involved in the operation explained. "We didn't want them to work in peace, so we used methods you could call a little 'mafiosi'—disrupting commercial operations, burning containers, blocking bank accounts, stealing their passports, and the police arrested them."[212]

Sometimes the operational ties between criminal activities like drug-running and terrorism cases became clear only after the fact, as in the 1996 arrest of Marwan Kadi (also known as Marwan Safadi), who was caught by US agents after conducting surveillance as part of a plot to bomb the US embassy in Asunción, Paraguay. Convicted in a Canadian court of smuggling cocaine from Brazil, Kadi came to the tri-border area after escaping from prison in Canada, possibly with the help of Hezbollah elements. He obtained an American passport under an alias and returned to the tri-border area, where Brazilian police arrested him for cocaine possession. Amazingly, he escaped from jail again and fled across the border to Paraguay. Following his surveillance of the US embassy, police arrested him at his apartment in Ciudad del Este, where they found explosives, firearms, counterfeit Canadian and American passports, and a large quantity of cash. However, after he was deported to the United States, prosecutors were only able to charge him with simple passport fraud. He would later be sent to Canada to serve out the remainder of his previous prison sentence.[213]

While Double Top operations continued through 2001, they succeeded only on the margins in part due to insufficient buy-in and coordination among countries in the tri-border area. Hezbollah operational activity continued through the 1990s and into the next decade. For example, Sobhi Fayyad, the Hezbollah military leader in the tri-border area who served as Assad Barakat's personal secretary, was arrested in 1999, like Kadi before him, for conducting surveillance of the US embassy in Asunción. That prosecution fizzled, but Fayyad later served time for tax evasion related to his illicit financial dealings, some of which supported Hezbollah.[214]

Just months after Hezbollah's surveillance was detected, photos surfaced in early 2000 of local Lebanese businessmen standing next to Iranian and Hezbollah al-Muqawama ("resistance") flags at a training camp allegedly located outside Foz do Iguaçu. Argentine intelligence believes that Hezbollah operated a weekend military and ideological training camp in the tri-border area.[215] According to a former FBI agent who worked on Hezbollah in South America, Hezbollah operatives have also engaged in military training in Panama and Venezuela.[216] Barakat himself is reported to have planned attacks on Jewish targets in Canada, Argentina, and Ciudad de Este. When a plot was broken up on December 22, 1999, Argentine intelligence arrested, but later released, suspected members of Hamas and Hezbollah, along with an Iranian intelligence agent.[217] In 2000, an FBI delegation traveled to Argentina to help with the renewed effort to investigate the AMIA bombing and coordinate with local authorities to deal with the Hezbollah presence in the region. Briefed extensively by Argentine intelligence in both Buenos Aires and the tri-border area, the FBI agent who led the delegation left convinced that local intelligence services "had the goods" on Hezbollah and its role in the AMIA bombing.[218] Still, Hezbollah's activity in the region would continue to thrive.

Hezbollah Narco-Terrorism

Abdallah el-Reda, Farouk Abdul Omairi, and Assad Ahmad Barakat, the players identified early on by Argentine intelligence, were suspected not only of membership in Hezbollah but also of a host of other criminal activities including "smuggling, support to terrorism, drug trafficking, weapons trafficking, documents counterfeiting, car thefts, forgery of products, and money laundering activities."[219] Sticking to the principle that the simpler the cover, the more effective the ruse, their preferred means of concealing their covert support for terrorism and criminal enterprises was to operate travel agencies and import-export companies. The potential for big money, however, came from involvement in drugs.

Hezbollah's growth into the narcotics industry began in the early 1980s but really took root later on. "Drug trafficking organizations based in the tri-border area have ties to radical Islamic organizations such as Hezbollah," according to the Drug Enforcement Administration's (DEA) senior intelligence officer.[220] Hezbollah's later involvement in the drug trade was a consequence of the growth in commercial narcotics cultivation in the Bekaa Valley in the late 1970s.[221] According to an Israeli daily, "The civil war virtually destroyed all other economic fields; however, the production of marijuana became a key import sector in which almost all the ethnic communities and forces involved in Lebanon played a part."[222] Over time, Lebanese Shi'a involved in narcotics in Lebanon began to work with criminal associates within the Lebanese Shi'a diaspora in South America.[223]

Starting in the 1980s, DEA agents noticed that so-called Lebanese Colombians were increasingly involved in the movement of drugs and money laundering for drug cartels through the port of Barranquilla on Colombia's Caribbean coast. Some were involved in the shipping business and sidestepped into drugs through their involvement in other trade-based money laundering schemes that depended on a reliable stream of foreign currency income. Working with the drug cartels provided this revenue stream and opened the door to money laundering and drug shipment.[224]

In 1986, President Ronald Reagan signed National Security Decision Directive No. 221, establishing drug enforcement as a US national security priority. Three years later, the DEA set up a bank of its own, Trans America Ventures Associates, for the express purpose of luring traffickers looking for a place to launder their drug money. Using this bank, DEA undercover agents and informants targeted drug kingpins' financial managers, money launderers, and associates in what became known as Operation Green Ice. More than 170 people were ultimately arrested and tens of millions of dollars seized.[225] Several of the individuals targeted in this sting were Lebanese. Regarding the development of Hezbollah's role in narcotics, DEA agents would later comment, "We were already looking at some of the same Lebanese guys [back then], but the Hezbollah link [we see now] is new to us."[226]

There is, however, no one model for Lebanese criminals involved in drugs and tied to Hezbollah. "Some belong to families tied to Hezbollah, some just pay money to Hezbollah because it represents 'the cause' [of resistance against Israel and the West]. Some of what we see is Hezbollah actively involved in drugs [as a group], some is just Lebanese Shia involved in drugs who happen to be sympathetic to Hezbollah" and support the group but are not members of or directed by Hezbollah.[227] Both baskets of Hezbollah supporters, however, whether members or sympathizers, were put at ease by a fatwa issued in the mid-1980s providing religious justification for the otherwise impure and illicit activity of drug trafficking. Presumed to have been issued by Iranian religious leaders, the fatwa read: "We are making drugs for Satan—America and the Jews. If we cannot kill them with guns, so we will kill them with drugs."[228] According to the FBI, "Hezbollah's spiritual leader has stated that narcotics trafficking is morally acceptable if the drugs are sold to Western infidels as part of the war against the enemies of Islam."[229]

While Hezbollah is involved in a wide variety of criminal activities, the connection between drugs and terrorism has grown particularly strong, especially in South America. In March 2009, Adm. James G. Stavridis, then commander of US Southern Command, testified before the House Armed Services Committee about the threat to the United States from illicit drug trafficking—"including routes, profits, and corruptive influence"—and "Islamic radical terrorism."[230]

One of the most significant takedowns to date was dubbed Operation Titan, a two-year investigation of a cocaine smuggling and money laundering operation in Colombia run by a Hezbollah figure named Chekry Harb who used the alias Taliban. The case began when agents overheard Harb talking to cartel members on wiretaps targeting a Medellín, Colombia, cartel called La Oficina de Envigado. By June 2007, an undercover DEA agent met Harb in Bogotá and learned details about Harb's smuggling routes, including one that involved shipping cocaine to Jordan's Aqaba port and then smuggling it overland to Syria. At one point, Harb bragged to the undercover agent that he could get 950 kilos of drugs into Lebanon within hours, prompting the agent to casually suggest he must have Hezbollah connections in order to operate so freely there. According to the agent, Harb just smiled and nodded.[231]

In time the undercover agent got close enough to the cartel to serve as one of its money launderers. The agent laundered some $20 million, enabling the DEA to follow the money and map out much of the cartel's operations. But before Harb could identify his Hezbollah contacts to the DEA undercover agent, the operation broke down, reportedly due to CIA interference.[232]

Over the course of the operation, Colombian and US agents arrested more than 130 suspects, seized $23 million, deployed 370 wiretaps, and monitored 700,000 conversations. Harb's network reportedly paid Hezbollah 12 percent of its narco-income. "The profits from the sales of drugs went to finance Hezbollah," Gladys Sanchez, lead investigator for the special prosecutor's office in Bogotá, commented after the October 2008 arrests. Among those reportedly cooperating in this narcotics and money laundering enterprise were members of the Northern Valley Cartel, right-wing paramilitary groups, and the Revolutionary Armed Forces of Colombia (FARC).[233] Despite the collapse of the intelligence operation, Harb was ultimately convicted on drug trafficking and money laundering charges and placed, along with several of his associates, on the US Treasury Department's list of Specially Designated Narcotics Traffickers.[234]

Authorities came to a similar conclusion in April 2009, when they arrested seventeen people in the Dutch Caribbean island of Curaçao for involvement in a "Hezbollah-linked drug ring."[235] The suspects included locals, as well as individuals from Lebanon, Cuba, Venezuela, and Colombia. According to the Dutch Prosecution Service, the drug network shipped containers of cocaine from Curaçao to the Netherlands, Belgium, Spain, and Jordan. Others were shipped from Venezuela to West Africa and from there onward to the Netherlands, Lebanon, and Spain. In still other cases, couriers smuggled smaller amounts of cocaine on flights from Curaçao and Aruba to the Netherlands. Drug profits were invested in real estate in Colombia, Venezuela, and Lebanon. According to prosecutors, "the organization had international contacts with other criminal networks that financially supported Hezbollah in the Middle East. Large sums of drug money flooded into Lebanon, from where [sic] orders were placed for weapons that were to have been delivered from South America."[236]

Iran's Expanded Footprint in South America

Iran's intelligence penetration of South America has expanded significantly since the AMIA bombing. Testifying before Congress in the weeks following the attack, the State Department's coordinator for counterterrorism expressed concern that Iranian embassies in the region were stacked with larger-than-necessary numbers of diplomats, some of whom were believed to be intelligence agents and terrorist operatives: "We are sharing information in our possession with other States about Iranian diplomats, Iranian terrorist leaders who are posing as diplomats, so that nations will refuse to give them accreditation, or if they are already accredited, to expel them. We have had some success in that respect, but we have not always succeeded."[237] Another witness recounted meeting with senior government officials in Chile, Uruguay, and Argentina regarding overrepresentation at Iranian embassies in the region in March 1995—eight months after the AMIA bombing. Officials in Chile and Uruguay, the countries of most concern regarding Iranian overrepresentation at the time, indicated that "the activities of those at the [Iranian] embassy were being monitored and that this was very clearly a concern."[238]

Fifteen years later, the commander of US Southern Command indicated the Iranian presence in the region had grown still larger, expanding from just a handful of missions a few years earlier to twelve by 2010. That, plus Iran's traditional support for terrorism, concerned Gen. Douglas Fraser. "Transnational terrorists—Hezbollah, Hamas—have organizations resident in the region," Fraser noted.[239] Just two years later, in a statement before the House Armed Services Committee, Fraser warned of Iran's success circumventing international sanctions by establishing modest economic, cultural, and security ties, mostly in nations like Venezuela, Ecuador, Bolivia, Nicaragua, and Cuba. Iran, Fraser added, also propagates its agenda through its thirty-six Shi'a cultural centers. The Fundación Cultural Oriente, for example, an Iranian outreach center dedicated to strengthening Iranian ties to Latin America, was run by the radical cleric Mohsen Rabbani. The cleric oversaw several media outlets and recruited students from the region to study in Iran.[240]

Over the next few years, evidence emerged that Rabbani's activism and involvement in terrorism targeting South America had not waned since Argentina indicted him and Interpol issued a Red Warrant arrest notice for his role in the AMIA bombing. In 2007, Rabbani helped four men who were plotting to bomb John F. Kennedy International Airport in New York (JFK), according to court documents. The four men had sought technical and financial assistance for their plot, which they code-named Chicken Farm.[241] Three of the plotters were Guyanese, including Russell Defreitas, a baggage handler at JFK who had become an American citizen. The last co-conspirator, Kareem Ibrahim, was an imam and leader of the Shiite Muslim community in Trinidad and Tobago. All four were ultimately convicted in federal court in the Eastern District of New York.

Four years later, around the same time the last defendants in the JFK Airport bomb plot were convicted, reports of Rabbani's continued activities in South America emerged in the Brazilian press. Security had become a priority in Brazil as the country began preparations to host first the 2014 World Cup and then the 2016 Olympic Games. But as security experts looked closely at Brazil, they expressed concern about the country's lax counterterrorism legal regime and weaker-still enforcement. In April 2011 *Veja*, a weekly newsmagazine, ran an article that discussed how Rabbani "frequently slips in and out of Brazil on a false passport and has recruited at least 24 youngsters in three Brazilian states to attend 'religious formation' classes in Tehran." In the words of one Brazilian official quoted by the magazine, "Without anybody noticing, a generation of Islamic extremists is appearing in Brazil."[242] As for Hezbollah, a former FBI agent who worked on Hezbollah and the AMIA bombing notes that Hezbollah's role in criminal activities and fraud has only grown. The group now engages in shipping fraud, for example, involving containers that enter Brazil at the port of São Paulo and then "disappear on their way up the river toward Foz in the tri-border area."[243]

To be sure, Iran and Hezbollah remain hyperactive in South America—a fact that has the full attention of US intelligence officials and their counterparts south of the border. Consider, for example, that the October 2011 IRGC Qods Force plot to kill the Saudi ambassador to Washington reportedly also included plans to attack the Saudi and Israeli embassies in Buenos Aires.[244] In a July 2012 report, the State Department concluded that although the department knew of no credible information indicating Hezbollah operatives were engaged in "terrorist training or other operational activity" in the tri-border area, Washington "remained concerned that these groups used the region to raise funds from local supporters."[245]

But even back in 1994, as Rabbani and his Hezbollah hit squad laid the groundwork for the AMIA attack, other groups of Hezbollah operatives were engaged in fundraising, procurement, and operational activities across the globe. In Saudi Arabia, one network was carrying out surveillance of US targets for still another spectacular bombing. In the United States, the FBI was knee-deep investigating Hezbollah cells from New York and Boston to Detroit and Los Angeles. And in Thailand, a Hezbollah plot targeting the Israeli embassy in Bangkok was well under way.

Notes

1. Buenos Aires, Argentina Judicial Branch, AMIA Indictment, Office of the National Federal Court No. 17, Criminal and Correctional Matters No. 9, Case No. 1156, March 5, 2003 (hereafter cited as AMIA indictment), 16–17.

2. Buenos Aires, Argentina Investigations Unit of the Office of the Attorney General, *Office of Criminal Investigations: AMIA Case*, report by Marcelo Martinez Burgos and Alberto Nisman, October 25, 2006 (hereafter cited as Burgos and Nisman), 20, 378.

3. Statements of Robert Bryant and Ambassador Philip Wilcox, *Terrorism in Latin America/AMIA Bombing in Argentina*.

4. Gabriel Levinas, "Report about the Investigation of the AMIA Attack."

5. Ambassador Philip Wilcox, *Terrorism in Latin America/AMIA Bombing in Argentina*.

6. Burgos and Nisman, 20.

7. The sketches were published in the Buenos Aires newspaper *Clarin* on August 1 and 6, 1994, and again on September 28, 1995; see copies of the paper and details in written answers to Question for the Record for Ambassador Philip Wilcox in Testimony at Hearing on *Terrorism in Latin America/AMIA Bombing in Argentina*, 111–17.

8. AMIA indictment, 62.

9. Burgos and Nisman, 14.

10. Ibid., 224–26.

11. Ibid., 243.

12. Ibid., 212; AMIA indictment, 130, 141.

13. "Report of the Task Force of the Federal Bureau of Investigation (FBI): Analysis of the Attack on the Seat of the Mutual Israeli Argentinean Association (AMIA), 18th of July, 1994, Buenos Aires, Argentina," August 1998 (original copy in Spanish, translated to English for the author by Yair Fuxman).

14. Burgos and Nisman, 245.

15. Burgos and Nisman's 2006 report states the suicide bomber likely came in through the tri-border area. But in a 2009 interview with the author, a senior Argentine law enforcement officer confirmed the investigation had "definitively" determined that Berro entered through the tri-border area. Author interview, senior Argentine law enforcement official, Washington, DC, August 16, 2009.

16. Burgos and Nisman, 14–15.

17. Ibid., 8.

18. Alexei Barrionuevo, "Inquiry on 1994 Blast at Argentina Jewish Center Gets New Life," *New York Times*, July 18, 2009.

19. Larry Rohter, "Iran Blew Up Jewish Center in Argentina, Defector Says," *New York Times*, July 22, 2002.

20. Burgos and Nisman, 3.

21. Ibid., 7.

22. Ibid.

23. Ibid., 8.

24. Claudio Lifschitz, *AMIA: Porqué Se Hizo Fallar la Investigación* (Argentina: New Press Grupo Impressor S.A., 2000), 24–31.

25. US Department of Justice, FBI, "International Radical Fundamentalism."

26. Jozami, "Manifestation of Islam in Argentina," 70–74; Brieger and Herszkowich, "Muslim Community of Argentina," 157–69.

27. Universal Strategy Group, *Directed Study of Lebanese Hezbollah*, produced for the United States Special Operations Command, Research and Analysis Division, October 2010, 54.

28. Burgos and Nisman, 227.

29. Ibid., 238.

30. Sebastian Rotella, "Jungle Hub for World's Outlaws," *Los Angeles Times*, August 24, 1998; US Department of State, Office of the Coordinator for Counterterrorism, *Country Reports on Terrorism 2009*, August 5, 2010.

31. US Department of State, *Country Reports on Terrorism 2009*.

32. Burgos and Nisman, 311.

33. AMIA indictment, 153.

34. Universal Strategy Group, *Directed Study of Lebanese Hezbollah*, 54.

35. AMIA indictment, 154.

36. *United States of America v. Bassam Gharib Makki*, United States District Court, Southern District of Florida, Miami Division, CR 98-334-01, February 12, 1999, Affidavit of FBI Agent James Bernazzani Jr., p. 13.

37. Ibid., 5.

38. US Department of the Treasury, "Treasury Targets Hizballah Fundraising Network in the Triple Frontier of Argentina, Brazil, and Paraguay," press release, December 6, 2006.

39. Burgos and Nisman, 311–12.

40. AMIA indictment, 190; Burgos and Nisman, 239.

41. Burgos and Nisman, 314–15; AMIA indictment, 154–55, 232.

42. AMIA indictment, 154.

43. Ibid., 158.

44. Larry Rohter, "South America Region under Watch for Signs of Terrorists," *New York Times*, December 15, 2002; "Hizbullah Gets Hit with the Conviction of a Collector," *ABC Color* (Paraguay), September 30, 2007; "Drop a Course Link in the Drug Trade to the East," *ABC Color* (Paraguay), May 6, 2006.

45. "Hizballah Captive in Brazil Participated in 1994 Argentine Attack," *Estadao* (Brazil), October 24, 2008.

46. US Department of the Treasury, "Treasury Targets Hizballah Fundraising Network."

47. Ibid.

48. US Department of the Treasury, "Treasury Designates Islamic Extremist, Two Companies Supporting Hizballah in Tri-Border Area," press release, June 10, 2004.

49. Jeffrey Goldberg, "In the Party of God: Hezbollah Sets Up Operations in South America and the United States," *The New Yorker*, October 28, 2002.

50. *United States of America v. Bassam Gharib Makki*, Affidavit of FBI Agent James Bernazzani Jr., pp. 2–5.

51. Goldberg, "In the Party of God: Hezbollah Sets Up Operations."

52. Burgos and Nisman, 314.

53. Blanca Madani "Hezbollah's Global Finance Network: The Triple Frontier," *Middle East Intelligence Bulletin* 4, no.1 (January 2002).

54. US Department of the Treasury, "Treasury Designates Islamic Extremist."

55. Ibid.

56. Marc Perelman, "U.S. Hand Seen in Paraguay's Pursuit of Terrorism Suspect," *Forward*, January 17, 2003.

57. AMIA indictment, 156.

58. US Department of the Treasury, "Treasury Designates Islamic Extremist."

59. Ibid.

60. Ibid.

61. Associated Press, "Brazil Probes Hezbollah Link in Murder of SLA Man's Cousin," *Haaretz* (Tel Aviv), March 13, 2002.

62. Perelman, "U.S. Hand Seen in Paraguay's Pursuit"; FBI Most Wanted Terrorists List, "Mohammed Ali Hamedei."

63. Rohter, "South America Region under Watch"; Jose de Cordoba, "Is Jungle Junction a Terrorist Hideaway?" *Wall Street Journal*, November 28, 2001.

64. Rohter, "South America Region under Watch."

65. Perelman, "U.S. Hand Seen in Paraguay's Pursuit."

66. Ibid.

67. Burgos and Nisman, 313.

68. Ibid.

69. US Department of the Treasury, "Treasury Designates Islamic Extremist."

70. Chilean Department of Foreign Affairs, Investigation Police (presentation, The Chilean-American Conference of Future Geopolitical Trends, Santiago, March 6–7, 2002).

71. Burgos and Nisman, 314.

72. "Film Piracy, Organized Crime, and Terrorism," Appendix B (Santa Monica, CA: RAND Corporation, 2009), 59.

73. Cordoba, "Is Jungle Junction a Terrorist Hideaway?"; Library of Congress, Federal Research Division, with the Department of Defense, "A Global Overview of Narcotics-Funded Terrorist and Other Extremist Groups," May 2002, 32.

74. US Department of the Treasury, "Treasury Designates Islamic Extremist."

75. "Chief Extremist Arrested in Foz Trying to Flee to Angola," *ABC Digital* (Paraguay); "Two Lebanese Suspects 'Key' to Hezbollah Tri-border Activity," *ABC Color* (Paraguay), November 27, 2002 (Spanish); Goldberg, "In the Party of God: Hezbollah Sets Up Operations."

76. "Hong Kong Mafia Was Linked to Hizbullah in the Tri-Border," *ABC Digital* (Paraguay), November 22, 2002 (Spanish); "Chief Extremist Arrested in Foz Trying to Flee to Angola," *ABC Digital* (Paraguay).

77. "Argentine Prosecutors Link Tri-Border Hizballah Leaders to AMIA Attack," *ABC Color* (Paraguay), May 28, 2003 (Spanish); Hudson, *Terrorist and Organized Crime Groups in the Tri-Border Area*, 13.

78. "Paraguay: Hizballah Financier Barakat Extradited from Brazil," Program Summary Excerpt from *Sistema Nacional de Televisión – SNT TV* (Paraguay), November 17, 2003; "Film Piracy, Organized Crime, and Terrorism," 64; *Asunción La Nación*, June 17, 2007, included in "Highlights: Paraguay Press 16–18 Jun 07," Paraguay OSC Summary, Open Source Center, June 18, 2007.

79. US Department of the Treasury, "Treasury Designates Islamic Extremist."

80. US Department of the Treasury, "Treasury Targets Hizballah Fundraising Network."

81. Cordoba, "Is Jungle Junction a Terrorist Hideaway?"

82. US Department of the Treasury, "Treasury Targets Hizballah Fundraising Network."

83. Government of Argentina, Arrest warrant for Samuel Salman el Reda, Buenos Aires, June 2009; AMIA indictment, 197.

84. Burgos and Nisman, 237–40; AMIA indictment, 232.

85. Arrest warrant for Samuel Salman el Reda.

86. AMIA indictment, 163.

87. Ibid., 165.

88. Ibid., 162–63, 232.

89. Ibid., 163; Burgos and Nisman, 238.

90. AMIA indictment, 165.

91. Arrest warrant for Samuel Salman el Reda.

92. Burgos and Nisman, 238–40.

93. Ibid., 246–47.

94. Ibid., 243.

95. Ibid., 244, 374.

96. Ibid., 91.

97. US FBI, "International Radical Fundamentalism."

98. Burgos and Nisman, 94.

99. Ibid., 108.

100. Ibid., 219.

101. Ibid., 243–45.

102. Mark S. Steinitz, "Middle East Terrorist Activity in Latin America," *Policy Papers on the Americas*, vol. 14, study 7, Center for Strategic and International Studies, July 2003.

103. AMIA indictment, Expert Opinions of Ariel Merari and Bruce Hoffman.

104. AMIA indictment, 28.

105. Burgos and Nisman, 189–90.

106. Ibid., 191.

107. AMIA indictment, 30.

108. Burgos and Nisman, 191–92.

109. Ibid.

110. AMIA indictment, 30; Burgos and Nisman, 192.

111. Burgos and Nisman, 193.

112. Ibid., 235–37.

113. US Department of the Treasury, "Fact Sheet: Designation of Iranian Entities and Individuals for Proliferation Activities and Support for Terrorism," October 25, 2007.

114. Burgos and Nisman, 235–37.

115. Ibid., 247.

116. Goldberg, "In the Party of God: Hezbollah Sets Up Operations."

117. Ranstorp, "Hizbollah's Command Leadership," 319–20.

118. US Department of Defense, Office of the Secretary of Defense, "Unclassified Report on Military Power of Iran," April 2010.

119. Burgos and Nisman, 175–76.

120. Ibid., 15, 175–76.

121. Ibid., 177–78.

122. Ibid., 176.

123. AMIA indictment, 71.

124. Burgos and Nisman, 174, 177.

125. Ibid., 242.

126. "Report of the Task Force of the Federal Bureau of Investigation (FBI): Analysis of the Attack on the Seat of the Mutual Israeli Argentinean Association (AMIA), 18th of July, 1994, Buenos Aires, Argentina," August 1998 (original copy in Spanish, translated to English for the author by Yair Fuxman).

127. Alexei Barrionuevo, "Inquiry on 1994 Blast at Argentina Jewish Center Gets New Life," *New York Times,* July 18, 2009.

128. Arrest warrant for Samuel Salman el Reda.

129. Ibid.

130. Goldberg, "In the Party of God: Hezbollah Sets Up Operations."

131. Burgos and Nisman, 310.

132. Library of Congress, "Global Overview of Narcotics-Funded Terrorist and Other Extremist Groups."

133. AMIA indictment, 234.

134. Goldberg, "In the Party of God: Hezbollah Sets Up Operations."

135. "Argentine Prosecutors Link Tri-Border Hizballah Leaders to AMIA Attack," *ABC Color* (Paraguay), May 28, 2003 (Spanish).

136. Burgos and Nisman, 328–30.

137. "Report of the Task Force of the Federal Bureau of Investigation (FBI): Analysis of the Attack on the Seat of the Mutual Israeli Argentinean Association (AMIA)."

138. Rohter, "South America Region under Watch."

139. Burgos and Nisman, 215.

140. Comments of FBI Special Agent James Bernazzani Jr. as cited in Burgos and Nisman, 312.

141. Burgos and Nisman, 328.

142. Rex Hudson, "Terrorist and Organized Crime Groups in the Tri-Border Area (TBA) of South America," A Report prepared by the Federal Research Division, Library of Congress, under an Interagency Agreement with the Crime and Narcotics Center Director of Central Intelligence, July 2003 (Revised December 2010), 14.

143. Presentation of Israeli intelligence official at a conference conducted under Chatham House Rule, December 2010.

144. Goldberg, "In the Party of God: Hezbollah Sets Up Operations."

145. Library of Congress, "Global Overview of Narcotics-Funded Terrorist and Other Extremist Groups," 19.

146. Burgos and Nisman, 216–17.

147. AMIA indictment, 71, 101, 135.

148. Burgos and Nisman, 207.

149. Arrest warrant for Samuel Salman el Reda.

150. Ibid.

151. Burgos and Nisman, 318.

152. Arrest warrant for Samuel Salman el Reda.

153. Burgos and Nisman, 15.

154. Arrest warrant for Samuel Salman el Reda.

155. Burgos and Nisman, 15.

156. Ibid., 320–21.

157. "Report of the Task Force of the Federal Bureau of Investigation (FBI): Analysis of the Attack on the Seat of the Mutual Israeli Argentinean Association (AMIA)."

158. Sebastian Rotella, "Deadly Blasts and an Itinerant's Tale," *Los Angeles Times*, April 17, 1999.

159. "Report of the Task Force of the Federal Bureau of Investigation (FBI): Analysis of the Attack on the Seat of the Mutual Israeli Argentinean Association (AMIA)."

160. Burgos and Nisman, 324–25.

161. Ibid.

162. Dos Santos, the shadowy figure warned that terrorists with whom his Iranian ex-girlfriend was involved were preparing to bomb a Jewish target in Buenos Aires, reportedly cultivated a romantic relationship with Fat Nora so he could smuggle goods across the border. See "Report of the Task Force of the Federal Bureau of Investigation (FBI): Analysis of the Attack on the Seat of the Mutual Israeli Argentinean Association (AMIA); See also Rotella, "Deadly Blasts."

163. Martinez may have been an employee of Telledin's, or the name may have been a fake. See "Report of the Task Force of the Federal Bureau of Investigation (FBI): Analysis of the Attack on the Seat of the Mutual Israeli Argentinean Association (AMIA)."

164. Ibid.

165. Burgos and Nisman, 15.

166. Ibid., 15, 21, 248; "Report of the Task Force of the Federal Bureau of Investigation (FBI): Analysis of the Attack on the Seat of the Mutual Israeli Argentinean Association (AMIA)."

167. Burgos and Nisman, 15.

168. Arrest warrant for Samuel Salman el Reda.

169. Ibid.

170. "Iran as a State Sponsoring and Operating Terror," Intelligence and Terrorism Information Center (Israel), Special Information Bulletin, April 2003.

171. Burgos and Nisman, 333, 337–39, 354–55.

172. Article in *Clarin* newspaper, as cited in Burgos and Nisman, 345.

173. Burgos and Nisman, 334; Marc Perelman, "Argentine Authorities Said to Seek Arrest of Iranians in 1994 Bombing," *Forward*, November 18, 2005.

174. Burgos and Nisman, 299; *United States of America v. Bassam Gharib Makki*, Affidavit of FBI Agent James Bernazzani Jr.; William R. Long, "Islamic Jihad Says It Bombed Embassy; Toll 21," *Los Angeles Times*, March 19, 1992; Bergman, *Secret War with Iran*, 170; US Department of State, *Patterns of Global Terrorism 1992*, Washington, DC, April 1993, 1, 9.

175. Bergman, *Secret War with Iran*, 170–71.

176. Burgos and Nisman, 301–2.

177. Bergman, *Secret War with Iran*, 171.

178. Burgos and Nisman, 301.

179. Long, "Islamic Jihad Says It Bombed Embassy."

180. *USA v. Bassam Gharib Makki*, Affidavit of James Bernazzani Jr.

181. Statement of Ambassador Philip Wilcox, *Terrorism in Latin America/AMIA Bombing in Argentina*.

182. Burgos and Nisman, 302.

183. US CiA, "Lebanon's Hizballah," 8–9.

184. Burgos and Nisman, 305–6.

185. AMIA indictment, 84–85.

186. Burgos and Nisman, 152.

187. Author interview, Alberto Nisman, March 21, 2010.

188. AMIA indictment, 31, 125.

189. Ibid., 166.

190. "Barakat Traveled to Iran with Paraguayan Passport" (Spanish), *ABC Color* (Asunción), June 9, 2003; Burgos and Nisman, 313.

191. Bergman, *Secret War with Iran*, 172.

192. Burgos and Nisman, 301.

193. US CIA, "Lebanon's Hizballah," 8.

194. Library of Congress, "Global Overview of Narcotics-Funded Terrorist and Other Extremist Groups," 21.

195. AMIA indictment, 231–32; Burgos and Nisman, 309.

196. *United States of America v. Bassam Gharib Makki*, Affidavit of FBI Agent James Bernazzani Jr.; Long, "Islamic Jihad Says It Bombed Embassy."

197. Burgos and Nisman, 305.

198. AMIA indictment, 139–40.

199. Bergman, *Secret War with Iran*, 171.

200. Ibid.

201. Burgos and Nisman, 239.

202. AMIA indictment, 102.

203. Burgos and Nisman, 228.

204. US CIA, "Lebanon's Hizballah: Testing Political Waters."

205. Burgos and Nisman, 377.

206. "Panama Jews Fear Sabotage in Crash," *Jerusalem Post*, July 21, 1994; "Bomb Caused Plane Crash, Panama Official Says," *New York Times*, July 21, 1994.

207. Statement of Ambassador Phillips, *Terrorism in Latin America/AMIA Bombing in Argentina*.

208. "Lebanese Group Claims Responsibility for AMIA and Panamanian Aircraft Bombing," Voice of Israel, July 23, 1994, acquired through *BBC Summary of World Broadcasts*, July 25, 1994.

209. US FBI, "International Radical Fundamentalism." See also the finding of Hezbollah expert Magnus Ranstorp that Hezbollah (with help from Iran) was behind attacks in Argentina, Panama, and London in the wake of the July 1994 peace agreement signed between Israel and Jordan. Magnus Ranstorp, "Hizbollah's Command Leadership."

210. Hudson, *Terrorist and Organized Crime Groups in the Tri-Border Area*, 35, 19.

211. "Two Lebanese Are Linked to Hezbollah in the East" (Spanish), *ABC Color* (Asunción), November 27, 2002; "Argentine Prosecutors Link Tri-Border Hizballah Leaders to AMIA Attack," *ABC Color* (Paraguay), May 28, 2003 (Spanish).

212. Perelman, "Clandestine Operation Targeted Arab Suspects," *The Forward*, January 17, 2003.

213. Rotella, "Jungle Hub for World's Outlaws." See also Hudson, *Terrorist and Organized Crime Groups in the Tri-Border Area*, 77. According to Hudson, Kadi is the same as Marwan Safadi who, according to the Nisman/Burgos AMIA report, may also have played

a role in the 1993 attack on the World Trade Center in New York (see Burgos and Nisman, 315). Re Kadi/Safadi, see also "Lebanese Prisoner in Miami Is the Cousin of Individual Involved in Attack" (Spanish), *ABC Color* (Asunción), February 24, 2010.

214. US Department of the Treasury, "Treasury Designates Islamic Extremist."

215. Hudson, *Terrorist and Organized Crime Groups in the Tri-Border Area*, 18; Goldberg, "In the Party of God: Hezbollah Sets Up Operations."

216. Author interview, former FBI agent, Washington, DC, February 23, 2011.

217. Allan Woods, "Ottawa Was Terror Target, U.S. Reports," *National Post* (Canada), February 9, 2004.

218. Author interview, former FBI agent, Washington, DC, February 23, 2011.

219. AMIA indictment, 154.

220. US Congress, House Committee on Oversight and Government Reform, *Transnational Drug Enterprises (Part II): Threats to Global Stability and U.S. Policy Responses: Hearing before the Subcommittee on National Security and Foreign Affairs*, 111th Cong., 2d sess., March 3, 2010, Statement of Anthony P. Placido.

221. Wege, "Hizballah's Bekka Organization," 29–38.

222. Ron Ben Yishai, "Hizbullah's Drug Link: The Ayatollahs Allowed Drug Traffic as a Weapon against Israel," *Yediot Ahronot* (Tel Aviv), June 6, 1997.

223. US Department of State, Bureau of International Narcotics and Law Enforcement, *International Narcotics Control Strategy Report* 1, 2011, 365.

224. Author interview, DEA agents, Washington, DC, June 18, 2010.

225. US Department of Justice, "Operation Green Ice (1992)," *DEA History Book 1990–1994*; Andelman, "Drug Money Maze," 94–108.

226. Author interview, DEA agents, Washington, DC, June 18, 2010.

227. Ibid.

228. Library of Congress, "Global Overview of Narcotics-Funded Terrorist and Other Extremist Groups"; Yishai, "Hizbullah's Drug Link."

229. US Department of Justice, Federal Bureau of Investigation, "International Radical Fundamentalism: An Analytical Overview of Groups and Trends," November 1994, declassified on November 20, 2008.

230. US Congress, Senate Armed Services Committee, Posture Statement of Admiral James G. Stavridis, United States Navy Commander, United States Southern Command, 111th Congress, 1st sess., March 17, 2009, 12.

231. Jo Becker, "Beirut Bank Seen as a Hub of Hezbollah's Financing," *New York Times*, December 13, 2011.

232. Ibid.

233. Chris Kraul and Sebastian Rotella, "Drug Probe Finds Hezbollah Link," *Los Angeles Times*, October 22, 2008.

234. US Department of the Treasury, "Treasury Designates Medellin Drug Lord Tied to Oficina de Envigado Organized Crime Group," press release, July 9, 2009.

235. Associated Press, "17 Arrested on Curacao for Involvement in Hezbollah-linked Drug Ring," *Guardian* (London), April 29, 2009.

236. "Police Crack Down on Curacao Drug Ring with Ties to Hizbullah," *Naharnet*, April 29, 2009.

237. Statement of Ambassador Philip Wilcox, *Terrorism in Latin America/AMIA Bombing in Argentina*.

238. Statement of Tommy Baer, *Terrorism in Latin America/AMIA Bombing in Argentina*.

239. Benjamin Birnbaum, "General in Latin America Trains Eye on Middle East," *Washington Times*, July 29, 2010.

240. US Congress, House Armed Services Committee, *Fiscal Year 2013 National Defense Authorization Budget Requests from U.S. Southern Command and U.S. Northern Command: Hearing before the House Armed Services Committee*, 112th Cong., 2d sess., March 6, 2012, Statement of Douglas Fraser.

241. Associated Press, "U.S.: 'Unthinkable' Terror Devastation Prevented," June 3, 2007.

242. "Exclusive: CIA Documents, the FBI and PF Show How the Acts of Islamic Terror Network in Brazil," *Veja* (Brazil), April 2, 2011; see also "Brazil Latest Base for Islamic Extremists," *Telegraph* (London), April 4, 2001.

243. Author interview, retired FBI agent, Washington, DC, February 23, 2011.

244. Reuters, "Report: Saudi Officials Warned of Iran Plot to Attack Israel Embassy in Argentina," *Haaretz* (Tel Aviv), October 14, 2011.

245. US Department of State, *Country Reports on Terrorism* 2011, July 31, 2012, 184.

5

A Near Miss in Bangkok

AS HE NAVIGATED his motorcycle taxi through Bangkok's notoriously congested streets, Boonserm Saendi likely had his eye out for oncoming traffic. It was about 9 AM on March 11, 1994, and rush hour was at its peak. Saendi drove a passenger to the Chidlom branch of the Central Department Store in the Lumpini neighborhood of the city's Patumwan district. Saendi was parked at an entry-exit zone when a truck turning left out of the department store's underground garage hit him. Little did he know it, but Saendi had just inadvertently foiled a Hezbollah plot, almost a year in the making, to bomb the Israeli embassy located just another 240 meters down the road.[1]

The truck continued down the road, showing no signs of stopping until two motorcyclists who witnessed the accident stopped the driver some fifteen to twenty meters down the street. Presumably, the driver wanted to reach his ultimate destination, dismayed at being stopped so close to his goal. When one of the motorcyclists approached the driver, objecting to his failure to stop at the scene of the accident, the driver said nothing but quickly reached out his window and offered the motorcyclist what he described as "three greenish foreign currency notes." Rejecting the money, the motorcyclist insisted the driver exit the truck, which he did. At this point, an agitated Boonserm Saendi insisted the truck driver return to the scene of the accident. But when the two got there, the driver, who spoke a foreign language, gestured that he had to make a phone call. He entered the shopping center and disappeared.[2]

Saendi filed a victim's complaint with the police concerning the accident, the police took the abandoned truck to the Lumpini police station, and no one thought much of the frustrating but not uncommon incident. So far as the police, the victim, and the witnesses were concerned, this was a simple hit-and-run fender bender.

Some time passed, and eventually the owner of the rented truck, Ms. Linchi Singtongam, was tracked down and summoned to claim her vehicle. When she arrived, the owner noticed odd, customized adjustments that had been made to the vehicle. The windows were tinted with filtering film, but only on the driver's side. Two posts were removed from the truck's platform, increasing the storage space, and an extra spring was attached to the chassis, enabling the truck to carry more than a ton of cargo. She informed the police of the unauthorized alterations, which led them to examine the vehicle more closely. What they found amazed them, yet remained largely unexplained for another five years.[3]

Inside the truck, police found a full, bolt-locked water tank, two oil containers, a battery, and a leather bag with Arabic writing on it. As soon as the police broke the lock on the water tank, a noxious odor of diesel fuel filled the truck, combined with a rotten smell. It was not water in the tank but rather "white granular objects," which, after further investigation, were determined to be approximately a thousand kilograms of fertilizer. About thirty centimeters into the tank, investigators found wires connected to metallic objects. As they emptied the tank, they found detonators connected to metal tubes and bottles filled with C4 explosives. A circuit and a 12-volt battery led to a wire threaded through the handle of the tank, then through the truck and into the front cabin, where it ended at two manual switches located beneath the driver's seat. The investigators were standing in a professionally built and highly combustible vehicle-borne improvised explosive device, or VBIED; in layman's terms, a truck bomb customized for a suicide bomber.[4]

Only when the Thai police removed the explosives from the water tank, which some police reports described as more of a metal drum, did they discover a dead body at the bottom of the drum, beneath the urea fertilizer and explosives. The owner of the truck recognized the murdered man as one of her company's drivers, and confessed to police that she had rented out the truck to a person who preferred not to provide the standard documents required to rent a vehicle, such as a driver's license or passport. The owner's only condition had been that one of her employees drive the rented truck. This employee had been strangled before being stuffed into the drum. Had the bomb plot gone off as planned, no evidence of the driver's death would have survived the blast.[5]

While Thai intelligence at the time named two Iranian nationals as the prime suspects in the case, they arrested only one person, an Iranian, whom the court referred to as Mr. S., who was charged with being "a member of an extremist Islamic group . . . whose goal was to carry out acts of terrorism and sabotage."[6] The man identified in media wires as Hossein Shahriarifar (alias Hossein Dastgiri) was convicted of murder, robbery, possession of explosives, and attempted sabotage by the Southern Bangkok Criminal Court and sentenced to death.[7] Shahriarifar was ultimately acquitted on appeal by the Supreme Court of Thailand, which ruled that conflicting eyewitness testimony failed to demonstrate beyond a reasonable doubt that he was the bomb-laden truck's driver.[8]

In retrospect, authorities recognized that the Bangkok truck bomb closely resembled those employed by Hezbollah in other attacks like the 1983–84 Beirut bombings and the 1992 bombing of the Israeli embassy in Buenos Aires. In Bangkok, the failed truck bombing led to a massive, joint covert operation involving the Philippines Directorate for Intelligence and its Israeli counterpart, among others, called Operation CoPlan Pink Poppy. None of this became public, however, until a fortuitous arrest in 1999.[9]

CoPlan Pink Poppy: Stumbling onto Hezbollah

Within minutes after stepping off Philippine Airlines flight 126 from Zamboanga City, in the southern Philippine island of Mindanao, to Manila in November 1999, Pandu Yudhawinata was approached by customs officials with drug-sniffing dogs and arrested for drug possession. The customs officials had no way to know, but their arrest interrupted an ongoing counterterrorism intelligence investigation centered on Pandu. But intelligence officials were focused on his activities related to Hezbollah, not drugs.

Philippine intelligence had launched Operation CoPlan Pink Poppy in October 1998, targeting Filipinos who were in telephone contact with al-Qaeda fixer Zayn al-Abidin Mohammad Hussein, better known by his nom de guerre Abu Zubaida. A Pakistan-based gatekeeper for new recruits stopping at al-Qaeda boarding houses en route to the group's Afghan training camps, Zubaida was originally thought to be the organization's number-three leader. US officials would later reassess him to be much lower down on the group's totem pole, but he was still purportedly a key liaison between al-Qaeda and many of the graduates of the group's training camps.[10] Operation CoPlan Pink Poppy was launched, more broadly, in response to a request by the French to uncover overlapping terrorist networks tied to al-Qaeda and Hezbollah.[11]

Terminated for lack of funds in 2000, the operation regained momentum after the September 11 attacks under the name Operation Kamikaze. But before it was shut down, what started as a search for global jihadists tied to al-Qaeda and an effort to keep tabs on local militant Islamist groups like the Moro Islamic Liberation Front inadvertently led investigators to uncover Hezbollah's Southeast Asian network.[12] For the record, Hezbollah had already demonstrated its operational capability in Thailand as early as 1988 by orchestrating the hijacking of Kuwait Airways flight 422 seized en route from Bangkok to Kuwait. But until Pandu's arrest in 1999, authorities had no idea just how developed Hezbollah's Southeast Asian network had become.

Born Krisna Triwibawa in 1958 in the city of Pontianak in Kalimantan, the Indonesian portion of the island of Borneo, Pandu Yudhawinata was an unlikely but impressively accomplished Hezbollah operative.[13] His case became public after his November 1999 arrest in Manila, on his return from the island of Mindanao, the home of a long-running Islamist insurgency.[14] But Pandu was no stranger to counterterrorism officials. Within weeks after his arrest, the Philippines Directorate for Intelligence informed the chief of the Philippines National Police that Mr. Yudhawinata "was a subject of [a] covert operation by [the] Directorate and Israeli counterparts."[15] Israeli counterterrorism officials confirmed that a joint operation led officials to a number of local cell members across Thailand who, when questioned in October 1999, provided key information that uncovered information about the failed 1994 bombing plot and exposed Pandu and his network. An Israeli intelligence report summarized the breakthrough:

> The scope of Hizballah's infrastructure in South East Asia . . . became evident with the questioning of the organization collaborators, mostly local recruits, in Thailand and the Philippines. The initial questionings were made in October 1999 in Thailand in three different areas of the country where there is a Shiite infrastructure—in Bangkok, the area west of Bangkok, and in the south of the country. The questioning in the Philippines and Thailand led, among other things, to the exposure of the fact that Hizballah, with the assistance of Iranian intelligence, was responsible for an abortive attack on the Israeli embassy in Thailand on 11 March, 1994.[16]

But that was not all. According to the Israeli intelligence report, the interrogation of the suspected Hezbollah operatives revealed that the group was planning other attacks targeting Israeli and US interests not only in Southeast Asia but in Europe as well.[17] This revelation appears to have picked up the pace of the joint operation to expose Hezbollah operational activities. Among active Hezbollah plots in both Southeast Asia and Europe—beyond conducting surveillance of potential targets in these two regions—were efforts to infiltrate operatives to execute attacks and collect intelligence in Israel.[18]

Philippine intelligence reports do not reveal the source of the information that led them to Pandu, but according to a memo marked "Reference: ODI COPLAN Pink Poppy," they received information on October 14, 1999, more than five years after the attempted attack, indicating that "an unidentified foreign national connected to Hezbollah" was staying in room 202 at the Hermosa Hotel in Zamboango City. The report added, somewhat mysteriously and offering no further context, that "two leaders of the group were expecting something very important from Pandu to accomplish in Mindanao." The Regional Intelligence and Investigation Division followed the tip that same day and confirmed that an individual they suspected was Pandu had checked into the hotel on the afternoon of September 29, using a Malaysian passport under the name P Yudha W. Only four days later, when he applied for an extension of his visa using his true Indonesian passport, did police confirm his real identity. From that time until his arrest at Manila's domestic airport, he was under intensive surveillance.[19]

Philippine police had arrested Pandu, however, not on charges related to terrorism or other security offenses but for drug possession. The plan, it seems, had been to follow him and collect further intelligence on his activities and accomplices, not to arrest him at the airport. Philippine police intimated the sudden change of plans in a report they filed the following day for the office of the prosecutor—the discovery of drugs in Pandu's checked luggage by a K-9 unit, the report said, had led to his "incidental" arrest.[20] What the drug-sniffing dogs homed in on in Pandu's luggage was an undetermined quantity of Shabu, a street name for methamphetamine hydrochloride in Asia.[21]

A full inspection of Pandu's checked luggage revealed a variety of documents with names and telephone numbers of individuals and organizations. These included five Philippine passports in the names of different people, a photocopy of a sixth Philippine passport, and bio-data for five more persons. In time, investigators found that one of Pandu's areas of specialization was procuring false passports for Hezbollah operatives. They quickly learned that Pandu had traveled extensively, including trips in 1993 to Johor Bahru, a city in Malaysia near Singapore, for the purpose of "trading/human smuggling" and to the Philippines for "processing passports." They also learned he had traveled to the Philippines for this very purpose at least twice in August and September in the weeks leading up to his arrest in November.[22] The urgency, they discovered, was operational. According to Philippine investigators, Pandu reportedly "was on a mission in the country to buy Philippine passports through the assistance of his local collaborators in Zamboanga City. These passports were intended to be used by [the] Lebanon-based international terrorist group known as Hezbollah (Party of God) for an impending terrorist attack at [a] still undetermined country in the Middle East."[23]

Pandu's own use of multiple fraudulent passports prompted Philippine police to request that the court defer his arraignment until they could provide the court with these other identities.[24] The day after his arrest, police turned him over to the Bureau of Immigration pending deportation—apparently before local law enforcement officials knew of the ongoing intelligence investigation into his activities on behalf of Hezbollah—but the very next day he made a failed attempt to escape custody and, because of this, was transferred to the custody of the Philippine National Police Criminal Investigation and Detection Group. Between the attempt to escape and the matter of his multiple passports, officials correctly surmised Pandu posed a significant flight risk. Once the interagency memos made their way through the Philippine bureaucracy and it became clear a senior Hezbollah operative had inadvertently been locked up, the focus shifted to questioning the suspect to determine the full scope of his activities and accomplices.[25]

What officials found was that Pandu played a major role in the failed 1994 truck bombing five years earlier and that he had been an active Hezbollah operative until his arrest—along with serving as a recruiter and document procurer for the group. Within days, Pandu admitted to maintaining arms caches in both Bangkok and metro Manila. Based on the information he provided, Philippine police uncovered a cache on the afternoon of November 23, 1999, including a submachine gun, two semiautomatic pistols, and ammunition. On the same day the weapons cache was found, the revelation that Pandu and his cohorts were planning current operations led to still wider information sharing among intelligence services. Referring to Hezbollah's Islamic Jihad Organization (IJO), Philippine intelligence officials reported that "tri-lateral cooperation with U.S. and Israeli counterparts is being worked out by this Directorate to monitor and neutralize the activities of members of the Islamic Jihad in Southeast Asia."[26] The more these services learned about Hezbollah's Southeast Asian pursuits, the more they realized just how much they had been missing. Much to their surprise, authorities discovered that such activities on the part of Iran and Hezbollah were nothing new in the region. As for Pandu Yudhawinata's journey as a Hezbollah operative, it had begun almost twenty years earlier.

Iran Builds the Foundations for a Hezbollah Network in Southeast Asia

Following the Iranian revolution, the new Islamic Republic of Iran proactively sought to export its version of Shi'a Islam beyond its national borders. Without this ideological underpinning, former president Akbar Hashemi Rafsanjani warned, Iran might become nothing more than "an ordinary country."[27] Iran's Supreme Leader, Ayatollah Ruhollah Khomeini, formulated the fundamental belief in this idea and enshrined it in the constitution of the Islamic Republic. So perhaps it should not surprise that two years after the 1979 revolution, Iran was already actively recruiting Islamist firebrands all over the world to study in Iran. An ideal such recruit was Pandu Yudhawinata.

According to a Philippine intelligence report dated December 8, 1999, Pandu traveled to Iran in 1981 "to take part in prayer activities in mosques. He and other participants proceeded to India to attend an Islamic conference for their indoctrination into the Islamic causes. After which, they went to Mecca for the Hajj."[28] But as the investigation into Pandu's activities grew, so did authorities' knowledge base on the genesis of his relationship with Iran. Just three months later, an updated intelligence report concluded that Pandu's relationship with Iran was less benign than originally thought: "Subject's involvement with the Islamic extremist group [Hezbollah] can be traced back as early as 1981 when he went into hiding in Iran after his expulsion from the university for his Islamic activism in Indonesia."[29]

Whatever precipitated his trip to Iran, these and other reports are unanimous on his path after his arrival. Over two years, Pandu received "military, ideological and language training." He reportedly submitted a request to his Iranian trainers to stay and fight in the Iran-Iraq War, but they denied him on the grounds that Iran already had too many volunteers for the war at home. What his trainers wanted was to send him back home, where he was to function as an agent of Iran's Ministry of Intelligence and Security (MOIS) station operating out of the Iranian embassy in Kuala Lumpur, Malaysia. So, once his training was complete, "he returned to Indonesia in 1983 and participated full time in mainstream activism and demonstrations against the Indonesian government."[30]

Investigators soon found more skeletons in Pandu's closet, including links to a series of attacks in the mid- to late 1980s: "He also formed a bomb squad with other members of the Indonesian cell of Hizballah. The squad was involved in several attacks in 1985 and 1986. In 1987, the group attempted another bomb attack on two discotheques but one of the bombs accidentally went off prematurely and a member was captured. [Pandu] went back to Iran after this incident and stayed there for four to five years."[31] In retrospect, this group appears to have been more of an Iranian-trained cell of local Islamist militants than a full-fledged Hezbollah cell, at the time.

The members subsequently became Hezbollah activists, raising funds, procuring false documents, conducting preoperational surveillance, and executing attacks on behalf of Hezbollah. This fits an established pattern, whereby Iran established Hezbollah cells not only to serve as a model for jihad against Israel and the West but also as "a proxy for Iranian efforts to export [the] revolution to other Muslim countries."[32]

Sometime after his arrest, Pandu conceded to investigators that while working with Iranian intelligence in the 1980s he had met Yutipum Sakatisha, described as "the most prominent activist in the Thai [Hezbollah] group," planting the seeds for his own membership and activism on behalf of the group. Yutipum may have served as a reference for Pandu, but his actual recruitment by Hezbollah was facilitated by an individual whom Pandu knew as Abu Mourtada. Abu Mourtada introduced Pandu to a Hezbollah operative named Hisham and to another named Bassam.[33]

According to Philippine intelligence, Bassam is "possibly a [Hezbollah] appara- tus activist who operated around Latin America and Australia."[34] An Israeli intelli- gence report stated that Bassam is Lebanese and credited him and another opera- tive with carrying out preoperational surveillance of the Israeli embassy in Bangkok prior to the failed 1994 plot targeting the embassy.[35] But the more interesting figure is Hisham.

Philippine intelligence identified Hisham as the leader of the Hezbollah network in Southeast Asia and Pandu's case officer. According to one report, "a certain Hisham was identified as the leader of the Islamic Jihad [Organization], a special attack unit of Hezbollah in Southeast Asia."[36] At one point Philippine officials tied him to a Brazil- ian passport issued in Beirut in 1997 with the name Mahmud Idris Charafeddine, a Spaniard born in 1961. According to their files, he fit the bill: Fair skinned with Euro- pean features, he speaks some English, French, Portuguese, and Spanish.[37]

Israeli intelligence provides a richer picture of a man known by many names, in- cluding Jaafer, Mustafa, and Abu al-Ful, along with Hisham.[38] By this account, the man we shall call Abu al-Ful is a senior operative within the IJO overseeing Hez- bollah's Southeast Asian networks. Based in Lebanon, he traveled to the region frequently—particularly Thailand, Malaysia, and the Philippines—using a variety of names and passports. To cover the true reasons for this travel, he engaged in busi- ness in the region selling religious books and clothing. He met with local recruits personally, providing them funds to cover logistical and operations costs, and assign- ing their missions. Hezbollah leadership dispatched operatives to procure authentic and forged passports, explosives, and other equipment; rent safe houses; and spot potential new recruits.[39] Philippine authorities concurred with the Israeli assess- ment, noting that Hezbollah "is set to carry out terrorist attacks in the region." Opera- tives used Philippine passports to facilitate their entry into the target countries, and new recruits used them to expedite travel to Lebanon for training.[40]

As for Pandu, he admitted to Philippine authorities that he was recruited by and worked for Iranian intelligence in Malaysia. For several years his efforts were over- seen by intelligence officers from Iran's MOIS station in Malaysia before he was turned over to Hezbollah. His first handler, according to Philippine reporting on

Pandu's interrogation, was Reza Afshar Moghadam, who served as a first secretary at the Iranian embassy in Kuala Lumpur. Moghadam, Pandu informed officials, "handled a group of Islamic activists, some of whom were from Zamboanga [on the island of Mindanao in the Philippines], that arrived at the Kuala Lumpur airport on 25 Oct. 1998. The group was to perpetrate a terrorist attack during the APEC [Asia-Pacific Economic Cooperation] Summit held in Malaysia." In time, Pandu reported, Moghadam was replaced by an officer named Hidri, who also served as Pandu's next handler.[41]

Looking back, Philippine investigators determined that both Moghadam and Hidri had traveled to Manila in the mid-1990s for unknown reasons. Arriving on January 21, 1995, Moghadam stayed in the Philippines for three days before returning to Kuala Lumpur.[42] While the particular reasons for his trip are unknown, it coincided with operational surveillance activity by Hezbollah agents in Singapore and followed efforts to recruit new Hezbollah operatives in the region before sending them to Lebanon and Iran for training. All this occurred following the botched attempt to bomb the Israeli embassy in Bangkok in March 1994.[43]

Hidri, for his part, was found by authorities to have traveled to the Philippines at least twice in 1997, arriving on January 15 and July 4. Both times, he later stopped in Bangkok (on January 24 and July 10) before returning to Kuala Lumpur.[44] This travel occurred at a time when Iranian agents and proxies were known to be conducting surveillance of American diplomatic facilities across the world. In 1997, the Clinton administration sent a "strong message" to Tehran demanding that Iran stop such activities immediately. The surveillance included noting where Americans parked their cars and which routes they traveled to and from work, and was especially prevalent in the Persian Gulf, Central Asia, and the Balkans. According to one official it was beyond "the normal spy vs. spy stuff" and could have been used to prepare attacks targeting Americans.[45]

These trips also coincided with a variety of Hezbollah activities in the region. Pandu Yudhawinata, for example, traveled to Lebanon for intelligence and military training in 1994 and again in 1997. According to Philippine authorities, "in between and after these trainings, Yudhawinata carried out smaller missions for the Hizballah," including arms and passport procurement, recruitment of new members, and surveillance of possible terrorist targets.[46] According to Israeli officials, investigators uncovered a "direct connection" between the local Hezbollah recruits and Hezbollah operatives in Lebanon, Iran, and Iranian embassies in Thailand and the Philippines.[47] Meanwhile another local recruit ran a parallel Hezbollah network, this one in Singapore.

Ustaz Bandei: From Bombing a Buddhist Shrine to Recruiting for Hezbollah

In the early 1990s, five Singaporeans, recruited by a Hezbollah spotter, were tasked with collecting preoperational surveillance of the US and Israeli embassies and a local synagogue. Typical of Hezbollah's business model, a local operative focused on recruiting individuals with local citizenship and passports. The new cell was a bonanza for Hezbollah, given that the cell consisted completely of local citizens who blended in easily with the rest of society in the city-state.[48]

The initial promise fizzled quickly. Afraid of getting caught, the recruits backed out.[49] Hezbollah operatives, however, were undeterred and conducted the surveillance themselves, later plotting attacks targeting American and Israeli ships either docked in Singapore or traversing the Singapore Straits or the Straits of Malacca.[50] "Among other things," a Singaporean official noted, "they went to a seafood restaurant in Pasir Gudang in Malaysia for the purpose of capturing video images of the Singapore coastline."[51] In June 2002, Singaporean intelligence released details of the Hezbollah network's activities in Singapore, acknowledging the activity had begun in the early 1990s and continued at least through 1998.[52] The following month press reports mentioned in passing a joint intelligence operation in which the Singaporean and South Korean services "uproot[ed] a Hezbollah operation misidentified publicly as exclusively al Qaeda."[53] Like the 1994 plot to bomb the Israeli embassy in Bangkok, however, this story has much deeper roots.

Once he had spotted and approached the five Singaporeans he hoped to enlist in Hezbollah, Ustaz Bandei introduced his recruits to an important figure in his own chain of command—an Iranian. Authorities never revealed the Iranian's identity, which they may not have even known, but they were closely focused on his role in the radicalization and recruitment of local Muslims to Hezbollah. It was the Iranian, officials confirmed, who "made [the recruits] pledge loyalty to Allah and obey instructions given to them, which included going to war."[54] From its inception, the Hezbollah cell in Singapore was the brainchild of Iranian intelligence.

The parallels between Iran's recruitment of Pandu Yudhawinata and Ustaz Bandei, both Indonesian radical Islamists, are noteworthy. Neither was Shi'a, but both left their early affiliations with radical Sunni elements in favor of operating first as Iranian agents and later as key Hezbollah operatives in Southeast Asia. Both spotted and recruited other Southeast Asian Muslims for Iran and Hezbollah, and both participated in Hezbollah plots in the region.

The story of one plot in which Bandei was involved takes us to the ninth-century Borobudur Buddhist temple in Magelang, in the center of the Java island, one of Indonesia's most visited tourist attractions. Abandoned in the fourteenth century with the decline of the island's Buddhist and Hindu kingdoms, the magnificent temple was buried under jungle growth and volcanic ash for decades. Rediscovered in 1814, it underwent several renovations over many years and was reopened to the public in 1983 after an eight-year, $20 million renovation.[55] In January 1985, Islamic extremists targeted the site in a bombing, claiming this "symbol of Java's pre-Islamic traditions" represented the worst kind of pagan, infidel influence amid the world's most populous Muslim country.[56] For Ustaz Bandei and his co-conspirators, the temple, located about 250 miles east of Jakarta, was also an apt target for retribution against the government.

The bombing of the Borobudur temple was carried out on January 21, 1985, by a group of radical Sunni Muslims. Eleven bombs were placed among the temple's seventy-six domes, nine of which exploded in the middle of the night.[57] No injuries were reported, but Abdulkadir Ali Alhabsyi and three others were promptly arrested for the attack. After a quick trial, Abdulkadir and another conspirator were sentenced to twenty years in prison; another participant was sentenced to thirteen years.[58]

Six years later, in 1991, Abdulkadir Ali Alhabsyi's brother, the blind Muslim cleric Husein Ali Alhabsyi, would be sentenced to life in prison for his role in the series of bombings in 1984 and 1985, including the Borobudur temple attack. Husein, who was arrested in 1989, was ultimately convicted for subversion, the bomb plots, inciting unrest, and undermining the government and national ideology (he was pardoned in 1999 and released from prison). An advocate for the establishment of an Islamic state in Indonesia, Husein chanted "Allah Akbar" upon hearing his sentence.[59]

Interestingly, Husein denied the accusations against him while on trial, insisting that the Borobudur temple bombing was the work of Muhammad Jawad, who went by the name Ibrahim and assembled the homemade bombs. According to Husein's brother, Abdulkadir, Jawad invited Abdulkadir and three other friends to go camping near the temple, and only then persuaded them to bomb the Buddhist shrine in response to the September 1984 shooting of Muslim protesters at Tanjung Priok. Jawad, Abdulkadir insisted, assembled the eleven bombs, each made up of two sticks of dynamite taped together and linked to a timer. Abdulkadir and the others, he insisted, merely placed the devices and pushed a button to activate the timer. Jawad remains a fugitive.[60]

Just a month after the September 11 attack in the United States, Prime Minister Goh Chok Tong of Singapore revealed that another militant Islamist was still wanted by Indonesian authorities for the Borobudur bombing. In a public address he said this militant recruited several Singaporeans into a terrorist cell.[61] At the time, the prime minister's listeners had no way to know the prime minister was referring to Ustaz Bandei.

The following year, Singapore's Internal Security Department (ISD) released more detailed information. ISD's suspicions were stoked in the early 1990s with "a few Hezbollah operatives recruiting a group of Muslims through religious classes in Singapore." Hezbollah leaders spotted and selected five Singaporeans for special classes, some of which were held in Singapore and some in Johor Bahru, Malaysia, located about fifteen miles north of the city-state. Then, the ISD reported, "they met a teacher, known as Ustaz Bandei, who was wanted by Indonesian authorities for the 1985 bombing of the Borobudur temple in Indonesia."[62]

When and how Ustaz Bandei was recruited to Hezbollah is not known, though he "and three other Hezbollah operatives continued to be active in 1998," according to a senior Singaporean official and the ISD report.[63] Other sources, however, noted that senior Hezbollah operations manager Abu al-Ful, also known as Hisham, actively vetted potential Hezbollah recruits on his trips to Indonesia from Lebanon. The report that Bandei, once recruited as a Hezbollah operative himself, brought several of his potential recruits to Johor Bahru, Malaysia, fits the common pattern of recruitment. Abu al-Ful's other senior operative, Pandu Yudhawinata, was also Indonesian and brought several recruits to meet Abu al-Ful in Jakarta. According to Philippine information, "Yudhawinata revealed that he was asked by Hisham, leader of the Hizballah Special Attack Apparatus, to recruit additional activists to the organization."[64]

Perhaps, following the crackdown after the Borobudur temple bombing, Bandei tired of attacking Buddhist and Christian targets in Indonesia and yearned to engage in jihad with a more global, substantial reach. Pandu had a similar experience, participating in local bomb plots in Indonesia in 1985–87 before returning to Iran for several years.[65] By the time he returned to the region, Pandu was working full time for Hezbollah. In Bandei's case, around the time his co-conspirator and spiritual guide Husein Ali Alhabsyi was sentenced to life in prison, Bandei made the shift from local Islamist militant to regional Hezbollah recruiter and operative. The fact that he, a radical Sunni, would be working with a radical Shi'a organization closely aligned with Shi'a Iran does not appear to have dissuaded Bandei in the least. The final stage of his recruits' indoctrination into Hezbollah involved their pledging loyalty to the group and to holy war before an unknown Iranian national.[66]

Final Preparations

Preparations for the March 1994 bombing began the previous summer, around the same time senior Iranian intelligence and security officials met in the Iranian city of Mashhad and gave the green light to another Hezbollah plot targeting a Jewish community center in Argentina.[67] In the summer of 1993, Pandu and Abu al-Ful traveled to Zamboanga City to procure two Philippine passports, one featuring Pandu's picture and the other a picture of Pandu's wife. These were used throughout the preparation for the attack and came from a particularly reliable source.[68]

For years after the failed 1994 bombing, Pandu and his cohorts continued to rely on one document procurer and forger more than any other, Majid Galad, a Christian Filipino convert to Islam based in Zamboanga City. When law enforcement officials interviewed Pandu after his arrest, he first referred to the forger as Philip, apparently the operational name he used with customers seeking false documents.[69]

Having picked up the new passports, Pandu and Abu al-Ful flew to Bangkok, where they found and rented a house just outside of town "which became their storehouse and safe house for the preparation of their terrorism mission." It was at the safe house that Pandu first met several other Hezbollah activists, including three who went by the names Mouhandes (meaning "engineer"), Muda, and Tony. According to what Pandu told investigators, Tony did not stay at the safe house but rather at an apartment in town near the Israeli embassy. The reason: Tony was to collect "information on security details and the physical environment" of the embassy.[70]

The cell members were careful to acquire the explosive precursor chemicals in small batches over a period of time, but before doing that they covered the windows of the safe house with newspapers to conceal their activities. They brought the chemicals to the safe house and stored them in a large metal drum that Pandu purchased himself.[71]

Meanwhile, over the next few months Pandu oversaw the cell's progress in Bangkok and met two or three times with Abu al-Ful at the Soi Nana restaurant in Bangkok's red light district near the Grace Hotel.[72] The hotel, one reviewer notes, "is frequently visited by Middle Eastern and Asian tourists for two main reasons: it is located in the center of the red light area and also close to the Bumrungrad Hospital."[73]

Using a forged Philippine passport in the name of Abraham Buenaventura, Pandu apparently traveled to Jeddah, Saudi Arabia, in July 1993. Investigations in Thailand later revealed that someone named Abraham Buenaventura was a primary suspect in the bombing.[74] He returned to Saudi Arabia several times over the next few years following the failed embassy bombing, even as he was actively engaged in other plots in Southeast Asia on behalf of Hezbollah. Authorities do not know the reason for this summer 1993 visit, though the fact that he visited Riyadh and Dammam (the capital of the Eastern Province of Saudi Arabia, dominated by Saudi Shi'a) in 1994, Jeddah at least twice and Riyadh once in 1995, and then Dubai in the United Arab Emirates in 1996 raises suspicions that he may have been in contact with elements tied to Saudi Hezbollah, a local Shi'a terrorist group also supported by Iran with close ties to Lebanese Hezbollah.[75]

Throughout the preparations for the 1994 embassy bombing, Pandu did much of the actual legwork himself, including searching for a truck to rent for the attack. His search took some time, since most reputable companies insisted he provide the necessary documentation, such as his passport. Eventually, he found in Ms. Linchi Singtongam someone willing to rent him a truck without paperwork.[76]

Then, in February 1994, after some six months of logistics and operational planning and with just weeks to go before the planned attack, Pandu left the country to meet with both Abu al-Ful and Bassam in Kuala Lumpur. Meeting there provided a measure of extra security, he understood in retrospect, because he was about to receive the C4 explosives for the truck bomb. At the time Pandu apparently did not know what to expect from the meeting. He told authorities that two Hezbollah operatives handed him "a bag filled with what seemed like candy bars" and that he was simply told to return to the safe house outside Bangkok with the bag. Only afterward did he realize the "candy bars" were high-grade explosives. Pandu stated that he believed Abu al-Ful and Bassam also caught a flight to Bangkok at that time.[77]

On March 10, 1994, the day before the bombing, Pandu had the rented truck driven to the safe house and told the driver to go home and return the following day. While Tony conducted surveillance of the embassy and Pandu oversaw procurement details, Musa (described as a welding expert) and Mouhandes (an explosives expert) prepared the explosive and, with the truck now delivered to the safe house, installed it in the truck. Abu al-Ful took part in each of these steps as well, at different points in the preparation, when he was in town.[78] Then, concerned about the operational security of allowing the driver, who had now seen the safe house and may have seen or at least wondered about the plans for his truck, Mouhandes decided to kill him. According to a Philippine report, Mouhandes strangled the driver from behind while Pandu rained punches on the driver's midsection. The group then helped carry the driver's body into the truck and buried it under the fertilizer and explosives in the metal drum. Pandu and Abu al-Ful then drove the truck into town, parking it overnight in a parking lot near the Israeli embassy.[79]

By this point the group was joined by the intended suicide bomber, and the final stage of the operation, planned for the following morning, was left to him. Pandu received instructions to leave the country for Indonesia, where he met Abu al-Ful. After the collision that derailed the attack, the only trail investigators found was that someone using a Philippine passport under the name Abraham Buenaventura had purchased the metal drum, rented the safe house, and bought the chemicals. But it was not until Pandu was captured five years later that they made the connection between Abraham Buenaventura and Pandu Yudhawinata. And until then no one else involved in the case was identified.[80]

In Jakarta, Abu al-Ful informed Pandu that their mission had failed and gave Pandu a ready-made Nigerian passport with his picture, on which he was instructed to travel to Lebanon via Cyprus. For reasons unknown, Cypriot authorities stopped Pandu and required him to stay at a hotel overnight, but he was cleared for travel the following day and proceeded to Lebanon, where he was told he should expect to remain, under the radar and under the care of Hezbollah, for four to six months. At some point during his stay, still in 1994, Pandu met another Indonesian Hezbollah recruit named Herman Mothar, who had previously studied in Iran and served as an operational facilitator for Hezbollah's terrorist wing.[81] By one account it was Pandu who first spotted Herman and introduced him to Abu al-Ful.[82] The two traveled to Baalbek, a Hezbollah stronghold in the Bekaa Valley where the group ran training camps. At the training camps, Pandu and Herman learned military tactics and received explosives training. When finished, they assumed new operational names: Abu Mohammad for Pandu, Hussein for Herman. Abu al-Ful ultimately determined that Herman was "not too bright" and broke off Herman's contact with Hezbollah.[83] And yet, even while the investigation into the Bangkok bombing was ongoing, Abu al-Ful himself continued to plot attacks against targets in the region.

Abu al-Ful's Networks Regroup

Pandu and Abu al-Ful's botched plot to bomb the Israeli embassy in 1994 did not dissuade them from attempting to carry out other attacks in the region. If anything, the near success of their effort appears to have convinced them of the potential of Hezbollah's Southeast Asian networks in terms of logistics, document procurement, and operations targeting Israeli and American interests.

In between Pandu's trips to Iran and Lebanon for additional training, Pandu's smaller missions for Hezbollah, according to Philippine investigators, involved "procurement of armaments in Indonesia and passports in other parts of Southeast Asia and the conduct of casings on terrorist targets and recruitment of members."

And although he was then living in Malaysia, he was also involved in storing weapons in Thailand and the Philippines, "presumably in preparation for future missions."[84]

Less than a year after Cypriot authorities detained Pandu, he returned to Cyprus. While there, Pandu sought a visa from the Iraqi embassy, apparently to obtain cover for other operational travel. He was denied and told to seek a visa from the country from which he would depart on his intended trip to Iraq. By one account, comprising a list of Pandu's known international travels and the purpose of each visit, Pandu went to Nicosia in 1994 simply "to obtain information regarding immigration."[85]

A more detailed accounting of his visit to Cyprus, however, reveals the trip had an operational purpose. According to Philippine information, Abu al-Ful sent Pandu to Cyprus "to collect operational intelligence on the security measures in the airport and matters regarding immigration." Abu al-Ful traveled to Cyprus himself and informed Pandu on arrival that "a member of the Hezbollah's Special Attack Apparatus wanted to meet him." Philippine authorities commented on the meeting: "This member appears to be a central figure in the group." Given that Abu al-Ful was a senior operative in Imad Mughniyeh's IJO, it appears that somebody high up the Hezbollah hierarchy wanted to meet Pandu. But the meeting never materialized, for unspecified reasons.[86]

Amid his international travels, Pandu continued to be "instrumental in recruiting members of the Hezbollah Special Attack Apparatus in the Southeast Asian region, particularly in Indonesia and Malaysia," according to Philippine investigators. In 1995, apparently while on another trip to the Malaysian-Singaporean border town of Johor Bahru, Pandu met a Malaysian man named Zainal who made a living selling homemade candies he and his wife prepared at home. It was Zainal's "sturdy build" that led Pandu to recruit him for Hezbollah and bring him to meet Abu al-Ful (using the name Hisham) at a restaurant in Johor.[87]

Four years later, Pandu would admit that while he was not aware of the details of Zainal and Abu al-Ful's relationship, he was "quite certain" that the two remained in direct contact.[88] In fact, it appears this Zainal may be Zainal bin Talib, who underwent operational and intelligence training in Lebanon in 1997 and traveled to Israel undetected in 1999 and 2000 to collect operational intelligence.[89] Zainal's trips to Israel may have been tied to an unconfirmed Hezbollah plot involving Southeast Asian operatives to carry out an attack in Israel in 2000. Reportedly, one plan involved "an attack of the special attack apparatus in Jerusalem against Jewish targets by next year [2000] after the Hajj."[90]

Using his well-worn Buenaventura passport, Pandu traveled from the Philippines to Dubai in 1996. "In between these monitored travels," notes one report, "his whereabouts remained unknown and he might have made other trips using other passports."[91]

By this time the Hezbollah network in the region had fully regrouped after the failed Bangkok bombing and was active on many fronts in multiple countries. New recruits were being brought in, logistical procurement networks were established, contact was maintained with associates abroad, and new plots were being planned. In 1996, for example, Mouhandes—an operative crucial in the Bangkok plot of

1994—was sent back to Thailand and elsewhere in the region "for the purpose of preparing the 'Five Contingency Attacks.' " The opaque reference to a plan for five attacks appears to have been made by a detained Hezbollah operative and is not further explained. It does, however, fit an established Hezbollah modus operandi of casing targets and preparing off-the-shelf operations that can be delivered as ordered.[92]

Southeast Asia as a Recruitment and Logistics Hub

As of 1997, Pandu had moved to Indonesia, where he intensified his recruitment activities, including visits to Syria and Lebanon via Dubai, ostensibly for business but actually to undergo further military training in Lebanon.[93] That year's visit to Lebanon was also aimed at securing training for some of his new recruits. According to investigators, in 1997 Pandu "helped in the recruitment of members of the Islamic Jihad, the special attack apparatus of the Hezbollah in Southeast Asia and went to Lebanon to assist in their subsequent training in Lebanon near Balbek."[94]

Pandu later told investigators that Abu al-Ful personally picked him up at the Syrian-Lebanese border and drove him to an apartment in Beirut. He was surprised to find two other Southeast Asian recruits, Zainal and another Malaysian named Norman Basha, already there. The three spent a week learning the arts of surveillance, countersurveillance, and communicating in code. Norman's training ended there, but Hezbollah operatives transferred Pandu and Zainal to engage in more military training at Hezbollah camps in the Bekaa Valley.[95]

Under interrogation Pandu reportedly also admitted to traveling to Iran, financed by Hezbollah, "where he stayed for almost a month supposedly for tourism." For this trip he used a fake Pakistani passport he obtained in Malaysia.[96] At least one other Southeast Asian Hezbollah recruit traveled to Iran that year: Salim Mesilam, a Filipino Shiite who had procured weapons for Hezbollah that were stored in Manila.[97]

Pandu had increased his recruitment efforts in response to a direct request from Abu al-Ful. Fearful of getting involved with political opposition groups that might arouse the ire of local authorities or unintentionally invite law enforcement scrutiny, Pandu proceeded carefully. Instead, he preferred to scope out potential recruits in mosques, not only in Indonesia but in Thailand and Malaysia as well. Pandu then met with the prospects "to check their suitability." And not all candidates passed muster. Under questioning, Pandu listed several people in Jakarta, for example, whom he interviewed but did not invite to join Hezbollah or meet Abu al-Ful.[98]

Nor was Abu al-Ful averse to recruiting non-Shi'a Muslims, despite Hezbollah's explicit Shi'a self-identification. While preferring Shi'a recruits, an Israeli report concluded, "Hizballah does not hesitate to recruit activists from among Sunni populations as well, despite the differences between the two Muslim religious groups— the Shiite and the Sunni. This was especially prominent in Southeast Asia, where the spotting pool is mostly Sunni and Hizballah's Islamic Jihad apparatus operated there very intensively."[99]

In tandem with their recruitment efforts, Abu al-Ful's Southeast Asian networks developed into a logistics hub with particular expertise in the procurement of forged and altered travel documents. The importance of such documents for a group like Hezbollah cannot be overstated. In Pandu's case, he confessed under questioning to "using different passports whenever he carried out different missions for the Hezbollah Special Attack Apparatus." By the time of his arrest in 1999, Pandu conceded, he had used Indonesian, Malaysian, Nigerian, Pakistani, and Philippine passports.[100]

In 1999, Pandu and Abu al-Ful traveled to Zamboanga City, Mindanao, to procure passports, but their "usual contact," Philip, was out of the country.[101] In his absence they turned to Talib Tanjil, another of Pandu's sources for false documents, who agreed to provide the necessary passports.[102] Tanjil too was more of a collaborator than a member of the Hezbollah network, but he was certainly sympathetic to its mission. In the 1990s, Tanjil reportedly went to Iran "to study Islam and its dissemination," and later he accepted tasks from Abu al-Ful such as spotting recruits and procuring weapons, above and beyond his standard services procuring passports for the group.[103]

Tanjil provided Pandu with at least five passports on that visit and was in the process of procuring six more at the time of Pandu's November 1999 arrest. Philippine police seized the five passports on Pandu's person that Tanjil had already provided. But signs suggest Tanjil did not approach his work with optimal stealth, involving both his wife and his girlfriend in his passport procurement business. According to Pandu, payment for the eleven passports was to be sent to Tanjil's wife's bank account. And yet at one point that same year, "Tanjil tried to procure three passports with the help of his girlfriend, Arlene 'Popsy' Abuda." That effort failed, however, after authorities detected "irregularities" in the applications, such as multiple birth certificates with the same serial numbers and documents that had clearly been subject to tampering. These included true data and photographs for the intended recipients, but with fictitious names. One of these flagged applications was for a passport bearing the name Diosdado Castro Galvez with the picture and identifying information for Zainal bin Talib, the Malaysian Hezbollah operative, who later did travel to Israel undetected in 1999 and 2000.[104]

In other cases, instead of applying for authentic passports for false identities, Tanjil would buy passports for 2,500 Philippine pesos (about $50) each from anybody willing to sell their authentic passport.[105] Other procurement agents worked with Tanjil to obtain false documents, such as Zainal Abedin Tan, a Chinese convert to Islam living in the Philippines who drove a three-wheeled cab for a living but moonlighted in the passport business and even helped procure weapons for the Hezbollah network in 1992.[106] Weapons procurement and storage was an ongoing theme in Hezbollah's Southeast Asian network. Philippine authorities recovered a variety of weapons and ammunition stored in Manila in 1999. And an assortment of people were enlisted to procure these weapons, including Tanjil's brother-in-law, Salim Mesilam.[107]

Renewed Operational Tempo

By 1997, Abu al-Ful's networks were itching to attempt another round of attacks against Israeli, American, and Jewish targets in the region. While Pandu, Zainal bin Talib, Norman Basha, and Salim Mesilam traveled to Lebanon and Iran for various types of training, Abu al-Ful and several of his key lieutenants oversaw operations, primarily from Indonesia and Malaysia. According to investigators, these lieutenants included someone referred to as Haj Zein as well as two key players in the 1994 Bangkok plot: Ibrahim and Osama.

According to Israeli sources, Osama, a Lebanese member of Hezbollah, worked closely with Abu al-Ful to build a network of operatives in Southeast Asia and carry out operations there. He traveled to Indonesia and Malaysia with Abu al-Ful to meet with local recruits and participated in casing potential targets in Indonesia and Singapore.[108] He also helped develop Pandu into a trained and trusted Hezbollah operative. In a sign of the increasingly significant role Pandu played for Hezbollah in Asia, when Pandu was in Lebanon in 1997 Osama provided him contact numbers for other members of Hezbollah's terrorist wing, which Pandu entered into his address book in code.[109] Upon examination, investigators found that Pandu's address book contained several numbers of particular interest. One was a "trunk line" provided only to members of Hezbollah's terrorist wing through which they could be connected to one another. This line, investigators noted, "has been associated to the Hezbollah special attack apparatus."[110] Other telephone numbers of interest included those of Iranian MOIS operatives in Malaysia and several of Pandu's Hezbollah recruits.[111]

Ibrahim, the other aide who accompanied Abu al-Ful to the region, maintained direct communication with Imad Mughniyeh. According to one report, Ibrahim "was with Abu Ful and Haj Zein in the Far East in 1997. There are traces of calls he made to Immad Mughaniya."[112]

Perhaps as part of the planning for Hezbollah's "Five Contingency Attacks," and leading up to a series of operations planned for 1998, Abu al-Ful's network accelerated its operational tempo in summer 1997. In June of that year, Abu al-Ful acquired a new Brazilian passport issued in Beirut under the name Mahmud Idris Charafeddine, which he would soon use for operational travel to the Philippines.[113] The following month Pandu's contact in Iranian intelligence, MOIS agent Hidri, traveled to Manila from his station in Kuala Lumpur. It was his second trip to the Philippines in six months and fit an established modus operandi of MOIS support to Hezbollah operatives.[114]

In retrospect, investigators would recognize the increased activity as preoperational preparations for a surge in attacks. In Singapore, Ustaz Bandei was joined by several other Hezbollah operatives, including Abu al-Ful, who collected intelligence for a maritime bombing plot targeting US Navy and Israeli merchant ships either docking in Singapore or sailing through the Malacca Straits. According to Singaporean officials, "Ustaz Bandei and three other Hezbollah operatives continued to be active in 1998." "The plan," investigators in Singapore determined, "was to use a small boat packed with explosives and ram it into the target vessel."[115]

Dissatisfied with their rudimentary surveillance in 1995, when they videotaped Singapore's coastline from a restaurant across the Johor Strait in Malaysia, they now actively searched for a site from which they could launch their attacks. To this end, they took a boat from Johor Bahru, Malaysia, just across the Johor Strait from Singapore, along the coastline and across the Singapore Strait to the Malaysian island of Batam.[116] One island in particular off the coast of Singapore was deemed an especially promising launching point for their explosives-laden skiffs.[117] One of the operatives involved in this plot may have been Zainal bin Talib, the Malaysian who trained in Lebanon with Pandu and who also conducted preoperational surveillance of a synagogue in Singapore around this time.[118] More interesting is that according to Israeli intelligence, Abu al-Ful and his lieutenant Osama both participated in this surveillance operation.[119]

Nothing came of the surveillance of the synagogue, possibly because the network was exposed in 1999 or perhaps because circumstances never demanded that the contingency planning be acted upon. Pandu did, in fact, share the plot with his interrogators. According to one report dated December 1999, Pandu "revealed the Hezbollah's intention to attack Israeli/Jewish targets in Singapore. To this end, operational intelligence was collected about the local synagogue and this assignment was levied on one of the Malaysian recruits in the past year."[120] Singaporean officials took the threat very seriously, however, and developed contingency planning of their own to thwart maritime terror attacks. In 2004, officials from the United Kingdom, Australia, New Zealand, Malaysia, Indonesia, and Singapore met ahead of a joint military exercise aimed at combating "non-conventional security threats to the maritime environment."[121]

Meanwhile, Pandu's network remained active. Pandu made his first trip to the Philippines to procure passports for members of his network in late 1998 using a Malaysian passport. In August 1999, he returned, this time using an Indonesian passport, though he traveled frequently in his pursuit of "clean" passports, including stops in Indonesia, Malaysia, Thailand, and Singapore.[122]

It was that summer, between June and July 1999, that Pandu was told "to collect operational intelligence on the U.S. [sic] in Jakarta as well as on U.S. diplomats residing in the city."[123] At some point that year Abu al-Ful and his operatives also collected intelligence on a synagogue in Manila. Perhaps in support of these operations, that same year the network procured and cached weapons in Manila and Bangkok.[124]

But operational planning within Southeast Asia was only one item on the network's agenda that summer and fall. Having successfully infiltrated operatives into Israel through Lebanon and Europe in 1996 and 1997, using operatives with foreign passports and nationalities, Hezbollah found it could use the tactic to either execute attacks or collect intelligence for future use.

Pandu and al-Ful planned to send operatives to Australia at some point, where they would stay long enough to acquire legitimate Australian passports. Later, when flying to Israel, they would appear less suspicious traveling on documents from a Western country friendly to Israel. An alternative notional plan, which was never acted upon, involved "the entry of three Indonesian members to Australia for [a] possible attack on American and Jewish targets during the Olympics 2000."[125]

The core plan was to get operatives into Israel through Australia, like Zainal bin Talib, who had already entered Israel undetected twice, in 1999 and 2000.[126] Three others were working-class Indonesians—a porter, a truck driver, and a farmer—recruited by Pandu for this specific mission. He wanted to send them to Lebanon for training first, then to Australia, and ultimately to Israel.[127]

The summer before his arrest, Pandu worked frenetically to see this plan through. In August 1999, he met Abu al-Ful in Singapore. Using the name Walid Rahal, Abu al-Ful transferred funds to Pandu's account to cover his projected expenses during his upcoming extended stay in the Philippines.[128] That same month, the two traveled to the southern Philippines, where they visited Talib Tanjil in their quest for "clean" passports. Registering at their hotel, Pandu used the name Martin Yutti while Abu al-Ful called himself Idris Charac.[129] Pandu remained in Zamboanga City until he obtained the passports for his recruits. In October, Pandu withdrew $1,000 (exchanged to 39,000 pesos) from a money transfer from Lebanon. While Abu al-Ful provided him funds to cover his expenses in the Philippines, the 39,000 pesos appear to have been intended to pay for the passports, which cost Pandu a total of 24,904.26 pesos.[130]

By November, Pandu had collected several passports bearing the names Rumar Catalon Merafuentes, Noel Ahay Gani, Rodney Salazar Ortega, Benjamin Mintan Lipada, and Ismael Balagting Dimson. The assumption is that the first four of these five passports, using Christian-sounding names, were intended for the Hezbollah recruits. The application for Ismael Dimson, investigators later determined, was for a renewal rather than a new passport. The intended destination for the upcoming travel listed on the application for Dimson was Malaysia. "It is quite possible," a Philippine report later concluded, "that he is part of the Hezbollah group that will operate in Malaysia."[131] On November 4, 1999, police confiscated these passports when they arrested Pandu on drug charges as he landed in Manila en route to Kuala Lumpur via Singapore to provide the passports to Abu al-Ful.[132] Of course, with the arrest, the plans never came to fruition.

The arrest disrupted Hezbollah's activities in the region, but the impact may have been only temporary. The CIA aggressively combated the group's activities as well, quietly arresting forty-five Hezbollah members in Southeast Asia in fall 1999.[133] Referring to "detainees"—in the plural—Israeli authorities suggested Pandu was not the only Hezbollah operative arrested and interrogated for information on Hezbollah activities in the region.[134]

In March 2000, a Philippine report stated—in the present tense—that "terrorist activities are being planned to be carried out by members of suspected Hizballah cells in Indonesia, Malaysia, Thailand, Myanmar, Philippines, Singapore and Australia." Authorities at the time suspected Hezbollah of plotting bombings of US embassies in Jakarta, Kuala Lumpur, and Makati City, Philippines. According to officials, Israeli embassies and companies as well as synagogues and Jewish communities also topped Hezbollah's list of targets. Intelligence further suspected the group of continuing to plot maritime attacks, especially against American and Israeli military or merchant vessels traveling through the Singapore Strait and the Strait of Malacca. Last, authorities believed the group had plans to attack the El Al Airlines office in Thailand along with vacation spots frequented by American and Israeli nationals.[135]

Hezbollah's off-the-shelf planning persisted in the region over the next decade. According to media reports, Israel informed Thai authorities in late 2011 that three Hezbollah operatives holding Swedish passports entered the country with the intention of carrying out attacks against Israeli targets.[136] In early 2012, Thai police arrested a suspected Hezbollah operative and seized a large cache of chemical explosives in a storage facility outside Bangkok.[137] Then, in February 2013, the Bulgarian government concluded that a bus bombing there the previous summer was carried out by Hezbollah, and that one of the operatives carried an Australian passport.[138]

Southeast Asian Afterword: Diplomats, Diamonds, and Saudi Hezbollah in Thailand

Pandu Yudhawinata's activities in Saudi Arabia hardly constitute the whole story of the connection between the group's Southeast Asian and Saudi wings. As far back as the late 1980s, Hezbollah was implicated in the murders of several Saudi diplomats in Thailand. These murders can be traced to the September 30, 1988, beheading of four members of Saudi Hezbollah on charges of subversive activity in the oil-rich Eastern Province.[139] To avenge these deaths, Saudi Hezbollah "declared war" on anyone employed by "the House of Saud," a reference to the Saudi government.[140]

In October 1988, the terror began when the second secretary at the Saudi embassy in Turkey, Abdel Gahni Bedewi, was shot dead as he returned to his apartment in Ankara, with Saudi Hezbollah claiming responsibility for the attack from Beirut.[141] Two months later, in late December, another diplomat, Ahmed al-Amri, the second secretary at the Saudi mission in Karachi, Pakistan, was seriously wounded by a gunshot.[142]

Finally, Hezbollah's Saudi affiliate claimed responsibility for another murder on January 4, 1989. The victim, Saleh Abdullah al-Maliki, the third secretary at the Saudi embassy in Bangkok, was shot outside his home in the Soi Pipat neighborhood. The crime was never solved. Two factions of Saudi Hezbollah claimed responsibility for the murder in statements released in Beirut under the names Soldiers of Justice and Holy War Organization in Hejaz. The statements said the attack was part of a coordinated campaign targeting Saudi diplomats abroad in retaliation for the execution of four of the group's members in September 1988.[143]

But the story gets more complex. Reportedly, Maliki, Bedewi, and al-Amri—the three Saudi diplomats targeted in Thailand, Turkey, and Pakistan—were Saudi intelligence operatives working under diplomatic cover.[144] Such intelligence logically suggested that Saudi Hezbollah had somehow infiltrated Saudi intelligence. According to one report, this forced the government "to overhaul its entire security services after apparent infiltration by a new alliance of terrorist groups which resulted in the assassination of two senior intelligence officers."[145]

In February 1990, matters turned bizarre when the murders of four more Saudis were tied to a case involving the theft of some 200 pounds of jewels from the palace of a Saudi prince. The audacious robbery—dubbed "the Great Jewelry Caper" by one publication—led not only to the murders of the Saudi diplomats in Thailand but also to the murder of a Thai jeweler's family and a diplomatic row that continues today. It involved such bizarre characters as a corrupt Thai police officer convicted of robbery and murder who led an Elvis-style jailhouse rock band while on death row and, oddly enough, helped shape one of Hezbollah's first operational forays into Southeast Asia. While this case did not immediately lead authorities to Hezbollah, evidence surfaced much later that the group was intimately involved in the cover-up.

In 1989, around a quarter million Thai foreign laborers worked in Saudi Arabia. One of them, Kriangkrai Techamong, was employed as a gardener at the palace of Saudi Prince Faisal, the son of King Fahd. One day that summer, Kriangkrai snuck into the palace through a second-story window while the prince was on vacation; broke open a safe with a screwdriver; disabled the electronic alarm; and stole 200 pounds of jewels. He stuffed jewels "the size of chicken eggs" into a vacuum cleaner bag. Among them, reportedly, was a nearly flawless 50-carat blue diamond, although the stone was never found or its existence proven. The statistics cited would make the gem larger than the Hope Diamond and one of the largest in the world.[146]

There is no debate, however, about the heist itself. The thief shipped the loot by airmail to his home address in the town of Phrae in northern Thailand, then boarded a flight to Thailand. Converting the stones to cash, however, presented a problem. Not only did the Saudi government quickly inform Thai officials of the theft and tip them off to Kriangkrai, but the thief apparently had no sense of the value of the gems he had stolen. Back home, he sold some of the priceless stones to Santi Srithanakhan, a local jeweler, for $30 apiece before being arrested by Thai police in January 1990. He was sentenced to five years in jail, and most of the jewels were recovered.[147] But they were not immediately returned to the Saudi prince.

In March 1990, Thai police handed loads of jewels back to Saudi authorities in a public ceremony aimed at demonstrating the efficiency and professionalism of the Thai police investigation and shoring up ties with the kingdom, which employed so many Thai laborers. But when the Saudis inspected the jewels, they found that 80 percent were missing. Worse still, some had been replaced by crude fakes. By one account, "most of those that had been given back were paste."[148]

In June 1991, Saudi pressure led Thai authorities to reopen the dormant investigation into the heist. Quickly, more of the stolen jewels were found, but not all. Some $127,000 worth of jewels was returned to the Saudis and four people were charged with receiving stolen property, but no actual perpetrators were arrested. Riyadh issued protest after protest, but to no avail.[149]

It turns out the policeman who tracked Kriangkrai down, Chalor Kerdthes, had gone rogue. A decade and a half later, in 2006, he would be convicted of conspiring with several other Thai police officers to steal the Saudi jewels. By that time he was in jail impersonating Elvis, sitting on death row for the August 1994 kidnapping and killing of Santi Srithanakhan's wife and fourteen-year-old son. Chalor apparently thought Santi, the jeweler who had initially bought gems from the thief, still had more jewels in his possession.[150]

Meanwhile, the Saudis sent several officials—widely assumed to have been intelligence agents—to Thailand to investigate. Within weeks they were killed. On February 1, 1990, the Saudi consul in Bangkok, Abdullah al-Besri, was shot execution-style in front of the Sriwattana Apartments on Yen Akar Road in the Sathon district.[151] Minutes later, two more Saudi diplomats—attaché Fahad Az Albahli and telex operator Ahmed Alsaif—were killed in similar fashion at another location. Two days later, a Saudi businessman, Mohammad al-Ruwaili, was kidnapped and never seen again.[152] By one account, Ruwaili was tortured, killed, and buried in a rice field.[153] According to another Saudi official sent to investigate the murders and the missing jewels, the three diplomats were shot after learning the names of the people who had stolen the gems from the original thief.[154]

Over time, rumors persisted of wives of senior Thai government bureaucrats seen at a charity gala wearing diamonds very similar to those stolen from the Saudi prince.[155] Coming after the murders of the Saudi investigators sent to probe the missing gems, the Saudis were none too pleased. Bilateral Thai-Saudi relations plunged, with the Saudi mission to Bangkok being downgraded from ambassador to chargé d'affaires. Riyadh stopped issuing visas to Thai laborers, and the number of Thais working in the kingdom plummeted to a mere 20,000—costing Thailand an estimated $14 billion in lost remittances.[156]

Despite its toll on Thailand, the investigation languished. In 2008, the Thai minister of justice personally visited Chalor, the police general who had turned death row inmate, seeking information on other corrupt police officials who may have been involved in the murders of the four Saudis.[157]

It took nearly twenty years, but in 2009 the Thai Department of Special Investigation (DSI) issued an arrest warrant for a vaguely described Arab man named Abu Ali. Believed to be "a citizen of a Middle East country," Abu Ali—likely a pseudonym—was accused of killing only al-Besri.[158] Asked to issue an international arrest warrant for its suspect, Interpol informed the Thai government it would first need more complete personal information.[159] Even today, investigators suspect the same gang was behind all three murders. According to the DSI director-general, Police Colonel Tawee Sodsong, "officials believed the murders could have resulted from conflicts between Saudi Arabia and other countries in the Middle East," a veiled reference to Saudi Hezbollah's track record of targeting Saudi officials.[160] According to an Iranian opposition group, the Foundation for

Democracy in Iran, the 1990 murders were the work of Iranian-sponsored hit squads.[161]

But there is no doubt that corrupt police officers and possibly other criminal elements were also involved in the 1989–90 murders. In January 2010, prosecutors finally arrested five policemen and charged them with the murder of Mohammad al-Ruwaili, the Saudi businessman who disappeared in February 1990 just days after the murder of his three colleagues, the Saudi diplomats.[162]

Despite the warrant from DSI for Abu Ali, no one has been arrested for the diplomats' murders. But clues exist. An Israeli intelligence report, for example, concluded that even before the failed 1994 bombing targeting the Israeli embassy in Bangkok, some of the same Southeast Asian Hezbollah recruits were involved in "contract liquidations" and were suspected "of involvement in the murder of three Saudi diplomats in Bangkok in February 1990."[163] A CIA report from 1990 came to similar conclusions some thirteen years before the Israeli report. In an apparent reference to the Saudi diplomats killed in Thailand in 1989 and 1990, the CIA report concluded, "It is possible that the Islamic Jihad Organization (IJO), a Hizballah element headed by Imad Mughniyah, carried out these assassinations."[164]

Through leaders like Ustaz Bandei and Pandu Yudhawinata, Hezbollah successfully established itself in new territory far from Lebanon. This is especially impressive since most Southeast Asian recruits came from communities of Sunni Muslims. What many view as a regional conflict between Israelis and Arabs had expanded across the continent, reaching even Sunni Muslims on the Pacific Rim. Hezbollah's reach, however, extends in many directions, including deep into the large Lebanese diaspora in North America, where Hezbollah supporters would engage in a broad scope of financial and logistical support activity for the group.

Notes

1. Buenos Aires, Argentina, Investigations Unit of the Office of the Attorney General, *Office of Criminal Investigations: AMIA Case*, report by Marcelo Martinez Burgos and Alberto Nisman, October 25, 2006 (hereafter cited as Burgos and Nisman).

2. Ibid., 48.

3. Ibid., 48–50.

4. Ibid., 48–49.

5. Philippine intelligence report, "TIR on Pandu Yudhawinata aka Yudha/Abu Muhammad; Reference: ODI COPLAN PINK POPPY," December 8, 1999, 6 (hereafter cited as TIR on Pandu Yudhawinata); Burgos and Nisman, 49–50.

6. Burgos and Nisman, 49; Buenos Aires, Argentina Judicial Branch, AMIA Indictment, Office of the National Federal Court No. 17, Criminal and Correctional Matters No. 9, Case No. 1156, March 5, 2003 (hereafter cited as AMIA indictment).

7. Agence France Presse, "Death Sentence on Embassy Bomb Suspect Upheld," June 10, 1997; Reuters, "Thailand Upholds Death Sentence on Iranian Terrorist," *Xinhua News Agency* (China), June 10, 1997.

8. US Department of State, *Patterns of Global Terrorism 1998*, Washington, DC, April 1999; AMIA indictment, 207–8.

9. Burgos and Nisman, 49; Philippine intelligence memorandum, Chief of the Philippines National Police to the Director for Intelligence, "Development Report re Arrest of Suspected Foreign Terrorist," November 23, 1999.

10. Ressa, *Seeds of Terror*, 129–32; US Department of Defense, Military Commission Proceedings at Guantanamo Bay, "Detainee Biographies: Zayn al-Abidin Abu Zubaydah," public release, undated; Peter Finn and Julie Tate, "CIA Mistaken on 'High Value' Detainee, Document Shows," *Washington Post*, June 16, 2009.

11. Ressa, *Seeds of Terror*, 129–32.

12. Ibid.

13. Philippine intelligence report, "Subject: Pandu Yudhawinata," March 13, 2000.

14. Philippine National Police memorandum, Acting Assistant Director for Intelligence to the City Prosecutor regarding the arrest of Mr. Pandu Yudhawitana, November 5, 1999.

15. Philippine intelligence memorandum, "Development Report re Arrest of Suspected Foreign Terrorist."

16. Israeli intelligence report, "Hizballah World Terrorism," undated, received by the author August 5, 2003.

17. Ibid.

18. Statement of Matthew Levitt, *Islamic Extremism in Europe*.

19. Philippine intelligence report, "TIR on Pandu Yudhawinata," 1.

20. Philippine National Police memorandum, regarding the arrest of Mr. Pandu Yudhawinata, November 5, 1999.

21. Karl Taro Greenfeld, "The Need for Speed," *Time*, March 4, 2001.

22. Philippine intelligence report, "TIR on Pandu Yudhawinata," 1, 3, 9–10.

23. Philippine intelligence memorandum, Director for Intelligence to the Officer-in-Charge, Philippine National Police, "Development Report re: Apprehension of a Suspected Foreign Terrorist," November 10, 1999.

24. *People of the Philippines v. Pandu Yudhawinata*, Motion from the Public Prosecutor to the Court, "Urgent Motion to Offer Arraignment," Criminal Case No. 99-2013, Regional Trial Court, National Capital Judicial Region, Pasay City.

25. Philippine intelligence report, "TIR on Pandu Yudhawinata," 1, 3, 6–11.

26. Philippine intelligence memorandum, "Development Report re Arrest of Suspected Foreign Terrorist."

27. As cited in Shmuel Bar, "Iranian Terrorist Policy and 'Export of Revolution,'" (working paper presented at Interdisciplinary Center (IDC) Herzliya, Israel, February 2009).

28. Philippine intelligence report, "TIR on Pandu Yudhawinata," 3.

29. Philippine intelligence report, "Subject: Pandu Yudhawinata."

30. Ibid.; Philippine intelligence report, "TIR on Pandu Yudhawinata," 4, 8–9.

31. Philippine intelligence report, "Subject: Pandu Yudhawinata."

32. Shmuel Bar, "Iranian Terrorist Policy and 'Export of Revolution.'"

33. Philippine intelligence report, "TIR on Pandu Yudhawinata," 4.

34. Ibid.

35. Israeli intelligence report, "Hizballah World Terrorism."

36. Philippine intelligence memorandum, "Development Report re Arrest of Suspected Foreign Terrorist."

37. Philippine intelligence report, "TIR on Pandu Yudhawinata," 4–6.

38. Philippine intelligence appears to confuse the various names and lists Hisham separately from "Osama—he is probably the activist known as Abu Ful (also identified as Jafer by Yudha [Pandu])." See Philippine intelligence report, "TIR on Pandu Yudhawinata," 5. According to Israeli intelligence, Hisham is in fact Abu al-Ful, and Osama is another senior Lebanon-based Hezbollah operative who "accompanies Abu al-Ful in his visits to Indonesia and Malaysia for meetings with local recruits" in the 1990s and engaged in surveillance in Singapore in 1998. See Israeli intelligence report, "Hizballah World Terrorism."

39. Israeli intelligence report, "Hizballah World Terrorism."

40. Philippine intelligence memorandum, "Development Report re Arrest of Suspected Foreign Terrorist"; Philippine intelligence report, "TIR on Pandu Yudhawinata," 8–10.

41. Philippine intelligence report, "TIR on Pandu Yudhawinata," 9.

42. Ibid.

43. Author interview with senior Singaporean official, April 2004; see also *Sunday Straits Times*, "Hizbollah Recruited Singaporeans," June 9, 2002; Israeli intelligence report, "Hizballah World Terrorism"; Israeli intelligence report, "Hizballah's International Terrorism and the Penetration of Hizballah Activists into Israel," undated, received by the author August 5, 2003.

44. Philippine intelligence report, "TIR on Pandu Yudhawinata," 9.

45. Robin Wright, "Iranian Leader Plans to Address the U.S. on TV," *Los Angeles Times*, December 31, 1997.

46. Philippine intelligence report, "Subject: Pandu Yudhawinata."

47. Israeli intelligence report, "Hizballah World Terrorism."

48. Author interview with senior Singaporean official, April 2004.

49. Ibid.

50. *Sunday Straits Times*, "Hizbollah Recruited Singaporeans."

51. Author interview with senior Singaporean official, April 2004; see also *Sunday Straits Times*, "Hizbollah Recruited Singaporeans."

52. *Sunday Straits Times*, "Hizbollah Recruited Singaporeans."

53. William Safire, "The Spook Awards," *New York Times*, July 11, 2002.

54. Author interview with senior Singaporean official, April 2004; see also *Sunday Straits Times*, "Hizbollah Recruited Singaporeans."

55. Dr. Soekmono, *Chandi Borobudur: A Monument to Mankind* (Paris: UNESCO Press, 1976); "Borobudur Temple Compounds," UNESCO World Heritage Center; "Major Temple Damaged by Bombs in Indonesia," *New York Times*, January 22, 1985.

56. "Major Temple Damaged by Bombs in Indonesia."

57. "1,100-Year-Old Buddhist Temple Wrecked by Bombs in Indonesia," *Miami Herald*, January 22, 1985.

58. Edwin Soluhuddin, "Borobudur Temple Bombed," *Vivanews.com*, January 21, 2009.

59. United Press International, "Borobudur Bomber Life Term," February 1, 1991; Soluhuddin, "Borobudur Temple Bombed."

60. "Bom Borobudur, 16 Tahun Kemudian," *Majalah Tempo* (Indonesia), May 17, 1999; Muhammad Saifullah, "Cerita Terorisme di Indonesia: Candi Borobudur Korban

Aksi Teror Kedua," *News.Okezone.com*, October 15, 2009. For Tanjung Priok see: Ulma Haryanto, "Death Toll from 1984 Massacre at Tanjung Priok Still Uncertain," *Jakarta Globe*, April 15, 2010.

61. Prime Minister Goh Chok Tong, speech, Dialogue Session with Union Leader and Members and Employers, Nanyang Polytechnic, October 14, 2001.

62. *Sunday Straits Times*, "Hizbollah Recruited Singaporeans."

63. Author interview with senior Singaporean official, April 2004; see also *Sunday Straits Times*, "Hizbollah Recruited Singaporeans."

64. Philippine intelligence report, "Pandu Yudhawinata, as of 05 January 2000."

65. Philippine intelligence report, "Subject: Pandu Yudhawinata."

66. *Sunday Straits Times*, "Hizbollah Recruited Singaporeans."

67. Burgos and Nisman, 13, 93–94.

68. Philippine intelligence report, "TIR on Pandu Yudhawinata," 4.

69. Ibid., 4–9; undated Israeli intelligence report, "Hizballah World Terrorism."

70. Philippine intelligence report, "TIR on Pandu Yudhawinata," 5.

71. Ibid.

72. Ibid.

73. "Grace Hotel Travel Reviews," Trip Advisor website.

74. Israeli intelligence report, "Hizballah World Terrorism"; Philippine intelligence report, "TIR on Pandu Yudhawinata," 6.

75. Philippine intelligence report, "TIR on Pandu Yudhawinata," 6–7.

76. Ibid., 5–6.

77. Ibid., 5.

78. Ibid., 5–6; Israeli intelligence report, "Hizballah World Terrorism."

79. Philippine intelligence report, "TIR on Pandu Yudhawinata," 6.

80. Ibid.

81. Ibid., 6–8.

82. Philippine intelligence report, "TIR on Pandu Yudhawinata," 7.

83. Ibid., 6–7.

84. Philippine intelligence report, "Subject: Pandu Yudhawinata."

85. Philippine intelligence report, "TIR on Pandu Yudhawinata," 3, 8.

86. Ibid., 8.

87. Ibid., 7.

88. Ibid.

89. Philippine intelligence report, "Pandu Yudhawinata, as of 05 January 2000"; Israeli intelligence report, "Hizballah's International Terrorism and the Penetration of Hizballah Activists."

90. Philippine intelligence report, "TIR on Pandu Yudhawinata," 9.

91. Ibid., 7.

92. Ibid., 4, 9–10; Responses to Questions for the Record dated July 26, 2002, Hearing on "Current and Projected National Security Threats to the United States," before the Senate Select Committee on Intelligence, February 6, 2002.

93. Philippine intelligence report, "TIR on Pandu Yudhawinata," 3; Philippine intelligence memorandum, "Development Report re Arrest of Suspected Foreign Terrorist"; Philippine intelligence report, "Subject: Pandu Yudhawinata."

94. Philippine intelligence report, "TIR on Pandu Yudhawinata," 4.

95. Ibid., 7, 10; Israeli intelligence report, "Hizballah World Terrorism."

96. Philippine intelligence report, "TIR on Pandu Yudhawinata," 4.

97. Israeli intelligence report, "Hizballah World Terrorism."

98. Philippine intelligence report, "Pandu Yudhawinata, as of 05 January 2000."

99. Israeli intelligence report, "Hizballah's International Terrorism and the Penetration of Hizballah Activists."

100. Philippine intelligence report, "TIR on Pandu Yudhawinata," 6.

101. Philip was also known as Mujid or Majid. See Philippine intelligence report, "TIR on Pandu Yudhawinata," 9.

102. Philippine intelligence report, "TIR on Pandu Yudhawinata," 9, 10.

103. Israeli intelligence report, "Hizballah World Terrorism."

104. Philippine intelligence report, "TIR on Pandu Yudhawinata,"10; Israeli intelligence report, "Hizballah's International Terrorism and the Penetration of Hizballah."

105. Philippine intelligence report, "TIR on Pandu Yudhawinata," 10.

106. Israeli intelligence report, "Hizballah World Terrorism."

107. Ibid.

108. Ibid.

109. Philippine intelligence report, "TIR on Pandu Yudhawinata," 7.

110. Ibid., 10.

111. Ibid., 11.

112. Ibid., 5.

113. Ibid., 4, 9–10.

114. Ibid., 9.

115. Author interview with senior Singaporean official, April 2004.

116. Ibid.

117. *Sunday Straits Times*, "Hizbollah Recruited Singaporeans."

118. Israeli intelligence report, "Hizballah World Terrorism"; Philippine intelligence report, "TIR on Pandu Yudhawinata," 9.

119. Israeli intelligence report, "Hizballah World Terrorism."

120. Philippine intelligence report, "TIR on Pandu Yudhawinata," 9.

121. Dow Jones Newswires, "Defense Chiefs Meet in Singapore; Focus on Terror at Sea," September 10, 2004.

122. Philippine intelligence memorandum, "Development Report re: Apprehension of a Suspected Foreign Terrorist."

123. Philippine intelligence report, "TIR on Pandu Yudhawinata," 9

124. Israeli intelligence report, "Hizballah World Terrorism."

125. Philippine intelligence report, "TIR on Pandu Yudhawinata," 9

126. Israeli intelligence report, "Hizballah's International Terrorism and the Penetration of Hizballah Activists."

127. Philippine intelligence report, "TIR on Pandu Yudhawinata," 8; Israeli intelligence report, "Hizballah's International Terrorism and the Penetration of Hizballah Activists."

128. Philippine intelligence report, "TIR on Pandu Yudhawinata." 11.

129. Ibid., 9.

130. Ibid., 10–11.

131. Ibid., 10.

132. Philippine intelligence memorandum, "Development Report re: Apprehension of a Suspected Foreign Terrorist."

133. Tenet, *At the Center of the Storm*, 124.

134. Israeli intelligence report, "Hizballah World Terrorism."

135. Philippine intelligence report, "Subject: Pandu Yudhawinata."

136. Barak Ravid, "Thailand Hunting Hezbollah Operatives Planning Terror Attacks against Jews, Israelis," *Haaretz* (Tel Aviv), January 15, 2012.

137. Ben West, "A Hezbollah Threat in Thailand," *Stratfor Security Weekly*, January 19, 2012; Mark McDonald, "Tracking the Hezbollah Connection in Thailand," *New York Times*, January 19, 2012.

138. Nicholas Kulish and Eric Schmitt, "Bulgaria Implicates Hezbollah in July Attack on Israelis," *New York Times*, February 5, 2013.

139. Ihsan A. Hijazi, "Pro-Iranian Groups Targeting Saudi Envoys," *New York Times*, January 8, 1989.

140. Ibid.

141. "Saudi Killed in Ankara," *Washington Post*, October 27, 1988; Adel Darwish, "Saudis Overhaul Secret Service after Terrorist Killings," *Independent* (London), January 14, 1989; Federal Court of Canada, In the Matter of Hani Abd Rahim al-Sayegh, and In the Matter of a referral of the Immigration Act, R.S.C. 1985, c. I-2, Court File: DES-1-97, Appendix B: "Terrorist Operations Attributed to Saudi Hizballah."

142. Hijazi, "Pro-Iranian Groups."

143. Ibid.; Veera Prateepchaikul, "Name Dropping in the Saudi Murder Case," *Bangkok Post*, August 6, 2009.

144. "Alleged Victims of Iranian Government 'Hit Squads,' 1979–1996," A Special Report from the Foundation for Democracy in Iran, May 6, 1996; Darwish, "Saudis Overhaul Secret Service."

145. Darwish, "Saudis Overhaul Secret Service."

146. Christopher Shay, "Thailand's Blue Diamond Heist: Still a Sore Point," *Time*, March 7, 2010; Philip Shenon, "Saudi Envoy Helps Expose a Thai Crime Group: The Police," *New York Times*, September 19, 1994.

147. Terry McCarthy, "Saudi Gems Theft Leaves Deadly Trail in Thailand," *Independent* (London), September 25, 1994; Shay, "Thailand's Blue Diamond Heist."

148. McCarthy, "Saudi Gems Theft"; Shenon, "Saudi Envoy Helps Expose a Thai Crime Group."

149. McCarthy, "Saudi Gems Theft."

150. Reuters, "Thai Cop Convicted of Saudi Gem Theft," June 29, 2006; Shay, "Thailand's Blue Diamond Heist"; Shenon, "Saudi Envoy Helps Expose a Thai Crime Group."

151. "Arab Man Wanted for 1990 Murder of Saudi," *Bangkok Post*, August 6, 2009.

152. Shay, "Thailand's Blue Diamond Heist."

153. "The Big Issue: The Blue Diamond Affair," *Bangkok Post*, January 17, 2010.

154. Shenon, "Saudi Envoy Helps Expose a Thai Crime Group."

155. Shay, "Thailand's Blue Diamond Heist."

156. McCarthy, "Saudi Gems Theft."

157. "A Law unto Themselves: Reforming a Corrupt and Politicised Police Force Will Be Tough," *Economist*, April 17, 2008.

158. "The Big Issue."

159. "Interpol Can't Help in Hunt for Abu Ali," *Bangkok Post*, February 2, 2010.

160. "Arab Man Wanted."

161. "Alleged Victims of Iranian Government 'Hit Squads,' 1979–1996."

162. "The Big Issue."

163. Israeli intelligence report, "Hizballah World Terrorism."

164. US CIA, "Iranian Support for Terrorism: Rafsanjani's Report Card." The text immediately preceding this quote in the CIA report is redacted, but the context makes it clear the report is referring to the murders in Thailand, not to the activities of Saudi Hezbollah in Saudi Arabia which are discussed before the redaction.

6

Beirut to the Blue Ridge

Hezbollah Comes to North America

ONE OF HEZBOLLAH'S first American recruits was a Vietnam veteran and convert to Islam who first fought for Amal and then, as Amal lost political ground and members to Hezbollah, trained Hezbollah operatives. He reportedly served as a bodyguard for Mohammad Hussein Fadlallah (a trusted position once occupied by Imad Mughniyeh) and by 1996 would be described by then–defense secretary William Perry as "a known American terrorist."[1]

The casualty of a broken home who fell in with street gangs in Southeast Washington, D.C., Clevin Holt dropped out of school at age fourteen and used forged papers to enlist in the US Army at age fifteen. Holt spent three months in Vietnam but never saw combat. Most of his tour as an Army Ranger was spent in South Korea, where he became a black nationalist and was involved in a race riot that left one US soldier dead. When the army discovered he had enlisted as a minor, he was given an honorable discharge and flown home. There, angry at the treatment of returning Vietnam veterans and the racism still pervading American society, Holt planned to find a good vantage point in Silver Spring, Maryland, and "start shooting white people." Unable to enact his plan, he was about to commit suicide when, as he retells it, an angel told him he would go to hell if he killed himself. Three days later, he met Musa Abdul Raheem, an African American convert to Islam, and he soon converted to Sunni Islam and took on the name Isa Abdullah Ali.[2]

Within a couple of years, however, Abdullah Ali would leave the Sunni tradition and embrace Shi'ism. Inspired by the Iranian revolution, he and his fellow convert and friend Dawud Salahuddin (David Belfield) took jobs at the Washington, D.C., embassy of the new Islamic Republic of Iran. Salahuddin would soon be recruited by the Islamic Republic to assassinate Ali Akbar Tabatabai, a former Iranian embassy press attaché who had become a vocal critic of Khomeini. Disguised as a postal carrier, Salahuddin shot Tabatabai three times with a handgun at Tabatabai's Bethesda, Maryland, home.[3]

Abdullah Ali would first come to the attention of US law enforcement following "the assassination of this criminal Tabatabai," as Abdullah Ali later described it, as a result of to his friendship with Belfield.[4] FBI officials later questioned Abdullah Ali, reporting that the "subject provided minimal information concerning the areas of FBI interests."[5] They ruled him out as a suspect, likely because by the time of the murder Abdullah Ali had already left the United States to fight in Afghanistan.

Abdullah Ali was forced by illness to leave Afghanistan after just a month, returning to the United States in August 1980, a month after the Tabatabai murder. But four months later, he left for another foreign jihad, this time to fight in Lebanon with the Amal militia. He stayed in Lebanon from December 1980 to October 1981, at which point he went to Iran for eight months. He returned just days before the Israeli invasion of Lebanon on June 6, 1982. Speaking to an American reporter in 1982, Abdullah Ali declined, "for political reasons," to specify what he did in Lebanon and Iran before the 1982 Lebanon war. Generally, he stated, "when advice is needed I give it. When it's not, I'm a sniper." By that time, he claimed to have killed at least nine Israelis.[6] Years later, he claimed he stopped counting the number of people he had killed when the number reached 173.[7]

Over time, Abdullah Ali appears to have moved along the spectrum of Shi'a militancy in Lebanon from Amal to Hezbollah. According to former State Department intelligence officer Louis Mizell, Abdullah Ali appears to have trained Amal and Hezbollah operatives while in Lebanon, including female recruits.[8] By the time he left Lebanon, he had also served as bodyguard for Fadlallah.[9] Perhaps most interesting, however, is his role in the October 1994 kidnapping of Tod Robberson, an American journalist in Beirut.

Working for the Beirut *Daily Star*, Robberson took particular interest in the February 11, 1984, kidnappings of American professor Frank Regier and Frenchman Christian Joubert, one of whom was Robberson's neighbor. Hezbollah kidnapped the two Westerners during the trial of the Kuwait 17 operatives charged with carrying out acts of terrorism in Kuwait. While most of the defendants were Iraqis, also on trial were Imad Mughniyeh's brother-in-law Mustapha Badreddine and the cousin of Hussein al-Musawi.[10]

About a month after the kidnappings, Robberson heard that Amal had rescued the two captives from Hezbollah. The kidnappers were caught by surprise peeling potatoes for their next meal, and the captives were found chained to a wall. Robberson smelled a story—Westerners held by one extremist Shi'a group and rescued by another—and began interviewing people in the Beirut southern suburb where Regier and Joubert had been held. What he found astounded him: The Amal raid on the Hezbollah safe house was directed by an American who instructed the Amal militiamen how to surround the house and led the operation. Robberson probed his Amal and US embassy contacts, seeking more information about this American Amal militia commander. By the time he got back to his office, the death threats had already arrived, prompting his publisher to press him to stop asking questions about the raid. "I dropped it for a while," Robberson later recalled; "the warning was I'd get myself killed, not just in trouble. But people kept giving me small pieces of information."[11]

It took the journalist some time to identify the American as Isa Abdullah Ali. According to information the US embassy provided him, the American was David Belfield (Dawud Salahuddin), the man wanted for the Bethesda assassination of Ali

Akbar Tabatabai. That assessment proved to be wrong, as Robberson found out firsthand not long after he left the *Daily Star* for Reuters's Beirut bureau. Shortly after the Beirut embassy bombing, Reuters asked Robberson to travel to the Bekaa Valley, where a fellow Reuters journalist, the Briton Jonathan Wright, had just been kidnapped, to pass out fliers seeking his release. (Wright escaped from his captors after a couple of weeks.)[12] Driving back to Beirut through the Shuf Mountains and Beirut's southern suburbs at nightfall, Robberson and his Lebanese driver came to a checkpoint unlike the many others they had encountered before. Usually Robberson would joke with the Amal militants manning the checkpoints, but this person was eerily serious. "There was no joking with this guy," Robberson recalled. "After we were waved through, my driver, clearly nervous, says, 'Do you know who that was? It was the American, Isa.'"[13]

This chance meeting rekindled Robberson's interest in Abdullah Ali. With his editor's blessing and admonition to be careful, Robberson resumed his investigation. He talked with two Amal officials, and while neither would speak about Abdullah Ali, they both warned him to stay away from the story. Still, "the story seemed too sensational to set aside," Robberson later wrote.[14]

A month later—just days after the US embassy in Beirut was bombed a second time within eleven months—Robberson was riding his motorcycle home from work through West Beirut shortly after midnight when a car full of gunmen tried to ram into him. "Terrified, I tried every possible Steve McQueen maneuver," he recalled, "but I couldn't shake them. When I suddenly slammed on the brakes, hoping to evade them, they pulled up right beside me, guns drawn." One gunman drove off on Robberson's motorcycle, while another shoved an AK-47 in his back and forced him into the car.[15]

A few minutes later, the car pulled up at an Amal checkpoint, where militiamen asked the driver why he had a frightened American in the back of his car. "We are Hezbollah," the driver responded. The car was waved through the checkpoint. "I remember thinking that their claiming to be Hezbollah was itself almost a threat," Robberson later reflected. A few minutes later, Robberson's captors stopped at a field and told him to walk to a wall at one end. "I was convinced he was going to shoot me, firing-squad style." But he didn't. His kidnappers drove away, leaving him there. About a week later someone delivered his wallet to the Reuters office, as if to make clear the kidnapping was no random motorcycle robbery.[16]

In 1989, Robberson tracked down Isa Abdullah Ali, not in Beirut but in Washington, D.C. In 1986, Abdullah Ali returned to Washington, D.C., after being targeted by a would-be assassin on a busy Beirut street. In the nation's capital he worked as a groundskeeper at Howard University and as a security guard at a bar.[17]

In a series of interviews in Robberson's living room, Abdullah Ali first denied any knowledge of the journalist's kidnapping, but one day toward the end of a long session, Robberson turned off his tape recorder and Abdullah stood up. "I have something to tell you," he said. "I knew about your kidnapping all along. I told them to do it." He dropped his head, apologized, and asked Robberson, "Are you mad at me?"[18]

Abdullah Ali recalled to Robberson that Hezbollah had contacted him to say the organization had heard Robberson was asking questions about him. In a sign of Abdullah Ali's relative importance to the group, they asked him what he wanted them to do about it.[19] It is not clear if Abdullah Ali was already serving as Fadlallah's bodyguard at this point, though such a role might explain Hezbollah's particular interest in his safety. He told the Hezbollah muscle to scare Robberson, which they did.

In summer 1995, Abdullah Ali left Washington, D.C., to fight in Bosnia. Years later, his Bosnian wife would recall that she and others were given training in "military stuff" by "some people from Iran."[20] In fact, Hezbollah operatives were also involved in training Bosnian fighters, according to Hezbollah leader Hassan Nasrallah. Appearing on an Arabic-language television news program (a copy of which was found in the home of a Hezbollah operative in North Carolina several years later), Nasrallah was asked if any Hezbollah fighters had defended Muslims in the former Yugoslavia. "A group went in the past," Nasrallah replied, "and had a martyr among them. Their main role was training and not participation."[21]

In February 1996, Secretary of Defense William Perry publicly pegged Abdullah Ali (Holt) as "a known American terrorist."[22] Perry told CNN that Holt "has been identified with terrorist groups in the past" and was wanted for questioning in the United States. "Therefore, we take his possible presence in [Bosnia] very seriously. We have alerted troops to look out specifically for him." The fear, a Pentagon spokesman added, was that Abdullah Ali, who "is viewed as a terrorist threat," could infiltrate an American base in Bosnia.[23]

In fact, Abdullah Ali settled down in Bosnia, where he still lives today with his wife and children. He reportedly travels back to the United States periodically, without incident, and after turning himself in to US authorities, was immediately released for reasons unknown.[24] Following the September 11, 2001, attacks, Robberson returned to Lebanon and interviewed a Hezbollah leader, who was impressed by his acquaintance with Abdullah Ali, but when told the story of Robberson's abduction, insisted it was not Hezbollah who kidnapped him. Robberson was not convinced.[25]

Bassam Makki's Return

In 1989, around when Robberson tracked down Isa Abdullah Ali in Washington, D.C., Bassam Makki was caught plotting to bomb Israeli targets in Germany. After serving time in a German jail, he was deported to Syria in 1990. Members of Makki's family remained active Hezbollah operatives, including some who resided in New York City. By 1994, the FBI would report that New York Hezbollah cell members were taking directives from the group's Beirut leadership, exhibiting security-conscious behaviors, and, at the instruction of Hezbollah leaders, increasing counterintelligence efforts aimed at identifying Lebanese nationals within the community who may be providing information to law enforcement.[26]

The FBI warned of an unstated number of actual Hezbollah members with "paramilitary training, including explosives and firearms training." According to the

FBI, members "initiated a 'neighborhood watch program' in order to alert cell members of an FBI presence." In another case, a Hezbollah cell in New York was instructed to divide into teams as a security precaution. "Teams were not to discuss Hezbollah matters outside of their team," the FBI reported. "Secret communications could no longer be carried by courier, and letters could not contain details such as the names of members." The FBI's bottom line was sobering: While Hezbollah leaders in Lebanon would be "reluctant to jeopardize the relatively safe environment its members enjoy in the United States by committing a terrorist act within the U.S. borders," in the event it decided to do so "Hezbollah has the infrastructure present to support or carry out a terrorist act."[27] As for Bassam Makki, he next resurfaced on the radar of counterterrorism officials in 1998, first in Paraguay.

Bassam's younger brother Mohammad Gharib Makki had become a US citizen and, together with his cousin Hassan Gharib Makki, lived in New York. Authorities arrested Mohammad on February 22, 1995, and charged him with mail and wire fraud violations. Targeting Mohammad's clothing business, Nadia Fashions, prosecutors accused him of engaging in insurance and credit card fraud, among other criminal activities, which served as fundraising schemes to benefit Hezbollah. By one account, Mohammad was the leader of a Hezbollah "New York cell" and a senior Hezbollah lieutenant who reported directly to Hassan Nasrallah.[28] Mohammad was released on $100,000 bail. Though his US passport was confiscated, Mohammad fled the country traveling on his Lebanese passport and remains a fugitive today.[29] Officials also describe Bassam and Mohammad Makki's cousin Hassan as a senior Hezbollah member. He, too, is believed to reside in Lebanon, having fled the United States after Mohammad's arrest.[30] Just a few months after Mohammad Makki's arrest, in October 1995, the seriousness of the Hezbollah threat in the United States was again brought to light through intelligence indicating that the organization "had dispatched a hit squad to assassinate National Security Advisor Tony Lake." Lake was temporarily moved into a safe house until the threat was run aground.[31]

Three years passed before FBI agents working out of the New York Joint Terrorism Task Force (JTTF) received word that Mohammad Makki had attempted to secure a US tourist visa for his American passport in Ciudad del Este, Paraguay. He was detained on September 18, 1998, by the Paraguayan National Police, who contacted their American counterparts. When American investigators arrived, they discovered that the man who presented Mohammad Makki's US passport in Paraguay, which had been issued in Damascus as a replacement, was not Mohammad. A fingerprint check indicated that the person using Mohammad Makki's passport was actually his cousin Hassan. He was arrested and flown back to the United States to stand trial in Washington, D.C., on charges of misusing a US passport. Matters then took yet another strange turn. At the bond hearing, prosecutors announced that further investigation revealed that the individual in custody was, in fact, neither Mohammad Makki nor his cousin Hassan Makki. It was Bassam Makki, who was back on assignment after his failed bombing attempt in Germany nine years earlier.[32]

During his trial Bassam claimed that he owned an internet service provider (ISP), "Internet Center," and that he worked with the "Computer Center" from 1992 to 1996. But investigators found no evidence for the purported business in Beirut. They checked with officials at the largest ISP in Lebanon, who confirmed that they had never heard of the defendant.[33] However, at his trial, defense lawyers presented advertisements in Lebanese newspapers for the purported business, as well as statements by co-owners affirming Bassam's position within the organization. According to a US embassy source, a business called Internet Center was located in a part of Beirut under Hezbollah control.[34] Any claim that Bassam Makki was simply looking to import computers to South America fell apart, though, as the investigation proceeded.

Investigators quickly learned that Bassam had used his brother's passport to travel from Lebanon to Asunción, Paraguay, on September 14, 1998, aboard an Air France flight. He was met by Hussein Ali Hmaied, a Lebanese resident of Ciudad del Este and an allegedly central Hezbollah figure in the tri-border area.[35] According to FBI special agent Hector Rodriguez, Makki "was accompanied by a key Hezbollah facilitator throughout his trip there."[36] Upon arrival, the two immediately went to the Brazilian consulate to apply for a tourist visa to Brazil. Suspicious Brazilian officials notified the US embassy, which then contacted the FBI.[37]

State Department Diplomatic Security agent Michael J. Hudspeth found that despite Makki's protestations to the contrary, his travel to South America was not related to opening an import-export business. In his affidavit to the court, Hudspeth declared that "whatever Bassam's activities were in Paraguay, Bassam was sent to Paraguay at the express direction of [Hezbollah secretary-general] Nasrallah and was executing specific functions of the Hezbollah."[38] According to a Lebanese Shi'a confidential informant, the FBI informed, "Makki was involved in the military arm of Hezbollah, primarily in the physical training of Hezbollah terrorists." While the specific purpose of Makki's presence in the tri-border area was unknown, the various figures he met with suggest the reasons behind his trip.[39]

On arrival in Paraguay, Makki was chaperoned by Hussein Ali Hmaied, who served as the liaison between the Abdallah and Barakat clans. Hmaied owned an office and warehouse at the Galeria Page shopping center, which was designated by the US Treasury Department as a Hezbollah front in December 2006. An informant identified Hmaied as a "trusted assistant" of Abdallah, the owner of Galeria Page, as well as a business partner of Hussein Ali Barakat, Assad Ahmad Barakat's right-hand man. These ties allowed Hmaied to operate as a bridge between the two factions. Hmaied himself admitted to accompanying Makki in a written statement to the Fifth Duty Magistrate in Ciudad del Este, though he denied having any connection to Hezbollah or knowing Makki well.[40]

During his brief time in the tri-border area, Makki reportedly met with several local Hezbollah leaders. Almost immediately after his arrival in Ciudad del Este, Makki met with Hussein Alawieh, a senior Hezbollah member who owned Fatima Import Export and Alawieh Import Export, as well as another business in Canada. The informant described Alawieh as the "primary connection and the most important family member with ties to the Hezbollah in Canada." Also, according to the informant, Alawieh had told his colleagues that a relative on his mother's side with the last name Makki had come from Lebanon to invest almost $2 million in the area.[41]

Agent Rodriguez's informant also personally witnessed Makki meeting with Ali Moussa Barakat—the father of Hussein Ali Barakat, Hmaied's business partner—at the Galeria Page shopping center, next to Hmaied's office. The informant stated that the elder Barakat was an arms trafficker who came to Paraguay in the 1970s because of "personal problems he had encountered in Lebanon." Later, he spent significant sums to "fix" those problems and lived in West Beirut.[42]

To some, Makki's travel to South America was specifically intended to mend ties between the region's two main Hezbollah factions. Getting them to put aside their rivalry was seen as critical to focusing on their shared commitment to support Hezbollah financially and, at times, operationally. Furthermore, some suspect Makki's meeting with Hussein Alawieh—fingered as a primary link between Hezbollah supporters in the tri-border area and those in Canada—may have focused on efforts to help Makki travel to Canada or to the United States through Canada.[43]

As often occurs with Hezbollah operatives, officials were ultimately unable to collect sufficient evidence for use in public court pointing to Makki's terrorist activities. On December 16, 1998, Makki pleaded guilty in Washington, D.C., federal district court to passport violations and served a few months in prison. In December 1999, he was transferred to Miami, where he pleaded guilty to making false statements to federal agents and served a few months more in prison. Finally, on March 7, 2000, he was deported to Lebanon.[44]

The connection between US-based Hezbollah figures and activity in the tri-border area remained on the US radar over the next several years. In 2007, for example, agents from the Miami JTTF learned of a serious breach of US sanctions related to Hezbollah. During the investigation, US law enforcement discovered that two Miami businessmen, Khaled T. Safadi and Ulises Talavera, along with Paraguayan businessman Emilio Jacinto Gonzalez-Neira, were exporting Sony-brand electronics through Miami to an electronics distributor in Ciudad del Este. What caught the attention of the JTTF was the location of the Paraguayan business, operated by Samer Mehdi, in the Galeria Page shopping center.[45] The 2006 Treasury Department designation of the center proscribed any transactions or financial dealings with US persons or companies.[46] Later, Khaled Safadi was revealed to be the cousin of Marwan Safadi, also known as Marwan Kadi, a Paraguayan national arrested in 1996 for plotting to bomb the US embassy in Asunción. Marwan was later extradited to Canada, where he was convicted on drug trafficking charges.[47]

The Miami investigation revealed that between March 2007 and January 2008, the defendants knowingly engaged in export violations by doing business with Galeria Page even after it was designated. To conceal the shipments, they filed Shipper's Export Declarations with false ultimate consignees and marked invoices with fake addresses. Wire transfer payments between Mehdi and the US-based Sony distributors were also routed in such a way as to mask their origins.[48] Over a period of about a week in 2007, three separate shipments netted nearly $400,000 in profits for those involved.[49]

On February 18, 2010, Safadi, Talavera, and Gonzalez-Neira were arrested by US law enforcement and indicted the next day. Though Samer Mehdi was also indicted, he remains a fugitive from justice.[50] After prosecutors agreed to drop charges relating to the Treasury ban on dealings with Galeria Page, Safadi pleaded guilty to lesser charges of conspiring to violate US export law. On January 21, 2011, he was sentenced to six months' home confinement along with six months' probation.[51]

Even as American intelligence and law enforcement agents ran informants who collected information on Hezbollah in places like South America, Hezbollah did the same in reverse. Once, agents from the FBI's New York office arrived in the tri-border area to quietly investigate Hezbollah activities. The trip was not made public, and even the host country was only informed of the visit just prior to the agents' landing. Yet as the agents were walking across the tarmac, only minutes after landing, their pagers went off with instructions to call home. Imagine their shock when they were informed by officers at the New York field office that photographs of the agents coming off the plane had just arrived on the FBI fax machine in New York. The pictures included no text but the message was clear: We knew you were coming, we know you are here. You may be watching us, but we are watching you, too.[52]

Although known to operate in major cities, Hezbollah maintained a presence in smaller communities as well. By 2003, the FBI would reportedly be investigating "hundreds of suspected Hezbollah members or sympathizers in the United States—including several dozen émigrés believed to be hard-core Hezbollah believers." These investigations were spread across the country, from New York and Boston to Los Angeles. "You could almost pick your city and you would probably have a [Hezbollah] presence," as one law enforcement official put it.[53] Among the lower-profile cities in which Hezbollah would stake out ground was Charlotte, North Carolina.

A Hezbollah Boy Scout Comes to Charlotte

By age fifteen, in 1989, Mohamad Youssef Hammoud was already serving in Hezbollah's military wing in Lebanon. In a picture taken at the time, Hammoud poses at a Hezbollah center in a military-style camouflage jacket with an AK-47 automatic weapon in front of a picture of Iranian Supreme Leader Ayatollah Khomeini. But to understand the young militant's path from the Levant to serving as a pizza delivery man and then the kingpin of an interstate smuggling ring, all the while keeping in touch with Hezbollah figures back in Lebanon, we must return to his place of origin.

Hammoud was born September 25, 1973, in Lebanon, at the Bourj el-Barajneh refugee camp south of Beirut.[54] Weeks later, the Middle East was engulfed in yet another Arab-Israeli war. In the war, the Israelis recovered from a surprise attack to come within striking distance of Damascus on the northern front, and Cairo to the south. Although Arab leaders proclaimed victory, the shame of their defeat would fuel Arab extremism in the region. For the Israelis' part, the technical win came with deep national wounds.

In 1975, civil war broke out in Lebanon, affecting Hammoud even more directly. The Palestine Liberation Organization (PLO) had become a de facto state within a state in Lebanon since the PLO leadership was kicked out of Jordan in 1970. The fifteen-year civil war—the backdrop for Hammoud's youth—devastated Lebanon. And it all played out in the Bourj el-Barajneh refugee camp, where his family lived along with many Palestinian refugees and poor Shiites. According to Mohamad, an Israeli rocket landed near a party of schoolchildren celebrating the end of the school year in 1982, knocking him unconscious and killing a friend.[55]

Hammoud described Bourj el-Barajneh as a "less than middle class area" that was at the center of violence for as long as he could remember. As a teenager, Mohamad was originally impressed with Amal. "They had very good principles ... fighting the occupation and helping poor people and all that good stuff." But over time Amal became corrupt, Mohamad explained. "If you see somebody wealthy in the area, you can tell that's an Amal figure because he would have the best car, the best house and everything." Amal, Mohamad recalled, was suddenly only interested in protecting the interests of certain segments of the Shi'a community and not others. In turn, Hezbollah's social service activities and its success fighting Israel earned Mohamad's admiration. He acknowledged knowing that Hezbollah also engaged in other activities, like blowing up buildings and kidnapping people and hijacking airplanes, but that did not stop him from joining Hezbollah's version of the Boy Scouts, the Imam al-Mahdi Scouts.[56] The scouts, Lebanon's *Daily Star* reports, "teaches young boys the basics of religion, jihad and the ways of the revolution as a prelude to carrying weapons in the anti-Israeli resistance in the South."[57]

The migration from Amal to Hezbollah was by no means unique to Mohamad. Pictures investigators seized from the homes of Charlotte Hezbollah cell members included shots of members posing with weapons in their roles as Amal militants taken when they were still in Lebanon. Most of the militants held automatic weapons, but some carried rocket-propelled grenade launchers and others posed while loading mortars into a launching tube.[58]

By the time the group had come to Charlotte, it had turned a full 180 degrees away from Amal and toward Hezbollah. On learning, in a telephone conversation captured by the FBI, that two Hezbollah fighters had been killed by Amal and not Israel, Hammoud curses the group: "May God damn them. I swear to the great God, they are a second Israel."[59] In a home video found in Mohamad's residence in Charlotte and presented as evidence at his trial, Mohamad's nieces and nephews are urged by an adult voice off-screen—identified by Mohamad as his sister—to tell their uncle who they are. In response the children raise their fists and yell, "Hezbollah! Hezbollah!"[60]

In the video, the children are wearing Martyrs Foundation sweatshirts. The foundation is a massive entity that openly concedes to supplying charitable funds to the families of Hezbollah suicide bombers. In July 2007, the Treasury Department designated the Martyrs Foundation as a terrorist entity tied to Hezbollah. Beyond the foundation's work raising funds for Hezbollah, Treasury identified several cases in which its officials were directly involved in supporting terrorism. The Treasury action also targeted the Dearborn, Michigan–based Goodwill Charitable Organization, exposing the charity as a front for the Martyrs Foundation. In some cases, Hezbollah leaders in Lebanon instructed members and supporters in the United States to send contributions for the group to Goodwill Charitable Organization.[61]

In 1990, Mohamad's older brother, Chawki Hammoud, obtained a temporary exchange visa issued at the US embassy in Damascus, and in August of that year he flew to New York's John F. Kennedy International Airport. Admitted into the country for six months, he overstayed his visa. He later entered into a sham marriage in order to obtain status as a lawful permanent resident, and moved to Charlotte.[62] Another brother, Bassam, was already in the United States.[63] The younger brother, Mohamad, would arrive not three months after the 1992 bombing of the Israeli embassy in Buenos Aires.

Mohamad Hammoud's travel to the United States appears to have been directed by Sheikh Abbas Harake, a Hezbollah military commander with whom Hammoud had worked in the past. Harake sent Hammoud to the United States to build a network that could raise funds and procure materials for Hezbollah. According to some analysts, his mission was more alarming still: to "help create a hidden network ready to spring into action when ordered."[64]

For reasons unclear, Mohamad was denied a US visa at the US embassy in Damascus three separate times. Undeterred, he and two of his cousins flew to Venezuela, where they lived with an uncle for forty days on idyllic Margarita Island, long identified as a hotbed of Hezbollah supporters and "a congested traffic point for Hezbollah operatives" entering or exiting South America.[65] Eventually, Hammoud made it to the United States on a fraudulent visa he purchased with the help of his uncle. Hammoud and two of his cousins, Ali and Mohamad Darwiche, then flew to New York on June 6, 1992.[66]

Hammoud would claim it was merely coincidental that the three traveled to New York on three separate flights that arrived all around the same time. Hammoud later testified that it was "a funny story" that admittedly was "hard to be believed": "I got lost in the airport and I went in the wrong airplane. All [that] I understood at that time, New York, I heard people saying in New York—and just I went. And all of a sudden I was coming to an airplane—I left my cousins in [a] different airplane and they went in a different one and I knew that I was completely in the wrong airplane and the wrong place."[67]

More likely, traveling on different flights signaled sophisticated terrorist tradecraft, a skill with which Hammoud was credited by law enforcement officers assigned to his case.[68] He kept below the radar, and meticulously stuck to the cover story, or legend, that he first laid out on arrival in New York in summer 1992. Describing Hammoud, Stanley Bedlington, a retired senior CIA counterterrorism analyst, said, "He is sharp as a tack. . . . Under cross-examination, he didn't wilt. He looked straight at the jury. He tried to charm them."[69]

At JFK Airport, immigration inspector Stephanie Gaines interviewed the three men attempting to enter the United States from Venezuela. She quickly determined that Hammoud's visa was a "pretty bad quality fraud," reached the same conclusion about his cousins' passports, and deemed all three men inadmissible to the United States.[70] But the three Hezbollah supporters had anticipated such an outcome and were well prepared for it. They petitioned for political asylum.

A complete fabrication, the cover story was plausible; like the best of lies, it had grains of truth and was set against a historically accurate scenario. Hammoud claimed to be caught between Hezbollah, which was forcibly recruiting youth like himself from the Shi'a slums he was trying to escape, and the Israeli army's Lebanese proxy militia, the South Lebanon Army (SLA). Hezbollah now suspected him of being an informant for the SLA and its Israeli masters.[71] At JFK Airport, Hammoud told inspector Gaines that he feared he would be harmed if he returned to Lebanon.[72]

Mohamad and his cousins were admitted to the United States and given a date for a hearing before an immigration examiner. Within hours, they were on the streets in New York, and not long after that in Charlotte. Like many others in the Hezbollah network Mohamad would soon head, he would enter into a sham marriage of convenience—some would enter several—to obtain permanent residency in the United States. All told, seven individuals were involved in twelve phony marriages in the Charlotte cell, including two men who married lesbian partners.[73] It took Mohamad Hammoud three tries before a marriage got him a green card in July 1998.[74]

Angie Tsioumas, the manager at the Domino's pizza franchise where Hammoud worked, noticed that several of her employees took off days or weeks at a time, sometimes months, and found out they were driving cigarettes up to Michigan for Hammoud. She wanted in, and soon was making runs to Detroit for $500 a trip. A month later, she quit her job at the pizza shop and started managing the cigarette smuggling. "She was the brains of the operation," investigators believed.[75] Soon she and Mohamad were married, even though both were married to other people at the time. Ten months later, Hammoud had his coveted green card in hand.

Angie Tsioumas was knee-deep in the cigarette smuggling operation, to be sure, but she also appears to have had at least some knowledge of her husband's ties to Hezbollah. Aside from the Hezbollah videos he would screen at their home, he also indicated that the FBI might have more than a passing interest in his activities. During her husband's trial, Tsioumas testified that when she told Mohamad they would need a background check to qualify for a Small Business Administration loan to purchase a gas station, her husband became uneasy and said, "I wonder how far in depth they search things." When she pressed him about his question, Mohamad mentioned that he was concerned that the FBI had files on him. When Angie pressed even further, however, Mohamad simply stated that there were some things his wife was better off not knowing about him.[76]

Operation Smokescreen

When prosecutors first began to put together a case targeting a group of cigarette smugglers of Middle Eastern descent, they thought the situation was pretty much cut and dried. Then the FBI came knocking and informed the prosecutors that the group of smugglers identified by local law enforcement officers as petty thieves was actually affiliated with Hezbollah. As early as 1991, the FBI had expressed interest in some of the more radical members of Charlotte's Shi'a community.[77] The FBI ran an intelligence investigation—running sources, tapping phone lines, the works—overseen by the bureau's International Terrorism Operations Section. "Operation Smokescreen" resulted in criminal charges being filed against twenty-six individuals for contraband cigarette trafficking, money laundering, racketeering, wire fraud, conspiracy, visa and marriage fraud, and material support to a terrorist organization. The financial investigation alone included some 500 bank and credit card accounts, and the overall investigation encompassed so many agencies that it led to the formation of the North Carolina JTTF.[78]

In early 1995, Detective Robert Fromme of the Iredell County Sherriff's Office was working off-duty as a security officer at the JR Tobacco store in sleepy Statesville, North Carolina, when he noticed a group of individuals of Middle Eastern descent entering the store with plastic grocery bags stuffed with tens of thousands of dollars in cash. Suspicious, he watched as they purchased enormous quantities of cigarettes almost daily, walking off with 1,000 to 4,500 cartons at a time. Each man purchased 299 cartons, just under the legal limit. He observed as they loaded their cars, vans, and trucks and got on the highway heading toward Virginia or Tennessee. To be sure they were in fact crossing state lines, potentially violating federal law, Fromme followed them to the North Carolina state line. Then he contacted federal counterparts at the Bureau of Alcohol, Tobacco, Firearms, and Explosives (ATF) and learned he had stumbled on a cigarette diversion ring, a pretty typical and lucrative criminal scheme in which cigarettes are purchased in bulk in places where tobacco tax is low and transported to states where the tax is high. "Typically," Fromme and his FBI counterpart Rick Schwein would later write, "a carton of cigarettes costing $14 in North Carolina would sell for $28 in Michigan," which is where the Hammoud brothers shipped theirs, making an average of $13,000 profit per van load.[79] At the height of its operation, the network ran three to four minivans loaded with cigarettes up to Michigan each week.[80]

Over time, the drivers were pulled over for various reasons by police in West Virginia, Kentucky, and Tennessee and found to be transporting 400 to 1,400 cartons of untaxed cigarettes. In response, white women were recruited to replace the young Middle Eastern men as drivers. Sometimes drivers were sent in pairs, a man and a woman posing as a couple. Often, bike racks were hitched to the vans to create the appearance of a family on vacation.[81] "Is it criminal activity? Yes," Rick Schwein noted. "But it's more. It's tradecraft."[82] According to the FBI, at least a dozen other Hezbollah cells across the United States were running operations similar to Hammoud's.[83]

Investigators calculated the Charlotte Hezbollah cell purchased more than $8.5 million worth of cigarettes, making an estimated $2 million in profits.[84] Based on receipts from charities tied to Hezbollah found in Mohamad Hammoud's home, prosecutors identified several small payments, totaling several thousand dollars, that Hammoud and his cousins sent to Hezbollah. One receipt, from the offices of Mohammad Fadlallah, thanked Mohamad Darwiche for a $6,600 donation.[85] Others included at least two donations of $1,300 from Mohamad Hammoud.[86] But even adjusting for operating costs, seized assets, monies the conspirators reinvested in more cigarette purchases, or purchases of personal and business properties, hundreds of thousands of dollars remained unaccounted for.[87]

The testimony of several members of the conspiracy drove home the central tenet of the prosecution's charges that some percentage of the funds raised through criminal activities or charitable contributions went to Hezbollah. According to Said Harb, in 1999 Mohamad Hammoud gave him an envelope containing $3,500 to deliver to Sheikh Abbas Harake, a Hezbollah military commander with whom Mohamad remained in regular contact.[88] The two were very close, Harb testified, adding, "Pretty much any money that Mohamad generated in here from anything went to Abbas."[89] On the day Harb was scheduled to arrive in Beirut with the funds, Hammoud placed dozens of phone calls to Harake, apparently to confirm receipt of the money. Testifying in his own defense, Hammoud would claim that it happened to be his birthday, so he was calling all his friends that day. In fact, he called Harake fifty-seven times over the course of two days.[90]

Interestingly, Harb did not deliver the money to Harake personally, because Harake had once beaten Harb's brother to the brink of death. He instead gave the envelope to his own mother to pass along to Hammoud's mother. In fact, Harb admitted to carrying money to Lebanon for Hammoud on many occasions. On Harb's yearly trips to the country, Hammoud sent up to $900 at a time with instructions to "give it to . . . my mom, my sister, whoever you find at the house," according to Harb's testimony.[91] Some of that money is presumed to have gone to Hezbollah. As Bassam Hammoud commented to Mohamad in reference to the Hammoud family, "It's known we're all in the Hizb."[92] If anyone wanted to be sure the money they sent went to Hezbollah, Mohamad's brother Chawki told a member of the Lebanese community in Charlotte, they should give it to him or his brother.[93] As Mohamad Hammoud put it, "It's our duty to help Hezbollah or our people back home. . . . That's how we play our part."[94]

"A One-Man Crime Wave"

Mohamad Hammoud, two of his brothers, and twenty-two others were indicted in 2000 in US District Court in the Western District of North Carolina on various criminal charges. Most pleaded guilty, but Hammoud and his brother Chawki stood trial and were ultimately convicted in June 2002 of providing material support to Hezbollah, racketeering, fraud, and other charges.[95] In the authorities' successful prosecution of the Charlotte Hezbollah network, one witness stood out. Said Harb, as one agent described him, was "a one-man crime wave."[96] Neither religious nor a blood relative as many of the others were, Harb was at the center of nearly all the network's criminal enterprises, from credit card and bank fraud to cigarette smuggling to dual-use procurement efforts. Given his profile, the amount of jail time he faced, and the evidence US and Canadian authorities had compiled, investigators were keen to "flip" Harb—that is, offer him a reduced sentence in return for testifying against the rest of the network.

Harb, however, did not see himself as a major player. He was surprised when so many agents participated in his arrest in 2000. "Why a SWAT team?" he asked. "It's not like I'm a terrorist or anything." Rick Schwein, a supervisory FBI agent on the scene, replied, "Well, we're going to talk about that."[97]

As it turned out, Harb was the critical link between the Charlotte cigarette smuggling ring and a Canadian dual-use procurement ring. One of the major players in the Canadian Hezbollah network was a childhood friend of Harb's, and Harb provided him with false IDs that the Hezbollah operatives in Canada used to replicate Harb's credit card bust-out scams. An expert in using multiple identities, Harb had four different ring tones on his cell phone, each for a different identity.[98] As prosecutor Kenneth Bell put it, this was all about tradecraft. "If you are Hezbollah it is convenient to have more than one name. It is convenient to have financial resources in more than one name."[99] Harb taught Mohamad Hammoud and others the trade. Angela Tsioumas, Hammoud's wife, testified that Mohamad had accounts in Michigan and Charlotte under the name of Ali Abouselah and they would regularly transfer money between these accounts and an account in their own names.[100] The real Abouselah was a friend of Mohamad's, a Saudi student at the University of North Carolina. When he returned to Saudi Arabia, Mohamad assumed his identity, including bank accounts in Abouselah's name, credit cards, a driver's license, and a post office box and accounts at the JR Tobacco outlet as well.[101]

Hammoud apparently provided some of these credit cards to others so that they too could charge purchases at the JR outlet on his cards. And he was aware this exposed him to potential law enforcement scrutiny. In one conversation about a card Hammoud provided to someone else, Hammoud suddenly reminded the person at the other end of the line to be careful about what he says "because the line is being monitored by police." The other person continued talking until Hammoud cut off the speaker again. "I am telling [you] over this telephone that I don't know what [you] . . . mean by this . . . because the line is being monitored. . . . I have a big problem here."[102]

Where Harb could make a buck, he would. He was involved in an internet pornography business that, he conceded, was "religiously . . . wrong," adding, "I'm not a religious person."[103] Some of the drivers who transported cigarettes to Michigan for Harb complained that he ripped them off. As one driver put it, "I mean, what was I going to do, go to the local police?"[104] When a female driver threatened to quit, Harb retorted that he would go to the restaurant where she worked and "kick everybody's ass" and blow it up.[105]

"Death to America!"

Alongside the funds Hammoud raised through criminal enterprises, he collected donations for Hezbollah at weekly Thursday evening prayer meetings he hosted in his home, according to several local Shi'a men who attended.[106] The men would pray, talk politics, watch Hezbollah videos, and donate money to the cause. Several of the videos included footage of actual Hezbollah suicide bombing attacks targeting Israeli checkpoints in southern Lebanon.[107] On one video, a "martyr squad," posing for the camera strapped with explosives, vows to "detonate ourselves to cause the earth to shake under the feet of our enemy, America and Israel."[108]

One tape seized at Hammoud's home contained footage of a Hezbollah parade. Following a Hezbollah anthem ("the hand of God gave us the weapons . . . surely, Hezbollah are the victorious . . . Israel will get its reprisal"), scout groups—like the one Hammoud himself belonged to as a youth—stomp on American and Israeli flags painted on the ground. "How little you are, America; how worthless you are, Israel," the speaker intones. "Our heroes are stepping on the both of you as the Mujahedeen stomp with their feet on the American and Zionist terrorism." Speakers next in line included the Iranian ambassador to Lebanon and the head of Palestinian Islamic Jihad, both just opening acts for the main attraction, Hassan Nasrallah, who quickly gets to his central point: "I scream loudly [at] our forever enemies, the Big Devil, the United States of America, and its cancerous gland, Israel." His speech is interrupted by chants from the crowd focused not on Israel but on a more fundamental theme: "Death to America! Death to America! Death to America!"[109]

After his arrest, Hammoud told FBI special agent Andre Khoury the videotapes brought "joy to his heart because the Resistance forces [were] trying to liberate Lebanon."[110] Hammoud, one law enforcement official commented, was a "Dr. Jekyll–Mr. Hyde type," who shed his soft-spoken demeanor and came alive at the weekly meetings he hosted.[111]

A theme that emerges in another tape is that of "economic jihad" (jihad bin mal): If one cannot fight as a martyr in the south of Lebanon, viewers are told, "you can fight by giving your money."[112] The theme is echoed in a letter Hammoud received from a Hezbollah supporter and convert to Islam, Abu Adam.[113] Then in Lebanon, Abu Adam once belonged to the Shi'a community in Charlotte and participated in Hammoud's Thursday night meetings. In the letter, Abu Adam reminds Hammoud of the need for supporters to raise funds for Hezbollah, but to do so with "complete secrecy." He then asks for the continued raising of funds at the meetings, to be delivered by local Lebanese visiting Lebanon. Abu Adam then notes that he has sent materials with another member of the Charlotte network that cover "the accomplishments of the Resistance" so that "the guys [at Hammoud's meetings] could see it and donate to the Resistance." Not to worry, he adds, "I will send you a receipt for any amount donated."[114]

What really charged the group, however, was propaganda targeting not only Israel but also the United States. In one video, produced by Mohamad Dbouk, a speaker harks back to the 1983 Hezbollah attack on the marine barracks in Lebanon and acknowledges that Hezbollah continues to look for suitable American targets in Lebanon and, if none are found there, then others abroad: "As I've said many times before, we don't fear America or Israel, but rather fear our internal domain. The same spirit with which the martyr brother entered the Marines headquarters and rubbed the Americans' nose in the dirt, this spirit still exists."[115]

"Our Guys" in Hezbollah

Hammoud and other members of his network maintained contact with senior Hez-bollah officials even once they left Lebanon for the United States. Their principal contact was Sheikh Abbas Harake, a Hezbollah military commander in southern Beirut. When FBI special agent Khoury interviewed Hammoud after his arrest, Hammoud admitted to knowing Abbas Harake and identified him as a sheikh who provided lectures, speeches, and other forms of support for Hezbollah. But he denied ever speaking to Harake while living in the United States.[116] Unfortunately for Mr. Hammoud, the prosecution was armed with the transcripts of those suppos-edly nonexistent calls. "Unbeknownst to Mr. Hammoud," Prosecutor Kenneth Bell noted, "the American intelligence community had a wiretap up on Mr. Hammoud's house in the first part of 2000. And we have Mohamad Hammoud talking on the phone with Sheikh Harake."[117]

Then there are the letters. The FBI seized and translated at least two letters from Harake to Hammoud, which show the two maintained a close relationship, had worked together in Lebanon in the past, and continued to work together once Ham-moud went to America. "When the letter is far away and the love is eternal and rela-tionship is strong, it is impossible for words to summarize or depict an accurate picture of the amount of love that I have for you," Harake wrote to Hammoud.[118] At trial, prosecutors asked Hammoud about his work with Harake. Kenneth Bell re-called that exchange for the jury in his closing remarks: "Did he ever squirm around on any question more than that? At the end of lots of squirming and wandering [Hammoud's only reply was], 'I don't know what he's talking about.'"[119] Later in his letter, Harake indicated that Hammoud was still involved in work for Hezbollah.[120] In turn Bell asked the jury to consider, "What sort of work do you do as a military commander in Beirut for Hezbollah?"[121]

In another letter, Harake provides Hammoud with a detailed report on the situ-ation facing Hezbollah in Lebanon, including sections on the status of military, political, educational, and organizational affairs. Later in the letter Harake sends regards to "all the guys," and assures Hammoud that while he cannot write about certain details owing to their sensitivity, "know that we are alright and stronger than we were, holding on to our weapons to protect the dignity of our nation." Harake makes clear that he sees America as no less an enemy than Israel. After praising Iranian Supreme Leader Khamenei, and singing the praises of Hezbollah martyrs like Abbas Mousawi, Harake takes aim at his enemies. "As I greeted the virtuous ones, I must damn the evil ones. Damn America the criminal, and the arrogant Israel that commits injustice and hostility; and Allah, you are the everlasting over the enemies of Islam."[122]

His closeness to the Hezbollah military commander Abbas Harake aside, Ham-moud also kept in contact with Mohammad Hussein Fadlallah. By this time, Fadlal-lah was no longer formally affiliated with Hezbollah, and by some accounts he was no longer the group's spiritual adviser, either. Yet he still ran charities that funneled money to Hezbollah, some of which were designated as Hezbollah charities by the US government. For example, Fadlallah's al-Mabarrat Charity Association maintained

intimate ties with Hezbollah at least until Fadlallah's death in July 2010, and its
Dearborn, Michigan, office was raided by the FBI in July 2007.[123] Hammoud received receipts from Hezbollah for at least some of his donations, including receipts
from Fadlallah's office.[124]

Hammoud's personal ties to Fadlallah went back to Beirut, where Hammoud attended Fadlallah's mosque. Hammoud told FBI special agent Khoury that he had
several telephone contacts with Fadlallah since moving to the United States. "Unless
you have direct knowledge or direct contact with [Fadlallah] in Lebanon, you will
not be able to contact him while you're outside," explained Khoury, who grew up in
Lebanon.[125]

In another sign of Hammoud's ties to powerful Hezbollah elements in Lebanon,
he threatened to "have somebody take care of" the family back in Lebanon of anyone who testified he was tied to Hezbollah. The threats came from his jail cell in
Mecklenburg County, North Carolina, after he and others involved in the conspiracy were arrested in July 2000.[126] The threats resonated; perhaps some of those
threatened were aware that Hammoud had Abbas Harake rough up Hammoud's
own nephew back in Lebanon at one point over the nephew's "bad" behavior.[127]

Hezbollah demonstrated a deep interest in Hammoud's case, underscoring the extent of his ties to the group. When one member of the network returned to Lebanon
after serving his eighteen-month sentence, Hezbollah detained him for two weeks.
They "especially want[ed] to know [the details of] this case" and who was working
with the American government, Samir Debk testified.[128]

When FBI agents raided Mohamad Hammoud's home on July 21, 2000, he
pulled a handgun but then wisely thought the better of the decision and put it down.
Authorities seized the handgun, as well as photographs of Hammoud and others
holding automatic weapons at what appears to be an outdoor target-practice session.[129] According to the FBI, although he was primarily a Hezbollah fundraiser,
Hammoud may well have been willing to use these or other weapons for an attack in
the United States if asked to do so. According to a US government affidavit, a confidential FBI source reported that "if Hezbollah issued an authorization to execute a
terrorist act in the United States, Mohamad Hammoud would not hesitate to carry
it out."[130]

Plotting to Assassinate "the Arrogant, Bastard Prosecutor"

On January 12, 2001, Andy Walcott, an inmate with Mohamad Hammoud at Mecklenburg county jail, contacted the Charlotte FBI. He claimed Hammoud told him he
planned to escape from jail, have assistant US attorney Ken Bell killed, and bomb the
US attorney's office in Charlotte in order to destroy the evidence against him. Moreover, he said that Hammoud had asked for a fake birth certificate and Social Security
card, and claimed that a female guard was being bribed to pass notes among Hammoud and his co-conspirators. While the FBI questioned Walcott's credibility—he
had numerous prior convictions, was facing deportation to his native Trinidad, and
failed his polygraph test—they deemed the allegations too serious to ignore.[131]

Although the information was tantalizing, the government was in a bind, unable to initiate discussions with Hammoud about the subject matter for which he was on trial and represented by legal counsel. Eventually, a plan was hatched to arm Walcott with a recording device and have him meet with Hammoud.

Walcott and Hammoud engaged in three separate conversations. The first was captured by a recording device and produced no useful information. The second was initiated by Walcott himself (in violation of the FBI's instructions) and was thus unauthorized by the FBI. However, after the conversation, Walcott contacted the FBI in order to turn over an unsigned letter written in Arabic that he claimed Hammoud had given him. According to the FBI, the letter introduced Walcott to unnamed individuals and said, in part: "I retained A.G. [Walcott's] service for a substantial fee, his assignment is to put bullets into the skull of the arrogant, bastard prosecutor." Alternatively, the letter suggested, he could blow up the evidence against Hammoud.[132] An FBI translator's analysis of the letter would later conclude that it was written by someone who was illiterate or had limited knowledge of Arabic—since the writer most likely copied from an Arabic writing table—and was inconsistent with other communications discovered during the Hammoud investigation.[133] Fingerprint analysis determined that the fingerprints on the letter were Walcott's and a third party's—the latter of which did not belong to Hammoud.[134] Did somebody write the letter for Hammoud, or was it all fabricated by Walcott?

At their third meeting, Walcott asked Hammoud to provide him with the potential victim's name. This time Hammoud was crystal clear, repeating and spelling out Bell's name (no spelling champion, he misspelled Bell's name as Bill).[135] When Walcott further mentioned that he had decided to shoot Bell rather than use an explosive device, Hammoud did not seem surprised and simply warned Walcott to be careful. However, Hammoud did not incriminate himself during any of the conversations: He made no direct statements ordering or requesting criminal activity, and when presented with the evidence against him, he denied his involvement and even offered to take a polygraph in order to prove his innocence.[136] He did, however, tell Walcott that he was worried about his younger brother because he was a member of Hezbollah and had come to the states only to satisfy his mother. Mohammad says of his brother and other Hezbollah members, "[People like] my brother . . . they hate to come here, you know. Those [are people] waiting for the one day when they [are] going to meet God." Furthermore, Hammoud told Walcott that his brother was happy when the visa application he filed at the US embassy in Beirut was denied and explained that he had to ask his wife for help in finding a wife for his brother so that he could legally enter the United States.[137]

Dual-Use Procurement, the Canada Connection

As the Charlotte case would show, Hezbollah is involved in arms trafficking and procurement not only in less-developed countries but in the West as well. "Ironically, the black market in developed countries also provides an excellent opportunity to engage in arms trafficking activities," according to a study of Hezbollah prepared for US Special Operations Command. "Both U.S. and Canadian authorities track

Hezbollah's procurement of proscribed high-tech military and other equipment," the study notes.[138]

Hezbollah has been especially active procuring items from North America. An early example is Fawzi Mustapha Assi, a naturalized US citizen from Lebanon. He ultimately pleaded guilty to charges of providing material support to a terrorist organization for his attempt to smuggle night-vision goggles, a thermal imaging camera, and two global positioning modules to Hezbollah. Described by US authorities as a Hezbollah procurement agent, Assi first fled the United States after his arrest in 1998 but returned and surrendered to authorities in May 2004.[139] Before his arrest, FBI agents watched as Assi tossed a variety of items into two different area dumpsters. A dumpster dive revealed that the items included literature on military equipment and remote-controlled aircraft, lists of Israeli government cabinet addresses downloaded from the internet, articles on the effects of napalm, and more.[140] And although he was caught in 1998—while attempting to transfer these items to Hezbollah at Detroit Metropolitan Wayne County Airport—he had apparently succeeded in the past. According to Dbouk's longtime friend Said Harb, Dbouk described Assi as "'the guy' for getting equipment on behalf of Hezbollah until he got caught and fled the U.S. to Lebanon." Dbouk continued, telling Harb that he, Dbouk, "personally met this individual [Assi] at the airport in Beirut to ensure Hezbollah got the equipment he obtained."[141]

In other cases, individuals found to be procuring weapons for Hezbollah in the United States had connections to Canada as well. Take the case of Ali Boumelhem, who bought several twelve-gauge shotguns over a two-year period at Michigan gun shows (despite having a criminal record). In late 2000, Boumelhem and others loaded a forty-foot-long shipping container with car parts outside their Detroit auto repair shop. The bill of lading listed the container's contents as car engines and transmissions, but the FBI was aware it held more. A cousin had tipped off authorities that Boumelhem was sending weapons to Hezbollah, and provided a videotape of him firing an assault weapon in the desert and voicing support for Hezbollah. As an FBI surveillance team watched, a truck transported the container to a railway yard in Detroit, where it was scheduled for transport to Montreal. The container was seized at the railway yard, where US customs agents searched its contents and found ammunition, a shotgun, and spare parts for automatic weapons all hidden in a car door. Another shotgun and a two-way radio were found elsewhere in the container. Boumelhem was arrested in mid-November 2002 at Detroit Metropolitan Airport holding a one-way ticket to Lebanon. After a one-week trial, he was convicted on seven federal counts.[142]

Hezbollah has long maintained a particularly active procurement effort in Canada. Not only does the group have a significant pool of members, supporters, and sympathizers in Canada, but the country's strong position in industry, trade, and finance make it an attractive place to procure dual-use items. The immigration case of Mohammad Hussein al Husseini, who was ultimately ordered deported from Canada in 1994, sheds significant light on Hezbollah's presence in the country. Interviewed by Canadian security officials, al Husseini provided information both on

Hezbollah attacks abroad and on the group's presence and activities in Canada. He specified that "Hezbollah has members in Montreal, Ottawa, Toronto—in all of Canada." Referring to the situation in Montreal, al Husseini implied that he could provide Canadian authorities information about cigarette and weapons smuggling if the Canadian government would cut a deal with him.[143]

Mohammad Hassan Dbouk and his brother-in-law, Ali Adham Amhaz, ran the Canadian portion of Hezbollah's funding and procurement network under the command of Haj Hassan Hilu Laqis (then Hezbollah's chief military procurement officer). Their activities were funded in part with money that Laqis sent from Lebanon, in addition to their own criminal activities in Canada.[144] Under the win-win scam, they procured materials for Hezbollah and still made a profit. While their credit card and bank frauds covered the cost of the items they bought for Hezbollah, they still received fifty cents on the dollar from Laqis for the materials they procured.[145] At one point Harb told Mohamad Hammoud about the Canadian dual-use procurement ring and asked if he wanted to help. "No," Hammoud replied, "I'm helping in my own way."[146]

The items that the Hezbollah procurement network purchased or discussed purchasing in North America for smuggling into Lebanon were used, according to a defense specialist who served as an expert witness, to increase Hezbollah's tactical capabilities on the battlefield. Commander James Campbell, a former Defense Intelligence Agency counterterrorism intelligence officer, said the list was ambitious and indicative of Hezbollah's increasing military sophistication: night-vision devices (goggles, cameras, and scopes), surveying equipment, global positioning systems (watches and aviation antennas), mine and metal detection equipment, camera and video equipment, advanced aircraft analysis and design software, and a variety of computer equipment including laptops, high-speed modems, processors, joysticks, plotters, scanners, and printers. Commander Campbell pointed out to the jury several video clips—from videos seized at Mohamad Hammoud's home—of Hezbollah militants using the kind of equipment Dbouk's network procured for Hezbollah in Canada.[147] Such examples were not coincidental, given that Hezbollah sought specific items its fighters needed in the field. For example, the procurement network was asked to send specific compasses because "the guys were getting lost, you know, in the woods, or whatever, and they need compasses."[148]

In one instance, Said Harb provided Dbouk with $4,000 toward the purchase of such items. As Harb later recalled in testimony, Dbouk once asked him, when the two met in Canada, "Would you like to get anything, you know, for the guys?" Instructed to explain this more clearly, Harb elaborated: "We were talking about Hezbollah. Hezbollah has social, military, political, different branches within Hezbollah. We were talking about the military branch. You know, The Resistance."[149]

In support of its procurement efforts for "the Resistance," the Canadian Hezbollah network considered supplementing its income through other schemes, including importing counterfeit $100 bills from Lebanon or taking out life insurance policies for Hezbollah operatives committing acts of terrorism in the Middle East.[150] Neither of these ideas were acted upon, in part because the network had more money than it needed through basic credit card bust-out schemes, but it demonstrates the ingenuity of Hezbollah logisticians. As for the insurance scheme, in effect, the Hezbollah network considered trying to take out a life insurance policy in Canada for a prospective Hezbollah fighter in Lebanon who might be killed carrying out a suicide attack, or otherwise engaging in combat from which he would not return. Concerned a Canadian insurance company would not honor the policy of a suicide bomber, Dbouk suggested a death certificate could be produced falsely claiming the person was a civilian killed while "sitting in his village."[151]

In the years since the July 2006 war, Hezbollah's procurement program has taken on renewed importance as the group has spent most of its time replenishing its weapons stocks. Big-ticket items, like missiles, are provided by Iran and sometimes Syria. But other items, from small arms and ammunition to shoulder-fired rockets and dual-use items, are also procured globally through Hezbollah networks. According to Sheikh Nabil Qaouq, a Hezbollah commander in southern Lebanon, "the resistance is using this period to prepare, to train, to strengthen capabilities, and the enemy itself can attest to this."[152] Speaking in December 2011, Nasrallah himself underscored the group's procurement efforts. "We will never let go of our arms," he said. "Our numbers are increasing day after day, and we are getting better and our training is becoming better and we are becoming more confident in our future and more armed. And if someone is betting that our weapons are rusting, we tell them that every weapon that rusts is replaced."[153]

"I Know Why You've Done This to Me . . . You Want Dbouk"

In 2001, Mohamad Dbouk was indicted in US federal court under Operation Smokescreen. According to US investigators, Dbouk is an Iranian-trained Hezbollah operative and "an intelligence specialist and propagandist [who] was dispatched to Canada by Hezbollah for the express purpose of obtaining surveillance equipment."[154] According to information collected by the Canadian Security Intelligence Service (CSIS) during its investigation into Mohamad Dbouk's activities in Canada, first in Montreal and then in Vancouver, Dbouk was acting under the direction of Hezbollah's then chief of procurement, Haj Hassan Hilu Laqis, who was based in Lebanon. Mohamad Dbouk reportedly lived in the Detroit area for about six months, taking his activities to the US side of the Ambassador Bridge linking Michigan and Ontario.[155]

Dbouk solicited the assistance of his friend Said Harb to help facilitate the purchase of dual-use equipment and to test a scheme to use counterfeit credit cards to purchase these materials.[156] According to CSIS intercepts, in 1999 Dbouk informed an unidentified male that he had known Harb for more than fifteen years and that the two had been jailed and beaten together (presumably during the Lebanese civil war).[157] Harb was already at the center of a laundry list of criminal enterprises and frauds, but it was his relationship with Dbouk that brought him to the attention of CSIS agents who were already monitoring Dbouk's activities.[158]

US Attorney Robert Conrad, whose office successfully prosecuted the Hezbollah case in Charlotte, testified before the US Congress that according to human source intelligence (HUMINT), "Dbouk is such a major player in the Hezbollah organization that on five separate occasions his application to be a martyr was rejected." Given his overall intelligence, his military training, and his expertise in information operations, Dbouk was too valuable a commodity to expend on a martyrdom mission.[159]

Dbouk appears to have accepted Hezbollah's refusal to send him on a martyrdom mission, and dove into his procurement responsibilities in an attempt to secure a place in heaven through devotion to his assigned task. According to the CSIS intercepts, in a conversation with someone named Said (last name unknown), Dbouk tried to discuss politics and Said said he wanted to be careful about what they discussed on the telephone. Ignoring the kind of operational security protocol for which Hezbollah is well known, Dbouk responded that "he did not care about anything and was committed to securing all the items for the brothers at any cost; he was attempting to avoid going to hell and secure a place in heaven by so doing."[160]

Another indication of Dbouk's seniority within Hezbollah is not only that he worked directly for Hezbollah's chief procurement officer Haj Hassan Hilu Laqis but that CSIS intercepts indicate the two were close. Moreover, Laqis clearly assessed that Dbouk played a key role for Hezbollah as a procurement agent in Canada, while others considered him important enough to be needed back in Lebanon.[161]

Others recognized Dbouk's seniority as well. At one point during an FBI interview, Said Harb asked the agent to stop taking notes and said, "I know why you've done this to me and my family; you want Dbouk—you want Hezbollah." Harb went on to identify Dbouk, who by this time had left Canada and returned to Lebanon, as well as Dbouk's wife, as salaried employees of Hezbollah's al-Manar television station.[162]

Back in Canada, members of the Hezbollah procurement group, now being run by Dbouk's brother-in-law Ali Amhaz, were also concerned their ties to Dbouk might be their undoing. One cell member worried Canadian law enforcement might "know that Dbouk was related to you. . . . They are not stupid, and when you take lenses to (Lebanon) you are helping Hezbollah[,] who would use them in operations."[163]

Other members of the network appear to have been keenly aware that the dual-use items they were providing Hezbollah were being used to improve the military capabilities of Hezbollah's Islamic Resistance militia. They also appear to have been aware of the important role Dbouk played in this procurement effort. For example, on February 28, 1999, Hezbollah operatives set off two roadside bombs as an Israeli military convoy drove by in southern Lebanon. An Israeli general was killed in the blast, along with two sergeants and a reporter. On hearing the news, Ali Amhaz congratulated Dbouk for his part in improving Hezbollah military capabilities.[164]

Dbouk appears to have recognized that his procurement efforts for Hezbollah came under the ultimate authority of Imad Mughniyeh. In April 1999, Dbouk sent a fax to Hezbollah procurement chief Laqis, informing him that payment was needed for several items Dbouk had purchased. Dbouk boasted that he had sent Laqis "a little gift" in the form of a Palm Pilot and a pair of binoculars, and added, "I'm ready to do any thing you or the Father want me to do and I mean anything!"[165] "The Father," according to US Attorney Robert Conrad, is a reference to Mughniyeh.[166]

In other instances, Dbouk made explicit references to Mughniyeh. On June 1, 1999, Ali Amhaz told Dbouk about an individual who was speaking openly about his past work for "Haj Imad Mough/Moug/Mugh (ph)," someone who was "down there" and "working with the young men." Dbouk described Imad as the "whole story" and cautioned Amhaz "to be careful and to pretend to know nothing." Dbouk was shocked when told that this individual had invited Amhaz to ask Haj Imad about him. "Would anyone bring up Imad's name [redacted], here (Canada) or in any other country, and stay alive?" Dbouk asked rhetorically.[167]

According to the testimony of Said Harb, before his time in Canada, Dbouk received "extensive military training" coordinated by the IRGC, including in special operations skills such as parachuting. "Dbouk's cover is that he works for the Hezbollah al Manar television station," Harb told the FBI. But Dbouk does more than just produce what Harb described as "Hezbollah propaganda videotapes." According to Harb, Dbouk told him "he is responsible for reconnaissance and surveillance operations," which he conducts "in advance of Hezbollah attacks."[168] In other words, Dbouk provided preoperational surveillance for Hezbollah attack squads working under the cover of Hezbollah's satellite al-Manar television station. The preoperational footage he recorded was used to plan Hezbollah attacks on Israeli positions prior to the Israeli withdrawal from Lebanon, and the live footage of the actual attack was then used to produce propaganda videos like those seized in the homes of the Charlotte cell members.[169] The US Treasury Department referred to Dbouk's preoperational surveillance when it listed al-Manar as a Specially Designated Global Terrorist Entity. According to the Treasury Department, "One al Manar employee [is] engaged in preoperational surveillance for Hezbollah operations under cover of employment by al Manar."[170] When agents searched the home of Charlotte cell leader Mohamad Hammoud in July 2000, they found "a virtual library of Hezbollah propaganda," including videotapes—some produced by Dbouk—and other literature, some of which talked about "establishing Hezbollah resistance cells around the world."[171]

Hezbollah in the Great White North

Mohammad Hussein al Husseini, Fawzi Ayub, Mohamad Dbouk—these were not outliers. Hezbollah has been active in Canada since the 1980s, raising money through criminal activities and charity, procuring dual-use items, and sometimes engaging in potentially preoperational surveillance of principally Jewish or Israeli targets.[172] The group also produces false travel documents in Canada, and in a few instances fugitive Hezbollah operatives wanted for their roles in terrorist activities have been found hiding in Canada.[173]

In 1991 during the Gulf War, Canada expelled several Iraqi diplomats for fear of possible Iraqi terrorist reprisal attacks abroad. Speaking anonymously to the press, a government official said the government believed the Iraqi diplomats "had infiltrated Arab nationalist groups in Canada on behalf of the Iraqi Intelligence Service." Specifically, they sought to "cultivate links with small cells of the Lebanese Shiite group, Hezbollah, in Montreal and Toronto," as well as with other extremist groups across the country.[174] While fears of an Iraqi-inspired revenge attack in Canada did not materialize, reports of an organized Hezbollah presence in Canada were confirmed two years later with the arrest and interrogation of Mohammad Hussein al Husseini.

According to a former senior Canadian intelligence official, by 1997 a covert network of fifty to a hundred Hezbollah operatives—above and beyond the significantly larger pool of Hezbollah sympathizers and supporters—was "directly involved in Hezbollah activities in Canada." Just a week before his comments, CSIS informed a Canadian court that Hezbollah had established an "infrastructure" in Canada involving individuals who "receive and comply with direction from the Hezbollah leadership hierarchy in Lebanon."[175]

The summer 2006 war between Hezbollah and Israel had immediate consequences, not only in the region but far beyond as well. In Canada, officials assessed the possible ripple effects back home of Hezbollah's militant escalation along the Israeli-Lebanese frontier. In an unclassified report, Canada's Integrated Threat Assessment Centre (ITAC) warned that while Hezbollah had not carried out an attack against Western interests in several years, the group "retains the capability to conduct terrorist attacks against Western targets in Lebanon, and a limited capability to do so internationally."[176]

Two days later, ITAC issued another report, this one highlighting the evacuation of Canadians from Lebanon amid the July 2006 war. More than 40,000 Canadians were resident in Lebanon, according to the report, and Ottawa was already in the process of evacuating thousands of them via marine vessels to southern Turkey and Cyprus. Hezbollah posed a threat even to this humanitarian mission, as punctuated by the advanced C-802 missiles Hezbollah fired at an Israeli naval vessel and Cambodian merchant ship off the coast of Lebanon.[177]

In the 1980s and 1990s, a third ITAC report on Hezbollah in as many weeks noted Hezbollah carried out terrorist attacks in Europe, South America, the Middle East, and Africa, but "these attacks have largely ceased since the mid-1990s." Yet Canadian intelligence and law enforcement officials remained very concerned about the activities of Hezbollah operatives and supporters in Canada.[178] Their concerns were well founded, especially given the frequent travel of Hezbollah supporters back and forth between Canada and Lebanon. Investigators pointed to one case involving several members of "a major Lebanese crime family with ties to Hezbollah" who obtained permanent residency in Canada through illicit means.[179] As Canadian officials watched the events in Lebanon in summer 2006, what they saw must have underscored their concerns: One of the Hezbollah spokesmen appearing before the media throughout the July 2006 war had lived in Montreal. He reportedly reminisced about missing the St. Lawrence River after he returned to Lebanon. Asked about this case, a Montreal-based analyst commented, "Montreal is like a Club Med for Hezbollah."[180]

In February 2008, Imad Mughniyeh was killed in Damascus. Attending Mughniyeh's funeral, Nasrallah accused Israel of the killing and promised an "open war, without boundaries." The meaning was clear, according to the Canadian intelligence report that followed these events: "Nasrallah [was vowing] to retaliate against Israeli interests anywhere in the world." Much of the Canadian report remains classified, but the declassified portion listed potential Israeli targets in Montreal and Toronto, indicating Canada was not reassured by the lack of a previous Hezbollah attack on Canadian soil.[181] ITAC issued a new report two weeks later, further analyzing the implications for Canada of Hezbollah's "open war" threat. The report pointed to past Hezbollah attacks in South America as evidence that the group had "engaged in large-scale, mass-casualty, attacks outside the Lebanese-Israeli theater to retaliate against Israel," and noted that Canada has the world's fourth largest Jewish population. Beyond the Israeli diplomatic presence in the country, the report added Canada has more than a hundred Jewish institutions, "including schools, synagogues, [and] cultural and political centers."[182]

In June 2008, reports emerged that Hezbollah had activated suspected sleeper cells in Canada aimed at carrying out an attack to avenge the death of Imad Mughniyeh four months earlier. According to this report, Canadian intelligence and law enforcement had some twenty suspects under surveillance. One subject, "a known Hezbollah weapons expert," was followed as he traveled to Canada and was "seen at a firing range south of Toronto, near the U.S. border."[183] Nothing came of this threat reporting, possibly due to Canadian counterterrorism measures, and Canadian intelligence officials have since played down the significance of this surveillance, saying it was not directed toward an imminent plot but rather to build a portfolio of targets for a possible Hezbollah attack in Canada at some later date. Those engaged in this surveillance, the intelligence officials stressed, were lower-level operatives tied to Hezbollah's Foreign Relations Department, which is responsible for setting up platforms in foreign countries, spotting potential recruits, and organizing the local Shi'a community to be sympathetic toward and to support Hezbollah. These were not IJO operatives who live in Lebanon and just travel abroad for particular missions.[184]

The following year, a Canadian citizen and Hezbollah IJO operative was reportedly involved in one of three Hezbollah plots foiled in Turkey.[185] Speaking in late 2009, just a few months after the foiled plot in Turkey, the commissioner of the Royal Canadian Mounted Police warned that Canada was in no way immune from Hezbollah terrorist plots. "While Hezbollah has not articulated any specific grievance with Canada," he explained, "from its perspective any state that supports Israel or Israeli interests is the enemy, which casts a wide net."[186]

At times events abroad have brought Hezbollah's grievances to Canada's streets. During Israel's 2008–9 Operation Cast Lead, pro-Hamas and pro-Hezbollah groups staged rallies in several of Canada's major cities. At one rally in Montreal on January 10, 2009, young people holding Hezbollah flags shouted, "O Nasrallah,

O Beloved, strike, strike Tel Aviv!" Protesters then began to light an Israeli flag on fire; as soon as the flag was lit, the crowd erupted in cheers. Individuals shouted, "We'll sacrifice our soul and shed our blood for you, al-Aqsa [mosque]!" as they burned another Israeli flag, tossed it up and down, and proceeded to stamp on it. Protesters waved the Hezbollah and Palestinian flags and shouted in unison, "Nasrallah! Hezbollah!"[187]

Canadian government officials sometimes refer to their overall program of vigilantly tracking Hezbollah's activities in the country as "The Hezbollah Investigation," as if it were one single case. In fact, the terminology signals the government's holistic approach to the organization, which is a proscribed terrorist group under Canadian law. As part of this government-wide effort, Ottawa appropriately recognizes that Hezbollah affiliation and support occur along a spectrum. The Royal Canadian Mounted Police itself produced a paper aimed at clarifying the types of activity likely to happen at different points on the spectrum, by people who may be Hezbollah sympathizers, supporters, members, and all the way to trained militants and terrorist operatives.[188] In July 2012, one such Canadian Hezbollah operative came to the attention of officials who determined he served as the organizer of a devastating bus bombing in Burgas, Bulgaria.[189]

On the whole, both American and Canadian officials believe that Hezbollah primarily sees North America as a lucrative place to raise funds, procure weapons and equipment, and engage in other types of logistical support activities. The group likely would not want to put these activities at risk by carrying out an attack in the United States or Canada. But in light of Hezbollah's ties to Iran and tensions over Iran's nuclear program, and given the Canadian intelligence reporting that Hezbollah has scouted potential targets in Canada for possible reprisal attacks if Iran's nuclear sites are hit, officials in neither country take much comfort in their countries' status as cash cows for Hezbollah leaders. Nasrallah's promise of an "open war" against Israel, and evidence of further surveillance in Canada tied to that pledge, is still further unsettling.

As the FBI concluded back in 1994, while Hezbollah's leaders in Lebanon might be reluctant to jeopardize the safe fund-raising and procurement environment its operatives now enjoy in North America, they could still decide to call for attacks in reaction to perceived threats to the group or its interests.[190] Two years after the FBI wrote this assessment, and a decade before the July 2006 war that led Canadian officials to seriously consider the whiplash effect Hezbollah's attacks abroad could have in Canada, Hezbollah executed one of its most sophisticated attacks ever, targeting US forces stationed in Saudi Arabia.

Notes

1. William Rosenau and Sara Daly, "American Journeys to Jihad: U.S. Extremism and Foreign Conflicts During the 1980s and 1990s," *CTC Sentinel* 3, no. 8 (August 2010): 17–20; *American Jihadist: The Life and Times of Isa Abdullah Ali*, DVD, directed by Mark Claywell (Philadelphia, PA: Breaking Glass Pictures, 2011).

2. *American Jihadist.*

3. Ibid.

4. William Branigin, "U.S. Sniper in Beirut: Abdullah from D.C. Hunts Israeli Targets," *Washington Post,* July 29, 1982.

5. *American Jihadist.*

6. Branigin, "U.S. Sniper in Beirut."

7. *American Jihadist.*

8. Ibid.

9. Rosenau and Daly, "American Journeys to Jihad."

10. Ranstorp, *Hizb'Allah in Lebanon,* 91–92.

11. Author telephone interview with Tod Robberson, April 6, 2012.

12. Ibid.; Associated Press, "British Journalist Foils Kidnap Attempt in Beirut," *Observer Report* (Greene County, PA), September 27, 1986.

13. Author telephone interview with Tod Robberson, April 6, 2012.

14. Ibid.; Tod Robberson, "Bad Night in West Beirut," *Washington Post,* December 16, 1990.

15. Robberson, "Bad Night in West Beirut."

16. Ibid.; author telephone interview with Tod Robberson, April 6, 2012.

17. Eric Friedman, "Our Man in Bosnia," *Washington City Paper,* February 9, 1996.

18. Robberson, "Bad Night in West Beirut."

19. Author telephone interview with Tod Robberson, April 6, 2012.

20. *American Jihadist.*

21. *United States of America v. Mohamad Youssef Hammoud, et al.,* "Maxell VHS Tape Containing Televised Interview with Hassan Nasrallah," Verbatim transcript, FD-302, file #265B-CE-82188, transcribed March 3, 2001.

22. Brian Blomquist, "'Terrorist' Was a Regular in Adams Morgan Bar," *Washington Times,* January 26, 1996.

23. Friedman, "Our Man in Bosnia."

24. *American Jihadist.*

25. Author telephone interview with Tod Robberson, April 6, 2012.

26. US Department of Justice, FBI, "International Radical Fundamentalism."

27. Ibid.

28. Diaz and Newman, *Lightning Out of Lebanon,* 101.

29. Ibid., 155–56.

30. *United States of America v. Bassam Gharib Makki,* United States District Court, District of Columbia, 98-334 (PLF), February 26, 1999 (affidavit by Special Agent Michael J. Hudspeth, US Diplomatic Security Service).

31. Coll, *Ghost Wars,* 276.

32. Diaz and Newman, *Lightning Out of Lebanon,* 97–100; *United States of America v. Bassam Gharib Makki,* United States District Court, Southern District of Florida, Miami Division, 99-3664-STB, November 4, 1999 (affidavit by Special Agent James D. Combs, US Diplomatic Security Service).

33. *United States of America v. Bassam Gharib Makki,* Presentence Investigation Report, United States District Court, Southern District of Florida, Miami Division, CR 98-334-01, February 12, 1999, p. 15.

34. *United States of America v. Bassam Gharib Makki*, Memorandum in Aid of Sentencing, United States District Court, District of Columbia, 98-334 (PLF), March 2, 1999.

35. "Unos 50 Supuestos Extremistas Fueron Investigados en las Tres Fronteras," *Asunción ABC*, July 17, 2005.

36. *United States of America v. Bassam Gharib Makki*, Opinion, United States District Court, District of Columbia, 98-0334(PLF), 47 F. Supp. 2d 25, April 20, 1999.

37. Diaz and Newman, *Lightning Out of Lebanon*, 99–100; *United States of America v. Bassam Gharib Makki*, Presentence Investigation Report, 3.

38. *United States of America v. Bassam Gharib Makki*, Opinion.

39. *United States of America v. Bassam Gharib Makki*, United States District Court, District of Columbia, 98-334 (PLF), March 1, 1999 (affidavit by FBI Special Agent Hector Rodriguez).

40. Ibid.

41. Ibid.

42. Ibid.

43. Diaz and Newman, *Lightning Out of Lebanon*, 104–5.

44. Ibid., 103.

45. United States Attorney's Office, Southern District of Florida, "Seven Charged with Illegal Export of Electronics to U.S.-Designated Terrorist Entity in Paraguay," press release, February 19, 2010.

46. US Department of the Treasury, "Treasury Targets Hizballah Fundraising Network in the Triple Frontier of Argentina, Brazil, and Paraguay," press release, December 6, 2006."

47. "Lebanese Prisoner in Miami Is the Cousin of Individual Involved in Attack" (Spanish) *ABC Color* (Asunción), February 24, 2010; Hudson, *Terrorist and Organized Crime Groups in the Tri-Border Area*, 77.

48. US Department of the Treasury, "Treasury Targets Hizballah Fundraising"; *United States of America v. Mehdi et al.*, US District Court, Southern District of Florida, Case No. 09-20852.

49. *United States of America v. Mehdi et al.*, US District Court, Southern District of Florida, Case No. 09-20852.

50. US Department of the Treasury, "Treasury Targets Hizballah Fundraising Network in the Triple Frontier."

51. Jay Weaver, "Export-Law Violator Sentenced," *Miami Herald*, January 22, 2011.

52. Diaz and Newman, *Lightning Out of Lebanon*, 93–94.

53. Timothy J. Burger and Elaine Shannon, "Hizballah Is Moving Up the Threat Chart," *Time*, February 25, 2003.

54. *United States of America v. Mohamad Youssef Hammoud and Chawki Youssef Hammoud*, June 14, 2002, p. 1779.

55. Ibid., 1784–85.

56. *United States of America v. Mohamad Youssef Hammoud and Chawki Youssef Hammoud*, June 13, 2002, pp. 1780, 1830–31.

57. Mohammed Zaatari, "Hizbullah Scout Movement Trains Young Soldiers," *Daily Star* (Beirut), August 24, 2004.

58. *United States of America v. Mohamad Youssef Hammoud and Chawki Youssef Hammoud*, Government exhibit, pp. 270–72; one photo not put into trial evidence; included in a PowerPoint presentation by Kenneth Bell, "Hizballah Fundraising in the American Heartland," PolicyWatch 700, Washington Institute for Near East Policy (Washington, DC), January 15, 2003.

59. *United States of America v. Mohamad Youssef Hammoud and Chawki Youssef Hammoud*, June 10, 2002, p. 1345; "VHS Tape Containing a Home Video of Mohamad Hammoud's Family in Lebanon," transcribed 03/06/2001, FD-302, 265B-CE-82188.

60. *United States of America v. Mohamad Youssef Hammoud and Chawki Youssef Hammoud*, June 14–18, 2002, pp. 1836, 2267.

61. US Department of the Treasury, "Twin Treasury Actions Take Aim at Hizballah's Support Network," July 24, 2007.

62. *United States of America v. Mohamad Youssef Hammoud and Chawki Youssef Hammoud*, May 23, 2002, pp. 158–59.

63. *United States of America v. Mohamad Youssef Hammoud and Chawki Youssef Hammoud*, June 14, 2002, pp. 1768, 1789.

64. Diaz and Newman, *Lightning Out of Lebanon*, 13.

65. Cyrus Miryekta, "Hezbollah in the Tri-Border Area of South America," *Small Wars Journal*, September 10, 2010.

66. *United States of America v. Mohamad Youssef Hammoud and Chawki Youssef Hammoud*, May 23–June 18, 2002, pp. 65–66, 2158.

67. Ibid., 1792.

68. Diaz and Newman, *Lightning Out of Lebanon*, 75.

69. Manuel Roig-Franzia, "Smuggler Denies Aiding Hezbollah; Jury Weighs Question of Funds for Terror," *Washington Post*, June 20, 2002.

70. *United States of America v. Mohamad Youssef Hammoud and Chawki Youssef Hammoud*, May 23, 2002, pp. 108–9.

71. Ibid., May 23–June 14, 2002, pp. 78–79, 108–9, 1843.

72. Ibid., 106.

73. *United States of America v. Mohamad Youssef Hammoud, et al.*, Bill of Indictment, July 31, 2000.

74. *United States of America v. Mohamad Youssef Hammoud and Chawki Youssef Hammoud*, June 14, 2002, p. 1796.

75. *United States of America v. Mohamad Youssef Hammoud and Chawki Youssef Hammoud*, June 3, 2002, pp. 654, 656–57, 660; Diaz and Newman, *Lightning Out of Lebanon*, 88–89.

76. *United States of America v. Mohamad Youssef Hammoud and Chawki Youssef Hammoud*, June 3, 2002, pp. 731–32.

77. Diaz and Newman, *Lightning Out of Lebanon*, 167.

78. Robert Fromme and Rick Schwein, "Operation Smokescreen: A Successful Interagency Collaboration," *FBI Law Enforcement Bulletin* 76, no. 12 (December 2007): 20–25.

79. Fromme and Schwein, "Operation Smokescreen"; Bell, "Hizballah Fundraising in the American Heartland."

80. Bell, "Hizballah Fundraising in the American Heartland."

81. *United States of America v. Mohamad Youssef Hammoud and Chawki Youssef Hammoud*, May 24, 2002, p. 244; Bell, "Hizballah Fundraising in the American Heartland."

82. David Kaplan, "Homegrown Terrorists: How a Hezbollah Cell Made Millions in Sleepy Charlotte, N.C.," *U.S. News and World Report*, March 10, 2003, p. 30.

83. Faye Bowers, "Terror-Cell Alliance at Work in US?" *Christian Science Monitor*, July 15, 2002.

84. *United States of America v. Mohamad Youssef Hammoud and Chawki Youssef Hammoud*, "Appendix: Summary of Cigarette Purchases, after Allocation of Unidentified Wholesale Account Purchases," June 10, 2002; this slide was included in the PowerPoint presentation that accompanied his lecture, Bell, "Hizballah Fundraising in the American Heartland."

85. *United States of America v. Mohamad Youssef Hammoud and Chawki Youssef Hammoud*, June 5, 2002, pp. 1002–3.

86. Ibid., 1011–13.

87. *United States of America v. Mohamad Youssef Hammoud and Chawki Youssef Hammoud*, June 18, 2002, p. 2156; Bell, "Hizballah Fundraising in the American Heartland."

88. *United States of America v. Mohamad Youssef Hammoud and Chawki Youssef Hammoud*, June 10, 2002, pp. 1502–3.

89. *United States of America v. Mohamad Youssef Hammoud and Chawki Youssef Hammoud*, June 10, 2002, p. 1497.

90. Ibid., 1890; Tim Whitmire, "Hammoud Testifies in Own Defense in Hezbollah Trial," Associated Press, June 15, 2002.

91. *United States of America v. Mohamad Youssef Hammoud and Chawki Youssef Hammoud*, June 10, 2002, pp. 1500–1504.

92. Ibid., June 14, 2002, pp. 1910–12.

93. Ibid., June 7, 2002, pp. 1287, 1289.

94. *United States of America v. Mohamad Youssef Hammoud and Chawki Youssef Hammoud*, June 7, 2002, p. 1235; Tim Whitmire, "Trio of Witnesses Tie Brothers to Hezbollah Donations," Associated Press, June 8, 2002.

95. US Department of Homeland Security, "Mohamad Youssef Hammoud Sentenced to 30 Years in Terrorism Financing Case," press release, January 27, 2011.

96. Kaplan, "Homegrown Terrorists," 30.

97. Ibid.

98. Ibid.

99. *United States of America v. Mohamad Youssef Hammoud and Chawki Youssef Hammoud*, June 18, 2002, pp. 2218–19.

100. *United States of America v. Mohamad Youssef Hammoud and Chawki Youssef Hammoud*, June 3, 2002, pp. 671–72.

101. *United States of America v. Mohamad Youssef Hammoud and Chawki Youssef Hammoud*, June 4, 2002, p. 850; Diaz and Newman, *Lightning Out of Lebanon*, 86; *United States of America v. Mohamad Youssef Hammoud and Chawki Youssef Hammoud*, May 23, 2002, pp. 82–83.

102. *United States of America v. Mohamad Youssef Hammoud and Chawki Youssef Hammoud*, "Micro Cassette Tape," summary of a recorded telephone conversation, transcribed January 28, 2002.

103. *United States of America v. Mohamad Youssef Hammoud and Chawki Youssef Hammoud*, June 10, 2002, p. 1457.

104. Ibid., May 29, 2002, p. 599.

105. Ibid., 552–53.

106. *United States of America v. Mohamad Youssef Hammoud and Chawki Youssef Hammoud*, June 7, 2002, pp. 1188–89.

107. *United States of America v. Mohamad Youssef Hammoud and Chawki Youssef Hammoud*, June 10, 2002, pp. 1487–88.

108. *United States of America v. Mohamad Youssef Hammoud and Chawki Youssef Hammoud*, June 7, 2002, p. 1126.

109. *United States of America v. Mohamad Youssef Hammoud and Chawki Youssef Hammoud*, "VHS Tape Containing Hizballah Parade in Celebration of 'Jerusalem International Day' Including Speeches for Nasserallah," FD-302, 265B-CE-82188, transcribed March 14, 2001.

110. *United States of America v. Mohamad Youssef Hammoud and Chawki Youssef Hammoud*, May 23, 2002, pp. 74–76, 81, 88.

111. Kaplan, "Homegrown Terrorists," 30.

112. *United States of America v. Mohamad Youssef Hammoud and Chawki Youssef Hammoud*, June 18, 2002, p. 2217.

113. *United States of America v. Mohamad Youssef Hammoud and Chawki Youssef Hammoud*, June 7, 2002, p. 1184.

114. *United States of America v. Mohamad Youssef Hammoud and Chawki Youssef Hammoud*, June 5, 2002, pp. 999–1000; *United States of America v. Mohamad Youssef Hammoud and Chawki Youssef Hammoud*, "Letter Written in Arabic to Mohamad from Abu Adam dated 2/15/97," FD-302, 265B-CE-82188, transcribed January 22, 2001.

115. *United States of America v. Mohamad Youssef Hammoud and Chawki Youssef Hammoud*, "VHS Tape Titled Words for Abbas Mousawy, an Interview with the Prisoners, an Investigative Report about the Martyrdom Operations, Poems," FD-302, 265B-CE-82188, transcribed March 13, 2001.

116. *United States of America v. Mohamad Youssef Hammoud and Chawki Youssef Hammoud*, May 23, 2002, pp. 67–68.

117. *United States of America v. Mohamad Youssef Hammoud and Chawki Youssef Hammoud*, May 23, 2002, p. 35.

118. *United States of America v. Mohamad Youssef Hammoud and Chawki Youssef Hammoud*, "Letter Written in Arabic to Mohamad (LNU) from Abbas alHaraka," 265B-CE-82188, transcribed January 23, 2001.

119. *United States of America v. Mohamad Youssef Hammoud and Chawki Youssef Hammoud*, June 18, 2002, p. 2196.

120. *United States of America v. Mohamad Youssef Hammoud and Chawki Youssef Hammoud*, "Letter Written in Arabic to Mohamad (LNU) from Abbas alHaraka."

121. *United States of America v. Mohamad Youssef Hammoud and Chawki Youssef Hammoud*, June 18, 2002, p. 2197.

122. *United States of America v. Mohamad Youssef Hammoud and Chawki Youssef Hammoud*, "Letter Written in Arabic to Mohamad Hammoud from Sheik Abbas Alaa, Not Dated," FD-302, 265B-CE-82188, transcribed January 29, 2001.

123. "Alleged Hezbollah Front Raided in Michigan," Anti-Defamation League, July 30, 2007.

124. *United States of America v. Mohamad Youssef Hammoud and Chawki Youssef Hammoud*, June 5, 2002, pp. 1011–12.

125. *United States of America v. Mohamad Youssef Hammoud and Chawki Youssef Hammoud*, May 23, 2002, pp. 69, 71.

126. *United States of America v. Mohamad Youssef Hammoud and Chawki Youssef Hammoud*, June 12, 2002, pp. 1640–41; Tim Whitmire, "Prosecutors Rest Case against Brothers Linked to Hezbollah," Associated Press, June 13, 2002.

127. *United States of America v. Mohamad Youssef Hammoud and Chawki Youssef Hammoud*, June 18, 2002, p. 2213.

128. *United States of America v. Mohamad Youssef Hammoud and Chawki Youssef Hammoud*, June 12, 2002, pp. 1609–12, 1621; Paul Nowell, "Hammoud Threatened Anyone Who Tied Him to Hezbollah," Associated Press, June 12, 2002.

129. *United States of America v. Mohamad Youssef Hammoud and Chawki Youssef Hammoud*, May 23, 2002, p. 90.

130. Burger and Shannon, "Hezbollah Is Moving Up the Threat Chart."

131. *United States of America v. Mohamad Youssef Hammoud et al.*, Letter from Andy Walcott addressed to "Ken" at the FBI Charlotte office, received February 14, 2001, file no. 265-CE-82188-T.

132. *United States of America v. Mohamad Youssef Hammoud et al.*, "United States' Response to Motion to Suppress/Motion for Sanctions/Motion for Immediate Sealed Hearing," filed March 21, 2001, unsealed November 11, 2002, p. 4.

133. *United States of America v. Mohamad Youssef Hammoud et al.*, "Defendant's Sealed Reply to Government's Sealed Response to Defendant's Sealed Motion in Limine," Docket No. 3:00 CR 147-1-MU, filed December 28, 2001, unsealed November 6, 2002.

134. *United States of America v. Mohamad Youssef Hammoud et al.*, "Defendant Mohamad Hammoud's Supplement to Sealed Motion in Limine," Docket No. 3:00 CR 147-1-MU, filed August 8, 2001, unsealed November 6, 2002.

135. Transcript of conversation between Andy Walcott and Mohamad Hammoud, FBI, recorded February 20, 2001, transcribed March 36, 2001, File No. 265-CE-82188-T.

136. *United States of America v. Mohamad Youssef Hammoud et al.*, "United States' Response to Motion to Suppress/Motion for Sanctions/Motion for Immediate Sealed Hearing," Docket No. 3:00 CR 147-1-MU, Filed March 21, 2001, Unsealed November 6, 2002.

137. *United States of America v. Mohamad Youssef Hammoud et al.*, Federal Bureau of Investigation FD-302 (Rev.10-6-95), Verbatim transcript of two separate consensually recorded conversations between a cooperating witness (CM) and Mohamad Youssef Hammoud, recorded February 8, 2001, transcribed February 14, 2001, File Number 265B-CE-82188, Docket No. 3:00 CR 147-1-MU, Exhibit Q.

138. Universal Strategy Group, *Directed Study of Lebanese Hezbollah*, produced for the United States Special Operations Command, Research and Analysis Division, October 2010, 85, 89.

139. *United States of America v. Fawzi Mustapha Assi*, Government's Sentencing Memorandum, Eastern District of Michigan, Southern Division, Criminal No. 98-80695, June 9, 2008.

140. Ibid.

141. *United States of America v. Mohamad Youssef Hammoud et al.*, FBI 302 interview of Said Mohamad Harb, August 18, 2000, Case No. 265B-CE-82188, p. 9.

142. *United States of America v. Ali Boumelhem*, Appeal from the United States District Court for the Eastern District of Michigan at Detroit, No. 00-81013, decided and filed August 12, 2003; Ronald J. Hansen, "Lebanese in Metro Detroit on Edge," *Detroit News*, January 2, 2002.

143. Federal Court of Canada, In the Matter of Hani Abd Rahim al-Sayegh, and In the Matter of a referral of the Immigration Act, R.S.C. 1985, c. I-2, Court File: DES-1-97; "Annex 'E' – Interview with Mohamad Hussein Al Husseini," September 23, 1993.

144. *United States of America v. Mohamad Youssef Hammoud et al.*, United States Court of Appeals for the Fourth District; Goldberg, "In the Party of God: Hezbollah Sets Up Operations in South America and the United States," *The New Yorker*, October 28, 2002.

145. Bell, "Hizballah Fundraising in the American Heartland."

146. *United States of America v. Mohamad Youssef Hammoud and Chawki Youssef Hammoud*, June 10, 2002, pp. 1487–88.

147. *United States of America v. Mohamad Youssef Hammoud and Chawki Youssef Hammoud*, June 12, 2002, pp. 1590–1600.

148. *United States of America v. Mohamad Youssef Hammoud and Chawki Youssef Hammoud*, June 10, 2002, pp. 1486–87.

149. Ibid., 1477.

150. *United States of America v. Mohamad Youssef Hammoud et al.*, "CSIS Summaries, Redacted Copy, Trial Testimony," Docket No. 3:00-cr-147, Trial Exhibit 304, p. 58.

151. Ibid., 35.

152. "Top Hizbullah Official in South Lebanon Nabil Qaouq: The Resistance Is Using This Period to Train and Strengthen Its Capabilities and Is Preparing for the Great Confrontation," *Al-Alam TV* (Iran) and *Future TV* (Lebanon), July 26, 2010.

153. Nada Bakri, "Hezbollah Leader Backs Syrian President in Public," *New York Times*, December 6, 2011.

154. Fromme and Schwein, "Operation Smokescreen."

155. Diaz and Newman, *Lightning Out of Lebanon*, 165.

156. Fromme and Schwein, "Operation Smokescreen."

157. *United States of America v. Mohamad Youssef Hammoud et al.*, "CSIS Summaries, Redacted Copy, Trial Testimony," p. 58.

158. Fromme and Schwein, "Operation Smokescreen."

159. Statement of Robert J. Conrad Jr., *Assessment of the Tools Needed to Fight the Financing of Terrorism*.

160. *United States of America v. Mohamad Youssef Hammoud et al.*, "CSIS Summaries, Redacted Copy, Trial Testimony," p. 11.

161. Ibid., 23.

162. *United States of America v. Mohamad Youssef Hammoud et al.*, FBI 302 interview of Said Mohamad Harb, July 21, 2000, Case No. 265B-CE-82188, p. 11.

163. *United States of America v. Mohamad Youssef Hammoud et al.,* "CSIS Summaries, Redacted Copy, Trial Testimony," p. 103.

164. Ibid., 5

165. Ibid., 22.

166. Statement of Robert J. Conrad Jr., *Assessment of the Tools Needed to Fight the Financing of Terrorism.*

167. *United States of America v. Mohamad Youssef Hammoud et al.,* "CSIS Summaries, Redacted Copy, Trial Testimony," pp. 42–43.

168. *United States of America v. Mohamad Youssef Hammoud et al.,* FBI 302 interview of Said Mohamad Harb, August 18, 2000, p. 9.

169. Mark Dubowitz, "Wanted: A War on Terrorist Media," *Journal of International Security Affairs* 17, Fall 2009.

170. US Department of the Treasury, "U.S. Designates Al-Manar as a Specially Designated Global Terrorist Entity; Television Station Is Arm of Hezbollah Terrorist Network," press release, March 23, 2006.

171. *United States of America vs. Mohamad Youssef Hammoud et al.,* Opening statement of Assistant US Attorney Kenneth Bell, May 23, 2002, p. 33.

172. Stewart Bell, "Canada May Be Terror Target," *National Post* (Canada), July 23, 2009.

173. Rudner, "Hizbullah: An Organizational and Operational Profile," 239.

174. "Canada Expels 4th Iraqi Diplomat," *Vancouver Sun,* January 23, 1991.

175. Bill Gladstone, "Ex-official: Hezbollah Network of Operatives Active in Canada," *Jewish Telegraphic Agency,* April 9, 1997.

176. Canada, Integrated Threat Assessment Centre (ITAC), "Hizballah: Capability to Conduct Terrorist Attacks, But No Intent," ITAC Intelligence Assessment, July 19, 2006.

177. Canada, Integrated Threat Assessment Centre (ITAC), "Evacuation of Canadians from Lebanon," ITAC Intelligence Assessment, July 21, 2006.

178. Author interview, Canadian intelligence, law enforcement, and policy officials, Ottawa, Canada, January 12, 2010.

179. Author interview, Canadian intelligence officials, Ottawa, Canada, January 12, 2010.

180. Author interview, Canadian analyst and community activist, Montreal, Canada, March 16, 2010.

181. Canada, Integrated Threat Assessment Centre (ITAC), "Hizballah Leader Threatens Israeli Interests Abroad," ITAC Threat Assessment, February 15, 2008.

182. Canada, Integrated Threat Assessment Centre (ITAC), "Hizballah's 'Open War': Implications for Canada," ITAC Intelligence Assessment, March 6, 2008.

183. Richard Esposito and Brian Ross, "Hezbollah Poised to Strike," *ABC News,* June 19, 2008.

184. Author interview, Canadian intelligence officials, Ottawa, Canada, January 12, 2010.

185. Author interview, Washington, DC, February 26, 2010.

186. Stewart Bell, "Hezbollah Cell Smashed as FBI Hits Arms Trade," *National Post* (Canada), November 25, 2009.

187. "Canadian Jewish Congress Exposes Incitement to Hatred and Violence at Pro-Hamas Rallies," Canadian Jewish Congress, accessed on YouTube June 30, 2010.

188. Author interview, Canadian intelligence officials, Ottawa, Canada, January 12, 2010.

189. Stewart Bell, "Bulgaria Bus Bombing Suspect had Real Canadian Passport, Lived in B.C. before Return to Lebanon at Age 12," *National Post* (Canada), February 6, 2013.

190. Author interview, Canadian intelligence officials, Ottawa, Canada, March 15, 2010; US Department of Justice, FBI, "International Radical Fundamentalism."

7

Bombing Khobar Towers

IT WAS JUNE 25, 1996, Brig. Gen. Terryl J. Schwalier's last day commanding US troops stationed in the Eastern Province of Saudi Arabia. The 4404th Wing of the US Air Force was a critical component of the coalition's enforcement of the no-fly and no-drive zones south of the 32nd parallel in southern Iraq under Operation Southern Watch following the 1991 Gulf War. General Schwalier had already packed his bags before venturing into Dhahran that evening for a dinner of Saudi-style Mexican food with Maj. Gen. Kurt B. Anderson, commander of Joint Task Force–Southwest Asia. General Anderson was visiting the Khobar Towers military housing complex to attend the change-of-command ceremony scheduled for the following day. Built by the Saudis in 1979, the Khobar complex was barely used until coalition forces operating in the Dhahran area first took up residence there during the Gulf War in 1990. By 9 PM, as the muezzin called the faithful to prayer just outside the compound, Gen. Schwalier was back at his desk writing a note for the man who would replace him.[1]

Elsewhere on the compound, Staff Sgt. Alfredo R. Guerrero, a security policeman and shift supervisor, was checking in on sentries posted throughout the compound. Khobar Towers was located in the middle of a residential area. To the east was a set of high-rise buildings and to the north were a parking lot, a city park, and a mosque under construction. Security was a full-time job at Khobar Towers, especially after a terrorist bombing in Riyadh the previous November and successive bombings in Bahrain—just a forty-minute drive across a causeway—in December, January, February, and March.

A few minutes before 10 PM, Staff Sergeant Guerrero made his way to the eight-story Building 131, located at the northern edge of the Khobar Towers compound. As Guerrero neared the northeast corner of the roof, where two other sentries were keeping watch, a 5,000-gallon tanker truck and a white Chevrolet Caprice sedan approached the compound, turning toward the parking lot opposite Building 131. Heading toward the lot, the white sedan flashed its headlights and a second car, which had parked in the lot just a few minutes earlier, flashed its lights in return. Seeing the "all clear" signal, the white sedan and tanker pulled into the lot.[2]

From the roof, Staff Sergeant Guerrero and the other police officers noticed the two vehicles enter the lot. They watched as the truck drove to the second-to-last row of parking spaces, turned left as if about to exit the lot, and then backed up into the hedges at the perimeter fence directly in front of Building 131. Two men jumped out of the truck and into the waiting sedan, which then sped away followed by the prepositioned signal car.[3]

One of the police officers alerted the security desk by radio, and all three began to evacuate the building in a top-to-bottom "waterfall" fashion. They knocked loudly on each door, yelling that everyone should evacuate immediately and pass along the message to residents on lower floors as they ran downstairs. It was 9:49 PM. Within minutes the top three floors were evacuated, but that was as far as they got. Even the loudspeaker warning system could not be activated in the six minutes between the terrorists' abandoning the tanker truck at the perimeter fence and the massive explosion that tore the entire north face off Building 131 at 9:55 PM.[4]

Carrying at least 5,000 pounds of plastic explosives, the tanker truck detonated with the power of about 20,000 pounds of TNT.[5] More than twice as powerful as the 1983 bomb Hezbollah used to destroy the US Marine barracks in Beirut, the blast was later determined to have been the largest nonnuclear explosion then on record.[6] The bomb left a crater eighty-five feet wide and thirty-five feet deep, damaged buildings across the Khobar Towers compound, and was felt twenty miles away in Bahrain.[7]

Nineteen US Air Force personnel were killed in the attack, and another 372 Americans were wounded.[8] A number of Saudi citizens unfortunate enough to be in the nearby park at the time of the bombing were also killed.[9] The wounded included Saudi, Bangladeshi, Egyptian, Jordanian, Indonesian, and Filipino citizens as well.[10]

Over the next five years the FBI would lead a massive, politically sensitive investigation that would ultimately prompt the indictment in US federal court of thirteen members of the Iranian-sponsored Saudi Hezbollah—and an unidentified Lebanese Hezbollah operative referred to in the indictment as John Doe.

In time, authorities would trace the meticulously organized plot to bomb Khobar Towers to 1993, when Ahmed al-Mughassil, who then headed the military wing of Saudi Hezbollah, instructed members of a Saudi Hezbollah terrorist cell to begin carrying out surveillance of Americans in Saudi Arabia.[11] The larger conspiracy, however, dates even further back and involves long-running tensions between Iran and Saudi Arabia, the condition of the Shi'a minority in Saudi Arabia, the radicalization of a segment of the Saudi Shi'a community, and its ties to Iran.

The Birth of Saudi Hezbollah

Representing roughly 10 to 15 percent of all Saudis, the kingdom's Shi'a population—along with its largest oil fields—is located primarily in the Eastern Province. While Saudi Shi'a from the region are employed in the oil industry, the wealth that results is primarily invested elsewhere in the kingdom. The inequality in the distribution of wealth follows decades of religious intolerance for the Shi'a—seen as heretics by many in Saudi Arabia's conservative Sunni society—that has translated into discrimination in education, employment, administration of justice, and more.[12]

Encouraged by Iran's Islamic Revolution, the Shi'a community in Saudi Arabia's Eastern Province was inspired to confront the Saudi government—sometimes peaceably, sometimes not. In 1979, riots and mass protests broke out after police responded to several thousand Shi'a who defied a government ban on commemorating the Shi'a holy day of Ashura. Already on edge over the occupation of the Grand Mosque of Mecca just days earlier by Sunni extremists, the Saudi National Guard responded to the Shi'a protests using lethal force, reportedly targeting demonstrators with helicopter gunships. About twenty people were killed in the initial clashes, and the Saudi government crackdown lasted well into early 1980. Many more Shi'a were arrested and several hundred fled into exile, primarily in Iran and Syria. Among those who fled, a Canadian report notes, "it is believed that some of these persons may have been trained by the Hizballah. Those individuals who received this training became the Saudi Hizballah."[13] The events of 1979–80, collectively known as the "intifada of the Eastern Province," would loom large in the collective memory of Saudi Shi'a. The crackdown convinced most radical Saudi Shi'a that a violent confrontation with the Saudi regime was not realistic, leading some to fight for other radical Shi'a groups in Bahrain and Iraq, or on Iran's side in the Iran-Iraq War. Already in the early 1980s, such groups enjoyed the support of the government of Iran through its Office of the Liberation Movements and the Islamic Revolutionary Guard Corps (IRGC).[14]

July 31, 1987, marked a tragic watershed for Saudi Shi'a. During the Hajj, the annual pilgrimage to the Grand Mosque in Mecca, more than 400 people, including many Iranian pilgrims, were trampled in a human stampede. Among the dead were Saudi policemen, and rumors spread that some of the Shi'a killed were tied to Saudi Shi'a organizations, leading Saudi and Iranian officials to engage in a cycle of recrimination over the clashes that led to the stampede.[15] As a result, Iran courted radical Shi'a in Saudi Arabia's Eastern Province to carry out attacks against Saudi targets. By one account, "Iran wanted to have small, controllable organizations that could be used as pressure tools on the Al Saud [ruling family] but would not endanger Iran's foreign policy objectives."[16] Just two months earlier, in May 1987, Saudi Hezbollah had been officially founded primarily in response to the quietist stance taken by other Saudi Shi'a groups and their less intimate ties to Iran. Some of the new group's members came from Tajamu Ulama al-Hijaz, a group that had been more focused on religious and political than violent activities. Others, including Ahmed al-Mughassil, who later headed Saudi Hezbollah's military wing and masterminded the Khobar Towers attack, as well as several US-educated Saudi Shi'a, were former members of other groups, like the Movement for the Vanguards Missionaries.[17]

Following the tragedy at the Hajj, Iran found a pool of radicalized Saudi Shi'a willing to carry out attacks against the Saudi regime in support of Iran—and they wasted no time in retaliating.[18] A week after the tragedy, Saudi Hezbollah issued its first official statement vowing to challenge the ruling Saudi family. The next month, in August 1987, Saudi Hezbollah carried out a bombing attack against a petroleum facility in Ras al-Juayma. Saudi Hezbollah claimed responsibility for the attack and, in communiqués issued in Beirut and Tehran, threatened further revenge attacks targeting Saudi officials.[19] The following month Saudi Hezbollah announced plans to attack US and Saudi interests worldwide.[20]

According to CIA reporting at the time, Iran had already "smuggled explosives into Saudi Arabia and conducted terrorist operations against Kuwait targets." Iran, the CIA concluded, would "keep the United States as a primary terrorist target" for itself and its surrogates for a variety of reasons, including the US military presence in the Gulf, the recent reflagging of Kuwait oil tankers, the seizure of an Iranian ship laying mines in the Gulf, and an attack on an Iranian oil platform used to support Iranian military operations. Iran, the report added, also alleged the United States was involved in the deaths of the Iranian pilgrims at the 1987 Hajj. Pointing to the 1983 and 1984 Beirut bombings, the CIA reported, "many Iranian leaders use this precedent as proof that terrorism can break U.S. resolve" and view "sabotage and terrorism as an important option in its confrontation with the United States in the Persian Gulf."[21]

Following the accidental downing of Iran Air flight 655 by the USS *Vincennes* in July 1988, the CIA warned that "Iranian-backed terrorists plan to attack U.S. facilities and personnel, and most posts have gone on a high state of alert, anticipating some sort of attack."[22] One intelligence report warned that terrorists supported by Iran could use the 1988 Seoul Olympics to carry out a bombing or hostage-taking operation targeting American, Iraqi, Saudi, and other Arab targets. Surprisingly, the report cautioned that "Iranian-backed terrorist groups also could act as surrogates for North Korea."[23] Those threats did not materialize, but Saudi Hezbollah did conduct a series of attacks targeting the Saudi petrochemical industry, which employed many Americans. In March 1988, Saudi Hezbollah claimed responsibility for an explosion at the Sadaf petrochemical plant in Jubayl. That attack involved a Hezbollah cell that included one former employee at the Sadaf plant and another, Ali Abdullah al-Khatim, who "fought with Hezbollah in Lebanon and received military training"—a trend that would apply to many of the Khobar Towers conspirators. More bombs exploded at the Ras Tanura refinery, while another apparently failed to detonate in Ras al-Juayma.[24]

Saudi authorities responded forcefully, arresting suspected Shi'a militants and engaging in one standoff with three members of Saudi Hezbollah that left a number of Saudi policemen killed or injured. The three militants and another cell member were arrested and later publicly beheaded.[25] Meanwhile, Saudi intelligence officers were dispatched abroad to pursue some twenty more Saudi Hezbollah operatives thought to have fled the kingdom.[26]

To avenge the deaths of its beheaded operatives, Saudi Hezbollah embarked on an assassination campaign abroad, including attacks on Saudi officials in Turkey, Pakistan, and Thailand. Commenting on one of these assassinations, a CIA analysis issued in December 1988 noted that "Riyadh is concerned that the assassination of a Saudi diplomat in Ankara on 25 October may be the opening round in a Shi'a terrorist campaign targeting Saudi officials and facilities."[27] At this early time, however, the CIA suspected the group was active only outside Saudi Arabia: "We suspect the groups claiming responsibility for the assassination use a number of names interchangeably, including 'Hizballah of the Hijaz' and 'Islamic Jihad of the Hijaz.' No evidence has appeared, however, that Hizballah of the Hijaz is a functioning organization inside Saudi Arabia. The group has surfaced only in connection with claims or threats made in support of Saudi Shi'a dissidents or Iranian pressure on Saudi Arabia."[28]

Then, in July 1989, a group of Kuwaiti and Saudi Shi'a affiliated with Hezbollah al-Kuwait—the parallel Hezbollah element Iran created in Kuwait, as it had done elsewhere in the Gulf—were caught smuggling explosives into the kingdom and placing them in the vicinity of Mecca's Grand Mosque. In September, sixteen Kuwaitis and four Saudis were beheaded for their roles in the plot, prompting Saudi and Kuwaiti Hezbollah to issue a call for vengeance at a press conference in Beirut, where they could speak freely in the company and protection of their Lebanese affiliate and mentor, Lebanese Hezbollah. Two months later they would claim responsibility for the assassination of a Saudi diplomat in Beirut using the "Holy War Organization" name long affiliated with Hezbollah. Already in the 1980s Saudi Shi'a extremists were fighting with Lebanese Hezbollah against Israel in southern Lebanon. Some Saudi Hezbollah members received training in Iran or Lebanon from the late 1980s onward, often using Damascus and the Sayyeda Zeinab shrine as a transfer hub and as cover for travel between Saudi Arabia and these training camps.[29]

Several of the Khobar bombing conspirators were recruited there, according to US prosecutors, who described the system this way: "The young men would frequently have their first contact with Saudi Hizballah during religious pilgrimages to the Sayyeda Zeinab shrine. There, they would be approached by Saudi Hizballah members to gauge their loyalty to Iran and dislike for the government of Saudi Arabia. Young men who wished to join Saudi Hizballah then would be transported to Hizballah-controlled areas in Lebanon for military training and indoctrination."[30] Investigators determined that the Khobar conspirators held a key planning meeting at the Sayyeda Zeinab shrine in June 1995, just days before the attack.[31]

A month after the Hajj, in August 1989 Akbar Hashemi Rafsanjani became president of Iran. Though he would later attempt rapprochement with Riyadh, complicating the investigation into the Khobar Towers bombing, attacks targeting Saudi interests resumed under Rafsanjani's leadership following the execution of the Kuwaiti Shi'a responsible for the July attack at the Hajj. Several of the executed Kuwaitis were of Iranian origin, and Iranian leaders called for these martyrs' deaths to be avenged with attacks targeting Saudi, Kuwaiti, and US interests. A CIA analysis published in August 1990 assessed that "these statements may have encouraged radical Shia elements to carry out a series of attacks against Saudi facilities and personnel." The CIA assessed that Iranian terrorist attacks carried out over the past year "were probably approved in advance" by the president and other senior Iranian leaders.[32]

The end of the Iran-Iraq War in August 1988 dimmed the hopes of Gulf Shi'a that an Iranian victory over Saddam Hussein's minority Sunni government would liberate Iraq's majority Shi'a population and lead to similar redemptions of Shi'a enclaves throughout the Gulf. This, combined with the death of Ayatollah Khomeini a year later in June 1989 and the Iraqi invasion of Kuwait a year after that led to a slow improvement in relations between Saudi Arabia and Iran. Still, Iran continued to support the anti-Saudi propaganda efforts of Saudi Shi'a groups, including Saudi Hezbollah.

The crackdowns on Saudi Hezbollah operatives at home and abroad by Saudi security services likely helped prompt the decline of violent attacks by the group. The group continued to attempt several attacks that were thwarted, including an aborted plot to blow up a Saudi Airlines plane flying from Islamabad to Riyadh.[33] Saudi Hezbollah also used this time to recruit additional operatives and send them abroad for training in Iran and Lebanon—including people who would later participate in the conspiracy to bomb Khobar Towers.[34] Ties among Iran's various proxy groups, especially Lebanese and Saudi Hezbollah, grew stronger at this time. For example, in fall 1989 a series of coordinated speeches was issued by Lebanese Hezbollah and the Supreme Council for the Islamic Revolution in Iraq (SCIRI) praising "the four martyrs" of Saudi Hezbollah beheaded a year earlier. Lebanese Hezbollah and SCIRI officials issued their statements at the Sayyeda Zeinab shrine outside Damascus, while the future leader of Lebanese Hezbollah, Hassan Nasrallah, made his speech in Qom, Iran. This and meetings between leaders of Lebanese and Saudi Hezbollah and senior Iranian officials "made clear that Hizbullah al-Hijaz was very well connected to and supported by Iran and Lebanese Hizbullah, among others."[35]

Several years later, in 1993, the Saudi government and leaders of some Saudi Shi'a opposition groups came to an agreement by which the Shi'a groups would stop their activities in opposition to the regime—especially the publication of anti-regime books and magazines by émigré activists in London and elsewhere outside the kingdom—in return for general amnesty and a government pledge to discuss the grievances of the Shi'a in Saudi Arabia. Riyadh released Shi'a political prisoners, some of whom had been incarcerated since the 1980s, and allowed hundreds of Shi'a exiles to return to Saudi Arabia.[36] Saudi Hezbollah, however, rejected the agreement. The group "vowed to continue on the path of jihad and revolution and invoked the example of the four martyrs of 1988."[37] That year the head of Saudi Hezbollah's military wing directed several operatives to initiate surveillance of Americans in Saudi Arabia, including at the US embassy in Riyadh.[38]

Nonetheless, Saudi Hezbollah members were among the released political prisoners and former exiles returning to their homes in the country's Eastern Province in 1993 and 1994.[39] Some of these activists now focused on religious and social activities, while others were deeply involved in terrorist activity such as recruiting operatives, training in Hezbollah camps in Lebanon, and conducting surveillance of the US embassy and American citizens in Saudi Arabia for possible targeting.[40] Consider the following Canadian assessment:

Although it is a distinct entity, Saudi Hizballah receives much support and assistance from Hizballah. For example, Lebanese Hizballah train fundamentalist Saudi Arabian Shiites of the Saudi Hizballah at their camps in the Bekaa Valley, Lebanon. The camps are used to teach advanced techniques such as surveillance and counter-surveillance, methods of secure electronic communications, and the production of false identification documents. They also provide instruction in foreign languages, the use of small arms, methods of border infiltration, and the making of car bombs.[41]

US intelligence reports echoed the Canadian finding, suggesting that the IRGC's Lebanon contingent provided unspecified training to "Shia oppositionists" from Saudi Arabia and Bahrain. According to other, more specific intelligence reporting, sixteen Saudi Shi'a attended a two-month military training course in Lebanon in summer 1995.[42] Such intelligence reports align with the testimony of a former CIA official who stated that planning for the Khobar Towers attack began around 1994, including planning meetings likely held in Tehran and operational meetings held at the Iranian embassy in Damascus. It was in 1994, according to this account, that the Supreme Leader of Iran, Ayatollah Khamenei, gave the order for the attack on the Khobar Towers complex.[43] While planning the attack, Shi'a extremists continued to carry out other plots, including the hijacking of a Saudi Airlines flight, also in 1994.[44]

Iran's Terrorist Agenda in the Gulf

Iran's support for terrorism was born with the 1979 Islamic Revolution and the new clerical regime's belief that it had a religious obligation to export the revolution. Writing in 1986, the CIA assessed that this obligation included the edict "to wage, by whatever means, a constant struggle against the perceived oppressor states." But the report continued, "Terrorism is also used to further Iranian national interests."[45] In the early 1990s these interests dictated an increase in operational activities in the Gulf. Violence by Shi'a extremists was primarily the consequence of Iran's geopolitical calculus and its continued enmity toward Sunni Gulf states.

The dominance of radical elements within the Iranian clerical leadership translated into significant Iranian hostility toward the West and little chance more pragmatic leaders would come to the fore. Creating tensions abroad shifted popular attention away from domestic problems, while the asymmetry of supporting terrorism provided Tehran with a potent weapon at a time when its military and economy were weak.[46] Tensions were so high at the time over the downing of Iran Air flight 655 that the CIA warned of the possibility that individual Hezbollah operatives could mobilize off-the-shelf operational planning and "freelance an operation" even without direction from Iranian or Hezbollah leaders.[47]

Underlying Iranian grievances made tensions with the West all the more acute. Iran was keen to drive US and Western influence from the Middle East, mitigate Western power projection in the region (which had increased significantly following Operation Desert Storm and the enforcement of a no-fly zone over southern

Iraq), punish the Saudis and other Gulf regimes for supporting Iraq in the Iran-Iraq War, and eliminate individuals and undermine governments opposed to the clerical regime in Tehran.

All these factors led Iran to proactively pursue terrorist operations targeting the United States in the region, especially Saudi Arabia. The use of non-Iranian proxies to execute Iranian-inspired attacks was not new. A 1988 CIA report stressed that Iran saw benefit in using non-Iranian proxy groups to carry out its attacks probably because this approach "provides access to strategic targets as well as the deniability needed to prevent retaliation."[48] To this end Tehran has traditionally seen Hezbollah as a strategic tool with which to project power without having to contend with the consequences of such activities. Thus the Khobar Towers indictment explains in its opening paragraph that beginning sometime in the 1980s, Hezbollah was the name used by several related terrorist groups operating in Saudi Arabia, Lebanon, Kuwait, and Bahrain, among other places. "The Hizballah organizations," it explained, "were inspired, supported, and directed by elements of the Iranian government."[49] Not only were Lebanese and Saudi Hezbollah inspired by the same pan-Shi'a, pro-Iranian ideology, both organizations "owe allegiance to Iran's supreme religious leader. . . . And that process is a formal oath taking process."[50]

Ultimately, the FBI would conclude that the Khobar attack was planned, organized, and sponsored by Iran and executed by Saudi Hezbollah operatives. Beyond the evidence presented in the public indictment of the conspirators, intelligence intercepts reportedly also pointed to Iran's role in directing the attack.[51] According to former FBI deputy director for counterterrorism Dale Watson, evidence the FBI collected to determine Saudi Hezbollah carried out the attack at Iran's behest included not only forensics and the statements of detained conspirators but also "a lot of other types of information that I'm not at liberty to discuss." According to Watson, whose tenure at the FBI spanned twenty-four years and included a stint as chief of the Iran-Hezbollah unit at FBI headquarters, Hezbollah does not carry out terrorist attacks internationally on its own. "It must be sanctioned, it must be ordered, and it must be approved and somebody has to fund it," Watson noted in explaining Iran's role in the attack.[52] According to Bruce Tefft, a twenty-year CIA veteran who helped set up the CIA's Counterterrorism Bureau in 1985, the Khobar Towers attack was planned and overseen by Iran's IRGC and Ministry of Intelligence and Security (MOIS) "acting on the orders of the Supreme Leader of Iran."[53]

Ironically, in recruiting a network of radical Saudi Shi'a to bomb American soldiers stationed at Khobar Towers, Iran targeted the UN-mandated mission tasked with protecting the Shi'a of southern Iraq from the regime of Saddam Hussein, Iran's sworn enemy. From this vantage point, the pan-Shi'a ideology that bound Iranian Qods Force commanders and Saudi Hezbollah operatives was tied more to the decidedly Iranian national interest of driving US forces out of the Gulf than those of the greater Shi'a community.[54]

While Iran was the driving force behind the Khobar operation, it also directed a number of other terrorist organizations using the name Hezbollah in Lebanon, Kuwait, and Bahrain, among other places.[55] Hezbollah, a 1994 FBI report would note, "is particularly interested in recruiting non-Lebanese Shiites," with members from a variety of countries but especially Iraq and Iran.[56] By the time the CIA penned its 1992 report, several of the Khobar Towers plotters had already joined Saudi Hezbollah and undergone terrorist training in Iran and Lebanon. For example, in 1989 or 1990, Saed al-Bahar and Ali al-Houri received military training in Iran; around 1989, Abdallah al-Jarash went to Lebanon in a Mercedes supplied by the Iranian embassy in Damascus to receive military training from Hezbollah.[57]

Along with Saudi Hezbollah leader Ahmed al-Mughassil, several other members recruited young Saudi Shi'a to join Saudi Hezbollah. Mughassil also arranged for the recruits to receive training in Iran and Lebanon, directed them to conduct surveillance of potential targets, and planned and supervised attacks, according to the US indictment. Ali al-Houri, Hani al-Sayegh, and Ibrahim al-Yacoub were all active recruiters as well. Al-Houri was not only a "major recruiter" for Hezbollah but also the group's liaison to the Iranian embassy in Damascus, which was a key logistics and support hub for Saudi Hezbollah members traveling to and from Lebanon. Al-Sayegh, a fluent Farsi speaker who "enjoyed an unusually close association with certain military elements of the Iranian government," helped arrange new recruits' military training at Hezbollah camps in Lebanon and Iran. Al-Yacoub was both a recruiter and a liaison between Saudi Hezbollah and "the Lebanese and Iranian Hizballah organizations."[58]

Five of the Khobar Towers conspirators were recruited in Damascus, most at the Sayyeda Zeinab shrine, over a period from the late 1980s to around 1992. Mughassil, Yacoub, Houri, and Sayegh were among the people they met in Damascus. When they recruited Abdallah al-Jarash there, Jarash was informed that the group's goal was "to target foreign interests, American in particular, in Saudi Arabia and elsewhere." Mustafa al-Qassab, in contrast, traveled to Iran to meet Mughassil sometime in the late 1980s, after which he joined the group. Saleh Ramadan and Mustafa Mu'alem were recruited back home in the Eastern Province of Saudi Arabia by Ali al-Marhoun—one of the operatives recruited at the Damascus shrine.[59]

Such activity continued at full pace in the years leading up to the Khobar Towers attack. In 1995, Saudi authorities arrested "a large number" of Saudi Shi'a in the Eastern Province suspected of being involved in a series of small-scale explosions and shootings in Bahrain that July.[60] The same senior Iranian officials reportedly were responsible for directing both the disturbances in Bahrain and the Khobar Towers attack, which was then in the making.[61] Also in 1995, the CIA reported, Iranian agents engaged in intentionally blatant surveillance of US interests in Kuwait—and elsewhere in Asia and Europe—sometimes using Iranian diplomatic vehicles.[62] According to former White House counterterrorism coordinator Richard Clarke, US intelligence reports documented how between 1994 and 1996 the IRGC Qods Force fostered Hezbollah-style groups in Bahrain, Kuwait, and Saudi Arabia and sent terrorists for training in Iran and Lebanon.[63]

During this same time period, other reports note, Tehran established an extensive network of terrorist training camps in Iran under the orders of President Rafsanjani. More than 5,000 militants reportedly passed through these camps a year. Each camp was reportedly established to fill a different terrorist niche. The Abyek camp at Qasvim was used for training would-be assassins, and the Nahavand camp in Hamadan was used by Lebanese Hezbollah. The Imam Ali training camp in east Tehran, meanwhile, was said to be the largest of some eleven training camps, and was the one used by Saudi Hezbollah.[64] Such training enabled Iran to strike at American interests through proxies without being directly implicated in the attacks. Writing in 1992, the CIA assessed that Iran "would be likely to support Hizballah's efforts to retaliate against the United States," dependent on its ability to maintain probable deniability.[65]

Lights Blinking Red

On November 13, 1995, Sunni extremists detonated a car bomb filled with 250 pounds of explosives in the parking lot outside the headquarters of the Saudi Arabian National Guard training support mission (OPM-SANG) in Riyadh. Five Americans and two Saudis were killed in the attack, which left two craters about thirty-nine feet from the front of the building.[66] The perpetrators of that attack would claim inspiration from a little-known Saudi extremist named Osama bin Laden, and bin Laden himself would later sing their praises.[67] Just weeks after the OPM-SANG bombing, the State Department issued a travel advisory urging Americans in Saudi Arabia to be cautious. "Unconfirmed information," it read, suggested that "additional bombings may be planned against western interests in Saudi Arabia, including facilities and commercial centers occupied and/or frequented by Americans." Attacks, the advisory continued, "could occur anywhere in the kingdom."[68] Another warning would be issued two months later, this one "noting that targets in Riyadh are especially at risk."[69]

The OPM-SANG bombing was not the first attack targeting US interests in the kingdom, but it was a watershed event. The terrorist threat in Saudi Arabia preceding the attack, as reflected in a later evaluation led by Gen. Wayne Downing, was benign until fall 1994. The only exceptions were three "isolated incidents" during Operation Desert Storm and the hijacking of a Saudi Airlines airbus in 1994.[70] As it happened, these isolated incidents began just a month after one Saudi Shia group called for the uprooting of US forces from Saudi Arabia.[71] On February 3, 1991, a US transport bus was doused in kerosene, and at about the same time, shots were fired at another US military bus. The following month, several shots were fired at a US Marine vehicle. Then, in 1994, the Downing Report found, "the volume and tone of reporting on potential terrorist threats became more ominous."[72]

Following the OPM-SANG bombing, the threat condition for US forces in Saudi Arabia was raised one notch from THREATCON ALPHA—the second lowest— to THREATCON BRAVO, and security was enhanced at all installations with an American presence throughout Saudi Arabia. At Khobar Towers, the security fence was repaired and upgraded for the first time since US forces occupied the complex in 1990.[73] Requests to extend the perimeter of the complex 100 to 150 feet away from the buildings located right along the fence were denied by Saudi authorities.

The Saudis also denied requests to trim vegetation along the perimeter to allow for better observation of the perimeter, citing the need for vegetation to prevent local Saudis from observing Americans' activities within the compound. A US civil engineering team trimmed the vegetation anyway, though military commanders would later be taken to task for being too cautious in their requests for support from the Saudis due to cultural sensitivities.[74] General Schwalier issued several Battle Staff Directives focused on improving security for the 4404th Wing at Khobar, including physical barriers, serpentine driving control patterns at checkpoints, and more.[75]

Sometime in spring 1996, US military and intelligence officials began to notice suspicious activities around Khobar Towers. From April to June 1996, officials noted ten events, including incidents of Arab men watching, photographing, or hiding near the compound's perimeter fence. In one case an Arab male accosted a British airman driving to Khobar Towers, and in three other cases vehicles spun their tires in the north parking lot. There was also an unconfirmed report of a sniper attack aimed at a Frenchman within the compound. These cases were investigated and in most cases determined to be unrelated to terrorist activity. For example, officials concluded the photographs may have been taken by visitors to Dhahran during the Hajj pilgrimage who were curious about Americans. "The most serious incident," one government report concluded, involved a car moving one of the Jersey barriers on the compound's eastern perimeter in May 1996. In what may have been an effort to test the compound's perimeter and base security, the car slowly approached a row of barriers and hit one barrier at four to six miles per hour, moving the barrier two to three feet. The car then backed up and drove away.[76]

The following month, the June 17 issue of the Defense Intelligence Agency's (DIA) *Military Intelligence Digest* summarized these incidents based on information provided by investigators from the Air Force Office of Special Investigations (AFOSI). AFOSI, Saudi military, and local police all investigated these incidents and determined no attack on Khobar Towers was imminent. Still, the DIA report indicated "an increased threat of a terrorist attack at Khobar Towers."[77] By this point the Hezbollah cell members were nearly ready to strike. Eight days later, they did.

But in the days and weeks following the 1995 OPM-SANG bombing, threat assessments focused on the likelihood of further attacks in the Saudi capital employing an explosive device of about the same size. "Everyone assumed . . . there would be another bombing," the US Consul General in Dhahran noted, but "the focus was Riyadh. No one really thought anything was going to happen in Dhahran." Nor did anyone suspect terrorists would construct a bomb anywhere near as large as the one used in Khobar Towers. According to the chief of the National Intelligence Support Team in Riyadh, the threat, he and others assumed, would be an explosive of "maybe 500 pounds but . . . we never went above 1,000 pounds" when assessing the potential threat. The assumption, therefore, was that the base must be defended against "an OPM/SANG type bomb," as one AFOSI officer put it.[78]

And while tactical intelligence on the date, time, place, and type of attack were lacking, the air force investigation into the Khobar Towers bombing ultimately determined that "a considerable body of information was available that indicated terrorists had the capability and intention to target US interests in Saudi Arabia, and the Khobar Towers was a potential target."[79] In fact, in March 1996, a senior intelligence official briefed General Schwalier on the "increasing amount of circumstantial information indicating that some terrorist activity could occur during and immediately after the Hajj. . . ." The following month, an air force assessment concluded that "security measures here [at Khobar] are outstanding, which in my view would lead a would-be terrorist to attempt an attack from a position outside the perimeter. . . . If a truck parks close to the fence line, and the driver makes a quick getaway, I think the building should be cleared immediately."[80]

Hezbollah Surveillance Operations, under the Radar

The fact that red lights started blinking only in 1994 and that an attack on US personnel in Saudi Arabia was deemed unlikely until 1995 is startling, given that Hezbollah operatives had been engaging in surveillance operations for the Khobar Towers plot around 1993. It was that year, the FBI concluded, that Ahmed al-Mughassil instructed Mustafa al-Qassab, Ibrahim al-Yacoub, and Ali al-Houri to start surveillance of Americans in Saudi Arabia. Al-Qassab and al-Yacoub then spent three months in Riyadh, where Hani al-Sayegh joined them, and conducted surveillance of American targets. Their surveillance reports were passed on first to Saudi Hezbollah military chief al-Mughassil, and then to the leader of Saudi Hezbollah, Abdel Karim al-Nasser, and then to officials in Iran. When their surveillance mission was done, al-Mughassil met with them in person to review their work. As 1993 wore on, the assignments began to trickle down the Hezbollah chain. Al-Yacoub instructed Abdallah al-Jarash to conduct surveillance of the US embassy in Riyadh and to "determine where Americans went and where they lived." Also at al-Yacoub's direction, al-Jarash and Ali al-Marhoun conducted surveillance of a fish market frequented by Americans, also located near the US embassy in Riyadh, and reported back to al-Yacoub with the results.[81]

It was not long before Hezbollah expanded its surveillance operations beyond Riyadh. In early 1994, al-Qassab initiated surveillance of American and other foreign sites in the Eastern Province of Saudi Arabia and provided his written reports to al-Nasser and Iranian officials. Al-Mughassil called for further surveillance of American sites in the Eastern Province, which was carried out around fall 1994 by al-Marhoun, Saleh Ramadan, and Mustafa al-Mu'alem. Their reports were passed on to al-Mughassil in Beirut. Around the same time, an Iranian military officer directed Saed al-Bahar to conduct parallel surveillance activities in Saudi Arabia, which al-Bahar did. Finally, in late 1994 after extensive surveillance in the Eastern Province of Saudi Arabia, several Saudi Hezbollah operatives specifically identified Khobar Towers as an important American military location. Informed of this conclusion, al-Mughassil quickly provided funds to Ramadan for the express purpose of finding a place where Hezbollah could store explosives in the Eastern Province.[82]

Meanwhile, Iranian officers tasked Saudi Hezbollah cell members with carrying out additional, parallel surveillance in support of future attacks targeting Americans in Saudi Arabia. In 1995, for example, al-Bahar and al-Sayegh conducted surveillance at the direction of an Iranian military officer in the area of Jizan, along the Saudi Red Sea coast near Yemen, and at American sites in the Eastern Province. Hani al-Sayegh, who had spent time in Damascus, where he was issued an international driver's license in 1994, provided the group's surveillance reports to the Iranian officer.[83]

In about April or May 1995, al-Marhoun underwent four days of live-fire drills sponsored by Hezbollah in Lebanon. While in Lebanon, he visited al-Mughassil's Beirut apartment. Al-Mughassil provided al-Marhoun $2,000 in hundred-dollar bills to support the Saudi Hezbollah cell's surveillance activity in Saudi Arabia—money al-Marhoun subsequently used to finance a trip to Riyadh with Saleh Ramadan to scout out additional sites frequented by Americans. Al-Mughassil insisted that they remain focused on Khobar Towers, however, and in June al-Marhoun, Ramadan, and al-Mu'alem began regular surveillance of Khobar. Briefed in Beirut by Ramadan on their successful regular surveillance, al-Mughassil directed them to continue.[84]

As it happened, another cell member, Fadel al-Alawe, came to Beirut at al-Mughassil's request around the same time Ramadan was there. While the two Saudi Hezbollah operatives did not see each other in Beirut, al-Alawe—who thought he was there to brief al-Mughassil on the cell's surveillance activities—must have been surprised to see surveillance reports from Ramadan on al-Mughassil's desk. In fact, al-Mughassil had another reason to summon al-Alawe to Beirut. As surveillance of Khobar Towers continued, al-Mughassil now needed to ensure he could smuggle the explosives for the operation from Lebanon, through Jordan, and into Saudi Arabia. It was time for a test run, though al-Alawe would be told it was the real thing. Al-Mughassil instructed al-Alawe to drive a vehicle he claimed contained hidden explosives from Lebanon to Saudi Arabia, which al-Alawe did. Only on his arrival back home did al-Alawe discover al-Mughassil had been testing him.[85]

Then, in late fall 1995 and again in late 1995 or early 1996, Ramadan returned to Beirut to confer with al-Mughassil about the planned operation targeting Khobar Towers. During the first of these meetings, Ramadan brought more surveillance reports to al-Mughassil and learned for the first time that Hezbollah would be attacking Khobar Towers with a tanker truck loaded with explosives and gasoline. At the second meeting, al-Mughassil began to lay out the operational roles of different cell members. Al-Mughassil discussed the need to accumulate enough explosives to destroy a row of buildings and noted that "the attack was to serve Iran by driving the Americans out of the Gulf region."[86]

In hindsight, we know that none of the cell's local surveillance, travel back and forth to Beirut, test drives from Lebanon to Saudi Arabia, or telephone or other communications was noticed by US or Saudi authorities. US intelligence was generally aware of increased Iranian surveillance of US personnel based on classified source reporting, but it lacked the details. In the days after the bombing, US intelligence would significantly underestimate the time it took to hatch the plot, speculating that this "well-executed attack may have been planned for several months."[87]

In all likelihood, what enabled the Saudi Hezbollah cell members to successfully execute these surveillance efforts undetected was their prior training in Lebanon and Iran. But they also enjoyed close oversight and support during the operation from senior Iranian and Lebanese Hezbollah officials. During the cells' surveillance activities, for example, al-Mughassil told al-Marhoun that he had received a phone call from a high-level Iranian government official inquiring about the progress of their surveillance activity. Later, al-Mughassil would further confide to al-Marhoun that "he had close ties to Iranian officials, who supplied him with money and gave him directions" for Saudi Hezbollah.[88] Former FBI director Louis Freeh would later testify about one particular conspirator who ultimately described to investigators the money and passports he received from IRGC officials, as well as their directions on target selection and the training he received and surveillance he conducted at their behest.[89]

Meanwhile, al-Mughassil's presence in Beirut facilitated his close coordination with Imad Mughniyeh's senior operational planners within Hezbollah's Islamic Jihad Organization (IJO). According to the CIA, Saudi authorities believed al-Mughassil held a Lebanese and possibly also an Iranian passport at the time of the Khobar attack. Saudi information also suggested he "has strong family ties to Lebanese Hezbollah and has been in contact with the office of the Supreme Leader Khamenei." According to Jordanian intelligence, as reported by the CIA, an alleged Hizballah leader named Amad Ali Zayb Zahir (whom, the CIA conceded, it could not identify) "stated on 26 June [the day after the bombing] that the bombing was carried out by Saudi Shias with links to Hizballah and Iran." Leading up to the bombing, the CIA knew of little more than the previous year's training by the IRGC in Lebanon of Saudi and Bahraini "Shia oppositionists," as the CIA reports described them.[90]

Mughniyeh was also reportedly in contact with Saudi Hezbollah throughout the 1990s through his deputy Talal Hamiyeh.[91] Stemming from a powerful Bekaa Valley clan, Hamiyeh is said to have partnered with Mughniyeh in the 1980s during the early days of Hezbollah kidnappings, and even served as point man for negotiating the release of some hostages held in Lebanon.[92] Implicated in the 1992 and 1994 Hezbollah bombings in Buenos Aires, he succeeded Mughniyeh as head of Hezbollah's IJO after the latter's February 2008 assassination.[93]

The Khobar Operation

Briefed in Beirut on the intelligence his cell collected on Khobar Towers through months of surveillance, al-Mughassil traveled in January or February 1996 to Qatif, not far from Dhahran and Khobar Towers, where he instructed one of his operatives to find places to stockpile and hide their explosives. Sites were apparently identified rather quickly, because sometime around February Ramadan returned to Beirut at al-Mughassil's direction and drove back to Saudi Arabia in a car stuffed with hidden explosives.[94] Though authorities were unaware of this successful smuggling run, they did have indications that terrorists were smuggling explosives. In March, US authorities came by unconfirmed intelligence indicating that "a large quantity of explosives was to be smuggled into Saudi Arabia during the Hajj," which ran from mid-April to mid-May that year.[95] In a briefing they received on April 12, General Schwalier and key members of his staff were told the current threat included reports of "a large quantity of explosives destined for coalition military targets with the potential for use in a bombing attack." This information, however, was deemed too sensitive to be released down the chain of command, making it largely useless. No changes were made to the existing security posture at the base as a result of this briefing.[96]

When he arrived in Qatif, Ramadan delivered the car to an unknown man whose face was veiled.[97] Most of the cell members knew one another. This, plus the fact that a Lebanese Hezbollah operative and bomb maker referred to in the US Khobar Towers indictment as John Doe played a key role in constructing the truck bomb, suggests the mysteriously veiled recipient of the explosives delivered from Lebanon may have been the Lebanese Hezbollah bomb maker himself.

But the following month Hezbollah suffered a serious operational setback. Having passed al-Mughassil's test run the previous June, al-Alawe was summoned back to Beirut in March 1996 and given the keys to a car stuffed with hidden explosives. Al-Alawe drove the car through Syria and Jordan, arriving at the al-Haditha crossing point on the Jordanian-Saudi border on March 28. But whereas Ramadan was able to smuggle explosives across the border in his earlier run, al-Alawe was arrested on the spot when Saudi border guards inspecting his car discovered thirty-eight kilograms of plastic explosives expertly hidden within its engine compartment. This in turn led to the arrests over three days in early April of al-Marhoun, al-Mu'alem, and Ramadan.[98]

Suddenly, al-Mughassil found himself without his key operatives and facing the prospect that some elements of the operation may be compromised. Undeterred, al-Mughassil quickly found replacements for his four detained operatives and assumed a hands-on role himself to see the operation through.

Sometime in late April or early May, al-Mughassil returned to Saudi Arabia to personally assemble a new hit squad. Traveling on a false passport and under the cover of a pilgrim on Hajj, he appeared unannounced at Abdallah al-Jarash's home in Qatif on May 1. Al-Mughassil briefed al-Jarash on the Khobar Towers bomb plot and on the arrests of the four cell members, and asked for his help executing the attack. Al-Mughassil must have assumed al-Jarash would answer in the affirmative, because before leaving he provided al-Jarash with a forged Iranian passport that must have been prepared in advance and told him to "be ready for a call to action at any time."[99]

Assuming the authorities were broadening their investigation after the arrests of his operatives, al-Mughassil again showed up unannounced at another cell member's home. Three days after visiting al-Jarash, he knocked on Hussein al-Mughis's door and, after recruiting him to the operation and briefing him on the plan, left him a timing device to hide at his home. At least twice in the months leading up to the Khobar bombing, another Saudi Hezbollah cell member, Ali al-Houri, turned up at al-Mughis's home seeking help to hide several fifty-kilogram bags and paint

cans filled with explosives at sites around Qatif. Then, with just about three weeks
to go until the planned attack, al-Mughassil and the unnamed Lebanese Hezbollah
operative (John Doe) who arrived to help assemble the bomb moved into al-Mughis's
home in Qatif.[100]

Al-Mughassil's heightened concern for operational security was well warranted.
Reporting in the days right after the attack, the CIA would note that following the
March arrests the Saudis quickly determined that al-Mughassil directed the explosives smuggling operation based on information obtained from the interrogation of
the detained Hezbollah operatives. At first the Saudis thought he had fled to Iran,
given their information showing he held Lebanese and possibly Iranian passports.
Subsequent information, however, suggested he was in Syria and Lebanon. "Riyadh," the CIA noted, "has been seeking Syrian assistance in extraditing Mughassil
from Lebanon since at least April for questioning about the shipment of explosives
to the kingdom."[101] These efforts to secure Syrian counterterrorism cooperation
failed, as they would again when redoubled after the Khobar Towers bombing.

Meanwhile, the plot continued apace. Using stolen identification, the cell purchased a tanker truck from a Saudi car dealership for about 75,000 Saudi Riyals, or
some $20,000. The cell then spent two weeks leading up to the attack converting
the tanker into a massive truck bomb at a farm in the Qatif area. Al-Mughassil was
part of the team at the farm, along with al-Houri, al-Sayegh, al-Qassab, and the
Lebanese Hezbollah operative, John Doe. Al-Mughis and al-Jarash came and went,
with al-Mughis retrieving the timing device he was given and the explosives he
helped hide and al-Jarash supplying the tools and wiring for the truck bomb assembly. The explosives were concealed within the gasoline tanker truck such that they
would be unseen even if the truck were stopped and inspected. Had someone
opened the hatch atop the tanker, he would have seen what appeared to be a tanker
full of gasoline. In fact, John Doe and his crew had secured a fifty-gallon drum to
the inside of the full 20,000-gallon tanker. But beneath the gasoline-filled drum,
the rest of the tanker was filled with at least 5,000 pounds of plastic explosives. Mughassil's ambitions did not end there: as he and his operatives built the truck bomb
for the Khobar attack, al-Mughassil discussed plans for an additional attack, this
one targeting the US consulate in Dhahran.[102]

With the operational details attended to, several of the conspirators met at the
Sayyeda Zeinab shrine in Damascus. The purpose of the meeting, held sometime
around June 7–17, was to confer with the senior leadership of Saudi Hezbollah, including the group's leader, Abdel Karim al-Nasser, and al-Mughassil, the group's
military chief. Also present were al-Houri, al-Yacoub, al-Sayegh, al-Qassab, and
other senior Saudi Hezbollah leaders. Al-Nasser, the boss, presided over the meeting, reviewing details of the bombing plot and making clear to all that al-Mughassil
was running the operation.[103] According to Bruce Tefft, a former CIA official, other
operational meetings also occurred in Damascus, including some at the Iranian
embassy there. The Iranian mastermind of the Khobar plot, IRGC brigadier general Ahmed Sharifi, oversaw much of the operation out of the Iranian embassy in
Damascus, according to Tefft. Within months of the attack, new intelligence reports

revealed the role of "an Iranian intelligence officer who goes by various code names, including 'Sherifi' and 'Abu Jalal,' [who] acted as a liaison between Teheran and Saudi Shiites in Lebanon."[104] According to Tefft, "By the time [the plot] advanced far enough to the stage where they were actually recruiting individuals to participate in the attack, and passing out false passports and funds, those in the meetings with the conspirators, the people who executed the attack, took place out of the Iranian embassy in Damascus, Syria."[105]

The case of Jaafar Chueikhat, a Saudi citizen and bombing suspect thought to be hiding in Syria after the attack, was a particular sticking point. Saudi officials long suspected Chueikhat of involvement in the transport of the explosives used in the Khobar bombing from the Syrian-controlled Bekaa Valley in Lebanon to Saudi Arabia. Saudi authorities tracked Chueikhat from Kuwait to Egypt to Syria after the bombing, and asked the Syrians to arrest him. Chueikhat, the Syrians insisted, had already fled to Iran. The Syrians later arrested him, after he supposedly returned to Syria from Iran. But Chueikhat committed suicide while in a Syrian prison, according to Syrian officials. Chueikhat's death occurred under mysterious circumstances, however, just a day before Saudi investigators were scheduled to question him for the first time.[106] When US officials pressed the Syrian foreign minister, Farouk Sharaa, to look into the matter of Chueikhat's death, Sharaa lost his temper and insisted Syria was not involved in the attack in Dhahran or any other acts of terrorism. In a terse comment to the press, a senior US administration official said, "We are not satisfied with what we learned and continue to press the case."[107]

Hani al-Sayegh spent significant time in Syria in the years leading up to the bombing, and would later insist to Canadian investigators and reporters that he could not have been involved in the bombing because he lived in Syria the two years before coming to Canada in August 1996. Stamps in his passport, he maintained, revealed he was in Syria, not Saudi Arabia, at the time of the bombing.[108] Investigators were unconvinced, however, given that Iran provided cell members with false passports. Confessions from his co-conspirators and intercepted telephone conversations convinced Canadian, American, and Saudi officials that al-Sayegh played a key role in the bombing and had maintained contact with Iranian officials—both in Iran and Canada—since the attack. For example, while in Canada, al-Sayegh talked with his wife in Saudi Arabia and, speaking in Farsi, with Iranian officials in Iran. "In these conversations he makes oblique references that suggest a possible involvement in the Dhahran bombing, and he intimates that some of his cohorts fled at one time to Iran."[109]

Whether the Syrian government played some role in the attack, such as knowingly providing safe haven to Saudi Hezbollah operatives before and after the attack, remains an open question. For example, in the months after the attack, reports emerged that Saudi Hezbollah official Husayn bin Mubarak was holding court in Lebanon's Bekaa Valley, which was firmly under Syrian control, publicly receiving Saudi Hezbollah members who escaped Saudi Arabia and made their way to Lebanon via Iran.[110] What is known is that a week after the go-ahead meeting in Damascus, al-Mughassil and the members of his cell had returned to Saudi Arabia and were ready to execute the attack. On the evening of attack they met at the farm in

Qatif, about five miles from Khobar Towers, to review final preparations. Present at this meeting were only the members of the actual operational unit, including al-Mughassil, al-Houri, al-Sayegh, al-Qassab, al-Jarash, and al-Mughis. They waited at the farm, the truck bomb ready to go, until dark.

Hani al-Sayegh left the farm first, shortly before 10 PM. Driving a Datsun, with al-Jarash in the passenger seat, al-Sayegh pulled into the parking lot adjoining Building 131 at Khobar Towers and parked in the far corner. Serving as scouts, al-Sayegh and al-Jarash scanned the area for patrols or anything else that might disrupt their attack. Having conducted extensive surveillance of the site, they likely expected no such interruptions. The use of a scout vehicle, for its part, indicated the professional training the perpetrators received leading up to the attack. A white Chevrolet Caprice sedan entered the lot next. Al-Mughis had borrowed this car from an acquaintance, who likely had no idea his car would serve as the getaway for the perpetrators of a massive terrorist bombing. On their signal, the truck bomb entered, driven by al-Mughassil himself with al-Houri in the passenger seat. They backed up the truck to the fence in front of Building 131, then jumped into the back seat of the waiting getaway car, which drove away, followed by the lookouts in the signal car. Within minutes, the bomb exploded.[111]

For reasons unknown, al-Jarash and al-Mughis returned home to Qatif. The remaining members of the cell, however, immediately left the Khobar area and made their ways out of Saudi Arabia, traveling on a variety of false passports. Most of the perpetrators are believed to have traveled to Iran. Al-Qassab went to Syria. Al-Sayegh, however, took a circuitous route to Canada, traveling from Kuwait to Rome to Boston to Ottawa. The complicated itinerary may have reflected the operational security he and his co-conspirators were trained to employ to evade detection. Or it may simply have been, as al-Sayegh later claimed, that he found a cheap ticket on Alitalia Airlines that took this route.[112]

The Investigation

In the first days after the bombing, the US government had little hard information on the perpetrators. A July 1996 CIA analysis explained that "the Saudi investigation apparently is focusing on a group led by a Saudi Shia resident in Lebanon, but some reports point to Saudi Sunni militants or Iran as credible culprits." Further hedging its bets, the CIA report included a text box noting that the Khobar attack occurred on the third anniversary of the US attack on the Iraqi Intelligence Service Headquarters and noted Iraq could not be ruled out as a suspect.[113]

The Iraqi connection would quickly be dismissed, but the theory that the attack was carried out by radical Sunni "Afghan Arabs"—veterans of the jihad in Afghanistan inspired by bin Laden, like the accused and beheaded perpetrators of the OPM-SANG bombing—persisted for some time. In the weeks following the bombing, Saudi authorities arrested scores of suspects, Shi'a and Sunni alike. The Saudis claimed to have evidence linking some of the detained suspects to OPM-SANG suspects. "Our mistake," one Saudi official quipped, "was to think that the first bombing was an isolated case."[114] Early reports suggested six "former Afghan-trained fighters" confessed to the bombing, possibly after being tortured. This focus on radical Sunnis should not surprise, given the recentness of the OPM-SANG bombing and Osama bin Laden's 1996 fatwa calling for war against the United States and its allies. According to Abdel Bari Atwan, the editor-in-chief of the newspaper *al-Quds al-Arabi* who interviewed bin Laden, in the course of their discussions the al-Qaeda chief claimed responsibility for the Khobar bombing.[115] Subsequent findings suggest this claim to have been bravado. But authorities have still not ruled out some kind of peripheral role by radical Sunni elements tied to al-Qaeda.

As a result of their meetings in the early 1990s, Iran and al-Qaeda reached an informal agreement to cooperate, with Iran providing critical explosives, intelligence, and security training to bin Laden's organization. In addition to providing training, the 9/11 Commission report points to operational cooperation in planning and executing attacks. Referring, for example, to the Khobar Towers bombing, the 9/11 Commission report concludes, "The operation was carried out principally, perhaps exclusively, by Saudi Hezbollah, an organization that had received support from the government of Iran. While evidence of Iranian involvement is strong, there are also signs that al Qaeda played some role, as yet unknown."[116]

As the investigation proceeded, Iran's role in orchestrating the bombing would become crystal clear. Ultimately, FBI director Louis Freeh would testify that "the attack was planned, funded and sponsored by senior leadership in the government of the Republic of Iran; that the IRGC principally had the responsibility of putting that plan into operation; and it was [implemented] with the use of the Saudi Hezbollah organization and its members."[117]

Within hours of the attack, FBI agents and forensic specialists were en route to Saudi Arabia to assist in the investigation. FBI agents conducted what FBI counterterrorism chief Dale Watson described as a soup-to-nuts crime scene investigation, measuring the crater and searching for bomb components and other physical evidence.[118] The FBI then helped track the vehicle identification number found on a piece of the chassis of the truck bomb. Armed with this information, Saudi authorities quickly identified the company that sold the truck and the Saudi Hezbollah facilitator who purchased it. Analyzing the explosives used in the Khobar blast and comparing those with the explosives seized at the Jordanian border back in March, the FBI laboratory determined they were from similar batches of C4 military-grade plastic explosive. Saudi authorities then went back to the cell members detained at the border in the months before the bombing. These fresh interrogations yielded still more information about the plot.[119]

Meanwhile, six of the Saudi Hezbollah bombers were among the many people rounded up by Saudi authorities after the attack. Even as FBI investigators were sifting through the rubble at the bomb site, Saudi intelligence obtained the first confessions from the bombers. According to Louis Freeh, "the bombers admitted they had been trained by the Iranian external security service (IRGC) in the Bekka Valley, and received their passports at the Iranian Embassy in Damascus, along with $250,000 cash for the operation from IRGC Gen. Ahmad Sharifi."[120]

The FBI was keen to compile sufficient evidence to indict the bombers in US court for the deaths of nineteen US soldiers, but was frustrated in its early attempts to gain direct access to the suspects in Saudi custody. Then, in March 1997, the arrest of al-Sayegh in Canada provided the Bureau with its first big break. Canadian intelligence and law enforcement authorities had been watching al-Sayegh based on a tip from the Saudis. Although they preferred to keep him under surveillance to build a stronger case against him and learn more about the activities of Saudi Hezbollah and Iran, they received information indicating he was preparing to leave the country. On March 18, Royal Canadian Mounted Police arrested him at the Queen Mary convenience store in Ottawa on joint orders of the minister of citizenship and immigration and the solicitor general, on the grounds that he posed "a security risk to Canada."[121] In May, al-Sayegh met with American officials and, after first claiming ignorance about the Khobar bombing, he soon confessed to having once belonged to the Saudi Hezbollah cell that carried out the bombing. Al-Sayegh informed officials that he was recruited by the IRGC and had participated not only in the Khobar bombing but also in another unspecified operation directed by Gen. Ahmad Sharifi.[122]

Al-Sayegh agreed to assist US officials investigating the bombing as part of a plea bargain. But once he arrived in the United States, he reneged on his agreement and sought political asylum in America. That effort failed, and in October 1999, al-Sayegh was deported to Saudi Arabia. Concerned that Hezbollah might retaliate against US interests for deporting al-Sayegh to Saudi Arabia, the State Department issued a worldwide warning advising US citizens "to take appropriate steps to increase their security awareness to lessen their vulnerability." The potential existed, US officials maintained, that "someone might try to take retaliatory action" for returning al-Sayegh to Saudi custody.[123]

In July, two months after al-Sayegh was arrested in Canada, the Syrian government turned Mustafa al-Qassab over to Saudi authorities.[124] Referring to al-Qassab, Freeh would later note that a detained suspect—one "who had been returned to Saudi Arabia from another country"—provided "key information which would later implicate senior Iranian government officials as responsible for the planning, funding and execution of this attack."[125] Soon after Mohammed Khatami was elected president of Iran in May 1997, Saudi crown prince Abdullah raised the issue of the Khobar bombing with outgoing president Rafsanjani at a meeting in Pakistan. According to one account, Abdullah told Rafsanjani, "We know you did it." Rafsanjani reportedly replied that he was not personally involved but that if any senior Iranian official was involved "it was he"—and he pointed upward in an understood reference to Supreme Leader Ayatollah Khamenei.[126] Rafsanjani's protestations of personal ignorance, however, contradict CIA reporting, which noted as early as 1990 that "the terrorist attacks carried out by Iran during the past year were probably approved in advance by President Rafsanjani and other senior leaders."[127]

Ultimately, a deal was brokered that granted FBI agents indirect access to the suspects, but only in 1998. The agents could submit questions that Saudi officials would pose to the suspects while the agents observed the interview behind a one-way mirror. On November 9, 1998, FBI agents asked eight suspects a series of 212 questions posed by Saudi agents at a Riyadh detention center. The Saudis also provided the transcripts of interviews with other detainees and other physical evidence they had collected. The net result, according to Freeh, amounted to "a devastating indictment."[128]

Yet the information collected remained insufficient for senior US officials. With the statute of limitations nearing for any prospective indictment, the FBI pressed again for direct access to the suspects detained in Saudi Arabia. Finally, in 2000 the FBI got to talk directly with the detainees, including the eight suspects they had questioned indirectly through a one-way mirror two years earlier and others, among them al-Qassab. Each of their statements corroborated other evidence that had been collected, as well as one another's statements. They provided detailed descriptions of the plot, including training, preparing the explosives, carrying money, hiding explosives, and the roles played by Iranian officials.[129] For Freeh, the details al-Qassab provided about Iran's role in the attack "tied the whole package together for good."[130]

In June 2001, with the statute of limitations about to expire, the Department of Justice indicted thirteen members of the Saudi Hezbollah cell, including the unidentified Lebanese Hezbollah operative referred to as John Doe, in US federal court. To date, none of these fugitives have been captured, though several are believed to be living in Iran, including al-Nasser, al-Mughassil, and others. According to a 2009 Amnesty International report, Hani al-Sayegh and eight other accused co-conspirators were jailed in al-Dammam Prison, reportedly held without trial.[131] In 2002, Saudi officials announced that some of the people involved in the Khobar Towers bombing had been tried and sentenced under Islamic law, but the officials would not specify who, or how many, or what the sentences were. The verdicts, a senior Saudi prince told the press, "must be announced at the right time."[132] That time has apparently yet to come.

Following the Khobar Towers attack, the Clinton administration sought additional intelligence about Iran's role and warned Tehran against engaging in further attacks against US interests. According to former CIA and National Security Council official Bruce Riedel, "The administration also took targeted actions against the Revolutionary Guards and Iranian intelligence personnel around the world." One of these, Operation Sapphire, was a CIA operation that identified Iranian intelligence officers operating abroad and disrupted their activities in early 1997.[133] A January 1997 cable sent from the Office of the FBI Director to the CIA, the White House, and several FBI Legal Attaché offices abroad, among others, provided intelligence it described as "sensitive and singular in nature" warning that Hezbollah was funding "Saudi opposition elements in Kuwait for possible support of terrorist operations." The warning was set against information that a Hezbollah spiritual leader had produced a videotape for distribution to opposition party members in Saudi Arabia, Bahrain, and Kuwait that reportedly called for "Hezbollah supported suicide operations in defense of the [tenets] of Islam in the Gulf region."[134]

Meanwhile, the activities of Iranian MOIS agents continued to worry US officials, prompting a disruption campaign targeting the MOIS in late 1999. Former CIA director George Tenet would later recount, "In one memorable example, John Brennan, our liaison to the Saudis, handled the local MOIS head himself. John walked up to his car, knocked on the window, and said, "Hello, I'm from the U.S. embassy, and I've got something to tell you."[135]

Such approaches spooked Iranian intelligence, Tenet notes. "Just being seen with some of our people might cause MOIS officers to fall under suspicion by their own agency." Nor was Iran concerned only about its own operational security. Even as it continued to target US interests, Iran feared that after the Khobar attack, US or other intelligence services would accelerate their efforts to collect information about, and possibly target, Hezbollah. According to an American intelligence report, in November 1996 the director of the counterintelligence directorate within MOIS personally visited Mughniyeh in Beirut to assess Hezbollah's security.[136] Such activity continues. Testifying before Congress in 2008, Adm. William J. Fallon, then–commander of US Central Command, noted that Iran employs surrogate terrorist groups in the region and continues to engage in "confrontational activity in the Gulf."[137]

Iran would increasingly use Hezbollah in the years to come as a strike force through which it could operate with probable deniability. In the 1990s, several such operations used Europe as a launching pad from which to deploy operatives into Israel to conduct attacks or collect operational intelligence. In fact, seven months before MOIS assessed Hezbollah's security, the first of a string of Hezbollah operatives to infiltrate into Israel through Europe would be caught red-handed assembling a bomb in an East Jerusalem hotel room. Undeterred, more Hezbollah operatives would soon follow.

Notes

1. US Department of Defense, Memorandum for the Secretary of Defense, Downing Assessment Task Force, "Report of the Assessment of the Khobar Towers Bombing," August 30, 1996 (hereafter cited as Downing Assessment); Rebecca Grant, "Khobar Towers," *Air Force Magazine* 81, no. 6 (June 1998), 41–47.

2. *United States of America v. Ahmed Mughassil et al.*, Indictment, United States District Court, Eastern District of Virginia, Alexandria Division, No. 01-228-A, June 2001; Federal Court of Canada, In the Matter of Hani Abd Rahim al-Sayegh, and In the Matter of a Referral of the Immigration Act, R.S.C. 1985, c. I-2, Court File: DES-1-97; US Congress, 104th Cong., 2d sess., House, National Security Committee Staff Report, "The Khobar Towers Bombing Incident," August 14, 1996; Grant, "Khobar Towers," 41–47; US Department of Defense, "Report of Investigation Concerning the Khobar Towers Bombing, 25 June 1996," Prepared by the Inspector General Lt. Gen. Richard T. Swope and the Judge Advocate General Byran G. Hawley, July 31, 1997.

3. *United States of America v. Ahmed Mughassil et al.*, Indictment; Federal Court of Canada, In the Matter of Hani Abd Rahim al-Sayegh; House, National Security Committee Staff Report, "Khobar Towers Bombing Incident"; US Department of Defense, "Report of Investigation Concerning the Khobar Towers Bombing."

4. House National Security Committee Staff Report, "Khobar Towers Bombing Incident"; Downing Assessment, 55; Grant, "Khobar Towers," 46–47.

5. US Department of Justice, FBI, "Terrorism Charges Have Been Brought against 13 Members of the Pro-Iran Saudi Hizballah," press release, June 21, 2001. For a discus-

sion on the analysis of the yield of the explosive, see Lt. Gen. James F. Record, USAF, "Independent Review of the Khobar Towers Bombing," (Washington, DC: Headquarters US Air Force), October 31, 1996.

6. US Department of Justice, FBI, "Terrorism Charges against 13 Members"; *Heiser et al. v. Islamic Republic of Iran* consolidated with *Campbell et al. v. Islamic Republic of Iran*, Memorandum Opinion, United States District, Court for the District of Columbia, December 22, 2006.

7. Federal Court of Canada, In the Matter of Hani Abd Rahim al-Sayegh.

8. *United States of America v. Ahmed Mughassil et al.*, Indictment.

9. Louis J. Freeh, "Khobar Towers," *Wall Street Journal*, June 23, 2006.

10. Federal Court of Canada, In the Matter of Hani Abd Rahim al-Sayegh.

11. US Department of Justice, FBI, "Terrorism Charges Have Been Brought."

12. International Crisis Group, "The Shiite Question in Saudi Arabia," *Middle East Report* no. 45, September 19, 2005; Human Rights Watch, "Denied Dignity: Systemic Discrimination and Hostility toward Saudi Shia Citizens," September 3, 2009.

13. Federal Court of Canada, In the Matter of Hani Abd Rahim al-Sayegh.

14. Teitelbaum, "Shiites of Saudi Arabia"; International Crisis Group, "Shiite Question in Saudi Arabia"; Matthiesen, "Hizbullah al-Hijaz."

15. J. E. Peterson, *Historical Dictionary of Saudi Arabia*, (Lanham, MD: Scarecrow Press, 2003), 122.

16. Matthiesen, "Hizbullah al-Hijaz."

17. Ibid.

18. Ibrahim, *Shi'is of Saudi Arabia*, 142.

19. The government claimed it was an accident, but it was later tied to Saudi Hezbollah. Matthiesen, "Hizbullah al-Hijaz; see also US CIA, "Saudi Diplomat Assassinated."

20. Federal Court of Canada, In the Matter of Hani Abd Rahim al-Sayegh, 13.

21. US CIA, "Iran: Uses of Terror."

22. US CIA, "Shootdown of Iran Air 655."

23. US CIA, "South Korea [redacted]."

24. Matthiesen, "Hizbullah al-Hijaz."

25. Ibid.

26. Adel Darwish, "Saudis Overhaul Secret Service after Terrorist Killings," *Independent* (London), January 14, 1989.

27. US CIA, "Saudi Diplomat Assassinated."

28. Ibid.

29. Matthiesen, "Hizbullah al-Hijaz."

30. *United States of America v. Ahmed Mughassil et al.*

31. Ibid.

32. US CIA, "Rafsanjani's Report Card."

33. Marschall, *Iran's Persian Gulf Policy*, 38.

34. *United States of America v. Ahmed Mughassil et al.*

35. Matthiesen, "Hizbullah al-Hijaz."

36. See International Crisis Group, "Shiite Question in Saudi Arabia"; Human Rights Watch, "Denied Dignity."

37. Matthiesen, "Hizbullah al-Hijaz." See also Ibrahim, *Shi'is of Saudi Arabia*.

38. *United States of America v. Ahmed Mughassil et al.*

39. Ibrahim, *Shi'is of Saudi Arabia.*

40. *United States of America v. Ahmed Mughassil et al.*

41. Federal Court of Canada, In the Matter of Hani Abd Rahim al-Sayegh.

42. US CIA, "Khobar Bombing [redacted]."

43. *Paul A. Blais et al. v. Islamic Republic of Iran et al.*, United States District Court for the District of Columbia, Civil Action No. 02-285, May 26, 2006, Testimony of Bruce D. Tefft.

44. Downing Assessment.

45. US CIA, Memorandum for the DCI, "Iranian Support for International Terrorism."

46. US CIA, "Iran and the Radical Palestinians."

47. US CIA, "Shootdown of Iran Air 655."

48. US CIA, "Attacks against Saudi Interests."

49. *United States of America v. Ahmed Mughassil et al.*

50. *Campbell et al. v. The Islamic Republic of Iran*, United States District Court for the District of Columbia, Case No. 00-CV-02104, November 25, 2003, Testimony of Patrick Clawson.

51. Ibid.

52. *Heiser et al. v. Islamic Republic of Iran*, United States District Court for the District of Columbia, Civil Action nos. 00-2329, 01-2104, December 18, 2003, Testimony of Dale Watson.

53. *Blais et al. v. The Islamic Republic of Iran et al.*, Testimony of Bruce Tefft.

54. FBI Director Louis Freeh underscored this point as well, noting that members of the 4404th Wing risked their lives to enforce the no-fly zone over southern Iraq "to stop Saddam Hussein from killing his Shiite people." See Freeh, "Khobar Towers."

55. *United States of America v. Ahmed Mughassil et al.*

56. US Department of Justice, FBI, "International Radical Fundamentalism."

57. *United States of America v. Ahmed Mughassil et al.*

58. Ibid.

59. Ibid.

60. Human Rights Watch, "Denied Dignity"; United Nations, High Commissioner for Refugees, Minorities at Risk Project, *Chronology for Shi'is in Bahrain*, 2004.

61. *Campbell et al. v. The Islamic Republic of Iran*, Testimony of Patrick Clawson.

62. US CIA, "Iranian Surveillance of US Persons and Facilities 1995."

63. Clarke, *Against All Enemies*, 113.

64. Con Coughlin, "Iran Builds Up Network of Terror Schools," *Daily Telegraph* (London), July 13, 1996; Jack Kelley, "Terrorist Camps Seen in Iran Likely Tied to Saudi Blasts," *USA Today*, August 2, 1996.

65. US CIA, "Lebanon's Hizballah."

66. US Department of Defense, "Report of Investigation Concerning the Khobar Towers Bombing."

67. National Commission on Terrorist Attacks upon the United States, *9/11 Commission Report*, released July 22, 2004, 60; Scheuer, *Through Our Enemies' Eyes*, 141.

68. "State Dept. Warns Americans to Be Careful in Saudi Arabia," *Washington Post*, December 10, 1995.

69. "U.S. Says Americans Threatened in Saudi Arabia," *Washington Post*, February 1, 1996.

70. Downing Assessment.

71. "Iranian Reports on the War in Brief: Saudi Ulema in Qom Call for Uprising against USA," *BBC Summary of World Broadcasts,* January 24, 1991.

72. Downing Assessment.

73. Ibid.

74. US Department of Defense, "Report of Investigation Concerning the Khobar Towers Bombing"; regarding criticism over how and when commanders made requests of the Saudis, see Record, "Independent Review of the Khobar Towers Bombing," 9.

75. Record, "Independent Review of the Khobar Towers Bombing."

76. US Department of Defense, "Report of Investigation Concerning the Khobar Towers Bombing."

77. Ibid.; Record, "Independent Review of the Khobar Towers Bombing."

78. US Department of Defense, "Report of Investigation Concerning the Khobar Towers Bombing."

79. Record, "Independent Review of the Khobar Towers Bombing."

80. Downing Assessment.

81. *United States of America v. Ahmed Mughassil et al.*

82. Ibid.

83. Ibid. Regarding al-Sayegh obtaining an international driver's license in Syria, see Federal Court of Canada, In the Matter of Hani Abd Rahim al-Sayegh.

84. *United States of America v. Ahmed Mughassil et al.*

85. Ibid.

86. Ibid.

87. US CIA, "Khobar Bombing [redacted]."

88. *United States of America v. Ahmed Mughassil et al.*

89. *Heiser et al. v. Islamic Republic of Iran,* Testimony of Louis Freeh.

90. US CIA, "Khobar Bombing [redacted]."

91. James Risen, "A Nation Challenged: A Suspect; US Traces Iran's Ties to Terror through a Lebanese," *New York Times,* January 17, 2002.

92. Nicholas Blanford, "Not If, but How," *NOWLebanon,* February 16, 2008.

93. Baer, *See No Evil,* 263; US Treasury Department, "Treasury Designates Hizballah Leadership," press release September 13, 2012.

94. *United States of America v. Ahmed Mughassil et al.*

95. US Congress, House, National Security Committee Staff Report, "Khobar Towers Bombing Incident," August, 14, 1996.

96. Downing Assessment.

97. *United States of America v. Ahmed Mughassil et al.*

98. Ibid.; US Congress, House, National Security Committee Staff Report, "Khobar Towers Bombing Incident."

99. *United States of America v. Ahmed Mughassil et al.*

100. Ibid.

101. US CIA, "Khobar Bombing [redacted]." The CIA report refers to a shipment of explosives from Lebanon to Saudi Arabia seized in March 1995, though that appears to be a typo that actually references the March 1996 seizure.

102. *United States of America v. Ahmed Mughassil et al.* Regarding the concealment of the bomb in the truck bomb, see *Blais et al. v. Islamic Republic of Iran,* Testimony of Bruce Tefft.

103. *United States of America v. Ahmed Mughassil et al.*

104. Thomas Friedman, "Stay Tuned," *New York Times*, March 25, 1997.

105. *Blais et al. v. Islamic Republic of Iran et al.*, Testimony of Bruce D. Tefft.

106. Thomas Friedman, "Where Is Jaafar?"; *New York Times*, January 8, 1997.

107. Elaine Sciolino, "U.S. Rebuffed by Syrians over Bombing," *New York Times*, March 26, 1997.

108. Ibid.

109. Friedman, "Stay Tuned."

110. Joshua Teitelbaum, "Holier than Thou: Saudi Arabia's Islamic Opposition," Washington Institute for Near East Policy (Washington, DC), 2000, p. 88.

111. *United States of America v. Ahmed Mughassil et al.*

112. Howard Schneider, "Jailed Saudi Denies Role in Bombing: Suspect in 1996 Attack Says He Was in Syria," *Washington Post*, March 25, 1997.

113. US CIA, "Khobar Bombing [redacted]."

114. Youssef M. Ibrahim, "Saudi Rebels Are Main Suspects in June Bombing of a U.S. Base," *New York Times*, August 15, 1996.

115. Atwan, *Secret History of al Qaeda*, 36.

116. National Commission on Terrorist Attacks upon the United States, *9/11 Commission Report,* released July 22, 2004, pp. 60–61.

117. *Heiser et al. v. Islamic Republic of Iran*, Testimony of Louis Freeh.

118. *Heiser et al. v. Islamic Republic of Iran*, Testimony of Dale Watson.

119. R. Jeffrey Smith, "Saudis Hold 40 Suspects in GI Quarters Bombing; Sources Say Riyadh's Evidence Suggests Iranian Role," *Washington Post*, November 1, 1996; Elsa Walsh, "Louis Freeh's Last Case," *New Yorker*, May 14, 2001.

120. Freeh, "Khobar Towers."

121. Sciolino, "U.S. Rebuffed by Syrians"; Anthony DePalma, "Canada Links Pro-Iranian Group to Saudi Attack on U.S. Barracks," *New York Times*, March 28, 1997.

122. Freeh, *My FBI*, 19.

123. "Suspect in Khobar Towers Bombing Fights Deportation to Saudi Arabia," *CNN*, October 5, 1999.

124. Freeh, *My FBI*, 19.

125. Statement of Louis J. Freeh, *Joint Investigation into September 11th,* October 8, 2002; see also Freeh, *My FBI*, 30–31.

126. Walsh, "Louis Freeh's Last Case."

127. US CIA, "Rafsanjani's Report Card."

128. Freeh, *My FBI*, 29.

129. *Heiser et al. v. Islamic Republic of Iran*, Testimony of Louis Freeh.

130. Freeh, *My FBI*, 31.

131. Amnesty International, "Saudi Arabia: Assaulting Human Rights in the Name of Counter-Terrorism," July 22, 2009.

132. "Saudi Militants Are Sentenced in '96 Bombing," *New York Times*, June 2, 2002.

133. Bruce Riedel, "The Clinton Administration," in Robin Wright, ed., *The Iran Primer: Power, Politics, and U.S. Policy* (Washington, DC: United States Institute of Peace, 2010), 139–42.

134. US Department of Justice, FBI, "Hizballah: International Terrorism Lebanon, Warning: Inform," January 28, 1997.

135. Tenet, *At the Center of the Storm*, 124.

136. James Risen, "A Nation Challenged: A Suspect; U.S. Traces Iran's Ties to Terror through a Lebanese," *New York Times*, January 17, 2002.

137. US Congress, Senate Committee on Armed Services, *Hearing: United States Central Command and United States Special Operations Command in Review of the Defense Authorization Request for Fiscal Year 2009 and the Future Years Defense Program*, 110th Cong., 2d sess., March 4, 2008, Statement of Admiral William J. Fallon.

8

Unit 1800

Targeting the Israeli Heartland

IN THE EARLY TO MID-1990S, with the Oslo peace accords signed and Palestinian autonomy slowly growing in the West Bank and Gaza Strip, opponents of peace funded, supported, and executed terrorist attacks to undermine the prospects for peace. Iran was especially active in promoting terrorism targeting Israel at this time. According to the Canadian Security Intelligence Service, "in February 1999, it was reported that Palestinian police had discovered documents that attest to the transfer of $35 million to Hamas from Iran's Ministry of Intelligence and Security (MOIS), money reportedly meant to finance terrorist activities against Israeli targets."[1] Iran's primary proxy group, however, has always been Hezbollah. It should therefore not be surprising that Hezbollah increased its support for Palestinian groups in the 1990s, invested in its own terrorist infrastructure in the West Bank, and went to great lengths to infiltrate operatives into Israel to collect intelligence and execute terror attacks. Hezbollah established a dedicated unit to pursue these goals—Unit 1800.

While Israel occupied southern Lebanon, Hezbollah largely satisfied itself with targeting Israeli forces there or at the border. Carrying out attacks along the border with Lebanon in Israel's far north was one thing, but to effectively undermine the peace process, Hezbollah leaders decided they needed to target key Israeli decision makers, symbolic sites, or ordinary Israeli civilians in downtown shopping districts. Hezbollah was out to hit the Israeli heartland.

For its part, Iran sought to intensify and coordinate the terrorist operations of the various Palestinian groups it supported through its primary proxy, Hezbollah. According to a Palestinian intelligence document dated October 31, 2001, officials from Hamas, Palestinian Islamic Jihad (PIJ), and Hezbollah met in Damascus "in an attempt to increase the joint activity inside [i.e., in Israel, the West Bank, and Gaza] with financial aid from Iran." The meeting was held "after an Iranian message had been transferred to the Hamas and Islamic Jihad leaderships, according to which they must not allow a calming down [of the situation on the ground] at this period." The Iranian funds, the report added, were to be transferred to these groups through Hezbollah.[2]

From Iran's perspective, only Hezbollah's direct involvement would guarantee a truly successful terror campaign targeting Israel. According to US officials, shortly after Palestinian violence erupted in September 2000, Iran assigned Imad Mughniyeh to bolster the operational capacity of Palestinian militant groups, specifically Hamas and PIJ. According to a former Clinton administration official, "Mughniyeh got orders from Tehran to work with Hamas."[3] In fact, to carry out the March 27, 2002, "Passover massacre" suicide bombing, Hamas reportedly relied on the guidance of a Hezbollah expert to build an extra-potent bomb.[4] Following the death of Palestinian leader Yasser Arafat in November 2004, Hezbollah was said to have received an additional $22 million from Iranian intelligence to support Palestinian terrorist groups and foment instability.[5]

This assignment surely struck a chord for Mughniyeh and his lieutenants, who already operated a program aimed at infiltrating operatives into Israel through third countries in order to collect intelligence, train local Palestinian groups, and execute spectacular terrorist attacks deep within Israeli territory. Beginning in 1995, a select group of operational leaders within Hezbollah's Islamic Jihad Organization (IJO) developed plans to penetrate Israel's defenses, in the process tapping their extensive support networks abroad. Starting in the mid-1990s—unlike in his earlier operational activity in Europe, which focused on carrying out attacks there—Mughniyeh tasked his European networks with providing clandestine support for operatives who would use Europe as a launch pad for infiltrating operatives into Israel. An Israeli intelligence report assessed that "the most dangerous component in Mughniyeh's activity and the arena in which he excels is building a Hezbollah operational infrastructure abroad. This enables him to send more and more attackers from various arenas in the world, while exploiting the international system and its laws to implement these missions."[6]

One of Mughniyeh's key deputies within Unit 1800 would be Qais Obeid, an Israeli Arab and experienced drug smuggler whose intimate knowledge of Israel would prove invaluable for realizing Mughniyeh's desire to take the fight into Israel's cities and towns.[7] Mughniyeh was now well positioned to pair his own international operations expertise with Obeid's extensive experience in the Palestinian and Israeli Arab communities in Israel, the West Bank, and Gaza. Under Mughniyeh's command, Obeid would become Hezbollah's point man for recruiting Palestinians and Israeli Arabs and, with the help of Hezbollah's European networks, infiltrating operatives into Israel through Europe.

For years, Mughniyeh—aided by a handful of lieutenants—personally oversaw Hezbollah's clandestine networks in Europe.[8] By 1995, Mughniyeh was ready to use this network once more—this time to help a highly educated, English-speaking, light-skinned Hezbollah devotee infiltrate Israel via Europe.

Sneaking into Israel through the
Front Door: Hussein Mikdad

At 7:15 AM on April 12, 1996, in room 27 of the Lawrence Hotel in East Jerusalem, a man quietly prepared a bomb on his bed. Without warning, the bomb detonated, shattering windows and ripping doors off their hinges, one of which only narrowly missed a sleeping child. Miraculously, only the man preparing the bomb was injured—although his injury was dire. Israeli police and first responders arriving at the scene assumed the explosion was the result of a gas leak. A deep crater in the man's room, however, indicated a less benign cause.[9]

The Shin Bet took over the investigation, suspecting the explosion was a bomb, but the agents were not yet clear why someone would target a small, two-star hotel in East Jerusalem. Searching the rubble, investigators found a shattered Sony radio and residue of military-grade C4 explosive, a type not commonly employed by local terrorists, who typically opted for crude, homemade explosives. Investigators also found a hair dryer and a blender—two appliances often used to mix raw explosives— and a pile of rusty nails, a common component in suicide bombs.[10]

Investigators found other puzzling evidence at the scene as well: sheets from a notebook listing phone numbers, accounting papers in English with a firm's address in London, a roll of undeveloped film, a round-trip plane ticket from Zurich to Tel Aviv on Swissair, travel brochures and tourist maps of Zurich, and a British passport. The passport bore an official visa entry to Israel and showed its owner had traveled to Europe, the United States, and South America.[11]

The passport belonged to Andrew Jonathan Charles Newman, a British citizen born in London in 1970. The Mossad contacted Scotland Yard about its findings and soon located the original owner of the passport. The real Andrew Newman had told police his passport was stolen on a camping trip to France.[12] Investigators would later determine that someone affiliated with Hezbollah subsequently purchased the passport on the black market.[13] Further, when the roll of film was developed, Israeli intelligence found two pictures of the man shown in the passport standing in front of the Dome of the Rock in Jerusalem. Other photos of public areas were also found on the developed roll, including the popular Dizengoff Center in Tel Aviv, the site of a suicide bombing a month earlier that left 16 people dead and wounded 130 others.[14]

The Lawrence Hotel affair had its roots in late 1995, when Hezbollah leaders decided to carry out an attack in a major Israeli city, a new type of operation. In September 1995, Israel and the nascent Palestinian Authority (PA) signed the Interim Agreement on the West Bank and the Gaza Strip, which marked the conclusion of negotiations on the implementation of the first part of the Oslo Accords. To those hopeful for a two-state agreement that would end the Israeli-Palestinian conflict, the interim agreement was a clear step in the right direction. To opponents of peace, foremost the Islamic Republic of Iran and its terrorist proxies, the agreement was a siren indicating the need to intensify attacks aimed at undermining the prospects for peace. Hezbollah would now use its global support network to infiltrate highly trained operatives deep into Israel as well.[15] In order to carry out the operation in Israel at Iran's behest, Hezbollah would need someone who fit a particular profile. The man they chose was Hussein Mikdad.

Hussein Mikdad was born in Lassa, a town some forty miles north of Beirut. The oldest of four siblings, Mikdad grew up alongside the Christians of his village. In 1975, as the Lebanese civil war began, the area's Shi'a Muslims fled for fear of sectarian violence. Mikdad, only twelve years old at the time, and his family landed in Haret Hreik, the Hezbollah stronghold in the Dahiya suburbs of southern Beirut.[16] Mikdad eventually entered the Lebanese American University, where he earned a bachelor's degree in business management. "When I was at the university, I adopted the ideas of revolution, of change, democracy, and justice," Mikdad said.[17] After he graduated in 1991, his Hezbollah connections helped him get a job as a teacher and then, two years later, as the chief accountant for Hezbollah's humanitarian, or social service, operations in Beirut.[18]

In September 1995, Mikdad was approached by a man who went by Abu Muhammad and who explained that he ran a section of Hezbollah's "overseas security apparatus"—the IJO—that handles intelligence and conducts overseas terrorist attacks. The IJO saw in Mikdad not only a fervent believer but also someone who could pass as a European. In recruiting Mikdad, Abu Muhammad appealed to his vanity: "You have many attributes we need. You have leadership qualities and a European appearance. You have an academic education and you speak English." Two days after his meeting with Muhammad, Mikdad was transferred to Hezbollah's security branch. He was now a special case recruit.[19]

In November 1995, Mikdad was driven by Hezbollah operatives to the Iranian-run Janta training camp in the eastern Bekaa Valley, where in just under two months he mastered the art of guerrilla warfare.[20] He learned how to fire submachine guns, evade and conduct surveillance, and transform the timer from a standard digital watch into a timer for a bomb.[21] He specialized in assembling explosive devices using C4. Only after completing his training was Mikdad informed of his selection to engage in a special mission for Hezbollah. Abu Muhammad personally escorted Mikdad from the training camp back to Beirut in January 1996, telling Mikdad that he was "now a member of the security apparatus . . . it is best not to talk about it, even to your family." Abu Muhammad told him to get a job in Beirut and await further instructions.[22]

Mikdad did not have to wait long. A couple of weeks later, in mid-January, Abu Muhammad gave Mikdad an urgent assignment: infiltrate Israel by walking through the front door of Ben Gurion International Airport. Mikdad, Abu Muhammad continued, would "serve as an example for later attacks" by being "the first in a line of fighters who [would] enter Israel in this way." To secure this legacy, however, his action must be "impressive."[23]

The photograph of Mikdad used for his forged passport was taken in March 1996 at the Iranian embassy in Beirut. According to Israeli intelligence, the theft and altering of such passports by Hezbollah operatives in Europe is widespread, and the documents are "used by the organization's activists in their travels all over the world."[24]

In one operation, according to a 1994 FBI report, Hezbollah members presented photo-substituted passports and fraudulent visa applications at a US embassy. Eighteen individuals successfully obtained passports in this manner.[25]

Abu Muhammad also provided Mikdad with a small clock radio that concealed bomb-making materials. The detonator was hidden in a hollow tube that ran into the antenna and was wired to the radio timer. Abu Muhammad made sure Mikdad received documents to support his cover story as a British accountant, as well as a new suitcase and new clothes. The explosive was vacuum-packed, making it difficult to detect. Only then, at the Iranian embassy, did Mikdad learn that the mastermind of his operation was the infamous Imad Mughniyeh.[26]

Hezbollah's plot was rooted in a broader strategy of infiltrating operatives into Israel through neutral third countries using doctored travel documents from similarly neutral countries. When the time came for him to depart on his mission, Mikdad told his wife he was traveling to Turkey to buy leather coats for an import business. Instead, he set off for Israel via Syria, Austria, and Switzerland.[27]

Fearing a cousin who worked at the Beirut airport would recognize him, Mikdad convinced Abu Muhammad the two should drive to Damascus and fly out of Damascus International Airport. After touching down in Vienna on Austrian Airlines flight 708 and parting ways with Abu Muhammad, Mikdad converted $200 into Austrian currency. From the airport, he took a taxi to Westbahnhof, Vienna's train station, where he met at a café with a Hezbollah contact who provided him with his false British passport. The two spent about an hour together, during which the Hezbollah contact likely reviewed other elements of the operation with Mikdad, who then caught a train to Zurich. Abu Muhammad's men were reportedly on board, secretly watching and protecting Mikdad, although without Mikdad's knowledge.[28]

On April 2, Mikdad arrived at Zurich's Flughaven railway station. At a booth in the station, he printed fifty business cards identifying him as an accountant from London. He then called the Regina Hotel, presumably to check for a vacancy and book a room but possibly to speak to another contact already there, took a taxi to the hotel, and checked into room 217. Abu Muhammad called to set up a meeting for the next day at 9 AM under the big clock at the central train station in the city's old town. For the next two days Mikdad and Abu Muhammad walked along Lake Zurich, talking about religion and philosophy and reviewing details of the plan. This would be their last opportunity to refine the operation, finalize code words, review the details of Mikdad's cover identity as Andrew Newman, and bolster his resolve. Mikdad's goal in the operation was to revive the momentum of attacks in Israeli cities, in essence spurring on Hamas and PIJ to carry out more of the spectacular suicide bombings to which Israel, as an open society, was so vulnerable.[29]

At the Swissair travel office in Zurich, Mikdad paid cash for a round-trip plane ticket to Tel Aviv. Back in his hotel room, he practiced penning Andrew Newman's signature. In Zurich, Abu Muhammad received names and phone numbers from Iranian agents of Palestinians who would assist Mikdad in Jerusalem by providing him with additional explosives and guiding him if needed. To put his operative at ease the night before his big operation, Abu Muhammad set out to show Mikdad a good time; witnesses claim to have spotted Mikdad out in Zurich escorted by an unidentified woman.[30]

On April 4, Abu Muhammad accompanied Mikdad to the airport to review last-minute details. He reiterated that Mikdad was about to make a name for himself. He would be famous. The two set fixed times for communication, twice a day from public phones. After arriving at the airport, Mikdad checked his bags at the counter but kept the radio in his carry-on, which was searched manually by airport security officers after passing through the scanner. The security measures included the use of a special vacuuming device capable of detecting explosives residue. Mikdad was asked to turn on the radio to ensure it was what it appeared to be, and the soft classical music convinced the security officers the device was harmless. Mikdad boarded his flight without further hassle, and a few short hours later Swissair flight 314 arrived in Tel Aviv at 5:05 PM. According to Mikdad, he cleared Israeli customs on his forged British passport with no problems. Suppressing his nerves at the security counter, he was relieved when the Israeli officer looked at his passport, signed and stamped it, and welcomed him to Israel.[31]

His first stop was not Jerusalem but Tel Aviv. Mikdad checked into the Center Hotel near the Dizengoff shopping mall in central Tel Aviv. No one at the desk noticed when he misspelled his own last name on the hotel forms, signing "Nemam."[32] For three days he scoped out Tel Aviv for prime spots to detonate bombs. Every night at 8:00, he called Abu Muhammad from the same public phone in Tel Aviv to one of two public phones just outside the Zurich central train station. Mikdad and Abu Muhammad spoke only in code. Abu Muhammad asked, "How are the girls in Tel Aviv?" to which Mikdad responded, "I haven't found the right one just yet." Mikdad then asked if it was a good time to get in touch with their friends in Jerusalem, and Abu Muhammad approved. The next morning Mikdad took a train to Jerusalem, where he met two local contacts. They took him to a local fruit and vegetable market, which Mikdad viewed as an ideal spot for a bombing. They drove to a modern shopping mall, but the mall was not crowded and security was tight. They then strolled through an outdoor pedestrian mall that was popular with diners and tourists. Confident he had found what he was looking for, Mikdad returned to Tel Aviv.[33]

On April 9, at 10:30 AM, Mikdad took a taxi back to Jerusalem, where he checked into the Lawrence Hotel, right outside the Old City.[34] Hotel employees would later describe Mikdad as polite and quiet, leaving in the mornings carrying maps and a tourist's camera, and returning at night.[35] Room 27, however, had become Mikdad's base of operations. One of his contacts brought him a kilogram of plastic explosives, a box of rusty nails, and some basic appliances. Mikdad then met another of his contacts to discuss the first attack and requested another five kilograms of explosives. That night, he joined prayers at the al-Aqsa mosque and had his photograph taken in front of the Dome of the Rock.[36]

On April 11, Mikdad held a final meeting in Jerusalem with his local collaborators. They chose the site for the first bombing and delegated assignments. Mikdad called to report to Abu Muhammad, who offered his approval and blessing.[37] Mikdad would strike a mighty blow against the Israelis. The preoperational surveillance he conducted at other sites could be used in future attacks by others who would follow in his footsteps.

On the morning of April 12, Mikdad sat on his bed and dismantled the clock radio. He removed the detonator from the antenna and clamped it to the cord. He was confident, having practiced this maneuver a dozen times, and attached the detonator to the C4, which abruptly exploded. Later, alive but maimed, Mikdad wondered how the accident had happened. What had he done wrong? Perhaps his contact provided low-quality or faulty material? Or perhaps the Israelis penetrated his small network of local facilitators? The Israelis, happy to let such questions hang in the open for future plotters to ruminate about, refused to answer.[38]

The night after the explosion, Mikdad's wife and daughter were quickly taken away from their home in Dahiya and brought to Lassa by Hezbollah. The family issued two statements, one denying any connection to the bombing and another denying Hussein Mikdad's very existence.[39] Mikdad spent two years in the Ayalon Prison in Ramla under constant medical observation.[40] The explosion had blinded him and blown off both his legs and one hand. Then, in summer 1998, Israel agreed to a prisoner exchange with Hezbollah through German mediation. Dozens of Hezbollah and Amal prisoners and the bodies of still more who died fighting Israel were swapped for the body of Itamar Ilya, an Israeli soldier killed in combat in Lebanon. Among the people released back to Hezbollah was Hussein Mikdad. As he crossed the Lebanese army checkpoint at Kfar Falous, his wife and mother rushed to greet him.[41]

The German Hezbollahi: Stephan Joseph Smyrek

Even as Hussein Mikdad sat in Israeli custody in 1997, two new recruits trained in Hezbollah camps were primed to infiltrate Israel. Unlike Mikdad, however, these recruits were not Lebanese operatives capable of passing as foreigners but foreigners selected for recruitment by Hezbollah spotters in Malaysia and Germany, respectively. Both would travel to Lebanon for training in 1997 in advance of their missions.

The Malaysian recruit, Zainal bin Talib, was tasked primarily with collecting intelligence. This surveillance may have been tied to unconfirmed threat reporting suggesting that Southeast Asian Hezbollah operatives were planning an attack in Israel in 2000. Bin Talib's intelligence collection was so successful that Hezbollah dispatched him to Israel twice within a year, first in late 1999 and then again in summer 2000. Israeli intelligence services did not learn of his visits until long after they had occurred. Three other Indonesian recruits were selected for similar infiltration missions to Israel, though the exposure of Hezbollah's Southeast Asian network prevented these recruits from being dispatched on their missions.[42]

The German operative, a convert to Islam named Stephan Joseph Smyrek (also known as Abdul Karim), was less successful. Forewarned about Smyrek by German security, Israeli authorities arrested him on arrival at Ben Gurion International Airport on November 28, 1997. Like Mikdad before him, Smyrek had a mission to open a new front in Hezbollah's war with Israel by carrying out a suicide bombing in a heavily populated Israeli city.[43]

Smyrek was born in Detmold, Germany. His parents divorced when he was four years old, and when his mother remarried, Stephan moved with her and his British stepfather to England, where he attended boarding school from 1982 to 1987. After graduating he returned to Germany, serving in the army (Bundeswehr) from 1989 to 1993. Smyrek reportedly served a short prison sentence for couriering drugs before his 1994 conversion to Islam. He may have been under police protection briefly after testifying against some of his former drug-dealer associates. In Braunschweig, the Lower Saxony city where he lived, he spent time with a conservative Egyptian woman, but the romance ended badly when the woman's father forbade her from continuing to see Smyrek. Apparently smitten, Smyrek wrote her love songs, including one hinting that he would be engaged in some kind of terrorist operation.[44] He studied Arabic, worked odd jobs, frequented a Turkish-owned pizza shop, and attended a mosque. It was there, without direction in life, that Smyrek was recruited into Hezbollah.[45]

Germany was long a center of Hezbollah activity in Europe, and German security officials saw Imad Mughniyeh, in close concert with Iran, as the key leader of the group's efforts related to "planning, preparing and carrying out terrorist operations outside of Lebanon."[46] Bassam Makki's 1989 plot to bomb Israeli targets in Germany offers one stark case in point (see chapter 3), but Hezbollah's activities in Germany did not end there. In 1994, for example, Germany issued a warning related to the possible entry into the country of "a group sent by Mughniyeh to carry out attacks against U.S. targets."[47] According to Hezbollah scholar Magnus Ranstorp, several senior Hezbollah commanders shared responsibility with Mughniyeh for the group's "special operations abroad" in Europe, including Hussein Khalil, Ibrahim Aqil, Muhammad Haydar, Kharib Nasser, and Abd al-Hamadi.[48]

Over time, the Hezbollah support network in Germany would grow. According to the annual reports of Germany's domestic intelligence service, the Federal Office for the Protection of the Constitution, some 800 members or supporters of Hezbollah lived in Germany in 2002. That number increased to around 850 by 2004 and to 900 by 2005. Among "Arab Islamist groups" in Germany, Hezbollah had become the second largest by 2005.[49] That year, a German court deported a Hezbollah member who had lived in the country for twenty years. Though Germany had not banned Hezbollah as a terrorist group, the Dusseldorf court ruled the man was "a member of an organization that supports international terrorism" and refused to extend his visa.[50] German security agencies "intensively watch" groups like Hezbollah and Hamas, German minister of interior Wolfgang Schaeuble commented in summer 2006. Clearly referring to Stephan Smyrek, he noted that one reason for his concern was that "in the past, there were attempts to recruit suicide attackers in Germany."[51]

According to Israeli intelligence, Smyrek was recruited by Hezbollah spotters in Germany who saw in him "the picture of a Christian European—blond hair, blue eyes."[52] He could travel more freely in the West than a Lebanese Hezbollah operative. His recruitment, an Israeli report concluded, was "made possible by a spotting pool operated by Mughniyeh in Europe, especially in Germany. It enables Hezbollah to spot and recruit Europeans who support and identify with the organization's goals."[53] At some point, Israeli intelligence believed, Fahdi Hamdar and his cousin

Mohammed, Hezbollah talent spotters, noticed Smyrek's "virulent [expressions of] hatred for Israel" at a Braunschweig mosque, recognized his yearning for focus and purpose in his life, and suggested he consider a trip to Lebanon to attend a Hezbollah military training camp.[54]

It is unclear when exactly the Hamdar cousins made their pitch or how long Smyrek took to consider it, but by the time his mother visited him in May 1997, his mind was made up. Smyrek told his despondent mother that he was going on a trip and wanted to break off all contact with her. Asked where he was going, he simply replied, "You better not know where I am going or what I am going to do." His mother had not seen him since he converted to Islam. "I didn't recognize him," she would later recount. "He had changed and behaved very strangely." Within weeks, Smyrek would be in Beirut, his first stop en route to a Hezbollah training camp.[55]

Wary he might be an informer and keen to see him prove his commitment to the cause, Hezbollah security officials insisted Smyrek visit them in Beirut before his admission to a Bekaa Valley training camp. He arrived in Beirut in August 1997, where he was questioned at length before being accepted as a Hezbollah recruit and sent on for training. Over two months Smyrek trained in weapons and explosives in the Bekaa Valley. Then, having passed the scrutiny of Hezbollah security and completed an intense course, Smyrek was ready to be deployed.[56]

In November 1997, Smyrek left Lebanon and returned to Germany. His Hezbollah handlers instructed him to travel to Amsterdam, where he claimed to have lost his passport and received a new German passport bearing no evidence of his recent trip to Lebanon.[57] Despite this precaution, however, German security services had already picked up on Smyrek's radicalization, his travel to Lebanon, his return to Germany, and his intent to carry out an attack in Israel. It remains unknown at what point along his journey from German soldier to Hezbollah recruit the German security services identified Smyrek as a person of interest, but by the time he attempted to board an El Al Airlines flight to Israel at Amsterdam's Schiphol Airport, his name had been added to Interpol's terrorist watch list.[58] Dutch security officials detained Smyrek only briefly at the airport, but by the time they released him he had missed his flight. Dutch authorities presumably used this time not only to question Smyrek but also to warn Israeli authorities of his pending arrival. Smyrek reportedly contacted his Hezbollah handlers, who insisted that the mission go ahead. He boarded the next flight to Israel, during which he reportedly sat next to undercover Israeli officers and was arrested on arrival at Ben Gurion International Airport.[59]

According to Israeli police, after conducting surveillance of possible attack sites, Smyrek was to meet his Hezbollah handler in Turkey. Based on his surveillance reports (and, presumably, the handler's assessment of his commitment to carrying out the attack), the handler would decide on Smyrek's final target and attack plan.[60]

According to his confession, ever since he converted to Islam and set his heart on becoming a suicide bomber, Smyrek's attack of preference was a suicide bombing in Tel Aviv or Haifa.[61] According to Israeli intelligence, Smyrek devised alternative plans, in the event he could not enter Israel, to carry out an unspecified attack targeting the Israeli embassy then in Bonn or murder Israeli diplomats abroad.[62] Smyrek's

Hezbollah handlers supported his suicide bombing proposal but instructed him to collect as much information as possible about these alternative targets so that they could make a fully informed decision on the final target at their meeting in Turkey.[63] As in Mikdad's case, local facilitators were to provide Smyrek with explosives for the attack.[64]

Smyrek's arrest disrupted these plans. According to Israeli police, Smyrek arrived with $4,000, a video camera, maps of Israel, and unspecified "electronic communication devices."[65] Videotape in his possession when he was arrested showed footage of himself delivering the message Hezbollah requested he make denouncing Israel and proclaiming his desire to be a martyr for Hezbollah.[66] Under interrogation Smyrek confessed to plotting a suicide attack, expressed no remorse, and pledged to "continue his efforts to kill Israelis" if given the chance.[67] He detailed the basic code he had developed to communicate with his Hezbollah handlers based on references to books he owned.[68] He was convicted by an Israeli court and sentenced to ten years in jail for aiding and abetting Hezbollah by planning a suicide attack on its behalf. State prosecutors in Hanover, Germany, also indicted Smyrek for "planning to take his own life and that of others in a bombing attack," but Israeli prosecutors chose to try him there instead of extraditing him to Germany—a move that created friction with their German counterparts.[69] Smyrek still expressed no remorse after his conviction, and declined an offer to serve his time in a German prison.[70]

Israeli prosecutors were unable to convince German authorities to arrest Fahdi and Mohammed Hamdar for spotting and recruiting Smyrek into Hezbollah. As one former Israeli official wistfully recalled, "The people who recruited Smyrek managed to escape capture. The Germans did not arrest them. It was pretty strange."[71]

At the time of Smyrek's arrest, Hezbollah denied any knowledge of him and insisted the entire incident was an Israeli fabrication.[72] But after six years in jail, Israel released Smyrek under the terms of a prisoner swap negotiated with Hezbollah to secure the release of a kidnapped Israeli. Before leaving Israel, Smyrek granted an interview to a German documentary filmmaker. "It is an honor to die for Islam and for Allah," he said in the interview. "When the order comes you have to carry it out and there is no time to ask if there is a God or not, or to think what will happen after you're dead, without feeling you simply have to lay down your life as Allah decreed."[73]

Smyrek returned to Germany after his release. Though he signed a document renouncing violence as part of his early release from prison, Smyrek had told the documentary interviewer he remained eager to carry out an attack. A purportedly free man, Smyrek reportedly was still subject to police observation while in Germany.[74]

German security services remain concerned about the activities of the nearly thousand-strong Hezbollah support network in the country. The group's supporters reportedly meet in some thirty cultural centers and mosques across the country, including five in the North Rhine–Westphalia region alone.[75] And while their primary activities focus on raising funds for the organization back in Lebanon, they also function as a logistical support network for the group's weapons procurement and operational activities.[76] From time to time, intelligence suggests Hezbollah operatives may be plotting attacks within Germany. In August 2008, for example,

Germany's federal criminal police chief warned that Hezbollah sleeper cells might have been planning an attack in Germany. Investigators were reportedly monitoring as many as 200 suspected Hezbollah militant sleeper cells in Germany at the time, according to the police chief.[77]

For its part, Hezbollah has sought to normalize its presence in Germany and elsewhere in Europe. From 2002 to 2003, for example, Hezbollah officials visited Britain, Denmark, Germany, Italy (twice), and Switzerland (also twice).[78] Hezbollah even reportedly attempted to purchase a building in Berlin's Neukoelln district in June 2002. "The building was declared intended to be a cultural-social-religious center," an Israeli intelligence report noted, "but it is actually designed to be the general headquarters for Hezbollah's operational activity in Europe, especially Germany."[79]

In the wake of the Smyrek episode, Hezbollah continued to recruit operatives and train them for infiltration missions into Israel. At the same time, the group pursued a parallel project aimed not at sending its agents into Israel but at luring Israeli targets to them. Ironically, Qais Obeid, the key person behind Hezbollah's abduction program, was himself a citizen of Israel.

Qais Obeid: Hezbollah's Chief Abduction Agent

The Obeid family had deep roots in the State of Israel, centered on Taibeh, a town in what is commonly referred to as the Arab Triangle, a block of Israeli Arab towns bordering the northeast corner of the West Bank. Diab Obeid served as a member of the Israeli Knesset, on the Arab List, which was affiliated with the Mapai Party (the forerunner of today's Labor Party) from 1961 to 1973.[80] These were turbulent times, including the 1967 Six Day War, which brought the West Bank, Gaza, the Golan Heights, and the Sinai Peninsula under Israeli control and prompted a sharp upswing in Palestinian and broader Arab nationalism, as well as eventually radical Islamist extremism. As Israeli Arabs growing up amid these competing emotional and political currents, some members of Diab Obeid's family drifted away from his liberal political leanings and toward crime and, ultimately, religious extremism.

Diab's son, Hassan, served as deputy mayor of Taibeh in the 1980s, and both father and son were said to be well connected within Israeli political circles. The third generation of the Obeid clan also seemed to be doing well. Hassan's five sons included a physician in Germany, a manager of the Taibeh branch of one of Israel's largest banks, and three business owners, including Qais, the youngest, who was in the jewelry business. But in 1989 Hassan was arrested for trafficking large quantities of drugs from Lebanon and sentenced to ten years in prison. Released three years early, he died a short time later.[81]

How or why Hassan drifted into the underworld of drug smuggling remains unclear. What is clear is that by the time he was arrested he was no small player. Not only did the counternarcotics operation that led to his arrest reportedly involve a significant quantity of drugs, but he was arrested along with Mohammed Biro, known as the "Middle East drug lord" for his oversized role in the narcotics underworld in Lebanon.[82] In a twist more common to spy novels than real life, Mohammed Biro, a one-time source for Israeli intelligence, switched allegiance and allied himself and his drug-running enterprise with Hezbollah. In 1989, Biro was sentenced to fifteen years in prison. Sometime after his own release from prison, Hassan asked his sons to visit Mohammed Biro in jail, which they did. Qais returned several times and developed a relationship of his own with Biro, and through him, with Qayed Biro, Mohammed's youngest son, and other members of the Biro family living in Lebanon.

Qais was facing difficulties at the time of his meetings with Biro. His jewelry business had taken a turn for the worse, leading him to dabble in several other ventures, some shady, including a check-cashing scheme. Qais slipped in and out of debt, regularly relying on his family to bail him out but never fully finding his footing. In 1996, Qais and Ofer Schneitman, his Jewish-Israeli partner who also owned a gun shop, were arrested on charges of conspiring to sell ammunition to Palestinians in the West Bank. Qais's accomplice was sentenced to thirteen months in prison for selling 2,000 rounds of ammunition to an undercover Shin Bet agent posing as a Palestinian. Qais got a lucky break and was released after a month's detention. A short time later, Qais was rearrested on charges of carrying a gun without a permit and spent about a year and a half in prison.[83]

As he stumbled from failed business endeavors to debt to criminal activities, Qais Obeid grew closer to the Biro clan. Qais and Qayed Biro met several times in Europe, providing—investigators would later surmise—Qais's entrée to Hezbollah. Over time, Qais found in the service of Hezbollah the meaning and success that eluded him as a businessman and criminal. For a few months, maybe a little over a year, he operated covertly out of Israel. Later, in September 2000, just as the second Palestinian intifada was breaking out in the West Bank and Gaza Strip, Qais left Israel and turned up in Beirut, where he assumed a senior leadership position in Hezbollah's newly minted Unit 1800, which was responsible for supporting Palestinian terrorist groups and abducting Israelis.[84]

Qais Obeid's first attempt to kidnap Israelis on Hezbollah's behalf took place in July 2000, while he was still in Israel. That month, Obeid met with Gaza businessman Faiz Shohan and Nasser Ayad, a member of the Palestinian Authority special operations Force 17, to iron out a plan to smuggle $100,000 worth of cocaine from Lebanon, to Europe, and onward to Israel's Ashdod port. Shohan would use his shipping permit to transport containers from Ashdod to Gaza. At the time, the three also considered kidnapping Israelis and smuggling weapons into Gaza. Then the second intifada erupted. Although Qais fled to Lebanon, Ayad and Shohan revised their plan, with Obeid providing input and oversight from abroad in his new position with Hezbollah's Unit 1800. By December 2000, the plan was for Obeid to coordinate the smuggling of weapons—fifty Kalashnikov and M-16 rifles, rocket-propelled grenade launchers, and tens of thousands of rounds of ammunition—into Israel from Lebanon. Shohan would earn $30,000 for using his shipping license to move the container of weapons to Ashdod and from there to Gaza.[85]

But the plot would be altered once more, this time by Obeid and his friend Qayed Biro, who devised a plot to kidnap an Israeli soldier or civilian hitchhiker and use the captive as a bargaining chip to negotiate the release of Qayed's father, Mohammed. The profile of their target victim was a hitchhiker in his or her early twenties, a common sight in Israel. The pressure to secure the release of a young Israeli, especially a soldier, would be immense for any Israeli government, maximizing the plotters' negotiating leverage. After sedating the victim, they planned to stuff the victim into a container and smuggle the container through the Karni checkpoint into Gaza. From there the victim would be transferred to a fishing vessel to be met at prearranged coordinates by a boat from Lebanon carrying Qayed Biro and Qais Obeid along with drugs and weapons. The drugs and weapons would be taken back to Gaza, while Biro and Obeid would accompany the prisoner to Lebanon. The plot never came off, however, because Israeli commandos detained Nasser Ayad in January 2001. Within days, an Israeli targeted rocket attack killed Iyad's father, Col. Mansur Iyad, a senior Force 17 official who was recruiting cells in Gaza to carry out attacks at Hezbollah's behest. That same month, Faiz Shohan was arrested as well.[86]

Qais Obeid was a busy man, however, and this was not the only or even the most daring abduction he was then plotting. Even before he departed for Beirut, Obeid began to lay the groundwork for a plot that would involve Hezbollah networks as far afield as Germany and Abu Dhabi and deliver to Hezbollah a retired Israel Defense Forces (IDF) colonel whose current business clients gave him access to highly sensitive Israeli intelligence. The abduction that commenced would not only prove an intelligence bonanza for Hezbollah, it would ultimately enable Hezbollah to secure the release of more than 400 prisoners from Israeli jails—an accomplishment that dramatically boosted the organization's political stature in Lebanon and throughout the Arab world. It would also reveal the breadth of Hezbollah's operational reach across two continents and into Israel itself.

Bait and Trap: Luring an Israeli Target to Beirut via Europe

Around August 2000, Qais Obeid visited the elderly Mohammed Biro in jail one last time before leaving for Lebanon. Biro still had years to serve on his prison term, even as age and infirmity were catching up with him. In September, just as the second intifada was gaining momentum in the West Bank and Gaza Strip, Obeid booked a flight to Germany, where his brother lived. At Ben Gurion International Airport, authorities allowed him to travel, but only once he signed a document declaring he had no intention of contacting a "foreign agent" or representative of an "enemy group" while abroad. The declaration, which bears consequences only for resident citizens subject to local law enforcement, suggests Israeli authorities expected Obeid to return home to Israel. But Obeid had no such plans.[87]

Obeid and an Israeli named Elhanan Tannenbaum first met as children, and their lives intersected from time to time as they grew up.[88] "Elhanan visited our village and we met him sometimes in Tel Aviv restaurants," Qais Obeid's brother Aqram noted.[89] In the 1990s, Israel's Channel 2 television reported, Tannenbaum "forged ties with several elements of the Israeli and Palestinian underworlds, Obeid among them."[90] From about 1995 on, Tannenbaum and Obeid partnered in a business working with Palestinian money changers in the West Bank. Despite having advantages in life—Tannenbaum rose to the rank of colonel as a reservist in the IDF—both men suffered business failures, fell into debt, and engaged in criminal enterprises. By 2000 they both reportedly owed large sums to the Palestinian money changers with whom they did business.[91] Tannenbaum reportedly convinced an army buddy to arrange for him to serve extra reserve duty, explaining he needed the extra pay.[92]

During his reserve duty Tannenbaum worked on a variety of sensitive military issues, even as his financial situation and links to Obeid increased his vulnerability to recruitment by enemy states or terrorist groups.[93] Until Israel redeployed its forces south of the Lebanese border in May 2000, Tannenbaum maintained business ties in Lebanon, primarily selling pharmaceuticals. It was during his business trips to Lebanon, police would later assess, that Tannenbaum first met the Lebanese drug dealers with whom he would later work.[94] Shortly after the Israeli-Lebanese border was closed, effectively ending that business opportunity, Obeid proposed that the two men go into business together by leveraging Obeid's Arab-world contacts and Tannenbaum's salesmanship.[95]

Told by Obeid that he needed to travel to Europe to finalize a part of this new business deal, Tannenbaum booked a flight to Brussels for October 4. As he prepared to leave, he offered only one sign of possible reservations about the trip. His daughter Keren would later recall his last words before leaving: "I will take care of myself."[96] As a reserve officer who still consulted for major arms industry companies, he had reason to be cautious. An official with one of the companies Tannenbaum worked with conceded the work dealt "with the [Israeli] Defense Ministry's most sensitive technologies." The firm had "outsourced [work to Tannenbaum] for a number of contracts," the company's security officer conceded.[97] Strangely, however, Tannenbaum exhibited little of the caution common among people working on sensitive, classified matters. He reportedly boasted about his high security clearance and, according to police statements, would wear his military uniform to impress people at business meetings.[98]

Tannenbaum felt he had built a relationship of trust with Obeid, and with accumulating gambling and business debts, he desperately needed the income promised by this new business partnership. He departed Israel for Brussels believing he was meeting with some of Obeid's business contacts. A few days later he was reported missing.[99]

Tannenbaum told a friend and sometimes business partner before he left that he was heading to London, not Brussels. "He went to Europe to bring cash to conduct a deal here in Israel," the partner said, insisting he could not have been mixed up in drugs.[100] To other friends he reportedly said he planned to visit an unnamed Arab country and might be gone some time finalizing a major deal.[101] Media reports would link Tannenbaum to "a number of drug deals in the six months prior to his abduction," though the International Crimes Unit of the Israeli National Police would only comment that he was never indicted for narcotics trafficking.[102]

In the days following his abduction, however, a special team was set up within this police unit and quickly determined Tannenbaum had been planning a major drug deal.[103]

On October 7, just days after Tannenbaum's disappearance, Hezbollah operatives disguised as United Nations officials attacked an Israeli military vehicle patrolling the Israeli side of the border with Lebanon and abducted three Israeli soldiers. A week later, at a conference organized to pressure the Arab League to support the continuation of the second intifada and reject peaceful compromise at its upcoming meeting, Hezbollah chief Hassan Nasrallah took to the podium. With Israeli leaders still reeling from the recent cross-border abduction, the conference participants expected Nasrallah to gloat over his recent operational success and goad Arab leaders to follow his example of unyielding military pressure on Israel. They did not expect him to announce yet another, still more audacious, abduction.

"I inform you gladly," Nasrallah told the conference participants, speaking into the cameras carrying his speech live on Hezbollah's own al-Manar satellite television station and the pan-Arab al-Jazeera network, "in a new qualitative achievement and in a complicated security operation, the Islamic resistance was able to take prisoner an Israeli Army officer with the rank of colonel who works with one of the Israeli security agencies." The audience rose in applause. "Let us not give any further details, to keep the Israelis in confusion." Turning to Selim al-Hoss, the Lebanese prime minister, who was sitting next to him, Nasrallah jokingly apologized for the calls the prime minister would likely soon field from the US secretary of state.[104] Later, citing its reasoning for proscribing Hezbollah's IJO (referred to here as the ESO, or External Services Organization), the British government would note that, among other attacks on British or Western interests, the "ESO is believed to have been instrumental in the kidnapping in December 2000 of the Israeli businessman Elhanan Tanenbaum and of Israeli soldiers from the Shaba farms region of Southern Lebanon/Syria."[105]

Investigators quickly assumed the seized individual was Tannenbaum, now disappeared for twelve days. But how did Tannenbaum get to Lebanon? According to Nasrallah, Tannenbaum "flew to Beirut from Brussels on a false passport and entered Lebanon legally. We arrested him when he arrived."[106] The truth—which would emerge over a long period marked by rampant media speculation—bore out Nasrallah's account of the abduction as a "complicated security operation." Drawn to Brussels on the pretense of meeting "businessmen" central to the success of a $200,000 drug deal, Tannenbaum left Israel of his own free will on a Sabena Airlines flight on the night of October 3.[107] He and Obeid had been in regular telephone contact leading up to the trip.[108] From Tannenbaum's perspective, this contact likely underscored their business partnership. In fact, Obeid was the point man for the kidnapping operation, receiving a service fee of $150,000 from Hezbollah for delivering a childhood friend and high-ranking military reservist who still worked on highly classified projects.[109]

Tannenbaum spent several days in Brussels. At the meeting itself, someone tied to Hezbollah told Tannenbaum he would need to visit the United Arab Emirates

(UAE) to close the deal. Tannenbaum's previous mentioning to friends of an Arab destination suggests he knew in advance that the meeting in Brussels was just a prelude to another meeting in an Arab country. Whether he knew where that meeting was to be held is unknown. In Belgium, Tannenbaum's Hezbollah contacts provided him with a false passport bearing his photograph and a name similar to his own. The time it took to finalize the forged passport, with Tannenbaum's true photograph and signature, likely explains the lag before his departure to the UAE on a flight connecting in Germany.[110]

After his eventual release,Tannenbaum would testify that he flew to Brussels and then on to the Emirates on his true passport, only assuming his cover identity when he arrived in Lebanon. By some accounts, Tannenbaum used his new false passport to travel to Dubai, with the document switch making sense given Israeli regulations precluding a senior reserve IDF officer from visiting an Arab country. Whether he used the forged passport or not, the sophistication of Hezbollah's network in Europe was made apparent by its quick procurement of such a document.[111]

Most press reports indicate that Tannenbaum flew to Abu Dhabi, but by his own account, he went to Dubai, the glitzy Emirate city just across the Gulf from Iran.[112] How he got from there to Lebanon is a matter of some debate, and a story that Tannenbaum has never fully told. Nasrallah insisted that Tannenbaum came to Beirut of his own accord. By one account he was "lured to Beirut by a female Hezbollah agent masquerading as a businesswoman."[113] In the media frenzy that accompanied the Tannenbaum affair, Israeli reporters revealed that Tannenbaum maintained at least two mistresses and fathered a child with one of them, lending some credence to the possibility that he might have been vulnerable to a "honey trap" operation.[114] But as Israeli counterintelligence officials pieced together how Tannenbaum ended up in Beirut, a very different picture emerged.

Tannenbaum, investigators determined, was lured to Dubai, where the ruse of a lucrative drug deal quickly degenerated into what Israeli officials described as a Mafia-style abduction.[115] In Dubai, Hezbollah operatives, believed to be aided by agents of Iran's Islamic Revolutionary Guard Corps (IRGC), brought Tannenbaum to a safe house where he was drugged. The IRGC is known to operate front companies and employ agents in Dubai, a critical trans-shipment point for goods—both legitimate and illicit—from around the world to Iran.[116] Several anonymous Israeli security sources confirmed to prominent Israeli intelligence correspondents that Iran supplied Hezbollah operatives with both a safe house and the plane on which they bundled their sedated Israeli captive, locked in a large crate. Tannenbaum was considered such a valuable commodity, according to this account, that the flight stopped first in Iran, where he was interrogated by IRGC agents, and then, after an undetermined period, flew on to Lebanon.[117]

While the details remain unconfirmed, senior Israeli officials involved in the affair at the time unanimously insist Tannenbaum was drugged and did not travel to Beirut of his own accord. In the words of then–foreign minister Silvan Shalom, "He did not reach Beirut under his own power—this must be made clear."[118] That was not always clear, however. Only after extensive investigation did Israeli officials rule out the claim that the drug deal was an elaborate ruse used to cover Hezbollah's actual recruitment of Tannenbaum as a willing agent. In time, investigators determined the kidnapping was not faked, but this outcome was not assumed from the start.[119]

Without confirming or denying Iran's role in this particular abduction, one retired senior Israeli official noted that many in the Israeli government were wary of publicly pointing fingers at Iran, even when the evidence of Iranian involvement was overwhelming, for fear of forcing the government into having to take some kind of retaliatory action against the Islamic Republic.[120]

While Tannenbaum remained in Hezbollah's custody for more than three years, Mughniyeh and his lieutenants ran multiple infiltration operations by sending undercover operatives into Israel via third countries. Qais Obeid's special abduction unit, for its part, developed a list of some twenty Israelis targeted for Tannenbaum-like entrapment and abduction. One target was Gonen Segev, a former Israeli minister of energy who had tried to work out a private business deal to import natural gas from Qatar after he left government service in 1995. In 2001, the Shin Bet warned Segev of intelligence indicating a plot to kidnap him.[121]

In 2002, Obeid reached out to several Israeli entrepreneurs and offered them partnerships in especially lucrative businesses. As in the Tannenbaum case, the entrepreneurs were told they would have to travel to Europe to close the deal. Another operational template Obeid employed involved recruiting Israeli Arabs like himself to lure Israelis to areas near the Lebanese border where they could be grabbed and taken to the other side, similar to the kidnapping of Israeli soldiers just before Tannenbaum traveled to Europe.[122]

Supporting, or perhaps complementing, Obeid's abduction efforts, in 2003 Hezbollah assigned Ahmad Ma'aniya, a veteran IJO operative, to kidnap Israelis abroad. Ma'aniya was said to have "past experience in abduction plots and hostage mediation, including the seizure of Westerners in Lebanon. Outside Lebanon, Ma'aniya operates cells that carry passports from South American countries and Iran."[123] The involvement of someone of Ma'aniya's caliber in Hezbollah's kidnapping operations signaled to Israelis the group's serious commitment to this strategy. Moreover, it led Israeli security officials to issue warnings that Israelis and even non-Israeli Jews should be wary of business offers that sounded too good to be true and could not be fully verified in advance. Reports that Ma'aniya was working on these plots with the financial and technical support of IRGC agents spooked Israeli officials even more, especially in light of reports that top IRGC figures were known to have funded and provided support to Ma'aniya and his operations in the past. The involvement of the IRGC prompted officials to leak a warning to the press suggesting that Iranian participation in such kidnapping operations would have "very serious repercussions." Under such circumstances "Israel would have no alternative but to respond forcefully."[124]

Recognizing that the Tannenbaum abduction provided not just an intelligence coup in Hezbollah's conflict with Israel but also a political boost at home, Hezbollah invested in efforts to seize still more Israelis. More captives, Hezbollah reasoned, would provide the group still greater leverage in the prisoner exchange negotiations then being mediated by Germany.

Against the backdrop of these security threats, German-mediated prisoner swap negotiations continued. Throughout 2002–3, periodic press reports detailed progress in the talks, but no concrete agreement emerged until January 2004. The parties agreed to a deal under which Israel would release some 435 prisoners, including senior Amal and Hezbollah officials Mustafa Dirani and Abdel Karim Obeid, as well as the bodies of sixty Lebanese killed in clashes with Israeli forces, in return for Tannenbaum and the bodies of three Israeli soldiers killed during the Hezbollah operation when the kidnappings occurred. The prisoner exchange was carried out on January 29, 2004, the same day a suicide bomber struck a downtown Jerusalem bus killing at least eleven people and wounding fifty.

In an interview with Hezbollah's al-Manar television taped just hours before his release, Tannenbaum claimed he was treated well, "almost without exception." Compelled to do the interview while still a captive, Tannenbaum told his Hezbollah interviewer, "They treated me well. They brought me food on time. They took care of my medical problems. I have no complaints." He also claimed that he went to Lebanon in part to "make some money for my family" and in part to find information on Ron Arad, a missing Israeli aviator shot down over Lebanon and believed to have been held captive in Iran and later Lebanon. This, anyway, is what Tannenbaum told his Hezbollah captors in a videotaped interview before his release. Piecing together the details of the Tannenbaum affair, however, would prove frustratingly difficult, even after his release.[125]

Once released, Tannenbaum was detained at the Neurim police facility for interrogation on suspicion of drug trafficking, use of a forged passport, and revealing classified intelligence to Iran and/or Hezbollah. The most pressing questions, however, revolved around what Tannenbaum told his captors. If he had revealed information, was it done only under interrogation, or was he selling secrets to Israel's enemies as part of his business deal? Further, what damage was done to Israeli security as a result of these revelations? As soon as military officials were aware he was kidnapped, they did what they could to contain the potential damage from Tannenbaum's security breach, but they could not know whether they had done enough without Tannenbaum's full cooperation. This they did not receive. Tannenbaum passed a polygraph exam that refuted the suspicion that he was willingly involved in espionage or treason, but he continued to maintain the whole episode grew out of a small-time drug deal. "For that he would not have had to travel on to Abu Dhabi," one official stated, exposing a chief flaw in Tannenbaum's stance.[126] The counterintelligence operation aimed at cleaning up what the press widely described as the Tannenbaum affair was code-named Genius, but from the start, the efforts did not live up to the moniker.[127]

It appears that the key factor behind Israel's willingness to complete the prisoner swap with Hezbollah, even at such a high cost, was concern about the highly classified information to which Tannenbaum had access. Investigators quickly assessed that Tannenbaum revealed extensive information to his captors. They additionally made any plea bargain with the government contingent upon his taking polygraph tests to verify his cooperation and truthfulness in the investigations. Concerns shot through the roof as he failed successive polygraph tests and left out details about his drug trafficking activities in an apparent effort to shield himself from prosecution.[128] Later, under cross-examination in an unrelated case in which he was called to testify about a former business partner, Tannenbaum would concede, "I did not tell my interrogators everything. I didn't tell them about the drug deal."[129]

Back in the weeks following his release, however, Israeli officials concluded Tannenbaum was not cooperating with counterintelligence investigators, and Shin Bet chief Avi Dichter told Israeli parliamentarians that investigators doubted Tannenbaum's story.[130] Despite his deceptive behavior, Israeli prosecutors signed an immunity agreement with Tannenbaum, because they were reliant on his cooperation—only he could tell them what they needed to know. However, he would be required to undergo further lie detector tests. This was a logical demand given the Knesset's subcommittee on Intelligence and Secret Services' conclusion that the Tannenbaum affair was "one of the gravest in Israel's history."[131] In June 2007, an Israeli military tribunal stripped Tannenbaum, now a taxi driver, of his rank, demoting him to private.[132]

Fawzi Ayub: The One Who Got Through

The case of Fawzi Mohammed Mustafa Ayub stands out for two reasons. First, he is one of the few Hezbollah infiltrators to successfully evade Israeli security and make his way into Israel undetected. Second, he was able to operate on the ground in Israel and the West Bank for about a year and a half before being detained. Coming off the failed efforts by Mikdad and Smyrek, Hezbollah worked hard to ensure the success of its next infiltration mission. In Ayub Hezbollah planners found a Hezbollah veteran who had taken part in sensitive operations abroad in the past.[133]

As a Shi'a teen growing up in war-torn Beirut at the start of the Lebanese civil war, Fawzi Ayub joined the Shi'a Amal militia in 1975. "The Christians oppressed us," he stated in testimony before a Tel Aviv court in 2002. "I saw dead people, women and children. It affected me. I saw that the miserable ones have to be protected."[134] In 1983, a year after Hezbollah's founding, Ayub followed a stream of religious Shi'a who left Amal for the more explicitly religious and radically militant Hezbollah. Ayub demonstrated his capabilities and rose within the ranks of Hezbollah's militia and terrorist wings. Just three years after joining the group, he was selected to participate in a sensitive terrorist operation abroad. In a sign of Hezbollah's early commitment to pan-Shi'a solidarity, the operation did not target Israel, America, France, or another multinational force, but Iraq—a fellow Arab state ruled by a minority Sunni regime that oppressed its majority Shi'a population and was at war with Iran.

In the mid-1980s, Ayub was convicted by a Romanian court for his role in a Hezbollah plot to hijack an Iraqi airliner set to depart from Bucharest in order to negotiate the release of Shi'a clerics detained in Iraq in exchange for the Iraqi passengers. Two operational teams—one primary and the other a backup—were assembled and dispatched to execute the hijacking. The redundancy served Hezbollah well since Romanian authorities uncovered the first team, which included Ayub. The point man for the first team, a man named Sh'alan, traveled to Bucharest a few days ahead of his associates to procure handguns for the hijackers, but he was caught and quickly confessed. "Sh'alan was supposed to meet us and give us weapons, a small handgun," Ayub told a Tel Aviv court after his arrest in Israel years later.[135] Romanian authorities arrested other members of the team, including Ayub, as they arrived in the country. The second team arrived undetected, however. It appears the hijackers flew from Romania to Iraq and then boarded Iraqi Airways flight 163 destined for Amman, Jordan. Iraqi security officers on board the plane tried to stop the hijacking, but two hand grenades went off, causing the flight to crash near Arar, Saudi Arabia. Of the 106 people on board, some 62 died as the plane crashed and split in two. Hezbollah's IJO claimed responsibility for the attack from Beirut, and the CIA identified one of the hijackers as Ribal Khallil Jalul, whose photo adorned a Hezbollah martyr poster found near a mosque in Beirut.[136] Ayub was sentenced to seven years in a Romanian prison, "but Hezbollah sent an agent to pay off the Romanians and he was released after just ten months."[137]

This was not Hezbollah's first operational venture in Romania. According to an April 1992 CIA report, as of late 1990, Hezbollah began planning a joint operation together with PIJ targeting Jewish émigrés at a Warsaw synagogue and the Budapest airport.[138] Over the years, reports would emerge indicating that Hezbollah operatives had long worked out of the Balkans, in general, and Romania, in particular. In October 2001, Moldovan intelligence accused Mahmoud Ahmad Hamoud, who left his native Lebanon when he was eighteen, of having close ties to Hezbollah. Hamoud, who lived in Romania from 1992 to 1997, married into the Moldovan political elite and served as Lebanon's honorary consul to Moldova. But authorities there alleged he "received 400,000 dollars from the leaders of the Hezbollah terrorist organization in order to consolidate the position of the organization in Romania" when he lived there. He was also accused of drug trafficking and smuggling women for prostitution.[139] The following year, Romanian intelligence sources reported that Hezbollah was active "in the country's main university cities, focusing on propaganda, economic and intelligence activities."[140]

Following his release from a Romanian prison in 1988, Ayub immigrated to Canada, sponsored by an uncle under a program reserved for refugees displaced by the Lebanese civil war. Family members living in Canada welcomed Ayub, and he became a Canadian citizen in 1992. Asked by an Israeli judge if he had told Canadian authorities about his conviction in Romania on terrorism charges, Ayub replied, "They didn't ask me."[141] And he never told.

At first glance, Ayub seemed to be leading a normal life in the Toronto area. He married a woman from the United States, just across the Ambassador Bridge linking Detroit to Windsor, Ontario. At some point the couple lived near Dearborn, Michigan, according to US prosecutors.[142] He worked at a grocery store during the day and took classes at night. But all the while Ayub remained an active Hezbollah agent, according to Israeli officials. While in Canada, Israeli officials note, Ayub "maintained contact with senior Hezbollah officials and carried out operations."[143]

After his first marriage fell apart, Ayub married an émigré from Lebanon in 1994. The new couple had several children, and Ayub worked for a computer company, but his wife was unhappy in Canada. In 2000 they moved back to Lebanon, where Ayub bought a bakery and ran a business selling building supplies. Around the time Ayub went into debt that same year, Hezbollah came calling. It sent senior members who knew Ayub from his early days in the group with a simple message: It was time for Ayub's next sensitive mission.[144]

Looking back, it is possible Ayub's travel to Canada was less a personal decision than a strategic move by Hezbollah. After just a few years, the group procured from Canada something far more valuable than the night-vision goggles or other dual-use equipment it usually shopped for in North America; it secured Canadian citizenship and a Canadian passport for a member of its elite IJO. "Fawzi Ayub is a very important guy for them," an Israeli official explained. "We have good information that he is connected to this [Islamic Jihad] apparatus. There are not many guys like that."[145] Armed with his Canadian passport, and trained to carry out sensitive missions abroad, Ayub was an ideal candidate for Hezbollah's most ambitious infiltration operation to date.

Ayub trained in the handling and preparation of explosives at secret Hezbollah facilities in Beirut apartments. He was also taught how to hide any trace of his Lebanese identity and given strict guidelines on how to behave once in Israel, including suppressing all aspects of his Arab identity and speaking only English at all times. Some of this training may have been carried out by Mughniyeh himself.[146] The purpose of his mission, according to the FBI, was to conduct a bombing on behalf of Hezbollah.[147] Israeli authorities believe his mission was to perpetrate multiple attacks in Israel in cooperation with operatives from Hamas and PIJ. This was presumably part of an effort to improve the Palestinian terrorist groups' bomb-making techniques just as the second intifada was gaining traction in October 2000.[148]

But that was not all. Israeli officials also believe that the bombing Ayub was to carry out by himself was to be an assassination attempt targeting the Israeli prime minister.[149] Like Hussein Mikdad before him, Ayub arrived in Israel just before an Israeli election with the possible objective of influencing the vote by targeting key officials or sensitive government buildings. While Ayub was in the country, another Hezbollah operative, Jihad Shuman, was arrested just 300 meters from the prime minister's Jerusalem residence. An Israeli intelligence report concludes, "By virtue of the similarities in their activity and the fact that the operatives concentrated on the area of Jerusalem containing many government buildings, it is possible that all three cases were attempts to harm the Prime Minister of Israel."[150]

After several months of training, Ayub traveled to an unknown European country on his Canadian passport. In an attempt to wrap their operative in an extra layer of operational security, Hezbollah planners decided Ayub would not travel on to Israel on his Canadian passport, which was apt to create suspicion with its Lebanese visa stamps. The high-quality forged American passport he received while in Europe featured Ayub's picture and the name Frank Boschi. Nine years later, in August 2009, Ayub would be indicted in US District Court in Detroit for willfully and knowingly using a false US passport to enter Israel "for the purpose of conducting a bombing on behalf of the Designated Terrorist Organization Hizballah."[151]

Now answering to the name Frank Boschi, Ayub traveled to Greece and boarded a boat to Israel. It was October 2000, just weeks into the violence of the second intifada, when the Hezbollah operations specialist disembarked at the Israeli port of Haifa. "Then I did what I was told to do," Ayub would later recount. "I went to Jerusalem, I stayed in hotels, and I bought a cellphone and called and said I was in Jerusalem."[152]

After a few days in Jerusalem, Ayub traveled to Hebron in the southern West Bank, where he contacted a local terrorist operative. Together, the two scouted possible sites for the prepositioning and concealment of weapons for future operations.[153] According to Israeli intelligence, Ayub did in fact prepare and hide explosives in caches in Israel for later use.[154] According to one report, Ayub intended to assemble a fragmentation bomb in Hebron, a feat that would have marked a qualitative improvement in the lethality of the explosives utilized by Palestinian terrorist groups until that point.[155] Fragmentation bombs have a thick outer layer designed to shatter into many pieces that then disperse in every direction at a very high velocity on detonation. To effect destruction at that level, Palestinian terrorists previously had to surround their explosives with nails, screws, and bolts.

Ayub's mission was interrupted, however, by his arrest—not by the Israelis but by Palestinian police in Hebron. For all his training in operational security, something about Ayub's behavior led Palestinian security officials to arrest him on suspicion of being an Israeli spy. Ayub claims Palestinian security officials blindfolded him, beat him, and accused him of being a member of the South Lebanon Army, whose members were sometimes deployed to the West Bank to spy on Palestinian groups and the Palestinian Authority on behalf of Israel. Perhaps it was Ayub's arrival on the scene just as the second intifada began that raised their suspicions. Whatever the reason, Ayub suddenly found himself in a Palestinian prison cell.[156] Ayub recounted his exchange with Palestinian police in testimony before an Israeli court:

> I told them, "I'm from South Lebanon." . . . They asked, "What organization?" I told them I was with Amal and then I moved to Hezbollah. Only when I told them I was with Hezbollah were they satisfied. They said, "You are in the resistance," and I said, "I am here in the resistance as well." Right away they brought me coffee and they left me alone; they were satisfied with me. They said they would bring me cigarettes and chicken. I said I was finished with being kicked and beaten up. . . . Later, one by one they came to me and asked me to tell them about my heroism.[157]

But the Palestinians did not release Ayub. A sympathetic officer named Younis reportedly looked after him and brought him coffee in return for the promise of several thousand dollars. After a period, however, Israeli forces arrested Younis. Another Palestinian officer chided Ayub for making a big mistake by cutting the deal with the arrested officer. Younis would surely tell the Israelis about the Hezbollah operative in their custody. On June 25, 2002, the IDF raided Hebron; in particular, they focused on the Palestinian police station and arrested Ayub.[158]

Ayub's arrest remained secret until late October 2002, when his trial was set to begin. In custody, Ayub reportedly admitted that part of his mission was to free the three key Shi'a militants discussed before—Mustafa Dirani, Abdel Karim Obeid, and Jihad Shuman—perhaps by kidnapping Israelis and bargaining for their release in exchange for the detained Hezbollah operatives.[159] On the stand, Ayub testified in February 2003 that he saw himself as being on a divine mission: "You want to know the reason I came here? I came here by an order from God. This is my religion. To defend the oppressed."[160] But one official, who questioned Ayub for several hours, concluded he was a "classic sleeper agent."[161]

Ayub's arrest and interrogation led Israeli authorities to amplify their intelligence collection focused on Hezbollah's terrorist activities in the Israeli heartland. Between this intelligence collection effort and the investigation and interrogation of Ayub, Israeli security officials maintained they were able to uncover and thwart still more Hezbollah operations in Israel.[162] Eleven months after his court testimony, Ayub landed in Germany on a flight from Israel as part of the Tannenbaum prisoner exchange. From there he flew to Beirut, where Hezbollah leader Hassan Nasrallah waited on the tarmac to greet and embrace him.[163]

Jihad Shuman: From Beirut to Jerusalem . . . via London

Even as Hezbollah handlers kept in regular contact with Fawzi Ayub—at least until his arrest in Hebron—they trained and dispatched another operative on a parallel infiltration mission to Israel. Jihad Aya Latif Shuman, a dual Lebanese-British citizen and graduate of the American University of Beirut with a degree in computer sciences, made his way to Israel from Beirut through London, where he benefited from the support of a Hezbollah facilitation network there. He arrived in Israel on New Year's Eve 2001, traveling on an authentic British passport bearing the name Gerard Shuman. He was arrested just six days later near the prime minister's residence in Jerusalem.[164]

Shuman was reportedly born to Lebanese parents in Sierra Leone in 1969 and inherited British citizenship from his father. Years later, Hezbollah's IJO recruiters saw in Shuman not just a run-of-the-mill candidate for recruitment but someone with a valid British passport who had lived abroad and could pass as a foreigner. His initial recruitment occurred on a visit to Lebanon, but at least some of the recruitment process and initial training reportedly took place during visits to his new Hezbollah handlers in Malaysia.[165] Shuman moved to Jouaiya, Lebanon, near Tyre, and studied at the American University of Beirut. While in Lebanon, Shuman would later concede, he was trained by Mughniyeh's international operations group to execute "strategic attacks," as Hezbollah described them.[166] When he was deemed ready, Shuman was sent from Lebanon to Britain on his Lebanese passport.[167]

Following the instructions he received in Lebanon, once Shuman arrived in London he left his Lebanese passport in a hidden dead drop located in a public place.[168] According to the British government, Hezbollah maintains "a small, overt" presence in the United Kingdom, "with extensive links to Hizballah's Foreign Relations Department (FRD)," the department responsible for overseeing the group's organized political, financial, and procurement efforts abroad. Beyond this overt presence, however, "there is some indication of occasional ESO [IJO] activity in the UK," a British government report notes.[169]

Hezbollah engages in fund-raising and propaganda activities in the United Kingdom, though its fund-raising there is fairly small compared with its fund-raising in North and South America, Africa, and elsewhere in Europe. According to an Israeli report, Hezbollah raises tens of thousands of dollars a year in Britain.[170] British experts say the Hezbollah presence in Britain includes not only fund-raising networks but also trained operatives ready to be called upon to support Hezbollah operations or even carry out revenge attacks in the West. Richard Kemp, a senior counterterrorism adviser to former Prime Minister Tony Blair and a member of the Cabinet Office's Joint Intelligence Committee, warned that "Hezbollah cells are operating in this country, in London. The big question is how capable Hezbollah groups are in Europe. What I can say is that Hezbollah is probably the world's most effective terrorist organization, and that includes al Qaeda."[171]

Iran has a record of dispatching terrorists, particularly Hezbollah members, to conduct attacks in or from Britain. Back in 1989, Mustafa Maza, a Hezbollah operative staying in a London hotel, was killed when explosives he was carrying in his suitcase detonated prematurely.[172] According to the Argentine indictment in the Asociación Mutual Israelita Argentina (AMIA) bombing, Iran and Hezbollah may have played a role in a pair of London bombings perpetrated by Palestinian terrorists on July 26 and 27, 1994, just days after the AMIA strike.[173] In 2003, British intelligence officials assessed that Hezbollah's political activity in Lebanon and the group's attempts to engage politically with European countries—including Britain—could lessen the likelihood of a Hezbollah attack in Europe. (In late May 2003, for example, Hezbollah parliamentarian Muhammad Fanish visited Britain, Switzerland, and Italy.)[174] In the event Hezbollah did plot an attack, however, British officials assess it would be a targeted attack against an Israeli official or institution, not an indiscriminate bombing.[175]

In the case of Shuman's infiltration operation, Hezbollah's London network needed only to provide basic logistical support for an attack planned not for the streets of London but for the streets of Jerusalem. Shuman's operational instructions in London were very clear and were intended to bolster his cover story before his travel to Israel on his British passport. He was told to rent an apartment in London, set up a voice mailbox there in case anyone called, and purchase a British cell phone. Having established these supports for his cover story, he purchased a plane ticket at a travel agency that allowed him to pay in cash.[176]

Shuman arrived in Israel on December 31, 2000. On arrival in Jerusalem, he checked in to the Novotel on the Arab side of Jerusalem's Route 60 north, a parkway leading out of the city and dividing its Arab eastern and Jewish western neighborhoods. Before he departed for Israel, Shuman's instructors made him memorize the location of dead drops in East Jerusalem's Wadi Joz neighborhood, which is located between Mount Scopus and the Old City. Soon after he checked into the Novotel, Shuman made his way to the dead drop and began digging. It is not clear if Shuman found what he was looking for—likely weapons, explosives, or preoperational surveillance information. He soon moved several blocks away, to the Dan Panorama, a hotel in West Jerusalem overlooking the walls of the Old City.[177]

Shuman later confessed to Israeli authorities that he called his Hezbollah handlers in Lebanon regularly to update them on his progress. That progress, however, was short-lived: on January 5, six days after arriving in the country, Shuman was arrested just 300 meters from the prime minister's Jerusalem residence.[178] At the time of his arrest Shuman carried Sierra Leonean travel documents along with his British passport.[179] A search of the items in his possession revealed Shuman had a *kippah* (a skullcap, often employed by terrorists to blend into Israeli society), a timer that could have been used for an explosive device, maps of Jerusalem, a large sum of money, a video camera, two disposable cameras, and several cellular phones purchased in Israel.[180]

Recruiting Israeli Arabs Abroad

Even as Hezbollah invested heavily in Palestinian terrorist networks, the group continued to recruit its own operatives to target Israel, often leveraging its foreign operations capabilities to that end. Israeli Arabs were of particular interest to Qais Obeid, especially following the Israeli withdrawal from southern Lebanon in May 2000, though earlier, in the late 1990s and early 2000, Hezbollah had focused on recruiting Israeli Arabs. Back then the group expressed particular interest in members of Israel's Bedouin communities, whose mobility provided an attractive cover for movement around the country. Both before and after 2000, Hezbollah focused on Israeli Arabs with clean security records.[181]

With the Israeli occupation of Lebanon over, Hezbollah lost its primary justification for maintaining its armed militia in continued and explicit violation of the Taif Accord, which ended the Lebanese civil war. Refocusing its effort on liberating a few disputed hilltops like the Shebaa Farms (determined by the UN to actually be in Syrian, not Lebanese, territory) could not suffice to maintain a culture of resistance and martyrdom. This explains Hezbollah's fixation on carrying out cross-border military attacks and its support for terrorism targeting Israel since 2000. Seeking much-needed intelligence and operational support networks south of the border, Hezbollah found Israeli Arabs "an especially attractive target for recruitment and handling," according to Israeli security sources.[182] As full citizens of Israel, Israeli Arab operatives enjoyed complete freedom of movement throughout Israel, enabling them to collect information on strategic locations, critical infrastructure, traffic arteries, and Israeli cities and towns. Beyond luring Jewish and Arab Israeli citizens into drugs for intelligence schemes, Hezbollah endeavored to spot and approach Israeli Arabs staying abroad for recruitment. Sometimes individuals would be considered based on their statements and political positions, whereas other times Hezbollah recruited on a "friend brings a friend" basis.[183]

Investigation into one such case led Israeli authorities to arrest Khalid Kashkoush, an Israeli Arab medical student from the Qalansua, an Arab city in central Israel, as he landed at Ben Gurion Airport in July 2008. Kashkoush had been studying in Göttingen, Germany, where a relative introduced him to a Lebanese doctor named Hisham Hassan, who headed the Orphaned Children Project Lebanon. Dr. Hassan, Israeli authorities charged, had spotted Kashkoush and put him in touch with a Hezbollah handler. German authorities were likely not surprised by the allegations, given that several German intelligence offices, among other government authorities, publicly identified the Orphaned Children Project's ties to Hezbollah and Hezbollah's Martyrs Foundation. Among these offices were those located in Baden-Württemberg and Bremen.[184]

Until the German government shut it down in 2002, the Martyrs Foundation operated in Germany as the al-Shahid Social Relief Institution.[185] The US Treasury Department followed suit in July 2007, designating the Martyrs Foundation (including its US office, the Goodwill Charitable Organization) as a terrorist entity. Senior Martyrs Foundation officials were not only involved in fundraising for Hezbollah, according to the Treasury Department; they were also "directly involved in Hizballah operations against Israel during the July–August 2006 conflict." In fact, Treasury noted, "a Lebanon-based leader of the Martyrs Foundation has directed and financed terrorist cells in the Gaza Strip that worked with Hizballah and PIJ."[186] The Orphans Project website was not coy about its ties to the Martyrs Foundation: The site informed donors that the funds it raised were directly transferred to the Lebanese Martyrs Foundation's bank account.[187]

According to Israeli authorities, Kashkoush would meet Dr. Hisham several times after their introduction in 2002. After a few meetings, Hisham suggested Kashkoush establish a business relationship with someone he called Rami. In December 2005, Kashkoush met Rami in Erfurt, Germany, where Kashkoush was instructed to buy a "clean" phone and to set future meetings by email. Rami, who identified himself now as Mazen, was actually Mohamad Hashem, an "experienced Hezbollah senior handler." According to Israeli officials, "Mohamad Hashem frequently visits in various countries for meetings with Hizbullah agents to give instructions and money and receive information."[188]

Kashkoush and Hashem met several times over the next couple of years, including in Erfurt in December 2006 and in Frankfurt in April 2007 and January 2008. Hashem asked for the names of other Israeli citizens studying abroad who might be possible targets for recruitment by Hezbollah. He also asked Kashkoush to supply information to Hezbollah about Israel and to identify addresses and public buildings in Qalansua on Google Earth maps. Moreover, he was told to try to get a job at an Israeli hospital, where he could collect information on hospitalized members of the Israeli security forces. He was given basic security training and paid €13,000 for his activities on behalf of Hezbollah. Once arrested, Kashkoush reportedly informed

Israeli authorities not only about his recruitment by Mohamad Hashem but also about the activities of another Hezbollah agent, Ayman Kamel Shihadeh, a Palestinian from Hebron who had already been the target of the Shin Bet's attention for his association with Hezbollah.[189]

One event that, interestingly, shook Kashkoush was the August 2009 arrest of Rawi Sultani, another Israeli Arab, on charges of spying for Hezbollah. A resident of Tira, a town just seven miles from Kashkoush's home in Qalansua, Sultani also lived near the home of then–IDF chief of staff Lt. Gen. Gabi Ashkenazi. Recruited by a Hezbollah speaker at a summer camp in Morocco run by the Israeli Arab Balad (National Democratic Assembly) Party, Sultani informed officials that he and the Israeli chief of staff worked out at the same gym.[190]

Keen to exact revenge for the previous year's assassination of Imad Mughniyeh, the Hezbollah recruiter—Salman Harb—asked Sultani for detailed information on Ashkenazi. Hezbollah had hoped to target a current or former senior Israeli official, someone roughly equal in rank and importance to Hezbollah's Mughniyeh. The sitting chief of staff made for a particularly attractive target.[191] Hezbollah had been gunning for Ashkenazi for years. Six years earlier, IDF Lt. Col. Omar al-Heib, a Bedouin tracker who lost an eye in an explosion in 1996 while on an IDF mission in Lebanon, was charged with espionage for providing Hezbollah with details about Israeli military installations in general and about General Ashkenazi, then head of Israel's Northern Command, in particular. Sentencing al-Heib to fifteen years in jail, a Tel Aviv court concluded that in return for drugs and money, al-Heib, a senior IDF officer, willingly supplied information to Hezbollah.[192]

Salman Harb must have marveled at his good fortune for having stumbled onto a potentially huge source—someone who went to the same gym as a longtime Hezbollah target. The information provided by this twenty-three-year-old participant in an outreach seminar represented an ideal operational opportunity, so Sultani and Harb kept in touch by phone, email, and Facebook after their meeting in Morocco. As it happened, Israeli intelligence operations eventually tagged Rawi Sultani as an Israeli citizen who was in communication with Hezbollah.[193] Informed of this discovery, the Shin Bet and the International Serious Crimes Unit of the Israeli police tracked Sultani's email and Facebook correspondence with Hezbollah, unraveling the plot to target Ashkenazi before it became operational.[194]

Authorities waited to arrest Sultani, however, until they were sure they had collected sufficient evidence to convict him.[195] In December 2008, Sultani flew to Poland to meet with a Hezbollah operative going by the name Sami. Sultani officially joined Hezbollah at this meeting and passed along information he had gathered about Ashkenazi and other Israeli officials and IDF bases.[196] Sultani was provided encryption software for his computer and a secure email address at which he could contact his handlers. (The same had been done for Kashkoush.) Once he returned to Israel, Sultani kept in touch with both Sami and Salman Harb. Later, a former senior Shin Bet official would assess that Iran was most likely kept informed of Hezbollah's efforts to collect intelligence on Ashkenazi.[197] Sultani's arrest came in late August 2009, and ultimately he was sentenced to five years and eight months for spying on the chief of staff and maintaining contact with a foreign agent.[198]

In more recent years, evidence has emerged indicating that a core group of Hezbollah operatives working with Qais Obeid—people like Mohamad Hashem, Ayman Shihadeh, and Salman Harb—have the responsibility of meeting Israeli Arab recruits abroad. Another such operative is Hassan Jaja, who recruited Israeli Arab political activist Ameer Makhoul, among others. Makhoul, who is from Haifa, headed the Union of Arab Community-Based Associations, which works to strengthen and expand the voluntary work of Arabs. Makhoul is an author and the brother of a former Knesset member, and his arrest sparked protests among Israeli Arabs. In custody, however, Makhoul reportedly admitted to meeting Hassan Jaja in Jordan in 2004, finding out Jaja was a Hezbollah operative soon after the July 2006 war, and agreeing to serve as a Hezbollah source two years later. In 2008, Makhoul reached out to Jaja and offered his services, which led to a meeting in Copenhagen, at which one of Jaja's men installed an encoding program on Makhoul's laptop and provided Makhoul cash to cover the cost of the trip to Denmark. Sitting at a Copenhagen café, the Hezbollah operative asked Makhoul to collect information about Israeli army bases, Shin Bet and Mossad offices, the home address of the head of the Shin Bet, security surrounding the prime minister's and defense minister's convoys, and information on the impact of terror attacks in Israel. Makhoul was also asked for information about Israeli Arabs and Israelis of Russian descent experiencing financial stress who might be open to a recruitment pitch by Hezbollah.[199]

Back in Israel, Makhoul reportedly sent Jaja at least ten encoded emails providing details on the precise location of two Shin Bet installations, including means of entry and security procedures; the location of a Mossad facility; information about the IDF's Nachshonim base (which Makhoul inexplicably thought was an American base); and the location of the Rafael Advanced Defense Systems factory off the Acre–Haifa highway. Ultimately, Makhoul was given a reduced sentence of nine years in prison as part of a plea bargain in which he confessed to espionage and related charges.[200]

Denmark, it turns out, had been central to at least one earlier Hezbollah recruitment gambit. In December 2004, a Danish citizen of Lebanese descent named Khaled Ashuah arrived in Israel on a Turkish Airlines flight. His newly issued Danish passport bore no markings from his trip to Lebanon to visit family the previous summer. While in Lebanon, Ashuah's brother introduced him to Hezbollah officials who recruited him as an agent and instructed him to travel to Israel to collect intelligence, much like Smyrek, Ayub, and Shuman had done before him. After three weeks of training and preparation, Ashuah returned home to Denmark with $2,000 and clear operational instructions from Hezbollah. Once his new passport arrived, he flew to Israel with plans to travel north, where he would stay with Israeli Arab relatives and identify suitable sites for future Hezbollah attacks. But while riding the train between Nahariya and Haifa, Ashuah apparently filmed security installations in a rather conspicuous manner. An Israel Railways security officer notified authorities, who arrested Ashuah.[201]

Under questioning, Ashuah admitted to being recruited by Hezbollah and said he had been sent to Israel to collect intelligence on security installations and army bases in the north of the country. He was also told to identify Israeli Arabs to be recruited, although he appears to have had time only to try to recruit a couple of people, including his cousin, Hussein Ashuah. Brashly, Ashuah told police he considered this first visit just a test for more important operations he planned to carry out on behalf of Hezbollah in the future.[202]

The aggressive and proactive posture of Hezbollah's Unit 1800 led Israeli intelligence to devote significant resources toward intelligence collection efforts targeting not only Imad Mughniyeh but also key deputies like Unit 1800 commander Haj Halil Hareb. At least once, senior officials considered responding to Hezbollah terrorist activity with targeted assassinations of such leaders, according to a study prepared for the US Air Force on the use of air operations in Israel's war against Hezbollah.[203] Nasrallah, for his part, warned that Hezbollah had its own "target bank" of Israeli military and critical infrastructure sites it could attack within minutes of any Israeli attack.[204] Such threats would have to be taken very seriously, given Hezbollah's success infiltrating its own operatives into Israel and recruiting Palestinians and Israeli Arabs to collect such intelligence for the group.

Qais Obeid's efforts to recruit Israeli Arabs and to infiltrate operatives into Israel continue as of this writing. In 2005, reports emerged that Obeid flew from Beirut to Egypt, where he held meetings with members of Fatah's al-Aqsa Martyrs Brigades— who at the time were practically operating as terrorist subcontractors for Hezbollah—in El Arish in the northern Sinai.[205] In late 2009, Obeid's name appeared in the press again, this time when he called to comfort the mother of a Fatah operative who had been killed by Israeli authorities after allegedly taking part in the shooting of an Israeli civilian, with promises that Hezbollah would "assist the family in anything she asked for." By this time not only Israel but the Palestinian Authority too feared that Hezbollah was actively trying to infiltrate Palestinian Authority ranks in order to recruit Fatah members.[206] Six months later, their suspicions were confirmed when Palestinian Authority security agencies arrested dozens of Hezbollah recruits in the West Bank. The young men, Palestinian officials reported, were part of an organized Hezbollah recruitment effort led by Qais Obeid to undermine the relative calm Israelis and Palestinians were then experiencing on the ground.[207]

In the winter of 2011, the IDF decided to renew Lt. Gen. Gabi Ashkenazi's security detail even though he had retired as chief of staff almost a year prior. Fresh intelligence suggested that Hezbollah was planning attacks on Israeli targets worldwide to avenge Mughniyeh's assassination. Due to Hezbollah's previous attempts to target Ashkenazi, and Ashkenazi's status as IDF chief of staff when Mughniyeh was assassinated, Israel was not taking any chances.[208] A few weeks later, in January 2012, the Israeli military announced again that it was tightening Ashkenazi's security. Nearing the anniversary of Mughniyeh's death, this second announcement came just days after Thai police arrested a suspected Hezbollah operative in Bangkok and a week after Bulgarian security officials found a suspicious package on a bus carrying Israeli tourists.[209]

Beyond Hezbollah's persistent efforts to recruit Israeli Arabs and its operational focus on infiltrating operatives into Israel, Hezbollah has engaged, as we have seen, in a variety of operational and support activities far away from the Blue Line separating Israel and Lebanon. Among the lesser-known stories of Hezbollah's global footprint are its activities in Africa.

Notes

1. Canadian Security Intelligence Service (CSIS), "Terrorist Group Profiler: Hamas," June 2002. See also Stewart Bell, "Hamas May Have Chemical Weapons: CSIS Report Says Terror Group May Be Experimenting," *National Post* (Canada), December 10, 2003.

2. Israeli Defense Forces, Military Intelligence, "Iran and Syria as Strategic Support for Palestinian Terrorism," September 2002. Report based on the interrogations of arrested Palestinian terrorists and captured Palestinian Authority documents.

3. Douglas Frantz and James Risen, "A Secret Iran-Arafat Connection Is Seen Fueling the Mideast Fire," *New York Times*, March 24, 2002.

4. Molly Moore and John Ward Anderson, "Suicide Bombers Change Mideast's Military Balance," *Washington Post*, August 17, 2002.

5. "Iran Expands Its Palestinian Control; Offers al-Khadoumi Five Million Dollars," *al-Watan* (Kuwait), December 13, 2004.

6. Israeli intelligence report, "Hezbollah's International Terrorism and the Penetration of Hezbollah Activists into Israel," undated, author's personal files, received August 5, 2003.

7. Kevin Peraino, "Death of a Hezbollah Leader: Attack Fells a Suspected Terrorist with a List of Enemies," *Newsweek*, February 12, 2008.

8. Ranstorp, "Hizbollah's Command Leadership."

9. Douglas Frantz, "The Accountant Is a Terrorist," *New York Times*, November 10, 1996.

10. *Mikdad: Into the Mind of a Terrorist*, DVD, Director Dan Setton, Direct Cinema Limited, 1998.

11. Ibid.

12. Ibid.

13. Frantz, "Accountant Is a Terrorist."

14. *Mikdad*.

15. For a detailed discussion of terrorism aimed at disrupting the Oslo peace process, see Matthew Levitt, *Negotiating under Fire: Preserving Peace Talks in the Face of Terror Attacks* (Lanham, MD: Rowman & Littlefield, 2008).

16. Frantz, "Accountant Is a Terrorist."

17. *Mikdad*.

18. Frantz, "Accountant Is a Terrorist." By another account, Mikdad joined Hezbollah in 1994 and began working as an accountant in one of Sheikh Fadlallah's charitable foundations. See Forest, *Making of a Terrorist*, 257.

19. Frantz, "Accountant Is a Terrorist"; *Mikdad*.

20. Forest, *Making of a Terrorist*, 257.

21. Frantz, "Accountant Is a Terrorist."

22. Ibid.

23. Ibid.

24. Israeli intelligence report, "Hizballah's International Terrorism," undated, received by the author August 5, 2003.

25. US Department of Justice, FBI, "International Radical Fundamentalism."

26. Frantz, "Accountant Is a Terrorist"; Israeli Ministry of Foreign Affairs, Jerusalem Police Spokesman, "Details of Lawrence Hotel Bombing Released," May 16, 1996; *Mikdad*.

27. Frantz, "Accountant Is a Terrorist."

28. *Mikdad*.

29. Ibid.; Frantz, "Accountant Is a Terrorist."

30. *Mikdad*.

31. Ibid.

32. Frantz, "Accountant Is a Terrorist."

33. *Mikdad*.

34. Ibid.

35. Frantz, "Accountant Is a Terrorist."

36. *Mikdad*.

37. Ibid.

38. Ibid.

39. Frantz, "Accountant Is a Terrorist."

40. *Mikdad*.

41. Forest, *Making of a Terrorist*, 258; Hussein Dakroub, "Prisoners Arrive Home After Israel and Lebanon Swap Bodies," Associated Press, June 26, 1998.

42. Philippine intelligence report, "TIR on Pandu Yudhawinata," December 8, 1999, 9; Israeli intelligence report, "Hizballah's International Terrorism."

43. Margot Dudkevitch, "Germany Warned Israel of Smyrek," *Jerusalem Post*, December 28, 1997; Justin Sparks, "Freed Terrorist Vows He'll Fulfill Suicide Mission," *Sunday Times* (London), February 8, 2004.

44. Author interview, former Israeli judiciary official, Israel, September 12, 2011.

45. Margot Dudkevitch and Douglas Davis, "German Terror Suspect's Mother Asks Forgiveness," *Jerusalem Post*, December 30, 1997; Dudkevitch, "Germany Warned Israel of Smyrek"; Forest, *Making of a Terrorist*, 258; Israeli intelligence report, "Hizballah's International Terrorism." By other accounts, Smyrek converted to Islam shortly after completing a third prison term for drug offenses. See Agence France-Presse, "English-Educated German among Prisoners to Go Free in Hezbollah Deal," January 27, 2004.

46. German government reports referenced in Buenos Aires, Argentina, Investigations Unit of the Office of the Attorney General, *Office of Criminal Investigations: AMIA Case*, report by Marcelo Martinez Burgos and Alberto Nisman, October 25, 2006, 305.

47. Ibid.

48. Ranstorp, "Hizbollah's Command Leadership," 309.

49. German Government, Federal Office for the Protection of the Constitution, *Annual Report of the Office for the Protection of the Constitution 2005 (Bundesamt für Verfassungsschutz, BfV)* 2005, 166, 191.

50. Agence France-Presse, "Lebanese Hezbollah Official Forced to Leave Germany," January 5, 2005.

51. "German Interior Minister 'Worried' about Islamist Radicalization," *Bild* (Hamburg), July 24, 2006.

52. Author interview, former Israeli judiciary official, Israel, September 12, 2011.

53. Israeli intelligence report, "Hizballah's International Terrorism." By another account, Smyrek approached Hezbollah operatives in Germany and volunteered to carry out a suicide attack on the group's behalf. See Intelligence and Terrorism Information Center at the Center for Special Studies, "Hezbollah, Part 1: Profile of the Lebanese Shiite Terrorist Organization of Global Reach Sponsored by Iran and Supported by Syria," Special Information Paper, July 2003, 76.

54. According to Israeli intelligence, Fahdi Hamdar doubled as a Hamas liaison in Germany. Israeli intelligence report, "Hizballah's International Terrorism"; Forest, *Making of a Terrorist*, 258. An Israeli official involved in Smyrek's prosecution noted "his life was out of focus, he was still looking for purpose." Author interview, former Israeli judiciary official, Israel, September 21, 2011.

55. Dudkevitch and Davis, "German Terror Suspect's Mother Asks Forgiveness."

56. Forest, *Making of a Terrorist*, 258.

57. Agence France-Presse, "German in Court over Planned Suicide Bombing in Israel," December 25, 1997.

58. Margot Dudkevitch, "Charges Pressed against German Suspected of Planning Suicide Attack," *Jerusalem Post*, December 26, 1997.

59. Forest, *Making of a Terrorist*, 258; Dudkevitch, "Charges Pressed against German"; Sparks, "Freed Terrorist Vows."

60. Dudkevitch, "Germany Warned Israel of Smyrek." By one account, Smyrek's initial entry into Israel was in part a training mission to test his commitment to carrying out a suicide bombing. See Yoram Schweitzer, "The Export and Import of Suicide Bombers," Jaffee Center for Strategic Studies, *Tel Aviv Notes* No. 77, May 11, 2003.

61. "Court Says German Suspected of Planned Suicide Attack 'Not Tortured,'" *Ma'ariv* (Tel Aviv), March 12, 1999, accessed via BBC Summary of World Broadcasts, March 15, 1999.

62. Israeli intelligence report, "Hizballah's International Terrorism."

63. Dudkevitch, "Charges Pressed against German."

64. Intelligence and Terrorism Information Center at the Center for Special Studies, "Hezbollah (part 1): Profile of the Lebanese Shiite Terrorist Organization of Global Reach Sponsored by Iran and Supported by Syria," June 2003.

65. Agence France-Presse, "German in Court"; Margot Dudkevitch, "German Sent by Hizbullah Nabbed Last Month," *Jerusalem Post*, December 25, 1997.

66. Dudkevitch, "German Sent by Hizbullah Nabbed"; Forest, *Making of a Terrorist*, 258.

67. Galit Lipkis Beck, "German Government May Seek Smyrek's Extradition," *Jerusalem Post*, January 23, 1998.

68. Author interview, former Israeli judiciary official, Israel, September 12, 2011.

69. "Germany Issues Arrest Warrant for Terrorist Suspect Held by Israel," Deutsche Presse-Agentur, March 23, 1998; author interview, former Israeli judiciary official, Israel, September 12, 2011.

70. Sparks, "Freed Terrorist Vows."

71. Author interview, former Israeli judiciary official, Israel, September 12, 2011.

72. Dudkevitch, "Charges Pressed against German."

73. Sparks, "Freed Terrorist Vows."

74. Ibid.; Associated Press, "Four Released Prisoners Ask for Asylum in Germany after Exchange between Israel and Hezbollah," January 30, 2004.

75. Alexander Ritzmann and Mark Dubowitz, "Hezbollah's German Helpers," *Wall Street Journal*, April 17, 2007; "Hezbollah's European Base," *Berlin Welt am Sonntag* (Germany), July 23, 2006.

76. Regarding procurement, see, for example, *United States of America v. Dani Nemr Tarraf*, 09-01902, US District Court, Eastern District of Pennsylvania.

77. "ICT Global Terrorism Brief: Mughniyeh Killing Triggers Spate of Hezbollah Alerts," International Institute for Counter-Terrorism, September 7, 2008.

78. Israeli intelligence report, "Hizballah Leader's Visits to Europe," undated, author's personal files, received August 28, 2003. See, for example, Nicole Winfield, "Hezbollah Denounces Terrorist Label," Associated Press, May 24, 2002.

79. Israeli intelligence report, "Hizballah World Terrorism," undated, received by the author, August 5, 2003.

80. Matthew Gutman, "Israeli Arab 'Sold' Tannenbaum for $150,000," *Jerusalem Post*, October 14, 2003; "To Lebanon via Car, Container and Fishing Boat," *Haaretz*, May 7, 2002.

81. "To Lebanon via Car, Container and Fishing Boat."

82. Matthew Gutman, "Court Denies Tannenbaum Family's Plea," *Jerusalem Post*, October 23, 2003.

83. "To Lebanon via Car, Container and Fishing Boat."

84. Ibid.

85. Amos Harel, "Kais Obeid Plotted to Abduct Other Israelis," *Haaretz*, March 24, 2004; "To Lebanon via Car, Container and Fishing Boat."

86. Ibid.

87. Yossi Melman, "Tannenbaum Suspects Met While Visiting Jailed Relatives," *Haaretz*, October 22, 2003.

88. "Tannenbaum: I Was in Lebanon for Drug Deal," *Jerusalem Post*, December 21, 2006.

89. Yossi Melman, "Tannenbaum: Failed Businesses and an Ostentatious Lifestyle," *Haaretz*, October 23, 2003.

90. Gutman, "Court Denies Tannenbaum Family's Plea."

91. Melman, "Tannenbaum."

92. Author interview with former Israeli judiciary official, Israel, September 12, 2011.

93. Ibid.

94. Baruch Kra, "Drug Deal Cited in Tannenbaum Case," *Haaretz*, October 23, 2003.

95. Gutman, "Court Denies Tannenbaum Family's Plea."

96. Ibid.

97. "AM Archive: Israel Questions Colonel Released by Hezbollah," *Australian Broadcasting Corporation* (radio), February 27, 2004.

98. Matthew Gutman, "Tannenbaum Rumors Grow," *Jerusalem Post*, October 26, 2003; Kra, "Drug Deal Cited."

99. Gutman, "Tannenbaum Rumors Grow."

100. Ibid.

101. Yossi Melman and Baruch Kra, "Iran Said to Have Aided Hezbollah in Tannenbaum Kidnap," *Haaretz*, October 22, 2003.

102. Gutman, "Court Denies Tannenbaum Family's Plea."

103. Kra, "Drug Deal Cited."

104. John Kifner, "Hezbollah Says It Seized an Israeli Colonel," *New York Times*, October 16, 2000.

105. UK Parliament, "The Terrorism Act 2000: Proscribed Organisations," Standard Note SN/HA/00815, House of Commons Library, December 7, 2011, p. 25.

106. Robert Fisk, "Middle East Crisis: Hizbollah Boasts of How It Lured Colonel to Beirut," *Independent* (London), October 17, 2000.

107. Yossi Melman and Baruch Kra, "Lifting the Tannenbaum Gag Order Still Leaves Many Questions Unanswered," *Haaretz*, October 23, 2003; "Tannenbaum: I Was in Lebanon for Drug Deal."

108. Author interview with former Israeli military official, Washington, DC, August 2, 2011.

109. Gutman, "Court Denies Tannenbaum Family's Plea."

110. Melman and Kra, "Lifting the Tannenbaum Gag Order"; Gutman, "Court Denies Tannenbaum Family's Plea."

111. "Tannenbaum: I Was in Lebanon"; Israeli intelligence report, "Hezbollah's International Terrorism and the Penetration of Hezbollah Activists into Israel."

112. Liat Collins et al., "The Tannenbaum Affair," *Jerusalem Post*, March 12, 2004.

113. Melman and Kra, "Iran Said to Have Aided Hezbollah."

114. Collins et al., "Tannenbaum Affair."

115. Kifner, "Hezbollah Says It Seized Israeli Colonel."

116. Con Coughlin, "Iran Using Dubai to Smuggle Nuclear Components," *Telegraph* (London), June 6, 2010; Richard Spencer, "UAE Moves Illegal Nuclear and Weapons Trade," *Telegraph* (London), July 1, 2010.

117. Zeev Schiff, "Iran Was Involved in Tannenbaum Kidnap," *Haaretz*, October 23, 2003; Melman and Kra, "Iran Said to Have Aided Hezbollah"; Gutman, "Tannenbaum Rumors Grow." The fact that Tannenbaum was drugged was confirmed to the author in an interview with a former Israeli military official, Washington, DC, August 2, 2011.

118. Melman and Kra, "Iran Said to Have Aided Hezbollah."

119. Author interview, former Israeli judiciary official, Israel, September 12, 2011.

120. Author interview, former Israeli military official, Washington, DC, August 2, 2011.

121. "To Lebanon via Car, Container and Fishing Boat"; Gutman, "Israeli Arab 'Sold' Tannenbaum."

122. Gutman, "Israeli Arab 'Sold' Tannenbaum."

123. Ze'ev Schiff, "Israeli Security Officials Warn Hezbollah Planning Kidnappings," *Haaretz*, August 17, 2003.

124. Ibid.

125. "Hezbollah TV Interviews Israeli Prisoner Prior to Release," *al-Manar Television*, January 29, 2004, accessed through BBC Summary of World Broadcasts, January 29, 2004.

126. Author interview, former Israeli judiciary official, Israel, September 12, 2011.

127. Ronen Bergman, "The Mystery of Elchanan Tannenbaum," *Yediot Ahronot*, February 20, 2004.

128. Ibid.

129. "Tannenbaum: I Was in Lebanon."

130. "Israel Doubts Freed Captive Story," *BBC News*, February 19, 2004.

131. "Israel Makes Deal with Ex-Hostage," *BBC News*, February 27, 2004.

132. Reuters, "Formerly Captive Israeli Officer Stripped of Rank," June 25, 2007.

133. Israeli intelligence report, "Hizballah's International Terrorism."

134. Bell, *Cold Terror*, 80.

135. Ibid., 80–81.

136. Baer, *See No Evil*, 113.

137. Bell, *Cold Terror*, 81.

138. US CIA, "Iran: Enhanced Terrorist Capabilities."

139. "Moldova Expels Former Lebanese Honorary Consul for Hezbollah Connections," *Bucharest Mediafax* (English), October 28, 2001, accessed through Foreign Broadcast Information Service, October 29, 2001.

140. Radu Tudor, "Terrorism in Romania, Hizballah, Commercial and Propaganda Operations in Romanian University Cities," *Bucharest Ziua* (Romania), February 13, 2002, accessed through Foreign Broadcast Information Service, February 13, 2002. Information confirmed for the author in interview with Romanian security official, Washington, DC, July 2004.

141. Bell, *Cold Terror*, 81–82.

142. *United States of America v. Faouzi Ayoub*, Indictment, Case 2:09-cr-20367, filed under seal August 5, 2009, unsealed July 2011; see also Robert Snell, "Dearborn Man Accused of Bomb Mission on FBI's Most Wanted List," *Detroit News*, July 6, 2011.

143. Israeli Government, Office of the Prime Minister, "ISA Arrests Senior Hizballah Terrorist," press release, October 30, 2002.

144. Bell, *Cold Terror*, 82.

145. Ibid., 80–82.

146. Stewart Bell, "Canadian a Suspect in Plot to Kill Israeli PM," *National Post* (Canada), April 5, 2003.

147. *United States of America v. Faouzi Ayoub*, Indictment; see also US Department of Justice, FBI, "Most Wanted Terrorists: Faouzi Mohamad Ayoub."

148. Israeli intelligence report, "Hizballah's International Terrorism."

149. Bell, "Canadian a Suspect in Plot to Kill Israeli PM."

150. Ibid.

151. *United States of America v. Faouzi Ayoub*, Indictment.

152. Bell, *Cold Terror*, 85.

153. Israeli Government, Office of the Prime Minister, "ISA Arrests Senior Hizballah Terrorist"; see also Israeli Ministry of Foreign Affairs, "Iranian Activities in Support of the Palestinian Intifada," press release, January 30, 2003.

154. Israeli intelligence report, "Hizballah's International Terrorism."

155. Bell, "Canadian a Suspect."

156. Bell, *Cold Terror*, 113.

157. Ibid.

158. Bell, *Cold Terror*, 113–14; Israeli intelligence report, "Hizballah's International Terrorism."

159. Adrain Humphryes, "Canadian Seen as Planner of Hebron Attack," *National Post* (Canada), November 18, 2002.

160. Bell, *Cold Terror*, 116.

161. Author interview, former Israeli judiciary official, Israel, September 12, 2011.

162. Israeli Government, Office of the Prime Minister, "ISA Arrests Senior Hizballah Terrorist."

163. Bell, *Cold Terror*, 116.

164. Etgar Lefkovits, "Terror Suspect Given Six Months' Administrative Detention," *Jerusalem Post*, February 22, 2001.

165. Bar, "Deterring Nonstate Terrorist Groups," 469–93; *Mikdad*.

166. Israeli intelligence report, "Hizballah's International Terrorism."

167. Israeli Ministry of Foreign Affairs, "Details of Arrest of Jihad Shuman," press release, February 21, 2001.

168. Ibid.

169. UK Parliament, Alexander Home, "The Terrorism Act 2000: Proscribed Organisations," Standard Note SN/HA/00815, House of Commons Library, December 7, 2011, p. 25.

170. Intelligence and Terrorism Information Center at the Center for Special Studies, "Hezbollah (part 1): Profile of the Lebanese Shiite Terrorist Organization of Global Reach Sponsored by Iran and Supported by Syria," June 2003.

171. Jason Groves, "Hezbollah Will Avenge Iran Strike," *Sunday Express* (London), November 25, 2007.

172. Anthony Loyd, "Tomb of the Unknown Assassin Reveals Mission to Kill Rushdie," *Sunday Times* (London), June 8, 2005; UK Parliament, "Pursue, Prevent, Protect, Prepare: The United Kingdom's Strategy for Countering International Terrorism," Her Majesty's Government, March 2009, 29 (presented to Parliament by the Prime Minister and the Secretary of State for the Home Department.)

173. Buenos Aires, Argentina Judicial Branch, AMIA Indictment, Office of the National Federal Court No. 17, Criminal and Correctional Matters No. 9, Case No. 1156, March 5, 2003, 39, 210–11, 275.

174. Israeli intelligence report, "Hizballah Leader's Visits to Europe," undated, author's personal files, received August 28, 2003.

175. Author interview, British intelligence officials, London, April 15, 2010.

176. Israeli Ministry of Foreign Affairs, "Details of Arrest of Jihad Shuman."

177. Ibid.; United Press International, "Israel Jails Hezbollah Man with British Passport," February 21, 2001.

178. Bell, *Cold Terror*, 85.

179. Schweitzer, "Export and Import of Suicide Bombers."

180. Israeli Ministry of Foreign Affairs, "Details of Arrest of Jihad Shuman."

181. Israeli intelligence summary, "The Logic of Action and the Mode of Operation of the Hezbollah," author's personal files, November 29, 2011.

182. Israeli Ministry of Foreign Affairs, "Arrest of Hizbullah Agent from Kalansua," press release, August 6, 2008.

183. Israeli intelligence summary, "Logic of Action."

184. Alexander Ritzmann, "Hezbollah's Fundraising Organisation in Germany: The Orphans Project Lebanon Promotes Martyrdom in Lebanon with German Taxpayers' Money," European Foundation for Democracy, July 2009.

185. Intelligence and Terrorism Information Center at the Center for Special Studies, "Hezbollah, Part 1: Profile of the Lebanese Shiite Terrorist Organization of Global Reach Sponsored by Iran and Supported by Syria," Special Information Paper, July 2003, 92.

186. US Department of the Treasury, "Twin Treasury Actions Take Aim at Hizballah's Support Network," July 27, 2007.

187. Israeli Ministry of Foreign Affairs, "Arrest of Hizbullah Agent from Kalansua."

188. Ibid.

189. Israel Security Agency, *Data and Trends in Palestinian Terror*, "Palestinian Terror in 2008: Statistics and Trends," December 2008; Israeli Ministry of Foreign Affairs, "Arrest of Hizbullah Agent from Kalansua."

190. Israel Defense Forces, "Israeli Arab Indicted in Hezbollah Plot to Assassinate Lt. Gen. Ashkenazi," August 31, 2009.

191. Ibid.

192. Amost Harel, Jalal Bana, Baruch Kra, "Bedouin Officer Says He's Innocent of Spying for Hezbollah, Drug Dealing," *Haaretz*, October 25, 2002; "Israeli Colonel Jailed for Spying," *BBC News*, June 19, 2006; author interview, former senior Israeli official, Washington, DC, August 22, 2011.

193. Author interview, former senior Israeli official, Washington, DC, August 22, 2011.

194. Yaakov Katz, "Israeli-Arab Indicted for Hizbullah Plot to Assassinate Ashkenazi," *Jerusalem Post*, August 31, 2009.

195. Author interview, former senior Israeli official, Washington, DC, August 22, 2011.

196. Israel Defense Forces, "Israeli Arab Indicted in Hezbollah Plot"; Katz, "Israeli-Arab Indicted for Hizbullah Plot to Assassinate Ashkenazi."

197. "Former Shin Bet Official: Iran Knew of Israeli Arab Shadowing Ashkenazi," *Jerusalem Post*, March 9, 2009.

198. Ofra Edelman, "Israeli Arab Gets 5 Years, 8 Months for Spying on IDF Chief," *Haaretz* (Tel Aviv), June 4, 2010.

199. Indictment of Ameer Makhoul in Haifa Regional Court (Hebrew), author's personal files. See also Dan Izenberg and Yaakiv Lappin, "Israeli Arab Charged with Spying," *Jerusalem Post*, May 27, 2010; "Makhoul Exposed Location of Mossad Facility," *Ynetnews*, May 27, 2010; Dan Izenberg, "Makhoul Sentenced to 9 Years for Spying for Hizbullah," *Jerusalem Post*, July 26, 2011.

200. Indictment of Ameer Makhoul; Izenberg and Lappin, "Israeli Arab Charged with Spying"; "Makhoul Exposed Location of Mossad Facility," *Ynetnews*; Izenberg, "Makhoul Sentenced to 9 Years."

201. Israel Security Agency, "Hizballa Activity Involving Israeli Arabs," undated report; Margot Dudkevitch and Yaakov Katz, "Dane Recruited by Hizbullah: Shin Bet Reveals He Filmed Security Sites from Train in North," *Jerusalem Post*, January 27, 2005.

202. Israel Security Agency, "Hizballa Activity Involving Israeli Arabs"; Dudkevitch and Katz, "Dane Recruited by Hizbullah."

203. Benjamin S. Lambeth, "Air Operations in Israel's War against Hezbollah: Learning from Lebanon and Getting It Right in Gaza," RAND Corporation, Project Air Force, Prepared for the United States Air Force, 2011, pp. 154–57.

204. Daniel Sobelman, *New Rules of the Game: Israel and Hizballah after the Withdrawal from Lebanon*, Memorandum No. 69, Jaffee Center for Strategic Studies, Tel Aviv University, January 2004.

205. Barak Ravid, "Senior Wanted Person Arrived 5 Minutes from the Philadelphia Corridor," *Maariv* (Hebrew), September 23, 2005.

206. Ali Waked, "PA Fears Hezbollah Infiltrating Fatah," *Ynetnews*, December 28, 2009.

207. Ali Waked, "Tennenbaum's Kidnapper Recruiting for Hezbollah," *Ynetnews*, August 26, 2010.

208. Yaakov Katz, "Hezbollah Threat Prompts Security for Ashkenazi," *Jerusalem Post*, December 22, 2011.

209. United Press International, "Israel Fears Hezbollah Targets Top General," January 16, 2012.

9

Finance and Logistics in Africa

AT THE ISRAELI National Security Council's Counterterrorism Bureau, located at a military base not far from Tel Aviv, one particular stream of threat reporting commanded the nearly singular focus of senior officials for several weeks in the summer of 2008: kidnappings. And those kidnappings were happening on one particular continent: Africa.

Ever since the October 2000 kidnapping of Elhanan Tannenbaum, Israeli intelligence regularly uncovered information suggesting that Hezbollah was planning more such kidnappings. The targets, as with Tannenbaum, were Israeli businesspersons, most of them former military officers or government officials. In February 2002, for instance, Hezbollah considered kidnapping an Israeli businessman in Belgium, and in April, Hezbollah agents planned to abduct an Israeli businessman in the Netherlands. Another plot, which spanned several months starting in November 2002 and running into 2003, targeted an Israeli national in Spain.[1]

By late 2003, Hezbollah operational planners shifted their attention south. In December 2003, they were plotting to kidnap an Israeli military-officer-turned-businessman in Cyprus.[2] The Cyprus plot was foiled, but Hezbollah planners were already focused on kidnapping opportunities in Africa. Perhaps contrary to conventional wisdom, targets in Africa proved plentiful.

In October 2003, Israeli intelligence officials warned of a Hezbollah plot to kidnap Israeli businesspersons and diplomats in the Horn of Africa.[3] The warning included both general threat information related to Hezbollah activity in East Africa—focused in particular on Eritrea, Ethiopia, Kenya, Somalia, and Tanzania—as well as detailed intelligence identifying at least one specific diplomat as a target. According to Israeli officials, the warnings came from a number of sources and were given extra attention in light of threats by Hezbollah secretary-general Hassan Nasrallah to "work day and night to abduct more and more Israelis" if a prisoner swap then being mediated by the Germans was not imminently concluded. (On January 29, 2004, the same day a Hamas suicide bomber struck downtown Jerusalem, Israel released several hundred prisoners in return for Tannenbaum and the bodies of three Israeli soldiers.) Asked in October 2003 if such a prisoner swap would not embolden Hezbollah to kidnap more Israelis in the future, Israeli prime minister Ariel Sharon replied, "If they could kidnap someone right now, you think they wouldn't do it? They would kidnap now and they will try to kidnap in the future."[4] Later that year, Hezbollah operatives sought to kidnap a former Israel Defense Forces (IDF) colonel and diamond trader in Cameroon.[5]

Israeli officials feared the kidnapping threat was especially acute in the Horn of Africa: "For Hezbollah, Africa constitutes a very comfortable base of operations. On the one hand, there is a strong base for extremist Islamic groups there and, on the other hand, the local security forces and intelligence agencies are very lenient."[6] Describing Hezbollah's financial support activity in West Africa, one US official cautioned that even such support networks are "always a bit operational."[7] It therefore should not surprise that Israeli Counterterrorism Bureau officials saw the development of an effective traveler-warning system—one that would protect sensitive sources and methods while earning and maintaining the Israeli public's trust—as one of its highest priorities. Officials built such a system and later partnered with a major Israeli research university to study whether the public trusted and followed the warning system. Sometimes the warnings were general; other times, they were incredibly specific and warranted a detailed briefing to the intended target. In one case, an Israeli living in Madrid was on Hezbollah's radar as an easy target. In another, the European lover of an Israeli businessman was working with friends in Hezbollah who planned to kidnap the Israeli when the two spent a weekend away.[8] Hezbollah's interest in kidnapping Israelis appears to have been an Islamic Jihad Organization (IJO) innovation—a new take on an old tactic—executed as a means of collecting intelligence and securing the release of comrades incarcerated in Israel's and other countries' jails, completely different from the classic model of kidnapping for ransom.

In summer 2008, six months after Imad Mughniyeh's assassination, the Israeli Counterterrorism Bureau issued a warning specific to Hezbollah plots to attack Israeli citizens in West Africa. Unlike in previous cases, the bureau did not issue a general travel advisory warning against traveling to Africa. Instead, Israeli security officials traveled to specific communities in West Africa to warn visiting or resident Israelis about actionable threat information related to specific persons or communities. By now, Israeli officials worried about not only attacks against prominent individuals and significant targets but also low-profile attacks on targets of opportunity. With hundreds of Israelis working across the continent in endeavors ranging from large construction projects to the diamond trade, Africa provided a target-rich environment.[9]

The following month Israeli military officials intentionally leaked to the press the recent foiling by the Israeli security services and their local counterparts of five Hezbollah kidnapping plots in West Africa, Europe, North America, South America, and Asia, respectively. The plots, Israeli security officials reported, were part of "a concerted effort by Hezbollah, backed by Iran," to avenge Mughniyeh's assassination. "Hezbollah is scouring for prey, and it's going country by country" looking for a target of opportunity, an official told the press. While the assumption was that the individuals in question were targeted for kidnapping, authorities feared some or all the plots may have been attempts on their lives. "Several businessmen owe their lives and their freedom to this emergency operation," one Israeli security source noted, adding that all the operations were conducted jointly with foreign intelligence agencies.[10]

Kidnapping threats persisted throughout 2009, with warnings issued about Hezbollah plots in Europe in April and in Egypt that summer. In the latter incident, only a technical malfunction saved a busload of Israeli tourists in the Sinai, en route from Taba to Sharm el-Sheikh, from a roadside explosive device that, if properly wired, could have killed dozens. Among the chief concerns of Israeli authorities at the time was the prospect that Hezbollah operatives would kidnap Israeli tourists, perhaps grabbing wounded survivors after a roadside attack, and smuggle them into the Gaza Strip through one of the many tunnels that snake their way under the border at Rafah.[11]

The large Lebanese diaspora in Africa has long made the continent a particularly rich source of financial and logistical support for Hezbollah. Whether their supporters in any given community are many or few, Hezbollah operatives can hide in plain sight within these communities. And they can operate with near impunity because crime and corruption are endemic to Africa. In one representative assessment, a senior law enforcement adviser for Africa at the United Nations Office on Drugs and Crime explained that Africa attracts international organized crime because it consists of weak states, often characterized by corruption, dominated by weak and uncoordinated law enforcement agencies, and accustomed to the involvement of high-level officials in criminal activity.[12] In several African countries, a 2010 US Federal Research Division survey found, Lebanese with suspected or known ties to Hezbollah were associating themselves with key military and government officials and even heads of state to become financial advisers and confidants. From this position, the study noted, they could "pilfer millions of dollars from government contracts, kickbacks, or mismanagement of state companies."[13]

Africa has served not only as a prominent cash cow for Hezbollah but also as a place where exhausted or injured Hezbollah fighters went to recuperate, reportedly including Imad Mughniyeh himself.[14] With connections in the lucrative diamond industry, ties to heads of state and other prominent decision makers, and extensive business interests in Africa, prominent Lebanese Shi'a living in Africa have proven to be a critical link in Hezbollah's foreign support network. And as the string of kidnapping plots suggests, from time to time Hezbollah operatives have tapped this network to carry out terrorist operations as well. In January 1988, a CIA intelligence assessment projected that "paralleling developments inside Lebanon, Hizballah probably will expand its influence with the Lebanese African communities."[15] How those communities migrated to Africa in the first place is a story in itself.

Hezbollah Support Networks and
the Lebanese Diaspora in Africa

Maronite Christian immigrants from Lebanon, in what was then the Ottoman Empire, first arrived in West Africa in the nineteenth century, particularly in what is now Sierra Leone. The migrants were predominantly entrepreneurs either seeking to prevent their sons from being conscripted in the army under a fading Ottoman banner or fleeing financial pressures that hit Lebanon in the mid-nineteenth century. Africa, however, was not their destination of choice. According to a US intelligence report, "many of these early migrants traveled to Africa because they could not meet the more stringent health requirements of the United States and because travel documents were not needed for the French and British colonies."[16]

With the onset of World War I, the pace of migration increased. Some, looking for economic opportunities, were drawn to West Africa in response to British and French colonial officials who sought a foreign business class to serve as middlemen between the colonial governments and local populations—the latter of which had questionable loyalty to their colonial governments.[17] Shi'a Muslim immigrants started arriving in 1903, largely in response to population pressure and poor agricultural yields in southern Lebanon, and they quickly surpassed the Lebanese Christian community in numbers. This new wave of Lebanese immigrants not only hailed from a different confessional element of Lebanese society; in some cases—like the Lebanese émigrés to the Ivory Coast—it was also largely uneducated and impoverished.[18]

During the first half of the twentieth century, the Lebanese Shi'a community continued to grow in numbers and political influence, especially in Senegal, the Ivory Coast, and Sierra Leone.[19] In several countries, the success of Lebanese businessmen bred widespread jealousy and hostility on the part of locals. In 1919, riots broke out targeting Lebanese merchants in Freetown, Sierra Leone, who were suspected of hoarding rice at a time when the staple was scarce.[20]

Beginning in the 1970s, the Lebanese communities in Africa became more politicized with the arrival of additional immigrants, almost all of whom were Muslim and a majority of whom the CIA assessed were "members of Shia sects that are in practice, or at least potentially, influenced by Iran."[21] Whereas in the 1960s Christians made up nearly half the Lebanese community in the Ivory Coast, by the late 1980s their proportion had fallen to 10 percent. And of the 30,000 Lebanese in Sierra Leone, the CIA reported in January 1998, "about half have arrived in the last decade, and the majority are impoverished former street-fighters from Beirut."[22]

Throughout the Lebanese civil war, the various factions and sectarian elements of the Lebanese communities in Africa sent money back home to fund their respective groups' militias. Setting the stage for the kind of fundraising tactics Hezbollah would later master, many of these factions engaged in a wide array of illicit financial dealings to raise the needed funds. Organized gangs sometimes attacked businesses in a Mafia-style racketeering scheme to pressure businessmen to "donate" to the cause.[23]

Particularly as Lebanese Shi'a gained visibility in West Africa, views of the Lebanese community deteriorated among existing inhabitants. By the 1980s "the [once] indispensable middlemen between town and country" in the Ivory Coast were seen as "racist . . . corruptors of others as well as being themselves corrupt." Ivorians feared local Lebanese, regarding them as "a fifth column working towards the disintegration of the state." The Lebanese, Ivorians feared, sought to "'Palestinize' or 'Lebanize' the Ivory Coast by securing a hold on key posts of the economy." Their activities, a further fear held, would turn the country into a "haven of anti-Western lackeys of Hizbollah."[24]

As Hezbollah gained ground and members at the expense of Amal back home in Lebanon, a similar trend occurred in Africa. Having set itself apart from Amal, and with other groups like Islamic Amal joining the Hezbollah fold, the choice between the two groups became increasingly stark. Writing in 1988, the CIA noted that "over the past two years—reflecting events in Lebanon—Hizballah's presence in Africa has grown at the expense of Amal and other Muslim Lebanese factions."[25] Beyond ideological differences, financial incentives contributed to defections from Amal to Hezbollah, with the emergent group now offering "not only the virtue of ideological simplicity and authenticity, but the rewards of hard cash." While Hezbollah enjoyed the benefits of generous funding from Iran, Amal relied on donations from Lebanese supporters even during the hard-hit economy of the 1980s.[26] The loss of donations from Amal's supporters among the Lebanese diaspora in Africa, therefore, not only paralleled defections from Amal to Hezbollah back home in Lebanon but may have contributed to the phenomenon in Africa as well.

In fact, Amal appears to have been forced to rely more heavily on coercive measures to raise funds in Africa as increasing numbers of supporters were drawn to Hezbollah. Threatening the welfare of relatives living back in Lebanon if "donations" were not paid, Amal, in 1986, was able to collect $1 million from Nigerian Lebanese, $500,000 from Ivorian Lebanese, and $400,000 from Liberian Lebanese. (In time, Hezbollah would adopt this tactic itself). As Amal and Hezbollah jockeyed for power back home, the CIA assessed that the "many Lebanese in Africa are likely to rally to Hizballah's side and provide the movement with financial and material support."[27] That they did.

Over time, Hezbollah's support networks in western and central Africa grew substantially. Africa analysts reported that Hezbollah, with the help of its networks in East Africa, operated in Sudan, Uganda, and Somalia, holding the most extensive presence of all terrorist groups active in the area.[28] This expanded presence was the result of a concerted effort reportedly spearheaded by Imad Mughniyeh to build support networks within Lebanese Shi'a diaspora communities. By one account Mughniyeh was "the architect who instituted the establishment of support cells" in Lebanese Shi'a communities outside Lebanon.[29]

By 1988, support for Hezbollah had already become so entrenched within the Lebanese immigrant community in Africa that the CIA's Directorate of Intelligence wrote an eighteen-page analytical report on the economic and political roles of Lebanese communities in sub-Saharan Africa. The report made clear that the US intelligence community was concerned not only about Hezbollah's fundraising activities in the region but about the prospects for Hezbollah terrorist operations in Africa as well. One issue the paper sought to address was "the radical, pro-Iranian Hizballah movement" and "the potential for terrorism against pro-Western governments and U.S. facilities and citizens in the region." Portions of the declassified report that remain redacted include "Coping with a Terrorist Threat" and "Hizballah's Links to Tehran and Tripoli."[30]

Hezbollah Operations in Africa: The Hijacking of Air Afrique Flight 56

On January 13, 1987, German authorities arrested Hezbollah operative Muhammad Hammadi at Frankfurt Airport as he attempted to smuggle liquid explosives into the country. Around the same time, another Hezbollah operative was arrested in Italy, but it was the arrest of Hammadi in particular that led to a series of Hezbollah terrorist operations aimed, at least in part, at securing his release. Hezbollah could tolerate the arrest of an average operative, but not the arrest of a member of the IJO's inner circle. Such was the case with Imad Mughniyeh's fixation on securing the release of his brother-in-law, Mustapha Badredinne, and the rest of the Kuwait 17, and such was the case now with the Hammadi clan.

Hezbollah quickly carried out several operations aimed at securing Hammadi's release, including the kidnapping of two German nationals in Beirut.[31] The kidnapping of the German businessmen in Beirut was allegedly carried out by Muhammad Hammadi's brother, Abbas Ali Hammadi. When that operation failed to secure his brother's release, Abbas traveled to Germany himself, presumably as part of some more serious plot to free his brother. But on January 26, 1987, just thirteen days after his brother's arrest, Abbas was also arrested at Frankfurt Airport as he landed.[32] That appears to be when Hezbollah called upon Hussein Ali Mohammed Hariri to hijack Air Afrique flight 56—a civilian airliner traveling from Brazzaville, Republic of the Congo, to a final destination of Paris, France—in an attempt to secure the release of both Hammadi brothers, as well as other detained Hezbollah operatives.

Hezbollah's clear commitment to seek Hammadi's release indicated how important a player he was within Hezbollah's IJO. A member of a clan closely tied to Hezbollah, Muhammad Hammadi already had an impressive terrorist resume. Most notably, in June 1985, he and Imad Mughniyeh, together with several other Hezbollah operatives, hijacked TWA flight 847 after it took off from Athens and redirected the plane to Beirut.

Air Afrique flight 56, a DC-10 jumbo jet, originated in Brazzaville on the evening of July 24, 1987. Its flight plan called for stops in Bangui in the Central African Republic and then Rome before arriving in Paris. While officials first assumed Hariri had boarded the flight in Brazzaville, they later learned his embarkation point was Bangui, where he brought on board an Italian 7.65-millimeter pistol and explosives.[33] Amazingly, he smuggled these possessions onto three different flights without incident or challenge. At Beirut International Airport, Hariri hid his weapons in a box supposed to have contained pastries. From there he flew to Lagos, Nigeria, where he transferred the weapons into a sports bag that was carried on board by an airport employee. (It remains unclear if the employee was a knowing accomplice or simply assisting a passenger.) From Lagos, Hariri flew to Bangui, where a small, token bribe greased the palms of a local customs official to allow Hariri to bypass security.[34] He may have had more organized help, though. According to the CIA, "Hariri almost certainly received some support in the Central African Republic (CAR) before he boarded the flight in Bangui."[35]

One can imagine Hariri, now seated on the flight, his weapons on board, sighing in relief at having gotten this far unimpeded. For the next several legs of the trip, he bided his time, perhaps steeling himself for the moment of truth when he would strap on his explosives and hijack the aircraft. That moment came shortly after the plane took off from Rome for Paris. As the flight flew over Milan, Hariri brandished his handgun, exposed the explosives now wrapped around his waist, and commandeered the aircraft. Threatening to shoot passengers or blow up the plane, he demanded the flight veer off course and land in Geneva, Switzerland, for refueling so that he could direct the plane to Beirut. It appears Hariri intended to replicate Hammadi and Mughniyeh's TWA hijacking from just two years earlier.[36]

The flight landed at Geneva's Cointrin International Airport with 164 people on board. Aside from fifteen crew members, the great majority of the passengers, sixty-four, were French, but Americans, Britons, a Canadian, and citizens of several African and Latin American countries were also represented. After conferring with French and Ivorian officials (because the airline was headquartered in the Ivory Coast and was due to land in France), Swiss authorities decided the plane would not be allowed to leave Geneva. Meanwhile, Hariri issued demands for the release not only of the Hammadi brothers but of other jailed Hezbollah and Palestinian terrorists as well. As Swiss security forces considered how to charge the plane, airport personnel began refueling it as slowly as possible to buy time.[37]

Apparently keen to the refueling ruse, Hariri became nervous or angry (or both) over the delay and shot a French businessman, Zavier Beaulieu, through the mouth. Passengers in the back of the plane did not hear the shot but grew nervous when Hariri sent crew members to collect passengers' passports. At the time, France and Iran were engaged in a heated diplomatic spat over France's effort to arrest an Iranian diplomat. US intelligence would assess that "Hizballah's desire to take revenge on France—which has a number of pro-Iranian terrorists under arrest—helps to explain why Hariri singled out French passengers first."[38]

The turning point came when passengers overheard Hariri saying, "It is in Beirut that my problem will be solved." Then, when an announcement over the intercom indicated that the hijacker planned to reroute the flight to Beirut, several passengers scrambled for the doors to try to escape. "Beginning then," one passenger recalled, "we felt really threatened." Luckily, a Congolese crew member was able to overwhelm Hariri, and passengers flung a side door open and slid down emergency chutes to the tarmac. The brave crew member was shot in the stomach and seriously wounded, but he survived. As the passengers escaped and more crew members wrestled the hijacker to the ground, Swiss security forces stormed and secured the plane.[39]

Hariri, it turns out, not only went through Hezbollah military training but had been detained for ten months by Israeli authorities in the early 1980s on suspicions of terrorism. Saying he was prepared to die for his religion, Hariri would tell the court that sentenced him to life in prison, "You say I am a fundamentalist. I accept."[40] Hariri admitted carrying out the hijacking on Hezbollah's orders, saying it was an honor to be a "fighter for Allah."[41] Seventeen years later, Swiss authorities released Hariri from jail and deported him to Lebanon, well short of his full life sentence. Even his seventeen-year sentence proved eventful, including two attempted jail-breaks, the first in 1992 and the second a decade later. Although his second escape was successful, after two months, authorities tracked him down in Morocco. In August 2003, after nine months of legal machinations, Hariri was extradited back to Switzerland. His release and deportation to Lebanon occurred after he became eligible for parole fourteen months later.[42] In line with the CIA's initial suspicion, however, Swiss authorities continued to investigate someone they believed may have helped Hariri during his escape. It was not clear if that someone was believed to be connected to Hezbollah or not.[43]

Expanded Operations in "Nontraditional" Venues like Africa

An October 1987 intelligence report noted that "the Air Afrique hijacking dovetails with information that suggests Hizballah has increased planning for operations outside the Middle East." One reason Hezbollah was looking abroad was that Western targets were growing scarce in Lebanon following Hezbollah's kidnapping campaign, and those few remaining targets had been significantly hardened against potential attackers. Meanwhile, improved security measures in Europe meant more restricted access to targets of interest there.[44]

Considering Hezbollah's commitment to terrorism and the permissive operating environment that pervades the African continent, US intelligence warned, "We believe that Hizballah will turn increasingly to Africa as a site for terrorist operations." One reason for this concern was the level of support Hezbollah enjoyed in Africa. "Hizballah already has political supporters in place in several West African countries, some of whom presumably could recruit terrorist operatives from local Lebanese communities." The CIA warning continued, "Local Hizballah support-ers—or, as in Hariri's case, relatives of Hizballah members—could provide logistic support to operatives sent from Lebanon for specific operations."[45]

In a late July 1988 piece weighing the likelihood of an Iranian-sponsored attack in retaliation for the accidental US Navy downing earlier that month of Iran Air flight 655, the CIA speculated that Hezbollah terrorists could hijack or bomb a US airliner. "They would probably try to mount this kind of operation from an Asian or African airport where security is lax, American targets are more accessible, and local support networks are in place," the CIA assessed.[46] Later reports confirmed such suspicions were on the mark. In December 1989, CIA analysts wrote that following the Hezbollah hijacking of a Kuwaiti airliner out of Bangkok in April 1988, "the group was linked to operational activity in Ivory Coast and elsewhere in Sub-Saharan Africa" in 1988 and 1989.[47]

Investigations into Hezbollah's activities in Europe and Africa in 1989 led to further revelations about Hezbollah's logistical support network in Africa. An investigation initiated that August led to the arrest of a former French vice consul to Conakry, Guinea, for selling fifty blank French passports to Shi'a extremists. According to a US intelligence report, the investigation began when British authorities found "an authentic, French passport, issued in Conakry, among the belongings of a Hizballah operative who was killed when the bomb he was assembling in his London hotel room exploded." In the ensuing investigation, British authorities determined that the consular officer sold the authentic but blank passports to extremists with ties to Hezbollah. "The incident," the report concluded, "is another sign that Hizballah has an infrastructure in Africa that can be tapped to support terrorist operations elsewhere in the world."[48]

US intelligence remained concerned about Hezbollah's growing international support structure and operational capabilities in places like Africa. Writing in July 1992, the CIA assessed that Hezbollah's expanded international support network improved its ability to carry out attacks in unlikely places: "Hezbollah's efforts to expand its international support infrastructure have enhanced the group's ability to target U.S. and Israeli interests, particularly in non-traditional venues such as Eastern Europe, Latin America, and Africa."[49] Nearly two decades later, this assessment would still ring true. On August 5, 2008, a Nigerian official learned from Moshe Ram, Israeli ambassador to Nigeria, that Hezbollah was planning an attack against Israeli targets in West Africa. This was no empty threat. According to Ram, "[we] got a security threat yesterday from Hezbollah that our embassies in West Africa will be attacked."[50]

Expatriate Remittances: The Revealing Case of UTA Flight 141

Hezbollah's institutionalized presence in Africa, a benefit of operating within large, long-standing Shi'a communities, presents the group with especially lucrative fundraising opportunities. "Hezbollah uses the region extensively to raise funds, recruit new members and launder money," Former *Washington Post* West Africa bureau chief, Doug Farah, noted. "Because it is part of a large community, its presence there is much greater than that of al Qaeda, and more institutional. Because of that, it is both easier to identify and more difficult to uproot."[51] To be sure, not all Shi'a and certainly not all Lebanese living in Africa support Hezbollah. "It is important to note," a 2011 Congressional Research Service report stressed, "that the Lebanese community in West Africa is not monolithically Muslim nor completely supportive of Hezbollah, but mirrors the same religious and political divisions present in Lebanon." Yet according to the report, the Lebanese diaspora communities in West and central Africa continued to provide Hezbollah "a significant amount of financing."[52] The vast majority of these funds are raised through expatriate donations, Mafia-style shakedowns, front companies, and even blood diamonds and drugs.

Hezbollah's well-oiled campaign to solicit charitable donations from expatriate communities in Africa is perhaps best illustrated by the tragic crashing of a Union des Transport Africaines (UTA) charter flight in December 2003. Technical problems delayed the flight's departure, which had originated in the Guinean capital Conakry, and stopped in Freetown, Sierra Leone, before making a stop in Cotonou, Benin, before the final leg to Beirut. That Christmas day, the Lebanese-owned UTA plane, flight 141, registered in Guinea, clipped a building just after takeoff at 2:55 PM. The plane then exploded and crashed into the shallow surf just off the Atlantic coast, killing 141 of the 161 passengers on board.[53] Most of the casualties were Lebanese businessmen working in West African nations; fifteen were Bangladeshi peacekeepers returning to Lebanon from missions in Sierra Leone and Liberia.[54] Ten of those killed came from Kharayeb, a small village in southern Lebanon. Among the village's 5,000 residents, 300 had immigrated to Benin, "where they work, mainly in the car trade between Germany and Africa," a village official explained. "Theirs was an economic success story. You can see the proof in the beautiful villas they had built here [in Kharayeb] on the flanks of the hillsides."[55]

One passenger stood out, however: Sheikh Ali Damush, described as a representative of Hezbollah.[56] According to press reports, a "foreign relations official of the African branch of the Lebanese Hezbollah party and two of his aides" were among those killed. These press reports also claimed the Hezbollah officials were carrying $2 million in contributions, raised from wealthy Lebanese nationals living in Africa, to the organization's headquarters in Beirut. Arab reports indicated further that the $2 million "represented the regular contributions the party receives from wealthy Lebanese nationals in Guinea, Sierra Leone, Liberia, Benin, and other African states."[57]

The final report emerging from the French investigation into the crash revealed suspicious handling of the flight from the outset. Not only was there no overall flight manifest recording the boarding and loading of passengers and baggage, but seven different manifests were found, "all badly completed." Moreover, the flight was weighed down with around three tons of unreported baggage. This extra weight, investigators concluded, had been the direct cause of the accident, as compounded by structural flaws and several other possible contributing factors. In the final analysis, the plane crashed because of "the difficulty that the flight crew encountered in performing the rotation with an overloaded airplane."[58] By some accounts, the unregistered weight may have included as much as $6 to $10 million in cash. In a veiled reference to Hezbollah, Druze leader Walid Jumblatt suggested a scandal lay behind the UTA service that could implicate "big names."[59]

The day after the crash, Lebanon's foreign minister flew to Benin, together with a Lebanese diving team, to collect the Lebanese bodies and escort them, along with the few survivors, back to Lebanon. Also on the flight, Hezbollah indicated in a public statement, was a Hezbollah envoy. While Hezbollah quickly denied any ties to the crash, the group's immediate dispatching of an envoy to Benin "to console the sons of the Lebanese community" indicated the value it placed on these expatriate communities.[60]

The transfer of millions of dollars at a time via human courier is remarkable in its audacity, but not uncommon. In 1998, Lebanese expatriates in Senegal attempted to smuggle approximately $1.7 million to Lebanon.[61] At the time, the Lebanese in Senegal claimed the smuggling operation was merely an attempt to evade Senegalese law, not to finance Hezbollah. Israeli sources, however, rank Senegal as the "secondary center for Hezbollah's fundraising activity in Africa" after the Ivory Coast.[62] In December 2010, three men were arrested when they landed at Charles de Gaulle International Airport in Paris. The individuals were attempting to fly from Benin to Beirut via Paris with $6.5 million and €48,500 in undeclared funds, and a business card for Ellissa Megastore, a car lot in Cotonou, Benin, was found on one of the men. Further, between 2007 and 2008, Ghanian customs officials reported that $1.2 billion in declared US currency had been imported across Ghana's border with Togo, $845 million of which was declared by Lebanese nationals.[63]

Whatever the precise numbers, which in any event surely fluctuate, one conclusion is clear: "Many in the Lebanese diaspora community in West Africa, numbering several hundred thousand, pay a portion of their earnings to support Hezbollah in Lebanon, with the knowledge and acquiescence of the host government."[64]

One person who reportedly facilitated such donations was Sheikh Abd al-Menhem Qubaysi, a Lebanese national living in the Ivory Coast. In May 2009, the Treasury Department designated Qubaysi as a terrorist financier who played a public and prominent role in Hezbollah activities in the Ivory Coast. According to intelligence released by Treasury at the time of the designation, Qubaysi served as Hassan Nasrallah's personal representative in West Africa. "Qubaysi communicates with Hizballah leaders and has hosted senior Hizballah officials traveling to Cote d'Ivoire and other parts of Africa to raise money for Hizballah," the Treasury added. Beyond fundraising, the Treasury found that Qubaysi helped establish an official Hezbollah foundation in the Ivory Coast "which has been used to recruit new members for Hizballah's military ranks in Lebanon."[65]

About two months after the Treasury designation, Ivorian authorities detained Qubaysi at the airport on his return to the Ivory Coast on a commercial flight from Lebanon. Since 2006, an Ivorian counterespionage unit reportedly had Qubaysi under surveillance for his role in recruiting youths to fight in Lebanon.[66] Though he had lived in the country for several years, Ivorian authorities denied him entry for "security reasons" and sent him back to Lebanon on the same flight on which he arrived.[67] Ivorian defense and security forces planned to search the offices of the al-Ghadur Cultural Association, an official Hezbollah foundation used to "recruit new members for Hezbollah's military ranks" that Qubaysi helped establish. Last-minute intervention by President Laurent Ghagbo reportedly prevented the search.[68]

Examples such as that of Qubaysi led the authors of one US government study to note that contributions by Lebanese Africans, often taking the form of religious tithes, are frequently paid in cash and collected by Hezbollah couriers transiting the region for this express purpose.[69] As is the case among all terrorist groups that raise funds under the cover of charitable giving, some donors are willing participants in Hezbollah's financing schemes while others are unwittingly defrauded into funding terrorism. Yet another source of funds is furnished by criminal enterprises and businesses serving as fronts for the organization.

Fronting for the Resistance: Hezbollah's "Cover Companies" in Africa

According to US intelligence, "Hezbollah maintains several front companies in sub-Saharan Africa."[70] More specifically, many Hezbollah activists in the tri-border area of South America relocated to Africa and elsewhere following sharpened attention on the group's activities after the 1992 and 1994 bombings in Argentina. For example, Paraguayan authorities arrested Hezbollah's Assad Ahmad Barakat in 2002 just as he was about to flee to Angola.[71] According to a Paraguayan intelligence official, some of the primary Hezbollah members active in the tri-border area in 1992–95 likewise moved on to Angola. "We don't really know why they decided to go to Angola," the official added.[72] The heavy presence of front companies in Africa, however, predated the arrival of these transplants.

In May 2009, the Treasury Department designated Kassim Tajideen as "an important financial contributor to Hizballah who operates a network of businesses in Lebanon and Africa."[73] According to Treasury's fact sheet, Tajideen contributed tens of millions of dollars to Hezbollah and funneled money to the group through his brother, a Hezbollah commander in Lebanon. Tajideen, a dual citizen of Lebanon and Sierra Leone, was joined by his brothers in running "cover companies" for Hizballah in Africa, Treasury revealed.[74]

In fact, Tajideen had already been under investigation six years earlier. In May 2003, after a four-month international investigation by Belgium's Economic Crimes Unit, Belgian Judicial Police raided the Antwerp offices of Soafrimex, a Lebanese export company owned by Kassim Tajideen; arrested several of its officials; and froze its bank accounts on charges of "large-scale tax fraud, money laundering and trade in diamonds of doubtful origin, to the value of tens of millions of Euros." Tajideen and his wife were also arrested in connection with the charges. A few months later, Belgian authorities informed officials from the Congolese embassy that an investigation conducted on the ground in the Democratic Republic of the Congo (DRC) demonstrated that "the company systematically undervalued its imports, shipping and insurance costs and that it filed false customs declarations."[75]

Eight months after Treasury designated Kassim, another aviation tragedy struck the Lebanese African community. On January 25, 2010, moments after taking off from Beirut's Rafiq Hariri International Airport, Ethiopian Airlines flight 409, en route to Addis Ababa, crashed into the Mediterranean, killing all ninety passengers on board. Compounding the sense of despair, many people from southern Lebanon who had lost relatives in the 2003 crash lost family members in the Ethiopian Airlines crash as well. Once again, one name stood out among the many innocents killed for his ties to Hezbollah. This time it was Kassim Tajideen's brother and business partner Hassan, who was flying back to Africa with four employees from Arosfram, the food import company he owned. Speaking to the press at "the Hezbollah equivalent of a state funeral," one of Hassan's cousins said Hassan "had been living in Africa for over 30 years. He was a very successful businessman, with ties to Hezbollah, a movement he strongly supported."[76] The extent of that support became clear later that year, when the Treasury Department targeted two more Tajideen brothers—Ali and Husayn—as Hezbollah financiers, designating them and several of their companies, including Arosfram.[77]

Described as "two of Hizballah's top financiers in Africa," the two brothers ran a multinational network that generated millions of dollars for Hezbollah, according to the US Treasury. The businesses targeted by the Treasury Department were located as far afield as The Gambia, Sierra Leone, the DRC, Angola, the British Virgin Islands, and Lebanon. Treasury added that Ali alone provided huge cash payments to Hezbollah, in amounts as large as $1 million. And while he was apparently a major donor to Hezbollah, Ali Tajideen was no mere fundraiser, Treasury stressed; he was also "a former Hizballah commander" in Lebanon.[78]

Treasury noted that the Tajideen brothers' multinational network, beyond fundraising, "secures strategic geographical strongholds for Hizballah." The statement, strangely ambiguous at first, makes sense as one reads further into Treasury's press statement, where Ali Tajideen is noted as "a major player" in Jihad al-Binna, or Construction Jihad, the construction company formed and operated by Hezbollah and designated as a terrorist entity by Treasury in 2007.[79] The Lebanese press also noted Ali's ties to Jihad al-Binna, describing him as the head of the construction company in southern Lebanon.[80] In this capacity, several scholars later noted, he played a key role in Hezbollah's efforts to buy up swaths of real estate in Druze and Christian areas in Lebanon. Al-Binna's goal was to help Hezbollah build geographic continuity among Shi'a areas and to establish "security zones" in which Hezbollah constructed training camps.[81] Jihad al-Binna selects projects "based on political considerations that serve the overall objectives of Hezbollah," according to a 1999 UN report.[82] Treasury explained in its February 2007 designation of the firm, "Jihad al-Bina receives direct funding from Iran, is run by Hezbollah members, and is overseen by Hezbollah's Shura Council."[83]

The Tajideen brothers reportedly engaged in similar behavior using one of their companies, Tajco Company LLC, "as the primary entity to purchase and develop properties in Lebanon on behalf of Hizballah," according to the US government. Under the company's name, Treasury reported, Ali Tajideen developed the properties and established mortgage loans. His brother Husayn owned half the company and served as its managing director.[84] According to longtime Hezbollah watcher Nicholas Blanford, Ali Tajideen was reportedly paid top dollar for each square meter of land, often paying sellers' initial asking price in cash. The land purchases were near a new highway built by an Iran-funded nongovernmental organization (NGO) that replaced a potholed road running between Jezzine and the southern Bekaa

Valley—traversing precisely the security pockets where Hezbollah was said to be building Shi'a communities aimed at linking Shi'a communities in the east near Nabatiyah with others in the west.[85]

Also designated by the Treasury Department in 2010 were six other companies, including a supermarket chain in The Gambia, an import company in the DRC, a trading company in the British Virgin Islands, and a holding company, a food import company, and a retail store in Angola.[86] In September 2011, Angola's foreign migration office expelled 140 foreign nationals, including sixteen Lebanese, on suspicions of involvement in terrorism and money laundering. Four members of the Tajideen family, including Ali, were arrested because of their ties to Hezbollah.[87]

Alongside his own business activities, Husayn Tajideen was described by the Treasury Department as "a primary Hizballah fundraiser and prominent Hizballah supporter in The Gambia."[88] A year later, the Treasury Department exposed another Hezbollah money laundering scheme in The Gambia (see chapter 11). In this case, drug proceeds were used to purchase used cars in the United States that were then shipped to West Africa, among other destinations. These transactions were facilitated through the Lebanese Canadian Bank (LCB) and its subsidiaries, including Prime Bank Limited, a private commercial bank in The Gambia. LCB owned 51 percent of Prime Bank, with the remainder owned by local and Lebanese partners, according to LCB's 2009 annual report. According to information released by the Treasury Department's Financial Crimes Enforcement Network, one of those other owners is "a Lebanese individual known to be a supporter of Hezbollah."[89] In another case, FBI agents recruited a cooperating witness who helped them document Hezbollah's criminal activities spanning from Benin, Africa, to Pennsylvania, Lebanon, and Venezuela's Margarita Island.[90] For Hezbollah experts, the geographic reach fit a long-standing pattern.

Mafia-Style Shakedowns: "It's Not Even an Open Secret; There Is No Secret"

Tactics used by Hezbollah and Amal to raise funds from Lebanese communities in Africa have included "appealing to their religious convictions, appealing to their Lebanese identity or using threats and even outright violence," according to one NGO report.[91] For those expatriates who have resisted solicitations to support various groups back home, including Hezbollah, the response has often been attacks on commercial properties by organized groups of Lebanese thugs.[92] The more continuous expense for legitimate Shi'a businessmen involves "taxes" levied by Hezbollah, with payment enforced through Chicago-style racketeering.

"At least once a year," sources interviewed by Doug Farah explained, "senior Hezbollah operatives travel through the region collecting the 'donations' to be returned to Beirut."[93] According to one US study, "with the aid of extensive social intelligence networks in Lebanon and abroad, Hezbollah knows which Lebanon-based families have diaspora relatives." While some of the money is used to support Hezbollah networks in Africa, the study noted, most of the extorted cash is "probably remitted or hand-carried to Hezbollah central in Lebanon."[94] Carrying the cash home on chartered flights, Hezbollah couriers avoid banking regulations and the potential financial scrutiny of law enforcement authorities. And annually or semi-annually, Farah found, Hezbollah officials inform Lebanese businesses across West Africa just how much their contribution should be, based on an assessment of each business's expected earnings. That Hezbollah is in a position to make such assessments signals how institutionalized its enforced donation program has become.[95]

In some parts of Africa, Lebanese businessmen have historically controlled large segments of particular industries, thus making shakedowns an especially lucrative way of raising funds. While most Lebanese were middle-class traders, Lebanese communities also included a small number of multimillionaires in import-export, manufacturing, and agro-industrial companies. Consider some examples, as described in a 1988 CIA intelligence report. Lebanese in the Ivory Coast owned about 70 percent of the gas stations and a quarter of the grocery stores in Abidjan. Next door, in Liberia, Lebanese dominated Monrovia's retail sector, where they owned some 500 businesses, including restaurants, hotels, and cement and furniture factories. In the 1970s and early 1980s, the close political connections of one prominent member of the Lebanese community in Sierra Leone, Nabih Berri's friend Jamil Mohamed, allowed him to "exercise relatively unchecked control over the lucrative diamond and fishing industries," according to the CIA. (Jamil later fled the country following allegations he funded a coup attempt against the government.) In the former Zaire, a small community of some 7,000 Lebanese reportedly controlled some 40 percent of the commercial business in the capital. In the Central African Republic, the Lebanese community of just 4,800 members had "a near monopoly" on ownership of pharmacies and bakeries and owned several of the country's largest factories.[96]

In 1988, when Hezbollah as a movement was still somewhat small and vying with Amal for dominance within the Shi'a community, US intelligence anticipated that "competition between Amal and Hizballah for the allegiance of Africa's Lebanese will remain intense." Though Amal collected more funds in Africa than Hezbollah at the time, the CIA assessed that if Hezbollah were to gain the upper hand in Lebanon—as it ultimately did—a majority of the Lebanese in Africa would support the group. Some of this support might be willing, but the CIA anticipated much would be compelled. If Hezbollah were to overtake Amal back home, the CIA projected, "we believe that a majority of Lebanese in Africa, seeking to protect remaining family and business interests in Lebanon, probably would believe they had no choice but to side with Hizballah."[97]

Fast-forward to 2000, when a European Union official pointed out how Hezbollah pressures Lebanese in Africa to contribute to its cause. "Hizbullah is active and deeply involved in many businesses across the region," he noted. "It is only a small part of the Lebanese community that is sympathetic, but many people contribute to them just to keep Hizbullah off their backs."[98]

In 2004, US diplomats in West Africa publicly charged that Hezbollah was "systematically siphoning profits" from the region's lucrative diamond trade, in part by threatening Lebanese merchants. The deputy chief of mission at the US embassy in Sierra Leone was emphatic: "One thing that's incontrovertible is the financing of Hezbollah." Citing interviews by embassy staff with the targets of Hezbollah racketeering schemes, the deputy mission chief said, "It's not even an open secret; there is no secret. There's a lot of social pressure and extortionate pressure brought to bear: 'You had better support our cause, or we'll visit your people back home.' "[99]

Blood Diamonds: Funding the "Resistance"

In 2003, the NGO Global Witness determined, "There is already widespread understanding within the diamond industry and among governments that groups such as Hizbullah—who wield considerable influence over certain sectors of the diamond trading community—use the diamond trade to obtain funds."[100] According to the report, the "open secret" of Hezbollah diamond trading activity occurred across the continent, including in Angola, Burkina Faso, Congo, the DRC, Guinea, the Ivory Coast, Liberia, Namibia, Sierra Leone, South Africa, Tanzania, Zambia, and Zimbabwe.[101]

Not only are diamonds a sound investment, but buying diamonds mined in conflict zones enables less scrupulous investors to make an especially good return on their investment. Diamonds are also ideal for hiding, moving, and laundering cash. "Diamonds don't set off alarms at airports, they can't be sniffed by dogs, they are easy to hide, and are highly convertible to cash. It makes perfect sense," as one US official put it.[102] And while the barriers to entry into the diamond business are high, groups like Hezbollah have been able to leverage relationships with businessmen who have overcome these barriers to gain access to the market. Such concerns led the US State Department to report to Congress in 2002 that "reports that terrorists may be buying and hoarding diamonds are cause for immense concern."[103]

Hezbollah is believed to have raised significant funds by dealing in so-called conflict diamonds in the 1980s and 1990s and even as recently as 2003. In their testimonies before the US Senate on the links between conflict diamonds and terrorism, the former US ambassador to Sierra Leone, Joseph Melrose Jr., and the former Sierra Leonean ambassador to the United States, John Leigh, confirmed that diamonds mined in Sierra Leone finance the activities of terrorist groups such as Hezbollah and al-Qaeda.[104] In 2003, David Crane, the American prosecutor for the Special Court in Sierra Leone, concluded, "Diamonds fuel the war on terrorism. [Liberian President] Charles Taylor is harboring terrorists from the Middle East, including al-Qaeda and Hezbollah, and has been for years."[105]

Given the central role of the city of Antwerp in the global diamond trade, it should not surprise that Belgian authorities took a particular interest in the issue of terrorist abuse of the diamond trade in general, and through the sale of blood diamonds in particular. A July 2000 Belgian military intelligence report, which addressed diamond smuggling from Angola to Antwerp, concluded, "There are indications that certain persons, the "Lebanese connection" mentioned in the diamond smuggling file, also put in an appearance in files on money laundering, the drugs trade and the financing of Lebanese terrorist organizations such as Amal and Hezbollah. This finding gives a whole new dimension to the issue of diamond smuggling, we are NO longer dealing simply with white-collar crime [emphasis in the original]."[106]

Though the start of the Angolan civil war (1975–2002) predated Hezbollah and its movement into the African diamond smuggling business, the group was well positioned to exploit the conflict and reportedly continued doing so despite international sanctions. Again, it was Belgian intelligence that "identified several Lebanese diamond traders as having links with Hizbullah and as having bought diamonds from UNITA (National Union for the Total Independence of Angola) before and after the imposition of the UN embargo in July 1988."[107] Between 1992 and 1998, the State Department reported, UNITA exported between $3 and $4 billion worth of diamonds.[108] Global Witness further noted that, according to the Belgian report, some of the same Lebanese diamond traders and companies were also tied to organized crime, money laundering, and drug trafficking. One such company was reportedly knee-deep in trading banned Angolan diamonds obtained from UNITA. The revenues from its diamond sales "were apparently transferred via Switzerland to Lebanon, Iran and Syria," according to Global Witness and the Belgian intelligence report.[109]

Later, when the United Nations investigated violations of the Angola sanctions, a collection of five Western and African intelligence agencies all "pointed to the involvement of a Lebanese diamond trading network that was buying diamonds from UNITA before and after the imposition of sanctions in July 1998." One Lebanese diamond trader cited in the Belgian report, whose family was reported to be "connected with Shi'ite organizations, in particular Hezbollah," was Imad Bakri. Interestingly, press reports identified his brother, Yousef, as one of eleven Lebanese diamond dealers executed for their alleged roles in the assassination of President Laurent Kabila in the DRC in January 2001. Hezbollah reportedly pressured the DRC government to return the bodies to Lebanon, suggesting some or all of the accused Lebanese plotters had ties to the group.[110]

Nor were Hezbollah's ties to conflict diamonds limited to Angola. According to a former US official with firsthand experience following Hezbollah activity in Africa, Sierra Leone has become "Hezbollah's center of gravity" in Africa.[111] In large part, blood diamonds explain why.

For more than a decade starting in 1991, the Revolutionary United Front (RUF), a rebel army renowned for fielding child soldiers and committing gross crimes against humanity, fought the central government in Sierra Leone with the generous support of Liberian president Charles Taylor. The RUF mined the diamond fields under its control, and reportedly used Lebanese diamond traders with ties to Hezbollah as middlemen.

Douglas Farah, whose 2001 *Washington Post* reports highlighted Hezbollah and al-Qaeda ventures in African conflict diamonds, identified the RUF's principal diamond dealer as Ibrahim Bah, a former Senegalese rebel–turned–Islamist militant. In the 1980s, Bah trained with Hezbollah in Lebanon's Bekaa Valley and fought with the group in southern Lebanon before returning to Libya, where he met and befriended a variety of African militants. From 1987 to 1988, Bah was in Afghanistan, training at a jihadi camp near Khost and fighting in the Afghan jihad against the Soviets. At one point during these early years of his militant career, Bah also served as a bodyguard to Libyan dictator Muammar Qadhafi. By the end of the 1980s, Bah was back in Africa fighting for Charles Taylor—one of the people with whom he trained in Libya—and his National Patriotic Front of Liberia.[112] In July 2000, a small-time diamond dealer, Ali Darwish, earned $50,000 for introducing Bah to Hezbollah supporter Aziz Nassour, Farah reported. Bah then contracted Nassour to manage large quantities of diamonds on behalf of RUF and al-Qaeda.[113] By 2001, intelligence sources and associates identified Bah as "a conduit between senior RUF commanders and the buyers from both al Qaeda and Hezbollah."[114]

Among the Lebanese businessmen with whom Bah worked, Aziz Nassour and Sammy Ossailly were identified as two of his "key brokers." Together, the three men signed a three-year lease on a four-bedroom house in Monrovia to be used as a safe house. There, in rooms decorated with Hezbollah posters and pictures of Osama bin Laden, the Senegalese hired to staff the safe house were said to watch videos of Hezbollah suicide attacks on Israeli troops.[115]

Starting in the late 1990s, an intelligence source told the *Washington Post*, the Congo in particular saw an influx of "hard-core Islamist extremists" in what was described as a new "Wild West." The intelligence source acknowledged "we know Hezbollah is here, we know other groups are here, but they can probably operate a long time before we know enough to stop them."[116] Shortly after Farah ran his first story on this issue in November 2001, the regional security officer at the US embassy in Abidjan, Ivory Coast, where Farah was living, shared with him two lines of a classified cable reporting credible threats against Farah's life for reporting the story. The next day Farah's editor received another warning from a different country's intelligence service that individuals were planning "to take care of the *Washington Post* reporter." A source of Farah's informed him further that Ibrahim Bah planned to plant drugs on Farah at the airport, forcing Farah and his family to be escorted onto their flight home by US embassy security personnel.[117]

Aziz Nassour and Sammy Ossailly's activities as blood diamond smugglers who pay for the stones with weapons used to fuel war in Africa are further documented in a Belgian police slide presentation. Marked "For Police Use Only," the presentation focuses on the two operatives' activities from 1999 to January 2002. Filled with detailed link-analysis charts and including handwritten notes and lists of weapons, the presentation is compelling.[118] In October 2002, Belgian Federal Police provided two different FBI field offices with information regarding the diamond smuggling activities of Sammy Ossailly and Aziz Nassour.[119] At one point, Belgian investigators sought the assistance of their American counterparts when one of the individuals they were investigating was found to be staying at a hotel in Miami.[120]

Expelled from Angola in 1998 after having been accused of helping UNITA, Nassour moved to Marbella, Spain, where he worked with Mohammed Derbah, a reported Amal member involved in weapons trafficking. In late 2001, Spanish authorities arrested Derbah "for involvement in arms trafficking and financing

Hizballah and AMAL." Seventeen additional people were arrested with Derbah, all tied to a Canary Islands–based ring associated with Amal and Hezbollah and involved in fraud, money laundering, forgery, and extortion. Two years later, Derbah was arrested again, this time for money laundering. The group, which Spanish judge Baltasar Garzon linked to Amal and Hezbollah, netted more than $10 million a year, primarily through an especially lucrative time-share scheme targeting German and British citizens.[121]

In 2002, both Nassour and Ossailly were arrested, this time in Belgium, and convicted of illicit diamond smuggling in 2003.[122] But even as authorities investigated their activities, others stepped in to keep Hezbollah's diamond pipeline intact. Another person whose company Belgian intelligence suspected of "possibly being connected to Hizballah" was Abdallah Ezziddeen. In spring 2002, Ezziddeen reportedly tried to buy a diamond-prospecting concession on the Namibian coast near South Africa. But when meeting with the owners of the concession, he expressed little interest in its production potential—he just wanted to buy in immediately. The exchange raised authorities' suspicions that Ezziddeen's interest may not have been in the excavation of Namibian diamonds per se, but in the ability to smuggle blood diamonds mined illegally elsewhere into Namibia and register them as having been found in Namibia. A common practice among illicit diamond smugglers, the scheme enables smugglers to declare and then legally export diamonds that would otherwise be subject to sanctions and strict export controls. Hearing news of the possible concession sale, Israeli security consultants reportedly met with the sellers and expressed a keen interest in Ezziddeen and the prospect of the sale going through. The sale did not go through, but Hezbollah's reach into the African diamond industry persisted.[123]

As recently as September 2006, a senior State Department counterterrorism official testifying about Hezbollah's global reach noted that "Lebanese traders are also very active in diamond exports, both as a business and in criminal exploitation."[124] In 2008, when reports emerged that Hezbollah might be targeting Israeli businessmen in Africa, Israeli diamond merchants were not surprised. "The big problem for Israelis in West Africa," an Israeli in the diamond business commented, "is that there are countries whose diamond industry is controlled by Lebanese locals, a majority of whom openly support Hezbollah."[125]

US officials confirmed the gist of the Israeli businessman's fears when, in December 2011, the United States Attorney for the Southern District of New York filed a forfeiture action and civil money laundering complaint against the Lebanese Canadian Bank (LCB), several money-exchange houses and other companies, and thirty US used car purchasers and dealerships. The civil action, based on a detailed Drug Enforcement Administration (DEA) investigation, found that among the Hezbollah-affiliated entities with which the Lebanese bank did business was a Belgian diamond trader of Lebanese origin named Ibrahim Ahmad. According to a UN panel of experts, the civil complaint noted, a company in which Ahmad was a principal purchased $150 million in diamonds from the DRC in 2001. Ahmad's clan, the UN report noted, had ties to Hezbollah and was involved in counterfeiting, money laundering, and diamond smuggling.[126] As auditors combed through the LCB's accounts, they found almost 200 accounts that, according to US officials, "appeared to add up to a giant money-laundering operation, with Hezbollah smack in the middle." At the center of many of the complex transactions they uncovered was one common theme: companies trading diamonds.[127]

Radicalization and Recruitment by Iran and Hezbollah in Africa

Committed to its constitutional directive to export the Islamic Revolution, the Islamic Revolutionary Guard Corps (IRGC) proactively recruits Shi'a in Africa by tapping the efforts of Iranian and Lebanese missionaries proselytizing across the continent. One of the most prominent clerics to come has been Sheikh Abdul-Munam Azzain, a former student of Ayatollah Khomeini who opened a Shi'a Islamic Center in Dakar, Senegal, in 1978. In Nigeria, Sheikh Ibrahim Alzakzaky has been described as "a protégé of Iran [who] is involved in disseminating Shiite theology and creating a radical socio-economic and military system that resembles that of Hezbollah in Lebanon."[128]

As early as 1985, the CIA was aware that Iran was known to "promote subversive activity" among remote countries with Shi'a populations, including Nigeria.[129] Three years later, a CIA report acknowledged the phenomenon was far more widespread than originally thought, highlighting Hezbollah's participation in efforts to spread Iran's Islamic revolutionary vision across Africa. Despite the group's relatively small size at the time, the CIA wrote in 1998, "We believe Hezbollah—sometimes acting in concert with Iran—will continue to seek the spread of its brand of fundamentalist Islamic revolution in Africa." Working both independently and together, the intelligence report anticipated, Hezbollah and local Iranian diplomatic missions would be "likely to focus attention on the African Muslim communities in West Africa, especially in pro-Western Liberia and Sierra Leone." And while unlikely to win many religious converts, Hezbollah and Iranian diplomats could be counted on to "expand their inroads among Africa's Christian and animist populations" by offering more of a populist than a religious message as a counterweight to Western influence in the region.[130]

Analysts and officials confirm that Hezbollah continues to partner with Iran to spread a shared ideological message of Islamic revolution. "In some parts of Africa," Doug Farah wrote in 2006 based on interviews with US and European intelligence officials in West Africa, "Hezbollah, through Iran, has also worked to recruit militants and develop a teaching network of radical Shi'ite imams and mosques to compete with the larger and more visible Saudi-funded Sunni Salafist efforts."[131] Sometimes such efforts are understated and coordinated through local institutions sponsored by Iran. For example, an Israeli report identified a mosque in Kinshasa, the capital of the DRC, that was financed by the Iranian embassy and suspected of serving as "a kind of umbrella framework for fundraising activity on behalf of Hezbollah."[132] Another report pointed to a similar institution, the Iranian Cultural

Center in Khartoum, Sudan, which "is used as a meeting place by Islamic networks and as a center for disseminating Iranian propaganda and Shi'ite literature."[133] Shortly after setting up its first diplomatic mission in Sierra Leone in 1983, "the Iranian embassy in Freetown acquired the reputation of being the centre of Iran's spy network for all West Africa," according to Global Witness. Suspicions were likely fed by the establishment of an Iranian cultural center in Freetown that was never actually opened to the public.[134] In 2009, the Moroccan government cut off diplomatic ties with Iran over Tehran's aggressive use of such proselytizing tactics in the North African state.[135]

In other cases—though rare—Hezbollah and Iran have engaged in more blatant, public radicalization efforts. In 2008, for example, press reports included pictures of a joint Hezbollah-Iran parade in Nigeria, where an unidentified Shi'a mullah was given full military honors by uniformed militiamen before a crowd sporting hundreds of yellow Hezbollah flags and giant posters of Hezbollah chief Hassan Nasrallah and Iran's late Ayatollah Khomeini and current leader Ayatollah Khamenei. "One can draw a number of similarities," one analyst noted, "between the Cuban 'volunteers' who were acting at the behest of the Soviet Union, promoting communism in Africa in the 1960s and 1970s and Hezbollah acting as Iran's proxy, advancing Tehran's Islamic revolution today."[136]

Often Iran recruits directly from the pool of Lebanese Shi'a communities across Africa. The Africa Division of the Revolutionary Guard's Qods Force has "built many cells in Africa," according to a 2011 report, "most of which rely on Shiite emigrants from Lebanon who live in Africa." Once spotted and recruited, these recruits are sent to Iran for training. According to a retired Israeli military officer, "Lebanese recruited for the Iranian intelligence efforts were invited to visit Iran, where they underwent training in the field of intelligence. Upon their return, they serve as a nucleus for recruiting others and provide a base for Iranian intelligence activity in their countries."[137]

Such efforts are not limited to Lebanese Shi'a. According to a study commissioned by the US military, Iran uses scholarships to African students as "a major recruitment tool." Iranian scholarships are offered to students across Africa as part of Tehran's "greater diplomatic effort to simultaneously promote the broader Hezbollah agenda in Africa and undermine Western influence and credibility across the continent." Wherever Iran has embassies in Africa, the report added, "it also sets up cultural centers that 'award' scholarships and 'study tours' to Iran."[138] One such effort, focused on the recruitment of Ugandan Shi'a for religious study—and military and intelligence training—in Iran was exposed in 2002.[139]

The Ugandan recruits, along with young Lebanese Hezbollah members, underwent a month-long basic training course "specially tailored by Iranian intelligence." The mixed group of Ugandan Shi'a and Lebanese Hezbollah recruits was then taught to use a variety of small arms, produce improvised explosive devices, collect preoperational intelligence "on installations and people for terrorist attacks," plan escape routes, and withstand interrogation techniques. The students were given fictitious covers, money, and means of communication and then "instructed to collect intelligence on Americans and Westerners present in Uganda and other countries."

Their Iranian handlers saw these new recruits as force multipliers, telling both Shafi Ibrahim, leader of a cell of Ugandan Shi'as working for Iran, and his partner Sharif Wadoulo to be attuned to the need to expand Iran's network in the region and "to recruit other Ugandan civilians for similar assignments."[140]

Smuggling Arms via Africa

Iran has a long history of smuggling weapons through Africa.[141] As case after case has demonstrated, Hezbollah enjoys greater operational flexibility and support in those places where Iran runs intelligence and logistical support networks. Iranian involvement in the *Karine A* weapons smuggling ship—intercepted by the Israeli Navy in the Red Sea in January 2003—is especially revealing not only in terms of the quality and quantity of the weapons being shipped, or in its intended recipient being the Palestinian Authority, but also in the hands-on role played by Hezbollah in the operation.

The naval commando raid had all the makings of a Hollywood script. As dawn broke on January 3, 2002, Israeli Navy commandos boarded the *Karine A* as it plied the waters of the Red Sea en route to the Suez Canal. The operation, executed in the high seas some 500 kilometers south of Israel, went forward flawlessly and without injury. In a press statement the following day, then–Israeli chief of staff Shaul Mofaz praised the "daring and complicated mission" executed by a task force made up of Israeli Navy commandos, air force fighter pilots providing air cover, and intelligence specialists.[142] The seized ship was rerouted to the southern Israeli port of Eilat, where its crew was arrested and contents seized. Spread out over the secured dock, the weapons arsenal was huge.[143]

Most weapons smuggled through this region would arrive by ship at Port Sudan, after which they would be smuggled north overland across the Egyptian border, through the Sinai, and into the Gaza Strip. Not in this case. Purchased in Lebanon in August 2001, the ship then sailed to Port Sudan, where over twelve days it was loaded with regular cargo and renamed the *Karine A*. Both the regular cargo and the name change were designed to provide cover for the ship's true mission, smuggling weapons. Also in Sudan, the ship's original crew was replaced with the smuggling team, including Omar Akawi, an officer in the Palestinian Authority's nascent navy. Over time, Port Sudan became well known as "a shipping point for Iranian arms to Hamas in Gaza and to Islamist organizations in both North and Sub-Saharan Africa."[144]

In November, the *Karine A* departed Port Sudan and sailed over four days to the port city of Hodeidah, Yemen. On the instructions of Adel Mughrabi, the Palestinian Authority's point man on the weapons smuggling operation, the ship then sailed for the Iranian island of Qish in December 2001. According to Israeli officials, since October 2000, Mughrabi had been in regular contact with the Iranian agents and Hezbollah operatives with whom he planned the smuggling plot.[145]

Near Qish, a ferry commanded by a Mughniyeh deputy, Hajj Bassem, approached the *Karine A* in Iranian waters, and the process of loading the weapons—stored in eighty large wooden crates—from the ferry to the *Karine A* began. Hajj Bassem personally oversaw the transfer, according to Israeli and US accounts. Meanwhile, one of Bassem's men aboard the ferry trained a member of the *Karine A*'s crew to configure the submergible flotation devices in which the weapons would ultimately be delivered.[146]

The plan was to pass through the Suez Canal and unload the weapons onto three smaller boats, which would then approach the coast and drop the waterproof containers off the shore of El Arish in the northern Sinai and the Gaza Strip just to its north. The containers, designed in Iran specifically for weapons smuggling, would float just below the surface, where they would remain until retrieved, all the while invisible from above water. But mechanical problems resulted in slight delays for the ship, including a return to the port of Hodeidah, Yemen. Unbeknownst to the smugglers, Israeli intelligence caught on to the plot and planned a raid several hundred kilometers away from the Suez Canal.[147]

The *Karine A* episode stands out not only for the magnitude and audacity of the arms Iran attempted to smuggle but for the quality of these weapons as well. The weapons seized aboard the *Karine A* were described as "force multiplier weapons systems" that would have drastically shifted the balance of power between Israeli forces and Palestinian militant groups. The weapons included 107- and 122-millimeter rockets and launchers with ranges of up to twenty kilometers, antitank launchers, 120-millimeter mortars, antipersonnel mines, and more. Some of these arms still bore serial number markings revealing they were produced in Iran in 2001. By some accounts the money needed to purchase both the ship and the arms was underwritten by Iran, while the ship's operational expenses (crew salaries, insurance payments, etc.) were covered by the Palestinian Authority.[148] But according to another account, the Palestinian Authority paid $15 million for the apparently discounted weapons themselves, but Hezbollah footed the $400,000 bill for the boat, purchased by a Palestinian Authority official.[149] Asked who he thought sent the weapons, the Palestinian captain of the *Karine A* replied, "I believe it was from Hizballah."[150] Speaking before the European Parliament in Strasbourg, France, in February 2002, European Union head of foreign affairs Javier Solana described the *Karine A* as "the link between Iran and the PA [Palestinian Authority]."[151]

While it is by far the biggest smuggling plot thus far funded by Iran, the *Karine A* incident is by no means the only one. Hezbollah and the Popular Front for the Liberation of Palestine–General Command were both involved in other maritime smuggling efforts involving the *Santorini* and the *Calypso-2*, which between them made three successful smuggling runs to Gaza and the Egyptian Sinai—in November 2000 and twice in April 2001—before a fourth attempt was thwarted by the Israeli Navy in May 2001.[152] In May 2003, the Israeli Navy intercepted the *Abu Hassan*, a fishing vessel on which Hezbollah was attempting to smuggle to Palestinian militants thirty-six CD-ROMs featuring bomb-making instructions, detonators, and a radio activation system compatible with rockets, suicide bombs, and remote-controlled explosives. The Israeli commandos also captured Hamad Abu Amar, a Hezbollah explosives expert, on board the boat.[153]

Six years later, in January 2009, Sudan's continued role as the preferred weapons smuggling route in the region was exposed when Israeli fighter-bombers, backed by unmanned drones, destroyed a twenty-three-truck convoy traveling through the Sudanese desert carrying arms destined for Hamas in the Gaza Strip. The arms arrived at Port Sudan and were loaded into the vehicles for the cross-desert trek. Iran's role in the plot was confirmed when news broke that several Iranians were reportedly killed in the airstrike.[154] Two years later, another Israeli airstrike targeted a car some fifteen kilometers south of Port Sudan, killing both passengers. One of them, according to press reports, was a Sudanese citizen; the other was a senior Hamas military commander.[155] In October 2012, four aircraft—presumably Israeli—bombed a Khartoum weapons factory reportedly run by the IRGC.[156] In the words of one analyst, Sudan offers "a very practical supply route for the Iranians to use." Sometimes it is not just a route for transporting weapons but also a place to procure them. "The arms market in Sudan is thriving and acts as a very easy way for Iran to send agents, mainly though Hezbollah, to come under false passports into Sudan, buy those arms, and transport them primarily via trucks across Sudan and into the Sinai Peninsula" and from there to the Gaza Strip.[157]

Colluding with Sunni Extremists in East Africa

By the late 1980s and early 1990s, Hezbollah operatives began appearing in areas where Sunni Islamist groups were operating. For example, a 1987 CIA report documented Hezbollah's propaganda ties to Egyptian extremists. "Although logistical ties probably are extremely limited and are likely to remain so," the CIA noted, "for Hezbollah and its Iranian patron closer public ties and apparent cooperation with radical Sunni groups constitute a valuable propaganda success underscoring their commitment to Islamic unity."[158] Within a few short years Hezbollah would be cooperating much more closely with Sunni extremist elements in Africa.

In November 1993, reports emerged indicating that several Hezbollah operatives, including car-bomb experts, had arrived in Mogadishu and "could be planning car bomb attacks on U.S. and U.N. forces in Somalia." According to US officials, hardline followers of Somali warlord Mohamed Farah Aideed had established ties to Hezbollah.[159]

Thirteen years later, a few months after the end of the July 2006 war between Israel and Hezbollah, the United Nations revealed that during the war Somalia's radical Islamic Courts Union (ICU) dispatched approximately 720 experienced militants to Lebanon to fight alongside Hezbollah against the Israeli military. "One of the criteria of the selection process," the UN monitoring group reported, "was individuals' combat experience, which might include experience in Afghanistan." Only eighty or so members of the Somali militant force returned to Mogadishu after the fighting ended, some of whom were wounded and received medical care at a private hospital the United Nations described as "operated and secured" by the ICU.[160]

In early September, the United Nations reported, around another twenty-five Somali fighters returned home, accompanied by five Hezbollah members. The UN report did not specifically say what business the five Hezbollah members had in Somalia, though it did note elsewhere that "the Hezbollah movement (operating in Lebanon) has provided military training to ICU and has made arrangements with other States on behalf of ICU for the latter to receive arms." Among the Somali fighters who had not returned home, the report added, "a number" extended their stays in Lebanon to attend advanced military training courses provided by Hezbollah.[161]

Hezbollah's presence in Somalia from the 1990s until the present day mirrored a larger shift in the group's operations and fundraising activities from West to East Africa, with a particular emphasis on Sudan. In the mid-1990s, according to former CIA chief George Tenet, Hassan Turabi, the leader of the Sudanese National Islamic Front, not only hosted terrorist conclaves and allowed terrorists to run training camps in Sudan but also facilitated the travel of North Africans to Hezbollah training camps in Lebanon.[162]

According to the State Department's 1999 global terrorism report, Sudan continued to serve as "a meeting place, safe haven, and training hub" not only for Hezbollah but for members of al-Qaeda, the Egyptian terrorist groups al-Jihad and al-Gama'a, and a variety of the Palestinian terrorist groups.[163] By rubbing shoulders in Sudan, where they enjoyed safe haven and openly engaged in terrorist training, such groups sometimes developed unlikely relationships.

One such relationship began when Hezbollah and Iran established contacts with senior al-Qaeda members in Sudan in the 1990s. According to the *9/11 Commission Report*, "while in Sudan, senior managers in al Qaeda maintained contacts with Iran and the Iranian-supported worldwide terrorist organization Hezbollah." Intelligence, the 9/11 Commission found, "indicates the persistence of contacts between Iranian security officials and senior al Qaeda figures after Bin Laden's return to Afghanistan." In fact, following the successful al-Qaeda attack on the USS *Cole* in Aden harbor in October 2000, Iranian officials reached out to al-Qaeda in a "concerted effort to strengthen relations," according to the *9/11 Commission Report*.[164]

In 1991 or 1992, the 9/11 Commission determined, "discussions in Sudan between al-Qaeda and Iranian operatives led to an informal agreement to cooperate in providing support—even if only training—for actions carried out primarily against Israel and the United States. Not long afterward, senior al Qaeda operatives and trainers traveled to Iran to receive training in explosives." Yet another delegation trained in explosives, intelligence, and security procedures in Hezbollah camps in Lebanon in fall 1993, the commission remarked.[165] As part of their agreement, the CIA noted, "experience from Hezbollah and Iran should be transferred to new nations/extremist groups who lack this expertise. This would then allow [bin Laden's] Islamic Army members [al-Qaeda] to gain the necessary experience in terrorist operations."[166]

Al-Qaeda and affiliated Egyptian terrorist groups sought to gain operational knowledge from Hezbollah and Iran in order to advance their own capabilities. Ali Muhammad, an Egyptian Islamic Jihad (EIJ) operative who was also involved in the 1998 East Africa embassy bombings, pointed to Hezbollah's success in the 1983 bombing of the marine barracks at Beirut International Airport and explained that both al-Qaeda and EIJ wanted to learn how to replicate such attacks.[167]

Seeking to achieve such objectives, al-Qaeda and EIJ operatives held a series of meetings in Sudan with their Iranian and Hezbollah counterparts. Ali Muhammad described one particular meeting between Hezbollah's international operations chief, Imad Mughniyeh, and bin Laden. According to Muhammad's testimony following the meeting, "Hezbollah provided explosives training for al-Qaeda and al Jihad [EIJ]. Iran supplied Egyptian Jihad with weapons. Iran also used Hezbollah to supply explosives that were disguised to look like rocks."[168]

Yet while Sudan and Iran built ever-closer ties, Khartoum's relationship with Hezbollah eventually seems to have soured. In summer 2006, just after Hezbollah's war with Israel, Sudanese president Omar al-Bashir publicly commended "the steadfastness of Hezbollah under the leadership of Nasrallah."[169] Three years later he praised Hezbollah again, saying, "We trust Hezbollah and its leadership and we consider them a genuine resistance group deserving respect and honor."[170] But in the same year, in a first-ever acknowledgment of Sudan as a weapons-smuggling route, a Sudanese diplomat in Egypt claimed that Sudanese rebel groups in the country's south may have partnered with Hezbollah to facilitate weapons smuggling through Sudan. "The suspicions of [Hezbollah] dealing with rebel groups that are spread all over Sudan are real since these movements do not recognize the national sovereignty in the first place," he said.[171] A year later, perhaps trying to placate the central government in Khartoum, Hezbollah came to President al-Bashir's defense after the International Criminal Court indicted him for the second time, this time for genocide. In a statement posted on a Hezbollah website, Hezbollah expressed "complete solidarity with Sudan—with its president, its government, and its people—over the new allegations leveled against the president of Sudan, Omar al-Bashir, by the International Criminal Court."[172]

But that was not all. Also in 2010, Hezbollah leader Hassan Nasrallah reportedly offered to put Hezbollah fighters at the disposal of the Sudanese government to confront what Nasrallah described as "the colonialist forces in Darfur." There is no evidence the offer, apparently made in a letter to the governor of Northern Darfur, was acted upon, but the governor seems to have responded positively. "Darfur is a land in which Islam runs deep and we are more than eager to support the Palestinian and Lebanese causes though Jihad and martyrdom," the governor reportedly replied. Echoing a typical Hezbollah mantra, he added, "This is not religious extremism, rather the defense of rights of the oppressed around the world."[173]

And then something changed, albeit quietly. No announcement was made, but sometime in 2010 Sudan reportedly added Hezbollah to its list of terrorist groups and organizations. According to press reports, a US diplomatic cable dated December 26, 2010, noted the addition to the secret Sudanese government lists, which, the cable stressed, are not published and are available only through personal connections with officials from Sudan's National Intelligence and Security Service.[174] At the time, Sudan was working hard to win Washington's good graces. Though weapons smuggling for Hamas, in particular, and other support for terrorism continued, the State Department reported in 2010 that Sudan remained a cooperative partner in actively targeting global jihadist terrorist groups like al-Qaeda.[175] Sudan remained on the State Department's list of state sponsors of terrorism, however, and it is not clear if Sudan's designation of Hezbollah—if, in fact, the cable documenting the unpublished list is accurate—ever led to any concrete action by Sudan targeting Hezbollah.

Information pointing to continued Hezbollah and al-Qaeda ties persisted through September 11. "Circumstantial evidence" indicates that senior Hezbollah operatives were "closely tracking" some of the September 11 hijackers' trips into Iran in late 2000. For example, in November 2000, September 11 hijacker Ahmed al-Ghamdi traveled to Beirut on the same flight as a senior Hezbollah operative. In addition, three of the September 11 hijackers, Wail al-Shehri, Waleed al-Shehri, and Ahmed al-Nami, flew from Saudi Arabia to Beirut and then to Iran. On their flight to Iran, a senior Hezbollah official traveled on the same plane. According to the commission report, "Hezbollah officials in Beirut and Iran were expecting the arrival of a group during the same time period. The travel of this group was important enough to merit the attention of senior figures in Hezbollah."[176] While the 9/11 Commission found no evidence that Iran was "aware of the planning for what later became the 9/11 attack," it cited "strong evidence" that Iran facilitated al-Qaeda members' travel— including that of some of the September 11 hijackers—through Iran to Afghanistan.

Hezbollah's African Narco-Terrorism Connection

One area in which groups affiliated with both Hezbollah and al-Qaeda are now active is smuggling drugs through Africa. A particularly lucrative means of terrorist financing, the African narcotics pipeline has secured the immediate attention of intelligence and law enforcement officials around the world. In late February 2012, Yuri Fedotov, head of the UN Office on Drugs and Crime, informed the UN Security Council, "The West African transit route feeds a European cocaine market which in recent years grew four fold, reaching an amount almost equal to the U.S. market. We estimate that cocaine trafficking in West and Central Africa generates some $900 million annually."[177]

A year earlier, in February 2011, US director of national intelligence James Clapper testified, "Drug trafficking continues to be a major problem in Africa." Speaking in the context of his annual US intelligence community worldwide threat assessment, Clapper highlighted "the emergence of Guinea-Bissau as Africa's first narco-state" in an effort to "highlight the scope of the problem and what may be in store for other vulnerable states in the region."[178] The drugs flowing through the small West African nation were not African in origin. With almost no drug cultivation or production of its own, Guinea-Bissau hosted only the corruption and lawlessness that made it an attractive transit route for traffickers of South American narcotics. Drugs from Brazil, Colombia, and Venezuela—and some from elsewhere in Africa—pass through Guinea-Bissau en route to southern Europe, according to the State Department's 2010 counternarcotics report.[179]

At least some of this activity, according to Interpol and UN reports, involves Hezbollah and other terrorist groups. "Cocaine traded through West Africa accounts for a considerable portion of the income of Hezbollah" and other terrorist groups, according to one report. Hezbollah leverages Lebanese Shi'a expatriate communities in South America and West Africa "to guarantee an efficient connection between the two continents."[180] Speaking in April 2009, Interpol secretary-general Ronald

Noble acknowledged that law enforcement efforts "dismantled cocaine-trafficking rings that used their proceeds to finance the activities of the FARC [Revolutionary Armed Forces of Colombia] and Hezbollah, while drugs destined for European markets are increasingly being channeled through West African countries."[181]

The drug smuggling threat came into focus in spring 2007, when two cocaine shipments from South America—each around 630 kilograms—were seized in Africa, one in Guinea-Bissau and the other in Mauritania.[182] By April 2010, the problem had become so endemic that the US Treasury Department felt compelled to designate Guinea-Bissau's former navy chief of staff and its then–current air force chief of staff as drug kingpins. Among other activities, the two officials were "linked to an aircraft suspected of flying a multi-hundred kilogram shipment of cocaine from Venezuela to Guinea-Bissau on July 12, 2008," according to the Treasury Department.[183] Then, in November 2009, an unmarked Boeing 727-200 commercial jet mysteriously crashed in the northern Mali desert some ten miles from a makeshift airstrip. Though completely burned out, the aircraft was suspected by authorities to be carrying a massive shipment of drugs, with a plane that size capable of carrying up to ten tons of narcotics. The mystery was compounded by the revelation that Mali's aviation authority was barred from investigating the crash for more than three weeks, and Mali's police counternarcotics unit was not allowed to investigate the crash at all. The entire investigation was run by Mali's secret intelligence service. In the wake of these episodes, American and British diplomats drafted cables expressing heightened fears about "the prospect of al-Qaida and Hezbollah exploiting the region's UN-estimated $1.3bn-a-year drug trade to fund terror."[184]

For those investigating the drug trade on the ground, the dangers are real. One journalist, Marco Vernaschi, recounted being dragged out of a Bissau hotel bar by six drunken Lebanese. "We all know what the foreign journalists look for in this country," the ringleader said. "And I know your name, Marco, so if I see anything published from you that mentions drug trafficking I will find you, wherever you are." Despite the threat, Vernaschi subsequently published content arguing that even considering the generous support the group received from Iran, "most of Hezbollah's support comes from drug trafficking, a major moneymaker endorsed by the mullahs through a particular fatwa." Vernaschi wrote that for a fee, Hezbollah facilitates drug trafficking for other smuggling networks, including those of the Colombian terrorist group FARC. Once shipments arrive at one of the ninety islands off the coast of mainland Guinea-Bissau, the cocaine is broken down into smaller batches and either sent by fast boat to Morocco or Senegal or trucked in armed four-wheel-drive vehicles across traditional Sahel (transcontinental corridor north of the Sahara) smuggling routes.[185]

"Mark my words," warned Michael Braun, the former head of the DEA's Special Operations Division, in congressional testimony in summer 2009, "as we speak here today, operatives from al Qaeda, Hezbollah and Hamas—perhaps others—are rubbing shoulders with Latin American and Mexican drug cartels, including the FARC, in West African countries and other places on the [African] Continent."[186] Together these illicit actors have become what Braun describes as "hybrid terrorist organizations," groups that he described from firsthand experience as "meaner and uglier than anything law enforcement or militaries have ever faced."[187] And they have developed mutually beneficial relationships of convenience. In Africa, Braun testified, "they are frequenting the same seedy bars and sleazy brothels, and they are lodging in the same seamy hotels. And they are 'talking business.' They are sharing lessons learned, sharing critically important contacts and operational means and methods."[188]

Adm. James Stavridis, then commander of US Southern Command, noted in 2009 that these syndicates' expanded presence in West Africa has become their "springboard to Europe."[189] In January 2010, *Der Spiegel* reported that in the previous year German authorities had arrested two Hezbollah members with ties to Hassan Nasrallah and other senior Hezbollah officials. The two had trained in Hezbollah camps but were arrested not for terrorist or militant activities but for cocaine trafficking on behalf of the group. The October 2009 arrests followed a pitched investigation that started in May 2008 when customs agents at Frankfurt Airport seized €8.7 million in cash and another half million later at the suspect's apartment. To their surprise, investigators found traces of cocaine on the bills along with the fingerprint of an infamous Dutch drug kingpin.[190]

A dramatic exposé of the full scope of both the African drug problem and Hezbollah's role in it appeared in January 2011 when the US Treasury Department blacklisted Lebanese narcotics trafficker Ayman Joumma along with an additional nine individuals and nineteen businesses involved in his drug trafficking and money laundering enterprise. With criminal associates and front companies in Colombia, Panama, Lebanon, Benin, and the Democratic Republic of Congo, Joumma's organization was truly transnational. But while his drug ties to South America and his terrorist ties to Lebanon were unsurprising, the African narco-terrorism link—and its direct connection to the United States—was a wake-up call. An extensive DEA investigation revealed that Joumma laundered as much as $200 million a month from the sale of cocaine in Europe and the Middle East through operations located in Lebanon, West Africa, Panama, and Colombia through money exchange houses, bulk cash smuggling, and other schemes.[191]

Another prominent Hezbollah operative involved in laundering drug money through Africa is Oussam Salhab, according to US officials. Court documents citing evidence collected during DEA investigations identify Salhab as "a Hizballah operative who, among other things, controls a network of money couriers who have transported millions of dollars in cash from West Africa to Lebanon." A close associate of his, Maroun Saade—who belongs to the Free Patriotic Movement, a Lebanese Christian group allied with Hezbollah—ran another major drug trafficking organization tied to Hezbollah in Africa. Along with several other defendants, Saade was indicted in February 2011 on narco-terrorism and other charges related to his alleged agreement to sell cocaine to people he believed were affiliated with the Taliban and to transport and distribute Taliban-owned heroin in West Africa.[192] In several instances, Saade reportedly bribed officials to close investigations into narcotics trafficking or to obtain the release of money couriers working for Salhab who were arrested by Togolese authorities for smuggling bulk currency across the border. In one case, in July 2010, Salhab himself was arrested along with one of his couriers, and Saade paid the bribes for their release. In another case, Saade bribed officials to close a narcotics investigation into the activities of Imad Zbib, described in US court documents as "a prominent Hizballah representative in Togo." According to US officials, Zbib is a close associate of Salhab and has transported loads of two to three metric tons of cocaine from South America to Togo, concealing the hauls in used cars purchased through lots he owns and transporting the drugs to Europe for sale.[193]

People like Ayman Joumma and Oussam Salhab appear to have been in the right place at the right time. As demand for narcotics increased in Europe and the Middle East, South American cartels started looking for new routes to these growing markets. One route went to Europe through West Africa, and another through Syria and Lebanon. The Middle East route benefited from Hezbollah's ties to Iran and Venezuela. According to Lebanon's drug enforcement chief, Col. Adel Mashmoushi, one way drugs were sent to Lebanon was on board the weekly Iran Air flight from Venezuela to Damascus and then overland by trucks to Lebanon. Confirming this route, US officials stressed that "such an operation would be impossible without Hizballah's involvement."[194]

Thanks to its support networks on both sides of the Atlantic, Hezbollah has a natural advantage vis-à-vis Latin American drug kingpins looking to transport their product to or through Africa. The only Spanish-speaking country on the African continent is Equatorial Guinea, and even the Portuguese dialect spoken in Angola differs from that spoken in Brazil. Long active as cargo aggregators, Lebanese merchants—including those with ties to Hezbollah—are well placed to use their existing logistical machinery to facilitate the movement of other products. From a trafficking perspective, it matters little whether the product being moved is frozen chickens, cigarettes, gasoline, or drugs.[195]

With several notable exceptions, Hezbollah has primarily relied on its formal and informal networks of operatives and supporters in Africa for just this kind of financial and logistical support, not as a preferred location for terrorist operations. The decision may seem counterintuitive given the lax law enforcement and gross corruption that plague so much of the continent. Moreover, the cost of getting caught red-handed engaging in operational activity in Africa, in addition to being unlikely, would be minimal since the region lacks many political or economic heavyweights to make Hezbollah pay the price for carrying out operations on their soil. Yet Africa presents Hezbollah financial and logistical opportunities few other areas can offer. Recognizing this, Hezbollah has preferred not to jeopardize its position on the continent unless presented with particularly attractive (and relatively low-risk) opportunities. Kidnapping operations, as well as cases like the Hezbollah network disrupted in Egypt in spring 2009, fall into this latter category.

Another reason Hezbollah may not have carried out more operations in Africa may be the influence of the larger Lebanese West African community. In an assessment considering the prospects for Hezbollah terrorism in Africa, the CIA considered that "the vast majority of Lebanese in West Africa—many of whom are prosperous members of the business community—reportedly would oppose terrorist activity by their countrymen out of fear that local governments would respond with a crackdown against the entire Lebanese community."[196] Hezbollah itself appears to have become increasingly self-constrained as Africa has grown ever more important as a cash cow feeding the group's coffers through mostly illicit funding channels. Such calculations undoubtedly factor into Hezbollah operational planning considerations. All the same, for more than twenty years, the group has balanced its sometimes competing interests toward achieving a variety of financial, logistical, and sometimes operational purposes.

Hezbollah has balanced similarly competing needs and influences in deciding how and when to operate in other places around the world as well, including in its own Middle Eastern backyard. In recent years, this balancing act has manifested itself most blatantly in the exposure of Hezbollah's activities in Iraq.

Notes

1. Author interview with senior Israeli counterterrorism official, Tel Aviv, November 16, 2004.

2. Ibid.

3. Author interview with Israeli official, Washington, DC, December 2003; also reported in Ellis Shuman, "Mossad Warns: Hezbollah Planning to Kidnap Israelis in Africa," *Israel Insider*, October 27, 2003.

4. Shuman, "Mossad Warns."

5. Author interview with senior Israeli counterterrorism official, Tel Aviv, November 16, 2004.

6. Shuman, "Mossad Warns."

7. Author interview with US intelligence official, Washington, DC, July 2003.

8. Author interview with senior Israeli counterterrorism official, Tel Aviv, August 4, 2009.

9. Amos Harel, "Officials: Hezbollah Planning Attack on Israelis in Africa," *Haaretz* (Tel Aviv), August 4, 2008.

10. Itamar Eichner, "Israel Foils 5 Attempted Abductions by Hizbullah," *Ynetnews* (Tel Aviv), September 2, 2008.

11. Barak Ravid, "Israelis in Europe Warned of Hezbollah Kidnap Threat," *Haaretz* (Tel Aviv), April 23, 2009; "Technical Glitch Stopped Terror Attack in Sinai," *Jerusalem Post*, September 23, 2009.

12. United Nations, Office on Drugs and Crime, Flemming Quist, Senior Law Enforcement Advisor for Africa, "Is Africa under Attack?" 2011.

13. Rex Hudson, "Lebanese Businessmen and Hezbollah in Sub-Saharan Africa: A Symbiotic Relationship," US Library of Congress, Federal Research Division, September 2010. For further discussion on corruption, see Elizabeth Blunt, "Corruption 'Costs Africa Billions,'" *BBC News*, September 18, 2002; "Africa Tops World Corruption Ranks," *Voice of America News*, October 26, 2010.

14. Douglas Farah, "Hezbollah's External Support Network in West Africa and Latin America," International Assessment and Strategy Center, August 4, 2006.

15. US CIA, "Lebanese in Sub-Saharan Africa."

16. Ibid.

17. Lansana Gberie, "War and Peace in Sierra Leone: Diamonds, Corruption and the Lebanese Connection," Occasional Paper no. 6, Partnership Africa Canada, International Peace Information Service, Network Movement for Justice and Development, November 2002; US CIA, "Lebanese in Sub-Saharan Africa."

18. Gberie, "War and Peace in Sierra Leone."

19. Farah, "Hezbollah's External Support Network in West Africa and Latin America."

20. Didier Bigo, "The Lebanese Community in the Ivory Coast: A Non-native Network at the Heart of Power?" in Hourani and Shehadi, eds., *The Lebanese in the World*, 1992.

21. US CIA, "Lebanese in Sub-Saharan Africa."

22. Ibid.

23. Gberie, "War and Peace in Sierra Leone."

24. Bigo, "Lebanese Community in the Ivory Coast."

25. US CIA, "Lebanese in Sub-Saharan Africa."

26. Norton, *Amal and the Shi'a*, 106.

27. US CIA, "Lebanese in Sub-Saharan Africa."

28. Hudson, "Lebanese Businessmen and Hezbollah in Sub-Saharan Africa."

29. Jacque Neriah, "Iran Steps Up Arming Hizbullah Against Israel," *Jerusalem Issue Briefs* 10, no. 21 (January 10, 2011), Jerusalem Center for Public Affairs.

30. US CIA, "Lebanese in Sub-Saharan Africa."

31. US CIA, "Iranian Support for Terrorism in 1987."

32. Edward Cody, "Hijacker Kills Plane Passenger; Gunman Captured by Crew in Geneva," *Washington Post*, July 24, 1987.

33. Craig Whitlock, "Hijacker Sought by U.S. Released," *Washington Post*, December 21, 2005; US CIA, "Prospects for Hizballah Terrorism in Africa."

34. Frances Williams, "Hizbollah Hijacker Gets Life," *Independent* (London), February 25, 1989.

35. US CIA, "Prospects for Hizballah Terrorism in Africa."

36. Cody, "Hijacker Kills Plane Passenger."

37. Ibid.; US CIA, "Prospects for Hizballah Terrorism in Africa."

38. Cody, "Hijacker Kills Plane Passenger"; US CIA, "Prospects for Hizballah Terrorism in Africa."

39. Ibid.

40. "Swiss Give Life Term to a Lebanese Man in a Fatal Hijacking," *New York Times*, February 25, 1989.

41. Williams, "Hizbollah Hijacker Gets Life."

42. "Lebanese Hijacker Freed after 17 Years in Prison," *New York Times*, October 18, 2004.

43. "Switzerland Deports Convicted Hijacker Back to Native Lebanon," Swiss Radio International's Swiss information website, October 17, 2004, obtained via BBC Summary of World Broadcasts, October 17, 2004.

44. US CIA, "Prospects for Hizballah Terrorism in Africa."

45. Ibid.; US Department of the Treasury, "Treasury Targets Hizballah Network in Africa," press release, May 27, 2009.

46. US CIA, "Shootdown of Iran Air 655."

47. US CIA, "Middle Eastern Terrorism: Retrospect and Prospect."

48. US CIA, "Former Consul Arrested for Selling Passports."

49. US CIA, "Lebanon's Hizballah."

50. "Israeli Embassies under Security Threat–Envoy," *Nigeria Daily News*, August 5, 2008.

51. Statement of Douglas Farah, *Fighting Terrorism in Africa*.

52. US Library of Congress, Congressional Research Service, *Hezbollah: Background and Issues for Congress*.

53. "Final Report Accident on 25 December 2003 at Conomou Cadjehous Aerodrome (Benin) to the Boeing 727-223 Registered 3X-GDO Operated by UTA (Union des Transports Africains)," *Bureau d'Enquêtes et d'Analyses* (BEA, France) December 15, 2010. The report caveats these numbers, noting "some doubts remain as to the total number of passengers." The 138-seat plane reportedly had more than 160 people on board. See "Mysterious Passengers, Loads of Cash Puzzle Investigators into Christmas Crash," *Naharnet* (Lebanon), January 8, 2004.

54. Hussein Dakroub, "Bodies of 77 Lebanese Killed in Benin Crash Flown Home," Associated Press, December 28, 2003.

55. Jihad Saqlaoui, "Lebanese Village in Mourning after Plane Crash in West Africa," Agence France Presse, December 26, 2003.

56. Ibid.

57. Hamid Ghiryafi, "Hezbollah Officials Carrying Donations Reportedly Killed in Lebanese Plane Crash," *al-Siyasah* (Kuwait), December 29, 2003.

58. "Final Report Accident on 25 December 2003 at Conomou Cadjehous Aerodrome (Benin) to the Boeing 727-223 Registered 3X-GDO Operated by UTA (Union des Transports Africains)," *Bureau d'Enquêtes et d'Analyses* (France: BEA), December 15, 2010.

59. Mysterious Passengers, Loads of Cash Puzzle Investigators into Christmas Crash," *Naharnet* (Lebanon), January 8, 2004.

60. Mariam Karouny, "Benin Plane Crash Deaths Rise to 111," Reuters, December 26, 2003; "Hizbullah Denies any Links to the UTA Plane Crash," *Daily Star* (Lebanon), January 14, 2004.

61. Intelligence and Terrorism Information Center at the Center for Special Studies, "Hezbollah (part 1): Profile of the Lebanese Shiite Terrorist Organization of Global Reach Sponsored by Iran and Supported by Syria," June 2003; author interview with Israeli intelligence official, Tel Aviv, July 2003.

62. Ibid.

63. Ibid.

64. Statement of Douglas Farah, *Confronting Drug Trafficking in West Africa*.

65. US Department of the Treasury, "Treasury Targets Hizballah Network in Africa," press release, May 27, 2009.

66. Hudson, "Lebanese Businessmen and Hezbollah in Sub-Saharan Africa."

67. US Department of State, Office of the Coordinator for Counterterrorism, "Country Reports on Terrorism 2009," August 2010; Agence France Presse, "Imam Deported from Abidjan, Accused by US of Funding Hezbollah," August 9, 2009.

68. Hudson, "Lebanese Businessmen and Hezbollah."

69. US Library of Congress, Congressional Research Service, *Hezbollah: Background and Issues for Congress.*

70. Author interview with US intelligence official, Washington, DC, July 2003.

71. "Chief Extremist Arrested in Foz Trying to Flee to Angola," *ABC Digital* (Paraguay), June 26, 2002.

72. Author interview conducted via email, March 24, 2004.

73. US Department of the Treasury, "Treasury Targets Hizballah Network in Africa."

74. Ibid.

75. "Coin in the Congo: The Moral Bankruptcy of the World Bank's Industrial Logging Model," *Carving Up the Congo* part 3, Greenpeace, April 11, 2007, p. 34.

76. Mona Alami, "Disproportionate Loss," *NOWLebanon*, January 27, 2010; Tony Badran, "Hezbollah Acts Local, Thinks Global," *NOWLebanon*, June 22, 2010.

77. US Department of the Treasury, "Treasury Targets Hizballah Financial Network," press release, December 9, 2010.

78. Ibid.

79. Ibid.

80. Ana Maria Luca, "Out of Africa," *NOWLebanon*, September 30, 2011.

81. Tony Badran, "Hezbollah Acts Local, Thinks Global," *NOWLebanon*, June 22, 2010; Blanford, *Warriors of God*, 424–29.

82. Palmer Harik, *Hezbollah: Changing Face of Terrorism*, 84.

83. US Department of the Treasury, "Treasury Designates Hizballah's Construction Arm," press release, February 20, 2007.

84. US Department of the Treasury, "Treasury Targets Hizballah Financial Network," December 9, 2010.

85. Blanford, *Warriors of God*, 424–25.

86. US Department of the Treasury, "Treasury Targets Hizballah Financial Network."

87. Ana Maria Luca, "Out of Africa."

88. US Department of the Treasury, "Treasury Targets Hizballah Financial Network."

89. US Department of the Treasury, Financial Crimes Enforcement Network, "Finding That the Lebanese Canadian Bank SAL Is a Financial Institution of Primary Laundering Concern," February 10, 2011.

90. *United States of America v. Hassan Hodroj et al.*, Smemo Affidavit, United States District Court, Eastern District of Pennsylvania, November 24, 2009.

91. Global Witness, "For a Few Dollars More: How al Qaeda Moved into the Diamond Trade," April 2003, 24.

92. Gberie, "War and Peace in Sierra Leone."

93. Douglas Farah, "Hezbollah's External Support Network in West Africa and Latin America," International Assessment and Strategy Center, August 4, 2006.

94. Hudson, "Lebanese Businessmen and Hezbollah."

95. Farah, "Hezbollah's External Support Network."

96. US CIA, "Lebanese in Sub-Saharan Africa."

97. Ibid.

98. Global Witness, "For a Few Dollars More," 24.

99. Associated Press, "Hezbollah Extorting Funds from West Africa's Diamond Trade," *Haaretz* (Tel Aviv), June 30, 2004.

100. Global Witness, "For a Few Dollars More," 9.

101. Ibid.

102. Douglas Farah, "Al Qaeda Cash Tied to Diamond Trade; Sale of Gems from Sierra Leone Rebels Raised Millions, Sources Say," *Washington Post*, November 2, 2001.

103. Statement of Alan W. Easthman, *U.S. Government Role in Fighting the Conflict Diamond Trade*.

104. US Senator Dick Durbin, "Durbin Hearing Confirms Conflict Diamond-Terrorist Link," press release, February 13, 2002.

105. Douglas Farah, "Liberian Is Accused of Harboring Al-Qaeda," *Washington Post*, May 15, 2003, A18.

106. Global Witness, "For a Few Dollars More," 20. Also see report endnote 53: "Angolan Diamond Smuggling: The Part Played by Belgium," *Service General du Renseignement et de la Security (Sgr)*, July 2000.

107. Global Witness, "For a Few Dollars More," 21.

108. Statement of Alan W. Easthman, *U.S. Government Role in Fighting the Conflict Diamond Trade*.

109. Global Witness, "For a Few Dollars More," 21.

110. Ibid., 21–24.

111. Author telephone interview with former US intelligence and law enforcement official, January 21, 2011.

112. Global Witness, "For a Few Dollars More," 42; Farah, "Al Qaeda Cash Tied to Diamond Trade." Global Witness places Bah in Afghanistan in the late 1980s, while Farah has him there in the early 1980s. While there is discrepancy regarding the specific dates, these and other sources concur on the places where Bah trained and fought.

113. Farah, *Blood from Stones*, 71–72.

114. Farah, "Al Qaeda Cash Tied to Diamond Trade."

115. Ibid.

116. Douglas Farah, "Digging up Congo's Dirty Gems: Officials Say Diamond Trade Funds Radical Islamic Groups," *Washington Post*, December 30, 2001.

117. Farah, *Blood from Stones*, 60–61.

118. Antwerp, Belgium, Belgian Police Diamond Section, GDA Antwerp, "Case LIBI," September 10, 2001.

119. United Nations, Special Court for Sierra Leone, Office of the Prosecutor, "Presence of al-Qaeda in West Africa: Independent Source Findings," 2004.

120. Author interview with Douglas Farah, email, November 23, 2011.

121. Global Witness, "For a Few Dollars More," 43–44; Peter Finn and Pamela Rolfe, "Calls Central to Spain's Sept. 11 Case: Indictment Reveals Cryptic References," *Washington Post*, November 21, 2001.

122. Farah, "Hezbollah's External Support Network."

123. Global Witness, "For a Few Dollars More," 24.

124. Statement of Frank C. Urbancic, *Hezbollah's Global Reach*.

125. Ora Cohen, "Israelis in West Africa: We Live in Hezbollah State," *Haaretz* (Tel Aviv), August 5, 2008.

126. *United States of America v. Lebanese Canadian Bank SAL et al.*, Verified Complaint, 11 CIV 9186, United States District Court, Southern District of New York, December 15, 2011.

127. Ibid.; Jo Becker, "Beirut Bank Seen as a Hub of Hezbollah's Financing," *New York Times*, December 13, 2011.

128. Jacque Neriah, "An Iranian Intelligence Failure: Arms Ship in Nigeria Reveals Iran's Penetration of West Africa," *Jerusalem Issue Briefs* 10, no. 35 (April 7, 2011), Jerusalem Center for Public Affairs.

129. US CIA, "Overview of State-Supported Terrorism in 1985."

130. US CIA, "Lebanese in Sub-Saharan Africa."

131. Farah, "Hezbollah's External Support Network."

132. Intelligence and Terrorism Information Center at the Center for Special Studies, "Hezbollah (part 1)," 91.

133. Intelligence and Terrorism Information Center at the Center for Special Studies, "Iran's Activity in East Africa, the Gateway to the Middle East and the African Continent," July 29, 2009.

134. Global Witness, "For a Few Dollars More," 24.

135. Agence France Presse, "Morocco Cuts Ties with Iran: Foreign Ministry," March 6, 2009.

136. Claude Salhani, "Special Report: Hezbollah Active in Nigeria," *Middle East Times*, June 3, 2008.

137. Neriah, "Iran Steps Up Arming Hizbullah against Israel."

138. Universal Strategy Group, *Directed Study of Lebanese Hezbollah*, produced for the United States Special Operations Command, Research and Analysis Division, October 2010, 41.

139. Israeli intelligence report, "Iranian Intelligence Activity in Uganda," undated. Corroborated in separate author interview with Israeli intelligence official, Tel Aviv, July 2003.

140. Ibid.

141. See, for example, United Nations Monitoring Committee, Panel of Experts Established Pursuant to Resolution 1929 (2010), final report, May 17, 2011; Neriah, "An Iranian Intelligence Failure."

142. Israel Ministry of Foreign Affairs, IDF Spokesman, "Shaul Mofaz Regarding Interception of Ship *Karine A*," January 4, 2002.

143. See Israel Ministry of Foreign Affairs, IDF Spokesman, "Seizing of the Palestinian Weapons Ship *Karine A*," January 4, 2002.

144. Choksy, "Iran Takes on the World," 62.

145. Israel Ministry of Foreign Affairs, "Seizing of the Palestinian Weapons Ship *Karine* A"; Intelligence and Terrorism Information Center, Israel Intelligence Heritage & Commemoration Center, "Iranian Support of Hamas," January 12, 2008, 16n9.

146. Amos Harel, "Hezbollah Paid for *Karine A*, PA Paid for Arms," *Haaretz* (Tel Aviv), February 1, 2002. A "senior U.S. official" confirmed then–Israeli defense minister Binyamin Ben-Eliezer's contention regarding Mughniyeh's role. See Matthew Lee, "Top Israeli Security Official Calls Palestinian Arms Ship Probe 'Absurd,'" Agence France Presse, January 10, 2002.

147. Israel Ministry of Foreign Affairs, "Seizing of the Palestinian Weapons Ship *Karine A*"; Intelligence and Terrorism Information Center, "Iranian Support of Hamas," January 12, 2008, 16n9.

148. Israel Defense Forces, Military Intelligence, "Iran and Syria as Strategic Support for Palestinian Terrorism," September 2002. Report based on the interrogations of arrested Palestinian terrorists and captured Palestinian Authority documents.

149. Harel, "Hezbollah Paid for *Karine A*."

150. Jennifer Griffin, "Prison Interview with Palestinian Ship Captain Smuggling 50 Tons of Weapons," *Fox News*, January 7, 2002.

151. Sharon Sadeh, "EU Says *Karine-A* Affair Changed Mideast Conflict," *Haaretz* (Tel Aviv), February 7, 2002.

152. Israel Defense Forces, Military Intelligence, "Iran and Syria as Strategic Support."

153. Greg Myre, "Israel Says Explosives Expert Was on Fishing Boat It Seized," *New York Times*, May 22, 2003.

154. "How Israel Foiled an Arms Convoy Bound for Hamas," *Time*, March 30, 2009.

155. Reuters, "Hamas Military Commander Killed in Sudan Air Strike," *Jerusalem Post*, April 6, 2011.

156. Amos Harel and Avi Issacharoff, "Sudan Opposition: Bombed Arms Factory Belongs to Iran's Revolutionary Guard," *Haaretz* (Tel Aviv), October 24, 2012.

157. "Alleged Israeli Attack Draws Attention to Sudan's Ties to Iran," *VOA News*, April 1, 2009.

158. US CIA, "Hizballah Ties to Egyptian Fundamentalists."

159. Aidan Hartley, "U.S. Says Hizbollah May Plan Car Bombs in Somalia," Reuters, November 15, 1993.

160. United Nations Security Council, Report of the Monitoring Group on Somalia pursuant to Security Council resolution 1676 (2006), S/2006/913, November 22, 2006.

161. Ibid.

162. Tenet, *At the Center of the Storm*, 352.

163. US Department of State, Office of the Coordinator for Counterterrorism, Office of the Secretary of State, "Overview of State Sponsored Terrorism," *Patterns of Global Terrorism 1999*, April 2000.

164. National Commission on Terrorist Attacks upon the United States, *9/11 Commission Report*, released July 22, 2004, 240.

165. Ibid., 61; US CIA, "Al-Qa'ida in Sudan, 1992–96."

166. US CIA, "Al-Qa'ida in Sudan, 1992–96."

167. *United States of America v. Ali Mohamed*, Guilty Plea in US Embassy Bombings, Criminal No. 1023, United States District Court, Southern District of New York, October 20, 2000.

168. Ibid.

169. "Wikileaks: Sudan Designates Hezbollah as a Terrorist Organization," *Sudan Tribune*, September 8, 2011.

170. Ibid.

171. "Sudan Says Rebels May Have Assisted Hezbollah in Arms Smuggling," *Sudan Tribune*, April 20, 2009.

172. Intelligence and Terrorism Information Center, "Hamas and Hezbollah Expressed Sympathy with President of Sudan," July 25, 2010.

173. Talal Ismail, "Hezbollah Places Army at the Disposal of Government in Darfur," *Al-Ahram* (Sudan), September 23, 2010.

174. "Wikileaks: Sudan Designates Hezbollah."

175. US Department of State, "Country Reports on Terrorism 2010," August 18, 2011.

176. National Commission on Terrorist Attacks upon the United States, *9/11 Commission Report*, released July 22, 2004, 240–41.

177. Edith M. Lederer, "UN: W. Africa Cocaine Trade Generates $900M a Year," Associated Press, February 22, 2010.

178. Statement of James Clapper, *Worldwide Threat Assessment of the U.S. Intelligence Community*, February 10, 2011.

179. US Department of State, Bureau for International Narcotics and Law Enforcement Affairs, "International Narcotics Control Strategy Report," *Drug and Chemical Control* 1, March 2010, 312–14.

180. Marco Vernaschi, "Guinea Bissau: Hezbollah, al Qaida and the Lebanese Connection," Pulitzer Center on Crisis Reporting (Washington, DC), June 19, 2009.

181. Ronald K. Noble, opening remarks, 20th Americas Regional Conference, Viña del Mar, Chile, April 1, 2009.

182. Ronald K. Noble, keynote speech, 9th Meeting of the West African Police Chiefs Committee, Accra, Ghana, October 3, 2007.

183. US Department of the Treasury, "Treasury Designates Two Narcotics Traffickers in Guinea-Bissau; Treasury Targets Emerging West African Narcotics Transit Route," press release, April 8, 2010.

184. Robert Booth, "Wikileaks Cables: US Fears Over West African Cocaine Route," *Guardian* (London), December 14, 2010.

185. Marco Vernaschi, "The Cocaine Coast," *Virginia Quarterly Review* 87, no. 1 (Winter 2010): 43–65.

186. Statement of Michael A. Braun, *Confronting Drug Trafficking in West Africa*.

187. Michael Braun, "Drug Trafficking and Middle Eastern Terrorism Groups: A Growing Nexus?" PolicyWatch 1392, Washington Institute for Near East Policy (Washington, DC), July 25, 2008.

188. Statement of Michael A. Braun, *Confronting Drug Trafficking in West Africa*.

189. Adm. James Stavridis, "U.S. Southern Command 2009 Posture Statement," US Southern Command, 2009, 15; see also Adm. James G. Stavridis, *Partnership for the Americas: Western Hemisphere Strategy and U.S. Southern Command* (Washington, DC: National Defense University Press, 2010), 11.

190. "Hezbollah Will Profit from the Cocaine Trade in Europe," *Der Spiegel* (Germany), January 9, 2010.

191. *United States of America v. Lebanese Canadian Bank SAL et al.*, Verified Complaint, 11 CIV 9186, United States District Court, Southern District of New York, December 15, 2011.

192. Ibid.; *United States v. Maroun Saade et al.*, Indictment, 11 Cr. 111 (NRB), United States District Court, Southern District of New York, February 8, 2011.

193. *United States of America v. Lebanese Canadian Bank SAL et al.*, Verified Complaint, 11 CIV 9186, United States District Court, Southern District of New York, December 15, 2011.

194. Jo Becker, "Beirut Bank Seen as a Hub of Hezbollah's Financing," *New York Times*, December 13, 2011.

195. Author interview with West Africa expert, Washington, DC, November 28, 2011.

196. US CIA, "Prospects for Hizballah Terrorism in Africa."

10

Unit 3800

Hezbollah in Iraq

IN THE EARLY EVENING OF JANUARY 20, 2007, American military officers and their Iraqi counterparts met at the Provincial Joint Coordination Center in Karbala, about thirty miles south of Baghdad, to coordinate security for the upcoming celebrations of the Shi'a holiday of Ashura. It was just after nightfall when a five-car convoy of black GMC Suburban trucks—the preferred vehicles of US government convoys—was waved through three checkpoints approaching the Coordination Center. The trucks carried about a dozen English-speaking men dressed in US military-style fatigues, carrying American-type weapons and fake identity cards. At the checkpoints, Iraqi soldiers assumed the convoy was just another US security team.[1] It was not.

The assailants, trained to carry out "terrorist-style kidnappings" by Iran's Islamic Revolutionary Guard Corps (IRGC) Qods Force and Lebanese Hezbollah, knew exactly where American soldiers would be situated on the compound and headed directly there.[2] After they entered the compound, the vehicles split up, with some parking in front and others circling to the back of the main building where the meeting was taking place.[3] Once near American soldiers, the assailants threw grenades and opened fire with automatic rifles. One US soldier was killed and three others were injured by a grenade that was thrown into the Coordination Center's main office, an upper-floor office that also contained the provincial Iraqi police chief's office. While some assailants attacked the Coordination Center's main building, others set off explosives throughout the compound, damaging three US military Humvees. After grabbing two soldiers and an unclassified US military computer inside the compound, the team jumped atop an armored US Humvee, captured two more soldiers, and fled the compound.[4] The convoy drove east, crossing into Babil province, where it sped through an Iraqi police checkpoint, prompting police to trail the suspicious vehicles. Continuing east, the convoy crossed the Euphrates River and then turned north toward Hillah. The attackers abandoned the five SUVs near the town of Mahawil and fled. Not far behind, Iraqi police caught up with the abandoned vehicles, where they also found uniforms, boots, radios, a rifle, and the four abducted US soldiers, only one of them still alive. Two of

the soldiers were found in the back of one of the SUVs, handcuffed and shot dead. A
third soldier was found dead on the ground, also shot. Nearby, the fourth soldier,
who had been shot in the head but was alive, was rushed to the hospital but died on
the way there.[5]

Just days after the attack, Lt. Col. Scott Bleichwehl, spokesman for Multi-National
Division–Baghdad, said, "The precision of the attack, the equipment used and the
possible use of explosives to destroy the military vehicles in the compound suggests
that the attack was well rehearsed prior to execution."[6] Bleichwehl's suspicions were
confirmed three months later when Hezbollah operative Ali Musa Daqduq and
Qais al-Khazali, leader of one of the radical Shi'a "Special Groups" that broke away
from Moqtada al-Sadr's Mahdi Army, were captured in southern Iraq on March 20.[7]
Documents captured with al-Khazali showed that the Qods Force had gathered detailed information on "soldiers' activities, shift changes and defenses" at the US base
in Karbala, "and this information was shared with the attackers."[8] One document
seized in the raid in particular caught the attention of US analysts: a twenty-two-page
memorandum that "detailed the planning, preparation, approval process and conduct
of the [Karbala] operation," among others.[9] Shortly thereafter, the trade magazine
Aviation Week & Space Technology reported, US spy satellites spotted a training center
in Iran complete with a mockup of the Karbala Provincial Joint Coordination Center.
"The U.S. believes the discovery indicates Iran was heavily involved in the attack,
which relied on a fake motorcade to gain entrance to the compound. The duplicate
layout in Iran allowed attackers to practice procedures to use at the Iraqi compound,
the Defense Department believes."[10]

In time, US forces would learn that the attack on the Karbala Provincial Coordination Center was commanded by Sheikh Azhar al-Dulaymi, a Sunni convert to
Shi'a Islam and wanted Iraqi militant tied to Qais al-Khazali. Al-Dulaymi, the military learned, was trained by Hezbollah operatives near the city of Qom, Iran, where
he learned how to execute military-style, precision kidnappings. The goal was to
kidnap US or British military personnel and take the captives to the Shi'ite stronghold of Sadr City in Baghdad.[11] Although a tactical success, the Karbala operation
was a strategic failure, given that the goal had been to kidnap, not kill. And in the
aftermath of the attack, coalition forces exposed the extent to which Iranian and
Hezbollah agents were involved in training, equipping, organizing, and in some
cases directing Shi'a militants in Iraq.

Hezbollah and the Qods Force in the Gulf

Hezbollah's activities in Iraq since the 2003 invasion are a function of the group's
close alliance with Iran in general and the Qods Force in particular. Iran's strategy
in Iraq—and Hezbollah's role in that strategy as Iran's primary militant proxy
group—is a logical extension of its covert activities in Iraq and the region throughout
the 1980s and 1990s.

In the years following the Islamic Revolution of 1979, the Tehran regime sponsored terrorist acts both to export the revolution and to further its national interests.

Iran gave special focus to its own backyard, where Shi'a minorities lived under Sunni monarchies that not only oppressed Iran's co-religionists but also stood in the way of the new regime's regional ambitions.

Throughout the Iran-Iraq War (1980–88), Iraq was a primary target of Iranian-sponsored terrorist groups. To this end, the CIA noted in 1986, "Iran trains and finances several Iraqi dissident groups, such as the Dawa Party, that are dedicated to overthrowing President Saddam Husayn."[12] In 1986, Kuwaiti Shi'a extremists bombed several Kuwaiti oil installations. More Kuwaiti oil installations were targeted six months later, in January 1987, and again in April and May of that year. In July 1987, two brothers blew themselves up while placing an explosive in front of a Kuwait City building housing the Air France ticket office. While the previous year the brothers had told Kuwaiti authorities that they had been abducted by Iran, the truth was that they were being trained in Iran as saboteurs. More attacks occurred over the course of 1987, including bombs that exploded in front of the Pan American Airlines ticket office, the Kuwaiti Ministry of the Interior, and the office of an American-owned insurance company.[13]

The Qods Force developed several proxy groups not only in Saudi Arabia but throughout the Gulf region as well. Often Iran used the expertise of Lebanese Hezbollah to train recruits from Saudi Arabia, Kuwait, Bahrain, and elsewhere. In some cases, such as the 1983 Kuwait bombings and the bombing of Khobar Towers, Hezbollah provided explosives and experienced operatives to help carry out specific attacks.

Lebanese Hezbollah and Iraqi Dawa operatives joined together again in a brazen attempt to assassinate the Kuwaiti emir in 1985. That attack was aimed at securing the release of the Kuwait 17, who by then had been sentenced for the 1983 bombings. The attack on the emir's motorcade occurred just days after Hezbollah's Islamic Jihad Organization (IJO) sent three letters to Beirut newspapers with pictures of kidnapped westerners held in an effort to get western governments to press Kuwait to release the Kuwait 17. In response to a US public statement rejecting negotiations with the kidnappers, an anonymous caller to a French news agency warned that "the U.S. Government should await the largest military operation it has ever known" and threatened attacks on Kuwaiti diplomats worldwide. A week later, a car filled with explosives rammed the emir's motorcade.[14] The emir suffered minor injuries, but three others perished in the explosion.

In 1986, Bahrain cracked down hard on Bahraini Hezbollah, and in 1987, fifty-nine of the group's members were put on trial. But a decade later, in March 1997, the arrest of thirteen Bahrainis and two Iraqis by the Kuwaiti State Security Service in Kuwait City proved the group was far from beaten. Those arrested apparently had ties to Saudi and Kuwaiti Hezbollah, the Kuwaitis told their Bahraini counterparts, and called themselves "Hezbollah Gulf." Correspondence seized at the suspects' homes revealed connections with people in Damascus, Syria, and Qom, Iran. The evidence, Kuwaiti officials stated at the time, suggests the cell may have operated on the directions of Iran's Ministry of Intelligence and Security (MOIS).[15]

Moreover, several of the Bahraini Hezbollah's top leaders were reportedly living in Kuwait. According to the CIA, Muhammad Habib Mansur Saffaf was "one of the group's top leaders" living in Kuwait City. "He reportedly has run a safe-house in Kuwait that served as [sic] key transit point between Bahrain and Lebanon, has engaged in weapons smuggling, and may still be involved in terrorist-related activities." According to Bahraini officials, around thirty-seven other known Bahraini Hezbollah members likely fled to Iran or Lebanon. The possible ties to Iran and the new name led CIA analysts to suggest that "Tehran may be working to create a new Hezbollah cell to oppose the Bahraini Government." The contact maintained between these radical Bahraini Shi'a and Lebanese Hezbollah suggested to the CIA "that Bahraini Hizballah retains an infrastructure in Bahrain as well." Underscoring this hypothesis was the fact that the individuals arrested in Kuwait were also raising money to send back to Bahrain.[16]

Iranian sponsorship of terrorism picked up pace as the Iran-Iraq War came to a close and US-Iran tensions increased. "No longer drained by fighting Iraq," former White House counterterrorism director Richard Clarke wrote, "[Iranian] aid to Hezbollah increased."[17] Iranian support to its proxies in the Gulf increased as well. Following the accidental downing of Iran Air flight 655 by the USS *Vincennes* on July 3, 1988, US diplomatic posts worldwide went on high alert in anticipation of a revenge attack by Iranian agents or their proxies. The CIA noted at the time that several posts reported individuals of Middle Eastern appearance conducting surveillance of US embassies. The risk of an attack on US interests in the Gulf was deemed especially high. In addition, the CIA noted, "Tehran could draw on its extensive assets in Dubai to rally protest demonstrations—which could easily turn to violence—or mount a terrorist operation."[18] Years later, an Iranian diplomat who defected to Europe in 2002 after serving as Iran's consul-general in Dubai would reveal that Iran used its consulate there as a regional intelligence hub through which it also funneled suitcases stuffed with millions of dollars to Hezbollah.[19] Such claims were given further credence two years later, when dozens of long-term Lebanese Shi'a residents were expelled from the United Arab Emirates on charges of being affiliated with Hezbollah.[20]

By 1992, articles in Hezbollah's own publications documented the group's support to extremist groups throughout the region, including "radical elements" in Tunisia, Kuwait, Saudi Arabia, Egypt, Pakistan, and Yemen. At the time, the CIA assessed that at least "some" of Hezbollah's support to these other extremist groups was taking place "at the behest of Iran, which is trying to expand its ties to extremist Islamic groups without jeopardizing its efforts to improve its political ties in the region."[21]

In the broader picture, the activities of Iran's terrorist proxies over the past two decades, and the Qods Force's role in nurturing them, reveal a number of trends. First, Iran has a long history of supporting Shi'a terrorist groups in the Gulf region that act as proxies for Tehran. On their own, and in cooperation with the Qods Force, local Hezbollah affiliates and groups like the Iraqi Dawa Party have engaged in terrorism and political violence in support of their own and Iranian interests.

Second, Iraqi Shi'a extremists feature prominently in Iran's arsenal of regional proxies. Some of the most proactive Iraqi Shi'a extremists to work with Iran in the post-2003 period began as Iranian proxies some twenty years earlier. Consider, for example, Jamal Jafar Muhammad Ali, better known as Abu Mahdi al-Muhandis, one of the Iraqi Dawa Party terrorists who partnered with Hezbollah to carry out the 1983 embassy bombings in Kuwait and the 1985 assassination attempt on the Kuwaiti emir. Convicted in absentia for his role in those attacks, Muhandis went on to lead the Badr Corps, the militant wing of the Supreme Council for Islamic Revolution in Iraq (SCIRI). The Badr Corps not only fought alongside Iranian forces in the Iran-Iraq War, it also engaged in acts of sabotage and terrorism targeting the Saddam regime. As head of the Badr Corps, Muhandis worked directly with the Qods Force and other militant Iraqi Shi'a targeting the Hussein regime.[22]

According to Iraqi documents captured by coalition forces, Muhandis's chief of staff in the Badr Corps was Hadi al-Ameri, who would go on to head the Badr Organization (so renamed in an attempt to rebrand the longtime militia as a political party) and serve as an Iraqi parliamentarian after Saddam's overthrow. At some point in the 1990s, Muhandis was succeeded by Mustafa al-Sheibani as commander of the Badr Corps.[23] Muhandis, who now also had Iranian citizenship, became an adviser to the commander of the Qods Force, Gen. Qassem Soleimani.[24] At one point Muhandis and Sheibani lived in the same IRGC compound. And all three, Muhandis, Sheibani, and Ameri, went on to become key Shi'a militant leaders in the post-2003 invasion period. "Today," a 2008 report published by the Combating Terrorism Center at West Point concluded, "some of Iraq's most wanted Shi'a insurgents share Badr Corps lineage with Iraqi politicians operating openly in Baghdad."[25]

Third, Iraqi Shi'a militant groups like the Dawa Party and Badr Corps have long histories of cooperation, training, and cross-fertilization with Lebanese Hezbollah. As noted before, Dawa operatives engaged in joint terrorist operations with Hezbollah. In fact, links between Hezbollah and the Dawa Party run deep. The Dawa Party in Lebanon, one of the precursor elements to what became Lebanese Hezbollah, was imported from Iraq in 1969 by followers of Iraqi cleric Mohammad Baqr al-Sadr. Hezbollah has long-standing ties to the Badr Corps as well. According to seized Iraqi intelligence documents, the Badr Corps employed a modus operandi— common among Iranian-sponsored groups—of establishing clandestine offices in businesses, hospitals, and nongovernmental organizations in Iraq. One undated Iraqi intelligence report explained that among the many functions of these fronts was to help "secure and support the Badr Corps, and the different groups belonging to the al-Qods Force, such as the movement of Hezbollah."[26]

Over the years, Iran has cultivated ties, both organizational and interpersonal, among its various proxies. That would continue in post-Saddam Iraq, where some of Iran's most prominent diplomats not only served in the IRGC but also had personal relationships with Hezbollah. Ambassador Hassan Kazemi Qomi, a former Iranian ambassador to Iraq, for example, previously served as an IRGC liaison to Hezbollah.[27]

Iranian Interests in Iraq

By forcing the collapse of the regime of Saddam Hussein, Operation Iraqi Freedom removed Iran's greatest enemy and longtime nemesis. The 2003 invasion therefore provided Iran with a historic opportunity to reshape its relationship with Iraq and, in the process, increase its influence in the region. To that end, Iran employed an "all elements of national power" approach in exploiting the outcome of this seminal event. This included both soft and hard power, from the use of political, economic, religious, and cultural leverage to the support of militant proxies.

In pursuing its goals in Iraq, Iran backed multiple, often opposing parties and movements in an effort to secure its interests no matter the outcome of the country's political developments. By hedging its bets, Iran was able to rely on different groups for different types of activities. For example, SCIRI and the Badr Organization quickly entered the political fray in Iraq, while other hard-line groups played a more strictly militant function. Understanding Iran's layered relationships with its Iraqi proxies is critical to understanding the role Hezbollah would come to play in Iraq. After all, even senior US and UK government intelligence analysts and policymakers themselves initially could not understand why Iran would need Hezbollah to act on its behalf in Iraq, let alone why Hezbollah would agree to do so.[28]

Working through its longtime proxies, Iran set out to achieve several goals in Iraq, the most important and overarching of which was the creation, in the words of then–Defense Intelligence Agency director Lowell Jacoby, of a "weakened, decentralized and Shi'a-dominated Iraq that is incapable of posing a threat to Iran."[29] In addition, the long-held Iranian desire to push the United States out of the Gulf region now extended to the large US and international military presence in Afghanistan to Iran's east and Iraq to its west. Iran sought to foster unity among Iraq's various Shi'a parties and movements so that they could consolidate Shi'a political control (Shi'a constitute about 60 percent of the country's population) over the new Iraqi government.[30]

Even as it pursued its political goal of seeking a weak federal state, dominated by Shi'a allies and vulnerable to Iranian influence, Tehran also sought to bloody coalition forces in Iraq. Careful not to provoke a direct confrontation with US and coalition forces, Iran armed, trained, and funded a variety of Shi'a militias and insurgent groups in an effort to bog down coalition forces in an asymmetric war of attrition. If the United States were humiliated in Iraq and forced out of the region in disgrace, the thinking went, the Americans would be deterred from pursuing similar military interventions in the region in the future.

Iran's plans to influence political developments in Iraq, as it happened, long predated the US invasion of 2003. This meant the Iranians were ready to fill the security vacuum immediately following the invasion, when, a US embassy cable would later note, "little attention was focused on Iran."[31]

In April 2008, General Petraeus and Ambassador Ryan Crocker, the most senior US military commander and diplomat in Iraq, respectively, testified before the Senate Armed Services Committee. In his testimony, Petraeus highlighted the flow of sophisticated Iranian arms to Shi'a militants in Iraq. The military's understanding of Iran's support for such groups crystallized, Petraeus explained, with the capture of a number of prominent Shi'a militants and several members of the Qods Force operating in Iraq as well. Ambassador Crocker, himself a former US ambassador to Lebanon, was undiplomatically blunt in assessing the implications of Iran's arming and training of extremist militia groups: "What this tells me is that Iran is pursuing, as it were, a Lebanonization strategy, using the same techniques they used in Lebanon, to co-opt elements of the local Shia community and use them as basically instruments of Iranian force."[32]

In the 1980s, Iran helped form what would become Hezbollah by drawing upon more radical members of the comparatively moderate Amal militia. The fact that a similar phenomenon was now playing out in Iraq was not lost on the country's Sunni population or its Sunni Arab neighbors. In the words of Vali Nasr, an Iranian-American scholar who later served as a senior adviser at the State Department, "SCIRI and its al-Badr Brigade—a force of some 10,000 that was trained by Iran's Revolutionary Guards to fight the Saddam regime—look too much like Lebanese Shia militias, Amal and Hezbollah, and prospects of their assumption of power evoke images of Lebanon's grueling civil war."[33]

Speaking to the Islamic Republic News Agency (IRNA) in January 2012, Qods Force chief General Soleimani expressed satisfaction with Iran's efforts to extend its influence over Iraq, much as it did over southern Lebanon. "In reality," Soleimani stated, "in south Lebanon and Iraq, the people are under the effect of the Islamic Republic's way of practice and thinking."[34] According to documents seized by coalition forces, alongside the Badr Corps operatives it sent to Iraq following the 2003 invasion, Iran "may have even funneled a few Lebanese Hizballah members into the country to provide expertise and training to its new would-be surrogates."[35]

In time, evidence of Hezbollah's presence in Iraq would be plentiful, as exemplified by the group's creation of an outfit, Unit 3800, dedicated to aiding the Shi'a insurgency in Iraq. Iraq became a core issue for Hezbollah, however, not because the country's affairs had anything to do with Lebanon but because gaining influence over Iraq and hegemony in the region was of primary concern to its Iranian sponsors. Before long, Unit 3800 trainers and operatives would be working alongside officers from the Qods Force's Department 9000, also known as the Ramazan Corps, targeting coalition forces in Iraq.

The Ramazan Corps: Qods Force Department 9000

In case General Petraeus was not clear that General Soleimani was calling the shots for Iran in Iraq, the head of the Qods Force reportedly sent the commander of coalition forces a message in early 2008 making this very point. Conveyed by a senior Iraqi leader, the message arrived just as Iraqi and coalition forces initiated Operation Charge of the Knights, an effort targeting Iraqi Shi'a militias in Baghdad and Basra. The message itself read, "General Petraeus, you should know that I, Qassem

Suleimani, control the policy for Iran with respect to Iraq, Lebanon, Gaza, and Afghanistan. And indeed, the ambassador in Baghdad is a Quds Force member. The individual who's going to replace him is a Quds Force member."[36] The message should have come as no great surprise, coming from a man aggressive in the belief that "offense is the best defense."[37] Indeed, the crux of the message was no surprise at all. Several months earlier, in October 2007, Petraeus confirmed to the press his "absolute assurance" that several Iranians detained by coalition forces were Revolutionary Guardsmen. "The Qods Force controls the policy for Iraq; there should be no confusion about that either," he noted, adding, "The ambassador is a Qods Force member."[38] In fact, by the time Petraeus made these comments, coalition forces had already arrested senior Qods Force officials on at least three occasions.

In the wake of the Iran-Iraq War, Tehran remained concerned about threats closest to home. The Qods Force's first four regional commands were therefore dedicated to Iraq (First Corps), Pakistan and Iran's border provinces (Second Corps), Turkey and Kurdish groups (Third Corps), and Afghanistan and Central Asia (Fourth Corps). According to seized Iraqi intelligence, by the early 1990s the Badr Corps was a fully functional militia backed by the Qods Force regional command in Iraq, better known as Ramazan Headquarters. By the mid-1990s, such reports stated, the Ramazan Headquarters operated three camps along the Iraqi border to support such activities.[39] By 2007, the multinational forces in Iraq assessed that the Ramazan Corps "is responsible for most of the Qods Force operations in Iraq."[40]

Gen. Qassem Soleimani succeeded Ahmad Vahidi as Qods Force commander in 1998.[41] In October 2011, Soleimani was designated as a terrorist by the US State Department, based on his role in the plot to assassinate the Saudi ambassador in Washington, DC. Qods Force activities in Iraq, mirroring those already enacted in Lebanon, would soon include providing IRGC and Hezbollah agents safe houses everywhere from Basra in the south to Irbil in the north.[42]

Sometime in 2006, at the height of sectarian violence then engulfing Iraq, Gen. Soleimani traveled secretly to Baghdad. Only after he returned safely to Iran did US intelligence and military forces discover he had been right in their backyard.[43] Washington's reaction was furious. Ever since the April 2005 election, Iranian-sponsored Shi'a militants had intensified attacks targeting coalition forces in Iraq. Now, Soleimani's confidence in his political and military proxies in Iraq was apparently so great that he felt secure paying a house call to Baghdad. Correspondingly, the Qods Force seemed to be riding high, deploying proxy groups in Iraq capable of striking at coalition forces with impunity and basking in Hezbollah's self-declared victory against the Israel Defense Forces in the July 2006 war.

That same summer, the White House began a process of reviewing its policy toward Iranian meddling in Iraq. Over the course of 2006, coalition forces detained dozens of suspected Iranian operatives in a "catch and release" program intended to signal to Iran the coalition's awareness of Tehran's aggressive activities in Iraq. DNA samples collected surreptitiously from the Iranian detainees were added to a database before the detainees were released after three or four days in custody. According to US intelligence, as many as 150 Iranian intelligence and IRGC operatives were deployed to Iraq at a time.[44]

"There were no costs for the Iranians," a senior administration official commented, explaining the reason for the policy review. The resulting presidential directive, or "finding," was signed by President Bush in November 2006 and authorized US forces to kill or capture Iranian operatives in Iraq. Coined "Counter Iranian Influence," the initiative included measures to roll back Iranian successes in five different theaters from Lebanon to Afghanistan and isolate the regime in Tehran. In Lebanon, for example, the White House authorized the intelligence community to engage in broadened operations targeting Hezbollah's engagement in a spectrum of activities called the Blue Game Matrix.[45]

In Iraq, the program to counter Iranian influence quickly bore fruit. The evening of December 19, 2006, a US military patrol stopped an official Iranian embassy vehicle in Baghdad and arrested three Iranians with diplomatic credentials and one Iraqi, presumably their driver. Two of the men were held for two days, the other two for four days.[46] The more significant arrests, however, came just a few hours later in a predawn raid of the Baghdad compound of Abdul Aziz al-Hakim, head of the SCIRI. US Special Forces detained ten men in this second raid, including two Iranians carrying diplomatic passports—passports later determined to have been issued under false identities. Neither of the Iranians, traveling in Iraq under aliases with false documents, was a diplomat in the traditional sense. In fact, they were important IRGC officials on a covert mission to Iraq. One, Mohsen Chizari, was the Qods Force's third-highest ranking officer. The Iranians quickly realized that US forces were holding one of Qassem Soleimani's most senior deputies.[47]

The evidence amounted to a "smoking gun," in one American official's description. "We found plans for attacks, phone numbers affiliated with Sunni bad guys, a lot of things that filled in the blanks on what these guys are up to."[48] Some of these detainees tried to destroy maps and other evidence as US Special Forces raided the house.[49] The evidence the military collected in the raid included maps, detailed weapons lists, reports of weapons shipped into Iraq, organization charts, telephone records, computers, and "other sensitive intelligence information."[50] According to US officials, some of this intelligence "dealt explicitly with force-protection issues, including attacks on MNF-I [Multi-National Force–Iraq] forces."[51] In other words, the Iranians were in possession of intelligence about weapons being smuggled into Iraq from Iran and about attacks on the Multi-National Force–Iraq by Tehran's proxy militias in Iraq.

Aside from Mohsen Chizari's high rank within the Qods Force, his capture was significant for underscoring a reality long known by the coalition, but only through extremely sensitive intelligence: that Iran was training Iraqi Shi'a militias to attack coalition forces and stoke sectarian tensions in Iraq. Further, this raid and others like it led US officials to refer to "a super-secret group called Department 9000," a part of the Qods Force that provided guidance and support to Iraqi insurgents and coordinated meetings between them and the IRGC.[52] In other words, the Ramazan Corps had been exposed.

Chizari's arrest clearly unnerved Iran. Over the next few days, an Iraqi official noted, the Iranian ambassador to Iraq desperately ran "around from office to office," in an effort to secure Chizari's release.[53] Iraqi leaders were also upset. The Iranians had reportedly come to Iraq at the invitation of President Jalal Talabani, leader of a prominent Iraqi Kurdish group. Under intense pressure from the Iraqis, the US military transferred the Iranian detainees to Iraqi custody. Days later they were "expelled" home to Iran, much to the frustration and dismay of US officials.[54]

A few days later, on January 11, 2007, former CIA director R. James Woolsey Jr. and former undersecretary of state Thomas Pickering appeared before the US House Foreign Affairs Committee to testify on "The Next Steps in the Iran Crisis." Just the day before, President Bush had given a national address, noting, "Iran is providing material support for attacks on American troops."[55] Then, just a few hours before the hearing, US troops arrested six more Iranians in an Iranian diplomatic office in Irbil in Kurdish-controlled northern Iraq. One individual was quickly released, but the other five were determined to be IRGC members, not diplomats. Publicly, the Iranian liaison office in Irbil processed papers for Iraqis attempting to travel to Iran. But intelligence indicated it doubled as a Qods Force base of operations. As US Special Forces entered, they found the Iranians frantically flushing documents down a toilet. Perhaps trying to pass themselves off as something other than Iranian Qods Force officers, the Iranians had recently shaved their heads. Soldiers carted away still more documents and computers for analysis, just as they had a few days earlier in Baghdad.[56] Mining data on seized cell phones indicated the officers were in direct contact with a wide array of insurgent groups. Analysts would find in the seized materials and devices evidence tying the Iranian officers to military operations carried out not only by Moqtada al-Sadr's Mahdi Army in places like Kirkuk but also by the al-Qaeda-affiliated Ansar al-Sunna group targeting Iraqi Kurds.[57]

A much clearer picture of Iran's policy of inserting "managed chaos" into Iraq was quickly emerging. Iran, US, and UK policymakers and intelligence officials concurred, hoped to raise the cost of US intervention in Iraq with an eye toward making Washington think twice about pursuing regime change elsewhere, especially in Tehran. While Iran insisted the five detained men held diplomatic immunity and demanded their release, the military held onto the five Qods Force operatives until May 2009. The Baghdad and Irbil raids came like a one-two punch, forcing the Iranians to reconsider the wisdom of putting their own people on the line in Iraq. According to one American military commander, with the Baghdad and Irbil raids the Iranians "realized we were coming after them. The Iranians didn't like doing much dirty work or getting their hands dirty. A lot of them would prefer the Arabs to do the dying."[58]

To that end, Tehran prioritized sending sophisticated weapons—especially explosively formed penetrators (EFPs)—to militants in Iraq. The uptick in attacks led US officials to decide the time had come to expose the breadth and lethality of Iranian arms smuggled to Iraqi Shi'a militias.

The press briefing was prepared for Sunday, February 11, 2007, in Baghdad's Green Zone. Laid out on the table were EFP launchers and their shaped metal charges, mortar shells, rocket-propelled grenades, and the false identification cards found on two of the Qods Force officials captured in the Irbil raid a month earlier. According to US officials, serial numbers on some of the grenades indicated they were manufactured in Iran in 2006.[59] The centerpiece of the weapons spread was the EFP, a deceptively simple-looking cylinder of PVC piping about eight inches long. What made the weapon so deadly was the concave-shaped soft metal slug, often made out of copper, launched with such force that it could penetrate the armor of a tank or Humvee. The briefing was more than just a show-and-tell, however. Though unable to share the intelligence underpinning the charge, the military and intelligence briefers insisted the Qods Force was responsible for the flow of arms to Shi'a militia groups. "We have been able to determine that this material, especially on the EFP level, is coming from the IRGC–Qods Force," the intelligence analyst stated. In reality, they report directly to the "supreme leader," a reference to Ayatollah Ali Khamenei.[60] The direction for this arming and smuggling operation, the analyst added, was "coming from the highest levels of the Iranian government."[61]

In September 2007, US forces in Iraqi Kurdistan arrested Mahmoud Farhadi, a "very senior member of the Qods Force." Posing as an Iranian trade representative, Farhadi's actual mission involved facilitating the transport of weapons into Iraq, according to a US military spokesman. In particular, he oversaw the smuggling of "weapons, people and money" across the border from Iran. "Multiple sources implicate Farhadi in providing weapon[s] to Iraqi criminal elements and surrogate[s] of Iran. We also know that for more than a decade he was involved in Iranian intelligence operation[s] in Iraq."[62] Officials were not surprised. In August 2004, for example, Qods Force Brig. Gen. Ahmed Foruzandeh drove a cache of explosives and other materials specifically designated for use in suicide bombings across the border into Iraq, according to US government information. In another case, he supplied a Shi'a militia with a specific target to hit.[63]

The capture of senior Qods Force officials, and the public airing of evidence demonstrating Iranian agents were arming and training Iraqi Shi'a extremists, embarrassed Tehran and appears to have accelerated Iran's efforts to put an Arab face on this mission. Using Hezbollah offered multiple advantages, not least the shared language of Lebanese Hezbollah operatives and Iraqi militants, Arabic. Farsi-speaking Iranian trainers could not communicate with their trainees as effectively, aside from the perception by some Iraqis that their Iranian trainers were aloof and patronizing. Reliable polling data would later reveal that Iranian intervention in Iraq faced "substantial popular resentment even among Iraqi Shiites, who are wrongly presumed to share Iran's interests due to their common sectarian background."[64]

The use by Hezbollah of Iranian-manufactured EFPs in Lebanon, before and during the July 2006 war, positioned Hezbollah operatives with in-the-field experience as ideal candidates to train Iraqi Shi'a in deploying this particular weapon.[65] A number of Iraqi Shi'a militants reportedly observed and trained alongside Hezbollah militants in Lebanon during the 2006 war, according to US intelligence.[66] Having seen Hezbollah in action, they would have been well situated to seek training from their Lebanese compatriots in the use of EFPs and other weapons and tactics.

The advantages of enlisting Hezbollah operatives as middlemen soon spurred action. But multinational forces would appreciate the full scope of this shift only when they arrested Ali Musa Daqduq, a senior Hezbollah official, along with key leaders of the Special Groups, in a Basra raid on March 20, 2007.

Unit 3800: Hezbollah's Support Mission in Iraq

"Generally," US military intelligence assessed in 2010, the Qods Force "directs and supports groups actually executing attacks, thereby maintaining plausible deniability within the international community."[67] This assessment proved as true in Iraq as it long had been in Lebanon. In Lebanon, the IRGC helped create Hezbollah. In Iraq, the Revolutionary Guards would do much the same for Iraqi Shi'a militias, sometimes on their own but often using Hezbollah to provide training and operational supervision on its behalf.

A variety of militant Shi'a groups in Iraq have benefited from Iranian and Hezbollah training and support, with the nature and extent of that support changing over time as these groups themselves evolved. Some groups supported by Iran, like SCIRI and the Dawa Party, focused primarily on establishing political influence in Iraq. And although Iran has supported both militant and political activities in Iraq, depending on its needs and assessments at a given time, its fundamental long-term goal has been establishing political influence in the country. At times, Iran appears to have temporarily curtailed support for militant activities when violence might undermine its political goals in Iraq, such as in the period before the January 2005 elections.[68]

But even as it supported political allies like SCIRI and Moqtada al-Sadr, Iran also backed the Badr Corps and Mahdi Army, the groups' respective military wings. When the renamed Badr Organization entered politics, Iran encouraged extremist militants to splinter off and form their own militant groups, echoing Iran's encouragement of Shi'a radicals years before to split from the Amal Party in Lebanon to form Hezbollah.[69] Both Mustafa al-Sheibani and Abu Mahdi al-Muhandis broke with Badr and founded terrorist groups that played central roles in Iran's proxy networks.[70] In 2005, when al-Sadr turned similarly to politics, radical members of his Mahdi Army, like Qais al-Khazali, who created Asaib Ahl al-Haqq, broke away to form splinter groups of their own, too.

Two years later, when British special forces detained Ali Musa Daqduq, the Hezbollah official, along with Qais al-Khazali and his brother Laith, they would find a document detailing a layered Iranian strategy to develop three distinct but overlapping categories of proxy groups. Iran wanted its proxies to vary in size and mission, with larger groups focusing on building grassroots support through political and social movements and using violence only intermittently as a means to secure political influence. Smaller groups would make more reliable militant proxies, focused as they were on securing social influence through violence alone. Still smaller, more radical groups would receive more sophisticated training and weapons.[71] Iran stuck to this strategy and in 2007, when even the League of the Righteous began engaging in Iraqi politics, formed yet another Special Group, Kata'ab Hezbollah (Hezbollah Brigades), which received the most sophisticated training and sensitive equipment. An Iraqi group with reported ties to longtime Dawa operative and Qods Force adviser Abu Mahdi al-Muhandis, the Hezbollah Brigades was distinct from Lebanese Hezbollah but would develop especially close ties with its Lebanese namesake.[72] Mirroring the creation of Unit 1800, a unit dedicated to supporting Palestinian terrorist groups and targeting Israel, Hezbollah created Unit 3800, a unit dedicated to supporting Iraqi Shi'a terrorist groups targeting multinational forces in Iraq.

The unit, established by Nasrallah at the request of Iran, trained and advised Iraqi militant groups.[73] Almost immediately following the US invasion of Iraq, reports emerged indicating Hezbollah operatives were reaching out to establish ties to Iraqi Shi'a groups. A July 29, 2003, US intelligence report citing Israeli military intelligence stated that Hezbollah "military activists" were trying to make contact with Moqtada al-Sadr and his Mahdi Army. By late August they had succeeded, according to a report prepared by a US military analyst. Based on information from a source with "direct access to the reported information," the report claimed Hezbollah had assembled a team of thirty to forty operatives in Najaf "in support of Moqtada Sadr's Shia paramilitary group." Hezbollah was both recruiting and training new members of the Mahdi Army, the report added.[74]

More reports documenting Hezbollah's then-still-small presence followed, including one citing multiple sources that said Hezbollah was "buying rocket-propelled grenades . . . antitank missiles" and other weapons for the Mahdi Army. Hezbollah's relationship with al-Sadr and his militia were not seen as ad hoc ties between individual Hezbollah and Mahdi Army members but as decisions made at the top of the respective organizations. A US Army report noted that "reporting also confirms the relationship between . . . Sadr and Hassan Nasrallah." According to unconfirmed information, the report added, a senior adviser to Nasrallah delivered funds to al-Sadr.[75] The connection rings true, given that "al-Sadr sought to model his organization on Lebanese Hezbollah, combining a political party with an armed militia and an organization providing social services."[76]

The American and Israeli intelligence services were not the only ones investigating Iran and Hezbollah's support to Shi'a militant groups at the time. In fact, one of the most prolific sources was also one of the most controversial: the Mujahedin-e Khalq (MEK), the Iranian exile group deeply and sometimes violently committed to the overthrow of the regime in Tehran. While the MEK has a track record of collecting critical intelligence later proven to be surprisingly accurate, it remained a US-designated terrorist group until September 2012 (it had already been removed from the European Union and British lists).[77]

The gist of the MEK's reporting on Hezbollah in Iraq would be corroborated by other sources. According to the MEK, some 800 Hezbollah operatives were on the ground in Iraq by January 2004, including assassination teams.[78] According to other MEK reports, nearly 100 Hezbollah members—including both "agents and clerics"—infiltrated postwar Iraq at Iran's behest. Following its established modus operandi in Lebanon, Hezbollah reportedly established charitable organizations in Iraq "to create a favorable environment for recruiting."[79] As early as October 2003, Israeli intelligence also warned their American counterparts that according to their information Hezbollah—at Iran's instruction—intended to help set up a "resistance movement," likely in the group's own image, that could conduct mass casualty attacks.[80]

Watching the phenomenon, the CIA reported in November 2003 not to have seen a "major influx" of Hezbollah operatives in the intervening months. "Hezbollah has moved to establish a presence inside Iraq," one administration official said, "but it isn't clear from the intelligence reports what their intent is."[81] It was clear, however, that they were traveling through Syria and crossing the long and porous Syrian-Iraqi border to gain entry to Iraq. In November 2003, Israel's defense minister Shaul Mofaz went public with information that a wide range of insurgents—from Sunnis affiliated with al-Qaeda to Shi'a tied to Hezbollah—were crossing Syria to fight coalition forces in Iraq.[82] A few months later, American officials came to the same conclusion, noting that the Syrian regime was believed to be knowingly allowing their passage through Syrian territory, supporting an Iranian initiative to inject battle-hardened foreign fighters into Iraq.[83]

By early 2005, the presence of Hezbollah operatives in Iraq would become an open secret when Iraqi interior minister Falah al-Naquib announced the arrest of eighteen Lebanese Hezbollah members on terrorism charges.[84] That summer, US military officials noted that Abu Mustafa al-Sheibani, the former Badr Corps commander, headed a network of Iraqi Shi'a insurgents created by the IRGC's Qods Force. Based out of Iran, Sheibani's express goal was targeting US and coalition forces in Iraq, often employing a new, more lethal type of EFP based on a Hezbollah design. A Sheibani network device reportedly killed three British soldiers in Iraq in July 2005 and was responsible for at least thirty-seven bombing attacks in the first half of 2005 alone. According to US officials, Sheibani's network of some 280 operatives was believed to train in Lebanon, in Baghdad's Sadr City, and, in an apparently veiled reference to Iran, "in another country."[85]

In London, British prime minister Tony Blair cited evidence linking Iran and Hezbollah to recent bombings in which British soldiers were killed in Iraq by a new type of explosive device. "The particular nature of those devices lead us either to Iranian elements or to Hezbollah, because they are similar to the devices used by Hezbollah, that is funded and supported by Iran," he noted.[86] Suddenly, Iran and Hezbollah's training and weapons smuggling programs had become a priority issue for coalition forces. Still two more years would pass before coalition forces would learn that sometime in 2005 "senior Lebanese Hezbollah leadership" directed an experienced Hezbollah commander "to go to Iran and work with the Qods Force to train Iraqi extremists."[87] Hezbollah was about to accelerate its Unit 3800 mission in Iraq, with deadly consequences.

Until this point, Hezbollah's ties were primarily with Moqtada al-Sadr's Mahdi Army, for which Hezbollah provided expertise and training. But the formation of a new Iraqi government in April 2005 brought Iran's Shi'a allies, SCIRI and the Dawa Party, into key leadership positions. Already in 2004, splits had begun to develop within the Mahdi Army, providing Iran and Hezbollah with a variety of new splinter groups—at this point more akin to neighborhood gangs than full-fledged militias—with which they could partner. For some of these splinter groups, al-Sadr's decision to align his movement with SCIRI and the Dawa Party under the United Iraqi Alliance (UIA) umbrella for the upcoming General Assembly election in December 2005 was a step too far. Though Sadr's political bloc gained control of key government ministries and therefore provided new sources of income and patronage, some Mahdi Army fighters fiercely opposed the movement's turn to politics.[88]

Meanwhile, Iran saw in the Mahdi Army splinter groups—later known as the Special Groups—an opportunity to reproduce the successful Hezbollah model from Lebanon, but with an eye toward the unique political and social realities in Iraq.[89] Beyond wanting to maintain plausible deniability for attacks in Iraq, Iranian leaders viewed Iraqi Shi'a groups as a mechanism through which they could influence Iraqi politics without arousing fears among Iraqi Shi'a and Sunnis alike that Iran, a longtime enemy of Iraq, still held animus and hostile intentions toward the new Iraqi government. Since direct Iranian support for Shi'a militants aroused concerns among Iraqis about Iran's long-term intentions, Lebanese (Arab) Hezbollah made an attractive proxy for Iranian support to Shi'a Iraqi militants. Some 100 Shi'a militants traveled to Lebanon in December 2005 for military training. "They didn't teach us anything about suicide bombings, they showed us real tactics and taught our snipers," one trainee commented.[90]

In early 2006, reports emerged that Imad Mughniyeh himself was seen in Iraq, in the southern city of Basra, organizing Mahdi Army fighters' travel to Iran for military training. By April, he had reportedly returned to Lebanon, where his skills were needed to plan the July 2006 kidnapping of Israeli soldiers that led to Hezbollah's war with Israel later that month. By some accounts, this visit would not have been Mughniyeh's first in Iraq. One of the many variations of Mughniyeh's biography, this one promoted by Iranian military leaders, has him completing three months of basic training in Iran in the early 1980s and then traveling "with other Lebanese young men to the Iranian front and [taking] part in several daring operations behind Iraqi lines."[91]

Whether or not Mughniyeh traveled to Iraq in 2006, by then American intelligence sources, as well as information gleaned from interviews with detainees in Iraq, revealed without a doubt that Hezbollah was training members of the Mahdi Army. A small number of Hezbollah trainers visited Iraq, according to a senior American intelligence official, but large-scale training for 1,000 to 2,000 Mahdi Army fighters took place in Lebanon. A midlevel Mahdi Army commander corroborated the US intelligence in summer 2006, when he conceded that some 300 Mahdi Army fighters were sent to Lebanon, apparently to fight alongside Hezbollah during the July 2006 war. "They are the best-trained fighters in the Mahdi Army," he added.[92] Meanwhile, back in Baghdad, hundreds of armed Shi'a militants marched in support of Hezbollah during the war with Israel. Heading into weekly Friday prayers, they chanted, "Here we are, ready for your orders, oh Muqtada and Nasrallah. . . . Woe to you, Israel! We will strike you!"[93]

The fact that the Iraqi trainees traveled to Lebanon through Syria, US officials added, suggested that at least some Syrian officials were complicit in the training program. Moreover, Syrian officials reportedly attended meetings together with Qods Force chief Qassem Soleimani and Hezbollah's Imad Mughniyeh to coordinate means of turning up the heat on US forces in Iraq.[94] Several months after Mughniyeh's assassination, a senior Mahdi Army commander in Baghdad—speaking anonymously because of the sensitivity of what he was about to reveal—said that Mughniyeh had, in fact, supervised Hezbollah operations in Iraq.[95]

In Washington, despite a consensus on the destructive role Iran was playing in Iraq in late 2006, debates still raged within the US intelligence community over whether Hezbollah was really on the ground in Iraq and whether the group was training Iraqi militias in Iran or Lebanon or both. Testifying before Congress in November 2006, then–CIA director Gen. Michael Hayden stated, "I'll admit personally that I have come late to this conclusion, but I have all the zeal of a convert as to the ill effect that the Iranians are having on the situation in Iraq."[96]

In early 2007, Iran's political allies in the Iraqi government actually issued a diplomatic demarche demanding Tehran scale back its support for the Iraqi Shi'a militias, which by then were posing a tremendous security risk in the country. Iraqi officials were being killed in internecine Shi'a violence, possibly the result of Iran's apparent decision to intensify Shi'a militia activity after Hezbollah's self-declared victory in its war against Israel. Speaking in January 2007, Hezbollah chief Hassan Nasrallah told his group's satellite television station, al-Manar, that "the American occupation poses a danger to the Iraqi people and to the region." He was crystal clear on his means of rectifying the situation: "We support the option of a comprehensive Iraqi resistance, with all its aspects, especially the military aspect. We believe that the solution in Iraq begins with adopting the option of armed resistance—jihad against the occupation forces."[97] Some in the Qods Force "sought to replicate [Hezbollah's self-perceived] victory [against Israel] in Iraq, opening the floodgates" and providing advanced EFPs and other weapons to a range of Shi'a factions.[98] By mid-2007, al-Sadr was no longer coy about his organization's ties to Hezbollah. "We have formal links with Hezbollah, we do exchange ideas and discuss the situation facing Shiites in both countries. . . . We copy Hezbollah in the way they fight and their tactics, we teach each other and we are getting better through this."[99]

In seeking to lead from behind and put an Arab face on its efforts, in 2007 the Islamic Republic sent a master trainer—Ali Musa Daqduq—to Iran to coordinate the training program and make periodic visits to Iraq. This use of the Hezbollah leader Daqduq would assuage any Iraqi unease about working under seemingly aloof and disdainful Iranian operatives.[100] Whereas Daqduq had been informed back in 2005 that he would be traveling to Iran to work with the Qods Force to train Iraqi extremists, he only went to Tehran in May 2006, accompanied by the Hezbollah official in charge of Unit 3800 activities in Iraq, Yusef Hashim. In Tehran,

Daqduq and Hashim met with the commander and deputy commander of Qods Force special external operations, who informed them of plans to monitor and report on progress in Iraq. In the year before British Special Forces captured Daqduq in Basra in late 2007, he made four trips to Iraq. He reported back to the Qods Force on the Special Groups' use of mortars and rockets, their manufacture and use of improvised explosive devices (IEDs), and kidnapping operations. His overall instructions were simple: "He was tasked to organize the Special Groups in ways that mirrored how Hezbollah was organized in Lebanon."[101]

Hezbollah's Training Programs for Iraqi Insurgents

So it was that Hezbollah, at Iran's behest, helped develop a sophisticated training program for Shi'a militants from Iraq. Some training occurred in Iraq, reportedly at the Deir and Kutaiban Camps east of Basra near the Iranian border. According to statements from detained Special Groups members, Hezbollah trainers numbered no more than ten at a time. Trainers, including Daqduq, always kept a low profile and never stayed in Iraq for very long, moving back and forth across the Iranian border.[102]

In Iran, Hezbollah and Qods Force instructors ran a well-organized training program in which Daqduq was directly involved.[103] The outsourcing of training to Hezbollah spoke volumes for Iran's regard for the group's professionalism as terrorist trainers. The use of Hezbollah also averted Iraqi militants' complaints about the religious indoctrination included in the Iranian training programs, which were generally uninspiring and taught by sheikhs who did not speak Arabic well.[104]

According to documents seized by coalition forces, a formal selection process for prospective trainees considered the needs identified by Special Groups leaders but also set minimal qualifications for admittance. Candidates had to be able to read and write, for example, but Special Groups leaders also sought open-minded, strong, mature, and responsible people who demonstrated acumen for organizational skills and were "not a problem."[105] The Qods Force and its Hezbollah instructors trained some twenty to sixty Iraqis at a time, in sessions generally lasting twenty days.[106]

Iraqi militants selected to train in Iran traveled to camps well inside the country through several well-organized ratlines, a mirror image of those moving weapons into Iraq. According to the statements of Iraqi detainees, Amara, a city in southeastern Iraq, served as a hub for the movement of militants into Iran. Iraqi militants flocked to Mahdi Army and Special Groups safe houses in Amara from the predominantly Shi'a areas where they were recruited. One Special Groups militant described the process, as summarized in a US intelligence report:

> When the training travel was ready, [redacted] would call the SG (Special Group) areas and have the trainees travel to Amara. The trainees would usually travel by taxi, a seven to eight passenger vehicle, to the Baghdad garage in Amara. Once in Amara, the trainees would contact [redacted] and inform him of their arrival. [Redacted] would arrange to have someone, usually [redacted][,] meet

the trainees and take them to an Amara SG safe house. [Redacted] would meet the trainees at the safe house where he would provide each 100 USD, brief them on their travel and what to be aware of, and verify their passports. The trainees would then wait at the safe house until [redacted] told them it was time to depart for Iran. The trainees would again use taxis, usually seven to eight person vehicles, in their travel to the Iranian and Iraqi border.[107]

Some trainees reported crossing the border legally, others illegally. Either way, once across they met Iranian guides who escorted them to safe houses and hotels in the nearby Iranian border towns of Ahvez and Kermanshah. From there, the Qods Force arranged for the trainees to catch flights to Tehran. Once in Iran's capital, Special Groups members stayed in apartments on the city's outskirts, where preliminary training took place indoors. Trainees also described riding a bus two or three hours away from Tehran to "military style training complexes manned by uniformed Iranian soldiers."[108]

Despite the pledges of senior Iranian leaders to cease such support, Defense Intelligence Agency director Burgess told Congress in 2010, "Iran continues to provide money, weapons and training to select Iraqi Shia militants and terrorists." In Iran, Gen. Ronald Burgess added, "the Qods Force or Lebanese Hezbollah-led training includes: small arms, reconnaissance, small unit tactics, and communications." The training that the Qods Force and Hezbollah provided shed significant light on the kinds of operations Iran sought to see proliferate in Iraq. In particular, the focus was on providing elite trainees the "training, tactics and technology" to conduct assassinations and kidnappings and handle IEDs and EFPs. Other training focused on intelligence and sniper operations.[109]

The twenty-day basic training course experienced by most trainees covered paramilitary skills and basic weapons training, including training with mortars, IEDs, and small arms. Among graduates, a smaller number would be selected for a more intense, advanced paramilitary course that stressed advanced operations and tactics. Trainees in this course would be expected to take on leadership roles, and the material therefore included topics such as logistics and support, weapons employment, explosives engineering, tactics, and information operations.[110]

For an even more select group, the Qods Force and Hezbollah offered two additional programs: a master trainer program and an elite Special Forces course. Given the cost, logistical barriers, and other risks associated with covertly bringing Iraqis to Iran for training, instituting a "train the trainer" component to the Qods Force/Hezbollah program just made sense. Far more trainees could be reached if Iraqi instructors could offer training courses in Iraq. As one Special Groups recruiter told a trainee selected for a third round of training in Iran, this time for the master trainer course, "I want to send you over there because you're an educated guy, so we'll send you to Iran. . . . You're gonna have some experiences and with this experience you're gonna pass it to your friends."[111] Iran did not want its fingerprints all over the training program, a detained Iraqi militant would later explain, seeking instead to develop an independent Iraqi training program that could not be traced back to the Islamic Republic.[112]

Over the course of 2006–7, several Special Groups members noted in their debriefings, sixteen operatives made several trips to Iran to take the master trainer course. Four specialized in EFPs; four in mortars and rockets; four in conventional weapons; and four in tactical and guerrilla warfare such as booby traps, kidnappings, and attacks on coalition bases and convoys.[113] In April 2008, a US senator asked General Petraeus if it would be fair to say that Iranian-backed Special Groups in Iraq were responsible for killing hundreds of American soldiers and thousands of Iraqi soldiers and civilians. "It certainly is," Petraeus answered.[114]

As for the Special Forces training, that seems to have been tailored to specific trainees or specific needs. Some detained militants described a thirty-day course that included swimming, diving, fitness, and driving. Others described a twelve-day course focused on tactics and use of the Iranian-produced Strella antiaircraft missile, courses on advanced sniper skills, and even the unenviable though critical courses in administration and management. Interestingly, some of these courses were offered in Lebanon as well as Iran.[115]

Some Iraqi Shi'a traveled through Iran en route to Syria and then Lebanon, where they were trained by Hezbollah experts. These trainees made their way to Tehran using the same facilitation networks as those remaining in Iran for training, but then caught flights to Syria and traveled overland from Damascus International Airport to and across the Lebanese border. Excerpts from a US intelligence report, which paraphrases a detained Iraqi militant's description of his travel to a training camp in Lebanon, document the operational security involved in transporting the Iraqi Shi'a militants from the Damascus airport to Lebanon. On his arrival in Damascus on a commercial flight from Iran, the detainee and his fellow Iraqi trainees were met halfway down the jetway by an unidentified male who collected their tickets and baggage tags. They were led away from the passenger terminal to the airport operations area, where they boarded a bus. After driving through farmland, the trainees were instructed to board different vehicles operated by Lebanese drivers.[116]

Some of the Iraqi trainees appear to have been selected for additional training in Lebanon after completing some training in Iran. In other cases, possibly those of more experienced fighters, candidates went straight to Lebanon without first training in Iran. Hezbollah and IRGC instructors both reportedly concurred that the paramilitary training Hezbollah provided in Lebanon was superior to the training provided in Iran.[117] Whereas most Iraqi trainees appear to have attended a three- to four-week course focused on management of paramilitary activities, others attended courses on management of personnel and project planning and still others on advanced intelligence training, with an emphasis on collecting intelligence on coalition forces in Iraq. Meanwhile, even as Hezbollah trained Iraqi militants in Lebanon on behalf of the Qods Force, the Qods Force continued to operate training camps of its own in Lebanon, where, the head of the Defense Intelligence Agency testified, it trains Hezbollah operatives "and other fighters."[118]

Wherever they trained, Iraqi militants could never have been as lethally effective as they were without the $750,000 to $3 million a month in funding and arms they received from Iran. "Without this support," US military authorities concluded, "these special groups would be hard pressed to conduct their operations in Iraq."[119] Asked the source of the 107-millimeter rockets Shi'a insurgents were firing on the Green Zone in Baghdad, General Petraeus replied succinctly, "They come from Iran." By early 2008, 107-millimeter rockets were turning up in seized weapons caches, with forty-five found in one cache alone, which also included several thousand pounds of explosives, all from Iran. Included among detainees who explained the Special Groups' process to officials were Qods Force operatives and Special Groups leaders and financiers.[120] Speaking in summer 2008, Iraqi president Jalal Talabani acknowledged that "there have been several occasions" when Hezbollah operatives or people who "claim to belong to Hezbollah" were detained in Iraq. Aside from Ali Musa Daqduq, Iraqi military sources noted the April 2008 arrest of a Hezbollah operative identified only as Faris.[121]

As a result of Iran and Hezbollah's training program, the Special Groups quickly became one of the most pressing security challenges in Iraq. "Unchecked," General Petraeus told the Senate Armed Services Committee in April 2008, "the special groups pose the greatest long-term threat to the viability of a democratic Iraq."[122] Over time, Hezbollah provided the Iraqi insurgents "with the training, tactics and technology to conduct kidnappings, small unit tactical operations, and employ sophisticated improvised explosive devices (IEDs), incorporating lessons learned from operations in Southern Lebanon," according to an April 2010 Pentagon report.[123] In Iraq, Shi'a militants were now far better trained in the specialized capabilities needed to carry out daring kidnapping and assassination attacks targeting coalition forces. It would not take long before Hezbollah operatives would begin directing Iraqi militants in the execution of exactly such operations.

Directing Attacks Targeting Coalition Forces

A 2009 report on Hezbollah's IJO (also known as the External Services Organization, or ESO) by the Australian attorney general is most interesting for its conclusion that Hezbollah's activities in Iraq went much further than simply training Iraqi Shi'a militants tied to Iran: "Hizballah has established an insurgent capability in Iraq, engaging in assassinations, kidnappings and bombings. The Hizballah units have been set up with the encouragement and resources of Iran's Revolutionary Guards al Qods Brigades. Hizballah has also established a special training cell known as Unit 3800 (previously known as Unit 2800) specifically to train Shia fighters prior to action in Iraq."[124] The Australian report provides no details regarding the assassinations, kidnappings, and bombings it attributes to Hezbollah in Iraq. But the US military also uncovered evidence, albeit limited, suggesting Hezbollah may have run operations of its own in Iraq. A US intelligence report includes the assessment of an Iraqi militant who believed one of his Hezbollah trainers in Iran seemed to have previously been involved in covert activities in

Iraq. Paraphrasing the Iraqi militant's statement, the intelligence report relayed the detainee's information:

> [Redacted] is the Lebanese Hezbollah trainer in charge of the training camp [Detainee] attended in Iran.... [Detainee] thinks [redacted] has operated in Iraq because [redacted] always used to talk about how Iraqi food is not good and how the Iraqis do not have good water. [Redacted] would drop hints like this to let the trainees know that [redacted] has worked in Iraq. [Redacted] was one of the more respectful of the LH [Lebanese Hezbollah] trainers, and appeared to demonstrate some knowledge of Iraqi culture. [Redacted] would say things about Iraq in a way that let the trainees know that [redacted] has been to Iraq before. There are two kinds of LH, the kind you see on television, and the secret underground kind. All the trainers in Iran were the secret LH. If [redacted] was in Iraq it would not be for a trip, [redacted] would only go to do secret LH work. [Redacted] spoke Iraqi dialect very well but it was still apparent that [redacted] was Lebanese.[125]

Nor were the Australians and Americans alone in their concern over Hezbollah operational activities in Iraq targeting their soldiers. British forces had a particular interest in Hezbollah activity in Iraq, beyond the fact that the area of southern Iraq under their control, and the city of Basra in particular, was a hotbed of Iraqi Shi'a extremist activity and a ratline for travel to training camps in Iran and Lebanon. In particular, while British officials first viewed the evidence skeptically, they ultimately concluded that "British soldiers were being killed by Shia special groups at a depressing and, it appeared, rising rate."[126] Then, on May 29, 2007, Hezbollah-trained Iraqi militants kidnapped five British citizens in a brazen attack on the Iraqi Ministry of Finance.

The operation began just before noon that Monday, when a convoy of SUVs of the type used by the Iraqi government pulled into the compound. In a flash, gunmen wearing Iraqi police uniforms abducted the five British civilians from the ministry—a technology consultant and his civilian security guards—without firing a shot.[127] The assault utilized the precise type of training Hezbollah had already been providing Iraqi Shi'a militants, so accusations of Hezbollah's supervision of the attack by two Iraqi parliamentarians came as little surprise.[128] In time, evidence would emerge strongly indicating that the hostages were quickly secreted across the border into Iran, where they were held in Qods Force facilities.[129]

Peter Moore, the British technology consultant, was reportedly targeted—according to a year-long investigation by the *Guardian* newspaper—because he was installing software specifically engineered to track the billions of dollars in international aid and oil revenue flowing through Iraqi government coffers. The investigation determined that a vast amount of international aid was being diverted to Iran's militant proxies in Iraq, prompting the operatives to kidnap Moore before the software installation was complete. According to a former IRGC member, Qods Force operatives participated in the raid itself.[130] "This was not a conventional kidnapping," an individual involved in the early investigation into the attack commented. "We were dealing with people who were obviously killers." The British embassy received a package with five fingers with a note saying the fingers belonged to the five British hostages. DNA testing proved the claim untrue, but the case clearly wore on British decision makers.[131] Ultimately, Moore was released after 946 days in captivity in exchange for Qais Khazali, the Shi'a militant leader who was detained in the same raid as Hezbollah's Ali Musa Daqduq.

In July 2008, the British government extended its proscription of Hezbollah's ESO (IJO) to include "the military wing of Hezbollah in its entirety, including the Jihad Council and all units reporting to it including the Hizballah External Security Organisation [ESO]." The explanatory memorandum to the proscription order, which underpins the action, stressed Hezbollah's "provision of training and logistical and financial support to terrorist groups in Iraq and Palestine." Prime Minister Gordon Brown emphasized that the broadened proscription order was issued "solely on the grounds of new evidence of its involvement in terrorism in Iraq and the occupied Palestinian territories."[132] Some of that evidence, it appears, centered on operations directed and supported by Hezbollah targeting British forces and civilians in Iraq, as in the May 2007 attack on the Iraqi Finance Ministry.

At the time of the British designation, senior US government officials met with their French counterparts in an effort to convince Paris to either issue its own proscription order banning Hezbollah or, at a minimum, signal to Iran and Hezbollah that any Hezbollah operational activity beyond Lebanon's borders would lead France to ban the group. France declined to do so, citing the group's status as an elected political party in Lebanon, much to the frustration of US officials.[133] Hezbollah had long ago been designated as a terrorist group in the United States, but in October 2007, the Treasury Department designated the IRGC Qods Force as a terrorist group as well. Aside from the Qods Force's support to Palestinian terrorist groups and the Taliban, Treasury noted that the group "provides lethal support in the form of weapons, training, funding, and guidance to select groups of Iraqi Shi'a militants who target and kill Coalition and Iraqi forces and innocent Iraqi civilians." The May 2007 Finance Ministry attack likely ranks among the events that contributed to the decision to designate the Qods Force. But that event did not occur in isolation. It followed the no-less-daring and bold January 20, 2007, attack on the Provincial Joint Coordination Center in Karbala and the March 20, 2007, British Special Forces raid that led to the arrest of Hezbollah operative Ali Musa Daqduq—along with the Khazali brothers—in Basra.

The Capture of Ali Musa Daqduq

In the world of counterinsurgency special operations, the material seized in each raid feeds the intelligence machine, which churns out further leads and targets. Not only are suspects detained and questioned, but everything from documents, cell phones, and computers to receipts, scraps of paper, and other "pocket litter" are seized and culled for actionable intelligence. It was just such a cycle of executing raids, processing intelligence, and executing more raids that led British Special Forces to raid a location in Basra, Iraq, looking for the Khazali brothers. This, plus "a lot of exploitation of human intelligence in southern Iraq over a period of eighteen months," enabled British forces to track militants' movement along key ratlines and pinpoint key locations along the way. When specific information surfaced about the Khazalis' whereabouts, an operation was quickly crafted to raid their location on the night of March 20, 2007.[134]

Members of the British Special Air Service (SAS) G Squadron stormed the Basra house where intelligence indicated the Khazalis were located, and they arrested the two brothers.[135] To the SAS commandos' surprise, they also encountered a middle-aged man who appeared to be deaf and mute. The man's ability to uphold the cover story for several weeks indicates the professionalism of his counterintelligence and resistance-to-interrogation (R2I) training. But ultimately, faced with evidence seized at the time of his arrest—including false identification and documents linking him to Hezbollah—the middle-aged man admitted to being a Lebanese national and senior Hezbollah operative by the name of Ali Musa Daqduq al-Musawi.[136]

"Someone with a Lebanese background is going to speak with a very specific Lebanese dialect," a US military spokesman noted, explaining why Daqduq pretended to be a deaf mute in an effort to conceal his affiliation with Hezbollah.[137] A central element of R2I training typically involves teaching operatives that while everyone ultimately breaks down and provides information under interrogation, the ability to resist providing this information for the first few days is critical, allowing accomplices time to escape, cover their tracks, and regroup. Daqduq lasted several weeks before he disclosed his true identity to coalition forces, but the trove of materials confiscated at his arrest had already led analysts from the Basra raid back to Hezbollah and the Qods Force and straight to a string of attacks targeting British and US forces, including the attack on the Karbala Provincial Joint Coordination Center.

In early July 2007, Multi-National Forces–Iraq (MNF-I) held a press conference to announce, among other things, the capture two and a half months earlier of the Khazali brothers and Ali Musa Daqduq. Aided by PowerPoint slides, the military spokesman described Daqduq as the commander of a Hezbollah special operations unit who "led Hezbollah operations in large areas of Lebanon" and had been a "Lebanese Hizballah senior leader since 1983."[138] As one of the early members of the group founded following the 1982 Israeli invasion of Lebanon, Daqduq, a member of the Musawi clan, would have had an inside track to Hezbollah's Special Security Apparatus, of which the IJO would become a key component.[139] By 2007, Daqduq had served in several high-level positions, including a stint as the coordinator of Hezbollah chief Hassan Nasrallah's security detail. According to several reports, material seized at Daqduq's arrest led authorities down a trail that ended at the front door of Imad Mughniyeh, who would be assassinated seven months after Daqduq's capture. Although impossible to confirm, Daqduq may have been a member of Mughniyeh's inner circle.[140]

When Daqduq was captured in Iraq, he held multiple false identity cards but claimed—while still pretending to be deaf and mute—to be an Iraqi named Hamad

Mohamed Jabarah Alami. In some of his false IDs he appeared wearing a black robe and turban, in others an open-collar dress shirt. His various ID cards featured his photograph and identified him as an employee of different Iraqi government agencies, including one for the Council of Ministers and another for the Ministry of Agriculture.[141] Daqduq, however, was neither an Iraqi citizen nor an employee of the Iraqi government. Instead "he was in Iraq working as a surrogate for Iranian Revolutionary Guard Corps Qods Force operatives involved with special groups."[142]

Most damning for Daqduq and the Khazali brothers was the collection of detailed documents in Daqduq's possession at the time they were captured. Daqduq, the documents revealed, was personally involved in violent operations in Iraq. For example, in his personal diary Daqduq recorded his involvement in a plot to kidnap a British soldier. "The operation is to infiltrate two brothers to the base to detain a British soldier in the first brigade from the bathrooms by drugging him," Daqduq wrote.[143] Daqduq noted meeting with Special Groups operatives who described the attack, which failed when Iraqi soldiers intervened. This was not the only attack targeting British forces in which he was involved—other documents refer to attacks on British bases at the Basra Palace and the Shatt al-Arab Hotel.[144]

In another entry, Daqduq recorded meeting with Special Groups operatives who were involved in attacks targeting fellow Iraqis as well as coalition forces in Diyala province with IED bombings and small arms fire. He wrote about IED bombings in the first person, suggesting he was either personally involved in the attacks on the ground or, at a minimum, saw himself as integral to the plot: "Met with the brothers[,] the observers of Diyalah province and I listened regarding the operations. . . . We conducted eight explosive charge operations on both sides."[145]

The documents in Daqduq's possession discussed a variety of attacks targeting coalition and Iraqi forces, including IED attacks, kidnapping plots, attacks on helicopters, and small arms assaults. As a master trainer, Daqduq played a hands-on role in preparing Special Groups operatives to execute attacks. A training manual he carried included very specific, tactical tips for successful operations. When conducting a rocket attack against a coalition convoy, for example, militants should (1) "Launch two rockets at the target and the third one for insurance"; (2) "Shoot the first and second vehicle"; (3) "Each vehicle shoots two rockets (four rockets for every vehicle)"; (4) "Secure the place using the weapon and shoot visible soldiers"; and (5) "Shoot single shots and don't shoot on automatic."[146]

But what most grabbed the attention of senior coalition leadership was an "in-depth planning and lessons learned document" about the attack on the Karbala Provincial Coordination Center. The document laid bare the extensive preoperational surveillance, logistical preparation, and tactical drills that were carried out prior to the attack. Later both Daqduq and Khazali would concede "that senior leadership within the Qods Force knew of and supported planning for the eventual Karbala attack." According to Daqduq, "the Iraqi special groups could not have conducted this complex operation without the support and direction of the Qods Force." It was now clear that Qais Khazali had authorized the Karbala operation and Azhar al-Dulaymi led the assault team.[147] "Dulaymi reportedly obtained his training from Hezbollah operatives near Qum, Iran, who were under the supervision of Iranian Islamic Revolutionary Guard Corps Quds Force (IRGC-QF) officers in July 2006," according to a US government report. After the Karbala attack, crime scene investigators found Dulaymi's fingerprints on the getaway car.[148] The role of senior Qods Force officials in planning and approving the attack was exposed as well. In September 2008, the US Treasury Department targeted Qods Force deputy commander Abdul Reza Shahlai for planning Special Groups attacks targeting coalition forces, including the Karbala attack.[149]

Daqduq's personal role in the attack, however, was unclear. He appeared to have played some role in the training and direction of the attack, but the details were sketchy. In late 2011, as US forces prepared to leave Iraq and detainees under US custody had to be turned over to Iraqi authorities, reports emerged that Daqduq— still being held by US authorities in Iraq as an enemy combatant—stood accused of "organizing" or "masterminding" the Karbala attack.[150] Indications also suggested a concrete Hezbollah role. For one thing, the Treasury action targeting Qods Force General Shahlai seemed to suggest that his role in the Karbala attack went through Hezbollah. "As of May 2007," Treasury noted, "Shahlai served as the final approving and coordinating authority for all Iran-based Lebanese Hezbollah training for JAM [Jaish al-Mahdi, or Mahdi Army] special groups to fight coalition forces in Iraq." In summer 2006, Treasury added, Shahlai "instructed a senior Lebanese Hezbollah official to coordinate anti-aircraft rocket training for JAM special groups."[151] Daqduq, we know from documents seized in his possession, specialized in just such training.[152]

Then, in February 2012, the US government went public with news that the previous month the Obama administration had approved the filing of military commission charges against Daqduq, who was still in Iraqi custody. The eight-page charge sheet, issued secretly just days after Daqduq was turned over to Iraqi authorities, provided the basis for his possible extradition to the United States. According to press reports, Daqduq confessed under interrogation to his role in the Karbala attack.[153] The military charge sheet accused Daqduq of murder, terrorism, and spying, among other charges, all related to his role in the attack. Not only did it accuse Daqduq of authoring the planning document for the operation and of maintaining—in both Iraq and Iran— a video clip of a US soldier kidnapped by insurgents and held by Khazali's group and another of various ambush and rocket attacks, it also accused Daqduq of the murders of the five US soldiers in the attack and the wounding of several more.[154] Whether the charge sheet meant that Daqduq pulled the trigger or orchestrated the attack was left unsaid. Either way, US authorities maintain he played a hands-on role in the murder of five American soldiers. In the words of one former CIA officer, Daqduq is "the worst of the worst. He has American blood on his hands. If released, he'll go back to shedding more of it."[155] In May 2012, an Iraqi court dismissed the terrorism and false document charges against Daqduq. Six months later, Iraqi authorities freed him and transferred him to Lebanon.[156]

But that was just the picture of one individual. The broader picture, which is all about Iran, implied a still more disturbing reality in the view of senior military and political officials. A US military spokesman put it this way:

> What we've learned from Ali Musa Daqduq, Qais Khazali and other special groups members in our custody expands our understanding of how Iranian Revolutionary Guards Corps Qods Force operatives are training, funding and arming the Iraqi special groups. It shows how Iranian operatives are using Lebanese surrogates to create Hezbollah-like capabilities and it paints a picture of the level of effort in funding and arming extremist groups in Iraq.[157]

More disconcerting still, Iran's increasing willingness to target US interests did not end at the Iraqi border. In October 2011, both General Shahlai and Qods Force commander Qassem Soleimani were targeted by the Treasury Department once more for their roles in a Qods Force plot to assassinate the Saudi ambassador to Washington.[158]

Notes

1. Multi-National Corps–Iraq, Public Affairs Office, "Update to Initial Findings from Karbala; Militant Attack Used Deception, US Army Type Uniforms," release no. 20070126-21a, January 26, 2007.
2. Rowan Scarborough, "Iraqi Insurgent Linked to Iran, Hezbollah," *Washington Examiner*, March 22, 2007; Multi-National Corps–Iraq, "Update to Initial Findings."
3. Steven R. Hurst and Qassim Abdul-Zahra, "Four Troops Abducted, Killed in Iraq Attack," Associated Press, January 27, 2007.
4. Hurst and Abdul-Zahra, "Four Troops Abducted, Killed"; Peter Capella, "Mahdi: Iraq Could Be Caught in US-Iran Crossfire," *Middle East Online*, January 27, 2007; "Karbala Attackers Posed as US Military Officials," *CNN*, January 22, 2007; "Military Confirms 4 Soldiers were Abducted during Attack in Karbala," *USA Today*, January 26, 2007.
5. Multi-National Corps–Iraq, "Update to Initial Findings from Karbala"; Hurst and Abdul-Zahra, "Four Troops Abducted, Killed."
6. Hurst and Abdul-Zahra, "4 Troops Abducted, Killed."
7. "U.S. Accuses Hezbollah of Aiding Iran in Iraq," *New York Times*, July 2, 2007; Associated Press, "US Alleges Iran using Lebanese Hezbollah as 'Proxy' in Iraq," *Haaretz* (Tel Aviv), January 2, 2007.
8. "U.S. Accuses Hezbollah of Aiding Iran."
9. US Department of Defense, Office of the Assistant Secretary of Defense, "News Briefing with Gen. Petraeus from the Pentagon," April 26, 2007.
10. Bill Roggio, "U.S. Finds Karbala PJCC Mockup Inside Iran," *Long War Journal*, June 9, 2007.
11. Scarborough, "Iraqi Insurgent Linked to Iran"; James Glanz et al., "The War Logs: Secret Dispatches from the War in Iraq," *New York Times*.
12. US CIA, "Iranian Support for Terrorism in 1985."
13. US CIA, "Iranian Support for Terrorism in 1987."

14. US CIA, "Lebanon: 'Islamic Jihad' Goes Public."

15. US CIA, "Bahrani Hizballah Still Active?"

16. Ibid.

17. Clarke, *Against All Enemies*, 103.

18. US CIA, "Shootdown of Iran Air 655."

19. Colin Freeman, "Iran Poised to Strike in Wealthy Gulf States," *Telegraph* (London), March 4, 2007.

20. Rita Daou, "UAE Accused of Expelling Lebanese Shiites," Agence France Presse, September 30, 2009.

21. US CIA, "Lebanon's Hizballah."

22. International Crisis Group, "Shiite Politics in Iraq: Role of the Supreme Council," *Middle East Report* no. 70, November 15, 2007; Joseph Felter and Brian Fishman, "Iranian Strategy in Iraq: Politics and 'Other Means,'" Combating Terrorism Center at West Point, October 13, 2008, 24.

23. Felter and Fishman, "Iranian Strategy in Iraq," 24.

24. US Department of the Treasury, "Treasury Designates Individual, Entity Posing Threat to Stability in Iraq," press release, July 2, 2009.

25. Felter and Fishman, "Iranian Strategy in Iraq," 24.

26. Ibid., 22.

27. Michael Rubin, "Bad Neighbor," *New Republic*, April 6, 2004.

28. Author interview with former senior US government official, Washington, DC, January 26, 2012; Urban, *Task Force Black*, 111.

29. US Congress, Senate Select Committee on Intelligence, *Current and Projected National Security Threats to the United States: Hearing before the Select Committee on Intelligence*, 109th Cong., 1st sess., February 16, 2005, Statement of Vice Adm. Lowell E. Jacoby.

30. Michael Eisenstadt, Michael Knights, and Ahmed Ali, "Iran's Influence in Iraq: Countering Tehran's Whole-of-Government Approach," Policy Focus 111, Washington Institute for Near East Policy (Washington, DC), April 2011.

31. Sam Dagher, "In Iraq, a Very Busy Iran," *Wall Street Journal*, November 30, 2010.

32. US Congress, Senate Committee on Armed Services, *The Situation in Iraq and Progress by the Government of Iraq in Meeting Benchmarks and Achieving Reconciliation: Hearing before the Committee on Armed Services*, 110th Cong., 2d sess., April 8–10, 2008, Statements of Gen. David H. Petraeus and Ambassador Ryan Crocker.

33. Vali Nasr, "Regional Implications of Shi'a Revival in Iraq," *Washington Quarterly* 27, no. 3 (Summer 2004): 7–24.

34. "Iran General's Remarks on South Lebanon Draw March 14 Ire," *Daily Star* (Lebanon), January 21, 2012; Hezbollah insisted Sulaimani's words were misunderstood. See "Hezbollah: Iran General's Words Twisted," *Daily Star* (Lebanon), January 26, 2012.

35. Felter and Fishman, "Iranian Strategy in Iraq," 26–27.

36. Institute for the Study of War, "Interview and Moderated Q&A with General David Petraeus," Washington, DC, January 22, 2010, 40–41.

37. Ali Alfoneh, "Iran's Most Dangerous General," *Middle Eastern Outlook*, no. 4, American Enterprise Institute, July 13, 2011.

38. Paul Von Zielbauer, "U.S. Calls Iranian Official Part of Elite Force," *New York Times*, October 8, 2007.

39. Felter and Fishman, "Iranian Strategy in Iraq," 17–18, 21.

40. Multi-National Forces–Iraq, Maj. Gen. Kevin Bergner and Brig. Gen. Michael Walsh, press conference, October 3, 2007.

41. Felter and Fishman, "Iranian Strategy in Iraq," 17.

42. US Department of the Treasury, "Treasury Sanctions Five Individuals Tied to Iranian Plot to Assassinate the Saudi Arabian Ambassador to the United States," press release, October 11, 2011.

43. Martin Chulov, "Qassem Suleimani: The Iranian General 'Secretly Running' Iraq," *Guardian* (London), July 28, 2011.

44. Dafna Linzer, "Troops Authorized to Kill Iranian Operatives in Iraq," *Washington Post*, January 26, 2007.

45. Linzer, "Troops Authorized to Kill Iranian Operatives in Iraq." See also Urban, *Task Force Black*, 205.

46. Sabrina Tavernise, "U.S. Says Captured Iranians Can Be Linked to Attacks," *New York Times*, December 27, 2006; James Glanz and Sabrina Tavernise, "U.S. Is Detaining Iranians Caught in Raids in Iraq," *New York Times*, December 25, 2006.

47. Sudarsan Raghavan and Robin Wright, "Iraq Expels 2 Iranians Detained by U.S.," *Washington Post*, December 30, 2006.

48. Eli Lake, "Iran's Secret Plan for Mayhem," *New York Sun*, January 3, 2007.

49. Author interview with former US Government Official, Washington, DC, January 19, 2012.

50. Raghavan and Wright, "Iraq Expels 2 Iranians."

51. Tavernise, "U.S. Says Captured Iranians Can Be Linked to Attacks."

52. "Tehran's Secret 'Department 9000,'" *Newsweek*, June 4, 2007.

53. Glanz and Tavernise, "U.S. Is Detaining Iranians."

54. Sabrina Tavernise and James Glanz, "U.S. and Iraq Dispute Role of Iranians But Free Them," *New York Times*, December 30, 2006; Raghavan and Wright, "Iraq Expels 2 Iranians."

55. "Text of President Bush's Speech on Troop Levels," *NPR*, January 10, 2007.

56. James Glanz, "U.S. Says Arms Link Iranians to Iraqi Shiites," *New York Times*, February 12, 2007; James Glanz, "G.I.'s in Iraq Raid Iranians' Offices," *New York Times*, January 12, 2007.

57. Eli Lake, "U.S. Deadlocked on Whether to Free Iranian Terror Suspects," *New York Sun*, January 19, 2007.

58. Urban, *Task Force Black*, 209.

59. Glanz, "Arms Link Iranians to Iraqi Shiites."

60. Ibid.; Tim Susman and Borzou Daragahi, "The Conflict in Iraq: Accusations of Interference; U.S. Makes Case That Iran Arms Flow into Iraq," *Los Angeles Times*, February 12, 2007.

61. Glanz, "Arms Link Iranians to Iraqi Shiites."

62. Multi-National Forces–Iraq, Maj. Gen. Kevin Bergner and Brig. Gen. Michael Walsh, press conference, October 3, 2007. Iraqi intelligence documents seized by coalition forces say Farhadi actually led the Ramazan Corps' Nasr Command, not Zafr Command. See Felter and Fishman, "Iranian Strategy in Iraq," 49n71.

63. US Department of the Treasury, "Treasury Designates Individuals, Entity Fueling Iraqi Insurgency," press release, January 9, 2008.

64. David Pollack and Ahmed Ali, "Iran Gets Negative Reviews in Iraq, Even from Shiites," Policy Watch 1653, Washington Institute for Near East Policy (Washington, DC), May 4, 2010.

65. Kimberly Kagan, "Iran's Proxy War against the United States and the Iraqi Government," Institute for the Study of War and *Weekly Standard*, May 2006–August 20, 2007, 3.

66. Michael R. Gordon and Dexter Filkins, "Hezbollah Said to Help Shiite Army in Iraq," *New York Times*, November 28, 2006.

67. US Congress, Senate Committee on Armed Services, *Iran's Military Power: Hearing before the Committee on Armed Services*, 111th Cong., 2d sess., April 14, 2010, Statement of Lt. Gen. Ronald L. Burgess Jr.

68. Felter and Fishman, "Iranian Strategy in Iraq," 37.

69. Eisenstadt et al., "Iran's Influence in Iraq," 8.

70. US Department of the Treasury, "Treasury Designates Individuals, Entity Fueling Iraqi Insurgency," January 9, 2008; US Department of the Treasury, "Treasury Designates Individual, Entity Posing Threat to Stability in Iraq," July 2, 2009.

71. Felter and Fishman, "Iranian Strategy in Iraq," 27.

72. US Department of the Treasury, "Treasury Designates Individual, Entity Posing Threat"; Michael Knights, "The Evolution of Iran's Special Groups in Iraq," *CTC Sentinel* 3, no. 11–12 (November 2010): 12–16; Rafid Fadhil Ali, "Iraq's Kata'ib Hezbollah Seek Greater Popularity through Threats to Kuwaiti Port Development," *Terrorism Monitor* 9, no. 33 (August 19, 2011), Jamestown Foundation.

73. US Department of the Treasury, "Treasury Designates Hizballah Commander Responsible for American Deaths in Iraq," November 19, 2012.

74. Edward Pound, "Special Report: The Iran Connection," *U.S. News & World Report*, November 14, 2004.

75. Ibid.

76. Marisa Cochrane, "The Fragmentation of the Sadrist Movement," *Iraq Report* 12 (January 2009), Institute for the Study of War.

77. Joby Warrick, "U.S. Officials to Remove Iranian Group from Terror List, Officials Say," *Washington Post*, September 21, 2012; Scott Peterson, "Iranian Group's Big-Money Push to Get off US Terrorist List," *Christian Science Monitor*, August 8, 2011; Bahman Kalbasi, "Iran Exile Group MEK Seeks US Terror De-Listing," *BBC Persian*, September 24, 2001.

78. Ibid.

79. Raymond Tanter, "Iran's Threat to Coalition Forces in Iraq," Policywatch 827, Washington Institute for Near East Policy (Washington, DC), January 15, 2004.

80. Pound, "Iran Connection."

81. James Risen, "A Region Inflamed: The Hand of Tehran; Hezbollah, in Iraq, Refrains from Attacks on Americans," *New York Times*, November 24, 2003.

82. "Israeli Warns of Terrorist Training," *Washington Times*, November 14, 2003.

83. Nathan Guttman, "U.S. Sources Claim Hezbollah Sending Combatants to Iraq," *Haaretz* (Tel Aviv), June 20, 2004.

84. Agence France Presse, "Lebanese Hezbollah Members Detained in Iraq: Minister," February 9, 2005.

85. Michael Ware, "Inside Iran's Secret War in Iraq," *Time*, August 15, 2005.

86. "UK-Iraq Relations," Joint News Conference with Prime Minister Tony Blair and President Jalal Talabani, *CSPAN*, London, October 6, 2005.

87. Press briefing with Brig. Gen. Kevin Bergner.

88. Cochrane, "Fragmentation of the Sadrist Movement."

89. Knights, "Evolution of Iran's Special Groups in Iraq"; Andrew Exum, "Comparing and Contrasting Hizballah and Iraq's Militias," Policywatch 1197, Washington Institute for Near East Policy (Washington, DC), February 14, 2007.

90. Nizar Latif and Phil Sands, "Mehdi Fighters 'Trained by Hizbollah in Lebanon,'" *Independent* (London), August 20, 2007.

91. Alireza Nourizadeh, "Imad Mughniyeh: Hezbollah's Phantom Killed," *Al Sharq al Awsat*, February 15, 2008.

92. Gordon and Filkins, "Hezbollah Said to Help."

93. "Hezbollah-Israeli Fight Stirs Shiite-Sunni Issues," *Seattle Times*, July 22, 2006.

94. Gordon and Filkins, "Hezbollah Said to Help."

95. Hamza Hendawi and Qassim Abdul-Zahra, "Hezbollah Said to Train Shiite Militiamen in Iraq," Associated Press, July 1, 2008.

96. Gordon and Filkins, "Hezbollah Said to Help."

97. Niles Lathem, "House of Jihad," *New York Post*, February 5, 2007.

98. Knights, "Evolution of Iran's Special Groups in Iraq."

99. Latif and Sands, "Mehdi Fighters."

100. Iraqi Shi'a resented and distrusted their Iranian sponsors and trainers. Hezbollah compensated for Iran's shortcomings. See Harmony document IR 012, cited in Felter and Fishman, "Iranian Strategy in Iraq," 69.

101. Press briefing with Brig. Gen. Kevin Bergner.

102. Hendawi and Abdul-Zahra, "Hezbollah Said to Train."

103. Press briefing with Brig. Gen. Kevin Bergner.

104. Harmony document IR 011, cited in Felter and Fishman, "Iranian Strategy in Iraq," 66.

105. Felter and Fishman, "Iranian Strategy in Iraq," 56–57.

106. Press briefing with Brig. Gen. Kevin Bergner.

107. Harmony document IR 007, cited in Felter and Fishman, "Iranian Strategy in Iraq," 57–58.

108. Felter and Fishman, "Iranian Strategy in Iraq," 59.

109. Statement of Lt. Gen. Ronald L. Burgess Jr., *Iran's Military Power*; press briefing with Brig. Gen. Kevin Bergner.

110. Harmony document IR001, in Felter and Fishman, "Iranian Strategy in Iraq," 63.

111. Quote from MNF-I debriefing, cited in Felter and Fishman, "Iranian Strategy in Iraq," 64.

112. Harmony document IR002, cited in Felter and Fishman, "Iranian Strategy in Iraq," 64.

113. Harmony documents IR009, IR016, IR013, and IR011, cited in Felter and Fishman, "Iranian Strategy in Iraq," 63.

114. Statements of Gen. David H. Petraeus and Ambassador Ryan Crocker, *Situation in Iraq*.

115. Harmony documents IR004, IR014, IR020, IR002, IR-016, cited in Felter and Fishman, "Iranian Strategy in Iraq," 66.

116. Harmony document IR014, cited in Felter and Fishman, "Iranian Strategy in Iraq," 68.

117. Harmony documents IR001, IR005, cited in footnote 61 in Felter and Fishman, "Iranian Strategy in Iraq," 69.

118. Statement of Lt. Gen. Ronald L. Burgess Jr., *Iran's Military Power.*

119. Press briefing with Brig. Gen. Kevin Bergner.

120. Statements of Gen. David H. Petraeus and Ambassador Ryan Crocker, *Situation in Iraq.*

121. Hendawi and Abdul-Zahra, "Hezbollah Said to Train."

122. Statements of Gen. David H. Petraeus and Ambassador Ryan Crocker, *Situation in Iraq.*

123. Unclassified Report on Military Power of Iran, Congressionally Directed Action, April 2010, 3.

124. Australian Government, Attorney General's Department, "Hizballah External Security Organisation," May 16, 2009.

125. Harmony document IR 005, cited in Felter and Fishman, "Iranian Strategy in Iraq," 69–70.

126. Urban, *Task Force Black*, 214.

127. Damien Cave, "Gunmen in Police Uniforms Kidnap 5 British Civilians," *New York Times*, May 30, 2007. In an interesting twist, the finance minister at the time was himself a senior SCIRI official and a former Badr Corps commander.

128. Duncan Gardham, "Hizbollah 'Planned Kidnap of British Workers in Iraq,'" *Telegraph* (London), July 2, 2008.

129. Mona Mahmoud, Maggie O'Kane, Guy Grandjean, "Revealed: Hand of Iran Behind Britons' Baghdad Kidnapping," *Guardian* (London), December 30, 2009.

130. Ibid.

131. Deborah Haynes, "Peter Moore Went for a Job—and Ended Up as a Hostage for 946 Days," *Times* (London), December 30, 2009.

132. Stephen Jones, "The UK Government's Decision to Proscribe the Military Wing of Hezbollah," Standard Note SN/IA/4791, International Affairs and Defence Section, House of Commons Library, July 10, 2008; Alexander Horne, "The Terrorism Act 2000: Proscribed Organisations," Standard Note SN/HA/00815, Home Affairs Section, House of Commons Library, December 7, 2011.

133. Author interview with former White House official, Washington, DC, January 26, 2012.

134. Urban, *Task Force Black*, 224.

135. Ibid., 222.

136. Press briefing with Brig. Gen. Kevin Bergner; US Military Commission Charge Sheet for Ali Musa Daqduq al Musawi, ISN Number 311933, January 3, 2012; Urban, *Task Force Black*, 224–25.

137. Press briefing with Brig. Gen. Kevin Bergner.

138. "Ali Musa Daqduq: False Identification Documents," slides accompanying press briefing with Brig. Gen. Kevin Bergner.

139. Press briefing with Brig. Gen. Kevin Bergner.

140. Universal Strategy Group, *Directed Study of Lebanese Hezbollah*, produced for the United States Special Operations Command, Research and Analysis Division, October 2010, 38; Daniel Byman, *A High Price: The Triumphs and Failures of Israeli Counterterrorism*, Oxford: Oxford University Press, 2011, p. 262.

141. "Ali Musa Daqduq: False Identification Documents," slides accompanying press briefing with Brig. Gen. Kevin Bergner.

142. Press briefing with Brig. Gen. Kevin Bergner.

143. "Ali Musa Daqduq: Translated Excerpt from Personal Journal," slides accompanying press briefing with Brig. Gen. Kevin Bergner.

144. Urban, *Task Force Black*, 225; "Attacks on "Palace" in Basrah," slides accompanying press briefing with Brig. Gen. Kevin Bergner.

145. "Ali Musa Daqduq: Translated Excerpt from Personal Journal," slides accompanying press briefing with Brig. Gen. Kevin Bergner.

146. "Ali Musa Daqduq: Translated Excerpt from Training Manual He Carried," slides accompanying press briefing with Brig. Gen. Kevin Bergner.

147. Press briefing with Brig. Gen. Kevin Bergner.

148. Michael R. Gordon and Andrew W. Lehren, "Leaked Reports Detail Iran's Aid for Iraqi Militants," *New York Times*, October 22, 2010.

149. US Department of the Treasury, "Treasury Designates Individuals and Entities Fueling Violence in Iraq," September 16, 2008.

150. Carrie Johnson, "As Iraq Hostilities End, Fate of Combatant Unclear," *NPR*, November 15, 2011; David B. Rivkin Jr. and Charles D. Stimson, "Obama and the Hezbollah Terrorist," *Wall Street Journal*, December 7, 2011.

151. US Department of the Treasury, "Treasury Designates Individuals and Entities Fueling Violence in Iraq."

152. "Ali Musa Daqduq: Documents Found in His Possession," slides accompanying press briefing with Brig. Gen. Kevin Bergner.

153. Charlie Savage, "Prisoner in Iraq Tied to Hezbollah Faces U.S. Military Charges," *New York Times*, February 23, 2012.

154. US Military Commission Charge Sheet for Ali Musa Daqduq al Musawi, ISN Number 311933, January 3, 2012.

155. Laura Jakes, "Hezbollah Commander Could Be Transferred in Days," Associated Press, July 20, 2011.

156. US Department of the Treasury, "Treasury Designates Hizballah Commander Responsible for American Deaths in Iraq," November 19, 2012; Thomas Joscelyn and Bill Roggio, "Iraq Frees Hezbollah Commander who Helped Mold Shia Terror Groups," *Long War Journal*, November 16, 2012.

157. Press briefing with Brig. Gen. Kevin Bergner.

158. US Department of the Treasury, "Treasury Sanctions Five Individuals Tied to Iranian Plot to Assassinate the Saudi Arabian Ambassador to the United States," October 11, 2011.

11

Party of Fraud

Hezbollah's Criminal Enterprise in America

IN THE SPRING OF 2012, the head of the FBI's counterterrorism office in Detroit told an audience at the local Jewish community center that while he knew of no specific Hezbollah threat to Jewish communities in metropolitan Detroit, he remained concerned about potential and "general" threats in the area, from Hezbollah and other violent extremists. "The Iranian issue . . . that is a huge deal," he said. "Their use of the proxy group Hezbollah—these are things we're very concerned about."[1] But while Detroit has seen its share of trained Hezbollah gunslingers pass through town, the vast majority of Hezbollah cases in Detroit and around the country revolve around financial and logistical support for Hezbollah through criminal enterprise.

"Hezbollah acts like a basic crime organization here in the United States," explained a former head of the FBI's Iran-Hezbollah unit.[2] Employing an "Al Capone" disruption model—getting the bad guys on whatever legitimate charges will most easily stick—can be an extremely effective means of disrupting terrorist activity. In fact, the vast majority of cases targeting Hezbollah supporters in the United States have been prosecuted in just such a fashion, without any mention of the group.

This was the strategy behind several Dearborn-based investigations that morphed into Operation Bathwater, a major case aimed at disrupting Hezbollah activities by focusing on the group's broad array of criminal schemes. While some bit players involved in the Hezbollah support network were caught up in the investigation, the FBI focused on the higher-level figures. "Some Hezbollah supporters [in the United States] are not actual members, they are just useful idiots who want to be associated with a glorious cause but don't need or want to know more," explained the former FBI unit chief.[3]

Operation Bathwater was predicated on information developed in January 1999 by US Secret Service agents assigned to the Detroit Joint Terrorism Task Force (JTTF).[4] Investigating a series of financial crimes, the agents stumbled onto what proved to be not only the largest credit card fraud scheme in the country at the time but also a Hezbollah fundraising enterprise. The scheme dated back to 1994, though authorities would become aware of it only in November 1998, when an off-duty

Toledo police officer moonlighting as a department store security guard arrested Nancy Paulino, a single mother from New York, for trying to purchase $1,600 in clothes with a counterfeit Visa credit card. A couple of days later, another New Yorker named Jose Diaz Jr. traveled to Toledo to post bond for Ms. Paulino's release and was himself arrested on outstanding theft warrants from Wisconsin. The two suspects quickly conceded their roles as shoppers in an elaborate credit card scam run out of Toledo by Dearborn resident Ali Nasrallah.[5]

What police officers and federal agents learned from their investigation amazed them. In 1994, Ali Nasrallah, then living in New York, approached Diaz with a business proposition: Nasrallah would provide Diaz with fraudulent credit cards and counterfeit identification to match, and Diaz would recruit shoppers—like Ms. Paulino—who would use the cards to buy electronic equipment for Nasrallah. In return, the shoppers would be paid 5 percent of the purchase price for the items they bought. Nasrallah's organization later expanded beyond New York, first to Florida and then to Michigan.[6]

Diaz walked federal agents through Nasrallah's scheme. In an effort to "keep the heat away from where he lived," Nasrallah used Toledo as his base of operations, away from his Dearborn home but close enough to make regular trips down Interstate 75.[7] Diaz would meet Nasrallah at a Knights Inn or an Olive Garden restaurant to pick up counterfeit credit cards and plan shopping trips. The shoppers, often single mothers from New York, drove across the country buying laptops in places like Oklahoma City; Fort Wayne, Indiana; and Jackson, Mississippi. The laptops were then shipped to one of several addresses in Michigan or Virginia. "The idea," the prosecutor explained, "was to move around, not get caught, and not stay anywhere too long."[8]

Nasrallah and his business partners obtained active credit card numbers from computer hackers who breached the security systems of some 138 financial institutions from New Zealand to Switzerland. They acquired more than 10,000 blank credit cards that were stolen from a security company in Nebraska, which they then embossed with legitimate but stolen credit card numbers, and produced false IDs to match. In the words of one prosecutor, "It was incredibly sophisticated, and it utilized the latest computer technology."[9]

Based on the information Diaz provided, authorities obtained a search warrant for Nasrallah's Dearborn home. They found ample evidence of his criminal enterprise—including a list of 1,300 credit card numbers issued by banks across the globe, just under $20,000 in cash hidden in socks, and store circulars from cities where the computers were purchased—but Nasrallah himself had fled south to Toledo just as the authorities were about to raid his home. What followed was a Hollywood-worthy chase down I-75, involving officers from fourteen police agencies. Eventually, Nasrallah was pulled over just short of a highway interchange in Toledo and arrested. Within months, he was convicted, sentenced to six years in prison, and fined $5.1 million.[10] According to Secret Service agent Dan Sullivan, who supervised the case, the full extent of the financial losses resulting from Nasrallah's scam will never be known, but the total for just two dozen of the affected financial institutions came to $1.7 million.[11]

The original investigation was conducted by state prosecutors because federal prosecutors passed on the case when it first arose in 1998. A Secret Service memo written for the US Attorney's Office noted that several of Nasrallah's associates were Hezbollah fund-raisers, but since the original criminal act involved only $1,600 in stolen charges, authorities did not appreciate the full extent of the case, as federal prosecutors later conceded.[12]

Later, in revisiting the case, federal authorities found that the Secret Service investigation had raised several disconcerting and unanswered questions. Several shipments of laptops were traced to southern Lebanon and one to Baghdad, but the ultimate recipients were unclear. Several wire transfers were also traced to southern Lebanon, but from there the money trail went cold. Finally, the Lucas County (Ohio) grand jury named two people as unindicted co-conspirators in the credit card fraud ring, Ali Farhat and Hussein Kassem. According to an assistant county prosecutor who investigated the case, the two were suspected of raising money for Hezbollah.[13]

While Ali Nasrallah's case was never explicitly connected to Hezbollah, members of the JTTF cite his case as an example not only of a successful disruption of a Hezbollah financial support scheme but also as the trigger for Operation Bathwater.[14] The investigation into Ali Farhat's criminal and terrorist support activities would be opened under the FBI's case management system as a "265"—Bureau-speak for a criminal case aimed at securing a conviction in federal court. The FBI understood all too well what Hezbollah operatives and supporters in America were up to; it was now time to put a stop to it.

Operation Bathwater

The Racketeer Influenced and Corrupt Organizations (RICO) Act of 1970, said by some to be named after the gangster protagonist in the 1931 movie *Little Caesar*, empowered federal prosecutors to target a criminal enterprise writ large, focusing not only on the criminal acts per se but also on the patterns of behavior that support the criminal activities. It also enabled prosecutors to hold the leaders of the conspiracy responsible for any involvement, whether direct or not, in the crimes they ordered as part of the conspiracy.[15] Originally used to prosecute Mafia dons and their organized crime networks, RICO has proven equally effective in targeting organized groups engaged in raising money for terrorist groups. In Detroit, the Bathwater investigation would lead to three rounds of indictments, targeting some fifty individuals for a variety of criminal activities.

Though they would not be the first to be indicted, the initial targets of the JTTF investigation were Dr. Ali Abdul-Karim Farhat and his brother, Hassan Karim Farhat. In March 2001, the FBI obtained approval for a Title III criminal wiretap—requiring a higher threshold than an intelligence wiretap authorized by the Foreign

Intelligence Surveillance Act (FISA) court—for Dr. Farhat's telephone lines. Two members of the JTTF oversaw the electronic surveillance portion of the investigation, which, together with traditional FBI surveillance and the recruitment of human sources, "morphed into an unprecedented global terrorist financing investigation," as one JTTF member described it.[16]

Investigators found that beginning in March 1999, Ali and Hassan Farhat and several members of the Berro family "conspired to defraud multiple banks and other issuers of credit cards of hundreds of thousands of dollars." The suspects used Ali Farhat's perfume distribution company, Sigma Distribution, Inc., and another conspirator's company, Byblous Distribution Investment, Inc., to process transactions on credit cards that they never intended to pay. Sigma and Byblous would be paid by the banks and credit card companies, and the members of the conspiracy would then declare bankruptcy to creditors who could not collect on the debts incurred. In an effort to hide their assets from bankruptcy court, several members of the group "sold" their homes to their wives or adult children. In total, they charged more than $1.7 million on more than 230 credit cards.[17]

Given that the Farhat-Berro branch of the investigation grew out of the Nasrallah credit card scam case, investigators were hardly surprised by the nature of what they found. What did surprise them was the extent to which the conspiracy involved extended members of a single family. Ali Farhat had married into the Berro family, the same clan to which Ibrahim Hussein Berro, the Hezbollah suicide bomber who struck the Asociación Mutual Israelita Argentina community center in Buenos Aires in 1994, belonged. So far, the Bathwater investigation had been pretty cut-and-dried—but it soon took a turn for the worse.

In December 2003, FBI agents secured a court order for a criminal wiretap of a suspected drug trafficker's cell phone. The suspect was believed to be a Nigerian bearing a Canadian immigration document involved in drug dealings with Ali and Hassan Farhat. Much of the drug trafficking investigation was run strictly by the book, including FBI surveillance, the use of undercover FBI agents, and telephone wiretaps. In June 2003, according to the evidence, which had overtones of a pulp detective novel, FBI agents watched as "a very large African man" who went by the name of Bull visited Ali Farhat's restaurant to emphasize, as only a large man named Bull could, that Farhat had to quickly repay overdue money he owed a more senior drug trafficker.[18] The Farhat brothers, in turn, were arrested in January 2004 on charges of conspiracy to distribute cocaine. According to the criminal complaint, Ali Farhat had been involved in trafficking of cocaine, as well as heroin and marijuana, for more than a decade. Within days, government filings made it clear agents saw the case as one involving narco-terrorism finance. According to two confidential informants, the document explained, the Farhat brothers were Hezbollah supporters. An affidavit used to secure search warrants for the Farhats' homes and businesses revealed agents were looking for evidence of possible ties to Hezbollah, including "Hezbollah-related books, videos and documents."[19] But the charges, borne of several years of investigation, quickly fell apart.

Ali Farhat was accompanied at his uncomfortable meeting with Bull by an FBI informant, usually a good thing, but not in this particular case.[20] While much of the most compelling evidence came from the court-approved wiretaps and FBI surveillance, a good deal came from confidential informants gone bad. In one instance, an informant reported seeing the Farhat brothers in possession of cocaine at Ali Farhat's perfume distribution company in early 2001. Yet another claimed Hassan Farhat once gave him four shopping bags filled with perfume and a Christmas gift containing cocaine.[21] But mishandling of two key sources by the FBI's Detroit field office caused these and many other claims to fall apart. One source admitted violating the law to collect information for his FBI handler, while the other was found to have fabricated events.[22]

Within weeks the Farhat brothers were released on bond and the drug charges dropped. "My clients feel vindicated," their lawyer told the press.[23] But the celebration was short-lived. The original credit card investigation was untainted by the scandal caused by the bad informants, leading a grand jury to approve new charges against twelve Dearborn residents, including Ali Farhat. Convicted on RICO charges, Farhat was ultimately sentenced to seventy-four months in prison and ordered to pay more than $660,000 in restitution, on top of forfeiting his business and more than $72,000 in cash. All told, sixteen people would be sentenced as part of this scheme.[24] The new case made no mention of Hezbollah when it was filed and none when argued in court, despite the case being a cornerstone of a law enforcement campaign by the FBI and US Attorney's Office to disrupt Hezbollah support networks in the Detroit area. Prosecutors made sure, however, to note the Hezbollah connection in their sentencing memorandum; for them this was always at heart a case of fundraising for Hezbollah through criminal activities.[25]

Charlotte Redux

One reason investigators were so convinced the Farhat case was at least as much a counterterrorism case as it was a white-collar crime case is that the Farhat investigation did not occur in isolation. At the very same time, other agents on the Detroit field office's counterterrorism squad were conducting related investigations. In fact, while the Hezbollah finance Bathwater investigations grew out of the Ali Nasrallah case and his ties to Ali Farhat, the first Bathwater case to be indicted—a full year before Ali Farhat was first indicted—was another case altogether.

In January 2003, prosecutors indicted Elias Akhdar, Hassan Makki, Salim Awde, and eight other individuals on RICO charges covering cigarette smuggling, possession of counterfeit cigarette tax stamps, credit card fraud, money laundering, arson, and witness tampering. Like several others, this criminal enterprise was bound together not only by physical locality (Dearborn) and common heritage (Lebanese) but by blood and marriage relations and a shared purpose of generating illegal income. Another commonality was the desire not just to enrich themselves but also to raise large sums of money for Hezbollah.[26]

Starting around May 1996, investigators determined, Akhdar and other members of this network ran a cigarette trafficking ring that was a counterpart to the Charlotte cell. By purchasing cigarettes from the Hammouds in North Carolina and from Akhdar's common-law American Indian wife, Brandy Jo Bowman, on the Cattaraugus Indian Reservation on Lake Erie in New York State and then slapping counterfeit tax stamps on them, the operators of the Dearborn cigarette scam made a hefty profit. In the context of his plea agreement, one participant indicated that the cigarette trafficking ring purchased more than $500,000 worth of cigarettes in North Carolina alone.[27]

Often, cell members used counterfeit credit cards to purchase their merchandise. They would take "fraud field trips" to North Carolina, New York, elsewhere within Michigan, and other locales where their shopping sprees would leave a path of defrauded retail and wholesale merchants in their wake.[28]

When Akhdar heard that the Charlotte cell was indicted in March 2001, he fled to the Cattaraugus Indian Reservation, where his estranged wife and her mother, both key members of his criminal enterprise, lived. Eager to rid himself of key pieces of evidence, and seeing one last opportunity for a profitable scam, Akhdar set fire to an Indian reservation tobacco shop he owned with his wife, Brandy Jo, who then submitted a claim on the shop's fire insurance policy. Another way Akhdar tried to obstruct the investigation into his criminal activities was to intimidate potential witnesses, in some cases while under FBI surveillance.[29]

One of Akhdar's partners, Salim Awde, threatened a potential government witness, saying, "If you are working with the FBI, I will blow you away."[30] According to authorities, Awde made multiple trips overseas in service of his fraudulent schemes. A Lebanese-Canadian, Awde was reportedly caught by authorities in Dubai holding counterfeit Social Security and credit cards in 2000 and was arrested again in Egypt in 2002.[31] Getting to the heart of the matter—the group's ties to Hezbollah—the government requested that Awde be detained without bond pending trial, stating that Hezbollah "would be motivated to assist Awde in fleeing the United States."[32] According to prosecutors, Awde "conspired with at least two individuals with strong ties to Hezbollah."[33]

In February 2003, prosecutors revealed Akhdar's ties to Hezbollah. He first received military training from Islamic Amal and later engaged in Hezbollah military campaigns within Lebanon. Once he built up his criminal enterprise, prosecutors added, he contributed a portion of his illicit profits to Hezbollah.[34] Hezbollah issued a statement denying any relationship to Akhdar, Makki, and Awde, but a few weeks later, still more evidence of the network's Hezbollah ties were revealed when prosecutors opposed bail for Hassan Makki.[35] One of the reasons Makki had joined the criminal conspiracy in the first place, prosecutors maintained, was to raise money for Hezbollah.[36] Once, he was stopped at the US-Canada border with half a million dollars in checks and cash, some of which was meant for Hezbollah.[37] He solicited money for Hezbollah from other members of the smuggling ring and admitted to holding "membership/official status with Hezbollah." He would "telephone Sheiks in Lebanon and in Iran to clear criminal acts that he was committing." Materials seized in a raid of Makki's home included a photomontage of Hezbollah leaders and spiritual figures, militants in battle fatigues, funeral processions, celebrations, tanks, rockets, and firearms.[38]

Little Blue Pills and the Zig-Zag Man

In March 2006, two and a half years after Makki pleaded guilty to raising money for Hezbollah through criminal activities related to the Akhdar cigarette smuggling ring, another one of Makki's criminal partners, Imad Hammoud, was publicly indicted along with eighteen other individuals in a parallel RICO case. In this case the Hezbollah connection would appear front and center, with five of the named defendants—Imad Hammoud, Hassan Al Moussawi, Hassan Nassar, Karim Nassar, and Ali Hammoud—described as "avid supporters" of Hezbollah.[39]

Imad Hammoud was one of Makki's partners in several overlapping cigarette smuggling rings. But when the State of Michigan imposed a cigarette tax stamp, Imad Hammoud and his co-conspirators branched out into other illegal moneymaking schemes, especially trafficking counterfeit and stolen goods.[40] "Imad Hammoud," investigators would conclude, "was a central conduit of virtually every aspect of the enterprise's unlawful activities."[41] As a result, they referred to the group as the "Hammoud enterprise."[42]

Hammoud's criminal enterprise crisscrossed the United States from Michigan, California, Florida, Georgia, Illinois, Kentucky, Missouri, New York, and North Carolina to West Virginia (and, prosecutors stressed, points in between) and spanned the globe from the United States and Canada to Lebanon, Brazil, Paraguay, and China. Members obtained counterfeit cigarette stamps from Paraguay and Brazil, prompting Detroit JTTF agents to travel to the tri-border area to investigate that end of the conspiracy's activities. The US agents' efforts enabled Brazilian authorities to apprehend a major counterfeit ring that manufactured not only false cigarette stamps but also passports, national identity cards, and more.[43] Other elements in the conspiracy involved the import of counterfeit Viagra pills from China and Zig-Zag-brand cigarette paper from Indonesia.[44] The Hammoud enterprise's primary source for counterfeit Zig-Zag paper was Tarek Makki, an ethnic Lebanese from Sierra Leone who was living in Dearborn and later pleaded guilty to Zig-Zag trafficking and money laundering charges filed in Michigan and Texas.[45] When agents learned that Tarek Makki's uncle was in the diamond business in Sierra Leone, where Hezbollah has long profited from blood diamonds, they sought evidence of Makki's involvement but could not substantiate their findings.[46]

With so many angles to the case, multiple agents were assigned to cover the various frauds in which Hammoud and Co. were involved. According to officials involved in the investigation, the period of 2002 and 2003 "was nuts. We were managing over a dozen sources and pursuing two to three different investigative tracks at a time."[47] While the cigarette tax stamp angle brought agents to South America, and the Zig-Zag file led to Indonesia, the counterfeit Viagra scheme drew agents' attention to China. Here too the profit margins were attractive, and the funding came directly from the profits of cigarette smuggling, illicit funds that had to be laundered anyway. By 2002, Hammoud and his crew were believed to be moving half a million dollars' worth of cigarettes a week across state lines. According to authorities, over a three-month period that year they bought more than 90,000 counterfeit Viagra pills. The knockoff little blue pills were easy money. "They're small, they're high in demand and they're easily transportable," explained a senior FBI agent who led the Iran-Hezbollah unit at FBI headquarters.[48] By 2009, knockoff versions of Viagra would be the most widely counterfeited drug in the world, as lucrative a criminal enterprise as narcotics.[49]

Hammoud's Viagra operation was by no means the only drug-related Hezbollah scheme uncovered in the United States. In August 2000, Drug Enforcement Administration (DEA) special agents arrested more than 140 people in eight cities as part of a three-phase operation dubbed Mountain Express targeting methamphetamine production. Investigators also traced large amounts of profit being sent to individuals in the Middle East with possible connections to terrorist organizations.[50] At the time, then–DEA administrator Asa Hutchinson said, "I am satisfied that portions of the drug sales have moved back to the Middle East and portions of that are going to support terrorist organizations. Clearly, this is the first time we have seen with [sic] drug transactions in the United States where proceeds are actually going back to fund terrorism."[51] The investigation found that many of the men arrested had ties to Jordan, Yemen, Lebanon, and other Middle East countries, and were sending portions of their proceeds back to accounts in the Middle East that have since been connected to terrorist groups, including Hezbollah.[52]

Back in Dearborn, Hammoud's criminal enterprise went where opportunities took it, including trafficking in stolen goods as varied as socks, toilet paper, and infant formula. On one day in July 2002, a member of the group took possession of 27,648 rolls of toilet paper; 10,560 pairs of socks; and 60 cans of Similac infant formula, all purportedly stolen.[53] In the words of one person involved in the Bathwater investigations, when it came to the amount of money made through cigarette smuggling and other schemes, "Ali Farhat was big but Imad Hammoud was huge." The totals, prosecutors estimate, were in the millions.[54]

Given the Hammoud group's direct ties to the Moussawi clan, and the avid support for Hezbollah held by its Dearborn ringleaders, investigators were little surprised to learn that individuals who were critical of Hezbollah were confronted and kicked out of the crew. Portions of the profits were reportedly delivered to Hezbollah, sometimes via Hammoud's uncle who lived just over the bridge in Ontario, Canada.[55] Hammoud and his partner Hassan Makki both charged a "resistance tax," an additional fee over the black market cost per carton of contraband cigarettes, which customers were told would go to Hezbollah. They also maintained collection boxes for Hezbollah donations and set aside other chunks of money for transfer to the group in Lebanon.[56]

Another reason prosecutors saw Hammoud as a priority target was his enterprise's close ties to senior Hezbollah leaders. One sign of this intimacy was that a conspiracy member, Beirut-based Hassan Ali Moussawi, is the brother of Islamic Amal founder and then Hezbollah leader Hussein Moussawi.[57] Now a Hezbollah Member of Parliament in Lebanon, Hussein's brother was caught raising money for Hezbollah by selling counterfeit Viagra in the United States. According to prosecutors, some of the funds raised for Hezbollah were sent to Lebanon through Hassan Moussawi, "who had a close personal relationship with upper echelon Hezbollah officials." While some of the conspirators were driven by personal gain and supported Hezbollah as a bonus, "Al-Mosawi's participation with the conspiracy was expressly for the purpose of benefitting Hezbollah; and virtually all of the conspirators' collaboration with al-Mosawi was to garner favor from Hezbollah."[58] In September 2012, the Moussawis would be tied to a similar scheme producing another counterfeit drug back in Lebanon.[59]

A close reading of the indictment reveals a particularly telling piece of information about the Hammoud enterprise's role in the overall Hezbollah network. "On or about February 22, 2001," the indictment reads, "Imad Hammoud wire transferred $47,000 through the Bank of New York to Fawzy Ayoub's bank account in Beirut Ryiad [sic] Bank in London, England."[60] Recall that Ayoub is a convicted Hezbollah operative who once lived in the Dearborn area as well as across the bridge in Canada (see chapter 6). At the time of the wire transfer, Ayoub had already arrived in Israel on a fictitious American passport for the purpose of carrying out a terrorist attack.

Hezbollah's 007 . . . in Detroit, via Mexico

In early February 2001, Mahmoud Youssef Kourani snuck into the United States through Mexico and made his way to Dearborn. Kourani, a highly trained Hezbollah operative whose brother was Hezbollah's military security chief for southern Lebanon, entered the United States completely undetected.[61] This is a vulnerability long on the radar of US intelligence. According to one intelligence report, "travelers associated with various terrorist groups—including Hezbollah, Hamas, and the Egyptian Islamic Jihad—are tapping into global alien smuggling networks to abet their movements around the world, including to the United States."[62]

Back in Lebanon, Kourani paid a Beirut consular official $3,000 for a Mexican visa and then paid Salim Boughader Mucharrafille, the owner of a Lebanese café in Tijuana, an additional $4,000 to smuggle him across the border into California. Four years after illegally entering the United States, Kourani pleaded guilty to materially supporting Hezbollah. According to an FBI affidavit, Kourani admitted raising at least $40,000 for Hezbollah, some of it through mortgage fraud and still more through solicitation of "charitable" donations.[63]

Whatever money he raised in the United States, Kourani was confident he could get it back to Hezbollah. Once, Kourani told an FBI informant that he had recently sent $40,000 in money orders and cash to Hezbollah and could send as much money back to Lebanon as he liked because a friend who worked at the Beirut airport helped smuggle the money into the country.[64] Nine different FBI informants independently identified Kourani as a Hezbollah operative, alternately describing him as a Hezbollah fundraiser, member, and fighter.[65]

To be sure, Kourani did much more than just raise funds for Hezbollah. For example, in Lebanon he oversaw the application process and detailed background checks of prospective Hezbollah recruits.[66] Later, Kourani would brag behind closed doors to like-minded friends in the Dearborn area that Hezbollah sent him to Iran for military training in the early 1990s, after which he took part in Hezbollah military actions against Israeli targets. In one instance, Kourani told someone he thought he could trust about his experience fighting the Israelis over sixteen days in 1996. Unfortunately for Kourani, the trusted friend was a well-placed FBI source.[67] According to prosecutors, Kourani had received "specialized training in radical Shiite fundamentalism, weaponry, spy craft, and counterintelligence in Lebanon and Iran."[68]

Kourani, whose familial ties to Hezbollah ran deep, was charged with conspiring with "individuals at the highest levels" of the group.[69] One brother, Haidar, was the group's chief of military security for southern Lebanon and was described by one FBI source as "the Chief of Staff for Hezbollah."[70] An unindicted co-conspirator, Haidar oversaw his brother's US activities on behalf of Hezbollah.[71] Mahmoud Kourani told FBI informants he was sending money to his brother for Hezbollah.[72] During an FBI interview, Kourani acknowledged Haidar's status within the Hezbollah hierarchy and added that two other brothers, Hussein and Abdullah, were also Hezbollah members.[73] Mahmoud and Haidar, an FBI source reported, "were members of a Hezbollah unit that claimed responsibility for the 1988 kidnapping, torture, and murder of Lt. Col. W. Higgins in southern Lebanon."[74]

Agents first arrested Kourani on charges of harboring an illegal alien after searching his Dearborn home in May 2003. In the search they found $8,000 in cash and checks hidden in his bedroom as well as audiotapes and pictures, one of which featured one of his young children wearing a large necklace with a picture of Hezbollah leader Hassan Nasrallah.[75] The tapes included songs glorifying Hezbollah violence. "We offer to you Hezbollah, a pledge of loyalty," went one refrain. "Rise for Jihad! Rise for Jihad! . . . I offer you, Hezbollah, my blood in my hand."[76] Indicted on those charges in November 2003, Kourani pleaded guilty and served six months in federal prison. All the while, federal agents were building a much more substantial case against him for providing material support to Hezbollah.[77] Kourani was awaiting deportation in an immigration holding facility when prosecutors unsealed a grand jury indictment laying out the terrorism charges in January 2004. Kourani pleaded guilty to conspiracy to provide material support to a Foreign Terrorist Organization and was sentenced to fifty-four months in prison.[78]

One question that still perplexes investigators is why someone of Kourani's stature within Hezbollah would come to the United States. Why allow him to take the risk? He clearly did not come to stay, considering that he left his wife and children back in Lebanon. There was the ever-present need for fundraising, which he apparently did successfully, but the group already had numerous capable financial supporters in the Dearborn area and across the country. The question persisted: Could he have come to the United States for some more critical purpose?

Though they had precious little incriminating information about him when they first opened their investigation, by the time he was indicted on terrorism charges, authorities believed keeping him detained pending trial was absolutely critical for two main reasons. The first reason was that they worried that Hezbollah could actively help Kourani flee the United States. "Hezbollah has loyalists and operatives in numerous countries, including Ontario, Canada and the Eastern District of Michigan," prosecutors informed the court. "Were Kourani to be released on bond, Hezbollah would have the full ability and tremendous incentive to assist Kourani in escaping from and eluding United States authorities, not only because of Kourani's family connections, but also to ensure that he could not be persuaded to cooperate with the government against other Hezbollah members within the United States and abroad."[79] Even within Hezbollah's higher echelons, it seems, trust went only so far.

The second reason prosecutors opposed bail for Kourani was more chilling. "Were Kourani to be released on bond," prosecutors argued, "he would be in a better position to help Hezbollah hunt the government's witnesses for elimination not only to prevent this case from going forward, but also to prevent witnesses from leading the government to other Hezbollah operatives in the United States."[80] The FBI's investigation into Kourani underscored the government's concern. According to one FBI source, "if Hezbollah tasked Kourani to do something in the United States, he would carry out the mission on behalf of the organization."[81]

Once Kourani was arrested, federal officials picked up information indicating that senior Hezbollah officials were worried about what government witnesses, sources, or telephone wiretaps might reveal about him in particular and Hezbollah's activities in general. In the wake of Kourani's arrest, authorities assessed that Hezbollah may have changed some of its standards allowing senior operatives to travel abroad so freely.[82]

Kourani was far from the only Lebanese national and Hezbollah member that the Tijuana café proprietor Mucharrafille smuggled across the US-Mexico border. Over a three-year period he successfully smuggled more than 300 Lebanese individuals into the United States, including a reporter for Hezbollah's al-Manar television station. "If they had the cedar on their passport, you were going to help them," Mucharrafille explained while imprisoned in Mexico City for his activities. "That's what my father taught me."[83]

In June 2010, North Carolina representative Sue Myrick sent a letter to Department of Homeland Security secretary Janet Napolitano urging the department "to do more intelligence gathering on Hezbollah's presence on our border." Myrick was specifically concerned with Hezbollah's presence, activities, and connections to gangs and drug cartels. In recent years, the ties between Hezbollah and drug cartels have grown, especially along the US-Mexico border. According to former DEA chief of operations, Michael Braun, "Hezbollah relies on the same criminal weapons smugglers, document traffickers and transportation experts as the drug cartel. . . .

They work together; they rely on the same shadow facilitators. One way or another they are all connected."[84]

Braun and other officials have noted that the terrain along the southern US border, especially around San Diego, is similar to that on the Lebanese-Israeli border. Intelligence officials fear drug cartels, in an effort to improve their tunnels, have enlisted the help of Hezbollah, which is notorious for its tunnel construction along the Israeli border. In the relationship, both groups benefit, with the drug cartels receiving Hezbollah's expertise and Hezbollah making money off its efforts. Relatedly, law enforcement officials across the Southwest are reporting a rise in imprisoned gang members with Farsi tattoos. While prisoners' tattoos, even in Arabic, are not uncommon, the rise in Farsi and Hezbollah imagery "implies a Persian influence that can likely be traced back to Iran and its proxy army, Hezbollah," argued Rep. Myrick.[85]

A Tucson Police Department memo from September 2010 cited similar concerns, stating that the relationship "bares alarming implications due to Hezbollah's long established capabilities, specifically their expertise in the making of vehicle borne improvised explosive devices (VBIED's)."[86] Around the same time, Arizona's Division of Emergency Management reported that border patrol agents had recovered military-style patches on clothing near the US-Mexico border. One patch contained the Arabic word for martyr, and another depicted a plane flying head-on into skyscrapers.[87]

The arrest in New York City of Jamal Youssef, a former member of the Syrian military, provides even more insight into Hezbollah's foothold in Mexico. Youssef, a known international arms dealer, attempted to sell military-grade weapons to the Revolutionary Armed Forces of Colombia (FARC). The weapons included automatic rifles, rocket-propelled grenades, hand grenades, M60 machine belt-fed guns, antitank munitions, and C4 explosives—all reportedly stolen from Iraq and stored in Mexico at the home of Youssef's relative, who he claimed was a Hezbollah member—to be sold in exchange for hundreds of kilograms of cocaine.[88]

Just over the California-Mexico border, the city of Tijuana hosts San Ysidro, the busiest land-border crossing in the world. It is there in summer 2010 that Mexican authorities reportedly foiled an attempt by Hezbollah to establish a network in Central America. According to press reports, Hezbollah operatives led by Jameel Nasr employed Mexican nationals who had family in Lebanon to set up a network targeting Israeli and Western interests. Nasr, who frequently traveled to Lebanon to meet with Hezbollah commanders, according to these reports, also routinely traveled throughout Latin America. In 2008, Nasr spent two months in Venezuela, a country with close ties to Iran and a well-established Hezbollah presence.[89]

Moving Dirty Money

With so many successful fundraising schemes at the ready, Hezbollah needed effective means of moving the proceeds of its criminal enterprises to Lebanon. Often operatives would send money back with friends, relatives, or others from the Lebanese community who were traveling to Lebanon. Some were couriers by happenstance, pleased to help a friend transport money home, possibly not even aware the money was intended for Hezbollah. Others were knowing participants who willingly carried funds to Lebanon for Hezbollah, either out of ideological devotion or for a fee. But Hezbollah never put all its eggs in one basket, using *hawala* dealers (informal value transfer systems based on trust), money-service businesses such as Western Union, charities, and various old-fashioned smuggling techniques to move money to Lebanon. In some cases, the means Hezbollah operatives used to move their money effectively laundered the money as well.

While Mahmoud Kourani boasted that his friend employed at Beirut International Airport helped smuggle cash into the country, Hezbollah supporters in the United States had access to an airport employee much closer to home. From 1999—three years after immigrating to the United States from Lebanon—until his arrest in 2007, Riad Skaff worked as a ground services coordinator for Air France at Chicago's O'Hare International Airport. With an active airport security badge, Skaff had full access to all secure areas of an international terminal. For a fee, Skaff smuggled bulk cash packages onto airplanes, circumventing security inspections. At one point Skaff told an undercover agent posing as an individual seeking to smuggle $25,000 in cash to Lebanon, "I am in charge of the plane, everything. . . . It is dangerous, if they catch [me], they take me to jail." Skaff did smuggle the money onto an Air France flight to Paris, noting to the undercover agent that millions of dollars pass through Paris to Lebanon daily. Skaff later smuggled $100,000 and a cellular jammer on another Paris-bound flight for the undercover agent. A month later he smuggled a package containing four night-vision rifle scopes and two night-vision goggles onto a Paris-bound flight.[90]

In a government sentencing memorandum filed after Skaff pleaded guilty to all the charges against him, prosecutors put Skaff's illicit conduct in the context of Hezbollah support activity. Arguing that Skaff's conduct "in essence was that of a mercenary facilitating the smuggling of large amounts of cash and dangerous defense items for a fee," prosecutors noted he was fully aware the items were destined for Lebanon, "a war-torn country besieged by the militant organization, Hezbollah."[91] Prosecutors never accused Skaff of being a Hezbollah supporter, just a criminal happy to accommodate the needs of potential Hezbollah supporters for a fee.[92]

In 2007, proactive investigative techniques exposed another illicit money transfer system that could have benefited Hezbollah, this time in upstate New York. Looking over currency transaction reports (CTRs) filed by financial institutions for transactions of more than $10,000, members of the Intelligence Collection and Analysis team at the Buffalo Office of Immigration and Customs Enforcement (ICE) found approximately 324 reports, representing a total of more than $12 million in transfers over approximately two years, all tied to the Social Security number of one person: Saleh Mohamed Taher Saeed, a Yemeni American. During the same period another batch of CTRs totaling more than $2.5 million was associated with the Social Security number of Yehia Ali Ahmed Alomari, another Yemeni American. The ensuing investigation led to money laundering charges against

Saeed, Alomari, and another Yemeni living in the Rochester area, Mohamed al-Huraibi. The three ran a money laundering conspiracy that transferred abroad large sums of money that they knew were or believed to be the proceeds of criminal activity.[93]

Based on statements of support for Hezbollah by a couple of Saeed's associates, ICE agents inserted a Lebanon-born undercover agent into the investigation who posed as a Hezbollah member. Shortly thereafter, in May 2006, the undercover agent and the informant met with the suspects at Saeed's store, where they discussed Hezbollah and the situation in the Middle East. Three months later they all met again, this time in a hotel room that law enforcement officials wired for audio and video surveillance. The undercover agent and the informant handed over some $60,000 they wanted to send to Lebanon, money they stressed was intended to help their own families and assist Hezbollah's efforts to rebuild Lebanon. Three months later they provided another $30,000 to be transferred to Lebanon, emphasizing this time that the money was the product of Hezbollah scams selling stolen and counterfeit goods and prescription drugs. Three months later, in February 2007, they were even more specific about the nature of their activities, telling Alomari and al-Huraibi that the $20,000 they now wanted to send "would be utilized by Hezbollah in Lebanon to re-arm and purchase military goods."[94] Lawyers for the defendants ultimately maintained their clients believed the money they were illegally transferring was to help fellow Yemenis, not fund Hezbollah, but nonetheless the three men pleaded guilty to money laundering in August 2009.[95]

The crime, in the case of Talal Chahine, owner of the famous La Shish restaurant chain in metropolitan Detroit, was one of massive tax evasion, with some $20 million secreted to Lebanon over a five-year period. Millions more were laundered through Lebanon and sent back to the United States. Chahine fled the United States in September 2005 and remains a fugitive, but his wife pleaded guilty to her role in the scheme in December 2006.[96] Federal prosecutors indicated they suspect a Hezbollah connection, noting that Chahine and his wife were guests of honor at an August 2002 fundraising event in Lebanon at which Chahine and Sheikh Mohammad Fadlallah were the keynote speakers. FBI agents seized a letter from the Chahine home thanking him for sponsoring forty Lebanese orphans, which prosecutors alleged was a "euphemism used by Hezbollah to refer to the orphans of martyrs." Agents also seized photographs of Chahine and his family posing in and around a Hezbollah outpost in Lebanon. Chahine, the government explained, had "connections at the highest levels" of Hezbollah.[97] In 2006, Chahine denied all charges in an emailed statement from his company's public relations firm, conceding he contributed to Fadlallah's al-Mabarrat Charity Association but noting the charity openly ran a branch in the Detroit area.[98] Al-Mabarrat's Dearborn office was raided, but not ultimately shut down, by the FBI in July 2007.[99]

The June 3, 2010, arrest of Hor and Amera Akl—dual US-Lebanese citizens living in Ohio—reflected more explicit attempts to transfer funds to Hezbollah. During recorded meetings with an FBI informant, Amera stated that she "dreamed of dressing like Hezbollah, carrying a gun and dying as a martyr," while Hor was recorded boasting that Hezbollah stored "artillery, firearms, and rockets" in his family home in Lebanon. The couple revealed that they had previously delivered money to Hezbollah representatives in Lebanon by hiding cash in magazines and on their person. With the informant, they discussed ways of clandestinely taking money out of the United States, as well as the requirements for Western Union money transfers. The June 2010 arrest of the couple occurred after they were observed by authorities concealing $200,000 in a Chevy Trailblazer they planned to ship to Lebanon.[100] Court documents indicate the couple was planning to send somewhere between $500,000 and $1 million to Lebanon and to charge about a 30 percent commission fee for the service.[101] The two pleaded guilty to terrorism charges in May 2011.[102]

A year later, the FBI would foil another scheme, this time in Virginia, to send money to Hezbollah hidden in the tires of used cars to be shipped to Lebanon. In 2010, Mufid Kamal "Mark" Mrad told an FBI source he had previously sent money and other contraband to Lebanon through a contact at the Lebanese embassy who gave him access to a diplomatic pouch and would return hashish from Lebanon through the same diplomatic pouch. As for sending money to Hezbollah? "What's a hundred thousand [dollars]? It's nothing." Sending money in cars was nothing new, but the higher ups had to be paid their cut, Mrad explained. The "Shiites are all sending [money] the same way. . . . How do you think the money from Africa is getting to Beirut?"[103]

Still more imaginative methods of transferring criminally obtained money have been uncovered by US investigators, such as the case of Ayman Joumma and the Lebanese Canadian Bank (LCB; see chapter 9). Authorities charged that as part of a money laundering scheme, funds were sent from Lebanon to the United States to purchase used cars. Subsequently, the used cars were shipped to and sold in West Africa, where the proceeds were mixed with proceeds from narcotics trafficking and transferred back to Lebanon.[104]

From 2008 to 2010, the Cybamar Swiss Family of Companies—a Michigan-based firm with several offices worldwide—reportedly shipped used cars worth more than $1 billion along with "hundreds of millions' worth of used cars purchased with funds from the Lebanese Banks" from the United States to the tiny West African nation of Benin.[105] In 2011, two Dallas-area car dealers were charged in a similar scheme to launder drug money through the purchase of used cars in the United States.[106] The cases were not entirely shocking: An earlier Hezbollah case on the East Coast involved shipping stolen cars from the United States to Benin and, in a few cases, receiving payment for other stolen property by wire transfer from Africa.[107] What did surprise was the explosive growth of the illicit used-car industry, with Google Earth images showing a tremendous increase in the size of car parks in Benin from 2003 to 2011.[108]

Based on information from law enforcement and other sources, the US Treasury Department reported that the LCB was complicit in international drug trafficking and money laundering activities. In one of the cases cited by the Treasury Department, an individual who used the LCB to exchange laundered funds was a Latin

America–based member of a Lebanese drug trafficking organization involved in moving large quantities of drugs from Latin America to destinations throughout Africa, Europe, and the Middle East. For more than a decade, according to information released by the Treasury Department, this individual and members of his family, all Hezbollah supporters, engaged in a variety of trade-based money laundering schemes involving American drug traffickers and Lebanese money launderers.[109]

Nine months after his designation as a narco-trafficker in February 2011, Ayman Joumma was indicted on charges of conspiracy to distribute narcotics and money laundering, including coordinating cocaine shipments for sale in the United States.[110] Joumma first emerged on DEA agents' radar when he placed a call to a phone tied to Chekry Harb, the Hezbollah-affiliated drug trafficker in Colombia (discussed in chapter 4). Joumma had arranged for the proceeds of cocaine sales to be picked up at a Paris hotel and then laundered back to Colombia, but the pickup turned out to be a sting operation. Listening in on the line, agents heard Joumma nonchalantly muse, "I just lost a million euros in France." Cell phones seized at the Paris hotel tied Joumma, himself a Lebanese Sunni Muslim, to Hezbollah. Meanwhile, Israeli intercepts documented Joumma's contact with a member of Hezbollah's Unit 1800. This contact worked for a senior Hezbollah operative named Abu Abdullah, who, Israeli officials believe, dealt with Hezbollah's drug operations. Abu Abdullah's name arose in the DEA intercepts too. In one conversation Chekry Harb complained about "the sons of whores I owe money to." In response, a relative from his hometown in Lebanon cautioned that the "people of Abu Abdullah, the people we do not dare have problems or fight with," were looking for him, and their money.[111]

A Beacon of Hatred in New York

Al-Manar (the Beacon), Hezbollah's satellite television station, aired its first broadcast on June 3, 1991.[112] Almost two decades later, two New York–based individuals would be sentenced for providing support to the station in exchange for thousands of dollars. As Hezbollah's primary mouthpiece and propaganda tool, al-Manar specializes in programming glorifying terrorism and inciting violence, racial hatred, and anti-Semitism. The self-declared "station of resistance," al-Manar promises to wage "psychological warfare against the Zionist enemy" and has called for violence against Americans in the Middle East.[113] Moreover, it has made the United States a key target of its programming and portrayed it as a global oppressor. In a September 2002 speech broadcast on al-Manar, Hezbollah secretary-general Hassan Nasrallah declared, "Our hostility to the Great Satan is absolute. . . . Death to America will remain our reverberating and powerful slogan: Death to America!"[114]

At the time of al-Manar's founding, the station reportedly received seed money from Iran and had a running budget of $1 million.[115] By 2002, its annual budget had grown to approximately $15 million.[116] Middle East analysts and journalists maintain that most of this funding comes from Iran. An assessment by former al-Manar program director Sheikh Nasir al-Akhdar, however, asserted that al-Manar receives a large portion of its budget through subsidies offered by Hezbollah and contributions from supportive individuals and institutions.[117]

Al-Manar is operated by Hezbollah members, reports directly to Hezbollah officials, and follows Hassan Nasrallah's orders.[118] As of 2000, most of the station's forty journalists were former guerrilla fighters.[119] Recall Mohammad Dbouk (see chapter 6), who used his al-Manar credentials to perform preoperational surveillance to plan Hezbollah attacks on Israeli soldiers. Dbouk accompanied Hezbollah units on their missions, filmed their live attacks, and used the resulting footage to produce propaganda videos. Some of these videos were later found in Hezbollah members' homes in Charlotte, North Carolina, where they were used to solicit funds at local gatherings.[120] In 2009, Arab media widely reported the discovery of an Egypt-based Hezbollah cell in late 2008 that contained at least one al-Manar employee who used his al-Manar credentials as a cover for collecting intelligence information for potential attacks.[121]

Prominent Hezbollah members have been major shareholders in al-Manar's parent company, the Lebanese Media Group, according to the US Treasury Department and corroborated by Nayef Krayem, al-Manar's third general manager and chairman of the board. Al-Manar, Krayem noted, "gets money from the shareholders [who] are leaders in Hezbollah. . . . [Al-Manar and Hezbollah] breathe life into one another."[122]

Hassan Fadlallah, the station's public relations director, once declared: "Neutrality like that of Al Jazeera is out of the question for us. We cover only the victim, not the aggressor. CNN is the Zionist news network, Al Jazeera is neutral, and Al Manar takes the side of the Palestinians. We're not looking to interview [former Israeli prime minister Ariel] Sharon. We want to get close to him in order to kill him."[123]

In response to al-Manar's incitement of racial hatred, many countries have banned the station from broadcasting, including France, Spain, the Netherlands, Germany, and Australia.[124] At a meeting of European Union member states in March 2005, media regulators agreed European satellites would no longer be allowed to carry the channel. In essence, this action banned al-Manar from broadcasting throughout the European Union.[125] The move was supported by the Palestinian Authority, which was frustrated with al-Manar's recruitment of suicide bombers out to sabotage the Palestinian Authority's fragile truce with Israel.[126]

While European countries banned Hezbollah's al-Manar because it incited hatred, the US ban focused on the channel's affiliation with Hezbollah. In December 2004, the US State Department added al-Manar to the Terrorism Exclusion List, effectively preventing the immigration and accelerating the deportation of non–US citizens associated with the station, as well as the removal of al-Manar from US television providers.[127] Two years later, the Department of the Treasury named al-Manar a Specially Designated Global Terrorist entity, noting that al-Manar supported fundraising and recruitment efforts by Hezbollah through advertisements and requesting donations on air. According to the Treasury Department, al-Manar broadcast an invitation from Hezbollah secretary-general Nasrallah for all Lebanese citizens to volunteer for Hezbollah military training. The station also provided support to Palestinian terrorist groups. In one example cited by the US

Treasury, al-Manar transferred tens of thousands of dollars to a charity controlled by Palestinian Islamic Jihad.[128]

Al-Manar's list of offenses included transferring funds to supporters in the United States. In 2006, two New Yorkers were arrested for supporting Hezbollah by conspiring to broadcast al-Manar programming to US customers. In exchange for thousands of dollars from al-Manar, Javed Iqbal and Saleh Elahwal allegedly provided satellite transmission services to al-Manar through the then–New York-based satellite transmission company HDTV Ltd.[129] In late 2005, Elahwal emailed a representative of al-Manar offering HDTV's services to broadcast the station in North and South America; within a month he would travel to Beirut to sign a contract with Hezbollah. Throughout 2005 and 2006, al-Manar wired funds to HDTV's bank account through a Manhattan bank. Subsequently, Iqbal and Elahwal shipped satellite receivers to al-Manar TV in Beirut and confirmed, in emails to al-Manar representatives, that HDTV would begin broadcasting al-Manar.[130] Ultimately, Iqbal and Elahwal were sentenced to sixty-nine and seventeen months, respectively, for providing material support to Hezbollah.[131]

Operation Bell Bottoms

Across the county, investigations into petty criminal activities, including food stamp fraud, misuse of grocery coupons, and sale of unlicensed T-shirts, have led to criminal fundraising plots tied to Hezbollah. As of 2002, US officials believed "a substantial portion" of the estimated hundreds of millions of dollars raised by Hezbollah and other Middle Eastern terrorist groups comes from the $20 to $30 million annually brought in by the illicit scam industry in America.[132]

In November 2007, after a two-year investigation centered on the Los Angeles garment district, a multiagency task force arrested a dozen suspects on narcotics trafficking, sale of counterfeit goods, and money laundering. The investigation, dubbed Operation Bell Bottoms, culminated in arrests of Ali Khalil Elreda and his associates. Elreda was detained at the Los Angeles International Airport attempting to smuggle $123,000 in money orders and cashier's checks to Lebanon stuffed in a child's toy.[133]

While public announcements about the November arrests made no mention of a terrorism connection, several sources close to the Elreda investigation claimed the ring smuggled criminal proceeds to Hezbollah. According to a Department of Justice press release, officers seized thirty kilograms of cocaine and hundreds of thousands of dollars' worth of counterfeit clothing during the investigation.[134] As a source told the press, "this was a classic case of terrorism financing, and it was pretty sophisticated how they did it."[135] In fact, while the case originated with the Los Angeles Sheriff's Department (LASD), it was turned over to the FBI when the terrorism angle became clear.[136] Focusing on a group of Lebanese immigrants living in the Los Angeles suburb of Bell, investigators noted certain local families had relatives who had fought (and died) with Hezbollah in the July 2006 war.[137]

In October 2006, a private trademark investigator contacted the LASD about an ongoing investigation of Hip Hop Connections, a retail store in Los Angeles County.

In coordination with the LASD, the investigator arranged to purchase a large number of Nike shoes from Mohammad Khalil Elreda, whose brother Ali owned the
store. The shoes were sent to Nike for a detailed examination and determined to be
counterfeit. Los Angeles law enforcement soon discovered that Ali Elreda was on
felony probation for dealing counterfeit goods.[138]

Two years earlier, another private investigator identified several counterfeit jerseys, T-shirts, and pairs of sweatpants at Hip Hop Connections over several visits.
When investigators returned to the store to serve Ali Elreda a cease-and-desist
notice in April 2004, he agreed to turn over the counterfeit items. According to
investigative reports, however, Ali's sister arrived as investigators inventoried the
counterfeit goods and belligerently insisted they were genuine. A few months after
this incident, the LASD arrested Ali Elreda for selling counterfeit goods and
seized $16,060 worth of retail items. A weapons charge was added when police
found a handgun in a front-counter cabinet and a semiautomatic rifle in a
storeroom.[139]

Counterfeiting crimes by Hezbollah supporters predate the Elreda group's arrest,
as affirmed in a 2005 congressional hearing by John Stedman of the LASD, who
recounted two notable instances in particular. In one instance, during a search of a
suspect's home in which thousands of dollars in counterfeit clothing were seized,
Stedman saw small Hezbollah flags displayed next to a photograph of Nasrallah.
When Stedman identified Nasrallah in the photo, the suspect's wife said, "We love
him because he protects us from the Jews." Also in the home were dozens of audio-
tapes of Nasrallah's speeches and a locket containing Nasrallah's picture. In 2004,
while serving a search warrant at a Los Angeles County clothing store, detectives
recovered thousands of dollars in counterfeit clothing and two unregistered firearms. The suspect was found to have a tattoo of the Hezbollah flag when he was
booked into custody.[140]

The financial rewards from petty crime like counterfeiting can be immense, but
the practice makes it difficult for a criminal network to use traditional banking prac-
tices. In a Los Angeles case, investigators discovered more than $800,000 in cash
throughout the suspect's home, hidden under the bed in trash bags and stashed in
trash cans and the attic, with over $10,000 in a child's piggy bank. In another case US
Customs officers at Los Angeles International Airport stopped a Lebanon-bound
woman with $230,000 in cash strapped to her body. The woman told the customs of-
ficers that she was heading to Lebanon for vacation. According to Stedman, authorities learned that the woman owned a chain of cigarette shops and seized more than a
thousand cartons of counterfeit cigarettes and an additional $70,000 in cash, along
with funds from wire transfers to banks throughout the world.[141]

"Take Down an F-16"

Bragging to a government informant about his ties to Hezbollah, Mahmoud
Kourani once let it slip that a few years before he had entered the country, another
Hezbollah supporter named Mohammed Krayem had sent money to his brother,

the Hezbollah military commander, to fund the purchase of military equipment from members of the United Nations Protection Forces in Lebanon.[142] In other cases, however, Hezbollah procurement agents sought to purchase weapons and military equipment in North America. Mohammad Dbouk and his associates in Canada focused on dual-use items (discussed in chapter 6), but others sought far more lethal equipment.

A case in April 2006 showed how sometimes the best leads come from the most unlikely places. In that affair a tipster reported to the Philadelphia police that at odd hours, suspicious-looking Middle Eastern men were loading carpet into white work vans with Michigan plates.[143] This particular tip was not given high priority, but when a state police detective assigned to the FBI's JTTF looked into the matter, a link to Hezbollah suspects involved in stolen property transactions piqued his interest. The investigation quickly led from a Hezbollah criminal enterprise in suburban Philadelphia to Dani Tarraf, a German-Lebanese procurement agent for Hezbollah with homes in Lebanon and Slovakia and significant business interests in China and Lebanon.[144]

Members of the Philadelphia JTTF introduced Sadek Koumaiha, one of the suspected Lebanese crooks, to an undercover officer posing as someone who could fence stolen goods, but Koumaiha and his crew never took to him. After a period of time the JTTF switched him out and inserted a new undercover officer with whom Koumaiha started doing business. Soon Sadek's cousin from Detroit, Hassan Koumaiha, called the undercover officer asking to be cut in on his cousin's deal but without his cousin's knowledge. With that, a massive Hezbollah criminal fundraising and weapons procurement case was all but delivered to investigators on a silver platter.[145]

Throughout the investigation Sadek Koumaiha and his co-conspirators engaged in a proactive fencing scheme buying and selling stolen and counterfeit property, laundering money, and more. But Sadek was more of a small-time crook than a terrorist financier, which explains why he and his network were indicted separately, not on terrorism charges. And yet hundreds of thousands of dollars were at stake in his schemes, involving, among other products, thousands of stolen cellular phones, hundreds of stolen Sony PlayStation 2 systems and laptops, and thousands of pairs of counterfeit Nike sneakers. Sadek also laundered funds presented as proceeds of criminal activity. The undercover agent gave him a McDonald's paper bag stuffed with more than $50,000, which Sadek was to launder for a fee of a few thousand dollars.[146]

Meanwhile, Sadek's cousin Hassan and others bought what they believed to be stolen property from the undercover agent and sent the merchandise to destinations as diverse as Michigan, California, Paraguay, Brazil, Slovakia, Belgium, Bahrain, Lebanon, Syria, and Iran. The money for these purchases came from Dani Tarraf, with whom the undercover agent met in Slovakia twice, in May and September 2008, and who wasted little time before asking whether the agent could supply guided missiles and 10,000 commando machine guns from the United States.[147]

In his meeting with the undercover agent, Tarraf expressed interest in a wide array of weapons needed, he explained, for urban fighting. Tarraf's wish list was long but focused, including M4 rifles and parts like specialized ninety-round magazines, Glock pistols, and antiaircraft and antitank missiles. Tarraf sought to impress the undercover agent, showing him around his Slovakian storage and shipping network and introducing him to his shipper, who would mislabel the weapons as "spare parts" before sending them on to Hezbollah. When Tarraf visited the United States in March 2009, the JTTF and its member agencies put on a similar show, giving him a tour of a fake criminal network capable of procuring many of the weapons Tarraf sought for Hezbollah through his company, Power Express. Law enforcement officers concluded that Power Express essentially "operated as a subsidiary of Hezbollah's technical procurement wing."[148]

Meeting in Philadelphia in June 2009, Tarraf was very clear about why he wanted these guided and shoulder-fired missiles: they had to be able to target helicopters and "take down an F-16." Tarraf showed the undercover agent exact weapons specifications on the internet as the FBI taped the conversations and captured the computer search records. Within weeks, Tarraf and the undercover agent met in Philadelphia again, where Tarraf paid the agent a $20,000 deposit toward the purchase of Stinger missiles and 10,000 Colt M4 machine guns. Tarraf noted that the weapons should be exported to Latakia, Syria, where Hezbollah controlled the entire port. Secrecy would be guaranteed there, because Hezbollah could shut down all the cameras when the shipment arrived. No shipping paperwork would be required once the items arrived in Syria, he promised.[149]

In November 2009, Tarraf visited the United States one last time to inspect the missiles and machine guns the undercover agent had procured for him. The FBI photographed Tarraf posing with a machine gun, looking down its sight as if he were about to shoot, and then again a few minutes later holding a shoulder-fired missile launcher. Sunglasses perched atop his shaved head, Tarraf looked like a man who had held weapons before.[150] On November 21, 2009, Tarraf was arrested on terrorism and other charges and quickly confessed in full, admitting to being a Hezbollah member, receiving military training from the group, and "working with others to acquire massive quantities of weapons for the benefit of Hezbollah."[151]

Major Case 251: Penetrating Hezbollah's Inner Core

Dani Tarraf and his co-conspirators were investigated as part of the interconnected Major Case 251. The four-year investigation led to the indictment of twenty-six individuals, including Tarraf and a slew of senior Hezbollah officials and operatives from locales ranging from Philadelphia and New York to Venezuela's Margarita Island to deep into the Dahiya, Hezbollah's stronghold in Beirut. Juggling these cases—running multiple human sources and undercover officers at once—challenged the interagency team and caused tension between field agents and headquarters supervisors struggling to keep up with the paperwork. Often, the paperwork and approval processes lagged far behind the natural flow of the operation, which slowed matters to a pencil-pusher tempo.[152]

Given Tarraf's global contacts, investigators saw him as the most valuable target of their operation. But their next priority was Dib Harb, the son-in-law of senior Hezbollah official Hassan Hodroj and a close associate of Hezbollah militant Hasan Karaki. While an undercover agent worked to build Tarraf's trust, an FBI source worked another angle of the case, building rapport with a naturalized US citizen from Lebanon who was knee deep in petty crime but also well connected to senior Hezbollah officials. Moussa Ali Hamdan was among the men moving carpets that night in April 2006, which is a little ironic given that he would later advise members of his criminal conspiracy to load their vans quickly to avoid being "exposed" to law enforcement. But Hamdan was likely already on investigators' radar; he had become a US citizen around 2005 by marrying an American woman who was arrested as part of the investigation into the Charlotte Hezbollah cell. Before moving to New Jersey, Hamdan lived in Dearborn, Michigan.[153]

On a cold winter day in late 2007, Moussa Hamdan pulled his high-end SUV into the parking lot of the Deptford Mall, the largest shopping mall in southern New Jersey, located just about twelve miles across the Delaware River from Philadelphia. The lunchtime meeting he would attend was his first with a fellow criminal who promised to deliver a reliable flow of bulk stolen goods—cell phones, laptops, game consoles, and automobiles—that Hamdan could resell for a nice personal profit. According to investigators, Hamdan smuggled some of the contraband into "a worldwide Hezbollah black market." Afraid of reselling stolen electronic goods in the United States due to tracking numbers stamped on the items, Hamdan and his co-defendants exported them to colleagues in Lebanon and a partner in Venezuela. The profit margins were such that they made about $12,000 moving 300 Sony PlayStations.[154]

But Hamdan's new supplier was actually an FBI source, who helped authorities unwind an extensive international Hezbollah network. Within weeks of their meeting, Hamdan started buying what he believed to be stolen property from the source. From January 2008 through May 2009, Hamdan and his associates purchased and transported 400 PlayStation 2 game systems, 1,781 cell phones, 3 cars, and 142 laptop computers. At the same time, they trafficked in counterfeit goods, moving 5,212 pairs of fake Nike sneakers and 334 knockoff sports jerseys.[155]

As the illicit business relationship between the two men grew, Moussa Hamdan introduced the FBI source to the Beirut-based Hezbollah official Dib Hani Harb. Hamdan had to get approval from his brother, a more senior operative, for the source to meet Harb, but once approved Hamdan vouched for the source as someone who could help Hezbollah sell counterfeit currency. In a conversation with the source, Harb explained that Iran produces high-quality counterfeit US and other currencies in facilities staffed by people working eighteen hours a day to crank out the fake bills for Hezbollah's use. The program is run by Iranian officials, Harb added, so Hezbollah officials would need approval to sell the source this particular type of high-quality counterfeit currency. At another point Harb clarified that the currency printer was located not in Iran but in Hezbollah's stronghold in Baalbek, Lebanon. The necessary approvals apparently came through, because two months later Hamdan and the source were hashing out the details of a deal for $1 million in counterfeit

US currency to be sold at around forty cents to the dollar. But when Hezbollah officials in Lebanon sent sample counterfeit notes to the source for inspection, something strange happened.[156]

Secreted in the inside cover of a photo album the source received in the mail in October 2008 were two $100 bills. The source provided the bills to his JTTF handlers, who passed them on to the US Secret Service, which unexpectedly found the bills to be genuine US currency. Law enforcement officers thought Hezbollah was trying to scam the source by passing off genuine bills as extremely high-end forgeries and then providing low-end forgeries when the deal actually came through. In fact, Hezbollah suddenly had an acute interest in dumping a stockpile of genuine currency stolen by Hezbollah supporters around the world. In support of its international terrorist activities, Hezbollah had a program in place through which Hezbollah supporters sent stolen currency to Iran for later use by Imad Mughniyeh and members of Hezbollah's IJO. The use of genuine, albeit stolen, currency instead of even high-end counterfeit bills was implemented to ensure operational security for Hezbollah's most sensitive activities. But in the wake of Mughniyeh's assassination in Damascus in February 2008, Hezbollah feared these bills might be traceable after all. Perhaps they were even part of the intelligence failure that led Hezbollah's enemies to Mughniyeh. As part of the damage assessment and counterintelligence investigation that followed Mughniyeh's death, a decision was made to sell the stockpile of stolen money.[157]

So it was in early December 2008, just about a week after Moussa Hamdan and the source met outside Philadelphia to discuss plans for the sale of counterfeit bills, that the source found himself on the phone with Dib Harb in Beirut discussing plans to buy stolen currency at a rate of about sixty-five cents to the dollar. The scene was now set for a meeting in person to firm up the relationships underpinning the source's illicit dealings with Hezbollah. After receiving another photo album containing a new batch of stolen currency, the source traveled to Beirut in mid-February to meet Harb's boss, Hasan Antar Karaki, who seemed at ease, unguardedly discussing Hezbollah and his own ties to the group. Hezbollah has access to data from an Iranian satellite, Karaki casually explained, which is capable of providing Hezbollah pictures of any place in Israel. Iran provides specialized military training for Hezbollah protection details, he continued, boasting that one of his brothers was responsible for all security in the Hezbollah-dominated Dahiya neighborhood in Beirut.[158]

The Karakis, according to US officials, are a family renowned for being "excellent fighters, crooks, and document forgers." The fighting component is emphasized by several Karaki brothers' adoption of the middle name Antar, a reference to an Arabian warrior-poet. Although known more as a crime family than a backer of any particular group, several Karakis have put their skills to use on behalf of Hezbollah. Aside from Hasan and his brother, the Dahiya security chief, there is Ali Mohammad Karaki, who—right around the time Hasan Karaki was scheming to sell counterfeit and stolen currencies in the United States—was arrested in Azerbaijan, where he was planning a Hezbollah attack in revenge for the assassination of Imad

Mughniyeh. A physically imposing man, Hasan Karaki is reportedly just as big of a braggart. According to law enforcement officials, he reportedly claimed that the FBI, Interpol, and even Lebanese law enforcement are all "after him." Lebanese undercover police once came to his house to arrest him, he claimed further, but he fought them off. Several reportedly left on stretchers.[159]

Hasan Karaki reiterated to the source that the stolen currency could not be spent in Lebanon because it was "blood money" Hezbollah stole abroad and then smuggled from Iran through Turkey and Syria into Lebanon. Some of the money—just under $10,000—was money stolen from Iraq, the source was told, explaining why Hezbollah was sensitive that the funds be spent in small amounts only, and not in Lebanon. In fact, US officials, using the serial numbers, traced the bills' movement through Germany to coalition forces in Iraq but never could determine if the bills were stolen, were paid out to insurgents tied to Iran as ransom, or made their way to Iran and Hezbollah through normal business transactions in Iraq. In any event, Karaki's assistant followed up on the meeting, sending the source samples of counterfeit American $100 bills and European €200 notes.[160]

A careful operative, Hasan Antar Karaki surprised nobody when he sent Dib Harb to an April 2009 meeting with the source and the source's purported Philadelphia crime boss in southern Florida. In fact, though investigators tried to lure Karaki to the United States, they learned that he was known in some circles as "the Lebanese Flag" for his refusal to leave Hezbollah's stronghold in Beirut's Dahiya neighborhood, let alone Lebanon. Despite his reputation for operational security, however, Israeli intelligence may have penetrated his inner circle: The source would later learn that the brother of Karaki's deputy, who also worked for Karaki, was arrested for reportedly spying on Hezbollah for Israel.[161]

At the April 2009 meeting in southern Florida, the part of the source's boss was played by an undercover FBI agent. The three men dined at fancy restaurants and negotiated terms for the sale of stolen US currency and multiple counterfeit currencies. According to Harb, the eighteen- to twenty-hour days worked by Hezbollah's representatives to counterfeit US dollars also included currency from "Kuwait, Saudi Arabia, and the European Union." All told, the Hezbollah officials provided the source a little less than $10,000 in counterfeit US currency.[162]

At one point Harb showed the undercover agent a Swedish krona bill with stains from a dye-pack security system used by banks to mark stolen funds. According to Harb, the bill was part of a $2 million bank heist Hezbollah supporters pulled off in Sweden. He explained that Hezbollah cells conduct robberies all over the world and send the money to Iran, where it is held before ultimately being distributed to Hezbollah in Lebanon.[163]

Keen to impress his hosts, Harb "threw the name Hezbollah all over the place." He himself was involved in the part of the group he described as "terrorism Hezbollah," which he said was active "all over the world." The medical clinic he ran in Dahiya was simply a cover for his Hezbollah activities, he noted, adding that the Dahiya is "all Hezbollah, terrorism Hezbollah." His own father-in-law, Hassan Hodroj, was involved with the smuggling of weapons, Harb boasted.[164]

When they got down to business, Harb explained that Karaki is a major figure in Hezbollah's forgery operations, a role that would also allow for the production of forged passports and visa stamps if desired. A couple of weeks after the meetings in Florida, Karaki and the source spoke by phone and Karaki instructed the source to send photographs for use in fraudulent passports to Karaki's home address and to fax the corresponding biographical information for each passport to Dib Harb. Less than two months later, Harb and Karaki delivered fraudulent British and Canadian passports to the source using the pictures and biographical information he had provided.[165]

The meetings in southern Florida went so smoothly that the source was invited back to Beirut to meet senior Hezbollah officials, including Karaki and Harb's father-in-law Hassan Hodroj. Even before the source traveled to Beirut, however, the conspiracy suddenly branched out to include weapons procurement. In mid-May 2009, Moussa Hamdan asked the source to provide pistols, to be concealed in stolen vehicles that would be shipped to Lebanon. There was good money to be made, Hamdan stressed, adding that he knew someone in Beirut who could move weapons through Beirut ports without being checked. He bragged that he could introduce the source to a buyer interested in bulk quantities of pistols and rifles.[166]

"We weren't ready for this," conceded one US official, speaking of the sudden request for weapons. On his arrival in Beirut in mid-June, Harb escorted the source to a meeting with an unnamed Hezbollah official, where they discussed firearms Hezbollah wanted to buy. When the source insisted on being assured by high-level Hezbollah officials that the weapons were bound for Hezbollah and would not be intercepted, Harb immediately phoned a senior Hezbollah official, who gave the necessary assurances. "The source expressed amazement that Harb could so easily contact a high-level Hezbollah figure," according to an FBI affidavit, prompting Harb to display an entry in his phone for a named "high-level Hezbollah official."[167]

Three days later, Harb and the source met in Beirut with Harb's father-in-law Hassan Hodroj, who served on Hezbollah's political council. In a sign of Hodroj's place in the Hezbollah hierarchy, Hezbollah leader Hassan Nasrallah had attended Dib Harb's wedding. Publicly described as a Hezbollah spokesman and the head of its Palestinian issues portfolio, Hodroj was also involved in Hezbollah's procurement arm.[168]

Hodroj knew what he wanted: 1,200 Colt M4 assault rifles, which the source said he could procure for $1,800 apiece. Hodroj added that payment would be made in cash to make it harder for authorities to track the payments back to Hezbollah. Hodroj told the source that Hezbollah had no need for the Glock pistols the source had told Harb he could also procure, explaining that Hezbollah needed only "heavy machinery" for the "fight against the Jews and to protect Lebanon." Like Dani Tarraf, Hodroj wanted the weapons shipped to the port of Latakia, Syria, which he described as "ours." But the source should move forward with caution, Hodroj counseled, because if caught dealing with Hezbollah, someone in America could "go to jail for 100 years."[169]

Before the meeting ended, Hodroj broached one more subject: Hezbollah's desire to procure still more sensitive items from the United States, specifically, communication and "spy" systems. Hodroj confided that he was involved in not only weapons but also technology procurement for Hezbollah and asked the source to keep his eyes open for technologies that could help Hezbollah secure its own and spy on its adversaries' communications. In the meantime, Hodroj directed the source to work through Dib Harb to complete the deal for the M4 machine guns.[170]

Within three days of his meeting with Hodroj, the source heard through Dib Harb that Hodroj had been impressed with the source. But the M4 deal was serious business, Harb warned, and the source must now deliver the promised weapons. The source swore to quickly get approval for the deal from his boss, the "Philadelphia crime boss," who would in turn run the deal by his own boss to guarantee the deal went smoothly.[171]

Over the following months, Harb, Hodroj, and the source spoke several times making arrangements for the M4 deal. The order was a Hezbollah priority, as became clear when the source returned to the United States. Only a few weeks passed before Harb sent the source a text message saying that the senior Hezbollah official he had met with in Beirut, the paymaster for the M4 deal, had called from Iran, where he was making headway—presumably on securing Iranian payment for the weapons—and was pushing for quick delivery of the machine guns, which he referred to in code as tires. "I just received a call from Iran from [the senior Hezbollah official] regarding the tires," Harb texted. "He is asking me where they are and telling me that we should not delay." A month later, Harb texted the source again stating that the M4 deal had been reviewed by "our group," adding, "They are very happy."[172]

While investigators in Major Case 251 succeeded in luring Dani Tarraf back to the United States, bureaucratic infighting undermined their effort to do the same for Dib Harb.[173] The case came to a head in November 2009, when authorities rolled out three sets of indictments and exposed a Hezbollah politician's role in global arms deals and criminal enterprises. But the multiyear investigation, which was significant enough to warrant two briefings to the president, was not quite done. Moussa Hamdan had moved out of New Jersey and settled in Brooklyn, but he fled the country to evade arrest. Had he stayed in Lebanon with Harb, Hodroj, and several of the other indicted fugitives, he likely would still be free today. Instead, he turned up in South America's tri-border area. At the FBI's request, Interpol issued an international arrest warrant for Hamdan. When someone applied for a Paraguayan national identity card on his behalf, officials were alerted to the outstanding warrant for Hamdan's arrest and picked him up in Ciudad del Este, Paraguay. Hamdan was extradited to the United States and officially charged in early 2011 with providing material support to Hezbollah.[174]

South of the Border: Venezuela

Moussa Ali Hamdan's partner in his criminal conspiracy was Latif Kamel Hazime, a resident of Venezuela's Margarita Island who, like Hamdan, once lived in Dearborn, Michigan. Hazime received stolen electronics for resale beyond the reach of

US regulators who might track the serial numbers stamped on them. Hamdan's contacts in Venezuela also gave him access to counterfeit networks there, leading Hamdan and his Venezuelan contacts to produce a fraudulent passport for an FBI source.[175]

A Hezbollah support network has long existed in Venezuela. According to a July 2003 report by Mark Steinitz, then–director of the terrorism analysis office in the State Department's Bureau of Intelligence and Research, "by the mid-1990s, Hezbollah had cells in Venezuela. Attention has focused on the group's presence among Lebanese Shia in the 12,000-strong Arab community on Margarita Island."[176] A free trade zone off the coast of Venezuela, Margarita Island is believed to be a location of choice for drug traffickers and Hezbollah and other Islamist extremists.[177] Several members of the Charlotte Hezbollah cell, including Mohammad Hammoud, entered the United States through Venezuela (see chapter 6).[178]

Officials remain concerned about the potential use of Venezuela as a stepping-stone from the Middle East into the Western Hemisphere. US officials say that Venezuelan officials have issued thousands of fake *cedulas* (the equivalent of Social Security cards) to individuals from Middle Eastern nations who do not qualify for them. In obtaining a *cedula*, an immigrant can then obtain a Venezuelan passport and subsequently an American visa.[179] Even if immigrants to Venezuela cannot find an official to bribe, they still have a good chance of gaining entry into the United States because Venezuelan passports can be forged with "child-like ease."[180]

In 2003, a study in *U.S. News & World Report* found that "thousands of Venezuelan identity documents are being distributed to foreigners from Middle Eastern nations, including Syria, Pakistan, Egypt, and Lebanon," and in 2006, the State Department divulged to Congress that border officials were seeing an increased number of third-country aliens carrying false Venezuelan documents.[181] "The systems and processes for issuing" Venezuelan passports and ID cards "are corrupted on various levels," according to State Department's Frank Urbancic. In early 2011, Tarek el-Aissami, the Venezuelan minister of interior and justice and a prominent figure in Hugo Chavez's government, was accused by the media of abusing his position by issuing passports to members of Hamas and Hezbollah.[182] Allegations also exist that el-Aissami, who was born in Lebanon to parents of Syrian descent, oversees the recruitment of young Venezuelan Arabs to train in Hezbollah camps in southern Lebanon.[183]

With regard to Venezuela, lax security and tolerance of Hezbollah raise security concerns well beyond North America. In February 2003, British authorities detained Mohammed Alan, a passenger arriving at London's Gatwick Airport from Caracas on a Venezuelan passport who had a grenade in his luggage. Venezuelan police subsequently told reporters that Alan's identity may be false and that members of his supposed family may be tied to a Hezbollah money laundering operation run out of Margarita Island.[184]

More recently, in June 2008, the US Department of the Treasury designated two Hezbollah operatives in Venezuela. One, Ghazi Nasr al-Din, was a Venezuelan diplomat who had been posted to the Venezuelan embassies in both Damascus and Beirut. According to the Department of the Treasury, Nasr al-Din "is a Venezuela-based Hezbollah supporter who has utilized his position as a Venezuelan diplomat and the president of a Caracas-based Shia Islamic Center to provide financial support to Hezbollah." Information available to the US government demonstrated that Nasr al-Din "counseled Hezbollah donors on fundraising efforts and has provided donors with specific information on bank accounts where the donors' deposits would go directly to Hezbollah." Undercutting the notion that distinct wings exist within Hezbollah, he also met with senior Hezbollah officials in Lebanon "to discuss operational issues" and "arranged the travel of Hezbollah members to attend a training course in Iran." Fawzi Kanan, the second Venezuelan individual targeted by the Treasury Department, is described as "a Venezuela-based Hezbollah supporter and a significant provider of financial support to Hezbollah [who also] facilitated travel for Hezbollah members." Kanan trained in Iran and met with "senior Hezbollah officials in Lebanon to discuss operational issues, including possible kidnappings and terrorist attacks."[185]

One example of the increasingly close Iran-Venezuela relationship is Iran Air flight 744, which travels from Caracas to Tehran with stops in Beirut and Damascus and is referred to by some investigators as "Aeroterror."[186] Most seats on this flight are reportedly not open to the public. "If you tried to book yourself a seat on this flight and it doesn't matter whether it's a week before, a month before, six months before—you'll never find a place to sit there," said former Israeli Shin Bet agent Offer Baruch. This is because the flight is reported to be reserved for Iranian agents, including Hezbollah, the IRGC, and other intelligence personnel. What concerns US intelligence officials most, though, is that when the plane lands in Caracas, its passengers do not go through Venezuelan customs or immigration, preventing any knowledge of who enters the country and what they bring with them.[187]

The southern border to the US homeland has been acknowledged as a weak point for decades. The threat that it poses gained unprecedented headlines following Iran's plot to assassinate Adel al-Jubeir, the Saudi ambassador to the United States in Washington, D.C. Manssor Arbabsiar, a dual US-Iranian citizen, allegedly told his cousin, a Qods Force official, that he did business on both sides of the US-Mexico border and knew a number of drug traffickers who could be of help. Once back in the United States, Arbabsiar contacted someone whom he called the Mexican, a figure whom he hired to kill the ambassador, who was in fact a DEA confidential informant.[188]

Although the plot to assassinate al-Jubeir was foiled, the incident was a wake-up call for the United States in two respects. First, it indicated that Iran is no longer hesitant to cross the proverbial redline and carry out operations on US soil. Second, Iran's attempt to recruit a Mexican hit man to assassinate the Saudi ambassador to the United States in a Georgetown café highlighted the breadth of cooperation that is possible along America's southern border.

Notes

1. "FBI: Radicalized Individuals, Hezbollah Are Potential Threats for Detroit-Area Jews," Jewish Telegraphic Agency, April 25, 2012.
2. Author interview with former FBI official, Washington, DC, February 23, 2011.

3. Ibid.

4. Author telephone interview with former FBI official, September 25, 2009; author email interview with former FBI official, April 29, 2010.

5. *State of Ohio v. Ali Abdul Nasrallah*, Court of Appeals of Ohio, Sixth District, Lucas County, No. L-99-1194, September 1, 2000; Michael D. Sallah, "Terror Links Sought in Credit Card Scam," *The Blade* (Toledo, OH), December 15, 2002.

6. *State of Ohio v. Ali Abdul Nasrallah*; Sallah, "Terror Links Sought."

7. Sallah, "Terror Links Sought."

8. *State of Ohio v. Ali Abdul Nasrallah*; Sallah, "Terror Links Sought."

9. Sallah, "Terror Links Sought."

10. *State of Ohio v. Ali Abdul Nasrallah*.

11. Sallah, "Terror Links Sought."

12. Ibid.

13. Ibid.

14. Author interview with former FBI official, Detroit, MI, September 25, 2009; author email interview with former FBI official, April 29, 2010.

15. Nathan Koppel, "They Call It RICO," *Wall Street Journal*, January 20, 2011. For background on the RICO Act, see Mark Gordon, "Ideas Shoot Bullets: How the RICO Act Became a Potent Weapon in the War against Organized Crime," *Concept Journal* 26 (2003).

16. Author email interview with former FBI official, April 29, 2010.

17. US Department of Justice, United States Attorney's Office, Eastern District of Michigan, bank fraud press release, April 26, 2004; US Department of Justice, United States Attorney's Office, Eastern District of Michigan, "Final Defendant Sentenced in 17-Member Complex Fraud Scheme," press release, February 21, 2007; Associated Press, "Grand Jury Indicts 12 Dearborn Residents in Credit Card Fraud Scheme," April 26, 2004.

18. *United States of America v. Ali Abdul-Karim Farhat*, Affidavit of FBI Agent Karen Pertuso, Affidavit in Support of Complaint, Case No. 04-80044, United States District Court, Eastern District of Michigan, January 14, 2004.

19. United Press International, "FBI Probes Drug Money for Terrorists Deal," January 21, 2004; Associated Press, "Michigan Brothers Charged in Drug Ring, Links to Hezbollah Alleged," January 21, 2004.

20. *United States of America v. Ali Abdul-Karim Farhat*, Affidavit of Karen Pertuso.

21. Associated Press, "Michigan Brothers Charged."

22. Robert E. Pierre and Allan Lengel, "Detroit FBI Chief Cleared in Drug Ring Leak Probe," *Washington Post*, February 6, 2004.

23. Associated Press, "Brothers Suspected of Hezbollah Ties Freed on Bond in Drug Case," February 4, 2004.

24. US Department of Justice, United States Attorney's Office, Eastern District of Michigan, "Final Defendant Sentenced in 17-Member Complex Fraud Scheme."

25. Author interview with federal officials, Detroit, MI, May 10, 2010.

26. *United States of America v. Elias Mohamad Akhdar et al.*, Indictment, United States District Court, Eastern District of Michigan, Southern Division, January 23, 2003; Jim Irwin, "Cigarette Smugglers Fed Money to Hezbollah, Feds Say," Associated Press, February 5, 2003.

27. *United States of America v. Elias Mohamad Akhdar et al.*, Indictment; David Shepardson, "Dearborn Resident Pleads Guilty to Terror Charges," *Detroit News*, September 19, 2003.

28. *United States of America v. Elias Mohamad Akhdar et al.*, Indictment.

29. Ibid.; *United States of America v. Elias Mohamad Akhdar*, Government's Written Proffer.

30. PoliceOne Critical Alert, "Terrorism-Related Arrests in Va., Mich; One Officer Shot," *Policeone.com*, February 5, 2003.

31. Stewart Bell, "Canadian Accused of Smuggling Cigarettes to Fund Lebanese Terrorism," *National Post* (Canada), February 5, 2003.

32. Irwin, "Cigarette Smugglers Fed Money."

33. Bell, "Canadian Accused of Smuggling."

34. *United States of America v. Elias Mohamad Akhdar*, Government's Written Proffer; *United States of America v. Elias Mohamad Akhdar et al.*, Indictment.

35. "Hizbullah Denies Connection with Three Lebanese Indicted in U.S.," *Daily Star* (Lebanon), February 17, 2003.

36. *United States of America v. Hassan Moussa Makki*, Government's Written Proffer in Support of Its Request for Detention Pending Trial, Criminal No. 03-80079, United States District Court, Eastern District of Michigan, Southern Division, April 4, 2003; *United States of America v. Elias Mohamad Akhdar et al.*, Indictment.

37. Shepardson, "Dearborn Resident Pleads Guilty."

38. *United States of America v. Hassan Moussa Makki*, Government's Written Proffer in Support of Its Request for Detention Pending Trial, Criminal No. 03-80079, United States District Court, Eastern District of Michigan, Southern Division, April 4, 2003; *United States of America v. Elias Mohamad Akhdar et al.*, Indictment.

39. *United States of America v. Imad Mohamad-Musbah Hammoud et al.*, Opinion and Order Denying Defendants' Motion to Dismiss Indictment, Criminal No. 03-80406, United States District Court, Eastern District of Michigan, Southern Division, May 16, 2008.

40. *United States of America v. Imad Mohamad-Musbah Hammoud et al.*, Indictment, Criminal No. 03-80406, United States District Court, Eastern District of Michigan, Southern Division, April 4, 2004.

41. Ibid.

42. *United States of America v. Imad Mohamad-Musbah Hammoud et al.*, Opinion and Order.

43. Author telephone interview with former FBI official, September 25, 2009.

44. *United States of America v. Imad Mohamad-Musbah Hammoud et al.*, Indictment; author telephone interview with former FBI official, September 25, 2009; see also *United States of America v. Tarek Makki*, Plea Agreement, Criminal No. 03-80617, Eastern District of Michigan, Southern Division, October 5, 2005.

45. *United States of America v. Tarek Makki*, Plea Agreement; *United States of America v. Tarek Makki*, Defendants' Sentencing Memorandum, Criminal No. 03-80617, Eastern District of Michigan, Southern Division, March 10, 2006.

46. Author telephone interview with former FBI official, September 25, 2009; author interview with federal officials, Detroit, MI, May 10, 2010.

47. Author interview with federal officials, Detroit, MI, May 10, 2010.

48. Michael Isikoff, "Nasrallah's Men inside America," *Daily Beast*, August 13, 2006.

49. Jaime Holguin, "Bogus Viagra Business Booms," *CBS News*, February 11, 2009.

50. United States Drug Enforcement Administration, *DEA History in Depth: 1999–2003,*"Operation Mountain Express I, II, and III (2000–2002)" (accessed May 14, 2012).

51. Greg Krikorian, "Terrorists Received Drug Money, U.S. Says," *Los Angeles Times*, May 10, 2002.

52. Associated Press, "Drug Money For Hezbollah?" *CBS News*, February 11, 2009.

53. *United States of America v. Imad Mohamad-Musbah Hammoud et al.*, Indictment; author telephone interview with former FBI official, September 25, 2009.

54. *United States of America v. Imad Mohamad-Musbah Hammoud et al.*, Indictment; author telephone interview with former FBI official, September 25, 2009; author interview with federal officials, Detroit, MI, May 10, 2010.

55. Author interview with federal officials, Detroit, MI, May 10, 2010.

56. *United States of America v. Imad Mohamad-Musbah Hammoud et al.*, Indictment.

57. Author email interview with former FBI official, April 29, 2010.

58. *United States of America v. Imad Mohamad-Musbah Hammoud et al.*, Indictment.

59. Roi Kais, "Hezbollah Funding Terror with Fake Medicine," *YnetNews*, September 10, 2012.

60. *United States of America v. Imad Mohamad-Musbah Hammoud et al.*, Indictment.

61. National Commission on Terrorist Attacks upon the United States, *9/11 Commission Report*, released July 22, 2004, pp. 240–41; *United States of America v. Mahmoud Youssef Kourani*, Indictment, Criminal No. 03-81030, United States District Court, Eastern District of Michigan, Southern Division, November 19, 2003.

62. US CIA, "Expanding Links between Alien Smugglers and Extremists."

63. *United States of America v. Mahmoud Youssef Kourani*, First Superseding Indictment, March 1, 2005; Pauline Arrillaga and Olga R. Rodriguez, "The Terror-Immigration Connection," MSNBC, July 3, 2005; Associated Press, "Hizballah Fundraiser Sentenced to Prison," *Los Angeles Times*, June 15, 2005.

64. *United States of America v. Sealed Matter*, Affidavit of FBI Agent Timothy T. Waters, Misc. No. 03-x-71722, United States District Court Eastern District Court, Eastern District of Michigan, Southern Division, April 15, 2004.

65. *United States of America v. Mahmoud Youssef Kourani*, Government's Written Proffer in Support of Detention Pending Trial, Criminal No. 03-81030, United States District Court, Eastern District of Michigan, Southern Division, January 20, 2004.

66. *United States of America v. Mahmoud Youssef Kourani*, Indictment.

67. *United States of America v. Sealed Matter*, Affidavit of Timothy T. Waters.

68. *United States of America v. Mahmoud Youssef Kourani*, Indictment.

69. *United States of America v. Mahmoud Youssef Kourani*, Government's Written Proffer.

70. *United States of America v. Mahmoud Youssef Kourani*, Indictment; *United States of America v. Sealed Matter*, Affidavit of Timothy T. Waters.

71. *United States of America v. Mahmoud Youssef Kourani*, Indictment.

72. *United States of America v. Sealed Matter*, Affidavit of Timothy T. Waters.

73. *United States of America v. Mahmoud Youssef Kourani*, Government's Written Proffer.

74. *United States of America v. Sealed Matter*, Affidavit of Timothy T. Waters.

75. David Shepardson, "Feds: Man Hid Terror Cash," *Detroit News*, January 16, 2004.

76. *United States of America v. Mahmoud Youssef Kourani*, Government's Written Proffer.

77. Author interview with federal officials, Detroit, MI, May 10, 2010.

78. *United States of America v. Sealed Matter*, Judgment, Criminal No. 03CR81030-1, United States District Court Eastern District Court, Eastern District of Michigan, Southern Division, June 20, 2005.

79. *United States of America v. Mahmoud Youssef Kourani*, Government's Written Proffer.

80. Ibid.

81. *United States of America v. Sealed Matter*, Affidavit of Timothy T. Waters.

82. Author interview with federal officials, Detroit, MI, May 10, 2010.

83. Associated Press, "Terror-Linked Migrants Channeled into U.S.," *Fox News*, July 3, 2005.

84. "Myrick Calls for Taskforce to Investigate Presence of Hezbollah on the US Southern Border," letter from US Congresswoman Sue Myrick to Secretary of the Department of Homeland Security Janet Napolitano, June 23, 2010.

85. Ibid.

86. Tucson Police Department, Tucson Urban Area Security Initiative, "International Terrorism Situational Awareness: Hezbollah," September 20, 2010.

87. "Border Security 2010: Year in Review, Open Source Reporting," Arizona Division of Emergency Management.

88. *United States of America v. Jamal Yousef*, Sealed Indictment, S3 08 Cr. 1213, United States District Court, Southern District of New York, July 6, 2009.

89. Jack Koury, "Mexico Thwarts Hezbollah Bid to Set up South American Network," *Haaretz* (Tel Aviv), July 6, 2010.

90. *United States of America v. Riad Skaff*, Government's Sentencing Memorandum, No. 07CR0041, United States District Court, Northern District of Illinois, Eastern Division, May 27, 2008.

91. *United States of America v. Riad Skaff*, Government's Sentencing Memorandum; *United States of America v. Riad Skaff*, Affidavit of ICE Special Agent Matthew Dublin, January 29, 2007.

92. *United States of America v. Riad Skaff*, Affidavit of Colonel Kevin M. McDonnell, April 24, 2008.

93. *United States of America v. Yehia Ali Ahmed Alomari et al.*, Case No. 07M4009, United States District Court, Western District of New York, February 24, 2007, Affidavit of ICE Special Agent James K. Crawford.

94. Ibid.

95. Associated Press, "3 Yemeni Business Men Who Sent $200,000 Overseas Plead Guilty in NY Court to Money Laundering," August 28, 2009.

96. *United States of America v. Talal Khalil Chahine et al.*, Indictment, No. 5:06-cr-20248, United States District Court, Eastern District of Michigan, Southern Division, May 19, 2006; *United States of America v. Elfat El Aouar*, Government's Sentencing Memo-

randum, Criminal No. 06-20248, United States District Court, Eastern District of Michigan, Southern Division, May 11, 2007.

97. *United States of America v. Elfat El Aouar,* Government's Written Proffer in Support of Detention Pending Trial, May 19, 2006.

98. Niraj Warikoo, "La Shish Chain Owner Denies Ties to Terror," *Detroit Free Press,* May 19, 2006.

99. "Alleged Hezbollah Front Raided in Michigan," Anti-Defamation League, July 30, 2007.

100. Wes Bruer, "Ohio Couple Plead Guilty to Supporting Hezbollah," *Long War Journal,* May 24, 2011.

101. *United States of America v. Hor I. Akl and Amera A. Akl,* Indictment, Case No. 3:10-CR-251, United States District Court, Northern District of Ohio, Western Division, June 7, 2010.

102. *United States of America v. Hor I. Akl,* Plea Agreement, May 23, 2011; *United States of America v. Amera A. Akl,* Plea Agreement, May 23, 2011.

103. *United States of America v. Mufid Kamal Mrad,* Affidavit in Support of a Criminal Complaint and Arrest Warrant, United States District Court, Eastern District of Virginia, Case No. 1:12mj363, May 30, 2012.

104. *United States of America v. Lebanese Canadian Bank SAL et al.,* Verified Complaint, United States District Court, Southern District of New York, 11 CIV 9186, December 15, 2011.

105. Ibid.

106. US Department of Justice, Office of Public Affairs, "Dallas Area Used Car Dealers Indicted in Money Laundering Scheme," press release, November 17, 2011.

107. *United States of America v. Hassan Hodroj et al.,* Affidavit of FBI Supervisory Special Agent Samuel Smemo Jr., United States District Court, Eastern District of Pennsylvania, November 20, 2009.

108. David Asher, "Party of Fraud: Hizballah's Criminal Enterprises," Policy Forum Presentation, Washington Institute for Near East Policy (Washington, DC), March 22, 2012.

109. US Department of the Treasury, Financial Crimes Enforcement Network, "Finding That the Lebanese Canadian Bank SAL Is a Financial Institution of Primary Money Laundering Concern," *Federal Register* 76, no. 33 (February 17, 2011).

110. *United States of America v. Ayman Joumaa,* Indictment, Criminal No. 1:11-CR-560, United States District Court, Eastern District of Virginia, November 23, 2011.

111. Jo Becker, "Beirut Bank Seen as a Hub of Hezbollah's Financing," *New York Times,* December 13, 2011.

112. Avi Jorisch, "Al-Manar: Hizbullah TV, 24/7," *Middle East Quarterly* 11, no. 1 (Winter 2004): 17–31.

113. Ibid., 17.

114. BBC Summary of World Broadcasts, "Hezbollah Leader Nasrallah Supports Intifada, Vows 'Death to America,'" September 27, 2002.

115. Jorisch interview with Lebanese Hezbollah expert, October 11, 2002, in Avi Jorisch, *Beacon of Hatred: Inside Hezbollah's al-Manar Television* (Washington, DC: Washington Institute for Near East Policy, 2004), 32.

116. Nicholas Blanford, "Hizbullah Sharpens Its Weapons in Propaganda War," *Christian Science Monitor*, December 28, 2001.

117. "Hizbollah Inaugurates Satellite Channel via ArabSat," al-Ra'y (Amman), May 29, 2000, BBC Summary of World Broadcasts, May 31, 2000; Robert Fisk, "Television News Is Secret Weapon of the Intifada," *Independent* (London), December 2, 2000.

118. Jorisch, *Beacon of Hatred*, 20.

119. Fisk, "Television News."

120. *United States of America v. Mohamad Youssef Hammoud and Chawki Youssef Hammoud*, trial transcript, Docket No. 3:00-cr-147, United States District Court, Western District of North Carolina, Charlotte Division, June 10, 2002, pp. 1487–88.

121. Intelligence and Terrorism Information Center at the Israel Intelligence Heritage & Commemoration Center, "Exposure of a Hezbollah Network in Egypt," April 28, 2009; Intelligence and Terrorism Information Center at the Israel Intelligence Heritage & Commemoration Center, "Egypt Exposes a Hezbollah Network on Its Soil," April 13, 2009.

122. Jorisch, *Beacon of Hatred*, 21.

123. Jeffrey Goldberg, "In the Party of God: Are Terrorists in Lebanon Preparing for a Larger War?" *The New Yorker*, October 14, 2002.

124. "France Pulls Plug on Arab Network," *BBC News*, December 14, 2004.

125. "International Approaches to the Regulation of Al-Manar Television and Terrorism-Related Content," *Australian Communications and Media Authority* (Sydney: Commonwealth of Australia, 2011), 9–10.

126. US Congress, House, Committee on International Relations, Statement of James Phillips, *Adding Hezbollah to the EU Terrorist List*.

127. Statement of Frank C. Urbancic, *Hezbollah's Global Reach*; US Department of State, "Addition of Al-Manar to the Terrorist Exclusion List," press release, December 28, 2004.

128. US Department of the Treasury, "U.S. Designates Al-Manar as a Specially Designated Global Terrorist Entity; Television Station Is Arm of Hezbollah Terrorist Network," press release, March 23, 2006.

129. US Department of Justice, US Attorney Southern District of New York, "U.S. Arrests Two for Supporting Hizballah," press release, November 20, 2006.

130. *United States of America v. Javed Iqbal and Saleh Elahwal*, Indictment, United States District Court, Southern District of New York, Criminal No. 06-CR-1054, November 2006.

131. US Department of Justice, US Attorney Southern District of New York, "Staten Island Man Sentenced to 69 Months in Prison for Providing Material Support and Resources to Hizballah," press release, April 23, 2009; US Department of Justice, US Attorney Southern District of New York, "New Jersey Man Sentenced to 17 Months in Prison for Providing Material Support and Resources to Hizballah," press release, June 23, 2009.

132. John Mintz and Douglas Farah, "Small Scams Probed for Terror Ties: Muslim-Arab Stores Monitored as Part of Post–Sept. 11 Inquiry," *Washington Post*, August 12, 2002.

133. US Department of Justice, United States Attorney's Office, Central District of California, "Operation Bell Bottoms Targets Counterfeiting, Drug Operation in Los Angeles–Area Clothing Stores," press release, November 6, 2007.

134. Ibid.

135. James Meek, "Busted Los Angeles Drug Ring Had Ties to Hezbollah," *New York Daily News*, November 9, 2007.

136. Author telephone interview with law enforcement officer, January 14, 2010.

137. Ibid.

138. Author interviews with suspects, Los Angeles, May 11, 2010; County of Los Angeles Sheriff's Department, Incident Report, "Sale of Counterfeit Trademark Merchandise," November 11, 2006.

139. Author interviews with suspects, Los Angeles, May 11, 2010; County of Los Angeles Sheriff's Department, Incident Report, "Sale of Counterfeit Trademark," October 8, 2004.

140. US Congress, Senate, Committee on Homeland Security and Governmental Affairs, Statement of John C. Stedman, *Counterfeit Goods: Easy Cash for Criminals and Terrorists: Hearing before the Committee on Homeland Security and Governmental Affairs*.

141. Ibid.

142. *United States of America v. Sealed Matter*, Affidavit of Timothy T. Waters.

143. Mike Newall, "Road to Terrorism Arrests Began at Deptford Mall," *Philadelphia Inquirer*, January 25, 2010.

144. Author interview with law enforcement officials, Philadelphia, PA, March 11, 2010.

145. Ibid.; *United States of America v. Sadek Mohamad Koumaiha et al.*, Indictment, United States District Court, Eastern District of Pennsylvania, November 23, 2009.

146. Author interview with law enforcement officials, Philadelphia, PA, March 11, 2010; *United States of America v. Sadek Mohamad Koumaiha et al.*, Indictment.

147. Author interview with law enforcement officials, Philadelphia, PA, March 11, 2010; US Department of Justice, "Arrests Made in Case Involving Conspiracy to Procure Weapons, Including Anti-Aircraft Missiles," press release, November 23, 2009; *United States of America v. Dani Nemr Tarraf et al.*, Indictment, Criminal No. 09-743-01, United States District Court, Eastern District of Pennsylvania, November 20, 2009.

148. Author interview with law enforcement officials, Philadelphia, PA, March 11, 2010.

149. Ibid.; US Department of Justice, "Conspiracy to Procure Weapons, Including Anti-Aircraft Missiles"; *United States of America v. Dani Nemr Tarraf et al.*, Indictment, November 20, 2009.

150. *United States of America v. Dani Nemr Tarraf et al.*, Supplement to Government's Motion for Pretrial Detention, Criminal No. 09-743-01, United States District Court, Eastern District of Pennsylvania, December 3, 2009; for photo, see trial exhibits.

151. *United States of America v. Dani Nemr Tarraf et al.*, Pretrial Detention Order.

152. Author interview with law enforcement officials, March 11, 2010.

153. *United States of America v. Hassan Hodroj et al.*, Affidavit of Samuel Smemo Jr.; Newall, "Road to Terrorism"; author interview with law enforcement officials, March 11, 2010.

154. *United States of America v. Hassan Hodroj et al.*, Indictment, United States District Court, Eastern District of Pennsylvania, November 24, 2009; Newall, "Road to Terrorism."

155. *United States of America v. Hassan Hodroj et al.*, Indictment, United States District Court, Eastern District of Pennsylvania, November 24, 2009.

156. Ibid.; Newall, "Road to Terrorism"; author interview with law enforcement officials, March 11, 2010; *United States of America v. Hassan Hodroj et al.*, Affidavit of Samuel Smemo Jr.

157. Author interview with law enforcement officials, March 11, 2010; *United States of America v. Hassan Hodroj et al.*, Affidavit of Samuel Smemo Jr.; *United States of America v. Hassan Hodroj et al.*, Indictment.

158. *United States of America v. Hassan Hodroj et al.*, Affidavit of Samuel Smemo Jr.

159. Author interview with law enforcement officials, March 11, 2010; Sebastian Rotella, "Azerbaijan Seen as New Front in Mideast Conflict," *Los Angeles Times*, May 30, 2009.

160. *United States of America v. Hassan Hodroj et al.*, Affidavit of Samuel Smemo Jr.; *United States of America v. Hassan Hodroj et al.*, Indictment; author interview with law enforcement officials, March 11, 2010.

161. *United States of America v. Hassan Hodroj et al.*, Affidavit of Samuel Smemo Jr.; author interview with law enforcement officials, March 11, 2010.

162. *United States of America v. Hassan Hodroj et al.*, Indictment; US Department of Justice, "Four Indicted for Conspiring to Support Hezbollah; Six Others Charged with Related Crimes," press release, November 24, 2009.

163. *United States of America v. Hassan Hodroj et al.*, Affidavit of Samuel Smemo Jr.

164. Ibid.

165. *United States of America v. Hassan Hodroj et al.*, Indictment; author interview with law enforcement officials, March 11, 2010.

166. *United States of America v. Hassan Hodroj et al.*, Affidavit of Samuel Smemo Jr.

167. Ibid.

168. Spencer Hsu, "Hezbollah Official Indicted on Weapons Charge," *Washington Post*, November 25, 2009; "Sayyid Nasrallah, Hamas Call for Resumption of Lebanese-Palestinian Dialogue," Al Manar TV, December 2, 2009 (transcript supplied by BBC Worldwide Monitoring); Stewart Bell, "10 People Charged with Supporting Hezbollah," *National Post* (Canada), November 24, 2009; author interview with law enforcement officials, March 11, 2010; *United States of America v. Hassan Hodroj et al.*, Affidavit of Samuel Smemo Jr.

169. *United States of America v. Hassan Hodroj et al.*, Affidavit of Samuel Smemo Jr.

170. Ibid.

171. Ibid.

172. Ibid.

173. Mike Newall, "Ex-Camden County Resident Indicted in Alleged Terror Cell Held in Paraguay," *Philadelphia Inquirer*, June 17, 2010.

174. Ibid.; Mike Newall, "Suspected Hezbollah Funder Appears in a Philadelphia Court," *Philadelphia Inquirer*, February 26, 2011.

175. *United States of America v. Hassan Hodroj et al.*, Indictment.

176. Mark Steinitz, "Middle East Terrorist Activity in Latin America," *Center for Strategic and International Studies*, Policy Papers on the Americas XIV, no. 7, July 2003.

177. The presence of Lebanese Hezbollah supporters in Venezuela should not be confused with Hezbollah Venezuela, also known as Hezbollah America Latina, also known as "Autonomía Islámica Wayyu," which emerged in July 2005 and gained prominence during the 2006 war between Israel and Hezbollah in Lebanon. Initially led by Teodoro Fafael Darnott, also known as Comandante Teodoro, a Marxist activist, the group is

mostly composed of an indigenous tribe, the Wayuu Indians, who embraced Shi'a Islam in the early twenty-first century. See Ely Karmon, "Hezbollah America Latina: Strange Group or Real Threat," *International Institute for Counter-Terrorism* (Herzliya), November 14, 2006.

178. Roger F. Noriega and José R. Cárdenas, "The Mounting Hezbollah Threat in Latin America," American Enterprise Institute, October 6, 2011; *United States of America v. Mohamad Youssef Hammoud and Chawki Youssef Hammoud,* trial transcript, May 23, 2002.

179. US Congress, House, *A Line in the Sand: Confronting the Threat at the Southwest Border,* report prepared by House Committee on Homeland Security, Subcommittee on Investigations, October 13, 2006, 31.

180. US Congress, House, Committee on International Relations, Statement of Edward Royce, *Venezuela:* Terrorism Hub of South America.

181. Ibid.

182. Statement of Frank C. Urbancic, *Venezuela: Terrorism Hub of South America;* Anna Mahjar-Barducci, "Venezuelan Minister Hangs out with Hezbollah," Gatestone Institute (New York, NY), February 11, 2011.

183. Robert M. Morgenthau, "The Link between Iran and Venezuela: A Crisis in the Making?" briefing, Brookings Institution (Washington, DC), September 8, 2009.

184. Martin Arostegui, "Analysis: Venezuela's Islamic Links," United Press International, September 1, 2003.

185. US Department of the Treasury, "Treasury Targets Hezbollah in Venezuela," press release, June 18, 2008.

186. Vanessa Neumann, "The New Nexus of Narcoterrorism: Hezbollah and Venezuela," Foreign Policy Research Institute (Philadelphia, PA), December 2011.

187. J. J. Green, "Iran's Secret Pipeline into the U.S.," WTOP 103.5 FM radio (Washington, DC), August 18, 2010.

188. US Department of Justice, Office of Public Affairs, "Two Men Charged in Alleged Plot to Assassinate Saudi Arabian Ambassador to the United States," press release, October 11, 2011; Jerry Markon and Karen DeYoung, "Iran behind Alleged Terrorist Plot, U.S. Says," *Washington Post,* October 11, 2011.

12

Shadow War

ON JULY 18, 2012, at the height of the summer tourist season, a group of Israelis landed at the Sarafovo Airport in Burgas, Bulgaria, and boarded buses for the thirty-mile drive south to a Black Sea beachfront resort. An affordable destination and a short flight away, Bulgaria had become popular with Israeli vacationers as a winter ski and summer beach destination. But on July 18—eighteen years to the day after the Asociación Mutual Israelita Argentina (AMIA) Jewish Community Center was bombed in Buenos Aires—a bomb destroyed one of the seven tour buses, killing the Bulgarian bus driver and five Israelis and wounding some thirty more.[1]

None of the travelers in the large group noticed when a Caucasian man in Bermuda shorts and a T-shirt, wearing a baseball cap and glasses and carrying a backpack, joined the crowd in the airport terminal and walked with them to the buses. Later, airport surveillance footage showed the man, apparently in his thirties, entering and exiting the terminal as he waited for the Israeli flight to arrive. At the time, he wore a long, blond wig, but a car rental clerk would recognize him from the video, recalling that he spoke English with an Arabic accent, had short hair, carried a wad of 500-euro notes, and seemed upset when he had rented a car.[2]

At first, authorities assumed a suicide bomber had detonated the device. But forensic investigation quickly determined that a Caucasian man placed the bomb in the bus's luggage compartment before it was then remotely denotated. It appears the bomber was not a knowing suicide bomber, though it remained unclear if something went wrong when he tried to plant the bomb on the bus or if he was a mule duped into carrying the backpack bomb and unaware his accomplices planned to use him as a delivery mechanism.[3] Either way, DNA tests of the bomber's remains failed to definitively identify him, though it determined he was related to a Canadian co-conspirator.[4] In time, Bulgarian investigators would conclude that the Burgas bomber's handlers traveled on Canadian and Australian passports, respectively, and returned to Lebanon after the bombing through Romania and Poland.[5]

Only one thing was clear: The American driver's license found on the bomber's body was a fake, and not a very good one at that—the Michigan license listed a

Louisiana address. As they searched for the bomber's accomplices, authorities determined that one carried another fake Michigan license, but at least this one listed a Michigan address. Suspicious about the license, one travel agency reportedly chose not to rent a car to the nervous accomplice.[6]

Even before they uncovered much about the bomber, Israeli intelligence apparently knew something about him from other sources. According to Israeli officials, whether he was a mule or not, the bomber was selected in part because he was not Lebanese "in order to avoid any suspicions."[7] From the outset, Israeli officials publicly insisted—and anonymous American and British officials confirmed—that Lebanese Hezbollah was behind the attack.[8] "We are confident," Israeli defense minister Ehud Barak told CNN, "without any doubt about the responsibility of Hezbollah [for] the actual execution of the operation—preparation, planning and execution." This judgment, he added, was based on "direct, hard evidence" that Israel had already shared with Washington and others.[9]

At least part of this evidence was apparently based on intercepted telephone calls between Lebanon and Bulgaria. For two months before the bombing, authorities listened in as Hezbollah officials in Lebanon plotted with unknown operatives on the ground in Bulgaria. These operatives must have been Hezbollah facilitators, because the bomber and an accomplice flew into the country only a month before the attack, one via Germany and the other through Belgium.[10] In the three days leading up to the bombing, the flurry of calls intensified. To protect sources and methods, Israel refused to publicly release details of these calls. The Hezbollah officials in Lebanon "shouldn't know that we know the numbers [they use] in Lebanon."[11] Nor, officials added, was the attack the work of rogue Hezbollah gunmen. "Nobody pushes the button in Burgas without Nasrallah's approval," explained an Israeli official close to the investigation.[12]

A similar plot targeting Israeli tourists in Bulgaria was thwarted a few months earlier, in January, just weeks ahead of the anniversary of Mughniyeh's assassination, when a suspicious package was spotted on a bus carrying Israeli tourists from Turkey to Bulgaria. Officials in Bulgaria subsequently honored Israeli requests to provide enhanced security for buses carrying Israeli tourists. Additional security was reportedly put in place at the country's premier ski resort as well. At the time Israeli officials had deemed airport security sufficient.[13] In fact, Western intelligence officials had long worried about Bulgaria as a potential venue for Hezbollah or Qods Force attacks. Five years earlier, Western intelligence indicated "that Hezbollah chiefs and Iranian intelligence officials had put Bulgaria on a list of nations propitious for developing plots against Western targets."[14]

The July Burgas attack came just days after the arrest of a suspected Hezbollah operative accused of plotting an eerily similar attack on Israeli tourists in Cyprus. On July 7, Cypriot authorities raided the hotel room of Hossam Taleb Yaakoub, a twenty-four-year-old Lebanese-Swedish man traveling on his European passport. While authorities recognized that Hezbollah members raised money in Sweden to finance terrorist activities elsewhere, European officials in particular were alarmed by the second arrest, within six months, of a dual Swedish-Lebanese citizen accused of participating in Hezbollah operations. In Cyprus, Yaakoub had in his possession photographs of Israeli targets, including information on buses carrying Israeli tourists and Israeli flights to and from the island nation.[15]

In court, Yaakoub testified that he conducted surveillance of Israeli tourists arriving on the island nation on flights from Israel and took note of the buses they boarded to their hotels. Cypriot police tracked the suspect before arresting him, and found in his possession information on arriving Israeli flights and buses taking Israeli tourists to their hotels. Though he initially denied ties to Hezbollah, Yaakoub later admitted being a Hezbollah operative sent to Cyprus to conduct surveillance for Hezbollah. Just four hours after insisting to police he was just in Cyprus on business, Yaakoub sat back down and conceded to police, "I did not tell the whole truth." He claimed he did not know what his reconnaissance was for, but knew "something weird was going on" and speculated it was "probably to bring down a plane, but I don't know, I just make assumptions." Later, he put it to police differently: he was not part of a terrorist plot in Cyprus at all: "it was just collecting information about the Jews, and this is what my organization is doing everywhere in the world." Further underscoring the European bent to the case, Yaakoub admitted that before sending him to Cyprus, first to create a cover story and then to conduct surveillance, Hezbollah initially used him as a courier to deliver or retrieve packages to or from Hezbollah operatives in places like Turkey, the Netherlands, and France.[16]

In Bulgaria, Hezbollah may have long relied on Lebanese drug and other criminal organizations to fund the group. A 2008 Bulgarian government commission concluded that profits from drug trafficking through the country support Hezbollah and other militant groups.[17] This was likely on the agenda when then–Mossad chief Meir Dagan visited Sofia in 2010 to meet with the Bulgarian prime minister.[18] Whatever the logistical details, most commentators (including this one) assumed the Burgas bombing was part of Hezbollah's declared commitment to avenge the assassination of Imad Mughniyeh.[19] It was not. To be sure, Hezbollah remained committed to avenging Mughniyeh's death, but the Burgas bombing represented something different, and more ominous: Hezbollah's entry into the shadow war raging between Iran and the West.

Tracking Hezbollah's Militant Trajectory

Hezbollah's anti-Western militancy began with attacks against Western targets in Lebanon, then expanded to attacks abroad intended to exact revenge for actions threatening its or Iran's interests, or to press foreign governments to release captured operatives. At times, such as the 1992 and 1994 bombings in Argentina, Hezbollah's own interests in carrying out attacks abroad were magnified by Iran's interest in the same. Their coincident interest led to joint operations—such as the bombing of Khobar Towers—that leveraged each party's strengths and maximized their combined capabilities.

Over the course of the always intimate relationship between Iran and Hezbollah, the head of the Qods Force or other senior Iranian leaders might have told Hezbollah to "jump" and the response would have been, "How high?" In part, this is a function of the close alignment between Hezbollah's senior leadership and Iran's clerical regime. Yet how firmly do Hezbollah leaders believe in *velayat-e faqih*, the Islamic Republic's principle of rule of the jurisprudent? According to Hezbollah leader Hassan Nasrallah, "the subject of the *velayat-e faqih* and the Imamate is at the heart of our religious doctrine, and any offense to it is an offense to our religion."[20] According to Hezbollah official Nawaf Musawi, Nasrallah reportedly has said that he would divorce his own wife if Iranian Supreme Leader Ayatollah Ali Khamenei were to make such an order; according to the theory of *velayat-e faqih*, one would do no less.[21] But the close relationship also persists because of Hezbollah's dependence on Iran for financial, material, and political support. For years Hezbollah relied almost exclusively on Iranian largesse, which hovered around $100 to $200 million a year or more.[22] Criminal and other funding enterprises initiated by expatriate supporters were a welcome bonus but were not considered central to Hezbollah's business model. Such generous state sponsorship, however, came with strings attached that Hezbollah, as Tehran's primary pan-Shi'a militant proxy group, could not easily ignore.

Over the years, American and other Western intelligence assessments have consistently judged that Hezbollah could attack their respective interests if the group, or Iran, perceived a direct threat to its interests. A British report issued prior to the July 2006 war Hezbollah fought with Israel warned "of an increased threat to the UK from Iranian state-sponsored terrorism should the diplomatic situation deteriorate."[23] Similarly, a July 2007 National Intelligence Estimate assessed that "Lebanese Hezbollah, which has conducted anti-US attacks outside the United States in the past, may be more likely to consider attacking the Homeland over the next three years if it perceives the United States as posing a direct threat to the group or Iran."[24] US intelligence officials believe that Hezbollah and Iran, through the Islamic Jihad Organization (IJO) and Iran's Revolutionary Guards, "had a list of American facilities around the world they were prepared to strike whenever they received orders from Tehran."[25]

Yet while it kept up its relentless campaign of military and terrorist activities targeting Israel and despite unabating tensions with the West, Hezbollah had not carried out a successful spectacular attack targeting Western interests since the 1996 Khobar Towers bombing. Moreover, Hezbollah worked hard under Mughniyeh to establish a measure of independence from Iran. In mid-2008, four months after Mughniyeh's death, an Israeli intelligence official concluded that "Hezbollah does not always do what Iran wants."[26] But under the leadership of Mughniyeh's successors, Mustapha Badreddine and Talal Hamiyeh, Iran's role seems to have hardened again. In February 2012, Director of National Intelligence James Clapper characterized the relationship between Hezbollah and Iran as "a partnership arrangement[,] with the Iranians as the senior partner."[27] This "strategic partnership," as the National

Counterterrorism Center director Matthew Olsen put it, is the product of a long evolution from the 1980s, when Hezbollah was just a proxy of Iran.[28]

To be sure, as demonstrated throughout this book, Hezbollah has consistently engaged in militant, terrorist, criminal, and other activities worldwide over the years. Its ability to continue to do so apace, however, was severely constrained by an act of terrorism not of its own making. Ironically, al-Qaeda's September 11 attacks proved to be a turning point for Hezbollah, the group responsible for the deaths of more Americans than any other terrorist group until September 11. Desperate not to be caught in the crosshairs of Washington's "war on terror," Hezbollah appears to have consciously decided to roll back its international operations and keep its efforts to strike at Israeli targets as focused and limited as possible. Coinciding with the second Palestinian intifada, Hezbollah leveraged its Unit 1800 efforts to support Palestinian terrorist groups in the West Bank, Gaza Strip, and Israel, while infiltrating its own operatives into Israel and targeting Israeli interests abroad.

At the time, domestic Lebanese considerations also limited Hezbollah's willingness to engage in terrorist activities abroad. Hezbollah first entered Lebanese politics in 1992, when it won twelve of 128 seats in Parliament.[29] Following the assassination of former prime minister Rafiq Hariri, Hezbollah participated in the 2005 general election. This time the party won all twenty-three parliamentary seats representing southern Lebanon, despite rising criticism from the populace from 2002 to 2004 over Hezbollah's activities in the absence of an Israeli occupation as a foil.[30] In 2009, Hezbollah's political bloc was invited to participate in Saad Hariri's national unity cabinet, an arrangement that lasted until 2011, when the Hezbollah ministers resigned, effectively collapsing the government, over the coming indictments of four Hezbollah members for Rafiq Hariri's assassination issued by the UN Special Tribunal for Lebanon in The Hague.[31]

Even after the ministers' resignation, the new government was dominated by Hezbollah and its coalition partners, making it the de facto ruling party in Lebanon. Western analysts see Hezbollah's emergence as a political player in Lebanon as another factor constraining its operational activities abroad. The repercussions of being implicated in a terrorist strike increased exponentially for a Hezbollah governing coalition, both in terms of the cost to its domestic standing and grassroots support and the possibility of a direct reprisal attack against not just the group's interests but the state's as well.[32] But the consequence was not a complete withdrawal from terrorist activity but a decision for the group's terrorist networks to operate at a greater length from the political party its parent organization had become. As a result, the Australian government noted, the IJO was encouraged to "become among the best organized terrorist networks in the world."[33]

In the wake of the July 2006 war, Hassan Nasrallah conceded that if he had known that Hezbollah's kidnapping two Israeli soldiers from across the border would lead to war, he would not have authorized the action.[34] Six months later he was more defensive still: "It could be that I made a mistake, only God doesn't make mistakes, and for that I apologized before the Lebanese nation and for that we paid a very heavy price in blood." Still, he maintained, "We do not hesitate to bring our boys into our just struggle."[35] After the war, Hezbollah was supremely focused on rebuilding Lebanon's destroyed infrastructure and Hezbollah's own fractured grassroots support.[36]

Local criticism arose once more in May 2008, after Hezbollah briefly seized control of part of West Beirut, turning the weapons purportedly maintained to "resist" Israel against fellow Lebanese and contributing, according to a senior US intelligence official, "to a dramatic increase in sectarian tensions."[37] Uninterested in opening up new fronts where it was unprepared to battle, Hezbollah reportedly made a "strategic decision" to avoid confrontation with the United States, US counterterrorism officials reported. The decision included two caveats, however: First, Hezbollah could still consider such an attack if Iran were threatened.[38] Second, the group would continue supporting other militant groups' efforts abroad, including Palestinian, Iraqi, and even Somali terrorist groups. US counterterrorism officials would later note that following the July 2006 war, Hezbollah engaged in "an increasingly aggressive terrorist campaign." This campaign, they added, was probably accelerated by the February 2008 assassination of Imad Mughniyeh.[39]

The US government's reaction was straightforward: "The world is a better place without this man in it. He was a coldblooded killer, a mass murderer and a terrorist responsible for countless innocent lives lost," the State Department spokesman said. "One way or another he was brought to justice."[40] But Mughniyeh's assassination led to the resurgence of activity by Hezbollah's international operations arm, which will no doubt regain its former potency in time—especially when paired with Iranian intelligence and Qods Force operatives. But as the IJO—now under the command of Mustapha Badreddine and Talal Hamiyeh—first set out to avenge Mughniyeh's death, Operation Radwan experienced a series of setbacks, which ultimately led both Iran and Hezbollah to reassess how they would each, separately and together, prosecute a three-tiered shadow war targeting Israeli, Jewish, American, Gulf, and sometimes British interests worldwide.

Reassessing Hezbollah's Place in Iran's Arsenal

Once Nasrallah promised an "open war" to avenge Mughniyeh's assassination, Israeli officials quickly took preventive action against what they deemed the three most likely scenarios: an attack on current or former senior Israeli officials traveling abroad; an attack on an Israeli embassy or other diplomatic mission abroad; or an attack targeting a location affiliated with a Jewish community abroad, such as the 1994 AMIA bombing. They knew better than to ignore Nasrallah's warning.

But however committed Hezbollah was to carrying out such attacks, the IJO was simply not up to the task. For one thing, Hezbollah leaders had actively pared down the IJO's global networks of operatives following the September 11 attacks. And the "strategic partnership" it had shared with Iran for the past decade or so appears to have focused on funding, training, and arming Hezbollah's increasingly effective standing militia, not on its cadre of international terrorists.[41] And so not only did Hezbollah lack the resources and capability to carry out a successful operation abroad, it also no longer had Mughniyeh around to quarterback operations.

Tightened security in the post–September 11 world also meant Hezbollah opted to operate in nations with comparatively lax security rather than vigilant Western nations. But even then, in places like Azerbaijan, Egypt, and Turkey, and even with significant support from Qods Force agents, Hezbollah suffered a series of embarrassing failures. First came the May 2008 fiasco in Baku, which led to the quiet release of Qods Force personnel but the public prosecution of two Hezbollah operatives. Operations were soon foiled in Egypt and Turkey too, as well as attempts to kidnap Israelis in Europe and Africa.

The foiled attack in Turkey in September 2009 was a watershed event for Hezbollah operational planners and their Iranian sponsors. Despite the massive logistical support Qods Force operatives provided for that plot, Hezbollah operatives still failed to successfully execute the attack. And by late 2009, Iran's interest in Hezbollah's operational prowess focused less on local issues like avenging Mughniyeh's death and more on the much larger issue of combatting threats to its nascent nuclear program. In April 2006, fifty centrifuges were destroyed at the Natanz nuclear facility when equipment—apparently tampered with by intelligence services—malfunctioned.[42] In January 2007, suspected Iranian nuclear scientist Ardeshir Hosseinpour died under mysterious circumstances, sparking speculation he was assassinated.[43] A few weeks later, reports emerged that Gen. Ali-Reza Asgari, a former Islamic Revolutionary Guard Corps (IRGC) official who worked with Hezbollah in Lebanon and later served as deputy defense minister, had disappeared—possibly defected—in Turkey.[44] In 2009, Iranian nuclear scientist Shahram Amiri disappeared while on pilgrimage in Saudi Arabia, by some accounts defecting and others being kidnapped.[45] Then, in January 2010, a remote-controlled bomb attached to a motorcycle killed Iranian physics professor Masoud Ali Mohammadi outside his Tehran home.[46]

According to Israeli intelligence officials, furious Iranian leaders reached two conclusions after Mohammadi's death: (1) Hezbollah's IJO had to revitalize its operational capabilities, and (2) the IRGC would no longer rely solely on Hezbollah to carry out terrorist attacks abroad—it would now deploy Qods Force operatives to do so on their own, not just as logisticians supporting Hezbollah hit men.[47] Even more than the loss of its scientists, Tehran sought to address its damaged prestige—the image of an Iran so weak it could not even protect its own scientists at home could not stand.

Much finger-pointing ensued between Hezbollah and the Qods Force regarding where the blame lay for the two years of failed operations, culminating in the botched attack in Turkey and then another failed plot in Jordan in January 2010. Humiliated, and under Nasrallah's instructions, Badreddine and Hamiyeh "undertook a massive operational reevaluation in January 2010, which led to big changes within the IJO over a period of a little over six months." During this period, IJO operations were put on hold and major personnel changes made. New operatives were recruited from the elite of Hezbollah's military wing for intelligence and operational training, while existing IJO operatives were moved into new positions. At the same time, the IJO invested in the development of capabilities and tradecraft that had withered on the vine since the 2001 decision to rein in operations.[48]

As part of its IJO shakeup, Hezbollah engaged in detailed talks with Iranian officials to lay out Hezbollah's role in Iran's larger plan for a coordinated shadow war targeting Israeli, American, British, and Gulf state interests. The coordinated plan, it was decided, would assign responsibility for specific types of attacks to Hezbollah or the Qods Force. These would include operations intended to achieve several different goals, including taking revenge for Mughniyeh's assassination, retaliating for attacks on Iran's nuclear program, and establishing a deterrent threat by convincing Western powers that an attack on Iran would result in—among other things—asymmetric terrorist attacks worldwide.[49]

To this end, Iranian decision makers settled on a campaign of violence based on three threat streams: targeting Israeli tourists, formal government targets (diplomats, retired officials), and targets broadly representative of Israel or the Jewish community (community leaders, prominent Israeli companies). It assigned the task of targeting Israeli tourists—a soft target—to Hezbollah, and maintained for the Qods Force operations targeting Israeli, American, British or Gulf states' interests. The latter would be carried out by a new Special External Operations Unit known as Unit 400.[50]

Iran's Three-Tiered Terror Campaign

At first, Iran's new terrorism strategy, and the IJO's overhaul, seemed to have little effect. In March and September 2010, authorities disrupted undisclosed Qods Force plots in Azerbaijan and Turkey, respectively.[51] In May 2010, Kuwaiti authorities arrested Kuwaiti, Lebanese, and other individuals on suspicion of spying, monitoring US military interests, and possessing explosives for attacks.[52]

Meanwhile, Hezbollah fared no better. Itching to prove their rejuvenated operational capabilities, IJO leaders reportedly pressed Nasrallah to allow them to carry out an attack abroad.[53] In April 2011, the Israeli Counterterrorism Bureau issued an advisory for Passover holiday travel to countries in the Mediterranean Basin and the Far East, warning of Iranian and Hezbollah plots.[54] In fact, the warning was a planned leak by Israeli intelligence aimed at exposing and therefore frustrating a budding Hezbollah plot to target Israeli tourists in Cyprus.[55] Officials went public not only with the travel warning but with details about the Hezbollah operatives involved. Under instructions from Nasrallah and Qods Force leader Qassem Soleimani, Hezbollah IJO chief Talal Hamiyeh was plotting the attacks with a small group of trusted lieutenants, Israeli officials told the press. These included Hamiyeh's "right-hand man and bodyguard, Ahmed Faid," as well as "explosives engineer Ali Najam al-Din and bomb assembly expert Malik Ovayad." False documents were reportedly produced by Majd al-Zakur, also known as the Forger, while logistics support came from Lebanese and Turkish businessmen.[56]

Given Hezbollah's role in the new three-tiered arrangement, Nasrallah was clearly uncomfortable with the notion that people might mistake Hezbollah attacks against Israeli tourists as the best the group could muster to avenge Mughniyeh's death. A few days after media reports exposed the Cyprus plot, Nasrallah gave an interview to a Kuwaiti newspaper underscoring Hezbollah's continued commitment to carry out an operation of equal standing to avenge the death of the IJO commander. The point was not retaliation for retaliation's sake, he stressed: "Had we wanted to, we could have retaliated by killing Israeli tourists in this or that country."[57] But that was not Hezbollah's calculus. Attacks on Israeli tourists were something different—the IJO's part in Iran's shadow war—a threat stream of its own, distinct from Operation Radwan.

In May 2011, Iranian agents shot and killed a Saudi diplomat in Karachi, Pakistan, foreshadowing a plot already under way targeting the Saudi ambassador to Washington, DC.[58] Ten days afterward, Qods Force and Hezbollah operatives carried out a far more complex operation targeting an Israeli diplomat in Turkey. Around 9:00 AM on May 26, 2011, a bomb exploded at a bus stop near one of Istanbul's upscale shopping centers, wounding eight people.[59] Placed underneath a bridge and secured to an electric bike, the bomb was structured to inflict maximum damage.[60] Turkish authorities originally assumed the attack was the work of the Kurdistan Workers Party (PKK), intended to impact upcoming Turkish parliamentary elections.[61] Within weeks, however, investigators determined the attack was a botched Hezbollah–Qods Force assassination attempt targeting the Turkish-born Israeli consul-general to Istanbul, Moshe Kimhi. According to *Corriere della Sera*, the Italian paper that broke the story, Qods Force operatives cased the area, recording Kimhi's routine, before Hezbollah operatives were called in to place the explosive along a route the diplomat was known to take. Intended as retribution for the assassination of Mohammadi, the Iranian physicist, the bombing injured random Turkish civilians instead.[62]

Within weeks the UN Special Tribunal for Lebanon in The Hague would indict the four Hezbollah operatives, including Mustapha Badreddine, for the February 2005 murder of the former Lebanese prime minister. Closer to home, Hezbollah operatives carried out two attacks that wounded French peacekeepers—six civilians and three soldiers—assigned to the UN Interim Force in Lebanon's (UNIFIL) mission in southern Lebanon, according to the State Department.[63] But the plot targeting the Saudi ambassador to Washington, then under way, was the most brazen of all.

On October 11, 2011, US attorney general Eric Holder announced that charges were filed in New York against a dual US-Iranian citizen and a Qods Force commander for their alleged roles in a plot to murder the Saudi ambassador, Adel al-Jubeir. The plot developed quickly over just a few months, starting in spring 2011 and culminating with the arrest of Manssor Arbabsiar, the Iranian-American man, in September. According to the Justice Department, Arbabsiar told a Drug Enforcement Administration (DEA) confidential source posing as an associate of a Mexican drug cartel that "his associates in Iran had discussed a number of violent missions for [the source] and his associates to perform, including the murder of the Ambassador."[64]

An opportunistic plot that fell into the lap of Qods Force planners just as they decided to unleash Unit 400 to attack the West, the scheme arose from an encounter between the dejected Iranian-American and a cousin working for the Qods Force, while the former visited family in Iran. Arbabsiar sent about $100,000 in wire transfers as a down payment for the assassination, which was deposited in an FBI undercover account he thought belonged to the assassin. At a meeting in Mexico in July, the DEA source raised the possibility that innocent bystanders might be killed in a lunchtime attack at a downtown restaurant. But Arbabsiar was clear on the instructions from his Qods Force handlers: "They want that guy [the ambassador] done [killed], if the hundred go with him f**k 'em." Later, after Arbabsiar was arrested and reportedly confessed to his role in the plot, he called Gholam Shakuri, the Qods Force commander (and his cousin), at the direction of law enforcement. With agents listening, Shakuri again confirmed that the plot should go forward and as soon as possible. "Just do it quickly. It's late," he said.[65] In October 2012, Arbabsiar pleaded guilty to charges related to murder-for-hire and conspiring to commit an act of international terrorism.[66]

Interestingly, the plot seems to have been launched shortly after a Saudi-led military intervention in Bahrain against Shiite protesters, which Iran objected to loudly but could not affect. According to a Saudi official, Shakuri was "an important Quds Force case officer who had helped organize militant Shiite protesters in Bahrain." Also according to this account, "Shakuri was among the Iranians who met Hasan Mushaima, a radical Bahraini Shiite cleric, during a stopover in Beirut last February, when Mushaima was on his way back home to lead protests in Bahrain."[67] Likely interpreted by Iran as the latest Western-backed salvo in a coordinated plot to hem in Iran, the Saudi intervention in Bahrain may have contributed to the calculus by which Iranian decision makers approved such an odd attack, involving the bombing of a popular Washington, DC, restaurant known to be frequented by US senators.

Signaling that US authorities had traced the plot to senior Iranian decision makers, the Treasury Department designated IRGC Qods Force commander Qassem Soleimani as a global terrorist for his role overseeing the officers involved in the plot.[68] British officials agreed, designating Soleimani and others involved in the plot themselves as well.[69] This plot against the Saudi diplomat, director-general of the UK Security Service (MI5) Jonathan Evans explained in June 2012, was likely tied to senior Iranian leadership. The plot was the work of the IRGC, he noted, adding, "And of course the IRGC leads straight back to the Iranian leadership."[70] In the assessment by Director of National Intelligence Gen. James Clapper, the Arbabsiar plot "shows that some Iranian officials—probably including Supreme Leader Ali Khamenei—have changed their calculus and are now more willing to conduct an attack in the United States in response to real or perceived U.S. actions that threaten the regime."[71]

Iran correctly perceived it was the target of a string of actions against its nuclear program and, by extension, the regime. In September 2010, Iranian computer networks linked to uranium enrichment at Natanz were infected with the Stuxnet virus, destroying some 1,000 centrifuges, reportedly part of an American-Israeli effort code-named Olympic Games.[72] The next month an explosion at an IRGC missile base leveled most buildings and killed seventeen people, including Gen. Hassan Tehrani Moghaddam, a founder of Iran's ballistic missile program.[73]

The Arbabsiar plot underscored Qods Force leaders' willingness to work with criminal elements to further operational planning, perhaps as a means of countering enhanced law enforcement and intelligence efforts. It was a trend officials would note several more times, perhaps most tellingly in Baku. In October 2011, signals intelligence intercepted emails suggesting Azeri criminal elements with known ties to Iranian intelligence and militant groups were planning to transfer weapons and explosives into Azerbaijan from Iran. Over the next few weeks, weapons and operatives—including at least ten Iranian recruits—were smuggled into Azerbaijan, where they met up with other Azeri criminal recruits. The Azeris were strictly in it for the money, which they were paid up-front, and used their knowledge of the area to conduct surveillance of a Jewish school, an American-owned fast food restaurant, the office of an oil company, the US embassy, and specific American diplomats. "They were going after individuals," a State Department official familiar with the investigation confirmed. "They had names [of employees]. And they were interested in family members, too."[74]

Over several months, the operatives planned what one investigator described as a "jumble of overlapping plots," including assassinating US diplomats and a local rabbi or striking other Jewish targets. One subplot involved snipers using rifles with silencers; in another, a car bomb would target US embassy employees or their families. One plot was planned for December 2011, another for February 2012. Together, these were intended to avenge the assassinations of Iranian scientists, the captured leader of the network would later tell investigators. Some two dozen accomplices were arrested in a series of raids in early 2012, most of whom were local criminal recruits. But US officials concluded the plots were overseen by the Qods Force, with possible support from Hezbollah, as part of a coordinated, thirteen-month campaign targeting foreign diplomats in at least seven countries.[75] According to a US law enforcement official, Hezbollah paid criminal gang members $150,000 each to target the Jewish school in Baku.[76]

Meanwhile, Hezbollah operatives were busy planning operations to fulfill their end of the three-tiered plan: targeting Israeli tourists abroad. Around the same time that authorities foiled the January 2012 plot targeting Israeli vacationers in Bulgaria, another Hezbollah plot was disrupted in Greece.[77] But it was halfway across the world, in Bangkok, where Israeli and local authorities broke up a far more ambitious Hezbollah bid to target Israeli tourists.

On January 12, 2012, acting on a tip from Israeli intelligence, Thai police arrested Hussein Atris—a Lebanese national who also carried a Swedish passport—at Bangkok's Suvarnabhumi Airport as he attempted to flee the country. Originally from southern Lebanon, Atris moved to Sweden, where he married a Swede and ran a hair salon in Gothenburg before returning to Lebanon some ten years before his arrest in Thailand. His family was well known within Hezbollah circles: According to press reports, a relative—Muhammad Atris—was involved in the 1992 Mykonos assassinations (see chapter 3). Another suspect, whose police composite portrait strongly resembled Naim Haris, a Hezbollah recruiting agent whose photo Israeli officials publicized a year earlier, escaped. Within days police would issue an arrest warrant for Atris's roommate, a Lebanese man who went by the name James Sammy Paolo.[78]

Israel first informed the Thai authorities on December 22 that three Hezbollah operatives were preparing to attack popular Bangkok tourist sites where they expected to find Israelis, and passed on more details of the plot as they became available. Long a popular destination for Israeli vacationers, and a country with a history of Hezbollah activity, Thailand likely featured on Israeli officials' list of possible venues for Hezbollah attacks on Israeli tourists. The investigation led authorities to Mr. Atris, identified by Thai officials as a Hezbollah member.[79]

Questioned over the weekend of January 13, 2012, Atris led police to a three-story building on the outskirts of Bangkok where he and his housemate had stockpiled some 8,800 pounds of chemicals used to make explosives. The materials were already distilled into crystal form, a key step in building bombs.[80] Information on international shipping found at the scene indicated at least some of the explosives—which were stored in bags marked as cat litter—were intended to be shipped abroad. Intelligence officials surmised that Hezbollah had been using Thailand as an explosives hub—Atris rented the space a year earlier—and decided to use its on-hand operatives and material to target Israeli tourists. The conclusion should not have surprised: US officials already determined that Hezbollah was known to use Bangkok as a logistics and transportation hub, describing the city as "a center for a [Hezbollah] cocaine and money-laundering network."[81]

Seeking to contain the damage to their tourist industry, Thai officials maintained that the shipping information indicated Thailand was merely a transit site, not a target itself. But Israeli officials insisted Thailand was the target of a "high—concrete threat." The US embassy in Bangkok posted an alert of its own informing citizens of terrorist threats targeting Bangkok tourist areas. According to an embassy spokesman, the warning was based on "specific, credible, not-counterable threats."[82]

Kooky Terrorists and Sticky Bombs

The American ambassador to Baku may have breathed a sigh of relief when the Qods Force plot targeting him and his staff was disrupted in February 2012, but that was only a small portion of what the Qods Force had planned. Five attacks targeting Western diplomats were scheduled to be carried out as close to the February 12 anniversary of Mughniyeh's assassination as possible. The plot in Baku was foiled; another in Turkey was delayed; others would play out in India, Georgia, and Thailand.

On February 13, twin bombings targeted personnel from the Israeli embassies in New Delhi, India, and Tbilisi, Georgia. In both cases Qods Force operatives encountered more sophisticated security arrangements than anticipated and so they settled for modest strikes. In India, an assailant on a motorcycle attached a magnetized "sticky bomb" to a car taking the Israeli defense attaché's wife to pick up her children at school. She was injured, along with her driver and two others. About three hours later in Georgia, a similar sticky bomb attack targeted a local citizen employed by the embassy but was discovered and defused before doing any harm.[83] Just a month earlier, the deputy director of Iran's uranium enrichment facility at Natanz, Mostafa Ahmadi Roshan, was killed in a nearly identical attack, also using a sticky bomb. Roshan was the fifth Iranian scientist to be assassinated, and the use of sticky bombs to target Israeli diplomats was a not-so-subtle message of retaliation from Iran.[84]

The next day in central Bangkok, police rushed to the scene of an explosion in the early afternoon at a home rented by a group of Iranians. Two barefoot men fled the house, but a third was injured and tried to hail a taxi to escape. When the taxi refused to stop, the injured man threw a bomb at the car, destroying half the vehicle and injuring the driver and four bystanders. Police soon cornered the injured suspect, who tried to throw another explosive at them but was too weak; the resulting explosion blew off both his legs. The other two men were soon caught—one was detained at the airport as he tried to catch a flight to Malaysia; the other managed to escape to Malaysia, where he was arrested boarding a flight to Iran. A fourth suspect, an Iranian woman who rented the house, was believed to have fled to Iran.[85]

Unlike the Hezbollah plot foiled just weeks earlier in Thailand, in this plot Qods Force operatives were targeting Israeli diplomats, Thai investigators determined. At the scene of the explosion, authorities found several undetonated devices, all homemade magnetic sticky bombs of the same type used in India and Georgia.[86] In time, investigators would tie the three attacks together not only based on the explosives used but through phone records, travel documents, and money transfers. About a dozen Qods Force operatives coordinated their preparations for the attacks, which began ten months earlier in April 2011—not long after press reports tied the Stuxnet virus to Israel and the United States and the sticky bomb assassination of Iranian nuclear scientist Majid Shahriari to Israel. That month, Iranian operatives traveled to India and Thailand to scope out targets, followed by more trips in the summer and fall of 2011 to rent apartments, hire local help, arrange finances, and conduct surveillance. During his 2011 reconnaissance visits to India, Houshang Afshar Irani, identified by Indian police as the assailant who attached the bomb to the Israeli diplomatic vehicle in New Delhi, used a cell phone number that was also used in June 2011 in Tbilisi, Georgia.[87] According to Israeli officials, cell phone calls and text messages among operatives in Thailand, India, and Baku also link the attacks.[88] Based on these findings and more, US counterterrorism officials concluded that Iran was tied to the terrorist plots in Azerbaijan, Georgia, India and Thailand.[89]

In the case of the Thailand plot, senior Qods Force commander Majid Alavi reportedly arrived on-scene on January 19, 2012, traveling through Malaysia on a diplomatic passport bearing a fictitious name. Responsible for Qods Force Unit 400, Alavi previously tracked Iranian dissidents in places as varied as London and

Los Angeles. It was Alavi who ordered the attacks on Israeli diplomats to occur as close to the anniversary of Mughniyeh's death as possible.[90]

Yet despite the hands-on oversight of senior Qods Force officers, the attacks not only failed but demonstrated sloppy tradecraft and operational security—the very strengths for which the Qods Force is usually known. Aside from reusing phone numbers and SIM cards across multiple operations, operatives traveled on Iranian passports, checked into hotels as Iranians, carried Iranian currency in their wallets, and in at least one instance took out time from their surveillance to party with prostitutes. A group photo on one of the women's cell phones helped identify accomplices who fled the country.[91] In the words of one flabbergasted analyst, "It's as if there's a systematic policy of Iran recruiting low-rent, downright kooky terrorists."[92]

Instead of restoring Iran's damaged prestige, the attacks only further underscored Iran's operational limitations. Following the Green Revolution in Iran, the Qods Force gained prominence at the expense of the Ministry of Intelligence and Security over the latter's perceived soft-handed approach to suppressing political protests in Iran. Within the Qods Force, quick promotions of mediocre managers diluted the group's professional capabilities at the management level.[93] The problem was compounded when, desperate to quickly implement its new attack strategy and exact revenge for covert attacks against its nuclear program, the Qods Force traded speed for tradecraft, cut corners, and reaped what it sowed. Qods Force planners were stretched thin by the rapid tempo of their new attack plan and were forced to throw together random teams of operatives who had not trained together.[94]

Worse, despite Iran's preference for signature attacks targeting embassies, diplomats, or other official targets—and despite concerns by US intelligence that Iran was developing contingency plans for such attacks targeting the United States and its allies—Iranian planners found their chosen targets too well protected and settled for less-hardened targets.[95] In the end, not one of the five planned attacks could be considered an operational success. Ever since, Israeli officials say, the frustrated Iranian operatives have been "trying harder than ever" to execute successful attacks.[96]

The operational tempo continued apace. In March 2012, the Israeli National Security Council's Counterterrorism Bureau warned of terrorist threats against Jewish and Israeli targets in Turkey. According to the Turkish press, the warning came less than a week after Israeli intelligence tipped off Turkish authorities about a Qods Force plot to be carried out by at least four individuals who crossed the border from Iran armed with weapons and materials.[97] The plot, again targeting Israeli diplomats, had originally been timed to coincide with the other plots in February but was postponed.[98] In May, yet another Hezbollah attack targeting Israeli tourists was thwarted, this time at the Johannesburg airport in South Africa.[99]

Also in March, forty-year-old Hamid Kashkouli, an Iranian PhD student at the University of Pune in India, was deported for spying on Israeli nationals, a Jewish center, and a synagogue. According to Indian police, Kashkouli, who worked as a paid undercover agent of the Iranian government, traveled regularly to the Iranian consulate in Mumbai, where Iranian government officials reportedly met him, according to his driver. Intercepted emails revealed he was providing Iranian officials with pictures of Jewish people in the area and reporting on their business dealings.[100]

In June 2012, authorities in Nairobi, Kenya, arrested two Iranian nationals, both of them purportedly Qods Force operatives.[101] Prior to the two men's arrest, Kenyan police reported, they had scouted out the Israeli embassy, the British High Commission, and other sites, leading authorities to conclude the pair was planning attacks targeting Israeli, American, British, or Saudi Arabian interests in Kenya or elsewhere in Africa.[102] The day after their arrest, one of the two operatives led authorities to thirty-three pounds of RDX explosives hidden under a bush at the Mombasa Golf Club, overlooking the Indian Ocean.[103] Seemingly to deflect attention from Iran, the Iranian operatives apparently partnered with al-Shabab, the al-Qaeda-affiliated terrorist group in Somalia. This tie underscored how desperate Tehran was to see successful attacks carried out. That interest has only grown more acute, as efforts to disrupt Iran's nuclear program—from sanctions to assassinations to covert sabotage of equipment—continue to gain momentum.

A month after the Kenya plot was exposed, a Hezbollah operative targeting Israeli tourists in Cyprus was arrested. In October 2012, the Cypriot secret service foiled another attempt against Israeli tourists on cruise ships arriving at the Limassol port.[104] Tragically, Israeli tourists in Burgas, Bulgaria, were less fortunate. In the months that followed, more threats arose, prompting travel advisories from Cyprus and Greece to Thailand, Bulgaria, and Ukraine.[105] All told, more than twenty terror attacks by Hezbollah or Qods Force operatives were thwarted over the fifteen-month period between May 2011 and July 2012; by another count, nine plots were uncovered over the first nine months of 2012.[106] The key to all these attacks, however, whether carried out by Hezbollah or the Qods Force, was deniability. Both Hezbollah and Tehran wanted attacks carried out, but neither wanted to invite a full-fledged military response targeting them back in Lebanon or Iran. Ever since the July 2006 war, Nasrallah has reportedly refused to approve any attacks along the Israeli-Lebanese border for fear of sparking another full-scale war with Israel.[107]

Contrary to conventional wisdom, however, while Hezbollah and the Qods Force have worked together on some plots—Baku in 2008 and Istanbul in 2009, among others—in other cases they failed to deconflict their operational activities and found themselves engaged in completely disparate operations in the same place. When Hezbollah operatives laid the groundwork for a bombing in late 2011–early 2012 in Bangkok, they were apparently unaware that the Qods Force was also preparing an attack there. Whether the Qods Force was, in turn, ignorant of Hezbollah's activities there is unclear, but the Iranians appear not to have known Hezbollah was using Bangkok as an explosives distribution hub. And even once Hezbollah operative Hussein Atris was arrested in January 2012, the Qods Force operation there was not suspended. Similarly, within days after the explosion in Burgas, Bulgaria—while the investigation into the bombing and the search for accomplices was at its height— Bulgarian authorities reportedly caught a Qods Force operative scoping out a synagogue in the country's capital, Sofia.[108]

Meanwhile, even as Hezbollah remains committed to exacting revenge for Mughniyeh's death, IJO leaders grudgingly began to appreciate the difficulty of hitting a high-level Israeli target abroad. Such targets are typically well protected, so while Hezbollah operational planners continued to search for viable targets abroad, they initiated parallel plans for attacks targeting Israeli officials inside Israel.[109] Leveraging networks of criminal associates who typically trade intelligence for drugs, and sometimes recruiting Israeli-Arabs through ideological appeals to spy for the group, Hezbollah pursued at least two plots targeting Israeli officials within the country within a three-month period in 2012, both of which were thwarted.

In June 2012, Israeli authorities arrested eleven men caught smuggling twenty kilograms of C4 explosives into Israel from Lebanon. According to authorities, the explosives crossed the border with the help of an Israeli-Arab resident from Ghajar, a small town that straddles the Blue Line demarcating Israel's northern border with Lebanon. The facilitator, who was known to authorities as a drug smuggler with ties to Hezbollah, hid the bag of explosives in a field he owned before passing it along in a series of exchanges among drug smugglers who believed, according to Israeli security officials, they were smuggling drugs, not explosives. Abed Zoabi, a drug smuggler from Nazareth who received the explosives, reportedly helped smuggle Israeli cell phone SIM cards through Jordan to Hezbollah operatives in Lebanon so that he and George Nimer, a Lebanese drug dealer with ties to Hezbollah, could communicate directly with greater security.[110] According to Israeli officials, the explosives were intended to be used in one or more attacks targeting Israeli officials within the country.[111]

September brought another arrest, this time of an Israeli-Arab accused of collecting intelligence for Hezbollah on Israeli public figures, army bases, defense manufacturing plants, and weapons storage facilities over a three-year period. Like several other Hezbollah spies before him, Milad Khatib was reportedly recruited by a Hezbollah agent in Denmark. The two would meet in several European countries, as well as Turkey, investigators said. According to Israeli officials, Israeli president Shimon Peres visited Khatib's village in August, at which time Khatib took note of Peres's security detail, his vehicle, and more. His indictment indicates that Khatib was arrested before he could pass this information over to his Hezbollah handlers.[112]

Hezbollah's Contradictions Expose Vulnerabilities

In July 2012, National Counterterrorism Center director Matthew Olsen warned that while Iran and Hezbollah had not yet hit targets in the United States, US officials worry that could soon change. "We're seeing a general uptick in the level of activity around the world," he noted, adding that "both Hezbollah and the Qods Force have demonstrated an ability to operate essentially globally." In fact, the Hezbollah–Qods Force threat has sometimes eclipsed that of al-Qaeda. "There are times when we are briefing the White House [on terror threats and] at the top of the list [is] Hezbollah or Iran," according to Olsen.[113]

To be sure, Hezbollah's international campaign brought unwanted attention to the group's terrorist activities. Meanwhile, Hezbollah has been engaged in a host of other activities that have also tarnished the group's image. Taken together, these events present Hezbollah with the greatest set of challenges it has ever faced, and offer the international community an opportunity to counter Hezbollah's militant capabilities and political appeal like never before.

Hezbollah's role in Iran's shadow war, along with its own interest in targeting senior Israeli officials, has cast the group as a dangerous terrorist network capable of operating everywhere from Europe to Africa and Asia to the Americas. As tensions continue to mount over Iran's nuclear program, Hezbollah's strategic relationship with Iran—and the role it has already played in Tehran's shadow war with the West—gives officials worldwide ample cause for alarm.

At home, too, Hezbollah remains a destabilizing force, refusing to relinquish its private stockpile of arms to the Lebanese Army, despite periodic explosions of poorly stored weapons in which Lebanese citizens are killed. "We consider our arms like blood flowing in our veins," Hezbollah Shura Council member Mohammad Yazbek explained in October 2012, pledging not to turn over the party's weapons "no matter what the costs are."[114] The indictment of the four Hezbollah members accused of assassinating Rafiq Hariri and the internecine Sunni-Shi'a violence in West Beirut in 2008 also stalk the group on the home front. In 2012, when the government of New Zealand blacklisted Hezbollah's military wing, it did so in part based on a determination that the group's "pre-planned and well-coordinated operation" to take over West Beirut, and the group's use of machine guns and rocket-propelled grenades during street battles, fit its definition of a terrorist act.[115]

But it is the group's destabilizing activities in Syria since the country's uprising began in 2011 that have, as a journalist in Lebanon put it, "torn away the party's mask of virtue."[116] Within weeks of the uprising, Nasrallah himself called on all Syrians to stand by the regime.[117] As reports emerged in May 2011 that the Qods Force was helping the Syrian regime crack down on antigovernment demonstrators, Hezbollah denied playing "any military role in Arab countries."[118] But by the following month, Syrian protesters were heard chanting not only for Assad's downfall but also against Iran and Hezbollah. Video footage showed protesters burning posters of Nasrallah.[119] According to a senior Syrian defense official who defected from the regime, Syrian security services were unable to handle the uprising on their own. "They didn't have decent snipers or equipment," he explained. "They needed qualified snipers from Hezbollah and Iran."[120]

Over time, Hezbollah increasingly struggled to conceal its on-the-ground support of the Assad regime. In August 2012, the US Treasury Department blacklisted Hezbollah, already on the department's terrorism list, this time for providing support to the Assad regime. Since the beginning of the rebellion, Treasury explained, Hezbollah had been providing "training, advice and extensive logistical support to the Government of Syria's increasingly ruthless efforts" against the opposition.[121]

Most funerals for those killed in the fighting were quiet affairs, as Hezbollah tried to keep a lid on the extent of its activities in Syria, but news began to leak. In August 2012, Hezbollah parliamentarians reportedly attended the funeral of military commander Musa Ali Shehimi, who "died while performing his jihadi duty."[122] A few weeks later another Hezbollah military commander, Ali Hussein Nassif, was killed in Syria, along with two bodyguards, also "while performing his jihadi duties," according to a Hezbollah newspaper.[123] Hezbollah's "resistance" rhetoric notwithstanding, US officials informed the UN Security Council in October 2012, "the truth is plain to see: Nasrallah's fighters are now part of Assad's killing machine."[124] Two months later, a UN report confirmed Hezbollah members were in Syria fighting on behalf of the Assad government.[125] Amid increasing concern that the struggle in Syria would engulf the region in conflict, Hezbollah set up training camps near Syrian chemical weapons depots in November 2012. According to one senior US official, "The fear these weapons could fall into the wrong hands is our greatest concern."[126]

For a group that has always portrayed itself as the vanguard standing up for the dispossessed in the face of injustice and that has always tried to downplay its sectarian and pro-Iranian identities, supporting a brutal Alawite regime against the predominantly Sunni Syrian opposition risked shattering a long-cultivated image. In the end, the strategic necessity of preventing the collapse of the Assad regime—which, if replaced by a regime representing the country's Sunni majority would, at the least, be far less friendly to Hezbollah and possibly oppose it outright—took precedence over the need to maintain the party's image.

Meanwhile, the rebellion in Syria has exacerbated Hezbollah's anxiety over the instability plaguing Iran ever since the Green Movement uprising in 2009. Flush with revenues from skyrocketing oil prices, Iran reportedly ramped up its funding to defray Hezbollah's soaring costs as it attempted to rebuild following its 2006 war with Israel.[127] The funds went toward fulfilling Hezbollah's unprecedented needs in areas such as restocking weapons supplies, investing in reconstruction, and buying favor within both the various sectarian communities and Lebanese towns and villages that suffered damage during the war. The 2009 elections provided another repository for funds, with Hezbollah increasingly desperate for support in order to compete with its Sunni political rivals, who were funded by Saudi Arabia. According to one report, as the election neared, Iran allegedly pledged as much as $600 million to Hezbollah for its political campaign.[128] In recent years, Israeli sources estimated, Iran had provided Hezbollah some $1 billion in direct military aid.[129]

With this influx of Iranian money, Hezbollah hired more people and invested in more programs, assuming the inflated support would persist. Yet, just as Hezbollah accustomed itself to a larger budget, Iran became a much less reliable donor. By mid-January 2009, oil prices had fallen to about $36 per barrel and remained under $60 until May, drastically reducing Iran's oil profits.[130] International sanctions against Iran's nuclear program, meanwhile, became harsher. Such factors combined with crippling subsidies for basic commodities and soaring inflation to severely hamper Iran's economic growth. Then, as the economy crashed, Tehran's ruling clerics blatantly stole the country's June 2009 elections, spurring months of protests by the Green Movement.

The economic pressures on Iran, according to Israeli intelligence, forced the regime to temporarily slash its annual budget for Hezbollah by up to 40 percent in early 2009.[131] As a result, Hezbollah was compelled to enact austerity measures, reducing salaries and paid staff and placing several building projects on hold. Hezbollah operatives feared for their jobs, and Hezbollah beneficiaries feared for their handouts. The ensuing cutbacks caused tension within the organization as certain programs and activities were prioritized over others.[132]

Suddenly constrained after years of abundant Iranian funding, Hezbollah turned to its preexisting criminal enterprises to boost its assets. The income earned through these illicit enterprises is viewed by the organization as critical for providing social services to an expanding swath of the Lebanese electorate, paying the families of its fighters, and investing in its growing arsenal of rockets and other advanced weapons. In diversifying its economic portfolio, Hezbollah also doubled down on its most lucrative criminal enterprises: drug trafficking and money laundering.

Taken together, all these activities—engaging in a worldwide terror campaign, threatening stability both at home in Lebanon and next door in Syria, and expanding its involvement in criminal activities—make Hezbollah increasingly vulnerable to the kind of serious, concerted international effort to counter its activities that it has successfully avoided to date. Many governments have shied away from taking action against Hezbollah on the pretext that the group is a duly elected political party and a key provider of social welfare services in Lebanon. But as the party muddies the waters between its more legitimate, public activities and its inherently illicit, clandestine pursuits, it invites ever-greater scrutiny.

Hezbollah should be judged by the totality of its actions. It cannot be forgiven its criminal, terrorist, or militant pursuits simply because at the same time it also engages in political or humanitarian ones. Hezbollah's leaders often insist the group does not maintain support networks around the world, let alone carry out attacks abroad. "We have not carried out operations anywhere in the world," Hezbollah secretary-general Hassan Nasrallah insisted in 2003.[133] But as the schemes and plots documented here demonstrate, Hezbollah can and has mobilized operatives for everything from criminal enterprises to terrorist attacks well beyond Lebanon's borders.

While Hezbollah is composed of multiple committees and branches, it operates as a singular entity. Hezbollah, the US intelligence community has determined, is "a multifaceted, disciplined organization that combines political, social, paramilitary, and terrorist elements" in which decisions "to resort to arms or terrorist tactics [are] carefully calibrated."[134] Hezbollah's Naim Qassem concurs: "We don't have a military wing and a political one; we don't have Hezbollah on one hand and the resistance party on the other. . . . Every element of Hezbollah, from commanders to members as well as our various capabilities, [is] in the service of the resistance and we have nothing but the resistance as a priority," Qassem insisted in October 2012.[135]

In light of its history of violence and extremism, its rapid expansion into organized criminal activities from narcotics trafficking to money laundering and more, its violent activities at home in Lebanon and next door in Syria, and above all else its continued and ongoing use of international terrorism, it is high time the international community conducted a thorough and considered discussion of the full range of Hezbollah's "resistance" activities, and what to do about them. With this book, I hope to kick-start that discussion.

Notes

1. "Israelis Killed in Bulgaria Bus Terror Attack, Minister Says," CNN, July 18, 2012.

2. Gordon Fairclough, "Bulgaria Releases New Image of Suspect," Wall Street Journal, August 1, 2012; "Struggle to Identify Bulgaria Bus Suicide Bomber," BBC, July 20, 2012.

3. Europol, The Hague, Netherlands, "Europol Supports Investigation into Terrorist Attack at Burgas Airport, Bulgaria," press release, February 5, 2013.

4. Stewart Bell, "A Family Affair: Canadian Suspected in Bulgaria Bus Bombing Was Related to Terrorist Who Died Planting Explosives," National Post (Canada), February 12, 2013.

5. Ibid.; Republic of Bulgaria, Ministry of the Interior, Statement of Minister Tsvetan Tsvetanov, press release, February 5, 2013.

6. Sebastian Rotella, "Before Deadly Bulgaria Bombing, Tracks of a Resurgent Iran-Hezbollah Threat," ProPublica and Foreign Policy, July 30, 2012.

7. Tom Kelly, "Was Bulgaria Bomber British?" Daily Mail (London), July 27, 2012.

8. Nicholas Kulish and Eric Schmitt, "Hezbollah Is Blamed for Attack on Israeli Tourists in Bulgaria," New York Times, July 19, 2012.

9. "Interview with Israeli Defense Minister Ehud Barak," CNN (The Situation Room), July 30, 2012.

10. Rotella, "Before Deadly Bulgaria Bombing."

11. Nicholas Kulish and Jodi Rudoren, "Plots Are Tied to Shadow War of Israel and Iran," New York Times, August 8, 2012.

12. Author interview with Israeli official, Tel Aviv, September 13, 2012.

13. Yaakov Katz, "Bulgaria Foils Terror Attack against Israelis," Jerusalem Post, January 8, 2012.

14. Rotella, "Before Deadly Bulgaria Bombing."

15. Barak Ravid, "Man Detained in Cyprus Was Planning Attack on Israeli Targets for Hezbollah," Haaretz (Tel Aviv), July 14, 2012; US Department of State, Office of the Coordinator for Counterterrorism, Country Reports on Terrorism 2009, August 2010, p. 105.

16. Cyprus Police, Hossam Taleb Yaakoub Deposition, Criminal Record Number 5/860/12, July 7, 2012; Joby Warrick, "Elaborate Surveillance Operation Raises Concerns

about Broader Hezbollah Attacks," *Washington Post,* February 26, 2013; Nicholas Kulish, "Hezbollah Courier Was Told to Track Israeli Flights," *New York Times,* February 21, 2013.

17. "Report of the Commission for Internal Security and Public Peace Regarding the Production and Distribution of Unauthorized Synthetic Drugs and the Problems Associated with the Ministry of Internal Affairs (MVR)," Commission for Internal Security and Public Peace, February 2008.

18. Yaakov Katz, "Analysis: Connecting the Dots from Bulgaria to Syria," *Jerusalem Post,* July 18, 2012.

19. Matthew Levitt, "Did Hezbollah Do It?" *Daily Beast,* July 18, 2012.

20. Tony Badran, "Hezbollah Is Being Elusive on Waliyat al-Faqih," *NOWLebanon,* June 24, 2009.

21. Dennis Ross and David Makovsky, *Myths, Illusions, & Peace: Finding a New Direction for America in the Middle East* (New York, NY: Viking Press, 2009), 256.

22. US Department of Defense, *Unclassified Report on Military Power of Iran,* "CDA—Military Power of Iran," April 2010.

23. "Ministers Warned of Terrorism Threat from Iran," *Guardian* (London), June 29, 2006.

24. US National Intelligence Council, "The Terrorist Threat to the US Homeland" (National Intelligence Estimate), July 2007.

25. James Risen, "Before Bin Laden, One of World's Most Feared Men," *New York Times,* February 14, 2008.

26. Author interview with Israeli intelligence official, Tel Aviv, June 3, 2008.

27. US Congress, Senate Committee on Armed Services, *Worldwide Threats to the National Security of the United States: Hearing before the Committee on Armed Services,* 112th Cong., 2d sess., February 16, 2012, Statements of James Clapper and Lt. Gen Ronald Burgess.

28. US Congress, Senate, Committee on Homeland Security and Governmental Affairs, Statement of Matthew G. Olsen, *Homeland Threats and Agency Responses.*

29. Norton, *Hezbollah: A Short History,* ch. 5.

30. Nora Boustany, "Hezbollah and Its Allies Celebrate Win in Regional Vote," *Washington Post,* June 7, 2005.

31. "Lebanese Government Collapses after Hezbollah Ministers Resign," *Fox News,* January 12, 2011.

32. Author interview with Australian intelligence officials, Canberra, May 25, 2009; author interview with British intelligence officials, London, April 15, 2010.

33. Australian Government, Attorney General's Department, "Hizballah External Security Organisation," May 16, 2009.

34. "Nasrallah: We Wouldn't Have Snatched Soldiers If We Thought It Would Spark War,"*Haaretz* (Tel Aviv), August 27, 2006.

35. Jack Khoury, "Report: Nasrallah Says Attacking Israel May Have Been a Mistake," *Haaretz* (Tel Aviv), February 3, 2007.

36. John Kifner, "Hezbollah Leads Work to Rebuild, Gaining Stature," *New York Times,* August 16, 2006.

37. Donald Kerr, "Emerging Threats, Challenges, and Opportunities in the Middle East," keynote address, Washington Institute for Near East Policy (Washington, DC), Soref Symposium, May 29, 2008.

38. Justin Walker and Leila Golestani, "Threat Analysis: Hamas and Hezbollah Sleeper Cells in the United States," Urban Warfare Analysis Center, US Army Research Laboratory, March 18, 2009.

39. US Congress, Senate, Committee on Homeland Security and Governmental Affairs, Statement of Matthew G. Olsen, *Homeland Threats and Agency Responses*.

40. Anthony Shadid and Alia Ibrahim, "Bombing Kills Top Figure in Hezbollah," *Washington Post*, February 14, 2008.

41. US Congress, Senate, Committee on Homeland Security and Governmental Affairs, Statement of Matthew G. Olsen, *Homeland Threats and Agency Responses*.

42. "Stuxnet: Targeting Iran's Nuclear Program," IISS *Strategic Comments*, International Institute for Strategic Studies, February 2012.

43. Yossi Melman, "U.S. Website: Mossad Killed Iranian Nuclear Physicist," *Haaretz* (Tel Aviv), February 4, 2007.

44. Muhammad Sahimi, "Report: Iranian Ex-Deputy Defense Minister, Missing 4 Years, in Israeli Jail," *PBS Frontline*, December 12, 2010.

45. "Profile: Shahram Amiri," *BBC*, July 14, 2010.

46. Alan Cowell, "Blast Kills Physics Professor in Tehran," *New York Times*, January 12, 2012.

47. Author interview with Israeli intelligence officials, September 13, 2012.

48. Ibid.

49. Ibid.

50. Author interview with Israeli intelligence officials, September 13, 2012; Rotella, "Before Deadly Bulgaria Bombing."

51. Author interview with Israeli intelligence officials, September 13, 2012.

52. Alexandra Sandels, "Kuwait: Media Banned from Reporting on Alleged Iran Spy Ring," *Los Angeles Times*, May 6, 2010.

53. Author interview with Israeli intelligence officials, September 13, 2012.

54. Attila Somfalvi, "Warning: Mediterranean Basin Dangerous," *Ynetnews* (Tel Aviv), April 10, 2011.

55. Author interview with Israeli intelligence officials, September 13, 2012.

56. Yaakov Lappin, "Hezbollah Terror Attack on Israelis Abroad 'Is Imminent,'" *Jerusalem Post*, April 21, 2011.

57. Abdullah Povian, "Nasrallah: All Who Referred to the 'Scud' Did So without Providing Evidence, but We Are Able to Meet Defense Commitments," *Al-Rai al-Aam* (Kuwait), April 30, 2010; see also "Nasrallah to Rai Aam: No Evidence Was Presented about Scuds," Mideast Wire, April 30, 2010.

58. David Ignatius, "Intelligence Links Iran to Saudi Diplomat's Murder," *Washington Post*, October 13, 2011.

59. Sebnem Arsu, "Bomb Wounds 8 in Heart of Istanbul," *New York Times*, May 26, 2011.

60. "Seven Injured in Etiler Explosion in Istanbul, Officials Say," *Dunya Times* (Istanbul), May 26, 2011.

61. "Bike Bomb Wounds 7 in Istanbul, Kurd Group Suspected," Reuters, May 26, 2011.

62. Oren Kessler, "Istanbul Bombing Was Hezbollah Strike on Israeli Envoy," *Jerusalem Post*, July 18, 2011.

63. US Department of State, Bureau of Counterterrorism, *Country Reports on Terrorism 2011*, July 2012, pp. 235–36.

64. US Department of Justice, Office of Public Affairs, "Two Men Charged in Alleged Plot to Assassinate Saudi Arabian Ambassador to the United States," press release, October 11, 2001.

65. Ibid.

66. US Department of Justice, Office of Public Affairs, "Man Pleads Guilty in New York to Conspiring with Iranian Military Officials to Assassinate Saudi Arabian Ambassador to the United States," October 17, 2012.

67. Ignatius, "Intelligence Links Iran."

68. US Department of the Treasury, "Treasury Sanctions Five Individuals Tied to Iranian Plot to Assassinate the Saudi Arabian Ambassador to the United States," October 11, 2011.

69. HM Treasury Department, *General Notice: Renewal of Final Designations, Terrorist Asset-Freezing etc. Act 2010*, October 10, 2012.

70. Jonathan Evans, Director General of the Security Service, Address at the Lord Mayor's Annual Defence and Security Lecture, London, June 25, 2012.

71. Statement of James R. Clapper, *Worldwide Threat Assessment of the U.S. Intelligence Community*, January 2012.

72. Ellen Nakashima and Joby Warrick, "Stuxnet Was Work of U.S. and Israeli Experts, Officials Say," *Washington Post*, June 1, 2012.

73. Ken Dilanian, "Mysterious Blasts, Slayings Suggest Covert Efforts in Iran," *Los Angeles Times*, December 4, 2011.

74. Joby Warrick, "U.S. Officials among the Targets of Iran-Linked Assassination Plots," *Washington Post*, May 27, 2012.

75. Warrick, "U.S. Officials among the Targets"; "Members of Group Accused of Terrorist Acts against Israeli Citizens Sentenced," *News.Az* (Azerbaijan), September 26, 2012.

76. Judith Miller, "Bagels and Plots: Notes on the NYPD's High Holy Days Threat Briefing," *City Journal* (New York), September 7, 2012.

77. Author interview with Israeli official, Tel Aviv, September 13, 2012.

78. Dudi Cohen, "Bangkok Threat: Terrorist's Swedish Connection," *Ynetnews* (Tel Aviv), January 15, 2012; "Second Terror Suspect Sought, Court Issues Warrant for Atris's Housemate," *Bangkok Post*, January 20, 2012.

79. Barak Ravid, "Thailand Hunting Hezbollah Operatives Planning Terror Attacks against Jews, Israelis," *Haaretz* (Tel Aviv), January 15, 2012; Thomas Fuller, "In Twisting Terror Case, Thai Police Seize Chemicals," *New York Times*, January 16, 2012.

80. James Hookway, "Thai Police Seize Materials, Charge Terror-Plot Suspect," *Wall Street Journal*, January 17, 2011; Rotella, "Before Deadly Bulgaria Bombing."

81. Fuller, "In Twisting Terror Case."

82. Attila Somfalvi, "CTB Issues Thailand Travel Advisory," *Ynetnews* (Tel Aviv), January 13, 2012; Embassy of the United States, Bangkok, Thailand, "Emergency Message to U.S. Citizens: Possible Terrorist Threat," press release, January 13, 2012; Hookway, "Thai Police Seize Materials"; Fuller, "In Twisting Terror Case."

83. Isabel Kershner and Michael Schwirtz, "Israel Blames Iran for Attacks in India and Georgia," *New York Times*, February 13, 2012.

84. Rick Gladstone, "Iran Tightens Its Security for Scientists after Killing," *New York Times,* January 17, 2012.

85. "Bangkok Blast Suspects 'Targeting Israeli Diplomats,'" *BBC,* February 16, 2012.

86. Joel Greenberg, "Israel Says Thai Bombs Similar to Those in India, Georgia," *Washington Post,* February 15, 2012.

87. Jason Burke, "Iran Was behind Bomb Plot against Israeli Diplomats, Investigators Find," *Guardian* (London), June 18, 2012.

88. Kulish and Rudoren, "Plots Are Tied to Shadow War."

89. Warrick, "U.S. Officials among the Targets"; US Congress, Senate, Committee on Homeland Security and Governmental Affairs, Statement of Matthew G. Olsen, *Homeland Threat Landscape and U.S. Response.*

90. Rotella, "Before Deadly Bulgaria Bombing."

91. Thomas Fuller, "Explosions in Bangkok Injure Suspected Iranian National," *New York Times,* February 14, 2012; Piyaporn Wongruang, "Suspects Partied in Pattaya," *Bangkok Post,* February 17, 2012.

92. Sebastian Rotella, "Azerbaijan Seen as New Front in Mideast Conflict," *Los Angeles Times,* May 30, 2009.

93. "Iran: IRGC Rise Increases the Influence of Radicals," Oxford Analytica, November 5, 2009.

94. Miller, "Bagels and Plots."

95. Statement of Dennis C. Blair, *Annual Threat Assessment of the Intelligence Community.*

96. Author interview with Israeli intelligence officials, September 13, 2012.

97. "Israel Warns of 'Attacks' in Turkey," *Hurriyet Daily News* (Turkey), March 8, 2012.

98. Author interview with Israeli intelligence officials, September 13, 2012.

99. Itamar Eichner, "South Africa Attack against Israelis Thwarted," *Ynetnews* (Tel Aviv), July 20, 2012.

100. Gitesh Shelke, "Iranian Spy was PhD Student at UOP," *Pune Mirror,* April 26, 2012.

101. Associated Press, "Officials: Iranians Targeted Israeli, US Interests," July 2, 2012.

102. Daniel Howden, "Iranian Agents Arrested in Kenya Were 'Looking for Foreign Targets,'" *Independent* (London), July 4, 2012; author interview with Israeli intelligence officials, September 13, 2012.

103. Zoe Flood, "Kenyan Police Arrest Iranians Suspected of Terror Plot," *Telegraph* (London), June 22, 2012.

104. "Cyprus Thwarts Terror Attack against Israelis," *Ynetnews* (Tel Aviv), October 18, 2012.

105. Gili Cohen, "Israeli Counterterrorism Bureau Warns of Attacks on Israelis during High Holidays," *Haaretz* (Tel Aviv), September 6, 2012.

106. Eichner, "South Africa Attack"; author interview with Israeli intelligence officials, September 13, 2012; Mark Hosenball, "New York Police Link Nine 2012 Plots to Iran, Proxies," Reuters, July 21, 2012.

107. Author interview with Israeli intelligence officials, September 13, 2012.

108. Ibid.

109. Ibid.

110. Yaakov Katz, Yaakov Lappin, and Ben Hartman, "Shin Bet Nabs Explosive-Smuggling Israeli-Arabs," *Jerusalem Post*, August 9, 2012.

111. Author interview with Israeli Intelligence officials, September 13, 2012.

112. Yonah Jeremy Bob, "Shin Bet Nabs Alleged Hezbollah Spy Living in North," *Jerusalem Post*, October 4, 2012.

113. Noah Shachtman, "'Hot War' Erupting with Iran, Top Terror-Watchers Warn," *Wired*, July 26, 2012.

114. Hussein Dakroub, "Hezbollah Buries Slain Fighters, Vows to Keep Arms," *Daily Star* (Beirut), October 5, 2012.

115. Government of New Zealand, "Case to Designate Lebanese Hizbollah's Military Wing."

116. Michael Young, "Syria Widens Hezbollah's Contradictions," *Al Arabiya News* (Dubai), October 4, 2012.

117. "Hezbollah Chief Calls on Syrians to Stand by Assad Regime," *Los Angeles Times*, May 26, 2011.

118. Joby Warrick, "Iran Reportedly Aiding Syrian Crackdown," *Washington Post*, May 27, 2011; Thomas El-Basha, "Nasrallah Blasts Obama, Urges Arabs Withdraw Peace Initiative," *Daily Star* (Beirut), May 25, 2011.

119. "Syrian Protestors Turn on Iran and Hezbollah," *France 24*, June 3, 2011.

120. Nate Wright and James Hidler, "Syrian Regime 'Importing Snipers' for Protests," *Australian*, January 26, 2012.

121. US Department of the Treasury, "Treasury Designates Hizballah Leadership," press release, September 13, 2012.

122. Babak Dehganpisheh, "Hezbollah Increases Support for Syrian Regime, U.S. and Lebanese Officials Say," *Washington Post*, September 26, 2012.

123. Elizabeth A. Kennedy, "Official: Hezbollah Fighters Killed in Syria," *Daily Star* (Beirut), October 2, 2012.

124. Edith M. Lederer, "US Says Hezbollah Is Part of Assad's War Machine," Associated Press, October 15, 2012.

125. United Nations, Office of the High Commissioner for Human Rights, *Independent International Commission of Inquiry on the Syria Arab Republic Established pursuant to United Nations Human Rights Council Resolutions S-17/1, 19/22 and 21/26*, December 20, 2012.

126. David Sanger and Eric Schmitt, "Pentagon Says 75,000 Troops Might Be Needed to Seize Syria Chemical Arms," *New York Times*, November 15, 2012.

127. Walid Phares, "Hezbollah's Billion Petrodollars," Human Events (Washington, DC), January 11, 2008.

128. Stratfor, "Iran: A Need for Budget Cuts," April 14, 2009.

129. Yaakov Katz, "Iran Said to Have Cut Hizbullah Aid by 40%," *Jerusalem Post*, December 16, 2010.

130. US Energy Information Administration, "U.S. FOB Costs of OPEC Countries Crude Oil," October 1, 2012.

131. Katz, "Iran Said to Have Cut Hizbullah Aid."

132. Author interview with former Israeli intelligence official, March 7, 2011.

133. Nicholas Blanford, "Hizbullah Chief Offers Carrot, Stick," *Christian Science Monitor*, July 31, 2003.

134. Statement of Dennis C. Blair, *Annual Threat Assessment of the Intelligence Community*.

135. "Party's Arms not for Internal Destabilitzation: Hezbollah," *Daily Star* (Beirut), October 7, 2012.

Afterword (2015)

SINCE THE ORIGINAL EDITION OF this book went to press in mid-2013, Hezbollah's international activities have continued apace. Thai security disrupted yet another planned attack in Bangkok in April 2014. Yemen and Bahrain are struggling with Shi'a rebellions aided and abetted by Hezbollah and the IRGC. Peruvian authorities arrested a suspected Hezbollah member in October 2014, who allegedly planned to attack Israeli and Jewish targets. And considerably more evidence has emerged in the case of Hossam Yaakoub, the Hezbollah operative in Cyprus, who is now serving a four-year sentence for helping to plan attacks against Israeli tourists on the island. As a result of this and several other cases, as well as Hezbollah's involvement in the war in Syria, the European Union added the military and terrorist wings of Hezbollah to its list of proscribed terrorist groups in July 2013.

Hearings also began at the United Nations' Special Tribunal for Lebanon in The Hague in January 2014. The Special Tribunal is investigating the 2005 killing of Rafiq Hariri, a former prime minister of Lebanon. In October 2013, prosecutors added a fifth suspect, Hassan Merhi, to the four men originally charged. The five Hezbollah members are all being tried in absentia. Hezbollah itself has slammed the tribunal as an American-Israeli plot and threatened to "cut off the hand" of anyone who tried to arrest its men.[1] And in January 2015, the special prosecutor investigating the 1994 bombing of the AMIA Jewish community center was found dead in his apartment under extraordinarily suspicious circumstances.

Still, in the past few years, Hezbollah's involvement in Syria has been its chief concern and will likely remain that way for some time. It is also of great concern to Hezbollah's Shi'a constituency, and indeed to Lebanese more broadly. The Lebanese army has now teamed up with Hezbollah to address security concerns, sparking accusations that the army is taking sectarian sides, most notably against Sunni militants in the town of Tripoli. Violent clashes between Hezbollah and Sunni jihadis such as Jabhat al-Nusra are flaring along the Lebanon-Syria border. Critics argue that the Shi'a organization is pulling Lebanon into Syria's war, while supporters argue that the violence in Lebanon would have been even worse had Hezbollah not stepped in. Either way, the group shows no sign of relenting.

Speaking in late May 2013, Hezbollah secretary-general Hassan Nasrallah declared that the battle in Syria was Hezbollah's fight: "We will continue along the road, bear the responsibilities and the sacrifices. This battle is ours, and I promise you victory."[2] To that end, Hezbollah went "all-in," fighting alongside Syrian leader Bashar al-Assad, his Alawite sect, regime loyalists, and Iranian Revolutionary Guardsmen against Syrian rebels.

There are several motivations for Hezbollah's presence in Syria. First, Hezbollah seeks to keep Assad in power for its own and Iran's interests. For years Syria has been a reliable patron of Hezbollah's, a relationship that only grew deeper under the rule of Bashar al-Assad.[3] While Bashar's father, Hafiz al-Assad, used Hezbollah as a proxy, he also kept the group at arm's length and at times used force to keep the group in line. In 1988, Syria issued a warrant for the arrest of Imad Mughniyeh, the head of Hezbollah's Islamic Jihad Organization.[4] By 2010, Syria was not just allowing the transshipment of Iranian arms to Hezbollah through Syria, but it was reportedly providing Hezbollah long-range Scud rockets from its own arsenal.[5] Nasrallah explained the nature of Hezbollah's alliance with Syria very clearly:

> I frankly say that Syria is the backbone of the resistance, and the support of the resistance. The resistance cannot sit with hands crossed while its backbone is held vulnerable and its support is being broken or else we will be stupid. Stupid is he who stands motionless while watching death, the siege and conspiracy crawling towards him. He would be stupid then. However, the responsible, rational man acts with absolute responsibility.[6]

Second, Hezbollah's support of the Assad regime is not just owing to a romantic sense of obligation. Hezbollah is keen to make sure that air and land corridors remain open for the delivery of weapons, cash, and other materials from Tehran. Until the Syrian civil war, Iranian aircraft would fly into Damascus International Airport, where their cargo would be loaded onto Syrian military trucks and escorted into Lebanon for delivery to Hezbollah.[7] Now, Hezbollah is desperate to either secure the Assad regime, its control of the airport, and the roads to Lebanon, or, at a minimum, establish firm Alawite control of the coastal areas so Hezbollah can receive shipments through the air and sea ports in Latakia. Over the past few years, FBI investigations into Hezbollah criminal enterprises in the United States and Europe have revealed at least two cases in which Hezbollah operatives planned to procure weapons—in one case MANPADs intended to take down Israeli airplanes—and ship them to Hezbollah through Latakia.[8] In one case, a European Hezbollah procurement agent told an FBI undercover agent that the weapons would be exported to Latakia, Syria, where Hezbollah controlled the port. Secrecy would be guaranteed there, he assured the undercover agent, because Hezbollah could shut down all the cameras when the shipment arrived and no shipping paperwork would be required once the items arrived in Syria.[9]

And third, Hezbollah is also fighting for the Assad regime in support of Iran's interests. Hezbollah's ideological commitment to Iranian ayatollah Ruhollah Khomeini's revolutionary doctrine of *velayat-e faqih* (guardianship of the jurist), which holds that a Shi'a Islamic cleric should serve as the supreme head of government, is a key source of tension since it means that the group is simultaneously committed to the decrees of Iranian clerics, the Lebanese state, its sectarian Shi'a community within Lebanon, and fellow Shi'a abroad.

In fact, Nasrallah was initially resistant to the idea of sending Hezbollah into Syria. US intelligence assessments noted that Nasrallah at first declined repeated requests from Iranian leaders, in particular Qods Force commander Qassem Soleimani, for Hezbollah to send large numbers of experienced fighters on behalf of the Assad regime. While some Hezbollah leaders were inclined to provide the fighters, others resisted what they (correctly) feared would prove to undermine their position in Lebanon and be, as one official put it, "bad for the brand." Nasrallah only acquiesced, officials explained, after receiving a personal appeal from the Iranian Supreme Leader, Ayatollah Ali Khamenei. Iran, the Supreme Leader made clear, not only expected Hezbollah to act, but to act decisively.[10]

Hezbollah Goes to War

Since the Syrian uprising began in 2011, Hezbollah's combatant role in the country has become more formal and overt. While Hezbollah initially performed more of an advisory and training role in Syria, it upped the ante when Assad appeared to be in serious danger of falling. Hundreds of Hezbollah's best were on the ground and directly participating in the fight for Qusayr, a strategically crucial town near the Lebanese border, in April 2013. The impact of Hezbollah's Syrian involvement cannot be overstated, as was seen most clearly in the battle for Qusayr, where Hezbollah gunmen reportedly fought house to house, took significant losses, and played the decisive role in turning the tide against the rebels who ultimately lost the battle. That battle also laid bare the myth that Hezbollah was not fighting in Syria. The successful regime offensive dealt the opposition a severe blow. Although Hezbollah has not taken on combat responsibility to the same degree since Qusayr, where coherent Hezbollah units took the lead in the battle, it remains strongly invested in the war, sending both fighters and trainers.[11]

Indeed, much like with Unit 3800, Hezbollah has invested considerable resources in training Syrian forces. Recruits to a new national paramilitary organization, the National Defense Force, received training in "basic combat skills, urban warfare, and guerrilla tactics, while others [were] taught specialized tactics such as infiltration, surveillance, and intelligence collection."[12] "When we first started helping the Syrians, it was true they had big problems with their army," said one Hezbollah fighter. "They had no skill, no discipline, and no leadership. Now, the men they have left have learned a lot and are very serious fighters. They've become more like Hezbollah."[13] Thanks to Hezbollah and its Shi'a allies adding much-needed manpower, Assad has been able to survive and even recover lost ground.

Yet many of these fighters were redeployed to Iraq in response to the takeover of Mosul by ISIS in June 2014, particularly after Grand Ayatollah Ali al-Sistani issued a call for Shi'a fighters to defend Iraq.[14] During Friday prayers on June 13, Sistani declared that it was "the legal and national responsibility of whoever holds a weapon, to hold it to defend the country, the citizens and the holy sites."[15] Qassem Soleimani reportedly ordered Hezbollah to send its own fighters to Syria to replace the departing Iraqi militants.[16] In Iraq, Hezbollah would likely dispatch only small numbers of trainers and special operators. Yet, given the group's past special operations and training activities in Iraq and its close ties with Iran's elite Qods Force, even a modest deployment would likely have a significant impact. As in the past, Hezbollah's contribution does not have to include hundreds of fighters, but only a limited number of experienced trainers and special operations "consultants." This type of contribution would not overstrain the organization, and it could facilitate far-reaching achievements for Iraqi Shi'a militias.

Unfortunately for Assad and Hezbollah, the redeployment of Iraqi Shi'a may well have a detrimental effect on their battle for Syria. Hezbollah, in attempting to backfill the ranks of the departing Iraqis, has had to resort to fielding less experienced fighters. Additionally, from March 2011 to July 2014, the Syrian Observatory for Human Rights estimated that more than five hundred Hezbollah fighters had been killed, including many "among Hezbollah's most elite fighters." A *Wall Street Journal* report interviewed a Syrian Shi'a fighting for Hezbollah, who expressed "surprise at what he saw as the greenness and naiveté of the recent Hezbollah recruits from Lebanon and their lack of arms and equipment."[17]

At the same time, intercommunal violence increased significantly in Lebanon, including gunfights between Sunni and Alawite militants in Tripoli, between Sunnis and Shi'a in Sidon, and bombings by Sunni militants—including the al-Qaeda affiliate Jabhat al-Nusra—in Shi'a neighborhoods in the cities of Beirut and Hermel. Hezbollah's stronghold in the Dahiyeh suburb of Beirut was struck on multiple occasions. Strictly Iranian buildings—an Iranian cultural center and the embassy itself—were also targeted. A double suicide bombing struck the Iranian embassy in November 2013, followed by a similar suicide bombing at the cultural center in February 2014. More than twenty people were killed at the embassy, including an Iranian diplomat. The Abdullah Azzam Brigades, an al-Qaeda affiliate based in Lebanon, took responsibility for both attacks, in addition to several other bombings in Hezbollah's stronghold in southern Beirut, as responses to the Shi'a organization's activities in Syria. It threatened more such attacks until Hezbollah withdrew. In a statement on its Twitter account, the Brigades warned, "We tell our people in Syria that Iran's party won't enjoy security in Lebanon until you restore security in Syria."[18] Jabhat al-Nusra claimed responsibility for other bombings. Protective sandbags and even concrete blast walls began to appear in Beirut.[19]

Losing Hearts and Minds

By siding with the Assad regime, its Alawite supporters, and Iran, and taking up arms against Sunni rebels, Hezbollah placed itself at the epicenter of a sectarian conflict that has nothing to do with the group's purported raison d'être: "resistance" to Israeli occupation. One Shi'a Lebanese satirist put it this way: "Either the fighters have lost Palestine on the map and think it is in Syria," he said, "or they were informed that the road to Jerusalem runs through Qusayr and Homs," locations in Syria where Hezbollah has fought with Assad loyalists against Sunni rebels.[20]

The implication is clear: for many Lebanese, Hezbollah was no longer a pure "Islamic resistance" fighting Israel, but a sectarian militia and Iranian proxy doing Assad and Ayatollah Khamenei's bidding at the expense of fellow Muslims. And it is therefore of no surprise that the pokes came from extremist circles too. In June 2013, the Abdullah Azzam Brigades released a statement challenging Hezbollah chief Hassan Nasrallah and his fighters "to fire one bullet at occupied Palestine and claim responsibility" for it. They could fire at Israel from either Lebanon or Syria, the statement continued, seeing as Hezbollah "fired thousands of shells and bullets upon unarmed Sunnis and their women, elderly and children, and destroyed their homes on top of them."[21]

But while taunts might be expected from radical Sunni extremist groups, Hezbollah now faced challenges it never would have anticipated just a few years ago. For example, the day before Nasrallah gave a speech in August 2013, Lebanese president Michel Suleiman called, for the first time ever, for the state to curtail Hezbollah's ability to operate as an independent militia outside the control of the government.[22]

Nevertheless, Hezbollah doubled down in its support for the Assad regime, even after bombs started going off in the Dahiyeh. Nasrallah was crystal clear: "If you are punishing Hezbollah for its role in Syria, I will tell you, if we want to respond to the Dahiyeh explosion, we would double the number of fighters in Syria—if they were 1,000 to 2,000, and if they were 5,000, they would become 10,000." Indeed, Hezbollah—and Nasrallah himself—has cast its lot with Assad to the end. "If," Nasrallah added, "one day came, and required that Hezbollah and I go to Syria, we will do so."[23] In fact, as the Treasury Department noted when it relisted Hezbollah as a terrorist group in August 2012, Nasrallah has personally overseen its activities in Syria.[24]

At one point, Nasrallah tried to paper over the fact that Lebanese Shi'a and Lebanese Sunnis were now openly battling one another in Syria, and threatening to drag that sectarian fighting across the border into Lebanon. After finally officially acknowledging Hezbollah's involvement in Syria in an April 30, 2013, speech, he proposed in May that Lebanese Shi'a and Sunnis agree to disagree over Syria. Addressing Lebanese Sunnis, Nasrallah said, "We disagree over Syria. You fight in Syria; we fight in Syria; then let's fight there. Do you want me to be more frank? Keep Lebanon aside. Why should we fight in Lebanon?"[25] But that pitch did not go over so well with Nasrallah's fellow Lebanese, who wanted an end to Lebanese interference in the war in Syria, not a gentleman's agreement that Lebanese citizens would only slaughter one another across the border.

In that same speech, Nasrallah addressed the "two grave dangers" facing Lebanon. The first, he argued, is "Israel and its intentions, greed, and schemes." The second danger is related to "the changes taking place in Syria." As for Israel, Nasrallah warned that it threatens Lebanon every day. And as for Syria, the regime there faces an "axis led by the United States, which is for sure the decision maker." The British, French, Italians, Germans, Arabs, and Turks are involved too, but "all of them work for the Americans." But what is the true force behind the "changes taking place in Syria"? "We also know that this axis is implicitly supported by Israel because the U.S. project in the region is Israeli *cum laude*." Hezbollah is not fighting in Syria as part of a sectarian conflict, Nasrallah insisted, but combating a radical Sunni, *takfiri* project with ties to al-Qaeda that "is funded and backed by America" out of an American interest to destroy the region. In other words, the war in Syria is no longer a popular revolution against a political regime but a place where America is seeking to impose its own political project on the region. Nasrallah concluded, "Well, we all know that the U.S. project in the region is an absolutely Israeli project." And so, by fighting in Syria, "today we consider ourselves defending Lebanon, Palestine, and Syria."[26] Syrian government officials reinforced this claim in January 2014, arguing that Hezbollah was "preemptively" defending Lebanon through its involvement in Syria.[27]

There are, however, few takers for the contorted logic that the Syrian rebellion is an American or Israeli scheme, or that participating in the Syrian civil war in any way benefits the Lebanese, outside Hezbollah's staunchest Shi'a supporters. And the proportion of Shi'a in Lebanon has fallen considerably since the war in Syria began. By February 2015, as many as an estimated 1.6 million mostly Sunni Syrian refugees had fled to Lebanon,[28] marking a significant shift in the sectarian balance of a state whose confessional political system is based on a sense of proportional representation (albeit outdated) among its confessional communities. This has, to say the least, exacerbated sectarian resentment. Not that Hezbollah has shown any sign of hoping to tamp down tensions; as late as July 2014, Western reporters were describing scenes such as the following:

> During a recent visit to [the Sayyeda Zeinab] shrine on the outskirts of Damascus, the effects of the accumulating losses were temporarily obscured by the unstinting enthusiasm of a group of children, some as young as 5 years old, standing at the shrine's entrance. . . .
>   They stood in military formation at the entrance of the golden-domed mausoleum and mosque where Shiites believe the Prophet Muhammad's granddaughter Zeinab is entombed. "Who are you?" the instructors shouted. "Hezbollah!" the children bellowed back.[29]

Hezbollah has suffered some serious personnel losses recently, both in Lebanon and in Syria. Hassan Laqis, Hezbollah's chief military procurement officer (see chapter 6), was assassinated in Beirut in December 2013. While the prime suspects are the Israelis, Sunni extremists have not been ruled out. Numerous high-ranking officers have been reported killed in Syria, most notably Fawzi Ayub, whose death Hezbollah announced in May 2014. Ayub, the naturalized Canadian citizen, would-be bomber, and longtime member of the IJO (see chapter 8), graced the FBI's Most Wanted Terrorists list. The death of a person in Syria of Ayub's stature within Hezbollah demonstrates the extent to which Hezbollah has gone "all-in" in its defense of the Assad regime.

The Shadow War Continues

Other operatives remain active abroad, though Hezbollah's commitment to Syria has tied up a major part of its operational "bandwidth." Increasingly, its abilities are becoming geared more toward outright military action than terrorism, as thousands of its fighters are active in Syria.[30] Yet while the group's international terrorism activities may have been largely placed on the backburner since the civil war began in 2011, they have not been shut down completely. In 2012, the US State Department noted, "Hizballah stepped up the pace of its terrorist plotting."[31] The killing of Israeli tourists in Burgas, Bulgaria, in July 2012 clearly demonstrated Hezbollah's continued interest in its shadow war. Three suspects have since been identified in the case. The bomber himself was identified as a dual Lebanese-French citizen named Mohammad Hassan El-Husseini, and died in the explosion. His two suspected accomplices were also dual citizens, a Lebanese-Australian, Meliad Farah, and a Lebanese-Canadian, Hassan El Hajj Hassan.[32] Given Hezbollah's history with recruiting Western citizens for such operations, none of the trio's dual citizenship should surprise.

As discussed in chapter 12, Hezbollah operative Atris Hussein was arrested by Thai authorities in Bangkok in January 2012, soon leading the police to a warehouse holding nearly 9,000 pounds of bomb-making material on the city's outskirts. Atris denied any ties to Hezbollah and was eventually sentenced in September 2013 to two years and nine months in jail for possessing explosive material.[33] Then, on April 1, 2014, Israel's Counter-Terrorism Bureau issued an updated travel advisory that recommended against visiting a number of countries, including Thailand.[34] Two weeks later, two men were arrested, a French-Lebanese named Daoud Farhat and a Filipino-Lebanese named Youssef Ayad, accused of links to Hezbollah and of planning to attack Israeli tourists during the Jewish holiday of Passover. One unnamed source suggested that the cell to which the two suspects belonged could have had up to nine members. Ayad reportedly confessed that the group entered Thailand with the intent of bombing Khao San Road, a popular tourist spot, and promised to lead investigators to a weapons stash in the Philippines.[35]

On the other side of the world, Nigeria's State Security Service seized weapons and arrested three Hezbollah operatives in May 2013. Among the weapons found in a warehouse in the northern city of Kano were submachine guns, antitank mines, and an RPG with twenty-one missiles. In a country better known for the terrorist group Boko Haram, it was "the first time that Nigerian authorities [had] alleged that Hezbollah has an operational interest in the country."[36] Authorities also asserted that the weapons were meant for attacks on American and Israeli targets. One of the men arrested was later sentenced to life in prison for illegal arms trafficking and possession, but the other two were freed on lack of evidence, as the judge noted that membership in Hezbollah was not in itself an offense in Nigeria.[37]

Since American and multinational forces withdrew from Iraq, Unit 3800 has been put to work elsewhere in the region, primarily in Yemen. There, Hezbollah and Qods Force personnel have helped the Houthis, a Zaidi Shi'a insurgent group, fight the government. In January 2013, Yemeni authorities intercepted a smuggler's boat from Iran, containing a variety of arms, explosives, and antiaircraft missiles. Both Yemeni and Western officials suspected the boat was intended for Yemeni militants. As far back as 2012, John Brennan, then the counterterrorism chief for the White House, said Iran and Hezbollah were "training militants in Yemen and Syria."[38] National Intelligence Director James Clapper reinforced this point in his January 2014 "Worldwide Threat Assessment," noting that "Iran will continue to provide arms and other aid to Palestinian groups, [Houthi] rebels in Yemen, and Shia militants in Bahrain to expand Iranian influence and to counter perceived foreign threats."[39] Worries have only increased with the takeover of the capital by Shi'a Houthi rebels in September 2014 and the release of suspected Hezbollah and IRGC members from Yemeni prisons.[40]

Back on Israel's doorstep, Jordan arrested eight men, including a Syrian fugitive, for Hezbollah activities in May 2013. They were charged in August 2014 with plotting to carry out terrorist attacks on US soldiers and the Israeli embassy in Jordan, as well as recruiting for Hezbollah.[41]

And finally, in October 2014, a Lebanese citizen named Mohammad Amadar was arrested in Peru. The suspected Hezbollah member had military-grade explosive materials in his home, including detonators, TNT, and gunpowder. More chemicals were found in the garbage outside. According to reports of his arrest, Amadar had gathered intelligence on potential Israeli and Jewish targets in Peru, such as the Israeli embassy and Chabad houses.[42]

The Cyprus Case Study: A Window into Hezbollah Recruitment and Training

In contrast to the aforementioned plots, a treasure trove of information has poured out of the trial in Cyprus of Hossam Yaakoub, the Lebanese-Swedish dual citizen and self-confessed Hezbollah operative arrested just days before the Burgas bombing.[43]

Arrested in his Limassol hotel room on the morning of July 7, 2012, just a few hours after returning from a surveillance operation at Larnaca Airport, Yaakoub was first interviewed by Cypriot police over a five-hour period starting within an hour of his arrest. At first, Yaakoub provided only basic background information about himself and insisted he was nothing more than a Lebanese businessman looking to import Cypriot goods into Lebanon. He had been to Cyprus three times, he explained, first as a tourist about three years earlier, then for business in December 2011, and now again in July 2012. Yaakoub stuck to his cover story throughout his first two police interviews on July 7 and July 11, 2012.

Several hours passed after the second interview, and as soon as Cypriot police began their third interview of Yaakoub later that same night the story began to change. "With regard to the previous deposition I gave to the police," Yaakoub said, "I did not tell the whole truth." Four deposition pages later, Yaakoub had changed his story, claiming to have been approached in Lebanon by a man named Rami in June 2012. He described clandestine meetings with Rami, always conducted during outdoor walks on which he was not allowed to bring his cell phone. Rami tasked Yaakoub with checking on the arrival of Israeli flights at Larnaca Airport. Whatever favors he asked, Yaakoub recalled Rami saying, would "be done for the sake of the religion and the 'end.'" Yaakoub detailed Rami's instructions to set up e-mail accounts through which he could contact Rami, to change his appearance and avoid cameras at the airport, and to collect leaflets from specific Cypriot hotels. Yaakoub said he took the $500 that Rami offered, traveled to Cyprus, wore a hat and glasses and avoided security cameras when he went to the airport to observe the arriving Israeli flights, and went to an internet cafe to create the new e-mail accounts per Rami's instructions.

Yaakoub described Rami as a thirty-eight-year-old Lebanese man, muscular and five foot eleven, with a fair complexion, green eyes, and blond hair. "I could recognize him from a picture," Yaakoub noted, adding, "I don't know if Rami belongs to Hizb Allah, he never mentioned such a word, but I suspected that he belongs to this organization." Yaakoub concluded by saying, "Everything I said in my deposition is the truth." It was not the truth, however. "Rami" never existed. Only later would Yaakoub admit that "the story I told you in a previous deposition about a guy called Rami, as you can guess, did not happen."

The next interview took place a couple days later and ran for two and a half hours in the middle of the night. By the time the interview ended at 3:15 AM, police had a much fuller picture of Yaakoub's recruitment by Hezbollah and the nature of his mission in Cyprus and his previous operations elsewhere in Europe. Again, Yaakoub opened the interview with a bombshell: "I am an active member of Hezbollah organization [sic] for approximately four years now. I was recruited by a Lebanese called Reda in 2007."

For a full week after his arrest, Yaakoub kept Cypriot police at bay first by sticking to his well-established cover story as a Lebanese merchant and then by conceding that he was asked to collect information on Israeli flights but making up a fake story about his recruitment. In fact, Hezbollah has a long history of teaching its operatives basic but effective resistance-to-interrogation techniques. In March 2007, the same year Hezbollah recruited Yaakoub, a seasoned Hezbollah operative was captured by British forces in Iraq. In that case, Ali Musa Daqduq al-Musawi pretended to be deaf and mute for several weeks before speaking and admitting to being a senior Hezbollah operative (see chapter 10).[44] From a counterintelligence perspective, misleading one's interrogators for a period of time enables other operatives to escape. The reason Yaakoub ultimately revealed the truth after a week of deceptive statements likely parallels Musawi's experience in Iraq: presented with hard evidence undermining his cover stories, and having bought time for accomplices to cover their tracks, there was no longer a need to mislead.

How Hezbollah spotted Yaakoub is unknown, although their interest in his European citizenship and import business was clear. Reda apparently called Yaakoub on the telephone suddenly, inviting Yaakoub for a meeting in his office at a Hezbollah bureau responsible for "student issues." It was there, not at a Hezbollah military or terrorist facility, that Yaakoub was told he was needed "for the secret mission of Hizb Allah." Yaakoub was flattered: "I accepted because I considered that he needed me for something great and I was for them the chosen one."

Reda immediately arranged for Yaakoub to meet his first Hezbollah trainer, Wahid, later that same day outside a Beirut storefront. Yaakoub worked with Wahid for two to three months before going to Sweden to visit his father. Yaakoub explained that "when I say 'work' I mean that Wahid explained to me roughly the secret operation, in which I would participate. He always pointed out that nobody should know anything, neither my family nor my friends." Wahid trained Yaakoub for another couple of months after he returned from Sweden, all of which was theoretical discussion focused on "explaining to me that my secret mission would be surveillance and undercover activities on behalf of Hezbollah." Then Wahid handed Yaakoub off to his next trainer.

A man named Yousef trained Yaakoub for another five to seven months, focusing on operational security concepts. Yousef taught Yaakoub "how to handle my personal life and my activities, so that people won't get information about me and so that I can work undercover and persuasively without giving rise to suspicions . . . he taught me how to create stories undercover."

Later, Mahdi took over the training regimen, which included Yaakoub's first test-run. In 2008, Yaakoub was given a large, thin envelope to deliver to someone in Antalya, Turkey, with specific instructions about the day, time, and place where the delivery was to be made. The meeting point was outside a Turkish department store, and the recipient recognized Yaakoub based on the specific hat and clothes Yaakoub wore, per his instructions. Once they exchanged the prearranged code words, the handoff was made. Yaakoub stayed in Turkey a couple of days more, at Hezbollah's expense, before returning to Lebanon. "I don't know what its contents was [sic] and I had not entitlement to ask, because everything is done in complete secrecy within the organization," he explained.

Having passed this test, Yaakoub was finally ready for military training and was assigned yet another instructor named Abu Ali, whom he first met at a secret meeting arranged by Mahdi. Abu Ali organized Yaakoub's military training over the next few years, which involved six to seven different training sessions each lasting for three to five days at a Hezbollah military camp. Yaakoub would get picked up at different spots in Beirut each time and was driven in closed vans so he and fellow trainees could not see where they were going. Once there, Yaakoub added, it was clear from the topography that they were in southern Lebanon.

Each military training group comprised ten to thirteen trainees, all of whom wore hoods—as did the instructors—to hide their identities from one another. They each slept in their own tent and trained at another site. Yaakoub described being trained in the use of multiple firearms, from handguns to shoulder-fired missiles, including the FN Browning, Glock, AK-47, M-16, MP-5, PK-5, and RPG-7. He also trained in the use of C4 explosives. Over the same period of time, while under the overall responsibility of Abu Ali, Yaakoub attended training sessions in Beirut basements focused on teaching surveillance techniques, how to work safely undercover, how to create a cover story, and resistance-to-interrogation techniques such as how to defeat a polygraph test.

In 2009, Yaakoub explained, Abu Ali sent him on a mission to Cyprus "to create a cover story for people to get to know me, to keep coming with a justifiable purpose and without giving rise to suspicions." He traveled to Cyprus via Dubai to strengthen his cover, and spent a week vacationing in Ayia Napa at Hezbollah's expense. When he returned to Cyprus two years later, he would be able to say that the idea for importing merchandise from Cyprus came to him while on vacation there in 2009.

Each time he returned from a mission, including this one, Yaakoub was debriefed by a Hezbollah security official who wanted to know where Yaakoub went, who he met, what the climate was like, how people live in the given location, and the state of the economy. On his return from his 2009 Cyprus vacation, Yaakoub was assigned to a new instructor, Aiman, who sent him on his next mission to Lyon, France, at Hezbollah's expense. His assignment: to receive a bag from one person and deliver it to someone else, all using the same tradecraft (identification signs and code words) he employed on his last courier mission in Turkey. Shortly thereafter, Aiman sent Yaakoub to Amsterdam, where he retrieved a cell phone, two SIM cards, and an unknown object wrapped in newspapers, and he brought them back to Aiman in Lebanon.

Then, in December 2011 and again in January 2012, Aiman sent Yaakoub back to Cyprus "to create a cover story" as a merchant interested in importing juices to Lebanon from a specific local company in Cyprus. He was also tasked with collecting information about renting a warehouse in Cyprus. "I did all these things after receiving clear instructions from Hizb Allah, so to have Cyprus as a basis [sic] and be able to serve the organization," he said. Yaakoub maintained he did not know why Hezbollah wanted this base of operations, but he speculated "perhaps they would commit a criminal act or store firearms and explosives."

For all of his European travels on behalf of Hezbollah, Yaakoub used his Swedish passport, which he had renewed for this purpose. Once his basic training was complete, Yaakoub became a salaried Hezbollah operative, earning $600 a month since 2010.

Yaakoub's next interview with Cypriot police occurred on July 16, 2012, in the late evening. His first words were: "My operational name, that is my nickname within Hezbollah, is Wael." Yaakoub offered more details about Hezbollah's operational security protocols, such as the need to answer a coded question each time he was picked up in Beirut for military training out of town. Aiman provided the updated passwords each time, and then different passwords would be provided by each instructor.

Yaakoub now admitted that his December 2011 visit to Cyprus actually involved several separate missions. First, Aiman tasked Yaakoub with gathering details on a parking lot behind the Limassol Old Hospital and near the police and traffic departments. Aiman wanted Yaakoub to take pictures and be able to draw a schematic of the area on his return. Yaakoub was to specifically look to see if there were security cameras, if payment was required on entry, if car keys were left with a parking attendant, and if there was a security guard, among other observations. Yaakoub was also told to find internet cafes in Limassol and Nicosia, which he marked on a map for Aiman, and to purchase three SIM cards for mobile phones from different vendors on different days, which he did. He also found good meeting places, such as at a zoo in Limassol and outside a castle in Larnaca. In the event a meeting was necessary, Yaakoub would receive a text message. A text about the weather meant to go to the Finikoudes promenade in Larnaca that day at 6 PM. If no one showed up, Yaakoub was to return the following day at 2:00 PM, and then again the next day at 10:30 AM. Aiman also wanted Yaakoub "to spot Israeli restaurants in Limassol, where Jews eat 'kosher,'" but an internet search indicated there were none. Later, in January 2012, Yaakoub was instructed to check out the Golden Arches Hotel in Limassol, collect brochures, and reconnoiter the area (he did survey the area, but the hotel was being renovated).

"Hizb Allah knows Cyprus very well," Yaakoub told police, adding he thought his tasks were intended to update the group's files "and create a database." He insisted that he was not part of any plot "to hit any target in Cyprus with firearms or explosives," and that he would have had the right to refuse the mission if asked to execute such an act.

Five days passed before Yaakoub's final police interview, which took place midday on July 22, 2012. Yaakoub conceded he was "aware of the ideology and the objectives of [the] Hizb Allah organization" and claimed that this was limited to protecting Lebanese territory "with all legal means"; this, he noted, included "armed struggle, military operations, and the political way." He opposed terrorism, he stressed, saying it was different from war. Yaakoub expressed support for "the armed struggle for the liberation of Lebanon from Israel," but he was "not in favor of the terrorist attacks against innocent people." Then, he added: "I don't believe that the missions I executed in Cyprus were connected with the preparation of a terrorist attack in Cyprus. It was just collecting information about the Jews, and this is what my organization is doing everywhere in the world."

On March 21, 2013, a Cypriot criminal court convicted Yaakoub of helping to plan attacks against Israeli tourists on the island in July 2012. In their eighty-page decision, the judges rejected Yaakoub's defense that he collected information for Hezbollah but did not know for what it would be used. There could be no "innocent explanation" of Yaakoub's actions, the court determined, reasoning that he "should have logically known" his surveillance was linked to a criminal act.[45]

Reason for Concern

Taken together, the Bulgarian and Cypriot cases present compelling evidence of Hezbollah's return to traditional tradecraft. As the Yaakoub case makes clear, several years before the Qods Force instructed Hezbollah to rejuvenate its IJO terrorist wing in January 2010, the group had already been recruiting operatives with foreign passports, and providing new recruits with military training and surveillance skills. Yaakoub was recruited in 2007 while Mughniyeh was still alive. Indeed, while Mughniyeh's assassination prompted the group to resume international operations in a way they had not since before 9/11, Hezbollah never stopped identifying and recruiting new operatives for a variety of different types of missions at home and around the world.

There is no question, however, that the operational failures that followed Mughniyeh's assassination demonstrated that the group's foreign operational capabilities had weakened over time. When Mughniyeh was killed, and later when Iran wanted Hezbollah to play a role in its "shadow war" with the West, Hezbollah was not yet fully prepared to do so. Yet the Bulgaria and Cyprus cases suggest that this may no longer be true. Yaakoub was no anomaly, as the Burgas attacks made clear. Like Yaakoub and the Burgas operatives, some of those new recruits are Western citizens. During one of his training sessions, Yaakoub heard another trainee speaking fluent Arabic with some English words mixed in. According to Yaakoub, the trainee spoke with a distinctly American accent.[46]

And in light of recent revelations, Americans may be in increased danger. On February 12, 2008, American spies on the ground in Damascus, Syria, conducted reconnaissance of a Hezbollah master terrorist and informed their Israeli counterparts, who pushed the button on a remote-controlled, custom-made American explosive device that instantly killed Imad Mughniyeh. The spies had to wait several days for a chance to detonate the bomb without anyone around in order to avoid collateral damage. In fact, they resisted the temptation to kill two dangerous birds with one stone when Mughniyeh was spotted walking the street with his Iranian counterpart, Commander Soleimani.[47]

The story, revealed by the *Washington Post* and *Newsweek* in January 2015,[48] reads like a paperback thriller—except this story is true and could lead Hezbollah to consider targeting American interests directly, as it had in the 1980s and 1990s. Writing in 1994, the FBI assessed that Hezbollah would be unlikely to carry out an attack in the United States—and put at risk its lucrative fund-raising, procurement, and other activities here—but the group could still decide to carry out reasonably deniable attacks targeting American or other Western interests in reaction to direct threats to the group or its own interests.[49] An American hand in the killing of Imad Mughniyeh would certainly seem to check that box.

To be sure, the group never completely stopped targeting American interests. As the director of the National Counterterrorism Center testified in September 2014, Hezbollah plots are not only Israel's concern: "Lebanese Hezbollah remains committed to conducting terrorist activities worldwide. . . . We remain concerned the group's activities could either endanger or target U.S. and other Western interests."[50] And now, with the CIA's role in the hunt for Mughniyeh revealed, it may not be long before Hezbollah once more puts Americans in the crosshairs of sniper attacks, or plants car bombs targeting US diplomats.

A Mysterious Death in Buenos Aires

In January 2015, Argentinean special prosecutor for the AMIA bombing Alberto Nisman released his latest report. A few days later he was found dead in his apartment under extraordinarily mysterious circumstances.

The story dates back to 2011, seventeen years after the AMIA bombing, when Iranian officials claimed they were prepared to "engage in constructive dialogue" with Argentina about the case, although they insisted that talk of an Iranian link was nothing more than "plots and political games."[51] The offer was roundly criticized, since the Argentinean investigation led by Mr. Nisman concluded beyond any shadow of a doubt that the attack was the work of Iranian and Hezbollah agents. Nonetheless, by January 2013, this Iranian willingness to look for any non-Iranian perpetrators of the plot had translated into a bilateral agreement between Tehran and Buenos Aires to jointly investigate the bombing.[52] For Mr. Nisman and his fellow prosecutors and investigators—whose tireless pursuit of justice in this case led to an exhaustive investigation and the issuing of arrest warrants and INTERPOL Red Notices for the arrest of several Iranian officials—this new deal was akin to inviting the fox into the henhouse.

Nisman continued to pursue the case, however, and in May 2013 released a 502-page report summarizing the findings of Argentinean investigators and accusing Iran of establishing covert intelligence networks throughout Latin America—including in Argentina, Brazil, Paraguay, Uruguay, Chile, Colombia, Guyana, Trinidad and Tobago, and Suriname—dating back to the 1980s. This latest report also included new evidence pointing to Mohsen Rabbani, the former Iranian imam turned cultural attaché in Argentina, as mastermind of the AMIA bombing. Moreover, it concluded that Rabbani's covert activities in the region had not ended with his indictment in Argentina. Instead, it identified him as the "coordinator of the Iranian infiltration of South America, especially in Guyana."[53]

But according to Nisman's latest report, it appears that the entire time he was investigating Iran and Hezbollah's roles in the AMIA bombings, others were actively conspiring to bury his investigation and redirect the investigation away from Iran and Hezbollah. According to one court-approved wiretap Nisman cites in his 2015 report, the conspirators plan was that "another hypothesis will come up, with different evidence." This new "evidence" would lead the prosecutor—Mr. Nisman—"high and dry, because he never saw it, the evidence, what's going to come up now." This would be accomplished by building up "a new AMIA enemy, someone new as the one responsible."[54] They rejected blaming "the Israel people" for the bombing—since that would be a stretch too far—but talked about concocting a "local fascist connection" to the bombing instead.[55]

Before Nisman filed his report with the court clerk in January 2015, an Argentinean court had already ruled the deal signed with Iran unconstitutional in May 2014, but the government of President Cristina Fernandez de Kirchner quickly appealed the ruling.[56] Then, events took a series of turns for the worse.

On January 14, 2015, Nisman filed his legal complaint formally accusing President de Kirchner and Foreign Minister Hector Timerman of trying to cover up Iran's role in the AMIA bombing. Kirchner and Timerman, Nisman claimed, were covering Iran's tracks in exchange for diplomatic and economic opportunities with Iran.[57] Four days later, a day before he was due to appear before Argentina's Congress to present new evidence backing up his accusations of a cover-up, Nisman was found dead in his apartment.[58]

After Nisman filed his complaint, Kirchner's administration insisted the charges "have no foundation,"[59] but neither those charges nor the sudden, suspicious death of the prosecutor who brought them would be the first time the case was marred by political corruption and illegal activities at the highest levels, as detailed in chapter 4.

Once Nisman was brought in as special prosecutor, his single-minded determination to see justice served and bring closure to the victims and their families energized the AMIA investigation and produced a thorough, compelling case file pointing to Iran and Hezbollah as the culprits. Given such a definitive conclusion by the government-appointed investigators, the deal between Buenos Aires and Tehran eight years later was suspect from the outset. And it was never clear how the joint investigation planned to contend with the extensive evidence of Iran's role in the attack, which had been documented in the government's own voluminous investigative files.

With Nisman's suspicious death, a deal with Iran may no longer be necessary to derail the investigation. Alberto Nisman was a uniquely determined and undeterred prosecutor. Argentine media quickly responded with rage and incredulity, and Buenos Aires and other cities saw thousands of protestors take to the streets with placards reading "#YoSoyNisman."[60] The reactions were not all harmonious, however. Anti-Semitic posters appeared in Buenos Aires one morning, around the time Nisman—who was Jewish—was buried in a local Jewish cemetery. "The good Jew is the dead Jew," the posters read. "The good Jew is Nisman."[61]

Now, in Nisman's absence, the public is left hoping for closure and justice not only for the victims of the AMIA bombing but for the man who tried more than anyone to bring them just that.

Syria's Foreign Legions

Yet the Syrian conflict remains Hezbollah's priority. With the prominence of violent Sunni outfits such as Jabhat al-Nusra and the Islamic State, much attention has been given to the extremists battling Assad. But Sunni extremism is only one side of the radical equation in Syria. In March 2014, FBI agents arrested Michigan-based Mohammad Hassan Hamdan at the Detroit Metropolitan Airport as he attempted to travel to Syria to fight alongside Shi'a Hezbollah.[62] Just as it did with Unit 3800 in Iraq, Hezbollah has also been once again instrumental in training Shi'a proxies for Iran. It has employed two of its Iraqi proxies, Asaib Ahl al-Haqq and Kata'ab Hezbollah, to build up auxiliary forces to assist the Assad regime.[63] The key militias that Hezbollah has assisted in Syria include Jaysh al-Shabi, Liwa Abu Fadl al-Abbas (the al-Abbas Brigade), Kata'ab Sayyid al-Shuhada, Liwa Zulfiqar, and Liwa Ammar ibn Yasir.[64]

Jaysh al-Shabi (The People's Army) is a US-designated terrorist organization and militia force that maintains a connection to the Assad regime's military apparatus,[65] highlighting how the regime has adapted its forces to fight an asymmetric and irregular war. According to the US Treasury Department, Jaysh al-Shabi "was created, and continues to be maintained, with support from Iran and Hizballah and is modeled after the Iranian Basij militia."[66]

In contrast to Jaysh al-Shabi, the other militias are not within Syria's security apparatus but are new independent proxies allegedly established with the assistance of the IRGC and Hezbollah.[67] Most of these groups use the same type of iconography and narratives that Hezbollah has put forward as it relates to the "resistance," its "jihadist duties," and protecting Shi'a shrines.

The attraction of Syria's war for Shi'a around the world raises worries of a Shi'a "foreign fighters legion." Before the summer 2014 campaign by IS, Iraqi Shi'a fighting in Syria were estimated to be as high as five thousand.[68] And Iranians are present in smaller support and advising roles. In April 2011, the entire Qods Force was designated by President Obama's Executive Order 13572 for human rights violations in Syria.[69] Shi'a from Saudi Arabia, Cote d'Ivoire, and Afghanistan have also flown to Syria to fight on behalf of the regime, and Yemeni Houthi fighters are reported to be going to Syria through Hezbollah camps in Lebanon to fight with the regime and Hezbollah.[70]

Combined with the influx of Sunni foreign fighters, the long-term implications for the region are dire. The Syrian war is a classic case of a proxy war, in this case between Saudi Arabia and other Sunni Gulf states on the one hand, and Iran on the other—with the additional, especially dangerous overlay of sectarianism. The sectarian vocabulary used to dehumanize the "other" in the Syrian war is deeply disturbing, and suggests both sides view the war as a long-term battle in an existential, religious struggle between Sunnis and Shi'a.[71]

Further, the war in Syria is now being fought on two parallel planes: one focused on the Assad regime and the Syrian opposition, and the other on the existential threats the Sunni and Shi'a communities each perceive from each other. The former might theoretically be negotiable, but the latter almost certainly is not. The ramifications for regional instability are enormous and go well beyond the Levant. But they are felt more immediately and more powerfully in Syria, in Lebanon to the west, and Iraq to the east, than anywhere else. Hezbollah is a central player in these events, fighting alongside the Assad regime and Iranian Qods Force. The outcome of this battle will shape not only the region for many years to come but the future of Hezbollah as well.

Notes

1. Kareem Shaheen, "Day of Justice for Lebanon," *The Daily Star,* January 16, 2014, http://www.dailystar.com.lb/News/Lebanon-News/2014/Jan-16/244209-day-of-justice-for-lebanon.ashx#axzz3I0mw7ldH.

2. Hasan Nasrallah, "Words on Eid al-Muqawama and the Liberation," al-Manar TV, May 25, 2013.

3. Ze'ev Schiff, "Don't Underestimate Assad Jr.," *Haaretz,* August 2, 2002, http://www.haaretz.com/print-edition/opinion/don-t-underestimate-assad-jr-1.37991.

4. Magnus Ranstorp, *Hizb'Allah in Lebanon: The Politics of the Western Hostage Crisis* (New York: St. Martin's, 1997) 71, 85–86.

5. Mark Lavie, "Israeli Officials: Syria Gave Hezbollah Scuds," Associated Press, April 14, 2010, http://www.nbcnews.com/id/36520789/ns/world_news-mideast_n_africa/t/israeli-officials-syria-gave-hezbollah-scuds/#.UfvwZ9LVCLp.

6. Hasan Nasrallah, "Words on Eid al-Muqawama."

7. Yossi Melman and Sof Hashavua, "In Depth: How Iranian Weapons Go through Syria to Hezbollah," *Jerusalem Post,* May 25, 2013, http://www.jpost.com/Features/In -Thespotlight/In-Depth-How-Iranian-weapons-go-through-Syria-to-Hezbollah -314312; Phil Alito, "Iran-Lebanese Hezbollah Relationship in 2008," *AEI Iran Tracker,* March 1, 2009, http://www.irantracker.org/military-activities/iran-lebanese-hezbollah -relationship-2008#_ednref12.

8. Author interview with law enforcement officials, Philadelphia, PA, March 11, 2010; US Department of Justice, "Conspiracy to Procure Weapons, Including Anti-Aircraft Missiles"; *USA v. Dani Nemr Tarraf et al.,* Indictment, November 20, 2009; Pretrial Detention Order, *United States of America v. Dani Nemr Tarraf,* US District Court, Eastern District, Pennsylvania, December 3, 2009; "Alleged Arms Dealer for Hezbollah Charged," *Philadelphia Inquirer,* November 24, 2009.

9. Author interview with law enforcement officials, Philadelphia, PA, March 11, 2010; US Department of Justice, "Conspiracy to Procure Weapons, Including Anti-Aircraft Missiles"; *USA v. Dani Nemr Tarraf et al.,* Indictment, November 20, 2009; Pretrial Detention Order, *United States of America v. Dani Nemr Tarraf,* US District Court, Eastern District, Pennsylvania, December 3, 2009; "Alleged Arms Dealer for Hezbollah Charged," *Philadelphia Inquirer,* November 24, 2009.

10. Adam Entous and Siobhan Gorman, "Behind Assad's Comeback, a Mismatch in Commitments," *Wall Street Journal,* December 31, 2013, http://online.wsj.com/news /articles/SB10001424052702303453004579292543464208138.

11. Nicholas Blanford, "Hezbollah Marks Major Triumph as Qusayr Tips Back into Assad Camp," *Christian Science Monitor,* June 5, 2013, http://www.csmonitor.com/World /Middle-East/2013/0605/Hezbollah-marks-major-triumph-as-Qusayr-tips-back-into -Assad-camp.

12. Marisa Sullivan, "Hezbollah in Syria," Middle East Security Report 19 (April 2014), 14, http://www.understandingwar.org/sites/default/files/Hezbollah_Sullivan _FINAL.pdf.

13. Ibid., 4–5.

14. Agence France Presse, "Iraq Shiite Volunteers in Syria Head Home to Fight Rebels: NGO," June 17, 2014, http://www.dailystar.com.lb/News/Middle-East/2014/Jun-17/260490 -iraq-shiite-volunteers-in-syria-head-home-to-fight-rebels-ngo.ashx#axzz34vTheKjl.

15. Alissa J. Rubin, Suadad al-Salhy, and Rick Gladstone, "Iraqi Shiite Cleric Issues Call to Arms," *New York Times,* June 13, 2014, http://www.nytimes.com/2014/06/14 /world/middleeast/iraq.html?_r=0.

16. "Hezbollah Displacing Iraqi Shiite Fighters in Syria," Ya Libnan, June 14, 2014, http://yalibnan.com/2014/06/14/hezbollah-displacing-iraqi-shiite-fighters-syria/.

17. Sam Dagher, "Syria's Allies Are Stretched by Widening War," *Wall Street Journal,* July 14, 2014, http://online.wsj.com/articles/syrias-allies-are-stretched-by-widening -war-1405383402?mod=fox_australian.

18. Anne Barnard and Hwaida Saad, "2 Deadly Blasts Rock Beirut, as Violence Seeps from Syria," *New York Times,* February 19, 2014, http://www.nytimes.com/2014/02/20 /world/middleeast/bombs-strike-southern-beirut.html?_r=0.

19. Loveday Morris, "Beirut's Southern Suburbs Become Targets as Syrian War Crosses Border," *Washington Post,* March 9, 2014, http://www.washingtonpost.com /world/Middle_east/beiruts-southern-suburbs-become-targets-as-syrian-war-crosses -border/2014/03/09/953dbc60-a454-11e3-b865-38b254d92063_story.html.

20. Sarah Birke, "Hezbollah's Choice," *New York Times,* August 6, 2013, http:// latitude.blogs.nytimes.com/2013/08/06/hezbollahs-choice/.

21. Thomas Joscelyn, "Online Jihadists Discuss Fate of al Qaeda Operative Held by Saudi Arabia," *Long War Journal*, June 27, 2013, http://www.longwarjournal.org/archives/2013/06/online_jihadists_dis.php.

22. Anne Barnard, "Pressed on Syria, Hezbollah Leader Urges Focus on Israel," *New York Times*, August 2, 2013, http://www.nytimes.com/2013/08/03/world/middleeast/under-fire-on-syria-hezbollah-leader-urges-focus-on-israel.html.

23. Ali Hashem, "Nasrallah Threatens to Double Hezbollah Forces in Syria," al-Monitor, August 16, 2013, http://www.al-monitor.com/pulse/originals/2013/08/nasrallah-double-forces-syria.html.

24. US Treasury Department, "Treasury Targets Hizballah for Supporting the Assad Regime," August 10, 2012, http://www.treasury.gov/press-center/press-releases/Pages/tg1676.aspx.

25. "Hezbollah Leader Hassan Nasrallah's Speech on Syria," Voltaire Network, May 25, 2013, http://www.voltairenet.org/article178691.html.

26. Ibid.

27. "Muallem: Hizbullah 'Preemptively' Defending Lebanon through Syria War Involvement," *Naharnet* (Beirut), January 31, 2014, http://www.naharnet.com/stories/en/116654.

28. "Japan Donates Additional $18 Million for Refugees in Lebanon," *Naharnet*, February 17, 2015, http://www.naharnet.com/stories/en/167865.

29. Dagher, "Syria's Allies Are Stretched."

30. David Horovitz, "5,000 Hezbollah Troops in Syria, with 5,000 More Set to Join Them," *Times of Israel*, May 26, 2013, http://www.timesofisrael.com/5000-hezbollah-troops-in-syria-with-5000-more-set-to-join-them/.

31. US State Department, "Hizballah," Country Reports on Terrorism 2013, April 30, 2013, 284.

32. "Bulgaria Identifies Bomber of Israeli Tourist Bus," Associated Press, July 18, 2014, http://www.timesofisrael.com/bulgaria-identifies-bomber-of-israeli-tourist-bus/?utm_source=dlvr.it&utm_medium=twitter.

33. "Swedish-Lebanese Man Jailed by Thai Court for Bomb Material," Reuters, September 18, 2013, http://www.reuters.com/article/2013/09/18/us-thailand-explosive-idUSBRE98H03T20130918.

34. "Israel Issues Passover Travel Warning for Sinai, Malaysia and Turkey," *Ynetnews*, April 1, 2014, http://www.ynetnews.com/articles/0,7340,L-4505711,00.html.

35. Wassayos Ngamkham, "Terror Suspect Admits Israeli Attack Plan," *Bangkok Post*, April 18, 2014, http://www.bangkokpost.com/news/local/405420/terror-suspect-admits-israeli-attack-plan.

36. "Nigeria: Hezbollah Armoury Discovered in Kano City," *BBC*, May 30, 2013, http://www.bbc.com/news/world-africa-22722948.

37. Tim Cocks, "Hezbollah Arms Suspect Gets Life in Nigeria, Two Others Freed," Reuters, November 29, 2013, http://www.reuters.com/article/2013/11/29/us-nigeria-hezbollah-idUSBRE9AS0N120131129.

38. Karen DeYoung, "Europe Should Label Hezbollah a Terrorist Group, U.S. urges," *Washington Post*, October 26, 2012, http://www.washingtonpost.com/world/national-security/europe-should-label-hezbollah-a-terrorist-group-us-urges/2012/10/26/780da3aa-1fa6-11e2-ba31-3083ca97c314_story.html.

39. Senate Select Committee on Intelligence, Statement for the Record: Worldwide Threat Assessment of the US Intelligence Community, 113th Cong., 2nd sess., January 29, 2014 (Testimony of James R. Clapper), http://www.odni.gov/files/documents/Intelligence%20Reports/2014%20WWTA%20%20SFR_SSCI_29_Jan.pdf.

40. Mohammed Ghobari, "Yemen Frees Members of Iran Revolutionary Guards: Sources," Reuters, September 25, 2014, http://www.reuters.com/article/2014/09/25/us -yemen-iran-idUSKCN0HK1GJ20140925.

41. Agence France Presse, "Jordan Charges 8 with Recruiting for Hezbollah," August 25, 2014, http://www.timesofisrael.com/jordan-charges-8-with-recruiting-for -hezbollah/.

42. Itamar Eichner, "Peru Foils Hezbollah Terror Plot against Israelis, Jews," Ynetnews, October 30, 2014, http://www.ynetnews.com/articles/0,7340,L-4586432,00.html.

43. All references to Hossam Yaakoub's interviews and depositions came from the official English translation of his police depositions. These were taken in Arabic, translated into Greek, and then into English by a certified translator. For details, see Depositions of Hossam Taleb Yaacoub (some spelled Yaakoub), Criminal Number Σ/860/12, File Page 35, 79, 85, 110, 134, 187, by interviewing police officer Sgt. Michael Costas. Depositions taken on July 7, 2012, July 11, 2012, July 11–12, 2012, July 14, 2012, July 16, 2012, and July 22, 2012.

44. See chapter 10.

45. Menelaos Hadjicostis, "Cyprus Court Convicts Hezbollah Member," Associated Press, March 21, 2013.

46. Depositions of Hossam Taleb Yaacoub (some spelled Yaakoub), Criminal Number Σ/860/12, File Page 187, by interviewing police officer Sgt. Michael Costas. Depositions taken on July 22, 2012.

47. Adam Goldman and Ellen Nakashima, "CIA and Mossad Killed Senior Hezbollah Figure in Car Bombing," Washington Post, January 30, 2015, http://www.washingtonpost .com/world/national-security/cia-and-mossad-killed-senior-hezbollah-figure-in-car -bombing/2015/01/30/ebb88682-968a-11e4-8005-1924ede3e54a_story.html.

48. Jeff Stein, "How the CIA Took Down Hezbollah's Top Terrorist, Imad Mugniyah," Newsweek, January 31, 2015, http://www.newsweek.com/2015/02/13/imad-mugniyah -cia-mossad-303483.html.

49. US Department of Justice, Federal Bureau of Investigation, Terrorist Research and Analytical Center, "International Radical Fundamentalism: An Analytical Overview of Groups and Trends," November 1994.

50. US Congress, House Committee on Homeland Security, Worldwide Threats to the Homeland: Hearing before the House Committee on Homeland Security, 113th Cong., 2nd sess., September 17, 2014, Statement of Matthew G. Olsen.

51. "Iran Agrees to Investigate Bombing of Buenos Aires Jewish Community Center," Haaretz, July 16, 2011, http://www.haaretz.com/jewish-world/iran-agrees-to-investigate -bombing-of-buenos-aires-jewish-community-center-1.373594.

52. Emily Schmall, "Deal Reached for Inquiry on Bombing in Argentina," New York Times, January 27, 2013, http://www.nytimes.com/2013/01/28/world/americas/argentina-and -iran-to-investigate-jewish-center-bombing.html?_r=0.

53. Guido Nejamkis, "Iran Set Up Terrorist Networks in Latin America: Argentine Prosecutor," Reuters, May 29, 2013, http://www.reuters.com/article/2013/05/29/us -argentina-iran-idUSBRE94S1F420130529.

54. Complaint of the General Prosecutor, Alberto Nisman, Prosecutorial Investigation Unit, January 13, 2015 (filed with the court clerk's office January 14, 2015), 230, http:// www.ptn.gov.ar/pdfs/Complaint%20Prosecutor%20Nisman.pdf.

55. Ibid., 174.

56. "Argentina Appeals Ruling Which Declared Iran Deal 'Unconstitutional,'" Buenos Aires Herald, May 30, 2014, http://www.buenosairesherald.com/article/160807/argentina -appeals-ruling-which-declared-iran-deal-unconstitutional.

57. Jonathan Gilbert, "Argentine President Accused of Cover-Up in Bombing Inquiry," *New York Times*, January 14, 2015, http://www.nytimes.com/2015/01/15/world/americas /argentine-president-accused-of-cover-up-in-bombing-inquiry.html.

58. Jonathan Gilbert and Simon Romero, "Puzzling Death of a Prosecutor Grips Argentina," *New York Times*, January 19, 2015, http://www.nytimes.com/2015/01/20/world /americas/alberto-nisman-found-dead-argentina-amia.html.

59. Gilbert, "Argentine President Accused of Cover-Up."

60. Agence France Presse, "Argentina Prosecutor Laid to Rest as Protesters Demand 'Justice for Nisman,'" January 29, 2015, http://www.theguardian.com/world/2015/jan /29/argentina-prosecutor-alberto-nisman-funeral-protesters-demand-justice.

61. Simon Romero, "Draft of Arrest Request for Argentine President Found at Dead Prosecutor's Home," *New York Times*, February 3, 2015, http://www.nytimes.com/2015 /02/04/world/americas/argentina-prosecutor-alberto-nisman-arrest-warrant-cristina -de-kirchner.html.

62. "Detroit-area Man Accused of Supporting Hezbollah," *Ynetnews*, March 18, 2014, http://www.ynetnews.com/articles/0,7340,L-4500195,00.html.

63. For more on these two Iraqi Shi'a militias, see "Kata'ib Hizballah," The International Centre for Political Violence and Terrorism Research, March 5, 2010; and Sam Wyer, "The Resurgence of Asa'ib Ahl al-Haqq," Middle East Security Report 7 (December 2012), http://www.understandingwar.org/sites/default/files/ResurgenceofAAH.pdf.

64. See Phillip Smyth's work at www.jihadology.net/hizballah-cavalcade.

65. "Treasury Sanctions al-Nusrah Front Leadership in Syria and Militias Supporting the Asad Regime," US Treasury Department, December 11, 2012.

66. Ibid.

67. Phillip Smyth, "Hezbollah's Fallen Soldiers," *Foreign Policy*, May 22, 2013, http:// foreignpolicy.com/2013/05/22/hezbollahs-fallen-soldiers/.

68. Jamie Dettmer, "Number of Shia Fighters in Syria Could Rise Following Fatwa," *Voice of America*, December 16, 2013, http://www.voanews.com/content/number-of -shia-fighters-in-syria-could-rise-following-fatwa/1811638.html.

69. US Executive Order 13572, "Blocking Property of Certain Persons with Respect to Human Rights Abuses in Syria," April 29, 2011, http://www.treasury.gov/resource -center/sanctions/Programs/Documents/13572.pdf.

70. Terrorist Groups in Syria: Hearing before the House Committee on Foreign Affairs, Subcommittee on Terrorism, Nonproliferation, and Trade, United States House of Representatives, 113th Cong., November 20, 2013 (Statement of Mr. Phillip Smyth), http://docs.house.gov/meetings/FA/FA18/20131120/101513/HHRG-113-FA18 -Wstate-SmythP-20131120.pdf; and Ariel Ben Solomon, "Report: Yemen Houthis Fighting for Assad in Syria," *Jerusalem Post*, May 31, 2013, http://www.jpost.com/Middle -East/Report-Yemen-Houthis-fighting-for-Assad-in-Syria-315005.

71. Aaron Zelin and Phillip Smyth, "The Vocabulary of Sectarianism," *Foreign Policy*, January 29, 2014, http://foreignpolicy.com/2014/01/29/the-vocabulary-of-sectarianism/.

Epilogue to the Updated Edition, 2024

THE WAR IN SYRIA has dramatically changed Hezbollah.[1] Once limited to jockeying for political power in Lebanon and fighting Israel, the group is now a regional player engaged in conflicts that have nothing to do with Israel and are far beyond its historical area of operations, often in cooperation with Iran.

This new epilogue updates our understanding of how Hezbollah has continued to evolve since the previous paperback edition of this book was published in 2015. While Hezbollah long denied that it carries out operations around the world, over the past few years the group has publicly embraced its regional and international operations. Speaking in 2015, the Hezbollah commander explained: "We shouldn't be called [the] Party of God. We're not a party now, we're international. We're in Syria, we're in Palestine, we're in Iraq, and we're in Yemen. We are wherever the oppressed need us. . . . Hezbollah is the school where every freedom-seeking man wants to learn."[2] Hezbollah's illicit activities and international terror plots remain key features of what the group does, which this epilogue covers as well. But the big change in Hezbollah's behavior over the past several years has been its new role as the de facto managing partner for Iran's network of militant proxies. Hezbollah assumed even more leadership responsibilities for Iran's network of proxies in the wake of the January 2020 targeted killing of Qods Force leader Gen. Qasem Soleimani.[3] After Soleimani's death, it was Hezbollah leader Hassan Nasrallah who called on Iran's proxies—the "Axis of Resistance," as he called them—to step up operations to force the US military out of the region.[4] He went on to state that Americans would now come to the region vertically (alive) and leave horizontally (dead).[5]

Hezbollah has emerged as a powerful regional actor, still seeking to destroy Israel and undermine Western influence in the region, but now partnering with Iran's Islamic Revolutionary Guard Corps (IRGC) Qods Force (QF) to aggressively reshape the region in Iran's favor. Consider, for example, Hezbollah's role in building up and supporting Iranian proxy groups in Gaza, Lebanon, Syria, Iraq, and Yemen, and how these groups each engaged Israel, US forces, or international maritime shipping in a loosely coordinated fashion that the late Qassem Soleimani envisioned as uniting the fronts. As early as 2015, Nasrallah called for "uniting the fronts against the Israeli occupation," speaking at the time about incorporating

Hamas into the Lebanese front by recruiting Palestinians from Lebanese refugee camps.[6] Indeed, Hezbollah remains engaged in a wide range of militant, terrorist, and criminal activities beyond Lebanon's borders. Developing a full appreciation of these activities—alongside its political, economic, social, and militant activities in Lebanon and its terrorist activities around the world—is fundamental to understanding the group in its totality. These regional activities include Hezbollah training other Iranian proxy groups and even deploying its key personnel and military units far beyond Lebanon's borders. These activities abroad, even more than its militia activity at home and its wars with Israel, have led countries around the world to task their law enforcement and intelligence agencies with countering Hezbollah's activities.

Hezbollah's Regional Deployments and Training Programs

Hezbollah's most pronounced regional adventurism has been its expeditionary deployment to Syria, but its forces have deployed elsewhere in the region as well. Moreover, no less significant are the group's advanced training regimen for other militants aligned with Iran, its expansive illicit financing activities across the region, and its procurement, intelligence, cyber, and disinformation activities. Together, these underscore the scale and scope of Hezbollah's all-in approach to transforming itself from a Lebanese party focused on Israel alone into a regional player active at Iran's behest, often in places and in ways that have nothing to do with either Lebanon or Israel.

As this book demonstrates in great detail, there are precedents for Hezbollah's regional activities, though the group has now taken these to a new level. As early as 1985, Hezbollah ran training camps for Shi'a militants from the Gulf,[7] and as early as December 1983, Lebanese Hezbollah and Iraqi Dawa operatives together attacked a series of targets in Kuwait (see chapters 2 and 7).[8] Now, as before, Hezbollah shifted much of its attention to the wider Middle East in response to a direct request from Iran. According to the US Treasury Department, sometime in 2005— even before Hezbollah's 2006 war with Israel—"Iran asked Hezbollah to form a group to train Iraqis to fight Coalition Forces in Iraq. In response, Hassan Nasrallah established a covert Hezbollah unit to train and advise Iraqi militants"[9] (see chapter 10). Then came Hezbollah's deployment to Syria, which was also the result of an Iranian request.[10]

Recognizing this growing regional threat, in 2016 the Gulf Cooperation Council branded Hezbollah a terrorist group, and the Gulf states have cracked down on Hezbollah supporters and financiers within their borders.[11] The Arab League and the Organization of Islamic Cooperation have issued statements condemning Hezbollah as well, leading to a war of words between the group and Gulf officials.[12] In 2018, Morocco broke diplomatic ties with Iran over reported Hezbollah ties to the Polisario Front.[13]

The first signs of Hezbollah's shift to a regional posture in support of Iranian interests were structural and involved moving key personnel from positions focused on Israel to those involving Iraq, Yemen, and Syria. As Hezbollah trained more Shi'a fighters from around the region, and then led them in battles across Syria, the group emerged as the leader and coalescing force for a broad range of Shi'a militants tied to Iran and the Qods Force. Hezbollah's roles in the wars in Iraq and Syria significantly changed the nature of how the group's alliance with Iran plays out in practice throughout the region. Over time, IRGC-QF commander Gen. Qassem Soleimani personally assumed more of a command leadership position over Hezbollah's fighting forces, at times at the expense of the group's own commanders. Then, after the January 2020 assassination of Soleimani alongside the Iraqi Shi'a militia leader Abu Mahdi al-Muhandis, Hezbollah assumed more of a leadership role coordinating the activities of a broad network of Shi'a militant proxies—the "Resistance Axis"—on behalf of Iran's IRGC-QF.[14] The US government issued a reward of up to $10 million for information about Muhammad Kawtharani, a member of Hezbollah's Political Council who, the State Department charged, is a senior leader of Hezbollah forces in Iraq and "assumed some of the political coordination of Iraq-based, Iran-aligned paramilitary groups formerly organized by now-deceased Islamic Revolutionary Guard Corps general Qassem Soleimani."[15] Suddenly, it was a Hezbollah official who promoted training, funding, and support for Iraqi Shi'a insurgent groups and who helped organize their travel to Syria to support the Assad regime.[16]

Hezbollah's Intelligence, Cyber, and Disinformation Operations

Beyond training and supporting Shi'a militants as "fighters without borders," Hezbollah has also stepped up its intelligence collection and cyber and disinformation operations across the region.[17] The case of the Iraq-based Hezbollah operative Muhammad Farhat offers a good example. According to the US Treasury Department, "as of 2017, Farhat was tasked with collecting security and intelligence information in Iraq and subsequently providing reports to senior Hezbollah and Iranian leadership." He also helped a Hezbollah and IRGC-QF effort "to analyze and report on the Iraqi security situation."[18]

In 2015, Kuwaiti authorities arrested a cell of several Kuwaiti operatives and one Iranian Shi'a operative on charges of spying for Iran and Hezbollah.[19] That same year, an Israeli airstrike in the Golan Heights in Syria targeted a joint Hezbollah and IRGC-QF intelligence collection effort, killing Hezbollah's Jihad Mughniyeh (son of the late Imad Mughniyeh), along with several other Hezbollah operatives and Iranian IRGC-QF Gen. Mohammad Ali Allahdadi.[20] Within a few short years, Israeli officials would reveal that the new head of this Golan operation was none other than Ali Musa Daqduq al-Mousawi, a senior Hezbollah operative previously detained in Iraq[21] (see chapter 10). In 2018, Bahraini authorities arrested a group of Shi'a suspected militants on charges of setting up a terrorist network in coordination with the Iranian intelligence services.[22] But perhaps the most glaring example of Hezbollah's regional intelligence operations is the case of the US military contract linguist Mariam Taha Thompson who, while stationed in Iraq, provided a Hezbollah contact with intelligence about human sources involved in the January 2020 assassination of IRGC-QF commander Soleimani. According to her plea, Thompson admitted to accessing and sharing dozens of intelligence files, including names of human assets, to provide to her

Hezbollah contact.[23] Tellingly, what Hezbollah intelligence officers sought from Thompson was not information specific to Israel or Lebanon, but information of particular interest to Iran and its proxy network.

Hezbollah's efforts to help other Shi'a militant groups establish media and propaganda outlets have increased in recent years, including television, radio, and online outlets. For example, both Kata'ib Hezbollah in Iraq and the Houthis in Yemen operate satellite television stations based in Beirut, with support from Lebanese Hezbollah.[24] Now, Hezbollah also supports the disinformation and cyber activities of Iranian proxy Shi'a militant groups across the region.

Separate from the cyber espionage and sophisticated malware operations in which Hezbollah has been implicated (typically in concert with Iran), the group also runs disinformation boot camps in Lebanon for the purpose of building up the "electronic armies" of Iran's proxy groups around the region.[25] "Since at least 2012," the *Telegraph* reported in August 2020, "Hizbollah has been flying individuals into Lebanon for courses teaching participants how to digitally manipulate photographs, manage large numbers of fake social media accounts, make videos, avoid Facebook's censorship, and effectively spread disinformation online."[26] Students from Bahrain, Iraq, Saudi Arabia, and Syria were among the thousands of "Iran-backed social media activists" who attended the ten-day courses, which were taught by Hezbollah specialists. In the words of an Iraqi politician who was involved in sending students to these courses, "The people we sent developed their skills in Beirut and when they returned they started training activists inside Iraq."[27] One of the groups that benefited from this Hezbollah training course was Kata'ib Hezbollah in Iraq, which now runs its own "online facade" group, Unit 10,000, which has developed its own "electronic armies capable of hacking, information operations, and open source intelligence gathering."[28] Iran and Hezbollah work together in the disinformation space in several other ways, as well, including Iran's creation of "the International Union of Virtual Media," established to promote Iranian and Hezbollah propaganda while obscuring the source of such information.[29] The US Treasury Department sanctioned cyber threat actors backed by Iran's Ministry of Intelligence, and the US Office of the Director of National Intelligence concluded that Iran engaged in a "multi-pronged covert influence campaign" targeting the 2020 US presidential election while Hezbollah "took some steps to attempt to influence the election."[30]

Managing Iran's Regional Proxies

The central theme running through the steady increase in Hezbollah's regional activism—be it in the form of fielding fighters to battlefields of strategic importance to Iran, training other Iranian proxies, collecting intelligence, engaging in illicit financial schemes, or promoting disinformation campaigns—is that it has been done at Iran's behest. Hezbollah's regional escalation coincided with a period when Iranian operatives began to play increasingly important decision-making roles for Hezbollah. As the Lebanese analyst Hanin Ghaddar has noted, Hezbollah's role as a regional actor did not start with its deployment to Syria; it was present in Iraq even earlier, "but it became more obvious and more structured in Syria—especially under IRGC [QF] commander Qassem Soleimani." Over time, Ghaddar explains, Soleimani became the one leading Hezbollah deployments and activities across the region.[31] Indeed, it was because of his dual-hatted role as head of the IRGC-QF and director of Iran's substate proxies that US government lawyers concluded Soleimani was a legitimate target for a targeted assassination in January 2020. The extent of his personal leadership of these proxies became clear as US analysts tracked his movements and mapped out his "pattern of life."[32]

Soleimani's force of personality and longtime connections made him uniquely qualified to oversee the management of Iran's growing proxy network. But since no single commander could replace him, the IRGC-QF is drawing on a brain trust of several of its more senior and experienced managers to collectively fill Soleimani's shoes at present. And as Iran's "strategic partner," Hezbollah leader Nasrallah and some of his key lieutenants are sure to play major roles. Indeed, the IRGC-QF officers who have stepped in to fill Soleimani's shoes are all longtime Hezbollah partners. Israel, for its part, has targeted several of the IRGC generals tasked with picking up where Soleimani left off, and others have died of natural causes. For example, Gen. Muhammad Hussein-Zada Hejazi was promoted to Qods Force deputy commander after serving in Lebanon but died suddenly of heart disease in 2021.[33] And in April 2024 an Israeli airstrike in Damascus killed Gen. Mohammed Reza Zahedi, the head of the Qods Force in Lebanon, along with his deputy and several others.[34] These Qods Forces losses have had the effect of making Hezbollah's role of providing stability and continuity during turbulent times all the more important.

Within weeks of Soleimani's death, the State Department issued a reward for information about Mohammad Kawtharani, Hezbollah's man on the ground in Iraq, noting that he "has taken over some of the political coordination of Iran-aligned paramilitary groups formerly organized by Qassim Sulemani after Sulemani's death in January. In this capacity, [Kawtharani] facilitates the actions of groups operating outside the control of the Government of Iraq that have violently suppressed protests, attacked foreign diplomatic missions, and engaged in widespread organized criminal activity." He also "assisted extremists transiting to Syria to support the Assad regime," according to the State Department.[35] A senior Iraqi Shi'a leader noted that Kawtharani "was trusted by Soleimani, who used to depend and call on him to help him in crises and in meetings in Baghdad."[36] Kawtharani's right-hand man is another Hezbollah official, his brother Adnan Hussein Kawtharani, who was also designated by Treasury in 2018. Adnan also "attended meetings in Iraq with sectarian armed groups and Hizballah officials."[37] In his new capacity, Mohammad Kawtharani chaired urgent meetings of Iraqi militia leaders in Iraq after Soleimani's death.[38]

Fighting Israel: The Road toward October 7, 2023

Meanwhile, Hezbollah actively has sought out ways to resurrect its active military engagement with Israel. When Hezbollah deployed the bulk of its forces to defend the Assad regime during Syria's civil war, it sought to buy time regarding its fight with Israel. This meant focusing on long-term projects that would improve its ability to attack Israel at a later date, such as investing in cross-border attack tunnels and importing and developing precision-guided missiles.[39] Hezbollah spent years and significant funds on the first project, building tunnels that Israel exposed in December 2018 and destroyed over the next few months.[40] The second project continues to pose a threat today, most recently evidenced by Hezbollah's near daily rocket launches into Israel since October 7, 2023, despite Israel's efforts to interdict missile-related transfers via Syria and to publicly reveal missile facilities operating in densely populated urban areas of Lebanon.[41]

Since 2019, with the vast majority of its forces back in Lebanon, Hezbollah has been eager to reestablish its "resistance" credentials—albeit in a way that minimizes the likelihood of a full-scale Israeli military retaliation. In the lead-up to the 2006 war, Secretary-General Hassan Nasrallah famously miscalculated how Israel would respond to the cross-border abduction of its soldiers.[42] According to Israeli analysts, however, he now believes he can predict the enemy's behavior more accurately, leading him to sharpen his rhetoric and approve a series of increasingly aggressive actions over the past several years.[43]

Previously, the unwritten understanding was that Hezbollah would not attack Israel so long as Israeli forces limited themselves to targeting its weapons shipments in Syria—the group's red lines would only be crossed if Israel struck targets on Lebanese soil or killed the group's personnel in any country. For example, on September 1, 2019, Hezbollah fired antitank missiles at an Israeli military ambulance driving between the border communities of Avivim and Yiron, an apparent response to a pair of Israeli attacks: an airstrike that killed two Hezbollah operatives in Syria, and a drone strike in Beirut that targeted a propellant mixer used in the manufacture of precision-guided missiles.[44]

At the same time, however, Hezbollah began taking steps to change the rules of the game. After the 2019 Beirut drone strike, Nasrallah vowed to shoot Israeli surveillance drones out of Lebanon's skies—whether or not they were involved in attacks.[45] By February 2022, he was boasting that Hezbollah's antiaircraft capabilities had forced Israel to drastically reduce its drone flights over south Lebanon and refrain from any such flights over the Beqa Valley for months.[46] Israeli Air Force chief Amikam Norkin seemed to confirm some of these claims that April—he acknowledged Hezbollah's aggressive air defenses, noted that the group had nearly shot down an Israeli drone in 2021, and described the resultant dampening of intelligence collection overflights, concluding that "Israel no longer has full freedom of action over Lebanon."[47]

Similarly, during the same August 2019 speech in which he threatened to down Israeli drones, Nasrallah warned Israeli soldiers stationed along the border to be on guard: "Starting today, you should stand on a leg and a half and wait for us." In July 2020, the military reportedly thwarted an attack by armed Hezbollah operatives who had crossed into Israeli territory.[48]

The August 2020 Beirut port explosion soon distracted Hezbollah from escalating tensions (at least beyond increasing its observation posts along the Blue Line), but the threatening rhetoric picked up again in 2021. When Iran sent a shipment of oil to Lebanon that August, Nasrallah publicly warned that any attack on the vessel would be considered an attack on Lebanese territory and therefore trigger a Hezbollah response—a risky statement in the midst of Israel and Iran's tit-for-tat escalation against each other's shipping interests.[49]

In July 2022, Nasrallah further upped the stakes by threatening to target Israel's offshore natural gas platforms if it began extracting from the Karish field before reaching a maritime border deal with Lebanon.[50] Soon thereafter, three Hezbollah drones were shot down en route to the Karish platform.[51] Although subsequent investigation indicated they were not armed, the message was clear—Nasrallah warned that these drones were "only the beginning" and pledged to go to war over the gas issue if necessary.[52] Hezbollah followed up with a propaganda video featuring drone footage of the Karish field apparently being targeted with a weapon.[53]

Nasrallah's willingness to risk conflict with Israel was partly driven by domestic economic and political pressures—he no doubt relished the opportunity to tell the Lebanese people that Hezbollah's weapons had protected the oil delivery from Iran and secured a better deal on the maritime border and gas field. Yet he also seemed to believe that Israel was unlikely to respond in a serious way to his threats, given Hezbollah's enlarged precision missile arsenal and air defense systems. Instead, he assessed that Israel would scale down its drone flights, refrain from attacking Iran's oil shipment, and delay gas extraction until the maritime agreement was concluded—and in each case, his assessment was correct. By March 2023, an internal debate among Israeli intelligence analysts asked whether this string of accurate assessments had emboldened Nasrallah to take even greater risks.[54]

Looking back, the road to the October 7, 2023, Hamas attacks appears to have started in earnest after the May 2021 rocket war between Hamas and Israel. At the time, the editor of a Lebanese newspaper affiliated with Hezbollah reported that Hamas, Hezbollah, and Iran coordinated the fighting from a "joint war room" in Beirut.[55] In the wake of that war, Hezbollah and the Qods Force met with Hamas officials to share strategic guidance to operationalize a long-held notional Hamas plot to storm across the Gaza border and attack Israeli communities. Tactical planning for the Hamas massacre began at least a year before the attack, according to Western and Middle Eastern intelligence officials, "with key support from Iranian allies"—that is, Hezbollah.[56] At the same time, Hezbollah itself prepared for potential attacks across the Blue Line border, published a video of a simulated attack on an Israeli outpost,[57] invited journalists to witness military training exercises, and increased efforts to obstruct UN Interim Force in Lebanon (UNIFIL) patrols in southern Lebanon.[58] By August 2023, the Emirati ambassador to the United Nations bluntly laid out the extent of Hezbollah's destabilizing activities in Lebanon[59]:

> The fact is, tensions on the Blue Line are at a level unseen since the 2006 war. Over the past year, . . . [Hezbollah] has erected concrete military outposts and observation towers; conducted military drills with live fire; and prevented UNIFIL's freedom of movement while brazenly attacking peacekeeping forces. . . . It has also actively perpetuated Lebanon's myriad crises, obstructed the investigation into the devastating Beirut Port explosion, and paralyzed key institutions of the State.[60] These extremely inflammatory actions threaten a dangerous escalation in our region.

This followed the July 2023 UN Secretary General's report on UNIFIL which documented Hezbollah actions damaging the security barrier along the Blue Line, setting up tents on the Israeli side of the Blue Line, expanding the illicit presence of armed Hezbollah personnel in the south (in violation of UN Security Council Resolution 1701), and conducting more than 600 intentional crossings into Israel in violation of the Blue Line.[61]

International Plots

But Hezbollah did not focus only on efforts along the Blue Line. In the years and months leading up to the October 7, 2023, Hamas attacks and the Hezbollah rocket war that followed, Hezbollah operations around the world also persisted.

In July 2013, when this book first appeared in hardcover, the Hezbollah operative Hossam Yaakoub had just been convicted in a Cypriot court for conducting surveillance for an attack targeting Israeli tourists in Cyprus—just one in a series of terrorist plots around the world tied to Hezbollah and Iran in 2012 (see the 2015 afterword).[62] Soon, the European Union would designate the military and terrorist wings of Hezbollah as a terrorist group (but not the group overall), based in part on Hezbollah's plots within the European Union—both the thwarted plot in Cyprus and the Burgas, Bulgaria, bus bombing. Commenting on Yaakoub's conviction, the US Department of State spokesperson noted:

> Over the past year, we have seen Hezbollah engage in increasingly aggressive terrorist activity around the world. In July 2012, just two weeks after Yaacoub's arrest, we witnessed the deadly impact of Hezbollah's commitment to terrorism in Burgas, Bulgaria. Today's verdict underscores the need for our European allies—and other governments around the world—to crack down on this deadly group and to send a strong message that Hezbollah can no longer operate with impunity, at home or abroad.[63]

Since then, Hezbollah has continued to engage in militant activities around the world. Consider, for example, the November 2023 case targeting Jewish and Israeli targets in Brazil. Brazilian police arrested at least five members of a terrorist cell—mostly local, non-Muslim Brazilians—who were recruited by Hezbollah to carry out attacks.[64] One of the arrested operatives, Lucas Passos Lima, reportedly conducted surveillance of two synagogues in Brasilia.[65] Looking through his phone's search history, investigators found that Lima was also collecting information on an unnamed Jewish community leader, as well as the Israeli Embassy in Brazil. One video on Lima's phone recorded someone in the vehicle with him saying "Bingo" while driving past Brasilia's Taguatinga Synagogue.[66]

Other Hezbollah plots took place directly on US soil. In June 2017, US authorities arrested Hezbollah operative Ali Kourani in New York, charging him with a number of terrorism-related crimes, including carrying out preoperational surveillance of potential targets.[67] According to the authorities, beginning in 2009, Kourani conducted surveillance of a wide variety of targets, focusing on New York City's critical infrastructure, US military and law enforcement facilities, and airports in New York and Toronto.[68] Kourani described himself as a long-term sleeper agent, who sought to identify Israelis in New York who could be targeted by Hezbollah and persons from whom he could procure small arms.[69] Kourani was convicted and sentenced to forty years in prison for his covert activities on behalf of Hezbollah.[70]

Hezbollah continues to use material culled from disposable ice packs to produce ammonium nitrate explosives, and at one point Hezbollah had Kourani travel to Guangzhou, China, on his American passport to "develop relationships that the [Islamic Jihad Organization] could rely on to obtain ammonium nitrate to be used as an explosive precursor chemical."[71] Around the same time but across the country, another person tied to Hezbollah was stockpiling ice packs for Hezbollah in Houston. Robert Assaf purchased hundreds of ice packs from local pharmacies and established a 300-pound cache of ammonium nitrate on Hezbollah's instructions, until he was ordered to destroy the explosives in August 2015.[72] Assaf ultimately pleaded guilty in 2017 to providing a false statement to the FBI and court documents revealing the ice pack purchases were unsealed.[73] Even as that plot was playing out in Texas, another Hezbollah operative was stockpiling ice packs in London.[74] In 2020, the State Department revealed that Hezbollah had been moving ammonium nitrate ice pack caches throughout Europe, including in Belgium, France, Greece, Italy, Spain, and Switzerland.[75]

The same day Kourani was arrested, US authorities also detained Samer El Debek, another Hezbollah sleeper agent based in Michigan. According to the Department of Justice, El Debek had a "high degree of technical sophistication" and was "trained in techniques and methods similar to those used to construct the improvised explosive device used in Hezbollah's 2012 Burgas, Bulgaria, bus bombing."[76] El Debek was instructed by his Hezbollah handler to travel to Panama, where he collected intelligence on the US and Israeli embassies, and to Thailand, where he reportedly removed "explosive precursor" material from a safehouse in Bangkok that Hezbollah believed to be compromised.[77] El Debek's case stands out in that he has not stood trial and nothing more was made public about his case since his arrest. However, a close reading of the criminal complaint in another Hezbollah-related case indicates that the reason for this secrecy is that El Debek appears to have pled guilty and become a cooperating witness working with the US government. That complaint refers to a cooperating witness who was arrested in the United States in June 2017, pled guilty to terrorism-related offenses, was a trained bomb maker, and traveled to Panama and Thailand on Hezbollah missions—all of which describes El Debek to a T.[78]

Then, in July 2019, US officials arrested the Hezbollah operative and naturalized US citizen Alexei Saab. Saab had cut his teeth with Hezbollah by observing Israeli and Lebanese military troop movements and positions in southern Lebanon, and he attended his first Hezbollah military training course in 1999. After that training, he was formally recruited into Hezbollah's Islamic Jihad terrorist unit in 2000 and moved to the United States that same year. In 2003, Saab's Hezbollah handlers instructed him to begin collecting preoperational surveillance on potential targets in the United States. According to the retired FBI special agent and former legal attaché at the US Embassy in Israel, Russel Rosenthal, Saab took photographs of a number of potential targets in New York City, including the New York Stock Exchange, Rockefeller Center, and 26 Federal Plaza, as well as other locations in Washington, DC, and Boston.[79] Saab traveled to Lebanon several times to participate in Hezbollah training; his indictment even described an incident in the early 2000s where he attempted to assassinate a suspected Israeli spy. Saab was sentenced in 2023 to twelve years for receiving military training from Hezbollah and other crimes.[80]

Hezbollah continues to engage in a wide range of illicit financial schemes, from laundering money through a casino in Argentina,[81] to laundering the proceeds of cocaine sales for Colombian cartels in Europe,[82] to shipping bricks of cocaine disguised as charcoal from Colombia to Lebanon.[83] One Hezbollah financial operative, Mohammad Ahmad Ammar, illegally moved $500,000 into Miami banks through a series of complicated financial transactions stretching from Australia to Europe.[84] Ammar underscores the transnational nature of Hezbollah's illicit financial activities. He was arrested on money laundering and other charges in California in September 2016,[85] held citizenship in four countries (Lebanon, Colombia, the United Kingdom, and the United States), and operated primarily from Colombia, where he laundered money for drug cartels. Authorities describe one case in which Ammar and others conspired to transfer funds from Australia to West Africa, the Netherlands, Spain, the United Kingdom, and the United Arab Emirates.[86] Meanwhile, Hezbollah operatives have stepped up to help Iran evade sanctions and enable the Qods Force to raise funds for itself, Hezbollah, and other Iranian proxies through sanctions-busting, illicit oil sales. Hezbollah has set up front companies to "finance, coordinate, and obscure" illicit oil shipments, according to the US State and Treasury Departments.[87]

Hezbollah also dabbles in a less common illicit market: luxury art. On April 18, 2023, the Department of Justice charged Nazem Said Ahmad and eight others with multiple crimes arising from a scheme to evade terrorism-related sanctions.[88] That same day, the Treasury Department designated Ahmad's money laundering and sanctions evasion network, describing Ahmad as a Hezbollah financier[89] (Ahmad himself was designated as a terrorist in December 2019).[90] The investigation and subsequent indictment revealed that Ahmad and his co-conspirators allegedly trafficked an estimated $160 million worth of artwork and diamond-grading services through the US financial system, routinely generated funds for Hezbollah through the blood diamond trade in Africa, and used a Beirut art gallery to launder money.[91] Hezbollah financiers have abused honorary consul status in foreign countries to benefit the group,[92] especially in places like West Africa where Hezbollah financiers have been particularly active in recent years.[93]

Conclusion

One theme of this book has been the fact that Hezbollah has multiple and sometimes competing goals. Balancing these, especially against the background of instability back home in Lebanon, is a complicated task. Even as Hezbollah carried out all these activities across the region and the world, its violent activities at home spiked as well.

In 2020, the UN's Special Tribunal for Lebanon found Hezbollah operative Salim Ayyash, a member of the group's assassination squad—Unit 121—guilty on all counts and sentenced in absentia to five life sentences in prison for his role in the 2005 assassination of Rafiq Hariri and others.[94] A year later, Hezbollah assassinated prominent Lebanese human rights activist and Hezbollah critic Lokman Slim, who was found shot dead in his abandoned car a mile from a UN compound.[95] Jawad Nasrallah, Hassan Nasrallah's son, posted on X shortly after Slim's death was announced: "The loss of some people is in fact an unplanned gain #sorrynotsorry."[96]

Consider also Hezbollah's overt obstruction of the investigation into the tragic August 2020 Beirut port explosion, which spoke volumes about the group's fears over where such an investigation might lead. In September 2021, Hezbollah security official Wafiq Safa threatened the judge investigating the Beirut port explosion, a week after the judge ordered the arrest of a former minister close to Hezbollah.[97] This would not be the only case in which an urban explosive stockpile put Lebanese civilians at risk. Hezbollah's precision-guided missile program is widely reported to be located under urban residential areas (using Lebanese civilians as human shields).[98]

It is against this backdrop that Hezbollah's role as a regional actor throughout the Middle East has grown so significantly, even as the group has also sought to expand its ability to strike Israel in ways it calculates would not spark full-scale war. In both these efforts, Lebanon's persistent economic-political crisis constrain Hezbollah's freedom of action since life in Lebanon is already difficult and most Lebanese are eager to avoid the kind of devastation such a war would bring.

Hezbollah's current quandary revolves around the push and pull of two different sets of frequently competing priorities: first, serving as a regional militant player as part of Iran's proxy network in tandem with the IRGC Qods Force; and second, the fact that the group is based in Lebanon and remains the most powerful Lebanese party and militia at a time when the crony-sectarian political system of which it is a key part has come under such tremendous pressure.[99] Hezbollah has long played a dominant role in Lebanon, extending its influence through political and social activism as well as terrorism, political violence, and military strength. But it has long insisted that it acts only with Lebanon's best interests at heart. In recent years, with its extensive militant commitments across the region and increased violence at home, Hezbollah had a hard time maintaining that fiction. As the majority of Hezbollah's forces returned home from Syria, the group sought to expand its capacity to attack Israel and reassert its "resistance" credentials after a grueling and controversial deployment to defend the Assad regime.

The Hamas attacks of October 7, 2023, provided Hezbollah the opening to engage in near-daily shelling of Israeli territory, leading almost 100,000 Israeli civilians to evacuate the north of the country. It also presented Hezbollah the opportunity to help coordinate efforts among Iran's various proxies to operationalize the vision of the late Iranian general Qassem Soleimani to "unite the fronts" in future battles against Iran's enemies. But it has also led to the destruction of most of Hezbollah's infrastructure along the Blue Line, the death of a significant number of Hezbollah fighters, and the evacuation of many Lebanese from homes on their side of the border.

The October 7 attacks are a watershed event, one in which Hezbollah has played a major role. While Hezbollah appears not to have known about Hamas's specific plans for October 7 in advance, it knew the group was planning an attack modeled after off-the-shelf Hezbollah plans for an assault on north Israel. For at least two years, Hamas and Hezbollah maintained a "joint operations room," as they called it, in Beirut.[100] And just three months before the October 7 attacks, Hezbollah released a video of a simulated Hezbollah attack on an Israeli military base on the Israel-Lebanon border.[101] However events transpire in the wake of the Hamas attacks and the war that followed, Hezbollah is bound to play a significant role. If history is prologue, then by virtue of providing the foundation for understanding Hezbollah's history, its war with Israel, and its regional and international operations, this book also provides a lens through which one can try to understand the ways Hezbollah is likely to act in the months and years to come.

Notes

1. Portions of this epilogue are drawn from the author's work published for the Washington Institute and the Middle East Institute, with permission from both. In particular, see Matthew Levitt, "Hezbollah's Regional Activities in Support of Iran's Proxy Networks," Middle East Institute, July 2021; and Matthew Levitt, "Hezbollah Infiltrates Israel (Part 1): Another Step Toward Changing the Rules of the Game," PolicyWatch 3715, Washington Institute for Near East Policy, March 21, 2023.

2. Erika Soloman, "Lebanon's Hizbollah and Yemen's Houthis Open Up on Links," *Financial Times*, May 8, 2015, www.ft.com/content/e1e6f750-f49b-11e4-9a58-00144feab7de.

3. Michael Crowley, Falih Hassan, and Eric Schmitt, "US Strike in Iraq Kills Qassim Suleimani, Commander of Iranian Forces," *New York Times*, January 2, 2020, www.nytimes.com/2020/01/02/world/middleeast/qassem-soleimani-iraq-iran-attack.html.

4. "Sayyed Nasrallah: Suleimani Revenge Is Long Track, Trump Biggest Liar in History of US Presidency," *al-Manar*, January 12, 2020, https://english.almanar.com.lb/913904.

5. Qassim Abdul-Zahra and Bassem Mroue, "Iraq Vote, Hezbollah Threat Leveled at US Troops in Mideast," Associated Press, January 5, 2020, https://apnews.com/article/us-news-ap-top-news-international-news-iraq-islamic-state-group-7c94f2ca6c51d9fd822444941893d4be.

6. Yigal Carmon and Y. Yehoshua, "From the Mediterranean to the Golan, Iran Builds Active Front and Direct Military Presence on Israel's Border to Deter Israel and Further Ideology of Eliminating the Zionist Regime," Middle East Media Research Institute, MEMRI Daily Brief 1146, February 16, 2015, www.memri.org/reports/mediterranean-golan-iran-builds-active-front-and-direct-military-presence-israels-border.

7. "Lebanon: Hezbollah Spreading the Word," Central Intelligence Agency, December 21, 1987, quoted by Matthew Levitt, "Hezbollah Acts as Tutor to the Gulf States," in *Lebanese Hezbollah Select Worldwide Activity Interactive Map and Timeline*, Washington Institute for Near East Policy, www.washingtoninstitute.org/hezbollahinteractivemap/#id=884.

8. Matthew Levitt, "Six Kuwait Sites Bombed," in *Lebanese Hezbollah Select Worldwide Activity Interactive Map and Timeline*, Washington Institute for Near East Policy, www.washingtoninstitute.org/hezbollahinteractivemap/#id=59\.

9. "Treasury Designated Hizballah Commander Responsible for American Deaths in Iraq," US Department of the Treasury, November 19, 2012, www.treasury.gov/press-center/press-releases/Pages/tg1775.aspx.

10. Matthew Levitt, "Waking Up the Neighbors: How Regional Intervention Is Transforming Hezbollah," *Foreign Affairs*, July 23, 2015, www.washingtoninstitute.org/policy-analysis/waking-neighbors-how-regional-intervention-transforming-hezbollah.

11. "GCC Designates Hezbollah as a Terrorist Organization," in *Lebanese Hezbollah Worldwide Activities Map*, Washington Institute for Near East Policy, www.washingtoninstitute.org/hezbollahinteractivemap/#id=602.

12. "Arab League Designates Hezbollah as a Terrorist Organization," in *Washington Institute Hezbollah Worldwide Activities Map*, Washington Institute for Near East Policy, www.washingtoninstitute.org/hezbollahinteractivemap/#id=603; "Islamic Summit Slams Hezbollah for 'Terrorism,'" Al Arabiya News, April 15, 2016, https://english.alarabiya.net/News/middle-east/2016/04/15/Islamic-summit-denounces-Hezbollah-for-backing-terrorism.

13. "Why Has Morocco Severed Its Diplomatic Relations with Iran?" *Al Arabiya*, May 2, 2018, https://english.alarabiya.net/features/2018/05/02/Why-did-the-Kingdom -of-Morocco-sever-its-diplomatic-relations-with-Iran-.

14. Timour Azhari, "Hezbollah Vows Retaliation Against US for Soleimani Killing," *Al Jazeera*, January 5, 2020, www.aljazeera.com/news/2020/1/5/hezbollah-vows -retaliation-against-us-for-soleimani-killing.

15. "Muhammad Kawtharani," Rewards for Justice, US Department of State, https://rewardsforjustice.net/rewards/muhammad-kawtharani/.

16. "Muhammad Kawtharani."

17. Matthew Levitt, "'Fighters without Borders': New Trends in Iran Threat Network Foreign Operations Tradecraft," Washington Institute for Near East Policy, February 27, 2020, www.washingtoninstitute.org/policy-analysis/fighters-without-borders -forecasting-new-trends-iran-threat-network-foreign.

18. "Treasury Sanctions Key Hizballah, IRGC-QF Networks in Iraq," US Department of the Treasury, November 13, 2018, https://home.treasury.gov/news/press -releases/sm546.

19. Matthew Levitt, "Hezbollah Operatives Storing Explosives Arrested in Kuwait," in *Lebanese Hezbollah Select Worldwide Activity Map*, Washington Institute for Near East Policy, www.washingtoninstitute.org/hezbollahinteractivemap/#id=577.

20. Levitt, "Hezbollah Operatives Storing Explosives Arrested."

21. Matthew Levitt, "Israel Exposes Hezbollah Cell in Syrian Golan Heights," in *Lebanese Hezbollah Select Worldwide Activity Map*, Washington Institute for Near East Policy, www.washingtoninstitute.org/hezbollahinteractivemap/#id=688.

22. Matthew Levitt, "169 Bahraini Hezbollah Members Indicted," in *Lebanese Hezbollah Select Worldwide Activity Map*, Washington Institute for Near East Policy, September 25, 2018, www.washingtoninstitute.org/hezbollahinteractivemap/#id=666.

23. "Defense Department Linguist Pleads Guilty to Transmitting Highly Sensitive Classified National Defense Information to Aid a Foreign Government," US Department of Justice, March 26, 2021, www.justice.gov/opa/pr/defense-department-linguist-pleads -guilty-transmitting-highly-sensitive-classified-national.

24. Michael Knights, "Back into the Shadows? The Future of Kata'ib Hezbollah and Iran's Other Proxies in Iraq," *CTC Sentinel*, October 2020, https://ctc.westpoint .edu/back-into-the-shadows-the-future-of-kataib-hezbollah-and-irans-other-proxies-in -iraq/; Michael Knights, "The Houthi War Machine: From Guerrilla War to State Capture," *CTC Sentinel*, September 2018, https://ctc.westpoint.edu/houthi-war-machine -guerrilla-war-state-capture/.

25. Jeff Moskowitz, "Cyberattack Tied to Hezbollah Ups the Ante for Israel's Digital Defenses," *Christian Science Monitor*, June 1, 2015, www.csmonitor.com/World/Passcode /2015/0601/Cyberattack-tied-to-Hezbollah-ups-the-ante-for-Israel-s-digital-defenses.

26. Wil Crisp and Suadad al-Salhy, "Inside Hizbollah's Fake News Training Camps Sowing Instability Across the Middle East," *The Telegraph*, August 2, 2020, www .telegraph.co.uk/news/2020/08/02/exclusive-inside-hezbollahs-fake-news-training -camps-sowing/.

27. Crisp and al-Salhy, "Inside Hizbollah's Fake News Training Camps."

28. Crispin Smith and Hamdi Malik, "Profile: Unite 10,000," Militia Spotlight Profiles, Washington Institute for Near East Policy, April 25, 2021, www.washingtoninstitute .org/policy-analysis/profile-unit-10000.

29. Jack Stubbs and Christopher Bing, "Iran-Based Political Influence Operation, Bigger, Persistent, Global," Reuters, August 28, 2018, www.reuters.com/article/us-usa -iran-facebook-exclusiveidINKCN1LD2R9.

30. "Treasury Sanctions Cyber Actors Backed by Iranian Intelligence Ministry," US Department of the Treasury, September 17, 2020, https://home.treasury.gov/news/press-releases/sm1127; "Foreign Threats to the 2020 Federal Elections," Intelligence Community Assessment, National Intelligence Council, Office of the Director of National Intelligence, March 10, 2021, www.dni.gov/files/ODNI/documents/assessments/ICA-declass-16MAR21.pdf.

31. Hanin Ghaddar, "Hezbollah's Regional Challenge," Middle East Focus, Middle East Institute, May 20, 2021, https://middleeastinst.libsyn.com/hezbollahs-regional-challenge.

32. Adam Entous and Evan Osnos, "Qassem Suleimani and How Nations Decide to Kill," *New Yorker*, February 10, 2020, www.newyorker.com/magazine/2020/02/10/qassem-suleimani-and-how-nations-decide-to-kill.

33. Matthew Levitt, "The New Iranian General to Watch," *Politico*, January 23, 2020, www.politico.com/news/magazine/2020/01/23/how-the-quds-force-is-filling-qassem-soleimanis-shoes-102820; "Top Iranian General Hejazi Dies at 65," RFE/RL, April 19, 2021, www.rferl.org/a/iran-general-hejazi-dies-/31210721.html.

34. Susannah George and Mohamad El Chamaa, "Israeli Strike on Iranian Consulate in Damascus Kills Key Commander, Iran Says," *Washington Post*, April 1, 2024, www.washingtonpost.com/world/2024/04/01/syria-iran-embassy-strike-israel/

35. "Lebanese Hizballah's Financial Network," Rewards for Justice, US Department of State, https://rewardsforjustice.net/rewards/disruption-of-hizballah-financial-mechanisms/.

36. "Tehran-Backed Hezbollah Steps In to Guide Iraqi Militias in Soleimani's Wake," Reuters, February 11, 2020, www.reuters.com/article/idUSKBN20520X/.

37. "Treasury Sanctions Key Hizballah, IRGC-QF Networks in Iraq," US Treasury Department, November 13, 2018, https://home.treasury.gov/news/press-releases/sm546.

38. "Tehran-Backed Hezbollah Steps In."

39. Katherine Bauer, Hanin Ghaddar, and Assaf Orion, "Iran's Precision Missile Project Moves to Lebanon," Policy Note 56, Washington Institute for Near East Policy, December 10, 2018, www.washingtoninstitute.org/policy-analysis/irans-precision-missile-project-moves-lebanon.

40. Collin Dwyer and Bill Chappell, "Israel's Army Says It Found Tunnels Dug by Hezbollah Beneath Border with Lebanon," NPR, December 4, 2018, www.npr.org/2018/12/04/673181288/israels-army-says-it-found-tunnels-dug-by-hezbollah-beneath-border-with-lebanon; "Israel Destroys Last Hezbollah Tunnel from Lebanon," Associated Press, June 3, 2019, https://apnews.com/article/31ad0d215a8641a2a776336c270f384e.

41. Hanin Ghaddar and Matthew Levitt, "Hezbollah's Urban Missile Factories Put Civilians at Risk," PolicyWatch 3024, Washington Institute for Near East Policy, October 4, 2018, www.washingtoninstitute.org/policy-analysis/hezbollahs-urban-missile-factories-put-civilians-risk.

42. "Nasrallah: Soldiers' Abductions a Mistake," CNN, August 27, 2006, www.cnn.com/2006/WORLD/meast/08/27/mideast.nasrallah/.

43. Author interview with Israeli analysts, Tel Aviv, March 2023.

44. Matthew Levitt and Samantha Stern, "Green Without Borders: The Operational Benefits of Hezbollah's Environmental NGO," Policy Note 79, Washington Institute for Near East Policy, May 14, 2020, www.washingtoninstitute.org/policy-analysis/green-without-borders-operational-benefits-hezbollahs-environmental-ngo.

45. "Hizbullah Secretary-General Hassan Nasrallah: We Will Confront Israeli Drones in Lebanon, Retaliate Against Israel," Middle East Media Research Institute, August 25, 2019, www.memri.org/tv/hizbullah-leader-nasrallah-we-will-confront-israeli-drones-lebanon-skies.

46. Assaf Orion, "Don't Look Down: The Struggle Over Lebanon's Airspace," Policy-Watch 3626, Washington Institute for Near East Policy, July 7, 2022, www.washington institute.org/policy-analysis/dont-look-down-struggle-over-lebanons-airspace.

47. "Outgoing Air Force Chief: Israel No Longer Has Full Freedom of Action Over Lebanon," *Times of Israel*, April 6, 2022, www.timesofisrael.com/outgoing-air-force-chief -says-israel-no-longer-has-freedom-of-action-of-lebanon/.

48. "IDF Thwarts Hezbollah Infiltration into Northern Israel," Israeli Defense Forces, July 27, 2020, www.idf.il/en/mini-sites/hezbollah-and-lebanon-an-in-depth -examination-under-hassan-nasrallah-s-leadership/idf-thwarts-hezbollah-infiltration -into-northern-israel/.

49. Bassem Mroue, "Hezbollah Says Iranian Fuel Tanker to Sail to Lebanon Soon," Associated Press, August 19, 2021, https://apnews.com/article/middle-east-business -iran-lebanon-iran-nuclear-4105371da0e473dcff364125b6602704; Assaf Orion, "Don't Look Down: The Struggle Over Lebanon's Airspace," PolicyWatch 3626, Washington Institute for Near East Policy, July 7, 2022, www.washingtoninstitute.org/policy-analysis /dont-look-down-struggle-over-lebanons-airspace; Matthew Levitt, "Iran and Israel's Undeclared War at Sea (Part 1): IRGC-Hezbollah Financing Schemes," PolicyWatch 3466, Washington Institute for Near East Policy, April 6, 2021, www.washingtoninstitute .org/policy-analysis/iran-and-israels-undeclared-war-sea-part-1-irgc-hezbollah -financing-schemes.

50. David Schenker, "Securing or Insecuring Israel? Assessing the Israel-Lebanon Maritime Agreement," Washington Institute for Near Institute Policy, March 7, 2023, www.washingtoninstitute.org/policy-analysis/securing-or-insecuring-israel-assessing -israel-lebanon-maritime-agreement.

51. Emanuel Fabian, "IDF Shoots Down 3 Hezbollah Drones Heading for Karish Gas Field," *Times of Israel*, July 2, 2022, www.timesofisrael.com/idf-says-it-shot-down-3 -hezbollah-drones-heading-for-karish-gas-field/.

52. Tobias Siegel, "Nasrallah Threatens War Over Israel-Lebanon Maritime Border Dispute," *Times of Israel*, July 13, 2022, www.timesofisrael.com/nasrallah-threatens-war -over-israel-lebanon-maritime-border-dispute/.

53. Emanuel Fabian, "Hezbollah Renews Threats on Israeli Gas Field: 'Playing with Time Is Useless,'" *Times of Israel*, July 31, 2022, www.timesofisrael.com/hezbollah -renews-threats-on-israeli-gas-field-playing-with-time-is-useless/.

54. Author interview with Israeli analysts, March 2023.

55. "Iran, Hamas and Hezbollah Coordinated Gaza Fighting in Joint War Room— Report," *Times of Israel*, May 29, 2021, www.timesofisrael.com/iran-hamas-and -hezbollah-coordinated-gaza-fighting-in-joint-war-room-report/.

56. Joby Warrick, Ellen Nakashima, Shane Harris, and Souad Mekhennet, "Hamas Received Weapons and Training from Iran, Officials Say," *Washington Post*, October 9, 2023, https://www.washingtonpost.com/national-security/2023/10/09/iran-support -hamas-training-weapons-israel/.

57. "Hezbollah Publishes Video of Simulated Attack on Israeli Outpost," in *Lebanese Hezbollah Select Worldwide Activity Map*, Washington Institute for Near East Policy, July 16, 2023, www.washingtoninstitute.org/hezbollahinteractivemap/#year=2023&id=1863.

58. "Hezbollah Stages Military Exercise for Media," in *Lebanese Hezbollah Select Worldwide Activity Map*, Washington Institute for Near East Policy, May 21, 2023, www .washingtoninstitute.org/hezbollahinteractivemap/#year=2023&id=1837.

59. Lana Nusseibeh, "UAE Explanation of Vote at the UN Security Council Meeting of UNIFIL," Permanent Mission of the United Arab Emirates to the United Nations, August 31, 2023, https://uaeun.org/statement/uae-unsc-unifil-31aug/.

60. Noam Raydan, "Lebanon's Port Risks: The Need for Action Against Substandard Ships," PolicyWatch 3768, Washington Institute for Near East Policy, August 9, 2023, www.washingtoninstitute.org/policy-analysis/lebanons-port-risks-need-action-against-substandard-ships.

61. "Implementation of Security Council Resolution 1701 during the Period from 21 February to 20 June 2023," United Nations Security Council, July 13, 2023, www.securitycouncilreport.org/atf/cf/%7B65BFCF9B-6D27-4E9C-8CD3-CF6E4FF96FF9%7D/2023.07.13%20S_2023_522.pdf.

62. Matthew Levitt, "Hossam Yaacoub Arrested for Plotting Attack Against Israeli Tourists," in *Lebanese Hezbollah Select Worldwide Activity Map*, Washington Institute for Near East Policy, July 7, 2021, www.washingtoninstitute.org/hezbollahinteractivemap/#id=506.

63. Victoria Nuland, "Cypriot Court Convicts Hezbollah Operative," US Department of State, March 21, 2013, https://2009-2017.state.gov/r/pa/prs/ps/2013/03/206525.htm.

64. Ricardo Brito, "Brazilian Hezbollah Suspect Cased Out Synagogues in Brasilia, Documents Show," Reuters, December 6, 2023, www.reuters.com/world/americas/brazilian-hezbollah-suspect-cased-out-synagogues-brasilia-documents-show-2023-12-06/.

65. "Brazilian Police Arrest Hezbollah Operatives for Plotting Attack on Israeli, Jewish Targets," in *Lebanese Hezbollah Select Worldwide Activity Map*, Washington Institute for Near East Policy, November 8, 2023, www.washingtoninstitute.org/hezbollahinteractivemap/#id=1883.

66. Leticia Cotta, "Quem é Mohamad Khir, suspeito de recrutar brasileiros para Hezbollah," *Metrópoles*, November 13, 2023, www.metropoles.com/brasil/mohamad-khir-recrutar-hezbollah.

67. Matthew Levitt, "Hezbollah Isn't Just in Beirut; It's in New York, Too," *Foreign Policy*, June 14, 2019, https://foreignpolicy.com/2019/06/14/hezbollah-isnt-just-in-beirut-its-in-new-york-too-canada-united-states-jfk-toronto-pearson-airports-ali-kourani-iran/.

68. "Criminal Complaint," *United States of America v. Ali Kourani*, 18.

69. Levitt, "Hezbollah Isn't Just in Beirut."

70. "Hizballah Operative Sentenced to 40 Years in Prison for Covert Terrorist Activities on Behalf of Hizballah's Islamic Jihad Organization," US Department of Justice, December 3, 2019, www.justice.gov/opa/pr/hizballah-operative-sentenced-40-years-prison-covert-terrorist-activities-behalf-hizballah-s.

71. "Hizballah Operative Sentenced."

72. "Hizballah Operative Sentenced."

73. "Robert Assaf Pleads Guilty to Providing False Statement to a US Agency," in *Lebanese Hezbollah Select Worldwide Activity Map and Timeline*, www.washingtoninstitute.org/hezbollahinteractivemap/#id=1675

74. Ben-Riley Smith, "Iran-Linked Terrorists Caught Stockpiling Explosives in North-west London," *The Telegraph*, June 9, 2019, www.telegraph.co.uk/news/2019/06/09/iran-linked-terrorists-caught-stockpiling-explosives-north-west/.

75. Nathan A. Sales, "Remarks at AJC Hizballah/Europe Event," US Department of State, September 17, 2020, https://2017-2021.state.gov/remarks-at-ajc-hizballah-europe-event/.

76. "Two Men Arrested for Terrorist Activities on Behalf of Hizballah's Islamic Jihad Organization," US Department of Justice, June 8, 2017, www.justice.gov/opa/pr/two-men-arrested-terrorist-activities-behalf-hizballahs-islamic-jihad-organization.

77. "Two Men Arrested."

78. *USA v Alexei Saab*, Criminal Complaint, Southern District of New York, July 8, 2019, www.justice.gov/usao-sdny/press-release/file/1203826/dl#:~:text=Ali%20Hassan%20Saab%2C-,%22Alex%20Saab%2C%22%20a%2Fk%2Fa%20%22Rachid,by%20the%20immigration%20laws%20and.

79. "Sleeper Cells and Surveillance in the US," *Breaking Hezbollah's Golden Rule*, Season 2, Episode 6, www.washingtoninstitute.org/media/6917.

80. "New Jersey Man Sentenced to 12 Years for Receiving Military-Type Training from Hizballah, Marriage Fraud, and Making False Statements," US Attorney's Office for the Southern District of New York, May 23, 2023, www.justice.gov/usao-sdny/pr /new-jersey-man-sentenced-12-years-receiving-military-type-training-hizballah -marriage.

81. Matthew Levitt, "Barakat Clan Uses Casino Iguazú for Hezbollah Money-Laundering Scheme," in *Lebanese Hezbollah Select Worldwide Activity Map*, Washington Institute for Near East Policy, January 1, 2015, www.washingtoninstitute.org /hezbollahinteractivemap/#id=845.

82. "DEA and European Authorities Uncover Massive Hizballah Drug and Money-Laundering Scheme," Drug Enforcement Administration, February 1, 2016, www.dea .gov/press-releases/2016/02/01/dea-and-european-authorities-uncover-massive -hizballah-drug-and-money.

83. Aurora Ortega, "Hezbollah in Colombia: Past and Present Modus Operandi and the Need for Greater Scrutiny," Washington Institute for Near East Policy, March 2022, www.washingtoninstitute.org/media/5546.

84. Sirwan Kajjo and Mehdi Jedinia, "Hezbollah-Linked Operative Extradited from Cyprus to US," Voice of America, July 21, 2020, www.voanews.com/a/extremism-watch _hezbollah-linked-operative-extradited-cyprus-us/6193213.html.

85. David Ovalle, "State: Hezbollah-Linked Group Laundered Drug Month Through Miami Banks," *Miami Herald*, October 11, 2016, www.miamiherald.com/news /local/crime/article107366182.html.

86. Callum Paton, "Lebanese National Accused of Laundering Drug Money for Hez-bollah Extradited from Cyprus," *The National*, July 19, 2020, www.thenationalnews.com /world/europe/lebanese-national-accused-of-laundering-drug-money-for-hezbollah -extradited-from-cyprus-1.1051446.

87. "Treasury Sanctions Oil Shipping Network Supporting IRGC-QF and Hizbal-lah," US Department of the Treasury, November 3, 2022, https://rewardsforjustice.net /rewards/disruption-of-hizballah-financial-mechanisms/.

88. "OFAC-Designated Hizballah Financier and Eight Associates Charged with Multiple Crimes Arising Out of Scheme to Evade Terrorism-Related Sanctions," US De-partment of Justice, April 18, 2023, www.justice.gov/usao-edny/pr/ofac-designated -hizballah-financier-and-eight-associates-charged-multiple-crimes.

89. "Treasury Disrupts International Money Laundering and Sanctions Evasion Network Supporting Hizballah Financier." US Department of the Treasury, April 18, 2023, https://home.treasury.gov/news/press-releases/jy1422.

90. "Treasury Designates Prominent Lebanon and DRC-Based Hizballah Money Launderers," US Department of the Treasury, December 13, 2019, https://home.treasury .gov/news/press-releases/sm856.

91. "Treasury Designates."

92. Evan Robinson-Johnson, "Ex-Honorary Consul Accused of Financing Hez-bollah Indicted on Money Laundering, Terrorism Counts," *ProPublica*, March 6, 2023, www.propublica.org/article/honorary-consuls-mohammad-ibrahim-bazzi-terrorism.

93. "OFAC-Designated Hizballah Financier and Eight Associates Charged with Multiple Crimes Arising Out of Scheme to Evade Terrorism-Related Sanctions," US Department of Justice, April 18, 2023, www.justice.gov/usao-edny/pr/ofac-designated-hizballah-financier-and-eight-associates-charged-multiple-crimes.

94. Stephanie Van Den Berg, "Hezbollah Man Convicted in 2005 Hariri Bombing Sentenced to Five Life Terms in Prison," Reuters, December 11, 2020, www.reuters.com/article/lebanon-tribunal-hariri-sentencing-idUKKBN28L15E/.

95. "Lokman Slim: Prominent Hezbollah Critic Shot Dead in Lebanon," BBC, February 4, 2021, www.bbc.com/news/world-middle-east-55933222.

96. Matthew Levitt, "Hezbollah Critic Lokman Slim Found Shot Dead in Hezbollah-Controlled Southern City," in *Lebanese Hezbollah Select Worldwide Activity Map*, Washington Institute for Near East Policy, February 4, 2021, www.washingtoninstitute.org/hezbollahinteractivemap/#id=1431.

97. Tamara Qiblawi, "Hezbollah Threatened Top Judge Probing Beirut Port Blast, Source Says," CNN, September 23, 2021, www.cnn.com/2021/09/23/middleeast/hezbollah-beirut-blast-probe-threat-intl/index.html.

98. Hanin Ghaddar and Matthew Levitt, "Hezbollah's Urban Missile Factories Put Civilians at Risk," PolicyWatch 3024, Washington Institute for Near East Policy, October 4, 2018, www.washingtoninstitute.org/policy-analysis/hezbollahs-urban-missile-factories-put-civilians-risk.

99. Matthew Levitt, "'Fighters Without Borders': Forecasting New Trends in Iran Threat Network Foreign Operations Tradecraft," *CTC Sentinel*, volume 13, issue 2, https://ctc.westpoint.edu/fighters-without-borders-forecasting-new-trends-iran-threat-network-foreign-operations-tradecraft/.

100. Jonathan Schanzer, "Iran-Hezbollah Intelligence Center May Help Hamas Target Israel," *Foreign Policy*, September 13, 2022, https://foreignpolicy.com/2022/09/13/iran-hezbollah-hamas-israel-beirut-lebanon-intelligence-sharing-center/.

101. "Hezbollah Publishes Video of Simulated Attack on Israeli Outpost," in *Lebanese Hezbollah Select Worldwide Activity Map*, Washington Institute for Near East Policy, July 16, 2023, www.washingtoninstitute.org/hezbollahinteractivemap/#year=2023&id=1863.

Selected Bibliography

Andelman, David A. "The Drug Money Maze." *Foreign Affairs* 73, no. 4 (1994): 94–108.

Atwan, Abdel Bari. *The Secret History of Al Qaeda*. Berkeley: University of California Press, 2006.

Azani, Eitan. *Hezbollah: The Story of the Party of God*. New York: Palgrave Macmillan, 2009.

Baer, Robert. *See No Evil: The True Story of a Ground Soldier in the CIA's War on Terrorism*. New York: Three Rivers Press, 2002.

Bar, Shmuel. "Deterring Nonstate Terrorist Groups: The Case of Hizballah," *Comparative Strategy* 26, no. 5 (October 2007): 469–93.

Bell, Stewart. *Cold Terror: How Canada Nurtures and Exports Terrorism to the World*. Toronto: Wiley, 2004.

Bergman, Ronen. *The Secret War with Iran: The 30-year Clandestine Struggle against the World's Most Dangerous Terrorist Power*. New York: Free Press, 2007.

Blanford, Nicholas. *Warriors of God: Inside Hezbollah's Thirty-Year Struggle against Israel*. New York: Random House, 2011.

Brieger, Pedro, and Enrique Herszkowich. "The Muslim Community of Argentina." *Muslim World* 92 (Spring 2002): 157–68.

Byman, Daniel. *Deadly Connections: States That Sponsor Terrorism*. New York: Cambridge University Press, 2005.

Chehabi, H. E., and Rula Jurdi Abisaab. *Distant Relations: Iran and Lebanon in the Last 500 Years*. New York: St. Martin's Press, 2006.

Choksy, Jamsheed K. "Iran Takes on the World." *Current Trends in Islamist Ideology* 11 (April 2011): 62–90.

Clarke, Richard. *Against All Enemies: Inside America's War on Terror*. New York: Free Press, 2004.

Clarridge, Duane R. *A Spy for All Seasons: My Life in the CIA*. New York: Scribner, 1997.

Coll, Steve. *Ghost Wars: The Secret History of the CIA, Afghanistan, and Bin Laden, from the Soviet Invasion to September 10, 2001*. New York: Penguin Press, 2004.

Davies, Barry, and Richard Tomlinson. *The Spycraft Manual: The Insider's Guide to Espionage Techniques*. St. Paul, MN: Zenith Press, 2005.

Deeb, Marius. "Shia Movement in Lebanon: Their Foundation, Ideology, Social Basis, and Links with Iran and Syria." *Third World Quarterly* 10, no. 2 (April 1988): 683–98.

Diaz, Tom, and Barbara Newman. *Lightning Out of Lebanon: Hezbollah Terrorists on American Soil.* New York: Ballantine Books, 2005.

Fadhil Ali, Rafid. "New Hezbollah Manifesto Emphasizes Political Role in a United Lebanon." *Terrorism Monitor* 7, no. 38 (December 2009): 3–4.

Farah, Douglas. *Blood from Stones: The Secret Financial Network of Terror.* New York: Broadway Books, 2004.

Fisk, Robert. *Pity the Nation: The Abduction of Lebanon.* New York: Macmillan International, 1990.

Forest, James J. F. *The Making of a Terrorist: Recruitment, Training, and Root Causes.* Vol. 2, *Training.* Westport, CT: Praeger, 2005.

Freeh, Louis. *My FBI: Bringing Down the Mafia, Investigating Bill Clinton, and Fighting the War on Terror.* New York: St. Martin's Press, 2005.

Geraghty, Timothy. *Peacekeepers at War: Beirut 1983—The Marine Commander Tells His Story.* Washington, DC: Potomac Books, 2009.

Gunaratna, Rohan. *Inside Al Qaeda: Global Network of Terror.* New York: Columbia University Press, 2002.

Hamzeh, A. Nizar. "Lebanon's Hizbullah: From Islamic Revolution to Parliamentary Accommodation." *Third World Quarterly* 14, no. 4 (June 1993): 321–37.

Hoffman, Bruce. *Recent Trends and Future Prospects of Iranian Sponsored International Terrorism.* Santa Monica, CA: RAND Corporation, 1991.

Hourani, Albert, and Nadim Shehadi, eds. *The Lebanese in the World: A Century of Emigration.* London: I. B. Tauris, 1992.

Ibrahim, Fouad. *The Shi'is of Saudi Arabia.* London: Saqi, 2006.

Jaber, Hala. *Hezbollah: Born with a Vengeance.* New York: Columbia University Press, 1997.

Jacobsen, David. *Hostage: My Nightmare in Beirut.* With Gerald Astor. New York: D. I. Fine, 1991.

Jozami, Gladys. "The Manifestation of Islam in Argentina." *The Americas* 53 (July 1996): 67–85.

Kepel, Gilles. *Jihad: The Trail of Political Islam.* 4th ed. London: I. B. Tauris, 2006.

Marschall, Christin. *Iran's Persian Gulf Policy: From Khomeini to Khatami.* New York: RoutledgeCurzon, 2003.

Matthiesen, Toby. "Hizbullah al-Hijaz: A History of the Most Radical Saudi Shi'a Opposition Group." *Middle East Journal* 64, no. 2 (Spring 2010): 179–97.

Norton, Augustus Richard. *Amal and the Shi'a: Struggle for the Soul of Lebanon.* Austin: University of Texas Press, 1987.

———. *Hezbollah: A Short History.* Princeton, NJ: Princeton University Press, 2007.

Palmer Harik, Judith. *Hezbollah: The Changing Face of Terrorism.* London: I. B. Tauris, 2004.

Pollack, Kenneth M. *The Persian Puzzle: The Conflict between Iran and America.* New York: Random House, 2004.

Qassem, Naim. *Hizbullah: The Story from Within.* London: Saqi Press, 2005.

Rabil, Robert. "Has Hezbollah's Rise Come at Syria's Expense?" *Middle East Quarterly* 14, no. 4 (Fall 2007): 43–51.

———. "Hezbollah: Lebanon's Power Broker." *Journal of International Security Affairs* (Fall 2008).

Ranstorp, Magnus. *Hizb'Allah in Lebanon: The Politics of the Western Hostage Crisis.* New York: St. Martin's Press, 1997.

———. "Hizbollah's Command Leadership: Its Structure, Decision-Making and Relationship with Iranian Clergy and Institutions." *Terrorism and Political Violence* 6, no. 3 (1994): 303–39.

Ressa, Maria A. *Seeds of Terror: An Eyewitness Account of Al-Qaeda's Newest Center of Operations in Southeast Asia.* New York: Free Press, 2003.

Rudner, Martin. "Hizbullah: An Organizational and Operational Profile." *International Journal of Intelligence and Counterintelligence* 23, no. 2 (2010): 226–46.

Scheuer, Michael. *Through Our Enemies' Eyes: Osama Bin Laden, Radical Islam, and the Future of America.* Washington, DC: Brassey's, 2002.

Shaked, Haim, and Daniel Dishon, eds. *Middle East Contemporary Survey.* Vol. 8, *1983–84.* Tel Aviv: Dayan Center for Middle Eastern and African Studies, Tel Aviv University, 1986.

Shaked, Haim, and Itamar Rabinovich, eds. *Middle East Contemporary Survey.* Vol. 9, *1984–85.* Tel Aviv: Dayan Center for Middle Eastern and African Studies, Tel Aviv University, 1987.

Shay, Shaul. *The Axis of Evil: Iran, Hizballah, and the Palestinian Terror.* New Brunswick, NJ: Transaction Publishers, 2005.

Tankel, Stephen. *Storming the World Stage: The Story of Lashkar-e-Taiba.* New York: Columbia University Press, 2011.

Teitelbaum, Joshua. "The Shiites of Saudi Arabia." *Current Trends in Islamist Ideology* 10 (August 2010): 72–86.

Tenet, George. *At the Center of the Storm: My Years at the CIA.* With Bill Harlow. New York: HarperCollins, 2007.

Testrake, John. *Triumph over Terror on Flight 847: A Story of Raw Courage That Shocked America and Changed Its Attitude on Terrorism.* With David J. Wimbish. Old Tappan, NJ: Fleming H. Revell Company, 1987.

Urban, Mark. *Task Force Black: The Explosive True Story of the Secret Special Forces in Iraq.* New York: St. Martin's Press, 2010.

Valiyev, Anar. "Alleged Iranian and Hezbollah Agents on Trial for Targeting Russian-Operated Radar Station in Azerbaijan." *Terrorism Monitor* 7, no. 20 (July 2009).

Wege, Carl Anthony. "The Hizballah Security Apparatus." *Perspectives on Terrorism* 2, no. 7 (April 2008): 11–17.

———. "Hizballah's Bekka Organization." *Perspectives on Terrorism* 4, no. 3 (2010): 29–38.

Wilhelmsen, Julie. "Islamism in Azerbaijan: How Potent?" *Studies in Conflict and Terrorism* 32, no. 8 (2009): 726–42.

Woodward, Bob. *Veil: The Secret Wars of the CIA 1981–1987.* New York: Simon and Schuster, 1987.

Wright, Robin. *Sacred Rage: The Wrath of Militant Islam.* New York: Touchstone, 2001.

Government Reports and Congressional Hearings

US Congress. House. Committee on International Relations. *Adding Hezbollah to the EU Terrorist List: Hearing before the Subcommittee on Europe.* 110th Cong., 1st sess., June 20, 2007 (Statement of James Phillips).

———. Committee on International Relations. *Fighting Terrorism in Africa.* 108th Cong., 2nd sess., April 1, 2004 (Statement of Douglas Farah).

———. Committee on International Relations. *Hezbollah's Global Reach: Hearing before the Subcommittee on International Terrorism and Nonproliferation and the Subcommittee on the Middle East and Central Asia.* 109th Cong., 2nd sess., September 28, 2006 (Statements of Christopher D. Hamilton and Frank C. Urbancic, Jr.).

———. Committee on International Relations. *Islamic Extremism in Europe: Beyond al-Qaeda–Hamas and Hezbollah in Europe: Hearing before Committee on International Relations.* 109th Cong., 1st sess., April 27, 2005 (Statement of Matthew Levitt).

———. Committee on International Relations. *Terrorism in Latin America/AMIA Bombing in Argentina: Hearing before the Committee on International Relations.* 104th Cong., 1st sess., September 28, 1995 (Statements of Tommy Baer, James L. Brown, Robert Bryant, and Ambassador Philip Wilcox).

———. Committee on International Relations. *Terrorism in Latin America/AMIA Bombing in Argentina: Hearing before the Committee on International Relations.* 104th Cong., 1st sess., September 28, 1995 (Report prepared by Gabriel Levinas).

———. Committee on International Relations. *Venezuela: Terrorism Hub of South America: Hearing before the Subcommittee on International Terrorism and Nonproliferation.* 109th Cong., 2nd sess., July 13, 2006 (Statement of Edward Royce and Frank Urbancic).

———. Permanent Select Committee on Intelligence. *Worldwide Threat Assessment of the US Intelligence Community: Hearing before the Permanent Select Committee on Intelligence.* 112th Cong., 1st sess., February 10, 2011 (Statement of James Clapper).

US Congress. Senate. Committee on Foreign Relations. *Assessing the Strength of Hezbollah: Hearing before the Subcommittee on Near Eastern and South and Central Asian Affairs.* 111th Cong., 2nd sess., June 8, 2010 (Joint Statement of Daniel Benjamin and Jeffery Feltman).

———. Committee on Foreign Relations. *Confronting Drug Trafficking in West Africa: Hearing before the Subcommittee on African Affairs.* 111th Cong., 1st sess., June 23, 2009 (Statement of Michael A. Braun and Douglas Farah).

———. Committee on Governmental Affairs. *Illicit Diamonds, Conflict and Terrorism: The Role of U.S. Agencies in Fighting the Conflict Diamond Trade.* 107th Cong., 2nd sess., February 13, 2002 (Statement of Alan W. Eastham).

———. Committee on Homeland Security and Governmental Affairs. *Counterfeit Goods: Easy Cash for Criminals and Terrorists: Hearing before the Committee on Homeland Security and Governmental Affairs.* 109th Cong., 1st sess., May 25, 2005 (Statement of John C. Stedman).

———. Committee on Homeland Security and Governmental Affairs. *Homeland Threats and Agency Responses: Hearing before the Committee on Homeland Security and Governmental Affairs.* 112th Cong., 1st sess., September 19, 2012 (Statement of Matthew G. Olsen).

———. Committee on Intelligence. *National Security Threats to the United States: Hearing before the Select Committee on Intelligence.* 108th Cong., 1st sess., February 11, 2003 (Statement of George Tenet, Director of Central Intelligence).

———. Committee on the Judiciary. *An Assessment of the Tools Needed to Fight the Financing of Terrorism: Hearing before Senate Committee on the Judiciary.* 107th Cong., 2nd sess., November 20, 2002 (Testimony of Robert J. Conrad Jr).

US Department of Defense. Downing Assessment Task Force. "Report of the Assessment of the Khobar Towers Bombing," *Memorandum for the Secretary of Defense,* August 30, 1996.

US Department of Defense, "Report of the DOD Commission on Beirut International Airport Terrorist Act, October 23, 1983," December 20, 1983.

US Department of Justice, Federal Bureau of Investigation (FBI), Terrorist Research and Analytical Center, "International Radical Fundamentalism: An Analytical Overview of Groups and Trends," November 1994.

US Library of Congress. Congressional Research Service. *Hezbollah: Background and Issues for Congress.* By Casey L. Addis and Christopher M. Blanchard, January 3, 2011.

———. Federal Research Division. *Terrorist and Organized Crime Groups in the Tri-Border Area (TBA) of South America.* By Rex A. Hudson, 2003.

———, under Interagency Agreement with the Department of Defense, Federal Research Division, *A Global Overview of Narcotics-Funded Terrorist and Other Extremist Groups,* May 2002.

"Report of the Task Force of the Federal Bureau of Investigation (FBI): Analysis of the Attack on the Seat of the Mutual Israeli Argentinean Association (AMIA), 18th of July, 1994, Buenos Aires, Argentina," August 1998 (original copy in Spanish, translated to English for the author by Yair Fuxman).

CIA FOIA Documents

US Central Intelligence Agency (CIA). Directorate of Intelligence. "Al-Qa'ida in Sudan, 1992–96: Old School Ties Lead down Dangerous Path." March 10, 2003.

———. "Attacks against Saudi Interests: Inspired by Iran [redacted]." *Terrorism Review,* June 2, 1988.

———. "Bahraini Hizballah Still Active?" *Terrorism Review,* May 1997.

———. "Beirut: Terrorist Mecca." *Terrorism Review,* January 13, 1987.

———. "Detainee Reporting Pivotal for the War Against Al-Qa'ida," June 3, 2005.

———. "Escape of the Dawa 15." *Terrorism Review,* September 6, 1990.

——— "Expanding Links between Alien Smugglers and Extremists: Threats to the United States." July 6, 2001.

———. "Former Consul Arrested for Selling Passports." *Terrorism Review,* November 2, 1989.

———. "Greece: The Tsoutsouvis Case." *Terrorism Review,* July 1, 1985.

———. "Hizballah Terrorist Plans against U.S. Interests." December 6, 1991.

———. "Hizballah Ties to Egyptian Fundamentalists." *Near East and South Asia Review,* April 24, 1987.

———. "Iran and the Radical Palestinians." *Terrorism Review,* June 1, 1989.

———. "Iran and the U.S. Hostages in Lebanon." August 1, 1998.

———. "Iran: Enhanced Terrorist Capabilities and Expanding Target Selection." April 1, 1992.

———. "Iran: The Uses of Terror." *Terrorism Review,* October 22, 1987.

———. "Iran-Hizballah-Israel: Inching toward a Hostage Release." *Terrorism Review,* June 27, 1991.

———. "Iran-Lebanon: Playing Politics with Western Hostages." *Terrorism Review,* March 21, 1991.

———. "Iranian Support for Terrorism in 1985." *Terrorism Review,* January 13, 1986.

———. "Iranian Support for Terrorism in 1987." *Terrorism Review,* February 25, 1988.

———. "Iranian Support for Terrorism: Rafsanjani's Report Card." *Terrorism Review,* August 9, 1990.

———. "Iranian Surveillance of US Persons and Facilities 1995." January 1996.

———. "Keenan's Release a Victory for Rafsanjani." *Terrorism Review,* September 6, 1990.

———. "Khobar Bombing: Saudi Oppositionists and Iran Major Suspects [redacted]." *Terrorism Review,* July 1996.

———. "Lebanese in Sub-Saharan Africa." January 1988.

———. "Lebanon: The Hizb Allah." September 27, 1984.

———. "Lebanon: Hizballah at the Crossroads." *Terrorism Review,* October 6, 1988.

———. "Lebanon: Hizballah at the Crossroads [redacted]." *Near East and South Asia Review,* August 26, 1988.

———. "Lebanon: 'Islamic Jihad' Goes Public on Hostages." *Terrorism Review,* June 3, 1985.

———. "Lebanon: Nabih Barri and Negotiations." *Middle East Africa Brief,* June 18, 1985.

———. "Lebanon: The Prospects for Islamic Fundamentalism." July 1987.

———. "Lebanon: The Theology of Power and the Power of Theology." *Near East and South Asia Review,* August 29, 1986.

———. "Lebanon's Hizballah: Testing Political Waters, Keeping Militant Agenda." July 1992.

———. "Lebanon's Khomeini: Muhammad Husayn Fadlallah." *Terrorism Review,* March 25, 1985.

———. Memorandum for the DCI, "Iranian Support for International Terrorism." November 22, 1986.

———. Memorandum for the Honorable Robert B. Oakley, Special Assistant to the President for National Security Affairs, from the Office of Near Eastern and South Asian Affairs, "Iran and the U.S. Hostages in Lebanon," August 1, 1988.

———. "Middle East Terrorism: The Threat and Possible US Responses." February 15, 1985.

———. "Middle Eastern Terrorism: Retrospect and Prospect." *Terrorism Review,* December 14, 1989.

———. "New Rash of Kidnappings in Lebanon." *Terrorism Review,* March 25, 1985.

———. "Overview of State-Supported Terrorism in 1985." *Terrorism Review,* January 13, 1986.

———. "Planning to Prosecute Shaykh for Bombing." *National Intelligence Daily,* February 13, 1998.

———. "Prospects for Hizballah Terrorism in Africa." *Terrorism Review*, October 22, 1987.

———. "Saudi Diplomat Assassinated." *Terrorism Review*, December 1, 1988.

———. "Shia Extremists Taste Own Medicine." *Terrorism Review*, March 25, 1985.

———. "Shootdown of Iran Air 655." *Terrorism Review*, July 28, 1988.

———. "South Korea: Terrorist Threats to the Seoul Olympics [redacted]." *Terrorism Review*, June 2, 1988.

———. "Spot Commentary: Status of TWA Hijacking/Hostages." June 26, 1985.

———. "Summary of Initiatives Known to DCI Hostage Location Task Force Which Have Been Taken to Secure the Release of US Hostages in Lebanon." December 18, 1986.

———. "Terrorist Use of Beirut International Airport." *Terrorism Review*, July 1, 1985.

———. "Two Jordanian Jets Hijacked for Opposing Reasons." *Terrorism Review*, July 1, 1985.

———. "Western Government Installations Targeted by Shia Terrorists." *Terrorism Review*, March 25, 1985.

———. "Western Hostages in Lebanon: Latest Developments and Implications." *Terrorism Review*, April 8, 1985.

———. "Wild, Wild West Beirut." *Terrorism Review*, April 8, 1985.

About the Author

Dr. Matthew Levitt is the Fromer-Wexler Fellow at The Washington Institute for Near East Policy where he directs the Institute's Reinhard Program on Counterterrorism and Intelligence. He is the author of *Hamas: Politics, Charity, and Terrorism in the Service of Jihad* (Yale University Press, 2006) and *Negotiating Under Fire: Preserving Peace Talks in the Face of Terror Attacks* (Rowman & Littlefield, 2008). Previously, Levitt served as deputy assistant secretary for intelligence and analysis at the U.S. Department of the Treasury and before that as an FBI counterterrorism analyst, including work on the Millennial and September 11th plots. Levitt is an adjunct professor at Georgetown University's School of Foreign Service and the Center for Jewish Civilization and has previously taught at Johns Hopkins University's Paul H. Nitze School of Advanced International Studies. Levitt is a member of the Council on Foreign Relations and sits on the advisory boards of several think tanks around the world.

Index